CRITICAL OPINIONS OF
SAMUEL JOHNSON

THE
Critical Opinions
OF
Samuel Johnson

Arranged and Compiled with an Introduction by
JOSEPH EPES BROWN, PH.D.

❧ A COMPILATION and Interpretation of Dr. Johnson's Principles of Criticism (*Part One*), and his Opinions of Authors and Works (*Part Two*).

New York

RUSSELL & RUSSELL

COPYRIGHT, 1926, 1963, BY PRINCETON UNIVERSITY PRESS
REISSUED, 1961, BY RUSSELL & RUSSELL
A DIVISION OF ATHENEUM PUBLISHERS, INC.
BY ARRANGEMENT WITH PRINCETON UNIVERSITY PRESS
L. C. CATALOG CARD NO: 60-6035
ISBN: 0-8462-0140-2
PRINTED IN THE UNITED STATES OF AMERICA

To
MY MOTHER

PREFACE

DICTIONARIES," wrote Johnson, "*are like watches, the worst is better than none, and the best cannot be expected to go quite true.*" This may, perhaps, serve both as justification for the present undertaking, and as apology for such "*casual eclipses of the mind*" of the compiler as may darken these pages.

It is hoped that the student of eighteenth century thought may here find in convenient form a considerable body of representative criticism, and that the Johnsonian may take delight in travelling over a corner of this robust mind, and re-discovering, perhaps, forgotten bypaths of wisdom and humour.

Completeness has been aimed at within certain limits. The whole Johnsonian canon has been covered, with the exception of a few pages of unpromising material (chiefly scarce "Dedications" and "Proposals"), which have not been available for examination. Every passage of a critical nature relating to original works whose primary aim is literary, rather than utilitarian or technical, is, I hope, either quoted in full, paraphrased, or, if unimportant, at least referred to, in the following pages. Comments on volumes of sermons, philosophical works, obscure translations or histories, and editorial undertakings, are not ordinarily included, unless the interest warrants. No attempt has been made to garner mere statements of fact which do not involve critical appraisal. In certain cases, however, where the material is not strictly critical, but of allied interest, I have exercised the right of selection without pretending to completeness.

The Index is divided into two sections, the first, setting forth Johnson's general critical principles; the second, recording his dicta regarding particular authors and works. Both parts are, however, related by numerous cross-references.

The aim has been to preserve as much as possible by actual quotation, not merely the kernel of thought, but that Johnsonian vigour of expression, which is, perhaps, at its best in his critical writings. In Part Two, however, the greater extent of the material has required some modification of method. Condensation and paraphrase have been more frequently resorted to, particularly when the original source is readily accessible, as in the case of "The Lives of the Poets." No attempt has been made to preserve entire Johnson's emendatory criticism of Shakespeare, or comment on particular passages. Only such notes have been quoted as seem to illuminate his critical principles, or his appreciation—or lack of appreciation—of Shakespeare.

The arrangement of the passages under each main heading is normally chronological, so that the development of Johnson's critical positions may easily be traced. Some modification of this procedure was necessary, however, in the index of authors and works, (Part Two), to permit a grouping of all passages relating to a given work.

The date which follows each excerpt or reference represents as far as practicable the year in which that opinion was held. In the case of Johnson's written works, unless otherwise stated, it has seemed sufficient to give the date of publication.

Remembering Johnson's own admission that "nobody,

at times, talks more laxly than I do," I have distinguished the Doctor's written, from his conversational, pronouncements by marking the latter with asterisks, that the heat of argument and the looseness of anecdote may be taken into consideration.

It gives me pleasure to record my indebtedness to Professor Tinker of Yale, who first turned my thoughts to the eighteenth century; and to Professor Osgood and Professor Root of Princeton, whose enthusiasm for matters Johnsonian, and whose helpful suggestions and encouragement have lightened the labour of "beating the track of the alphabet." Professor Root, indeed, has guided the work from its inception, and shared in the burden of proof-reading. I gratefully acknowledge also the friendly advice and encouragement of Mr. E. Byrne Hackett, of the Brick Row Book Shop, New York, and Mr. R. W. Chapman, of the Oxford University Press, England. It is fitting to close with mention of my wife, who has had a part in every page of this work.

JOSEPH E. BROWN

Princeton, New Jersey

ABBREVIATIONS
of Johnson's Works and Johnsoniana

Adv.
   THE ADVENTURER. Ed. Hawkins. (*Wks.* 9.1-161.)

Bibliog.
   BIBLIOGRAPHY OF JOHNSON. By William Prideaux Courtney. Oxford, 1915. (*Oxford Historical and Literary Studies*, volume 4)

Bos.
   BOSWELL'S LIFE OF JOHNSON, INCLUDING BOSWELL'S JOURNAL OF A TOUR TO THE HEBRIDES AND JOHNSON'S DIARY OF A JOURNEY INTO NORTH WALES. Edited by George Birkbeck Hill, Oxford, 1887. Six volumes.

D'Arblay, Diary and Letters.
   DIARY AND LETTERS OF MADAME D'ARBLAY. Edited by Austin Dobson, London, 1904. Six volumes.

Dict.
   A DICTIONARY OF THE ENGLISH LANGUAGE. London, 1755. Two volumes.

Falk. Isl.
   THOUGHTS ON THE LATE TRANSACTIONS RESPECTING FALKLAND'S ISLANDS. Ed. Hawkins. (*Wks.* 10.34-79.)

Hebrides.
   Boswell's JOURNAL OF A TOUR TO THE HEBRIDES. Ed. Hill. (*Bos.* 5.1-425.)

Idl.
>THE IDLER. Ed. Hawkins. (*Wks.*, volume 8.)

John. Misc.
>JOHNSONIAN MISCELLANIES. Arranged and edited by George Birkbeck Hill, Oxford, 1897. Two volumes.

Jour. to W. I.
>A JOURNEY TO THE WESTERN ISLANDS OF SCOTLAND. Ed. Hawkins. (*Wks.* 10.313-522.)

Letters.
>LETTERS OF SAMUEL JOHNSON. Collected and edited by George Birkbeck Hill, New York, 1892. Two volumes.

Lives.
>LIVES OF THE ENGLISH POETS. Edited by George Birkbeck Hill, Oxford, 1905. Three volumes.

Observ. on Macb.
>MISCELLANEOUS OBSERVATIONS ON THE TRAGEDY OF MACBETH. Ed. Hawkins. (*Wks.* 14.59-114.)

Ram.
>THE RAMBLER. Ed. Hawkins. (*Wks.*, volumes 5-7.)

Ras.
>THE PRINCE OF ABISSINIA [RASSELAS]. Ed. Hawkins. (*Wks.* 11.1-144.)

Shak.
>THE PLAYS OF WILLIAM SHAKESPEARE . . . TO WHICH ARE ADDED NOTES BY SAM. JOHNSON. London, 1765. Eight volumes.

Shak., Raleigh.
>JOHNSON ON SHAKESPEARE. ESSAYS AND NOTES SELECTED . . . BY WALTER RALEIGH. Oxford University Press, 1915.

Wks.
>THE WORKS OF SAMUEL JOHNSON, ed. Hawkins, London, 1787, eleven volumes; together with *Debates in Parlia-*

ment, issued by Stockdale in 1787 as volumes twelve and thirteen; a supplementary volume [fourteen] issued by Stockdale in 1788; and a supplementary volume edited by George Gleig [referred to as volume fifteen] issued in 1789.

Wks. ed. Oxford, 1825
  THE WORKS OF SAMUEL JOHNSON. Printed for William Pickering, London, and Talboys and Wheeler, Oxford, 1825. Nine volumes. [Oxford English Classics.] Supplementary volumes ten and eleven contain the *Debates.*

INTRODUCTION

Literature seems indeed drawing apace to its dissolution."[1] Thus Gray in 1747 expressed the dissatisfaction which the mid-eighteenth century in England was beginning to feel towards the Republic of Letters. Perhaps "crystallization" rather than "dissolution" would have been the right word, for the trouble with literature lay precisely in its lack of fluidity and solubility. It was suffering from a hardening of the arteries. The springs of Helicon had become but distilled water, refined to be sure, but lacking those living bacteria which prevent insipidity. As a writer in the *Monthly Review* for 1750[2] complained: "But in our later times, so large has been the inundation of rhiming trumpery from the press, that even the name of a poet, and of poetry, are become so cheap, so contemptible, and, in some instances, so abominable, that a real genius is often ashamed to be ranked among the sons of the muses, tho' in company even with *Homer*, *Horace*, and *Milton*."[3] Prose, to be sure, fared somewhat better. But in general the tendency to turn the art of

---
[1] Gray's *Letters*, ed. Tovey, 1.164
[2] 4.29
[3] cf. also *The Adventurer* No. 115: "The present age, if we consider chiefly the state of our own country, may be stiled with great propriety THE AGE OF AUTHORS; for, perhaps, there never was a time, in which men of all degrees of ability, of every kind of education, of every profession and employment, were posting with ardour so general to the press."

writing into a cookery book with a set recipe for every dish, had attracted a horde of literary homunculi, and the consequent over-production had inevitably resulted in mechanical inferiority and imitation.

Criticism, both a cause and effect of this state of affairs, had likewise become formularized and imitative. "There's not a drawer, a chair or hackney coach-man," wrote Shenstone in 1740, "but is politician, poet and judge of polite literature. Chimney sweepers damn the Convention, and black-shoe-boys cry up the genius of Shakespeare." [4] The Dick Minims of criticism canted from the Coffee Houses of Nature and Manners and Unities and Aristotle *ad nauseam*.[5] "We live in the days of writing by rule," as Thomas Warton summed it all up.[6]

Of course even by 1750 there were disintegrating forces at work upon neo-classicism. One is apt to forget, for instance, that the two chief literary enthusiasms of the eighteenth century, after the death of Pope, concerned two pronounced liberals in thought or expression, judged by the conventional standards of the age: Shakespeare and Milton. It is sometimes amusing to follow the apostles of orthodoxy in their attempts to justify the

---

[4] *Wks.*, ed. 1769, 3.15
[5] See *infra* under CRITICISM: TYPES OF CRITICS. Fielding in *The Tragedy of Tragedies* (ed. Hillhouse, 159–61), satirized "the Fable, the Moral, Catastrophe, Unity, Probability, Poetick Justice, true Sublime, Bombast, Simplicity, Magnificence, and all the critical Jargon, which is learn'd in a quarter of an hour, and serves to talk of one's whole Life after." cf. also Goldsmith's bookseller in *Citizen of the World*, letter LI: "Of all kinds of writings that [criticism] goes off best at present."
[6] *Observations on the Faery Queen*, ed. 1807, 1.21. Lord Kames, too, refers to "the despotism of modern critics [regarding 'the unities']." *Elements of Criticism*, ed. 1851, p. 432; see also *ib.* p. 16

irregularities of their favourites. Shakespeare was easily pardoned on the score of the rudeness of his age, though an occasional voice ventured to suggest that had he known the rules, the gain might not have compensated for the loss.[7]

Milton's appeal was a varied one. The conservatives judged his epic to their satisfaction by Aristotelian canons, gloried in the didactic and classical elements of his work, and indulged in grandiose diction and turgid sentences, which was their conception of the Miltonic style. The radicals found in him a champion of both political and poetical freedom, and seriously damaged the prestige of the heroic couplet by exalting Milton's blank verse. Admiration for Milton and Shakespeare, however misguided in certain aspects, could have but one result in the long run: it inevitably made for tolerance and a relaxation of the severities of neo-classicism. It is significant that at no period did English criticism follow the goose-step of the rules with quite the whole-heartedness of the French, whose favourites were less radical.

Another author whose influence on the whole proved salutary, was Longinus. This critic brought a semblance of fire and feeling to an age of Reason, and yet lent them respectability through his authority as a classic. Echoes

---

[7] See Young's *Conjectures on Original Composition*, ed. Steinke, p. 64. In the *Gentleman's Magazine* for 1743 (p. 379) is the following anonymous stanza:

> "To shine th' enervous poet tries,
> By rules of art confin'd;
> See *Shakespear's* genius tow'ring rise,
> And leave those rules behind."

of Longinus are audible in nearly every eighteenth century critic of importance, notably in Addison and in Young's *Conjectures* (1759).

Other emotional forces beat against the barriers of reason with greater insistence as the century wore on. Such were the novel of sensibility, the sentimental comedy, the poetry of the graveyard school and the "Gothic" tale of horror. In the realm of philosophy and social theory, the writings of Rousseau, the cult of the "noble savage"[8] and such humanitarian movements as that against slavery (in which Johnson early joined[9]) and the founding of the Magdalen charity for repentant prostitutes[10] —all these are but symptoms, frequently diseased, which nevertheless mark the final breaking up of habits of thought which had dominated for nearly a century.

We come now to a force rational rather than emotional, which notwithstanding played a conspicuous part in disintegrating this tradition of dogma. That force was the criticism of Dr. Johnson himself. He is commonly pictured as the last sturdy defender of a dying neoclassical faith. But a candid examination of the selections in this index reveals several interesting facts. In

---

[8] *Nature's Simple Plan*, by C. B. Tinker, gives some amusing instances of this phase of eighteenth century thought. The rise and development of this cult in French literature are traced by Gilbert Chinard in *L'exotisme américain dans la littérature française au XVIe siècle d'après Rabelais, Ronsard, Montaigne*, etc., Paris, 1911, and in *L'Amérique et le rêve exotique dans la littérature française au XVIIe et au XVIIIe siècle*, Paris, 1913.

[9] See *Bos.* 2.478 ff. (App. B.)

[10] W. R. Fisher has written an interesting unpublished thesis on *The Unfortunate Female; a Study of the Penitent Prostitute Type in English Literature of the Third Quarter of the Eighteenth Century*, Princeton University, 1922.

the first place, we find that Johnson was not sympathetic with the bulk of the literary output of his age. And this is true not merely with respect to various manifestations of sensibility—one would expect hostility toward these. Johnson also attacked with vigour many—perhaps most—of the prevailing fashions of the old established school of poetry.

What, for example, was the favourite poetic pabulum of the mid-century? Imitations account for much of the activity, for they were a logical outcome of the neoclassical position. But in Johnson's earliest utterance on the subject—it concerned the copying of Roman inscriptions by modern writers of epitaphs—he struck out boldly for independence.[11] To be sure, he himself soon afterwards wrote two imitations of Juvenal; but from the time of the *Rambler* essays until his death he maintained a fairly consistent critical barrage against "the servility of imitation."[12] "No man ever yet became great by imitation" challenged Johnson at a time when the practice was perhaps at its very height.[13] Pastoral imitators "numbers without number" transmitted "the same images in the same combination from one to another, till he that reads the title of a poem, may guess at the whole series of the composition."[14] Mythological fictions borrowed from the ancients, with which contemporary poetry was clogged, he declared obsolete. Spen-

[11] EPITAPH 1
[12] IMITATION 2
[13] 1751. See IMITATION 8 and 12
[14] PASTORAL 1

serian imitations, which consisted chiefly in affecting his antique language, as Joseph Warton observed,[15] became the fashion—and a target for Johnson. Pindaric imitators, whose odes were legion, fared little better. And the popular Miltonic blank verse effusions—which for the most part were really not Miltonic at all—naturally came in for their share of censure.

Then there was occasional verse including personal satire. Johnson never rated such productions highly on account of their temporary nature. Sacred poetry—and the press teemed with it—seemed to him pale and ineffectual beside the realities of the Christian religion and its Scriptures. The human imagination could not hope to compete with the divine. And to enlarge upon such material bordered on sacrilege.

That leaves little serious contemporary verse to be accounted for, except a considerable mass of purely didactic poetry. As might be expected, this type of verse would not be uncongenial to one of Johnson's temper. Here at least he appears to have been one with his age, although his insistence that poetry must please as well as instruct excluded the worst perpetrations of this school.[16]

The second field which neo-classicism dominated was the drama. We find little sympathetic criticism of the contemporary stage from Johnson. The monotonous correctness of tragedy, its inability to stir the passions, its

---

[15] *Essay on . . . Pope*, ed. 1806, 2.35
[16] See under AIM OF WRITING

"perpetual tumour of phrase" were justly singled out for censure.[17] Even his own tragedy of *Irene*, guilty on all of these counts, though composed strictly according to "Reason's rules,"[18] was later repudiated. "Sir, I thought it had been better" remarked Johnson at a reading of his play, and left the room.[19]

Indeed, beginning with the *Rambler*, we are faced with a questioning of those very doctrines which were peculiar to neo-classicism. And the tyranny of the rules—of the unities, of the necessity for poetic justice, or for an arbitrary division into five acts—these he ultimately repudiated.

Finally, Johnson's approach to the problems of criticism was not, in theory at least, neo-classical. Frequently his result coincided with that of the orthodox school, but his method of arriving at that result was not commonly its method.

These assertions need more careful analysis. Without attempting a formal definition of neo-classicism, we may safely say that its distinguishing feature was its concept of authority. Back of all was the recognition of the ancient classical writers as infallible guides in literary matters, since their works were supremely grounded in reason and nature. There followed from this premise belief in the authority of Aristotle and of Horace as the best interpreters of the practice of the ancients, and finally

[17] DRAMA 27
[18] DRAMA 57
[19] JOHNSON 14

faith in the authority of certain modern critics who codified this body of criticism into immutable law, in much the same way as the early Church Fathers crystallized Christianity into creeds. On such a hierarchy of authority were based the rules, unities, decorums, doctrines of kinds and imitation which go to make up the elaborate structure of neo-classicism.

Johnson too had a conception of authority, but it was not the authority of the ancients, nor that of their interpreters, Aristotle and Horace, nor of such moderns as Boileau, Rapin, etc. All such authority he distinctly repudiated, as being in no sense final. "I cannot receive my religion from any human hand" wrote Johnson.[20] Nor could he so receive his criticism. Johnson's knowledge and love of the classics were profound.[21] But his system of criticism did not rest on any such basis as their practice, much less on the assertion of their modern interpreters. One has only to read through the selections in this index under ANCIENT WRITERS to see how for nearly half a century Johnson fought the spirit of "blind reverence" [22] for antiquity. Instead, his Supreme Court of Literary Judicature was life itself or "nature." Literature must be tested by a direct appeal to experience, by its truth to human nature, by its effect upon man's mental, emotional, and sensory faculties. And to aid us in determining and applying such tests reason is called

---

[20] *Letters* 1.48
[21] With the notable exception of Greek drama, *q. v.*
[22] ANCIENT WRITERS 8, 12

to the aid of experience. This is not the subjective approach of the Romanticist critic who appeals to his own personal reaction to a work. It is rather truly classical, in that it is an appeal to general human nature which is "always the same." [23]

On such a foundation Johnson based his famous attacks on the dramatic rules. For example, we are to differentiate between "the accidental prescriptions of authority" and "the laws of nature"; between those "invincibly supported by their conformity to the order of nature and operations of the intellect" and others "formed by accident, or instituted by example. . . . It ought to be the first endeavour of a writer to distinguish nature from custom; or that which is established because it is right, from that which is right only because it is established."[24] The following week he returns to the attack in *Rambler* No. 158: "The rules hitherto received, are seldom . . . adapted to the natural and invariable constitution of things; but will be found upon examination the arbitrary edicts of legislators, authorised only by themselves." Fourteen years later in his stimulating preface to the works of Shakespeare (1765) he once more takes up the cudgels by a similar appeal to experience. "There is always an appeal open from criticism to nature," he writes, defending tragi-comedy. Moreover, how is the spectator really affected by a violation of the unities? Does his imagination really take offence? And

---

[23] See Nature 18, 24, etc.
[24] Rules 7

in answering these questions Johnson makes that vital distinction which the neo-classicists failed to do, between the actuality of life and a dramatic imitation of life, which compels us to accept certain conventions from the moment we enter the playhouse. "The truth is, that the spectators are always in their senses, and know . . . that the stage is only a stage, and that the players are only players." [25]

As a logical outcome of such an approach to criticism, we find Johnson asserting that the public's judgement of a work is usually right in the long run. If, for example, a work has long continued in favour it means that it is "adequate to our faculties, and agreeable to nature."[26] Hence he declares that "the common voice of the multitude uninstructed by precept, and unprejudiced by authority . . . in questions that relate to the heart of man, is, in my opinion, more decisive than the learning of Lipsius." And in regard to Gray's *Elegy* he writes over thirty years later: "I rejoice to concur with the common reader; for by the common sense of readers uncorrupted with literary prejudices, after all the refinements of subtilty and the dogmatism of learning, must be finally decided all claim to poetical honours." [27]

Theoretically this was all very well. But Johnson was no democrat by nature, whether in politics or in criticism. And the upshot of it was that he evidently consid-

---
[25] DRAMA 46 and 47
[26] CRITICISM 62
[27] POPULAR JUDGEMENT 10 and 36

ered the taste of his own generation at least as pretty thoroughly given over to the tyranny of fashion and corrupted by prejudice.[28] Johnson's remark on Milton's independent spirit applied equally to his own: "He was naturally a thinker for himself, confident of his own abilities and disdainful of help or hindrance." [29]

So much has been said in the past of Johnson's orthodoxy that it is well to keep in mind the critic militant. As we have already intimated, he was constantly challenging public opinion. The most notable instance was his *Life of Milton*. "We have had too many honeysuckle lives of Milton" he told Malone, and asserted that "his should be in another strain." [30] Still earlier, at a time when Milton was becoming the fashionable idol, he proceeded to point out the defects in *Samson Agonistes*. This was not from any perverse delight in taking the opposite side—Johnson confined such mental gymnastics to his conversational tilts—but solely in the interest of truth. A celebrated writer should be examined with particular care lest his authority "make error venerable." [31] Whether his criticism be right or wrong we shall not here inquire. The point is that it took courage to say these things and Johnson knew it. "He that attempts to shew," he wrote, "however modestly, the failures of a celebrated writer, shall surely irritate his admirers, and incur the imputation of envy, captiousness, and malignity. With

---

[28] See, for example, POPULAR JUDGEMENT 4, 6, 7 and 12
[29] *Lives* 1.194
[30] *Lives* 1.84 n1
[31] *Wks*. 6.430. (*Ram*. 139)

this danger full in my view, I shall proceed to examine the sentiments of *Milton's* tragedy."[32] It took courage also to attack a reigning favourite such as Gray, as the storm of criticism which followed soon showed.[33] And his damnatory faint praise of the poetry of a peer of the realm, who had recently died, Lord Lyttelton, caused the estrangement of Mrs. Montagu and other influential friends.[34] Of Prior, Cowper wrote that his "reputation as an author . . . stood unshaken till Johnson thrust his head against it."[35] Blackmore—included in *The English Poets* at Johnson's request—"has been exposed to worse treatment than he deserved," declared Johnson.[36] Virgil's pastorals are examined "without any inquiry how far my sentiments deviate from established rules or common opinions."[37] And this is by no means an exhaustive list of instances which show Johnson's heterodoxy.[38]

---

[32] *Wks.* 6.436. (*Ram.* 140)
[33] Johnson "deviates so widely from the general opinion [of Gray as a poet]." *Monthly Review*, 1782, p. 284. See also *ib.*, pp. 288, 290; and 1783, p. 371: Johnson's "partial and uncandid mode of criticism" in this life, which gave "general, and indeed just, offence" to Gray's numerous admirers.
[34] For a review of this quarrel, see *The Salon and English Letters* by C. B. Tinker, pp. 199 ff.
[35] Cowper's *Wks.*, ed. 1836, 4.175. See also *Monthly Review*, 1781, pp. 254 ff.: regarding Prior's poetry, Johnson "in more instances than one, deviates from the general opinion of its excellence."
[36] BLACKMORE I
[37] VIRGIL 12
[38] His friends testified to the independence of his criticism, e.g., Murphy wrote: "In matters of criticism, Johnson is never the echo of preceding writers. He thinks and decides for himself." (*John. Misc.* 1.469) And Tyers commented on the *Lives of the Poets*: "He took no critic from the shelf, neither Aristotle, Bossu, nor Boileau. He hardly liked to quote, much more to steal. He drew his judgments from the principles of human nature . . . before the *Elements of Criticism*, by Lord Kames, made their appearance." (*John. Misc.* 2.372)

Such independence indicates both Johnson's strength and his weakness as a critic. It shows a fearless zeal for the truth and a freedom from the fads and fancies of the day. But as Johnson unfolds his reasons for differing from the general verdict, we sometimes find him gradually building up a structure of dogmatism hardly less positive—and not always more tenable—than that of the neo-classicists themselves. Superficially it may seem to be their creed. But the foundations, let us not forget, were quite different.

The fault lay not in his fundamental position of a direct appeal to human nature and human experience in judging literature, but in his application of that doctrine, in his narrow and inflexible interpretation of mankind's tastes and aspirations. Human nature is unalterable, always the same, he postulates. And on this assumption he would reduce criticism to an exact science. But he fails to take sufficiently into account the infinite complexity of human nature, the variety of forces which govern its behaviour, and especially the variable factor of the interpreter himself. For in practice he tended to identify his own somewhat limited tastes with the one unalterable standard of truth to human nature. Here is the classicist seeking the one in the many—and overreaching himself.

Most of Johnson's limitations as a critic spring from this source. Such a method may produce sound criticism when the subject falls within the range of the critic's own appreciation. In the case of Johnson it did produce a magnificent body of criticism of permanent value. Such are his lives of Pope and Dryden, his Shakespearean preface (in part), and that splendid piece of pioneer work on the metaphysical poets, the *Life of Cowley*. Here was material suited to his own particular genius. But the method becomes dangerous when the self-reliant critic is subject to blind spots—and does not realize it.

To clarify this basic weakness in a great critic, let us examine Johnson's attitude to the problems of prosody. His paragraphs on versification have excited the scorn of succeeding critics. They are usually dismissed as thoroughly neo-classical. And indeed the conclusions reached usually coincide with those of the orthodox school. But, as in the case of Johnson's other basic principles, the approach is not neo-classical in method, for it is theoretically a direct appeal to the experience of the senses. "Where the senses are to judge, authority is not necessary, the ear is sufficient to detect dissonance." [39] On the ground that "harmony is the end of poetical measures" he discusses the cæsura in the heroic line and the effect on the ear of pauses variously placed.[40] Stanzaic forms are similarly judged. The involved and irregular forms of the ode are "perplexing to the ear."[41] The Spenserian stanza "is at once difficult and unpleasing; tiresome to the ear by its uniformity, and to the attention by its

---

[39] VERSIFICATION 2
[40] *Ib.* 7
[41] See ODE 4, and VERSIFICATION 29

length."[42] In other words, to Johnson's ear, "the essence of verse is regularity." Both Dryden's and Pope's odes for St. Cecilia's Day, he objects, "want the essential constituent of metrical compositions, the stated recurrence of settled numbers."[43] Naturally, then, to him the heroic couplet is "the most perfect fabrick of English verse." And to those who censure the poetry of Pope "as too uniformly musical, and as glutting the ear with unvaried sweetness," Johnson replies: "I suspect this objection to be the cant of those who judge by principles rather than perception."[44] Here is the clue to Johnson's weakness. What apparently he did not suspect—or was not willing to acknowledge—was the possibility that another ear than his own might prefer with equal reason harmony of a different sort. One might as reasonably insist that the simple rhythm of the dance was the only true music, to the exclusion of the subtler effects of the symphonic tone-poem. Boswell tells an anecdote that illuminates this defect. Miss Monckton "insisted that some of Sterne's writings were very pathetick. Johnson bluntly denied it. 'I am sure (said she) they have af-

---

[42] VERSIFICATION 10. This was a familiar cry. In the *Monthly Review* for 1751 (4.520) we find that Spenser's "labour'd stanza [is not] at all agreeable to those who love *ease* in reading; it is mere slavery to many to preserve at once clear ideas of his sense, and of the *mechanism*, order, and jingle of his versification and rhimes." Dryden likewise referred to Spenser's "ill-choice of his stanza", although he admitted that he achieved variety and harmony, in spite of this obstacle. (*Discourse concerning . . . Satire*, ed. Ker, 2.28–9.) And Spenser's enthusiastic commentators, John Hughes and Thomas Warton, both expressed themselves similarly. (Spenser's *Wks.*, ed. Hughes, 1715, 1. xciii–xciv, and *Observations on the F.Q.* 1.168)
[43] VERSIFICATION 26 and 29
[44] *Ib.* 30

fected *me.*' 'Why (said Johnson, smiling, and rolling himself about,) that is, because, dearest, you're a dunce.' "[45] Those few whose ears were attuned to the melodies of blank verse or to the more delicate lyric measures were apt to be called in effect dunces for their superior sensibility. The truth is that Johnson, who had no ear for music, provided a poor standard by which to judge any but the simpler and more regular forms of versification. Here was one critical blind spot.

Another was his conception of poetry. Nowhere are the critical limitations of Johnson—and of his age in general—more manifest than in the selections below under this heading. It was on the whole an elevated conception—Imlac's discourse on the poet in *Rasselas*[46] shows that—but how inadequate! As with all writing, so with poetry: truth to nature is the basic test of poetic excellence. So far all is well. But again the trouble lies in Johnson's tendency to interpret such principles in too narrow and arbitrary a fashion. Thus he objects to the "piscatory" eclogues of Sannazaro because of "the ignorance of maritime pleasures, in which the greater part of mankind must always live. . . . They have, therefore, no opportunity of tracing in their own thoughts, the descriptions of winding shores, and calm bays, nor can look on the poem in which they are mentioned, with other sensations than on a sea chart, or the metrical

---

[45] *Bos.* 4.109
[46] Ch. X. See POETRY 14: "To a poet nothing can be useless," etc.

geography of *Dionysius*."⁴⁷ In short, the conception of poetry as a chariot whirling us heavenward in glory above the commonplaces of daily life, was not his. Nor did one emotionally so reticent choose to regard it as a catharsis for the emotional life of the poet and his circle of readers. Yet "truth to nature" in a larger sense is observed in such conceptions of poetry—truth to human desires and aspirations and needs. Poetry "doth raise and erect the mind"—so runs that noble passage from Bacon—"by submitting the shows of things to the desires of the mind; whereas reason doth buckle and bow the mind unto the nature of things." ⁴⁸

"And therefore, Sir," one may imagine Johnson countering, "is Reason to be exalted. The poet—nay, the man of letters of whatsoever species—who teaches acquiescence in the universal order, or, as you say, 'buckles and bows the mind unto the nature of things,' is surely a more useful member of society than he who unsettles us for the business of living. No, Sir, the acceptance of life here and now is a consummation devoutly to be wished." And the concluding words, we may be sure, would have been uttered with fervour by one who was perpetually at war with himself. For if the imaginative sphere in which Johnson moved seem restricted, it is not from "stark insensibility." ⁴⁹ Surely it represents in part the triumph of reason and religion over "that hunger of imagination

---
[47] PASTORAL 1 *f*
[48] *Advancement of Learning*, ed. W. A. Wright, 1900, p. 102
[49] *Bos.* 1.60

which preys incessantly upon life."⁵⁰ The moralist feared the potentialities of emotional and fictional writing precisely because he himself felt and feared their effect upon his own essentially emotional nature. One recalls Percy's testimony that this lexicographer and moral essayist was "immoderately fond of reading romances of chivalry," to the "extravagant fictions" of which, however, Johnson attributed an "unsettled turn of mind."⁵¹ One remembers the extraordinary effect upon him of the *Dies iræ, Dies illa*;⁵² and his resolves recorded in that diary of a battle-scarred soul, "to reclaim imagination."⁵³ His intimate friend, Sir Joshua Reynolds, knew this side of his nature when he wrote: "Were I to write the Life of Dr. Johnson I would labour this point, to separate his conduct that proceeded from his passions, and what proceeded from his reason, from his natural disposition seen in his quiet hours."⁵⁴ Even his learning and scholarship were the products of "violent irruptions into the regions of knowledge"⁵⁵ rather than of placid, methodical search. To the alert reader of Boswell's *Life* it is clear that this "rough, tormented craggy soul"⁵⁶ was buffeted by "the conflict of opposite principles"⁵⁷ even as he

⁵⁰ *Rasselas*, Ch. XXXI
⁵¹ *Bos.* 1.49
⁵² *John Misc.* 1.284. (Piozzi). To the imagination in its lighter, more delicate aspects, he was, of course, far less sensitive.
⁵³ *John. Misc.* 1.25. (*Prayers and Meditations*)
⁵⁴ *John. Misc.* 2.228
⁵⁵ *Bos.* 1.97
⁵⁶ Quoted from an admirable poem by Christopher Morley, "On a Portrait of Dr. Samuel Johnson, LL.D." dealing with this side of his nature. See *Parson's Pleasure*, p. 58
⁵⁷ *Bos.* 1.411

himself buffeted his books. And if Johnson, the critic, seems to know not, in Lamb's phrase, "the twilight of dubiety," is it not perhaps because in his writings Reason could enunciate principles with greater ease than the practitioner of life could follow them? Indeed, we are tempted to query, is not the uncompromising finality of his remarks at times an attempt to overawe the enemy with a superior show of force? And not only was the enemy within the gates—from without a variegated army of emotionalists was even then storming with alarming success the fortress of Reason and Common Sense.

Johnson, then, by principle if not wholly by nature, was a classicist, who shunned the vagaries of emotion and sought life in its universal and permanent aspects. "The business of a poet . . . is to examine, not the individual, but the species." Then follows the familiar passage in which he warns the poet not to "number the streaks of the tulip." Rather is he to "rise to general and transcendental truths." [58] Neither he nor the age in general, however, visioned the possibility of rising "to general and transcendental truths" by seeing the true significance of the tulip's streaks or of the flower in the crannied wall. It needed the further impulse of science to bridge this gap. Once more, the trouble lay, not in Johnson's postulate that the poet should seek general truth, but in his limited conception of the way thither. There are many roads to universal truth. One leads

[5] [8] POETRY 14

among common, everyday things. Another winds upward to the heights of personal emotion. The eighteenth century preferred the level high-road of elegant didacticism. The ideal humanist will be familiar with them all.

Like most men of settled principles, Johnson sometimes failed to appreciate the complexity of interest of a work. If it did not measure up to a certain one of his rigorous—though usually sound—standards of reason and truth, there was a tendency on his part to damn it forthwith, "and there's an end on't." Compensating beauties were often passed over in silence. In this fashion he dismissed *Tristram Shandy* with a contemptuous "Nothing odd will do long,"[59] a principle sound enough by itself, but unsound when applied to a work which has lived by reason of its genuine humour and the vitality of its characters. Of course such a method was contrary to Johnson's oft-expressed principles that a work should be judged as a whole, and with the writer's end in view, and not with the microscope of criticism.[60] But by this time, it has become evident that precept and practice with this critic were not always one. One might apply to him his own remark on Polonius: "Such a man excels in general principles, but fails in the particular application." [61]

There are other blind spots, sins of omission or of imperfect appreciation, growing out of these basic limita-

---

[59] STERNE 2
[60] See CRITICISM 44, 45, 46, 50, 53, 59, 75
[61] SHAKESPEARE 99

tions. Usually they are defects of vision shared by the age in general. His curious neglect of the Greek dramatists, ("his studies had not lain amongst them," Johnson confessed) did not then excite the comment that it would today.[62] His Shakespearean criticism now seems strangely insensible to the more poetical qualities of the dramatist. But the age of Johnson, which adored Shakespeare almost to the point of idolatry, worshipped him less as a poet than as a moralist, the great searcher of the heart and mind of man. Dante,[63] Chaucer and other writers of the "Gothic" or "barbarous"[64] ages receive scant mention. Even the Elizabethans, outside of Spenser and Shakespeare, are sadly neglected.[65] But such critical aridities should be viewed in historical perspective, remembering the insufficient data of the age.

It is easy to see now why Johnson is so frequently rated as the last great defender of the neo-classical faith. Its doctrines were often his doctrines; its critical vocabulary was likewise his. But his principles were tested by other standards. If that which distinguishes false from true classicism be essentially a reliance upon an infallible and fixed code of literary laws, formulated on the authority of the ancients and certain of their interpreters, as opposed to a direct reliance upon nature in an attempt to imitate life in its more universal and permanent phases—then Johnson cannot be called a neo-

---

[62] GREEK DRAMATISTS 1 and foot-note.
[63] See DANTE 1 note, for illustration of the attitude of the age.
[64] See GOTHIC
[65] See ELIZABETHAN AGE

classicist. Certain of the laws of this school he found to be "adapted to the natural and invariable constitution of things."[66] These he accepted. Others—and these included most of the rules on which neo-classicism really rested—upon examination he declared in no uncertain terms to be "the arbitrary edicts of legislators, authorised only by themselves, who, out of various means by which the same end may be attained, selected such as happened to occur to their own reflexion, and then, by a law which idleness and timidity were too willing to obey, prohibited new experiments of wit, restrained fancy from the indulgence of her innate inclination to hazard and adventure, and condemned all future flights of genius to pursue the path of the *Meonian* eagle."[67] This is Johnson Militant. And if we are to judge him by his carefully formulated principles and not by his deviations from them in practice, then he belongs with those independent spirits of revolt from things as they are—with the denouncers of sham, and the destroyers of creeds outworn. But his remedy was not the remedy of the radical who repudiates the past. Rather was it a looking backward to the eternal sanities of true humanism.

* * *

One qualification of this conclusion needs still to be made. So strongly did the Christian religion colour Johnson's outlook upon life and literature that he might well

---

[66] Rules 8
[67] *Ib.*

be called a great *Christian* humanist. Few men have ever taken their religion more seriously, as that agonized confessional, *Prayers and Meditations*, proves so clearly. His belief in Christianity has never been sufficiently related to his criticism, for in the last analysis every fundamental critical tenet held by Johnson is the logical outgrowth of a moral or religious tenet. Those who base his criticism on Common Sense and Reason, on Truth and Nature, have but half stated the case. He tested literature by these standards, because he believed that a work which did not survive those tests was not convincing to the generality of mankind, and in so far as it failed to convince, it failed to serve the chief aim of all writing —the betterment of the human race and its equipment for a higher life. And while the moral function of art was also a classical conception, with Johnson it sprang directly from his intense religious convictions. Reason, he tells us in the *Vision of Theodore*, is but the handmaid of Religion, perhaps the chief handmaid, but not the all-powerful mistress which the eighteenth century was often prone to accept as a substitute for religion. "There are laws of higher authority than those of criticism" he wrote, when censuring Shakespeare's profane expressions."[68] And some years later: "there are thoughts . . . which no observation of character can justify, because no good man would willingly permit them to pass, however transiently, through his own mind."[69] Such a state-

[68] DRAMATIC PROPRIETY 3
[69] *Ib.* 6. See also 7, 8

ment as "the poet's art is selection"[70] now becomes clearer. He should follow nature—but avoid its grosser aspects. "The poet . . . having the subject in his own choice . . . ought always to consult the interest of virtue."[71] Likewise the writer of fiction should seek a true representation of actual life, but he ought to select events and characters in the interest of virtue. "If the world be promiscuously described, I cannot see of what use it can be to read the account: or why it may not be as safe to turn the eye immediately upon mankind as upon a mirrour which shows all that presents itself without discrimination."[72] Later, Johnson modified this theory of artistic selection sufficiently to enable him to declare that poetic justice need not be observed, that the wicked may prosper in drama and "the virtuous miscarry"[73] since life is so ordered. But it must have been a hard decision to the great moralist. And his preference for "the final triumph of persecuted virtue"[74] is clearly indicated.

The narrow range of Johnson's poetic taste likewise becomes more explicable. In part the effect of constitutional limitations, in part doubtless the temper of the age, it was also, as we have already suggested, a logical result of his interpretation of the moral basis of art. The imagination needs the restraint of judgement. " 'Incred-

[70] PASTORAL 15. See also SELECTION
[71] PASTORAL 2
[72] FICTION 1. The whole of this passage should be read.
[73] DRAMA 33
[74] *Ib.*

ulus odi.' To select a singular event, and swell it to a giant's bulk by fabulous appendages of spectres and predictions, has little difficulty, for he that forsakes the probable may always find the marvellous. And it has little use: we are affected only as we believe; we are improved only as we find something to be imitated or declined. I do not see that [Gray's] *The Bard* promotes any truth, moral or political."[75] Obviously poetry's wings are straitly clipped. Again the fault lies in a too literal interpretation of terms. He failed to distinguish between morality in the widest sense and mere didacticism. The world has but too often been loath to accord to beauty and the soarings of the human spirit the odour of sanctity.

We are now in a position to understand Johnson's extraordinary dislike for *Lycidas*. It really has nothing whatever to do with prejudice, if by prejudice we mean unreasoned opinion. In the first place, its form is pastoral, which implies a conventional imitation remote from life itself. This alone, to Johnson, is bad enough. But when pastoral is united with elegy it borders on cant and insincerity. Moreover, as part of the pastoral convention, *Lycidas* contains mythological fictions which Christianity has rendered obsolete. "Let fiction, at least, cease with life, and let us be serious over the grave," he wrote on another occasion.[76] And a still "grosser fault" lies in the fact that "with these trifling fictions are

[75] FICTION 12
[76] FICTION 6

mingled the most awful and sacred truths, such as ought never to be polluted with such irreverent combinations."[77] Here and elsewhere, Johnson's criticism suffers from what may seem to us a misconception of the realities of religion. Yet his deep sincerity deserves our respect.

Because Christianity meant more to him than to most men, Johnson likewise objected to sacred poetry. "The ideas of Christian Theology are too simple for eloquence, too sacred for fiction, and too majestick for ornament; to recommend them by tropes and figures is to magnify by a concave mirror the sidereal hemisphere."[78]

One suspects, too, that Christianity played no small part in causing him to break with neo-classical tradition. Such reverence as he had for the authority of the ancients was doubtless tempered by the knowledge that they had not the advantages of the Christian religion. "The ancient epick poets, wanting the light of Revelation, were very unskilful teachers of virtue: their principal characters may be great, but they are not amiable." We find "few precepts of justice, and none of mercy."[79] Nor should they be imitated without due discrimination. Johnson early pointed out the absurdity of copying that which is inconsistent with Christianity or with changed customs, and warned against "echoing the songs of the ancient bacchanals, and transmitting the maxims of

---

[77] MYTHOLOGY 14
[78] SACRED POETRY 4
[79] ANCIENT WRITERS 19

past debauchery."[80] Here his religious beliefs made for greater independence.

Obviously then Johnson preferred compositions with a decided didactic slant. That does not mean that he was in favour of spreading the age's "epidemical conspiracy for the destruction of paper,"[81] by the publication of those poetical dissertations on "Commerce," "Wisdom," "Benevolence," "Science," the "Immensity of the Supreme Being" and "The Present State of Europe," so dear to the heart of the average eighteenth century reader.[82] On the contrary, the aim of writing is to please as well as to instruct. The one function is seldom mentioned without the other. Ornament, variety, harmony and all the elegancies of style are highly necessary ingredients. Why? Because, the moralist replies, "they obtain an easier reception for truth."[83] "That book is good in vain which the reader throws away. He only is the master who keeps the mind in pleasing captivity."[84] Horatian sentiments, to be sure, but not inconsistent likewise with a common-sense Christianity.

Finally, as we have seen, Johnson's dislike for all the literary manifestations of sensibility, is based on ethical grounds. The passions and enthusiasms of man are lawless forces inconsistent with reason, and hence to be mis-

---

[80] EPITAPH 1 and ANCIENT WRITERS 3. See also ANCIENT WRITERS 17, 21, 22, 25, 30
[81] *Wks.* 9.119
[82] The titles are taken from a single volume of the *Monthly Review*—that for 1750.
[83] ORNAMENT 9
[84] AIM OF WRITING 20

trusted. Indeed, they are dangerous, for they tend to undermine virtue. With such premises, no wonder Johnson wanted Rousseau sent to the plantations! No wonder he failed to appreciate that arch-connoisseur of feeling, Laurence Sterne! We even see why he called Fielding a blockhead, and heatedly upbraided Hannah More for reading "so vicious a book" as *Tom Jones*; for was not the novel a glorification of the "natural" man, swayed by emotion rather than reason? Yes, when it came to the school of sensibility, he used strong language.

Thus Johnson's criticism springs out of his own outlook on life. Everywhere we turn, we are met by the great Christian moralist. On the whole this influence was narrowing, pointing away from catholicity of taste and a tolerance embracing the fact that truth (in Lord Morley's words) "dwells in divers mansions and wears vesture of many colours, and speaking strange tongues."

* * *

In the course of this formulation of Johnson's critical profession of faith the reader may have wondered at the absence of any indication of the evolution of this creed. Evidence of his stand on critical matters is drawn from the *Rambler* essays or from the *Lives of the Poets* indiscriminately, with little or no regard to the fact that nearly thirty years separated the two works. Generalizations based on such scattered material would be quite worthless in the case of Dryden, for example, whose critical opinions were in a state of constant flux. But

Johnson, unlike his friend Goldsmith, had "settled notions"[85] on life and letters, and the chronological arrangement of the material in this compilation proves that his critical notions for the most part had taken final shape by the publication of the *Ramblers*. Before their appearance he had been content, in his *Irene*, his imitations of Juvenal, and his hack-work for the periodicals, to follow the beaten track of letters, differing from his confrères rather in degree of excellence than in kind. One exception to this tendency should be noted: his *Life of Savage*, first published in 1744, is highly original and forecasts his later methods of writing biography and criticism. After the middle of the century, however, he appears to respect popular taste only when it coincides with his own private judgement. Undisturbed by eddies of fashion, he drifts with the current only when it happens to be going in his own chosen direction. His course is clear and pursued with vigour to the end. One detects in his *Lives of the Poets* a mellowness of utterance in pleasing contrast with the unrelieved severity of the *Rambler* essays. His later criticism, for example, lays an increasing stress on the vital necessity of the author to please, though he never for long loses sight of the writer's ultimate duty, to instruct. But if his own blows are delivered with more grace, there is no loss of force.

In one way, therefore, the writer on Johnson's criticism finds his task simplified. When erecting the struc-

---

[85] GOLDSMITH 14

ture of his criticism it is not necessary to ticket his utterances as those of youth, old age, or of some transitional period. It would be difficult to differentiate the *dicta* of these periods on other than stylistic grounds.

Even in the heat of conversation, Johnson seldom talked laxly on literary matters. His intimates, Miss Burney recorded, "know how little of his solid opinion was to be gathered from his accidental assertions."[86] And the Doctor himself admitted as much.[87] Nevertheless it is surprising how few actual inconsistencies appear when his written and his spoken criticism are placed side by side.[88] There is seldom a difference in the general conclusion reached, but the seismic shocks recorded in conversation are generally more violent. When "in the humour of opposition"[89] conversationally he might call Gray "dull in company, dull in his closet, dull every where. He was dull in a new way, and that made many people think him GREAT. He was a mechanical poet."[90] When writing for posterity, his tone changes to: "I hope not to be looked on as an enemy to his name if I confess that I contemplate it [his poetry] with less pleasure than his life."[91] Johnson's "settled notions" are nowhere more pronounced than in his criticism.

* * *

[86] *Diary and Letters of Madame D'Arblay*, ed. Dobson, 1905, 4.477
[87] *Bos.* 5.352
[88] In the following index, the more casual criticism of conversation is indicated by asterisks.
[89] *Bos.* 3.407
[90] GRAY 3
[91] GRAY 6

It is this rigidity of opinion that is perhaps chiefly responsible for the usual classification of Johnson as a neo-classicist. But in his case it was no *rigor mortis*. There was a vital humanistic principle at the heart of his creed, however crabbed its fruit at times. But other more powerful forces were at work which finally produced a renaissance of a quite different sort. It is well to pause here and ask ourselves what was Johnson's relation to the chief English critics of this new order.

One point at least they had in common: all, Johnson included, expressed a common dissatisfaction with the state of affairs in the so-called Republic of Letters, which had in fact for some time past been a veritable Tyrant State. Furthermore, there was small inclination to break away from genuine classical tradition. Like Johnson, they were mainly seeking to relieve literature of the dead wood of a false classicism and thus promote a more vigorous growth. Many sought further to graft new shoots on the old limbs, and such graftings were frequently denounced as unnatural excrescences by Johnson. But it is nevertheless surprising how much he shares in common with the leading liberal critics of his age.

Take for example those heralds of the Romantic Movement, Thomas and Joseph Warton. In 1754, appeared Thomas Warton's *Observations on the Faery Queen of Spenser*, revolutionary in its attempt to judge Spenser's poetry in relation to the age which saw its birth. Such an historical approach to criticism, although not unheard of,[92] was then decidedly novel. Yet Johnson was quick to see its soundness and in a letter to the author commended his method highly.[93]

Thomas Warton's antiquarianism did not leave Johnson wholly cold. His *History of English Poetry*, which began to appear in 1774, "has set a noble example" the latter declared, in seeking to revive the best in "antiquated literature."[94] Moreover he must have appreciated much in Warton's attacks on modern poetry, refined to the point of exhaustion by rules and "that bane of invention, IMITATION."[95] Johnson also touches the medieval revival through his connection with Percy's famous *Reliques*. His interest and aid in this important ballad anthology were considerable,[96] although neither he nor Percy appreciated the full significance of the work. The tone of Percy's *Preface* is apologetically appreciative, and Johnson later parodied the ballad manner.[97]

What Johnson did *not* relish in all this revival of inter-

---

[92] See *J. G. Ph.* 16.156 ff. and an article by Karl Young, "Samuel Johnson on Shakespeare," *Univ. of Wisconsin Studies*, No. 18. Pope hinted at the method in his *Essay on Criticism*, ll. 118 ff. Perhaps the most notable use of this method occurs in Blackwell's *Enquiry into . . . Homer*, 1735. This remarkable essay, with its underlying thesis that "every kind of writing . . . depends upon the Manners of the Age when it is produced," its recommendation to the poet to write of what he sees and knows, and its emphasis on poetic enthusiasm, deserves rescue from oblivion. Johnson himself employed the historical approach even earlier than T. Warton, but never consistently. See under CRITICISM: HISTORICAL METHOD
[93] See CRITICISM 16
[94] See WARTON, THOMAS, 2
[95] *Hist. of Eng. Poetry*, ed. Price, 1840, 3.20–1
[96] See under PERCY
[97] See BALLADS

est in the past was its immediate effect upon poetry. Imitations in the antique manner, archaic expressions, unnatural inversions and other paraphernalia of this school were felt by this classicist to be passing affectations of little permanency. Such grounds account in part for his hostility to much of the poetry of Collins, Shenstone, T. Warton and Gray himself.

Thomas Warton's brother, Joseph, a radical by reputation, is nevertheless a critic strikingly like Johnson in many respects. Both were reformers of false taste, denouncing slavish imitation and pleading for a return to the true spirit of the ancients. Following the lead of Johnson, Warton, too, differentiated rules based merely on custom and authority from those founded on reason and nature. Warton went farther than his friend in his insistence on imaginative fire and poetic enthusiasm as the *sine qua non* of genuine poetry. But even these qualities after all find classical authority in Longinus, Horace and the masterpieces of Greek poetry. Indeed in none of the major critics of this period do we find any disposition to break loose from all tradition and rules. That Johnson accompanied the younger critic a considerable distance on the road to reform is indicated by his attitude to the most radical of Warton's critical writings, his *Essay on the Writings and Genius of Pope*, the first volume of which appeared in 1756. This attack on neo-classical tendencies with its attempt to remove Pope from his pedestal to a juster elevation, was called by Johnson "a just specimen of literary moderation." [98] The latter, to be sure, in reviewing this *Essay* took issue on many minor points, but on the whole appears to have agreed with Warton's criticism. In fact, there seems to have been considerable mutual admiration between these two critics.[99]

Another important document of the so-called Romantic School is Young's *Conjectures on Original Composition*, published in 1759. After a half century's output of more or less conventional poetry and criticism Young, possibly influenced by Warton's *Essay on . . . Pope*, produced this fine declaration of literary independence, a stirring challenge to cast aside "the soft fetters of easy imitation" and, catching a "noble contagion" from the works of the ancients, trust to our own powers of originality. Johnson, who heard the author read his essay at the house of Richardson, and commented upon it, "was surprized to find Young receive as novelties, what he thought very common maxims."[100] And indeed Young's plea for poetic originality was in substance that of the author of the *Rambler* and of the tenth chapter of *Rasselas*.[101]

Lord Kames' *Elements of Criticism* (1762), long a text-

---

[98] WARTON, JOSEPH 2
[99] See under WARTON, JOSEPH. For Warton's appreciation of Johnson, see, for example, *Essay on . . . Pope*, ed.1806,1.120, 192, 380n; 2.229; *Adventurer*, No. 133
[100] YOUNG 7
[101] Brandl suggests that this passage in *Rasselas* on the high calling of a poet may have stimulated Young to write his *Conjectures* which appeared only a few weeks later. (*Shakespeare Jahrbuch* 39.12-13). But W. Carpenter (*Young in Germany*) takes the position that Young's essay was written in 1756.

book on esthetics, likewise clears the ground of much of the rubbish with which critics in the name of authority had long littered the field of criticism. Kames would build up a system of criticism founded not on "authority" but on "human nature" or the mental and physical laws of our being. The result is far from satisfying: a new series of laws arises, often hardly less dogmatic and formulated on questionable postulates. But on the whole, the work was a liberalizing influence and Johnson seems to have recognized it as such.[102] In fact, it may be considered a more systematic development of Johnson's own central position—his appeal to human nature and common experience. This also is a main doctrine of Burke's *Philosophical Inquiry into . . . the Sublime and Beautiful*, published a few years before the *Elements of Criticism*. "True criticism," Johnson called Burke's essay.[103] Richard Hurd's medievalism, his conception of the poet's world as a realm where "all is marvellous and extraordinary,"[104] and of the poet's chief function as the giving of pleasure rather than instruction[105]—these properly align him with the dissolvents of neo-classicism and the forces which prepared the way for the Romantic Movement. But this did not mean the abandonment of classical principles by any means. He was a devoted student of the classics, editor of Horace and disciple of Aristotle. Following Addison's method, he tactfully

[102] See under KAMES
[103] BURKE 6
[104] *Letters on Chivalry and Romance*, Letter X
[105] *Wks.*, ed. 1811, 1.251. 2.26. etc

sought to restore the age of chivalry to good repute, by showing that its manners were similar to those described by Homer.[106] But classical authority, valuable as it is, should not be mechanically obeyed. There are kinds of poetry to which Aristotelian principles and Horatian precepts do not apply. And sound rules, in fact—and this is thoroughly Johnsonian—"are indeed nothing else but an appeal to *experience*; conclusions drawn from wide and general observation of the aptness and efficacy of certain *means* to produce those *impressions*."[107] Thus Hurd seeks to enlarge the horizons of poetry and criticism, while holding on to that which is valuable from the past.

Such a review as we have just given of the major literary prophets of the third quarter of the eighteenth century is of course most cursory and subject to many qualifications. But it is, perhaps, sufficiently full and accurate in its general outlines to show that Johnson was no last stubborn defender of the lost cause of neo-classicism. On the contrary, he was an important motive force behind that tidal wave of revolt which eventually was to engulf this outworn creed. And in the chief critical documents of this discontent he found much to his liking. This is most emphatically no attempt to make an incipient romanticist out of Johnson except in this negative aspect of revolt. It indicates rather that these critics met John-

---

[106] *Letters on Chivalry and Romance*, Letter IV
[107] *Notes on Horace's Epistle to Augustus*. (Hurd's *Wks*., ed. 1811, 1.390)

son more often than is generally realized on common classical ground. After all, there is little in their writings that is inconsistent with ancient doctrine and practice, liberally interpreted. Classicism had fallen into a decline and they sought to rescue it from pernicious anemia by fresh transfusions of blood. Naturally these critical doctors differed professionally in the exact methods to be employed. But their diagnosis was fairly harmonious. At any rate they had no desire to kill off their classical patient.

There were excesses, of course, in this general reaction from aridity of soul. But these should be sought in the literary practice of the day rather than in its critical code. These early manifestations of the romantic temper, whether in poetry or fiction, inclined toward affectation, obscurity, lawlessness, excess of feeling and enthusiasm. As such they were anathema to Johnson—often not without good reason, one might add. Their ultimate value as dissolvents of a false classicism and as experiments in new fields, Johnson failed to see.

* * *

But after all it is less important to understand Johnson's relations to his contemporaries, than it is to grasp his significance for our own age. "To judge rightly of the present," remarked Imlac, "we must oppose it to the past; for all judgment is comparative, and of the future nothing can be known."[108]

[108] *Rasselas*, Ch. XXIX.

In many ways the second half of the eighteenth century in literature reminds one of our present age. The reaction from neo-classicism saw excesses of taste and feeling roughly comparable to our present revolt from the repressions of the Victorian age. How modern a ring has Beattie's remark in 1769 that it used to be allowed "that the study of the Classic Authors was a necessary part of polite education. This, however, has of late been not only questioned, but denied. . . . [Several authors of essays] seem to think, that the human mind, being now arrived at maturity, may safely be left to itself; and that the Classic authors . . . are become an incumbrance to the more sprightly genius of the present."[109] To those, whether of the past or present, who wave aside the rich stores of the ages, and mistake novelty for originality and identify success with excess, Johnson has much to say of corrective value. "The mental disease of the present generation, is impatience of study, contempt of the great masters of ancient wisdom, and a disposition to rely wholly upon unassisted genius and natural sagacity. . . . But though the study of books is necessary, it is not sufficient to constitute literary eminence. . . . No man ever yet became great by imitation."[110] In passages such as this the great humanist who finds in the past, not stagnation, but a vitalizing principle of progress speaks to our needs today. Truth and

---

[109] *Essays*, ed. 1779, pp. 453-4
[110] See ANCIENT WRITERS 10 and INVENTION 1

sincerity are his favourite weapons. He wages war uncompromisingly with all temporary short-cuts to fame, with affectation and cant and shallow novelty-seeking—not unknown in this twentieth century. There is something refreshing too for a theory-ridden modern in his sturdy common sense (when properly applied) and general sanity. We find it especially in his *Preface* to Shakespeare (in his directions for example on reading this dramatist),[111] in much of his practical advice to authors and critics, in his keen analysis, divertingly modern, of the different types of critics,[112] in his remarks on books of travel, on biography, on style—in short, on a hundred topics which are pertinent to the reader and author of every age. If much of this seem obvious today, most of it bears repetition, especially when expressed in the vigorous style of Johnson at his happiest. His critical writings are seldom what Lowell calls "penitential reading."

And that brings us to a quality of his criticism which should be especially appreciated today. If it is a corrective to excesses, it is likewise frequently provocative, stimulating. Not after the manner of those moderns who cultivate the art of sending nicely calculated shocks to our esthetic or moral systems. But from the sheer independence of its critical judgements and the confident fearlessness with which these are uttered. Criticism of that type, the product of a well-stored mind relying

---

[111] SHAKESPEARE 45 and 46
[112] See under CRITICISM: TYPES OF CRITICS

mainly on its own native powers and unbiased either by fear or favour, will always be challenging—and will always be needed. Such is Johnson's criticism at its best.

Literature today seems to be passing through an experimental stage. Pioneers are searching, after the manner of scientists, for fresh data, new raw material. And they have followed their gleam even into the psychopathic ward and the biologist's laboratory.

Strange are the bed-fellows of Art these days, and draggled the garment of Truth. Positive artistic achievement seems as yet small. But in our impatience at the vagaries of these enthusiasts, let us not forget the service they are rendering. Their raw material is after all life—and who shall say that art may not follow where human experience leads?

If, dazzled by new facets of experience, they omit those processes of selection and synthesis and transmutation which bring meaning and order and beauty into the facts of life and lift them into the realm of art, let us remember that others, greater than they, may carry on where they left off. It is seed time. And if the harvest is to come at all, it will be the finer and come the sooner if cultivated with those classical sanities of form, restraint, order, the glimpse of the one in the many—in short, the humanistic view of life and art which we find animating the criticism of Samuel Johnson.

TABLE OF CONTENTS

PREFACE	vii
ABBREVIATIONS OF JOHNSON'S WORKS AND JOHNSONIANA	xi
INTRODUCTION	xv

PART ONE
Principles of Criticism

ACADEMY	1
AIM OF WRITING	1
ALLEGORY	5
AMERICAN POETRY	6
AMOROUS VERSES	6
AMUSE	8
ANACHRONISMS	8
ANCIENT WRITERS. (CLASSICAL)	9
ANCIENT WRITERS. (NOT CONFINED TO CLASSICAL)	13
ANECDOTES	15
ANNOTATIONS	16
ANONYMITY	16
ANTHOLOGIES	16
ANTIQUE STYLE	17
APHORISMS	17
ARCHAIC STYLE. SEE ANTIQUE STYLE	
ARTIFICIAL	17
AUTHORS: MEN VS. WOMEN	18
AUTHORS, PITFALLS FOR	18

AUTHORS, POPULAR	18
AUTHORS: QUALIFICATIONS OF AN AUTHOR	18
AUTHORS, SELF-CONFIDENCE OF	19
AUTHORS, VALUE OF	19
AUTHORITY	20
AUTOBIOGRAPHICAL ELEMENT IN AN AUTHOR'S WORKS	20
AUTOBIOGRAPHY	20
BALLADS	20
BARBARISM	21
BEGINNING OF A WORK. SEE OPENING OF A WORK	
BIOGRAPHY	21
BLANK VERSE AND RHYME	27
BURLESQUE	31
CADENCE	32
CÆSURA	32
CANDOUR	32
CANT	33
CHANCE	33
CHANGE OF OPINIONS	33
CHARACTERS	34
CLARITY. SEE OBSCURITY	
CLASSIC (N.)	34
CLASSICAL; CLASSIC (ADJ.)	34
CLOSE (ADJ.)	34
COMEDY. SEE DRAMA: COMEDY	
COMMON SENSE. SEE GOOD SENSE	
COMPILATIONS	34
COMPOSITION	35
CONCATENATION	40

CONCEIT	40
CONVERSATION, RELIABILITY OF	40
CORRECTNESS	41
CRITICISM: THE AUTHOR AS SELF-CRITIC	41
CRITICISM, DRAMATIC	43
CRITICISM, THE EFFECT OF	43
CRITICISM: HISTORICAL METHOD	44
CRITICISM, PRINCIPLES AND FUNCTION OF	46
CRITICISM: THE PUBLIC AS CRITIC. SEE POPULAR JUDGEMENT	
CRITICISM, SATIRICAL	53
CRITICISM, TIME AS AN AID TO	53
CRITICISM: TYPES OF CRITICS	53
CURIOSITY	58
DECENCY	58
DECORUM	58
DEDICATIONS	58
DESCRIPTION	60
DIALOGUE	62
DIARIES	62
DICTATORS, CRITICAL	63
DICTION	63
DICTION, PURITY OF	69
DICTIONARIES	70
DIDACTIC POETRY	71
DIDACTICISM	72
DILIGENCE	72
DIVERSITY. SEE VARIETY	
DRAMA: ACTORS AND ACTING	72
DRAMA, AIM OF	73
DRAMA: BALLAD OPERA	74
DRAMA: BATTLES ON THE STAGE	74

DRAMA: BURLESQUE. SEE BURLESQUE	
DRAMA: CHARACTERS	74
DRAMA: COMEDY	75
DRAMA, DEFINITION OF	77
DRAMA: DIALOGUE	77
DRAMA: DIVISION INTO ACTS	78
DRAMA: ENDINGS	78
DRAMA: FARCE	78
DRAMA, MODERN	78
DRAMA: PLAY-WRITING	79
DRAMA: POETIC JUSTICE	79
DRAMA, RESTORATION	81
DRAMA: RULES	81
DRAMA, SPANISH	87
DRAMA: TRAGEDY	87
DRAMA: TRAGI-COMEDY	90
DRAMA: UNITIES	91
DRAMA: VERSIFICATION	91
DRAMATIC NARRATIVE	92
DRAMATIC PROPRIETY	92
ECLOGUE. SEE PASTORAL	
ELEGANCE	93
ELEGY	93
ELIZABETHAN AGE	95
EMENDATION, TEXTUAL	96
ENDINGS	96
ENGLISH LANGUAGE	96
ENGLISH LITERATURE	97
ENTHUSIASM	97
EPIC AND HEROIC POETRY	98
EPIGRAM	99
EPITAPH	99

Contents

EPITHET	102
ESSAYS	102
EXAGGERATION	103
EXPERIENCE. (CONTACT WITH THE WORLD)	103
EXPERIENCE. (AS A CRITICAL TEST)	104
FABLE	105
FAME, LITERARY	106
FAMILIAR STYLE	107
FANCY	107
FARCE. SEE DRAMA: FARCE	
FEELING	108
FICTION	109
FIRST IMPRESSIONS	113
FLORID	113
FRENCH LITERATURE	114
GENERAL AND THE PARTICULAR, THE	115
GENIUS	118
GOOD SENSE	124
GOTHIC	124
HARSH	125
HEROIC POETRY. SEE EPIC	
HISTORICAL METHOD OF CRITICISM	126
HISTORY	126
HISTORY, NATURAL	130
HUMAN NATURE. SEE NATURE	
HUMANIST	130
HUMOURIST	130
IAMBIC	130
IDYL	130

IMAGERY	131
IMAGINATION	131
IMITATION	133
INSPIRATION	138
INVENTION	138
ITALIAN LITERATURE	139
ITALIAN OPERA	140
JUDGEMENT	140
JUST	140
KNOWLEDGE	140
LABOUR. SEE COMPOSITION	
LAMPOON	141
LATIN POETRY, MODERN WRITERS OF	141
LEARNING. SEE KNOWLEDGE	
LETTER-WRITING	141
LIBERTY OF THE PRESS	144
LICENTIOUS	145
LITERATURE	145
LOVE	145
LOW	145
LYRIC POETRY	145
MACCARONIC VERSES	146
MARVELLOUS, THE	146
MASK	147
MEDIEVAL. SEE MIDDLE AGES	
MEMOIRS	147
MEMORY	147
METAPHORS	148
MIDDLE AGES	149

Contents lxi

MODERNS VS. ANCIENTS	149
MONEY, WRITING FOR	149
MORAL ELEMENT	149
MORALITY PLAYS. SEE MYSTERIES	
MYSTERIES. (MORALITY PLAYS)	154
MYTHOLOGY	154
NARRATION	160
NATURE. (INANIMATE)	160
NATURE. (GENERAL HUMAN NATURE AND HUMAN EXPERIENCE)	161
NATURE. (THE "RETURN TO NATURE" MOVEMENT)	167
NERVOUS	167
NOVEL, THE	167
NOVELTY	168
NUMBERS	171
OBSCURITY	171
OCCASIONAL WORKS	172
ODDITY. SEE NOVELTY	
ODE	176
ONOMATOPOEIA	176
OPENING OF A WORK	176
ORIGINALITY	178
ORNAMENT	180
PAMPHLETS AND SMALL TRACTS	181
PANEGYRIC	181
PARTICULAR, THE. SEE GENERAL AND THE PARTICULAR	
PASSIONS. SEE FEELING	
PAST, THE	181

PASTORAL	182
PATRIOTISM, LITERARY	188
PEDANTRY	188
PERIODICAL WRITINGS	188
PINDARIC VERSE	189
PLAGIARISM	191
PLEASE, AUTHOR MUST	193
PLEASE, BOOKS WHICH MERELY	193
PLEASING, ART OF	193
PLEASURE OF WRITING	194
PLOT. SEE FABLE	
POET LAUREATES	194
POETIC JUSTICE. SEE DRAMA: POETIC JUSTICE	
POETRY	194
POPULAR JUDGEMENT	204
POSTHUMOUS COMPOSITIONS	210
PRACTICE	210
PRAISE	211
PRECEDENTS	212
PRECEPT AND PRACTICE	212
PREFACES	213
PREJUDICE	213
PROBABILITY	213
PROPRIETY. SEE DECORUM	
PROSE	214
PROSODY. SEE VERSIFICATION	
PUNS AND VERBAL CONCEITS	214
QUAINT	214
QUOTATION	214
RACE	215

Contents

lxiii

READING	215
REALISM	216
REASON	216
RELIGIOUS POETRY. SEE SACRED POETRY	
RENAISSANCE, THE	217
"REPRESENTATIVE METRE" (ONOMATOPOEIA)	217
REVIEW	217
REVIEWERS	217
RHETORIC	217
RHYME	218
ROMANCES	218
ROMANTIC	220
ROMANTIC MOVEMENT	221
RULES	221
SACRED POETRY	226
SATIRE	229
SCOTCH WRITERS	230
SELECTION	231
SENSE. SEE GOOD SENSE	
SENSES	232
SENSIBILITY	232
SENTENCES	233
SENTIMENT	233
SERMONS	234
SHORT COMPOSITIONS	234
SIMILES	235
SONNET	236
SPANISH LITERATURE	236
SPENSERIAN IMITATIONS	236
STRUCTURE	236
STYLE	237
SUBJECTS	241

SUBLIME, THE	243
SUICIDAL ENDINGS	244
SYMPATHY. SEE FEELING	
TALES	244
TASTE	244
TEDIOUSNESS	244
TEMPORARY POEMS	244
TERSE	244
TIME. SEE CRITICISM, TIME AS AN AID TO	
TRAGEDY. SEE DRAMA: TRAGEDY	
TRANSLATION	245
TRAVEL, BOOKS OF	248
TRUTH	250
UNITY	253
UNNATURAL, THE	253
VARIETY	253
VERSIFICATION	255
VERSION	266
VULGAR	266
WIT	266

TABLE OF CONTENTS

PART TWO
Authors and Works

ADDISON, JOSEPH. (GENERAL CRITICISM)	269
ADDISON. (WORKS)	272
AESCHYLUS	277
AKENSIDE, MARK	277
ALABASTER	279
ANACREON	279
ARBUTHNOT, JOHN	280
ARIOSTO	280
ARISTOTLE	281
ASCHAM, ROGER	281
BACON, FRANCIS	282
BARETTI, GIUSEPPE	283
BARNES, JOSHUA	283
BEATTIE, JAMES	283
BEHN, AFRA	284
BENTLEY, RICHARD	284
BIRCH, THOMAS	285
BLACKLOCK, THOMAS	285
BLACKMORE, SIR RICHARD	285
BLACKWELL, THOMAS	287
BLAIR, HUGH	287
BOCAGE, MME. DU	288
BOCCACCIO	288
BOETHIUS, HECTOR	288

BOILEAU-DESPRÉAUX, N.	288
BOLINGBROKE, HENRY ST. JOHN, FIRST VISCOUNT	289
BORRICHIUS	290
BOSSU, RENÉ LE	290
BOSSUET, J. B.	290
BOSWELL, JAMES	290
BOUHOURS, FATHER DOMINIC	291
BOURDALOUE, L.	291
BROOME, WILLIAM	291
BROWN, THOMAS	292
BROWNE, SIR THOMAS	292
BUCHANAN, GEORGE	294
BUCKINGHAM, GEORGE VILLIERS, SECOND DUKE OF	295
BUCKINGHAM, JOHN SHEFFIELD, DUKE OF. SEE SHEFFIELD	
BUNYAN, JOHN	296
BURKE, EDMUND	296
BURMAN, PETER	297
BURNET, GILBERT	297
BURNEY, DR. CHARLES	298
BURNEY, FRANCES. (MME. D'ARBLAY)	298
BURTON, ROBERT	300
BUTLER, SAMUEL	301
CALLIMACHUS	302
CALPURNIUS. SEE NEMESIANUS	
CAMOENS, LUIS	303
CAPELL, EDWARD	303
CARLETON, GEORGE	303
CARLISLE, FIFTH EARL OF	303
CARO	304

CARTE, THOMAS	304
CARTER, MRS. ELIZABETH	304
CASIMIR	304
CASTIGLIONE	304
CAVE, EDWARD	304
CERVANTES	305
CHAMBERS, EPHRAIM	305
CHAPMAN, GEORGE	305
CHAPONE, MRS. SEE MULSO	
CHATTERTON, THOMAS	305
CHAUCER, GEOFFREY	306
CHESTERFIELD, FOURTH EARL OF	306
CHEVY CHASE	307
CHILLINGWORTH, WILLIAM	307
CHURCHILL, CHARLES	307
CIBBER, COLLEY	308
CICERO	309
CLARENDON, FIRST EARL OF	309
COLLIER, JEREMY	310
COLLINS, JOHN	310
COLLINS, WILLIAM	311
COLMAN, GEORGE, THE ELDER	312
COMMONSENSE JOURNAL	312
CONGREVE, WILLIAM	312
CONNOISSEUR, THE	316
CORNEILLE, PIERRE	317
COWLEY, ABRAHAM	317
CRABBE, GEORGE	322
CREECH, THOMAS	322
CRITICAL REVIEW	322
CROUSAZ	323
CUMBERLAND, RICHARD	323

DALRYMPLE, SIR JOHN	323
DANTE	324
D'ARBLAY, MME. SEE BURNEY, FRANCES	
DAVIES, SIR JOHN	324
DEFOE, DANIEL	325
DELANY, PATRICK	325
DENHAM, SIR JOHN	325
DENNIS, JOHN	326
DERRICK, SAMUEL	327
DIGBY, SIR KENELM	327
DIONYSIUS OF HALICARNASSUS	328
DODDRIDGE, PHILIP	328
DODSLEY, ROBERT	328
DONNE, JOHN	328
DORSET, CHARLES SACKVILLE, SIXTH EARL OF	329
DRAYTON, MICHAEL	329
DRYDEN, JOHN. (GENERAL CRITICISM)	329
DRYDEN, JOHN. (WORKS)	335
DU BOS, ABBÉ	343
DU HALDE, J. B.	343
DUKE, RICHARD	343
DYER, JOHN	343
EDWARDS, THOMAS	344
ERASMUS	344
EURIPIDES	345
EVANS, LEWIS	345
FARQUHAR, GEORGE	345
FÉNELON, ARCHBISHOP	345
FENTON, ELIJAH	345
FIELDING, HENRY	346

FRACASTORIO	348
FRANCIS, PHILIP	348
FREDERICK THE GREAT	348
GALILEO	348
GARRICK, DAVID	348
GARTH, SAMUEL	349
GAY, JOHN	350
GENTLEMAN'S MAGAZINE	352
GLOVER, RICHARD	352
GOLDSMITH, OLIVER	352
GOWER, JOHN	357
GRAHAM, REV. GEORGE	357
GRAINGER, JAMES	358
GRANVILLE, GEORGE, BARON LANSDOWNE	359
GRAY, THOMAS	361
GREEK DRAMATISTS	367
GREVILLE, RICHARD FULKE	367
GREY, DR. ZACHARY	367
GROTIUS, HUGO	367
GROVE, HENRY	368
GRUB-STREET JOURNAL	368
GUARINI	368
HALIFAX, CHARLES MONTAGU, EARL OF	368
HAMILTON, WILLIAM	368
HAMMOND, JAMES	368
HAMPTON, JAMES	369
HANMER, SIR THOMAS	369
HANNES, DR. EDWARD	369
HANWAY, JONAS	370
HARRIS, JAMES	370
HAWKESWORTH, DR. JOHN	370

HAYLEY, WILLIAM	370
HERVEY, REV. JAMES	370
HILL, AARON	370
HOLYDAY, BARTEN	371
HOME, HENRY. SEE KAMES	
HOME, JOHN	371
HOMER	371
HOOKE, NATHANIEL	374
HOOLE, JOHN	374
HORACE	374
HUGHES, JOHN	375
HUME, DAVID	376
HURD, RICHARD	376
IL PALMERIN DE INGLATERRA	376
JACK THE GIANT-KILLER	377
JEFFREYS, GEORGE	377
JENYNS, SOAME	377
JEPHSON, ROBERT	377
JOHNSON, SAMUEL	377
JOHNSTON, ARTHUR	382
JOHNSTONE, CHARLES	382
JONSON, BEN	382
JOURNAL DES SAVANS	383
JUNIUS	383
JUVENAL	384
KAMES, HENRY HOME, LORD	384
KELLY, HUGH	385
KEMPIS, THOMAS A	385
KENRICK, WILLIAM	385

Contents

KING, WILLIAM	385
KNOLLES, RICHARD	386
LA BRUYÈRE, JEAN DE	387
LA ROCHEFOUCAULD, FRANÇOIS DUC DE	387
LANGBAINE, GERARD	387
LANSDOWNE. SEE GRANVILLE	
LAW, WILLIAM	387
LEE, NATHANIEL	387
LEWIS, DAVID	387
LOBO, JEROME	388
LONDON CHRONICLE	388
LONGINUS	388
LOPEZ DE VEGA	388
LUCAN	388
LUCAS, HENRY	388
LUCIAN	389
LYTTELTON, GEORGE, FIRST BARON	389
MACKENZIE, HENRY	390
MACPHERSON, JAMES	390
MADDEN, DR. SAMUEL	391
MALLET, DAVID	392
MANDEVILLE, BERNARD	393
MANDEVILLE, SIR JOHN	393
MARANA, I. P.	393
MARLOWE, CHRISTOPHER	394
MARTIAL	394
MASON, WILLIAM	394
MASSILLON	395
MAY, THOMAS	395
METAPHYSICAL POETS	395
MILBOURNE, REV. LUKE	396

MILTON, JOHN. (GENERAL CRITICISM)	397
MILTON, JOHN. (VERSIFICATION AND STYLE)	398
MILTON, JOHN. (WORKS)	401
MIRROR, THE	410
MOLIÈRE	411
MONTAGU, CHARLES. SEE HALIFAX	
MONTAGU, MRS. ELIZABETH	411
MONTAGU, LADY MARY WORTLEY	412
MONTESQUIEU, C. DE SECONDAT DE	412
MONTHLY REVIEW	412
MORE, HANNAH	412
MULSO, HESTER. (MRS. CHAPONE)	413
MURPHY, ARTHUR	413
NAVAGERO	414
NEMESIANUS	414
OGILVIE, JOHN	414
OSBORNE, FRANCIS	414
"OSSIAN." SEE MACPHERSON	
OTWAY, THOMAS	414
OVID	416
PARACELSUS	416
PARNELL, THOMAS	416
PASSERATIUS	417
PERCY, BISHOP THOMAS	417
PERGOLESI	418
PETRARCH	418
PETRONIUS	418
PETVIN	418
PHILELPHE	419

PHILIPS, AMBROSE	419
PHILIPS, JOHN	420
PINDAR	421
PITCAIRNE, ARCHIBALD	421
PITT, CHRISTOPHER	421
POLITIAN	422
POMFRET, JOHN	422
POPE, ALEXANDER. (COMPARED WITH DRYDEN)	422
POPE, ALEXANDER. (GENERAL CRITICISM)	425
POPE, ALEXANDER. (VERSIFICATION AND STYLE)	426
POPE, ALEXANDER. (WORKS)	429
PRIOR, MATTHEW	447
RABELAIS, FRANÇOIS	452
RACINE, JEAN	452
RALEIGH, SIR WALTER	452
RAMSAY, ALLAN	452
RAPIN, PAUL DE	452
REDI	453
REED, JOSEPH	453
RICHARDSON, SAMUEL	453
ROBERTSON, WILLIAM	456
ROCHESTER, JOHN WILMOT, SECOND EARL OF	457
ROSCOMMON, WENTWORTH DILLON, EARL OF	457
ROUSSEAU, J. J.	458
ROWE, MRS. ELIZABETH	459
ROWE, NICHOLAS	459
RYLAND, [? JOHN]	462
RYMER, THOMAS	462

SALLUST	462
SALMASIUS	462
SANDYS, GEORGE	463
SANNAZARO	463
SARPI, FATHER PAUL	463
SATYR TO HIS MUSE	463
SAVAGE, RICHARD	463
SCALIGER, JOSEPH	467
SCARRON	467
SCOTT, JOHN, OF AMWELL	468
SELDEN, JOHN	468
SETTLE, ELKANAH	468
SEWARD, MISS ANNA	468
SHAKESPEARE. (GENERAL APPRECIATION OF)	468
SHAKESPEARE. (ANALYSIS OF HIS WORK IN GENERAL)	470
SHAKESPEARE. (INDIVIDUAL PLAYS)	487
SHEBBEARE, JOHN	504
SHEFFIELD, JOHN, DUKE OF BUCKINGHAM	504
SHENSTONE, WILLIAM	505
SHERIDAN, MRS. FRANCES	506
SHERIDAN, R. B.	507
SHERIDAN, THOMAS	507
SIDNEY, SIR PHILIP	507
SKELTON, JOHN	507
SMART, CHRISTOPHER	507
SMITH, EDMUND	507
SMOLLETT, TOBIAS	508
SOMERVILLE, WILLIAM	508
SOPHOCLES	509
SPECTATOR, THE	510

Contents lxxv

SPENCE, REV. JOSEPH	512
SPENSER, EDMUND	512
SPRAT, THOMAS	513
STATIUS	513
STEELE, SIR RICHARD	513
STEPNEY, GEORGE	513
STERNE, LAURENCE	514
SUCKLING, SIR JOHN	514
SWIFT, JONATHAN	515
TACITUS	521
TASSO	521
TATLER, THE	521
TEMPLE, SIR WILLIAM	521
THEOBALD, LEWIS	522
THEOCRITUS	522
THOMSON, JAMES	523
THORNTON, BONNELL	525
TICKELL, RICHARD	525
TICKELL, THOMAS	525
TOWNLEY, JAMES	527
TRAPP, JOSEPH	527
TUCKER, JOSIAH	527
VANBRUGH, SIR JOHN	527
VIDA	527
VIRGIL	528
VIRGIL. (COMPARED WITH HOMER)	531
VOITURE, V.	532
VOLTAIRE	532
WALLER, EDMUND	533
WALSH, WILLIAM	535

WALTON, IZAAK	536
WARBURTON, WILLIAM	536
WARTON, JOSEPH	540
WARTON, THOMAS	541
WASSE, CHRISTOPHER	543
WATTS, ISAAC	543
WEST, GILBERT	545
WEST, RICHARD	546
WHITEHEAD, PAUL	546
WHITEHEAD, WILLIAM	546
WILLIAMS, SIR CHARLES	546
WOODHOUSE, JAMES	546
WORLD, THE	547
WYCHERLEY, WILLIAM	547
YALDEN, THOMAS	547
YOUNG, EDWARD	547

PART ONE
Principles of Criticism

PART ONE
Principles of Criticism

Academy

1. See TRANSLATION 1 for attack on Academies.   1755
2. Plan for an academy of criticism satirised: one of Dick Minim's schemes. *Wks.* 8.244-5. (*Idl.* 61)   1759
3. J. thinks Swift's proposal for an academy impracticable. Stability, which S. thinks would follow, contrary to all experience. *Lives* 3.16. See also *Lives* 1.233
                                                                            1781

Aim of Writing. See also DRAMA, AIM OF; DRAMATIC PROPRIETY; MORAL ELEMENT

1. "The Character of an Author must be allowed to imply in itself something amiable and great; it conveys at once the Idea of Ability and Good-nature, of Knowledge, and a disposition to communicate it. To instruct Ignorance, reclaim Error, and reform Vice are Designs highly worthy of Applause and Imitation." *Gent. Mag.* 1739, p. 3   1739
2. Boerhaave "knew that but a small part of mankind will sacrifice their pleasure to their improvement, and those authors, who would find many readers, must endeavour to please while they instruct." *Wks.* 4.354
                                                                             1739
3. "The task of an author is, either to teach what is not known, or to recommend known truths by his manner of adorning them; either to let new light in upon the mind, and open new scenes to the prospect, or to vary the dress and situation of common objects, so as to

give them fresh grace and more powerful attractions, to spread such flowers over the regions through which the intellect has already made its progress, as may tempt it to return, and take a second view of things hastily passed over or negligently regarded. Either of these labours is very difficult, because that they may not be fruitless, men must not only be persuaded of their errors, but reconciled to their guide; they must not only confess their ignorance, but, what is still less pleasing, must allow that he from whom they are to learn is more knowing than themselves." *Wks.* 5.14. (*Ram.*3. Cf. Johnson on Goldsmith's art of pleasing. GOLDSMITH 22, 24, etc.) 1750

4. Periodical writer must please in order to gain many readers. *Wks.* 5.155. (*Ram.* 23) 1750

5. Ancient poets "intent rather upon giving pleasure than instruction." See ANCIENT WRITERS 3 1750

6. ". . . no species of writing seems more worthy of cultivation than biography, since none can be more delightful or more useful." See BIOGRAPHY 3. For practical value of biography, see also *ib.* 5, 9, 12, 14, 19 1750

7. "Whoever desires, for his writings or himself, what none can reasonably contemn, the favour of mankind, must add grace to strength, and make his thoughts agreeable as well as useful." *Wks.* 7.168. (*Ram.* 168) 1751

8. ". . . he that communicates truth with success, must be numbered among the first benefactors to mankind." *Wks.* 9.79. (*Adv.* 95) 1753

9. Popular authors. See AUTHORS 3. 1753

10. ". . . by pleasing only he can become useful." (Not applied specifically to literature.) *Wks.* 9.148. (*Adv.* 131) 1754

11. "The author is not wholly useless, who provides innocent amusements for minds like these [who seek a

refuge from vacuity]. There are in the present state of things so many more instigations to evil, than incitements to good, that he who keeps me in a neutral state, may be justly considered as a benefactor to life." *Wks.* 9.153. (*Adv.* 137.) See also AMUSE   1754

12. "Of the productions of the last bounteous year, how many can be said to serve any purpose of use or pleasure? The only end of writing is to enable the readers better to enjoy life, or better to endure it." *Wks.* 10.245   1757

13. To "move . . . with delight or terrour"; to convey "moral or religious truth." See POETRY 14   1759

14. Every author "undertakes either to instruct or please, or to mingle pleasure with instruction." *Wks.* 8.386 (*Idl.* 97)   1760

15. "The end of writing is to instruct; the end of poetry is to instruct by pleasing." *Shak. Pref.*, Raleigh, 16   1765

16. Shakespeare's indefensible lack of conscious moral purpose. ". . . it is always a writer's duty to make the world better." See SHAKESPEARE 34   1765

17. Shakespeare "has perhaps excelled all but *Homer* in securing the first purpose of a writer, by exciting restless and unquenchable curiosity and compelling him that reads his work to read it through." *Shak. Pref.*, Raleigh, 33   1765

18. * Ornaments justified: "they obtain an easier reception for truth." See ORNAMENT 9   1776

19. J. defends Milton's digressions (*Par. Lost.* Bks. 3, 7 and 9): Perhaps no passages more frequently read, and, "since the end of poetry is pleasure, that cannot be unpoetical with which all are pleased." *Lives* 1.175   1779

20. *Books should please:* Judge work as a whole, not individual lines. "Works of imagination excel by their allurement and delight; by their power of attracting

and detaining the attention. That book is good in vain which the reader throws away. He only is the master who keeps the mind in pleasing captivity; whose pages are perused with eagerness, and in hope of new pleasure are perused again; and whose conclusion is perceived with an eye of sorrow, such as the traveller casts upon departing day. By his proportion of this predomination I will consent that Dryden should be tried: of this, which, in opposition to reason . . ." gives Ariosto and Shakespeare their high rank. *Lives* 1.454   1779

21. The function of epic poetry is "to teach the most important truths by the most pleasing precepts." See Epic 6   1779

22. *Tediousness:* Prior's *Solomon* "wanted that without which all others are of small avail, the power of engaging attention and alluring curiosity. Tediousness is the most fatal of all faults; negligences or errors are single and local, but tediousness pervades the whole: other faults are censured and forgotten, but the power of tediousness propagates itself. He that is weary the first hour is more weary the second; as bodies forced into motion, contrary to their tendency, pass more and more slowly through every successive interval of space."

An author least able to discover this. "We are seldom tiresome to ourselves." (See Criticism 5.) *Lives* 2.206
Ptd. 1780

23. Referring to Akenside's *Odes:* it is not necessary to examine such compositions singly, for "when they are once found to be generally dull all further labour may be spared, for to what use can the work be criticised that will not be read?" *Lives* 3.420   1781

24. "But Dryden never desired to apply all the judgement that he had. He wrote, and professed to write, merely for the people; and when he pleased others, he contented himself." *Lives* 3.220   1781

25. The charge that Pope's *Iliad* is "not Homerical": "Elegance is surely to be desired if it be not gained at the expence of dignity. A hero would wish to be loved as well as to be reverenced. To a thousand cavils one answer is sufficient; the purpose of a writer is to be read, and the criticism which would destroy the power of pleasing must be blown aside. Pope wrote for his own age and his own nation: he knew that it was necessary to colour the images and point the sentiments of his author; he therefore made him graceful, but lost him some of his sublimity." *Lives* 3.239-40. See also *Lives* 3.240, *n* 1 1781

26. * A good work should please the general public and satisfy the learned. *Letters* 2.440. (Windham's *Diary*) 1784

27. According to Hawkins, (*Life of Johnson*), J. projected the *Lives of the Philosophers*, "written with a polite air, in such a manner as may divert as well as instruct." *Wks.* 1.82 n Date ?

Allegory

1. J. speaks of "the agreeable fiction" of Savage's *The Triumph of Health and Mirth*. ("Mirth" searches for "Health" to aid Lady Tyrconnel, etc.) *Lives* 2.370 1744

2. ". . . allegory is perhaps one of the most pleasing vehicles of instruction." *Wks.* 6.325. (*Ram.* 121) 1751

3. *Allegory:* "A figurative discourse, in which something other is intended, than is contained in the words literally taken; as, *wealth is the daughter of diligence, and the parent of authority.*" *Dict.* 1755

4. "To exalt causes into agents, to invest abstract ideas with form, and animate them with activity has always been the right of poetry. But such airy beings are for the most part suffered only to do their natural office,

and retire. Thus Fame tells a tale and Victory hovers over a general or perches on a standard; but Fame and Victory can do no more. To give them any real employment or ascribe to them any material agency is to make them allegorical no longer, but to shock the mind by ascribing effects to non-entity. In the *Prometheus* of Æschylus we see Violence and Strength, and in the *Alcestis* of Euripides we see Death, brought upon the stage, all as active persons of the drama; but no precedents can justify absurdity." *Lives* 1.185[1] 1779

5. ". . . . allegories drawn to great length will always break." *Lives* 1.436-7   1779

6. J., in commending Pope's new supernatural machinery in *Rape of the Lock*, remarks: "The employment of allegorical persons always excites conviction of its own absurdity: they may produce effects, but cannot conduct actions; when the phantom is put in motion, it dissolves; thus Discord may raise a mutiny, but Discord cannot conduct a march, nor besiege a town." *Lives* 3.233   1781

7. * Cf. J.'s reported remark on allegorical paintings: "I had rather see the portrait of a dog that I know, than all the allegorical paintings they can shew me in the world." *John. Misc.* 2.15   Date ?

American Poetry

1. Conspicuous by its absence. See GRAINGER 2   1764

Amorous Verses. Compare LOVE

1. * "Nonsense can be defended but by nonsense." See PRIOR 1   1769
2. Waller's "amorous verses have this to recommend them, that they are less hyperbolical than those of

---

[1] Addison had made substantially the same criticism in *Spectator* No. 357; also John Hughes, Ed. Spenser's *Wks.*, 1715, 1. xliii.

some other poets. Waller is not always at the last gasp; he does not die of a frown, nor live upon a smile. There is however too much love, and too many trifles. Little things are made too important; and the Empire of Beauty is represented as exerting its influence further than can be allowed by the multiplicity of human passions and the variety of human wants. Such books therefore may be considered as shewing the world under a false appearance, and, so far as they obtain credit from the young and unexperienced, as misleading expectation and misguiding practice." *Lives* 1.287

1779

3. J. attacks the alleged obligation of poets to compose "amorous ditties" to prove themselves poets: "But the basis of all excellence is truth: he that professes love ought to feel its power. . . . This consideration [Cowley's love poems not based on reality] cannot but abate in some measure the reader's esteem for the work and the author . . . it seems as reasonable to appear the champion as the poet of an 'airy nothing,' and to quarrel as to write for what Cowley might have learned from his master Pindar to call the 'dream of a shadow.' It is surely not difficult, in the solitude of a college or in the bustle of the world, to find useful studies and serious employment. No man needs to be so burthened with life as to squander it in voluntary dreams of fictitious occurrences. The man that sits down to suppose himself charged with treason or peculation, and heats his mind to an elaborate purgation of his character from crimes which he was never within the possibility of committing, differs only by the infrequency of his folly from him who praises beauty which he never saw, complains of jealousy which he never felt, supposes himself sometimes invited and sometimes forsaken, fatigues his fancy, and ransacks his memory, for images which may exhibit the gaiety of hope or the gloominess of despair, and dresses his

imaginary Chloris or Phyllis sometimes in flowers fading as her beauty, and sometimes in gems lasting as her virtues." *Lives* 1.6-8. See also *ib.* 41-2   1779

4. Prior's love verses censured "for they are not dictated by nature or by passion, and have neither gallantry nor tenderness . . . the dull exercises of a skilful versifier resolved at all adventures to write something about Chloe, and trying to be amorous by dint of study." Their "despicable" mythological fictions. *Lives* 2.202.   Ptd. 1780

Amuse. Compare AIM OF WRITING 11

1. *Definition.* "To entertain with tranquillity; to fill with thoughts that engage the mind, without distracting it. To *divert* implies something more lively, and to *please*, something more important. It is therefore frequently taken in a sense bordering on contempt." *Dict.* See also G. B. Hill's note on this word, *Lives* 2.219, *n* 2   1755

Anachronisms. See SHAKESPEARE: *Anachronisms;* see also ANTIQUE STYLE; and under IMITATION for anachronisms in Spenserian and other imitations of the antique

1. ". . . if we suffer them [shepherds in pastoral poetry] to allude at all to things of later existence, which, perhaps, cannot with any great propriety be allowed." *Wks.* 5.241. (*Ram.* 37)   1750
2. Milton's anachronisms in *Samson Agonistes.* *Wks.* 6.437. (*Ram.* 140)   1751
3. Anachronistic "modern terms" in *Memoirs of the Court of Augustus* censured. *Wks.* 10.188   1756
4. Anachronisms in Pope's sketch of his proposed epic on Brutus. See EPIC 9   1781

Ancient Writers. (CLASSICAL.) See also MYTHOLOGY, RULES, ARISTOTLE, HOMER, HORACE, THEOCRITUS, VIRGIL, etc.

1. Absurdity of moderns copying what is inconsistent with Christianity or with changed customs. See EPITAPH 1   1740
2. The ancient writers placed above those of Renaissance. See RENAISSANCE 1   1742
3. "The ancient poets are, indeed, by no means unexceptionable teachers of morality; their precepts are to be always considered as the sallies of a genius, intent rather upon giving pleasure than instruction. . . ." They are to be excused; "but surely those who are acquainted with the hopes and fears of eternity, might think it necessary to put some restraint upon their imagination, and reflect that by echoing the songs of the ancient bacchanals, and transmitting the maxims of past debauchery, they not only prove that they want invention, but virtue, and submit to the servility of imitation only to copy that of which the writer, if he was to live now, would often be ashamed." However, even the "incitements to pleasure" of ancient authors are generally mingled with reflections upon life worth treasuring. *Wks.* 5.188-9. (*Ram.* 29)   1750
4. Difficult "to improve the pastorals of antiquity, by any great additions or diversifications." See PASTORAL 1 [g]   1750
5. "In writing or judging of pastoral poetry, neither the authors nor criticks of latter times seem to have paid sufficient regard to the originals left us by antiquity." For a model of pastoral poetry, J. goes to Virgil. See VIRGIL 11. *Wks.* 5.238. (*Ram.* 37)   1750
6. Imitation of the ancients justified. See PLAGIARISM 1   1751

7. Inversion of accents in heroic measure censured: contrary to the practice of the ancients. "But where the senses are to judge, authority is not necessary, the ear is sufficient to detect dissonance." *Wks.* 6.96. (*Ram.* 86) 1751
8. "But many beauties of this kind [arising from onomatopœia], which the moderns, and perhaps the ancients, have observed, seem to be the product of blind reverence acting upon fancy." *Wks.* 6.147. (*Ram.* 94) 1751
9. Very few additions have been made to ancient fable. "The wars of *Troy*, and the travels of *Ulysses*, have furnished almost all succeeding poets with incidents, characters, and sentiments. The *Romans* are confessed to have attempted little more than to display in their own tongue the inventions of the *Greeks*. There is, in all their writings, such a perpetual recurrence of allusions to the tales of the fabulous age, that they must be confessed often to want that power of giving pleasure which novelty supplies; nor can we wonder that they excelled so much in the graces of diction, when we consider how rarely they were employed in search of new thoughts." Even Virgil "seduced by imitation" on occasion. (See VIRGIL 15.) *Wks.* 6.322-4. (*Ram.* 121) 1751
10. "The mental disease of the present generation, is impatience of study, contempt of the great masters of ancient wisdom, and a disposition to rely wholly upon unassisted genius and natural sagacity . . . But though the study of books is necessary, it is not sufficient to constitute literary eminence. . . . No man ever yet became great by imitation." "Invention in the design or the execution" necessary. (See INVENTION 1.) *Wks.* 7.82-7. (*Ram.* 154) 1751
11. Rules "dictated by reason and necessity" distinguished from those "enacted by despotick antiquity." See RULES 7 1751

12. "Blind reverence" for ancient writers as sources of critical authority attacked. See RULES 8   1751
13. *Ancients vs. moderns:* The superiority of the ancients to the moderns in composition: partly from the superior graces of their language, partly from "priority, which put them in possession of the most natural sentiments, and left us nothing but servile repetition or forced conceits"; but chiefly from their modesty and labour: hasty productions few. *Wks.* 7.171-3. (*Ram.* 169)   1751
14. ". . . the dictates of common sense and common honesty, names of greater authority than that of *Horace.*" *Wks.* 10.186   1756
15. "Of the ancients, enough remains to excite our emulation, and direct our endeavours. . . . Such is the general conspiracy of human nature against contemporary merit, that if we had inherited from antiquity enough to afford employment for the laborious, and amusement for the idle, I know not what room would have been left for modern genius or modern industry." *Wks.* 8.264-5.(*Idl.* 66)   1759
16. "We see how little the united experience of mankind have been able to add to the heroick characters displayed by *Homer*"; even "the fertile imagination" of the Italians has added few new incidents. *Wks.* 8.265. (*Idl.* 66)   1759
17. * "Had the ancients been serious in their [religious] belief, we should not have had their Gods exhibited in the manner we find them represented in the Poets." *Bos.* 3.10   1776
18. * *Ancients vs. moderns:* "Modern writers are the moons of literature; they shine with reflected light, with light borrowed from the ancients. Greece appears to me to be the fountain of knowledge; Rome of elegance." *Bos.* 3.333   1778
19. "The ancient epick poets, wanting the light of Reve-

lation, were very unskilful teachers of virtue: their principal characters may be great, but they are not amiable." Inspire active or passive fortitude, or prudence, but furnish "few precepts of justice and none of mercy." *Lives* 1.179   1779

20. "It could only be by long prejudice and the bigotry of learning that Milton could prefer the ancient tragedies with their encumbrance of a chorus to the exhibitions of the French and English stages." *Lives* 1.188-9
1779

21. Waller borrows too much "from the old mythology, for which it is vain to plead the example of ancient poets:" the deities were to them realities, to a certain extent. See MYTHOLOGY 10   1779

22. Dryden defends immorality on ground of precedent of ancients "which is only to say, that he was not the first nor perhaps the greatest offender." *Lives* 1.347
1779

23. ". . . reason wants not Horace to support it." *Lives* 1.423   1779

24. Cowley did not sufficiently inquire "by what means the ancients have continued to delight through all the changes of human manners." *Lives* 1.56   1779

25. ". . . no precedents can justify absurdity." See ALLEGORY 4   1779

26. Addison's writings in cause of virtue. "This is an elevation of literary character, 'above all Greek, above all Roman fame.'" *Lives* 2.126   Ptd. 1780

27. Pindar of questionable value as a precedent for irregular verse. See PINDARIC VERSE 6   1781

28. "In their similes the greatest writers have sometimes failed." Faulty similes in Ovid and Virgil. See SIMILES 5. (But cf. SIMILES 1 for praise of ancients)
1781

29. For J.'s belief that "time and place will always enforce regard," see CRITICISM 23   1781

30. * "The machinery of the Pagans is uninteresting to us." See MYTHOLOGY 34. Date ?
31. * J. "acknowledged that his studies had not lain amongst them [the Greek dramatists]" *John. Misc.* 2.78 (Cumberland) Date ?

Ancient Writers. (NOT CONFINED TO CLASSICAL)

33. Ancient Northern or Gothic writers: their particular claim on Englishmen to veneration. *Wks.* 9.344 1743
34. Superior claim of ancient writers to our regard. See CRITICISM 62 1751
35. Obscure passages "in books . . . made venerable by the uniform attestation of successive ages," not to be hastily censured: their obscurity often the result of contemporary allusions meaningless to modern ears. Illustrations from Horace. *Wks.* 9.32-9. (*Adv.* 58) 1753
36. "When, therefore, an author declares, that he has been able to learn nothing from the writings of his predecessors, and such a declaration has been lately made, nothing but a degree of arrogance unpardonable in the greatest human understanding, can hinder him from perceiving that he is raising prejudices against his own performance; for with what hopes of success can he attempt that in which greater abilities have hitherto miscarried? or with what peculiar force does he suppose himself invigorated, that difficulties hitherto invincible should give way before him?" *Wks.* 9.62-3. (*Adv.* 85) 1753
37. *Ancients vs. moderns:* "'. . . it fills me with wonder, that, in almost all countries, the most ancient poets are considered as the best: whether it be that . . . poetry is a gift conferred at once; or that the first poetry of every nation surprised them as a novelty, and retained the credit by consent which it received by accident at first: or whether, as the province of poetry

is to describe Nature and Passion, which are always the same, the first writers took possession of the most striking objects for description, and the most probable occurrences for fiction, and left nothing to those that followed them, but transcription of the same events, and new combinations of the same images. Whatever be the reason, it is commonly observed that the early writers are in possession of nature, and their followers of art: that the first excel in strength and invention, and the latter in elegance and refinement.'" Imlac in *Rasselas* (Ch. X). *Wks.* 11.29-30   1759

38. *Ancients vs. moderns:* The superior reverence paid to ancient writers that have stood the test of time justified on rational grounds. "To works . . . of which the excellence is not absolute and definite, but gradual and comparative . . . no other test can be applied than length of duration and continuance of esteem. What mankind have long possessed they have often examined and compared; and if they persist to value the possession, it is because frequent comparisons have confirmed opinion in its favour . . . in the productions of genius, nothing can be stiled excellent till it has been compared with other works of the same kind. . . . The reverence due to writings that have long subsisted . . . is the consequence of acknowledged and indubitable positions, that what has been longest known has been most considered, and what is most considered is best understood." *Shak. Pref.*, Raleigh, 9-10   1765

39. *Ancients vs. moderns:* "It may be observed, that the oldest poets of many nations preserve their reputation, and that the following generations of wit, after a short celebrity, sink into oblivion. The first, whoever they be, must take their sentiments and descriptions immediately from knowledge; the resemblance is therefore just, their descriptions are verified by every eye, and their sentiments acknowledged by every

breast. Those whom their fame invites to the same studies, copy partly them, and partly nature, till the books of one age gain such authority, as to stand in the place of nature to another, and imitation, always deviating a little, becomes at last capricious and casual." *Shak. Pref.*, Raleigh, 39   1765

40. "When he [Pope] entered into the living world it seems to have happened to him as to many others that he was less attentive to dead masters: he studied in the academy of Paracelsus, and made the universe his favourite volume. He gathered his notions fresh from reality, not from the copies of authors, but the originals of Nature. Yet there is no reason to believe that literature ever lost his esteem," etc. *Lives* 3.216   1781

41. "These benefits of nature [good sense, genius] he [Pope] improved by incessant and unwearied diligence; he had recourse to every source of intelligence . . . he consulted the living as well as the dead." *Lives* 3.217   1781

42. * "I am always angry when I hear ancient times praised at the expence of modern times." *Bos.* 4.217
     1783

43. * "He loved, he said, the old black letter books; they were rich in matter, though their style was inelegant; wonderfully so, considering how conversant the writers were with the best models of antiquity." *Bos.* 2.120. (Maxwell's *Collectanea*)   Date ?

Anecdotes. See also BIOGRAPHY

1. * J. enters a plea for anecdotes in Boswell's forthcoming *Account of Corsica*: "Give us as many anecdotes as you can." *Bos.* 2.11   1766

2. * ". . . I love anecdotes. I fancy mankind may come, in time, to write all aphoristically, except in narrative; grow weary of preparation, and connection, and illustration, and all those arts by which a big book is made.

If a man is to wait till he weaves anecdotes into a system, we may be long in getting them, and get but few, in comparison of what we might get." *Bos.* 5.39. (*Hebrides*, 16 Aug.) 1773
3. * Anecdotes of literature among his favourite topics. *John. Misc.* 1.451. (Murphy) Date?

Annotations. See CRITICISM 38

Anonymity

1. ". . . it may be prudent for a writer, who apprehends that he shall not inforce his own maxims by his domestick character, to conceal his name, that he may not injure them." *Wks.* 5.93. (*Ram.* 14) 1750
2. "I have always thought it the duty of an anonymous author to write, as if he expected to be hereafter known." *Wks.* 7.394-5. (*Ram.* 208) 1752
3. J. in a friendly way chides J. Warton for publishing his *Essay on Pope* anonymously: "That way of publishing, without acquainting your friends, is a wicked trick." *Letters* 1.162-3. See *ib.* 63 *n* 1 for J.'s practice of omitting his name from the title page. 1756
4. * "A name immediately draws censure, unless it be a name that bears down everything before it." *Bos.* 3.43. See CUMBERLAND 1 for context. 1776
5. J. would not criticise an anonymous work, "for why should I put my name in the power of one who will not trust me with his own." *Letters* 2.235 1781

Anthologies. See also COMPILATIONS

1. * "He [J.] was a great friend to books like the French *Esprits d'un tel*; for example, *Beauties of Watts*, &c. &c. at which, said he, a man will often look and be tempted to go on, when he would have been frightened at books of a larger size and of a more erudite appearance." *John. Misc.* 2.2. (Hawkins's *Apophthegms*) Date ?

Antique Style. See also under IMITATION for Spenserian Imitations.
1. The "Dorick" pastoral language of "obsolete terms and rustick words" attacked. The principle of decorum upheld. See PASTORAL 2   1750
2. * Thomas Warton's bad antique style. See WARTON, T. 3, 4   1777
3. Obsolete forms of words attacked. See VERSIFICATION 20   1779
4. The *Proeme* to Gay's *Shepherd's Week* "written with such imitation as they could attain of obsolete language, and by consequence in a style that was never spoken nor written in any age or in any place." *Lives* 2.269   1781
5. Collins's diction "often harsh, unskilfully laboured, and injudiciously selected. He affected the obsolete when it was not worthy of revival; and he puts his words out of the common order." *Lives* 3.341   1781

Aphorisms. Compare EPIGRAM
1. "But, perhaps, the excellence of aphorisms consists not so much in the expression of some rare or abstruse sentiment, as in the comprehension of some obvious and useful truth in a few words . . . he may therefore be justly numbered among the benefactors of mankind, who contracts the great rules of life into short sentences, that may be easily impressed on the memory, and taught by frequent recollection to recur habitually to the mind." *Wks.* 7.206. (*Ram.* 175)   1751

Archaic Style. See ANTIQUE STYLE

Artificial
1. *Definition.* "3. Artful; contrived with skill." *Dict.*[1]   1755

[1] J. normally uses the word throughout his criticism in this favourable sense; e.g., "The parts seem artificially disposed, with sufficient coherence," etc. *Lives* 3.417.

Authors: Men vs. Women

1. ". . . the faculty of writing has been chiefly a masculine endowment." The "superiority of writing" of men. *Wks.* 5.117. (*Ram.* 18) 1750

Authors, Pitfalls for

2. The uncertainty of literary fame; demands of the public, of literary task-masters; dangers of patronage of the great, of success, etc. *Wks.* 5.140-143. (*Ram.* 21) 1750

Authors, Popular. See also AIM OF WRITING; FAME, LITERARY; OCCASIONAL WORKS

3. ". . . the author . . . who has judgement to discern the taste of his contemporaries, and skill to gratify it, will have always an opportunity to deserve well of mankind, by conveying instruction to them in a grateful vehicle." *Wks.* 9.79. (*Adv.* 95) 1753

Authors: Qualifications of an Author. See also AIM OF WRITING

4. ". . . he who has not obtained the proper qualifications of an author, can have no excuse for the arrogance of writing, but the power of imparting to mankind something necessary to be known." *Wks.* 9.120. (*Adv.* 115) 1753

5. Qualifications: "a perfect knowledge of the subject"; mastery of the language in which he writes; "a style clear, pure, nervous,[1] and expressive" "if he treats of science and demonstration"; "elegance and imagery" and "the colours of varied diction, and . . . the musick of modulated periods" necessary, "if his topicks be probable and persuasory." A careful study of the best authors the foundation of knowledge and style.

---

[1] See NERVOUS for note on this word.

"No man is a rhetorician or philosopher by chance."
Wks. 9.121-2. (*Adv.* 115)   1753

Authors, Self-Confidence of. See also under CRITICISM: *The Author as Self-Critic*

6. "There is something captivating in spirit and intrepidity [in the opening of a work], to which we often yield, as to a resistless power; nor can he reasonably expect the confidence of others, who too apparently distrusts himself." See OPENING 1   1750

7. "I know not whether, for the same reason [to avoid the distraction of conflicting advice] it is not necessary for an author to place some confidence in his own skill, and to satisfy himself in the knowledge that he has not deviated from the established laws of composition, without submitting his works to frequent examinations before he gives them to the publick. . . . It is, indeed, quickly discoverable, that consultation and compliance can conduce little to the perfection of any literary performance; for whoever is so doubtful of his own abilities as to encourage the remarks of others, will find himself every day embarrassed with new difficulties, and will harass his mind, in vain, with the hopeless labour of uniting heterogeneous ideas. . . ." *Wks.* 5.150-1. (*Ram.* 23)   1750

Authors, Value of. See also AIM OF WRITING

8. The exalted character of an author. See AIM OF WRITING 1   1739

9. Their importance, even when inferior, to the public welfare. *Wks.* 9.150-5. (*Adv.* 137)   1754

10. "The chief glory of every people arises from its authors." *Wks.* 9.227. (*Pref. Dict.*)   1755

11. * "Intellectual pre-eminence, he observed, was the highest superiority; and that every nation derived their highest reputation from the splendour and dignity of their writers." (Maxwell's *Collectanea.*) *Bos.* 2.125
                                         Date ?

Authority. See ANCIENT WRITERS; RULES

Autobiographical Element in an Author's Works. See also PRECEPT AND PRACTICE

1. "The biographer of Thomson has remarked that an author's life is best read in his works: his observation was not well-timed." Not true of Thomson. *Lives* 3.297-8   1781

Autobiography. Compare BIOGRAPHY. See DIARIES; MEMOIRS

1. Autobiography superior to biography. See BIOGRAPHY 5   1759

Ballads. See also under PERCY

1. The *Rambler* correspondent "Vivaculus" (presumably J.) satirises antiquarians, among them "Cantilenus," the collector of old ballads, who "considered them as the genuine records of the national taste. He offered to shew me a copy of *The Children in the Wood*, which he firmly believed to be of the first edition, and by the help of which, the text might be freed from several corruptions, if this age of barbarity had any claim to such favours from him." *Wks.* 7.218 (*Ram.* 177)
   1751
2. * "The ballad of Hardyknute has no great merit, if it be really ancient. People talk of nature. But mere obvious nature may be exhibited with very little power of mind." *Bos.* 2.91   1769
3. * J. treats modern imitations of ancient ballads "with that ridicule which he always displayed when that subject was mentioned." *Bos.* 2.212   1773
4. "In *Chevy Chase* there is not much of either bombast or affectation; but there is chill and lifeless imbecility. The story cannot possibly be told in a manner that shall make less impression on the mind." *Lives* 2.147-8
   Ptd. 1780

5. Abrupt beginning of *The Bard* "has been celebrated; but technical beauties can give praise only to the inventor. It is in the power of any man to rush abruptly upon his subject, that has read the ballad of *Johnny Armstrong*." *Lives* 3.439. See also OPENING 3 for similar remark. 1781
6. * "*Chevy Chase* pleased the vulgar, but did not satisfy the learned; it did not fill a mind capable of thinking strongly." A good work should do both. *Letters* 2.440, Appen. D. (Windham's *Diary*) 1784
7. * J. parodies modern ballad imitations, including one from Percy's *Reliques*.[1] See PERCY: *Reliques* for similar parodies. *John. Misc.* 1.192 Date?
8. * J. burlesques Percy's *Reliques*. *Wks.* 1.389-90. (Hawkins) Date ?

Barbarism

1. *Definition.* "A form of speech contrary to the purity and exactness of any language." *Dict.* 1755

Beginning of a Work. See OPENING OF A WORK

Biography. Compare AUTOBIOGRAPHY; DIARIES; MEMOIRS; HISTORY

1. ". . . the disposition generally found in writers of lives, to exalt every common occurrence and action into wonders. Are not indexes daily written by men who neither receive nor expect very loud applauses for their labours?" *Wks.* 4.478 *n* 1741
2. "The moderate . . . know that Princes have their Foibles as Mortals; but they know too, that it is the Duty of good Subjects to conceal them, and not to display those Weaknesses, which hurt that exalted Character, whence the Person who publishes them de-

---

[1] J., however, encouraged Percy to publish these ballads. See PERCY: *Reliques.*

rives her highest Honours." *Gent. Mag.* 1742, p. 298

1742

3. [a] *Superiority of biography:* "It is not easy for the most artful writer to give us an interest in happiness or misery, which we think ourselves never likely to feel, and with which we have never yet been made acquainted. . . . Those parallel circumstances and kindred images, to which we readily conform our minds, are, above all other writings, to be found in narratives of the lives of particular persons; and therefore no species of writing seems more worthy of cultivation than biography, since none can be more delightful or more useful, none can more certainly enchain the heart by irresistible interest, or more widely diffuse instruction to every diversity of condition. . . ." [b] *Its educational value:* "I have often thought that there has rarely passed a life of which a judicious and faithful narrative would not be useful. For, not only every man has, in the mighty mass of the world, great numbers in the same condition with himself, to whom his mistakes and miscarriages, escapes and expedients, would be of immediate and apparent use; but there is such an uniformity in the state of man, considered apart from adventitious and separable decorations and disguises, that there is scarce any possibility of good or ill, but is common to human kind. . . . We are all prompted by the same motives, all deceived by the same fallacies, all animated by hope, obstructed by danger, entangled by desire, and seduced by pleasure."

[c]*Proper subjects for biography:* not necessarily the man of public eminence, since "the business of the biographer is often to pass slightly over those performances and incidents, which produce vulgar greatness, to lead the thoughts into domestick privacies, and display the minute details of daily life, where exterior appendages are cast aside, and men excel each other only by prudence and virtue. . . . There are many

invisible circumstances which, whether we read as enquirers after natural or moral knowledge . . . are more important than publick occurrences." Examples: Sallust's description of the way Catiline walked, reveals character; a story of Melanchthon's punctuality "affords a striking lecture on the value of time," etc. [d] *Mistaken biographical methods:* many biographers "rarely afford any other account than might be collected from publick papers, but imagine themselves writing a life when they exhibit a chronological series of actions or preferments; and so little regard the manners or behaviour of their heroes, that more knowledge may be gained of a man's real character, by a short conversation with one of his servants, than from a formal and studied narrative, begun with his pedigree, and ended with his funeral. If now and then they condescend to inform the world of particular facts, they are not always so happy as to select the most important. I know not well what advantage posterity can receive from the only circumstance by which Tickell has distinguished Addison from the rest of mankind, *the irregularity of his pulse*," etc. [e] *A biographer's obstacles:* "If a life be delayed till interest and envy are at an end, we may hope for impartiality, but must expect little intelligence; for the incidents which give excellence to biography are of a volatile and evanescent kind, such as soon escape the memory, and are rarely transmitted by tradition. We know how few can pourtray a living acquaintance, except by his most prominent and observable particularities, and the grosser features of his mind; and it may be easily imagined how much of this little knowledge may be lost in imparting it, and how soon a succession of copies will lose all resemblance of the original. If the biographer writes from personal knowledge, and makes haste to gratify the publick curiosity, there is danger lest his interest, his fear, his gratitude, or his tenderness, overpower his fidelity, and tempt him to conceal, if not to invent. . . . If we owe regard to the memory of the dead, there is yet more respect to be paid to knowledge, to virtue, and to truth." *Wks.* 5.381-6. (*Ram.* 60)   1750

4. "Of every great and eminent character, part breaks forth into publick view, and part lies hid in domestick privacy." The former, "may, at any distance of time, be traced and estimated; but silent excellencies are soon forgotten; and those minute peculiarities which discriminate every man from all others, if they are not recorded by those whom personal knowledge enables to observe them, are irrecoverably lost." *Wks.* 4.604
     1756

5. "Biography is, of the various kinds of narrative writing, that which is most eagerly read, and most easily applied to the purposes of life." Romances appeal chiefly in youth; history of little use in regulating life. But biographies "which are levelled with the general surface of life, which tell not how any man became great, but how he was made happy; not how he lost the favour of his prince, but how he became discontented with himself,"—these the most useful to mankind. "Those relations are therefore commonly of most value in which the writer tells his own story." The biographer of another, commonly "endeavours to hide the man that he may produce a hero"—or a villain. "But he that speaks of himself has no motive to falsehood or partiality except self-love, by which all have so often been betrayed, that all are on the watch against its artifices."[1] *Wks.* 8.339-42. (*Idl.* 84)
     1759

6. * ". . . the biographical part of literature, which is what I love most." *Bos.* 1.425   1763

---

[1] The opening paragraphs of Goldsmith's *Life of Richard Nash* (published in 1762) are indebted to this essay both for matter and even, in several instances, for phraseology.

7. "The little things which distinguish domestick characters are soon forgotten: if you delay to enquire, you will have no information; if you neglect to write, information will be vain." *Bos* 2.17   1766
8. * ". . . nobody can write the life of a man, but those who have eat and drunk and lived in social intercourse with him." *Bos.* 2.166   1772
9. * "MONBODDO. 'The history of manners is the most valuable. I never set a high value on any other history.' JOHNSON. 'Nor I; and therefore I esteem biography, as giving us what comes near to ourselves, what we can turn to use.' BOSWELL. 'But in the course of general history, we find manners. . . . JOHNSON. 'Yes; but then you must take all the facts to get this; and it is but a little you get.' " *Bos.* 5.79. (*Hebrides*, 21 Aug.)   1773
10. * "M'Leod asked, if it was not wrong in Orrery to expose the defects of a man [Swift] with whom he lived in intimacy. JOHNSON. 'Why no, Sir, after the man is dead; for then it is done historically.' " *Bos.* 5.238. (*Hebrides*, 22 Sept.)   1773
11. * J. "did not think that the life of any literary man in England had been well written. Beside the common incidents of life, it should tell us his studies, his mode of living, the means by which he attained to excellence, and his opinion of his own works." *Bos.* 5.240. (*Hebrides*, 22 Sept.)   1773
12. * "If a man is to write *A Panegyrick*, he may keep vices out of sight; but if he professes to write *A Life*, he must represent it really as it was." e.g. Parnell's drinking would act as a warning to others. *Bos.* 3.155   1773
13. * "It [biography] is rarely well executed. They only who live with a man can write his life with any genuine exactness and discrimination; and few people who have lived with a man know what to remark about him." *Bos.* 2.446   1776

14. * "Sir, there is no doubt as to peculiarities: the question is, whether a man's vices should be mentioned . . . so that more ill may be done by the example, than good by telling the whole truth." *Bos.* 3.155
1777

15. "The necessity of complying with times and of sparing persons is the great impediment of biography. . . . What is known can seldom be immediately told, and when it might be told it is no longer known. The delicate features of the mind, the nice discriminations of character, and the minute peculiarities of conduct are soon obliterated; and it is surely better that caprice, obstinacy, frolick, and folly, however they might delight in the description, should be silently forgotten than that by wanton merriment and unseasonable detection a pang should be given to a widow, a daughter, a brother, or a friend." J., about to describe his contemporaries in his *Lives*, feels himself "'walking upon ashes under which the fire is not extinguished,' and coming to the time of which it will be proper rather to say 'nothing that is false, than all that is true.'" *Lives* 2.116   Ptd. 1780

16. "From any minute knowledge of his [Addison's] familiar manners the intervention of sixty years has now debarred us." *Lives* 2.124. (cf. *Lives* 1.408)
Ptd. 1780

17. * J., defending his life of Lyttelton, observed "that it was the *duty* of a biographer to state *all* the failings of a respectable character." *John. Misc.* 2.417. (Pepys)   1781

18. *J.'s defence of his severely criticized *Life of Lyttelton*: "Sir, I considered myself entrusted with a certain portion of truth. I have given my opinion sincerely; let them shew where they think me wrong." *Bos.* 4.65
cir. 1781

19. * "If nothing but the bright side of characters should

be shewn, we should sit down in despondency, and think it utterly impossible to imitate them in *any thing.* The sacred writers (he observed) related the vicious as well as the virtuous actions of men; which had this moral effect, that it kept mankind from *despair."* Bos. 4.53 *cir.* 1781

20. * "When accused of mentioning ridiculous anecdotes in the lives of the poets, he [J.] said, he should not have been an exact biographer if he had omitted them. The business of such a one, said he, is to give a complete account of the person whose life he is writing, and to discriminate him from all other persons by any peculiarities of character or sentiment he may happen to have." *John. Misc.* 2.3. (Hawkins's *Apophthegms*)
cir. 1781

21. * J. "was extremely fond of reading the lives of great and learned persons." *John.Misc.* 2.8. (Hawkins's *Apophthegms*) Date ?

22. * "Biography was a kind of writing that he delighted in." *Wks.* 1.151. *Life* by Hawkins. See also Murphy's similar testimony, *John. Misc.* 1.451 Date ?

Blank Verse and Rhyme. See also under VERSIFICATION

1. * "He enlarged very convincingly upon the excellence of rhyme over blank verse in English poetry. . . . JOHNSON. 'Sir, I was once in company with [Adam] Smith, and we did not take to each other; but had I known that he loved rhyme as much as you tell me he does, I should have HUGGED him.'" *Bos.* 1.427-8
1763

2. The "interposition of a long paragraph of blank verses [in a poem written in heroic couplets] is unwarrantably licentious." *Lives* 1.237 1779

3. Dryden "made rhyming tragedies till, by the prevalence of manifest propriety, he seems to have grown ashamed of making them any longer." *Lives* 1.337-8
1779

4. The greater difficulty of rhyme. *Lives* 1.237-8   1779
5. "Versification, free, like his, [Milton's] from the distresses of rhyme." *Lives* 1.139   1779
6. "Easier than rhyme." *Lives* 1.192-4   1779
7. " 'Rhyme,' he [Milton] says, and says truly, 'is no necessary adjunct of true poetry.' But perhaps of poetry as a mental operation metre or musick is no necessary adjunct; it is however by the musick of metre that poetry has been discriminated in all languages, and in languages melodiously constructed with a due proportion of long and short syllables metre is sufficient. But one language cannot communicate its rules to another; where metre is scanty and imperfect some help is necessary. The musick of the English heroick line strikes the ear so faintly that it is easily lost, unless all the syllables of every line co-operate together; this co-operation can be only obtained by the preservation of every verse unmingled with another as a distinct system of sounds, and this distinctness is obtained and preserved by the artifice of rhyme. The variety of pauses, so much boasted by the lovers of blank verse, changes the measures of an English poet to the periods of a declaimer; and there are only a few skilful and happy readers of Milton who enable their audience to perceive where the lines end or begin. 'Blank verse,' said an ingenious critick, 'seems to be verse only to the eye.' Poetry may subsist without rhyme, but English poetry will not often please; nor can rhyme ever be safely spared but where the subject is able to support itself. Blank verse makes some approach to that which is called the 'lapidary style'; has neither the easiness of prose nor the melody of numbers, and therefore tires by long continuance. Of the Italian writers without rhyme, whom Milton alleges as precedents, not one is popular; what reason could urge in its defence has been confuted by the ear. But whatever be the advantage of rhyme I cannot prevail on myself to wish that Milton

had been a rhymer, for I cannot wish his work to be other than it is; yet like other heroes he is to be admired rather than imitated. He that thinks himself capable of astonishing may write blank verse, but those that hope only to please must condescend to rhyme." *Lives* 1.192-4   1779

8. "Blank verse left merely to its numbers has little operation either on the ear or mind: it can hardly support itself without bold figures and striking images. A poem frigidly didactick without rhyme is so near to prose that the reader only scorns it for pretending to be verse." *Lives* 1.237   1779

9. J. Philips in *Cyder* "unhappily pleased himself with blank verse, and supposed that the numbers of Milton, which impress the mind with veneration, combined as they are with subjects of inconceivable grandeur, could be sustained by images which at most can rise only to elegance. Contending angels may shake the regions of heaven in blank verse; but the flow of equal measures and the embellishment of rhyme must recommend to our attention the art of engrafting, and decide the merit of the 'redstreak' and 'pearmain.'" *Lives* 1.319-20   1779

10. "His [Fenton's] translation from Homer into blank verse will find few readers while another can be had in rhyme." *Lives* 2.264   Ptd. 1780

11. "Sublime and solemn prose gains little by a change into blank verse." *Lives* 2.264   Ptd. 1780

12. Pope adopted blank verse for his projected epic "with great imprudence." See EPIC 9   1781

13. Watts "writes too often . . . in blank verse." *Lives* 3.311   1781

14. Dyer's *The Fleece*: ". . . the disgust which blank verse, encumbering and encumbered, superadds to an unpleasing subject, soon repels the reader." *Lives* 3.346   1781

15. Shenstone's "blank verses, those that can read them may probably find to be like the blank verses of his neighbours." J. adds, concerning Shenstone's *Love and Honour*: "I wish it well enough to wish it were in rhyme." *Lives* 3.358　　　　　　　　　　1781
16. Mallet's *Amyntor and Theodora* has "copiousness and elegance of language, vigour of sentiment, and imagery . . . But it is blank verse." *Lives* 3.406　　　1781
17. Somerville's *Chace* undertaken "in his maturer age, when his ear was improved to the approbation of blank verse. . . . With still less judgement [than in his choice of subject] did he chuse blank verse as the vehicle of *Rural Sports*. If blank verse be not tumid and gorgeous, it is crippled prose; and familiar images in laboured language have nothing to recommend them but absurd novelty which, wanting the attractions of Nature, cannot please long. One excellence of *The Splendid Shilling* is that it is short. Disguise can gratify no longer than it deceives." *Lives* 2.319-20
　　　　　　　　　　　　　　　　　　　　1781
18. Thomson's *Seasons* "is one of the works in which blank verse seems properly used; Thomson's wide expansion of general views, and his enumeration of circumstantial varieties, would have been obstructed and embarrassed by the frequent intersection of the sense, which are the necessary effects of rhyme." *Lives* 3.299　　　　　　　　　　　　　　　　1781
19. Young's *Night Thoughts* "is one of the few poems in which blank verse could not be changed for rhyme but with disadvantage. The wild diffusion of the sentiments and the digressive sallies of imagination would have been compressed and restrained by confinement to rhyme." *Lives* 3.395　　　　　1781
20. "Praise should not be denied" to the blank verse in Akenside's *The Pleasures of Imagination*. "In the general fabrication of his lines he is perhaps superior to any other writer of blank verse; his flow is smooth

and his pauses are musical, but the concatenation of his verses is commonly too long continued, and the full close does not recur with sufficient frequency. The sense is carried on through a long intertexture of complicated clauses, and as nothing is distinguished, nothing is remembered. The exemption which blank verse affords from the necessity of closing the sense with the couplet, betrays luxuriant and active minds into such self-indulgence that they pile image upon image, ornament upon ornament, and are not easily persuaded to close the sense at all. Blank verse will therefore, I fear, be too often found in description exuberant, in argument loquacious, and in narration tiresome. . . . He is to be commended as having fewer artifices of disgust than most of his brethren of the blank song. He rarely either recalls old phrases or twists his metre into harsh inversions. The sense, however, of his words is strained. . . . And the pedant surely intrudes—but when was blank verse without pedantry?—when he tells how 'Planets absolve the stated round of Time.' " *Lives* 3.417-18   1781

21. * His "usual contempt for blank verse" illustrated. See DODSLEY 2   Date?

22. * "He was no admirer of blank-verse, and said it always failed, unless sustained by the dignity of the subject. In blank-verse . . . the language suffered more distortion, to keep it out of prose, than any inconvenience or limitation to be apprehended from the shackles and circumspection of rhyme." *Bos.* 2.124. (Maxwell's *Collectanea*)   Date ?

23. * Pope could translate Homer more easily into rhyme. J.:—"Sir, when Pope said that, he knew that he lied." *John. Misc.* 2.332. (Stockdale)   Date ?

Burlesque. For Johnson's parodies, see BALLADS 7, 8

1. Some exaggeration permitted in burlesque. See NATURE 17   1752

2. *Definition of Burlesque* (*adj.*): "Jocular; tending to raise laughter, by unnatural or unsuitable language or images." *Dict.* 1755
3. ". . . such probability [of action] as burlesque requires." *Lives* 1.216 1779
4. "Burlesque consists in a disproportion between the style and the sentiments, or between the adventitious sentiments and the fundamental subject," and therefore contains a principle of corruption. "All disproportion is unnatural; and from what is unnatural we can derive only the pleasure which novelty produces. We admire it awhile as a strange thing; but, when it is no longer strange, we perceive its deformity. It is a kind of artifice, which by frequent repetition detects itself." *Lives* 1.218 1779
5. Burlesquing Scriptures condemned. *Lives* 2.247 and 3.215 1780-81

Cadence

1. *Definition.* "The flow of verses, or periods." *Dict.*
1755

Cæsura

1. *Definition.* "A figure in poetry, by which a short syllable after a complete foot is made long."[1] *Dict.*
1755

Candour

1. *Definition.* "Sweetness of temper;[2] purity of mind; openness; ingenuity; kindness." (No other meanings given.) *Dict.* 1755

---

[1] J. uses the word in the sense of pause, in "their break or *cæsura*." (*Lives* 1.467) See VERSIFICATION 23 for similar use of the term.

[2] e.g., *Wks.* 6.141: "Criticism has so often given occasion to the envious and ill-natured of gratifying their malignity, that some have thought it necessary to recommend the virtue of candour without restriction, and to preclude all future liberty of censure."

Cant[1]

1. *Definition.* "2. A particular form of speaking peculiar to some certain class or body of men. . . . 3. A whining pretension to goodness, in formal and affected terms. . . . 4. Barbarous jargon." *Dict.*   1755

Chance. Compare COMPOSITION

1. * "Colman never produced a luckier thing than his first Ode in ridicule of Gray. A considerable part of it may be numbered among those felicities which no man has twice attained." Johnson, quoted by Steevens. *John. Misc.* 2.320. See also *ib.* 2.254 and *Bos.* 2.334. For the partnership of genius and chance, see GENIUS 7, 16, 17, 25   Date?

Change of Opinions

1. Excuses for change of heart toward a person, though "often plausible and sometimes just . . . are very seldom satisfactory to mankind, and the writer, who is not constant to his subject, quickly sinks into contempt, his satire loses its force, and his panegyrick its value, and he is only considered at one time as a flatterer, and as a calumniator at another. To avoid these imputations it is only necessary to follow the rules of virtue, and to preserve an unvaried regard to truth." Doing so, there will be occasional deceptions, but infrequent errors; "and it will be allowed that the name of an author would never have been made contemptible had no man ever said what he did not

---

[1] A favourite Johnsonian weapon of attack, illustrated by such phrases as: "the despicable cant of literary modesty," (*Lives* 2. 98); "the cant of an author," (*ib.* 3. 91); "the Verses cant of shepherds and flocks," (*ib.* 3. 446); "the cant of those who judge by principles rather than perception," (*ib.* 3. 248); "'Idalia's velvet-green' has something of cant," (*ib.* 3. 436); "such cant of sensibility," (*ib.* 3. 106); "the common cant of superficial satirists," (*ib.* 3. 266); "this fugitive cant [of commerce and business]," (*Wks.* 9. 221). For other instances of its use, see *Bos.* 4. 221 *n* 1. R. P. McCutcheon has traced the earlier history of the word in "A Note on Cant," (*Mod. Lang. Notes*, 36. 22 *ff.*).

think, or misled others but when he was himself deceived." *Lives* 2.359-60. Compare CRITICISM 83

1744

Characters. See under DRAMA and DRAMATIC PROPRIETY. For historical characters, see HISTORY 11, 19; and for pastoral characters, see PASTORAL 2C

Clarity. See OBSCURITY

Classic (N.)
1. *Definition.* "An author of the first rank: usually taken for ancient authors." *Dict.* 1755

Classical; Classic (ADJ.)
1. *Definition.* "1. Relating to antique authors; relating to literature." "2. Of the first order or rank." *Dict.*

1755

Close (ADJ.)
1. *Definition.* "6. Concise; brief; without exuberance or digression." *Dict.* 1755

Comedy. See under DRAMA

Common Sense. See GOOD SENSE

Compilations
1. Compilations have their use, but a multiplicity of them apt to indicate an age of literary stagnation. Their fame usually temporary. *Wks.* 8.343-6. (*Idl.* 85) 1759

COMPOSITION

Composition. See also DRAMA: *Play-Writing;* GENIUS; CHANCE; IMAGINATION; INVENTION. For rules of composition, see under RULES

1. *Diligence:* Inequality of performance of an author not obviated by ability or industry. *Wks.* 5.141. (*Ram.* 21) 1750
2. *Effect of seasons on composition:* "To the men of study and imagination the winter is generally the chief time of labour. Gloom and silence produce composure of mind, and concentration of ideas." *Wks.* 6.57. (*Ram.* 80) 1750
3. "Wit depends upon a thousand casualties . . . it is very little in a man's power. That no man can appoint an hour in which he will be witty. . . . The first principle of wit out of our power. . . . Misery of writing without the vein then flowing. The happy have their days, and the unhappy, and the genius the happy, who has flows often and knows their value. The little power men have over their effusions Genius made ancients attribute to impulse." J.'s "Adversaria" or notes for the *Rambler,* partly worked up in *Rambler* 101: (*Wks.* 1.457n) *cir.* 1750
4. *Writing for money justified. Wks.* 1.268 n.
cir. 1750
5. *Diligence:* The relation between diligence and genius in composition. See GENIUS 5 1751
6. *Hasty compositions perishable:*[1] Labour and study but rarely superseded by transcendent abilities. A chief cause of the superiority of the ancients to the moderns is the former's diligence. "Delay opens new veins of thought, the subject dismissed for a time appears with a new train of dependent images, the accidents of reading or conversation supply new ornaments or al-

---

[1] This apparent contradiction of Johnson's own practice of haste, is clarified if we make the distinction between compositions hastily *conceived* and those hastily *executed.* See *infra,* 36.

lusions, or mere intermission of the fatigue of thinking enables the mind to collect new force, and make new excursions." Obscurity one of the most pernicious effects of haste. *Wks.* 7.169-74. (*Ram.* 169) 1751
7. The distresses of composition for periodicals. See PERIODICAL WRITINGS 4 1752
8. *Diligence and style:* "No man is a rhetorician or philosopher by chance." See AUTHORS 5 1753
9. *Diligence:* "Composition is, for the most part, an effort of slow diligence and steady perseverance, to which the mind is dragged by necessity or resolution, and from which the attention is every moment starting to more delightful amusements." The difficulties of composition described. *Wks.* 9.158. (*Adv.* 138) 1754
10. *Diligence:* Pope's epitaph *On Mr. Gay* "probably written with an uncommon degree of attention; yet it is not more successfully executed than the rest, for it will not always happen that the success of a poet is proportionate to his labour. The same observation may be extended to all works of imagination, which are often influenced by causes wholly out of the performer's power, by hints of which he perceives not the origin, by sudden elevations of mind which he cannot produce in himself, and which sometimes rise when he expects them least." *Lives* 3.268 1756
11. *Diligence:* ". . . is never wholly lost." *Lives* 3.338
 1763
12. * *Writing for money:* "I look upon this [edition of Shakespeare] as I did upon the dictionary: it is all work, and my inducement to it is not love or desire of fame, but the want of money, which is the only motive to writing that I know of." *Wks.* 1.362. (Hawkins's *Life*) *cir.* 1764
13. *Rapid composition:* ". . . neither genius nor practice will always supply a hasty writer with the most proper diction." *Shak.*, Raleigh, 194 1765

14. *Diligence:* ". . . success in works of invention is not always proportionate to labour." *Shak.*, Raleigh, 113
   1765

15. *Seasons and composition:* "Between Easter and Whitsuntide, having always considered that time as propitious to study, I attempted to learn the Low Dutch language." *Bos.* 2.263. cf. *Idl.* 11
   1773

16. * ". . . a man may write at any time, if he will set himself *doggedly* to it." *Bos.* 5.40. (*Hebrides*, 16 Aug.)
   1773

17. * *J.'s method of composition:* "It was easier to him to write poetry than to compose his *Dictionary*. His mind was less on the stretch in doing the one than the other." *Bos.* 5.47. (*Hebrides*, 17 Aug.)
   1773

18. * *Rapid composition:* J. advises the novice to acquire the habit of rapid composition. *Bos.* 5.66-7. (*Hebrides*, 19 Aug.)
   1773

19. * *J.'s rapid composition:* "I have begun a sermon after dinner, and sent it off by the post that night. I wrote forty-eight of the printed octavo pages of the *Life of Savage* at a sitting; but then I sat up all night. I have also written six sheets in a day of translation from the French." *Bos.* 5.67. (*Hebrides*, 19 Aug.) See also *John. Misc.* 1.446-7
   1773

20. "The lucky moments of animated imagination" cannot be waited for by the occasional writer. See OCCASIONAL WORKS 12
   1779

21. ". . . those felicities which cannot be produced at will by wit and labour, but must arise unexpectedly in some hour propitious to poetry." *Lives* 1.79
   1779

22. *Diligence:* "It happened to Waller, as to others, that his success was not always in proportion to his labour." *Lives* 1.287
   1779

23. Effect of poverty on composition. See DRYDEN 10
   1779

24. *Climate and composition:* J. scoffs at connection, speaking of Milton. *Lives* 1.137-8. For instances, however, where J. acknowledges the influence of the weather on human actions, see *Letters* 1.346; 2.233; *Bos.* 4.360   1779
25. The pleasure of composition makes it difficult for an author to detect his own tediousness. See CRITICISM 5 and other passages under CRITICISM: THE AUTHOR AS SELF-CRITIC   Ptd. 1780
26. *Advice on the composition of sermons:* ". . . in the labour of composition, do not burthen your mind with too much at once; do not exact from yourself at one effort of excogitation, propriety of thought and elegance of expression. Invent first, and then embellish. The production of something, where nothing was before, is an act of greater energy than the expansion or decoration of the thing produced. Set down diligently your thoughts as they rise, in the first words that occur; and, when you have matter, you will easily give it form: nor, perhaps, will this method be always necessary; for by habit, your thoughts and diction will flow together." *Bos.* 3.437   1780
27. Gray's "fantastick foppery" in thinking he could write only "at certain times, or at happy moments." *Lives* 3.433   1781
28. *Diligence:* ". . . what is easy is seldom excellent." *Lives* 3.247   1781
29. *Diligence:* Watts's "poems on other subjects . . . have different degrees of value as they are more or less laboured." *Lives* 3.310   1781
30. *Different methods of composition:* Pope's method: "He was one of those few whose labour is their pleasure," etc. See POPE 15. See also *Bos.* 2.99; 4.219   1781
31. *J.'s method of composition: Lives of the Poets* written "in my usual way, dilatorily and hastily, unwilling to

work, and working with vigour and haste." *John. Misc.* 1.96   1781

32. * *J.'s method of composition:* J. doubts that the writing of poetry is pleasurable at the time: "I know when I have been writing verses, I have run my finger down the margin, to see how many I had made, and how few I had to make." *Bos.* 4.219   1783

33. * "What is written without effort . . . is in general read without pleasure." *John. Misc.* 2.309. (Seward's *Biog.*)   Date ?

34. * J. would not "distinguish between those writings which are the effect of a natural impulse of genius, and those other that owe their existence to interested motives. . . . I have, more than once, heard him assert, that he knew of no genuine motive for writing, other than necessity." *Wks.* 1.27. (Hawkins's *Life.*) See also *Wks.* 1.84 for similar statement by Hawkins.   Date ?

35. **J.'s method of composition:* "He [J.] told him [Reynolds] that he had early laid it down as a fixed rule to do his best on every occasion, and in every company; to impart whatever he knew in the most forcible language he could put it in; and that by constant practice, and never suffering any careless expressions to escape him, or attempting to deliver his thoughts without arranging them in the clearest manner, it became habitual to him." *Bos.* 1.204
    Date ?

36. * *J.'s method of composition:* Perfects his compositions in his mind, before committing them to paper. *John. Misc.* 2.215-6. (Percy.) See also *ib.* 2.313-4
    Date ?

37. * *Early composition:* "A man, he observed, should begin to write soon; for, if he waits till his judgement is matured, his inability, through want of practice to express his conceptions, will make the disproportion so

great between what he sees, and what he can attain, that he will probably be discouraged from writing at all." *Bos.* 4.12. (Langton's *Collection*) Date ?

Concatenation

1. *Definition.* "A series of links; an uninterrupted unvariable succession."[1] *Dict.* 1755

Conceit. For "Verbal Conceits" see PUNS

1. "1. Conception; thought; idea; image in the mind . . . 2. Understanding; readiness of apprehension . . . 3. Opinion, generally in a sense of contempt; fancy; imagination; fantastical notion . . . 4. Opinion in a neutral sense . . . 5. A pleasant fancy . . . 6. Sentiment, as distinguished from imagery . . . 7. Fondness; favourable opinion; opinionative pride."[2] *Dict.* 1755

Conversation, Reliability of

1. ". . . nor would it perhaps be wholly just [to relate the result of Mr. Savage's inquiry into the merits of the great], because what he asserted in conversation might, though true in general, be heightened by some momentary ardour of imagination," or imperfectly remembered or reported. *Lives* 2.372 1744

2. "The graces of writing and conversation are of different kinds . . . as many please by extemporary talk, though utterly unacquainted with the more accurate method, and more laboured beauties, which composition requires; so it is very possible that men, wholly accustomed to works of study, may be without that

---

[1] e.g., "the concatenation of his verses is commonly too long continued," (*Lives* 3.417); Young's style "is sometimes concatenated and sometimes abrupt ["unconnected"—*Dict.*], sometimes diffusive and sometimes concise." (*ib.* 3.393.)

[2] J. normally uses the word in its third sense: "fantastical notion," e.g., "Nothing can be more disgusting than a narrative spangled with conceits." (*Lives* 1.51); "remote conceits" unsuited to tragedy. See SENTIMENT 2.

readiness of conception, and affluence of language, always necessary to colloquial entertainment." *Wks.* 5.94. (*Ram.* 14) 1750

3. ". . . a man heated in talk, and eager of victory, takes advantage of the mistakes or ignorance of his adversary, lays hold of concessions to which he knows he has no right, and urges proofs likely to prevail on his opponent, though he knows himself that they have no force.[1] . . . To fix the thoughts by writing, and subject them to frequent examinations and reviews, is the best method of enabling the mind to detect its own sophisms, and keep it on guard against the fallacies which it practises on others: in conversation we naturally diffuse our thoughts, and in writing we contract them; method is the excellence of writing, and unconstraint the grace of conversation. To read, write, and converse in due proportions, is, therefore, the business of a man of letters." *Wks.* 9.66-7. (*Adv.* 85) 1753

Correctness

1. "Accuracy; exactness; freedom from faults." *Dict.* For modern interpretations of the term, see *Lives* 2.145 *n* 3, and *ib.* 3.93 *n* 3 1755
2. "The work of a correct and regular writer" compared to the superior, though unequal, beauties of Shakespeare. See SHAKESPEARE 76 1765
3. Prior's correctness described. See PRIOR 3 Ptd. 1780

Criticism: The Author as Self-Critic. See also AUTHORS 6, 7; Compare POPULAR JUDGEMENT

1. The highest genius liable to misjudge himself: "that judgment which appears so penetrating, when it is employed upon the works of others, very often fails where interest or passion can exert their power. We

---

[1] For J's inconsistency in conversation, see Hawkins's charge (*Wks.* 1.257), and Mrs. Piozzi's (*John Misc.* 1.185).

are blinded in examining our own labours by innumerable prejudices. Our juvenile compositions please us, because they bring to our minds the remembrance of youth; our later performances we are ready to esteem, because we are unwilling to think that we have made no improvement; what flows easily from the pen charms us, because we read with pleasure that which flatters our opinion of our own powers; what was composed with great struggles of the mind we do not easily reject, because we cannot bear that so much labour should be fruitless. But the reader has none of these prepossessions. . . ." *Wks.* 5.143. (*Ram.* 21) 1750

2. The partiality of an author towards his own work. *Wks.* 9.160. (*Adv.* 138) 1754

3. Milton preferred *Paradise Regained* to *Paradise Lost*: "Many causes may vitiate a writer's judgement of his own works. On that which has cost him much labour he sets a high value, because he is unwilling to think that he has been diligent in vain: what has been produced without toilsome efforts is considered with delight as a proof of vigorous faculties and fertile invention; and the last work, whatever it be, has necessarily most of the grace of novelty. Milton, however it happened, had this prejudice, and had it to himself." *Lives* 1.147 1779

4. ". . . of the plan and disposition, and all that can be reduced to principles of science, the author may depend upon his own opinion; but . . . in those parts where fancy predominates self-love may easily deceive." *Lives* 1.340 1779

5. "Unhappily this pernicious failure [to please: See AIM OF WRITING 22] is that which an author is least able to discover. We are seldom tiresome to ourselves; and the act of composition fills and delights the mind with change of language and succession of images: every couplet when produced is new, and novelty is the great source of pleasure. Perhaps no man ever

thought a line superfluous when he first wrote it, or contracted his work till his ebullitions of invention had subsided. And even if he should controul his desire of immediate renown, and keep his work *nine years* unpublished, he will be still the author, and still in danger of deceiving himself; and if he consults his friends, he will probably find men who have more kindness than judgement, or more fear to offend than desire to instruct." *Lives* 2.206-7. See also ROBERTSON 5
                                                      Ptd. 1780

6. Pope not hasty about publication of his work. "He suffered the tumult of imagination to subside, and the novelties of invention to grow familiar. He knew that the mind is always enamoured of its own productions, and did not trust his first fondness. He consulted his friends, and listened with great willingness to criticism; and, what was of more importance, he consulted himself, and let nothing pass against his own judgement." *Lives* 3.220   1781

7. "Upon this great poem [Thomson's *Liberty*] two years were spent, and the author congratulated himself upon it as his noblest work; but an author and his reader are not always of a mind . . . none of Thomson's performances were so little regarded. The judgement of the publick was not erroneous," etc. *Lives* 3.289   1781

8. Danger in solitude of judgement, but "it was the felicity of Pope to rate himself at his real value." *Lives* 3.89   1781

Criticism, Dramatic. See under DRAMA

Criticism, The Effect of

9. "It is not unpleasing to remark with what solicitude men of acknowledged abilities will endeavour to palliate absurdities and reconcile contradictions, only to obviate criticisms to which all human performances must ever be exposed, and from which they can never

suffer, but when they teach the world by a vain and ridiculous impatience to think them of importance." *Wks.* 5.201. (*Ram.* 31) 1750
10. The harmful example set by critics who perpetually censure. *Wks.* 8.12. (*Idl.* 3.) cf. *infra* 53, 54, 75
1758
11. "No genius was ever blasted by the breath of criticks." *Wks.* 8.238. (*Idl.* 60) 1759
12. * The value of hostile criticism to authors, especially "in subjects of taste, where you cannot confute." *Bos.* 5.273-5. (*Hebrides*, 1 Oct.) 1773
13. (To Mrs. Thrale): "Never let criticisms operate upon your face or your mind; it is very rarely that an author is hurt by his criticks. The blaze of reputation cannot be blown out, but it often dies in the socket; a very few names may be considered as perpetual lamps that shine unconsumed." *Letters* 2.148. For similar expressions of opinion and for J.'s own insensibility to hostile criticism, see *Bos.* 2.61 *n* 4; 1.199-200; 5.400-401 1780

Criticism: Historical Method

14. If Savage's *Tragedy of Sir Thomas Overbury* not perfect, consider circumstances surrounding production: its faults "must rather excite pity than provoke censure." *Lives* 2.339 1744
15. J. defends Shakespeare's use of the witches in *Macbeth* on the ground that "in order to make a true estimate of the abilities and merit of a writer, it is always necessary to examine the genius of his age, and the opinions of his contemporaries." The credulity of Shakespeare's audience not over-burdened by such enchantment. *Wks.* 14.60, 64. (*Observ. on Macb.*)
1745
16. Letter to Thomas Warton on receiving his *Observations on The Faery Queen of Spenser:* "You have shewn to all, who shall hereafter attempt the study of

our ancient authours, the way to success; by directing them to the perusal of the books which those authours had read. Of this method, Hughes and men much greater than Hughes, seem never to have thought. The reason why the authours, which are yet read, of the sixteenth century, are so little understood, is, that they are read alone; and no help is borrowed from those who lived with them, or before them. Some part of this ignorance I hope to remove by my book [the *Dictionary*]." *Bos.* 1.270   1754

17. "Authors are often praised for improvement, or blamed for innovation, with very little justice, by those who read few other books of the same age." *Wks.* 9.233-4. (*Shak. Proposals*)   1756

18. An historical method of approach to Shakespeare advocated: one must understand the manners, superstitions, traditions, language, and literature of his age in order to clarify Shakespeare. This the underlying thought of J.'s *Proposals for Printing the Works of Shakespeare. Shak.*, Raleigh, pp. 1 *ff.*   1756

19. "Every man's performances, to be rightly estimated, must be compared with the state of the age in which he lived, and with his own particular opportunities; and though to the reader a book be not worse or better for the circumstances of the authour, yet . . . as the enquiry, how far man may extend his designs, or how high he may rate his native force, is of far greater dignity than in what rank we shall place any particular performance, curiosity is always busy to discover the instruments, as well as to survey the workmanship, to know how much is to be ascribed to original powers, and how much to casual and adventitious help." *Shak. Pref.*, Raleigh, 30-1   1765

20. "Those who have no power to judge of past times but by their own, should always doubt their conclusions." *Lives* 1.143   1779

21. Waller's thoughts may have been novel in his own

time—"Let not the original author lose by his imitators." *Lives* 1.294-5   1779

22. "To judge rightly of an author we must transport ourselves to his time, and examine what were the wants of his contemporaries, and what were his means of supplying them." *Lives* 1.411   1779

23. J. meets the charge that Pope's *Homer* not Homerical: ". . . it must be remembered that 'necessitas quod cogit defendit,' that may be lawfully done which cannot be forborne. Time and place will always enforce regard. In estimating this translation consideration must be had of the nature of our language, the form of our metre, and, above all, of the change which two thousand years have made in the modes of life and the habits of thought." The progress of learning is from simplicity to refinement: "What was expedient to Virgil was necessary to Pope . . . Pope wrote for his own age and his own nation: he knew that it was necessary to colour the images and point the sentiments of his author; he therefore made him graceful, but lost him some of his sublimity." *Lives* 3.238-40
     1781

Criticism, Principles and Function of. See *infra* CRITICISM, TIME AS AN AID TO; and *supra* CRITICISM: *Historical Method.* See also AIM OF WRITING; EXPERIENCE (AS A CRITICAL TEST); RULES; POPULAR JUDGEMENT; and for dramatic criticism, under DRAMA

24. "Though I would not often assume the critic's privilege, of being confident where certainty cannot be obtained. . . ." *Wks.* 14.88. (*Observ. on Macb.*)
     1745

25. J. censures Fenton's criticism of Roscommon as "too general to be critically just." *Wks.* 14.417 *n.* (*Life of Roscommon*)   1748

26. *Allegory on Criticism:* [a] Criticism, eldest daughter of Labour and of Truth, cared for by Justice in the palace of Wisdom. Appointed the governess of Fancy, and impowered to beat time to the chorus of the Muses. Carries sceptre given by Justice, and an unextinguishable torch, which shows everything in its true form: exposes sophistry, rhetoric disguising falsehood, "disproportion of parts," etc. Works with such faults are refused immortality or destroyed by oblivion. [b] *Time as an aid to Criticism:* In doubtful cases, Time decides. "The proceedings of TIME, though very dilatory, were, some few caprices excepted, conformable to justice." Criticism withdraws, leaving Time to combat Prejudice and False Taste, "contenting herself thenceforth to shed her influence from afar upon some select minds, fitted for its reception by learning and by virtue." Fragments of her sceptre seized by Flattery, Malevolence and their slaves, who are subject to Power or Interest or seek only faults; while "TIME passes his sentence at leisure, without any regard to their determinations." *Wks.* 5.16-19. (*Ram.* 3) 1750

27. Minerva sends Criticism to the aid of Learning, attacked by the poisoned arrows of "Satyr". Criticism "generally broke the point of SATYR's arrows, turned them aside, or retorted them on himself." *Wks.* 5.147-8. (*Ram.* 22; Allegory on Wit and Learning) 1750

28. "It is, however, the task of criticism to establish principles; to improve opinion into knowledge; and to distinguish those means of pleasing which depend upon known causes and rational deduction, from the nameless and inexplicable elegancies which appeal wholly to the fancy, from which we feel delight, but know not how they produce it, and which may well be termed the enchantresses of the soul. Criticism reduces those regions of literature under the dominion of science, which have hitherto known only the anarchy

of ignorance, the caprices of fancy, and the tyranny of prescription." *Wks.* 6.129. (*Ram.* 92) 1751

29. Causes which tend to invalidate the judgements of critics: vanity, negligence, human fallibility, self-interest, and prejudice. The prejudice of "literary patriotism": "There is . . . seldom much respect due to comparative criticism, when the competitors are of different countries, unless the judge is of a nation equally indifferent to both." The particularly plausible prejudice of tenderness to authors, especially to celebrated names: tenderness to living writers more warranted than to dead authors, but "the faults of a writer of acknowledged excellence are more dangerous, because the influence of his example is more extensive; and the interest of learning requires that they should be discovered and stigmatized, before they have the sanction of antiquity conferred upon them, and become precedents of indisputable authority. It has, indeed, been advanced by *Addison*, as one of the characteristicks of a true critick, that he points out beauties rather than faults. But it is rather natural to a man of learning and genius, to apply himself chiefly to the study of writers who have more beauties than faults to be displayed: for the duty of criticism is neither to depreciate, nor dignify by partial representations, but to hold out the light of reason, whatever it may discover; and to promulgate the determinations of truth, whatever she shall dictate." (cf. *infra* 31, 32.) *Wks.* 6.139-43. (*Ram.* 93) 1751

30. The difficulty of critical definition. See RULES 5
1751

31. Obscure or wholly bad works may be properly disregarded by criticism. "But if there is any writer whose genius can embellish impropriety, and whose authority can make error venerable, his works are the proper objects of critical inquisition." (Examination of defects in *Samson Agonistes* follows. cf. 29, 32.) *Wks.* 6.430. (*Ram.* 139) 1751

32. "... he that attempts to shew, however modestly, the failures of a celebrated writer, shall surely irritate his admirers, and incur the imputation of envy, captiousness, and malignity. With this danger full in my view, I shall proceed to examine the sentiments of *Milton's* tragedy [*Samson Agonistes*]." (cf. 29,31) *Wks.* 6.436. (*Ram.* 140)   1751

33. "The eye of the intellect, like that of the body, is not equally perfect in all, nor equally adapted in any to all objects; the end of criticism is to supply its defects; rules are the instruments of mental vision, which may indeed assist our faculties when properly used, but produce confusion and obscurity by unskilful application." *Wks.* 7.213. (*Ram.* 176)   1751

34. "... criticism, which, in my opinion, is only to be ranked among the subordinate and instrumental arts." *Wks.* 7.396. (*Ram.* 208)   1752

35. "Arbitrary decision and general exclamation I have carefully avoided [in *The Rambler*], by asserting nothing without a reason, and establishing all my principles of judgment on unalterable and evident truth." *Wks.* 7.396. (*Ram.* 208)   1752

36. "There remains yet an objection against the writings of Browne, more formidable than the animadversions of criticism: [the charge of atheism or deism.]" *Wks.* 4.613. cf. *infra* 55   1756

37. "Barely to say that one performance is not so good as another, is to criticise with little exactness." Pope's direction followed: "in every work regard the writer's end." *Wks.* 15.471. For context, see Pope 73   1756

38. J. questions the pleasure or use of Shakespearean annotations which point out faults and beauties within "common understanding, or common observation", since "they preclude the pleasure of judging for ourselves, teach the young and ignorant to decide without principles; defeat curiosity and discernment, by leaving them less to discover; and at last shew the

opinion of the critick, . . . without affording any
light by which it may be examined." (cf. *infra* 56)
Wks. 9.237-8. (*Shak. Proposals*) 1756

39. ". . . a remark [in J. Warton's *Essay on* . . . *Pope*]
which deserves great attention: 'In no polished nation,
after criticism has been much studied, and the rules of
writing established, has any very extraordinary book
ever appeared.'" *Wks.* 15.476 1756

40. * "You *may* abuse a tragedy, though you cannot write
one. You may scold a carpenter who has made you a
bad table, though you cannot make a table. It is not
your trade to make tables." *Bos.* 1.409 1763

41. Comparison with works of the same kind necessary
in judging the productions of genius. See ANCIENT
WRITERS 38 1765

42. "His [Shakespeare's] adherence to general nature has
exposed him to the censure of criticks, who form their
judgments upon narrower principles." See SHAKE-
SPEARE 53 1765

43. Shakespeare's profane expressions censured: "There
are laws of higher authority than those of criticism."
See SHAKESPEARE 142. cf. *supra* 34 1765

44. "No other unity [in Shakespeare's 'histories'] is intended, and therefore none is to be sought." See SHAKE-
SPEARE 44. cf. *supra* 37; *infra* 45; 46; 58; 59; 60
1765

45. "When *Shakespeare's* plan [in mingling tragic and
comic scenes] is understood, most of the criticisms
of *Rhymer* and *Voltaire* vanish away." *Shak. Pref.*,
Raleigh, 18. cf. *supra* 37; 44; *infra* 46; 58; 59; 60
1765

46. "*Rowe* has been clamorously blamed [as editor of
Shakespeare] for not performing what he did not un-
dertake, and it is time that justice be done him." *Shak.
Pref.*, Raleigh, 43. cf. *supra* 37; 44; 45; *infra* 58; 59;
60 1765

CRITICISM 51

47. * An example of "true criticism" based on knowledge of human nature. See BURKE 6   1769

48. Dryden's "general [critical] precepts, which depend upon the nature of things and the structure of the human mind" safer than his "particular positions." *Lives* 1.413   1779

49. Questions on unity of action of *Paradise Lost*, whether it is heroic, and who is hero, "are raised by such readers as draw their principles of judgement rather from books than from reason." *Lives* 1.175-6   1779

50. *Criticize work as a whole:* "It is not by comparing line with line that the merit of great works is to be estimated, but by their general effects and ultimate result. It is easy to note a weak line, and write one more vigorous in its place . . . but what is given to the parts may be subducted from the whole, and the reader may be weary though the critick may commend. . . . That book is good in vain which the reader throws away." J. consents to try Dryden by his power of pleasing. (See AIM OF WRITING 20) *Lives* 1.454
1779

51. Dryden "the writer who first taught us to determine upon principles the merit of composition." *Lives* 1.410. See also DRYDEN 12   1779

52. J., commending Spence's criticism of the Pope-Fenton-Broome *Odyssey* as "commonly just," adds: "What he thought, he thought rightly, and his remarks were recommended by his coolness and candour. In him Pope had the first experience of a critick without malevolence, who thought it as much his duty to display beauties as expose faults; who censured with respect, and praised with alacrity." *Lives* 3.143
1781

53. "The Works of Pope are now to be distinctly examined, not so much with attention to slight faults or petty beauties, as to the general character and effect

of each performance." cf. *supra* 10; *infra* 54; 75.
Lives 3.224   1781

54. Crousaz, critic of Pope's principles in the *Essay on Man*, "was accustomed to argument and disquisition, and perhaps was grown too desirous of detecting faults; but his intentions were always right, his opinions were solid, and his religion pure." *Lives* 3.265. cf. *supra* 10; 53; *infra* 75   1781

55. A discussion of Akenside's poetry does not involve his philosophical or religious tenets. *Lives* 3.417. See also *supra* 36   1781

56. ". . . the cant of those who judge by principles rather than perception." (cf. *supra* 38) *Lives* 3.248   1781

57. "When Swift is considered as an author it is just to estimate his powers by their effects. [i.e., what he accomplished.]" *Lives* 3.50   1781

58. Little opportunity for critic in Swift's poetical works, which are usually light. "They are, for the most part, what their author intended . . . all his verses exemplify his own definition of a good style, they consist of 'proper words in proper places.' To divide this Collection into classes . . . would be to tell the reader what he knows already, and to find faults of which the author could not be ignorant, who certainly wrote often not to his judgement, but his humour." *Lives* 3.65-6. cf. *supra* 37; 44; 45; 46; *infra* 59; 60   1781

59. "To charge these *Pastorals* [by Pope] with want of invention is to require what never was intended . . . the writer evidently means rather to shew his literature than his wit." J. justifies this aim of Pope's, considering his age (sixteen). *Lives* 3.224. cf. *supra* 37; 44; 45; 46; 58; *infra* 60   1781

60. Warburton's search for what was never in Pope's mind. See POPE 26. cf. *supra* 37; 44; 45; 46; 58; 59   1781

61. * J. applies to *Chevy Chase* and Shakespeare, an Italian author's test of a good work: that it must be

one "with which the vulgar were pleased, and of which the learned could tell why it pleased." *Letters* 2.440. App. D. (Windham's *Diary*) 1784

Criticism: The Public as Critic. See POPULAR JUDGEMENT

Criticism, Satirical. See under SATIRE

Criticism, Time as an Aid to. See also POPULAR JUDGEMENT 13, 14, 17, 26, 33; FAME; and *supra* 26

62. Since beauty in compositions is largely relative, ("they have something which we agree, for whatever reason, to call beauty, in a greater degree than we have been accustomed to find it in other things of the same kind") it follows, as *"Boileau* justly remarks, that the books which have stood the test of time . . . have a better claim to our regard than any modern can boast, because the long continuance of their reputation proves that they are adequate to our faculties, and agreeable to nature." (cf. *supra* 42) *Wks.* 6.129. (*Ram.* 92) 1751

63. "What has been longest known has been most considered, and what is most considered is best understood." See ANCIENT WRITERS 38 1765

64. ". . . time quickly puts an end to artificial and accidental fame." See GENIUS 18 Ptd. 1780

Criticism: Types of Critics

65. *The malevolent critic:* ". . . there is a certain race of men, that either imagine it their duty, or make it their amusement, to hinder the reception of every work of learning or genius, who stand as centinels in the avenues of fame, and value themselves upon giving IGNORANCE and ENVY the first notice of a prey." *Wks.* 5.15. (*Ram.* 3) 1750

66. *Critical barkers:* ". . . modern criticks, who, if they

have not the eyes, have the watchfulness of ARGUS, and can bark as loud as CERBERUS, though, perhaps, they cannot bite with equal force . . ." *Wks.* 5.15. (*Ram.* 3) 1750

67. The self-appointed authority of "this virulent generation" not in accord with the true nature of Criticism, which J. portrays by means of an allegory. (See CRITICISM 26.) *Wks.* 5.15-16. (*Ram.* 3) 1750

68. *Flatterers:* Satire on the fawning flatteries of critics. *Wks.* 5.105-7. (*Ram.* 16) 1750

69. *The canting and carping critic:* Tendency of critics toward fault-finding—especially in manuscripts submitted. The critic who judges by pre-conceived opinions echoes without understanding cant phrases: "Taste and Grace, Purity and Delicacy, Manners and Unities, sounds which, having been once uttered by those that understood them, have been since re-echoed without meaning, and kept up to the disturbance of the world, by a constant repercussion from one coxcomb to another." He seeks objections from vanity; overlooks possibilities for variety in every work of imagination: "Every man who is called to give his opinion of a performance . . . first suffers himself to form expectations, and then is angry at his disappointment. He lets his imagination rove at large, and wonders that another, equally unconfined in the boundless ocean of possibility, takes a different course." There is always "an appeal from domestick criticism to a higher judicature, and the publick, which is never corrupted, nor often deceived, is to pass the last sentence upon literary claims." (See POPULAR JUDGEMENT.) The author should go his own ways, undisturbed by such contrarieties of opinion. *Wks.* 5.150-5. (*Ram.* 23) 1750

70. *The fault-finder:* The critic determined to find faults needs little sagacity. See VARIETY 1 1750

71. *The canting critic:* Misocapelus, in *The Rambler* (*No.*

123), learned "the cant of criticism, and talked so loudly and volubly of nature, and manners, and sentiment, and diction, and similies, and contrasts, and action, and pronunciation, that I was often desired to lead the hiss and clap." *Wks.* 6.336   1751

72. *Roarers, whisperers and moderators in criticism:* the last the most dangerous type. *Wks.* 7.24-7. (*Ram.* 144)   1751

73. *The vain critic:* "In criticism, as in every other art, we fail sometimes by our weakness, but more frequently by our fault. We are sometimes bewildered by ignorance, and sometimes by prejudice, but we seldom deviate far from the right, but when we deliver ourselves up to the direction of vanity." *Wks.* 7.214. (*Ram.* 176)   1751

74. Critics whose diversion is the baiting of an author described. *Wks.* 7.211-12. (*Ram.* 176)   1751

75. *Microscopic or telescopic criticism:* "Some seem always to read with the microscope of criticism . . . . As they discern with great exactness, they comprehend but a narrow compass, and know nothing of the justness of the design, the general spirit of the performance, the artifice of connection, or the harmony of the parts; they never conceive how small a proportion that which they are busy in contemplating bears to the whole, or how the petty inaccuracies with which they are offended, are absorbed and lost in general excellence. [cf. *supra*, 10; 53; 54.] Others are furnished by criticism with a telescope. They see with great clearness whatever is too remote to be discovered by the rest of mankind, but are totally blind to all that lies immediately before them. They discover in every passage some secret meaning, some remote allusion, some artful allegory, or some occult imitation which no other reader ever suspected; but they have no perception of the cogency of arguments, the force of pathetick sentiments, the various colours of diction, or the

flowery embellishments of fancy; of all that engages the attention of others, they are tôtally insensible, while they pry into worlds of conjecture, and amuse themselves with phantoms in the clouds." *Wks.* 7.213-4. (*Ram.* 176) 1751
76. *Petty modern critics:* ". . . whom neither any exuberant praise bestowed by others, nor any eminent conquests over stubborn problems, have entitled to exalt themselves above the common orders of mankind." Their hasty condemnation of obscure passages in ancient writers, when such obscurity often caused by modern ignorance of events referred to. Illustrations from Horace. *Wks.* 9.32-9. (*Adv.* 58) 1753
77. *"Disturbers of human quiet":* ". . . as the caprice of man is always starting from too little to too much, we have now amongst other disturbers of human quiet, a numerous body of reviewers and remarkers." *Wks.* 9.372 1757
78. *Periodical reviewers:* (Aims of the *London Chronicle* set forth by J.) "We shall repress that elation of malignity, which wantons in the cruelties of criticism, and not only murders reputation, but murders it by torture. . . . Our intention is not to pre-occupy judgment by praise or censure, but to gratify curiosity by early intelligence." *Wks.* 9.372 1757
79. *Satire on little great critics:* Dick Minim, the brewer's apprentice, who rises to the dignity of a critical oracle by a judicious use of the fashionable cant phrases of criticism. *Wks.* 8.238-47. (*Idl.* 60, 61)[1] 1759
80. *Dictators:* "Judgement, like other faculties, is improved by practice, and its advancement is hindered by submission to dictatorial decisions, as the memory

---

[1] These two *Idler* essays are particularly interesting in that they evidently summarize the prevailing critical tenets of the day. The satire is not, however, directed primarily against these judgements, for Johnson himself accepts many of them, but rather against the tribe of critics who repeated these cant phrases, parrot-like, without comprehending their meaning.

grows torpid by the use of a table book." *Shak. Pref.*, Raleigh, 54   1765

81. *"There are three distinct kinds of judges upon all new authors or productions; the first are those who know no rules, but pronounce entirely from their natural taste and feelings; the second are those who know and judge by rules; and the third are those who know, but are above the rules. These last are those you should wish to satisfy. Next to them rate the natural judges; but ever despise those opinions that are formed by the rules." D'Arblay, *Diary and Letters* 1.183-4   1779

82. Dryden "has been described as magisterially presiding over the younger writers, and assuming the distribution of poetical fame; but he who excels has a right to teach, and he whose judgement is incontestable may, without usurpation, examine and decide." *Lives* 1.396   1779

83. *The changeable critic:* J. defends Warburton's change of heart toward Pope's work: this not necessarily "hypocritical inconstancy"—"surely to think differently at different times of poetical merit may be easily allowed. Such opinions are often admitted and dismissed without nice examination. Who is there that has not found reason for changing his mind about questions of greater importance?" (Compare CHANGE OF OPINIONS 1) *Lives* 3.167   1781

84. "Those who like only when they like the author, and who are under the dominion of a name, condemned it [Pope's *Essay on Man*, Epistle I]; and those admired it who are willing to scatter praise at random, which while it is unappropriated excites no envy." *Lives* 3.161   1781

85. "It is pleasant to remark how soon Pope learned the cant of an author, and began to treat criticks with contempt, though he had yet suffered nothing from them." *Lives* 3.91   1781

86. ". . . the gravity of common criticks may be tedious,

but is less despicable than childish merriment." *Lives* 3.240   1781

Curiosity

1. "Curiosity" nearly always bears a favourable connotation, when applied by J. to literary and scholarly matters. e.g., "Curiosity is, in great and generous minds, the first passion and the last." *Wks.* 7.59. (*Ram.* 150)   1751

Decency. See DECORUM

1. *Definition:* "2. Suitableness to character; propriety." *Dict.* (e.g., "*Voltaire* perhaps thinks decency violated when the *Danish* Usurper is represented as a drunkard." *Shak. Pref.*, Raleigh, 15)   1755

Decorum. See also DRAMATIC PROPRIETY and under DICTION

1. ". . . it is an established principle, that all ornaments owe their beauty to their propriety." Applied to epitaphs. (See EPITAPHS 1.) *Wks.* 9.441-2. See also GOOD SENSE 3   1740
2. Decorum of language and thought in pastoral poetry upheld. See PASTORAL 2   1750
3. Decorum or propriety of sentiments advocated. See SENTIMENT 1 and DRAMA 12[1]   1751
4. Passages in *Henry V* in which royalty uses mean diction.[1] *Shak.*, Raleigh, 130, 131, 133   1765

Dedications. Compare OCCASIONAL WORKS; PRAISE

1. Savage's *Dedications* censured: "flattery . . . without . . . elegance or invention." See SAVAGE 5   1744

---

[1] Although J. accepts for the most part the Aristotelian and Horatian doctrine of decorum or propriety, he breaks with neo-classical tradition in such a passage as his defence of Shakespeare's portrayal of the drunken king in *Hamlet*, and of Menenius, senator of Rome, who plays the buffoon in *Coriolanus*. (See SHAKESPEARE 53).

2. "Praise, like gold and diamonds, owes its value only to its scarcity. . . . Nothing has so much degraded literature from its natural rank, as the practice of indecent and promiscuous dedication; for what credit can he expect who professes himself the hireling of vanity, however profligate, and without shame or scruple celebrates the worthless, dignifies the mean, and gives to the corrupt, licentious, and oppressive, the ornaments which ought only to add grace to truth, and loveliness to innocence? Every other kind of adulteration, however shameful, however mischievous, is less detestable than the crime of counterfeiting characters, and fixing the stamp of literary sanction upon the dross and refuse of the world." Yet responsibility shared by patrons. "Praise is the tribute of merit . . . no private views or personal regard can discharge any man from his general obligations to virtue and to truth." *Wks.* 6.412-16. (*Ram.* 136) 1751

3. *Dedication defined:* "2. A servile address to a patron." *Dict.* 1755

4. * "Studied conclusions" of dedications more elegant, and, when addressed to persons of high rank, more respectful. *Bos.* 5.239. (*Hebrides*, 22 Sept.) 1773

5. * "I do not myself think that a man should say in a dedication what he could not say in a history. However, allowance should be made; for there is a great difference. The known style of a dedication is flattery: it professes to flatter. There is the same difference between what a man says in a dedication, and what he says in a history, as between a lawyer's pleading a cause, and reporting it." *Bos.* 5.285-6. (*Hebrides*, 4 Oct.) 1773

6. * "He told me [Boswell] . . . it was indifferent to him what was the subject of the work dedicated, provided it were innocent. . . . In writing Dedications for others, he considered himself as by no means speaking his own sentiments." *Bos.* 2.2   Date ?

Description. See also NATURE. (INANIMATE)

1. Small opportunity for variety when describing nature. "Poetry cannot dwell upon the minuter distinctions, by which one species differs from another, without departing from that simplicity of grandeur which fills the imagination," etc. See PASTORAL 1c, d, f, g   1750
2. ". . . descriptions, which are definitions of a more lax and fanciful kind, must always have in some degree that resemblance to each other which they all have to their object." *Wks.* 7.15. (*Ram.* 143. J.'s discussion of plagiarism, *q.v.*)   1751
3. Descriptions of spring, night, poetical groves, etc. which will please, however trite, "as long as human nature shall remain the same." *Wks.* 9.103-4. (*Adv.* 108)   1753
4. J. comments on the justness of J. Warton's observation, in the latter's *Essay on Pope*, that the young genius generally turns to descriptive poetry before he has studied human nature and passions, and quotes Warton's example of this: "'Some of Milton's most early as well as most exquisite pieces are his Lycidas, l'Allegro, and Il penseroso, if we may except his ode on the nativity of CHRIST, which is indeed prior in order of time, and in which a penetrating critic might have observed the seeds of that boundless imagination which was one day to produce the Paradise Lost.'" Warton also (adds J.) "justly ridicules those who think they can form just ideas of valleys, mountains, and rivers, in a garret of the Strand. For this reason I cannot regret with this author, that Pope laid aside his design of writing American pastorals; for as he must have painted scenes which he never saw, and manners which he never knew, his performance, though it might have been a pleasing amusement of fancy, would have exhibited no representation of nature or of life." *Wks.* 15.471-2   1756
5. "One of the great sources of poetical delight is descrip-

tion, or the power of presenting pictures to the mind."
Lives 1.51   1779

6. A plea for "the grandeur of generality": "Thus all the power of description is destroyed by a scrupulous enumeration." See GENERAL 10 (cf. *ib*. 12)   1779

7. *Structural weakness:* "The objection made by Dennis [to Pope's *Windsor Forest*] is the want of plan, of a regular subordination of parts terminating in the principal and original design. There is this want in most descriptive poems, because as the scenes, which they must exhibit successively, are all subsisting at the same time, the order in which they are shewn must by necessity be arbitrary, and more is not to be expected from the last part than from the first. The attention, therefore, which cannot be detained by suspense, must be excited by diversity, such as his poem offers to its reader. But the desire of diversity may be too much indulged." e. g., Father Thames and Lodona in *Windsor Forest*. (See MYTHOLOGY 31.) *Lives* 3.225   1781

8. *Structural weakness:* "The great defect of *The Seasons* is want of method; but for this I know not that there was any remedy. Of many appearances subsisting all at once, no rule can be given why one should be mentioned before another; yet the memory wants the help of order, and the curiosity is not excited by suspense or expectation." *Lives* 3.299-300   1781

9. "Blank verse will therefore, I fear, be too often found in description exuberant. . . ." See BLANK VERSE 20
                                                          1781

10. Appreciation of Thomson's descriptions of nature in *The Seasons*. *Lives* 3.299   1781

11. *Description falls short of reality. "Description only excites curiosity: seeing satisfies it." *Bos.* 4.199   1783

12. ". . . description is always fallacious, at least till you have seen realities you cannot know it to be true." *Letters* 2.331   1783

Dialogue. For dramatic dialogue, see DRAMA: *Dialogue*

1. "It is indeed much more easy to form dialogues than to contrive adventures. Every position makes way for an argument, and every objection dictates an answer." Harder to end, than to continue. *Lives* 1.211   1779

2. The dialogue of *Hudibras:* "Some power of engaging the attention might have been added to it, by quicker reciprocation, by seasonable interruptions, by sudden questions, and by a nearer approach to dramatick spriteliness; without which fictitious speeches will always tire, however sparkling with sentences and however variegated with allusions." *Lives* 1.211-2   1779

Diaries. Compare AUTOBIOGRAPHY

1.* Boswell records that J. told him "that he had twelve or fourteen times attempted to keep a journal of his life, but never could persevere. He advised me to do it. 'The great thing to be recorded, (said he), is the state of your own mind; and you should write down every thing that you remember, for you cannot judge at first what is good or bad; and write immediately while the impression is fresh, for it will not be the same a week afterwards.'" *Bos.* 2.217   1773

2. J.'s advice to Mrs. Thrale: "Do not omit the practice of writing down occurrences as they arise, of whatever kind, and be very punctual in annexing the dates. Chronology you know is the eye of history; and every man's life is of importance to himself. Do not omit painful casualties, or unpleasing passages, they make the variegation of existence; and there are many transactions, of which I will not promise with Æneas, *et hæc olim meminisse juvabit.* Yet that remembrance which is not pleasant may be useful." Avoid "intemperate attention to slight circumstances." *Letters* 2.27. See also *Letters* 1.361-2   1777

3. * Mrs. Thrale objects to publishing an autobiography of Sir R. Sibbald: "'To discover such weakness, ex-

poses a man when he is gone.' JOHNSON. 'Nay, it is an honest picture of human nature. How often are the primary motives of our greatest actions as small as Sibbald's, for his re-conversion.' MRS. THRALE. 'But may they not as well be forgotten?' JOHNSON. 'No, Madam, a man loves to review his own mind. That is the use of a diary, or journal.'" *Bos.* 3.228   1778

Dictators, Critical. See CRITICISM 80, 82

Diction. See also DICTION, PURITY OF; ENGLISH LANGUAGE. Compare STYLE; DRAMA: *Dialogue.* For J.'s dislike of obsolete words and Spenserian diction, see ANTIQUE STYLE and IMITATION

1. Milton's melodious use of proper names. See MILTON 16   1751
2. *Mean diction:* [a] "Every man, however profound or abstracted, perceives himself irresistibly alienated by low terms; they who profess the most zealous adherence to truth are forced to admit that she owes part of her charms to her ornaments; and loses much of her power over the soul, when she appears disgraced by a dress uncouth or ill-adjusted. . . . No word is naturally or intrinsically meaner than another. . . . Words become low by the occasions to which they are applied, or the general character of them who use them; and the disgust which they produce, arises from the revival of those images with which they are commonly united. . . . Words which convey ideas of dignity in one age, are banished from elegant writing or conversation in another, because they are in time debased by vulgar mouths, and can be no longer heard without the involuntary recollection of unpleasing images." [b] Mean diction illustrated by passage from *Macbeth* ["Come, thick night!" etc., I.v. 51 *ff.*]: The poetry of the passage weakened by "an epithet now seldom heard but in the stable [dunnest], and

dun night may come or go without any other notice than contempt," and "by the name of an instrument [knife] used by butchers and cooks in the meanest employments . . . who does not, at last, from the long habit of connecting a knife with sordid offices, feel aversion rather than terror?" Macbeth's wish to escape the eye of providence "is so debased by two unfortunate words, that while I endeavour to impress on my reader the energy of the sentiment, I can scarce check my risibility, when the expression forces itself upon my mind; for who, without some relaxation of his gravity, can hear of the avengers of guilt *peeping through a blanket?* These imperfections of diction are less obvious to the reader, as he is less acquainted with common usages." e.g., to the foreigner or the "solitary academick." Hence the importance to an author of "an early entrance into the living world." *Wks.* 7.164-7. (*Ram.* 168) 1751

3. *Mean diction:* ". . . he that will not condescend to recommend himself by external embellishments, must submit to the fate of just sentiment meanly expressed, and be ridiculed and forgotten before he is understood." *Wks.* 7.168. (*Ram.* 168) 1751

4. *Poetic diction:* A poetic diction which distorts words from their original meanings censured. e.g., misuse by the poets of term "poverty," which "in the epick language, is only not to command the wealth of nations, nor to have fleets and armies in pay." *Wks.* 7.359-60. (*Ram.* 202) 1752

5. The importance to an author of study of diction. *Wks.* 9.159. (*Adv.* 138) 1754

6. *Definition of diction:* "Stile; language; expression." *Dict.* 1755

7. The "colloquial licentiousness" of "illiterate writers" condemned. *Wks.* 9.225. (*Pref. Dict.*) 1755

8. *Colloquialisms:* "Much less ought our written language to comply with the corruptions of oral utterance,

or copy that which every variation of time or place makes different from itself." *Wks.* 9.198. (*Pref. Dict.*)   1755

9. *Colloquial diction:* ". . . the familiar and colloquial part of our language being diffused among those classes who had no ambition of refinement, or affectation of novelty, has suffered very little change." *Dict.* (*Hist. of Eng. Lang.*)   1755

10. Faults of diction in Blackwell's *Memoirs of the Court of Augustus:* Gallicisms. Technical terms: "words that every other polite writer has avoided and despised." (cf. *infra* 19, 21.) Low words in serious composition: those "appropriated to jocularity and levity." Grand and burlesque expressions sometimes mixed together. Coined words and phrases. (cf. *infra* 34.) Gaudy or hyperbolical epithets. Sonority which draws attention from the meaning. *Wks.* 10.190-3   1756

11. "Sentiment and language" must differentiate the "subdivisions of passion." Versification unequal to this. See VERSIFICATION 15   1756

12. ". . . exclamation seldom succeeds in our language, and I think it may be observed that the particle O! used at the beginning of a sentence always offends." *Lives* 3.266   1756

13. "Many words easily understood on common occasion, become uncertain and figurative when applied to the works of Omnipotence." e.g., "subordination." *Wks.* 10.236   1757

14. Hard words defended. See OBSCURITY 3   1759

15. Words used in an uncommon sense in poetry censured. (cf. *infra* 27.) *Wks.* 8.309. (*Idl.* 77)   1759

16. *Colloquialisms:* "These accidental and colloquial senses are the disgrace of language, and the plague of commentators." (Referring to certain obscure colloquialisms used by Shakespeare.) *Shak.*, Raleigh, 95
   1765

17. "Every language of a learned nation necessarily divides itself into diction scholastick and popular, grave and familiar, elegant and gross; and from a nice distinction of these different parts arises a great part of the beauty of style." A few writers secured "delicacy of selection," instinctively without need of rules. Every other (before Dryden) "took for every purpose what chance might offer him." *Lives* 1.420   1779

18. *Mean diction:* ". . . words being arbitrary must owe their power to association, and have the influence, and that only, which custom has given them. Language is the dress of thought . . . so the most heroick sentiments will lose their efficacy, and the most splendid ideas drop their magnificence, if they are conveyed by words used commonly upon low and trivial occasions, debased by vulgar mouths, and contaminated by inelegant applications. Truth indeed is always truth, and reason is always reason; they have an intrinsick and unalterable value, and constitute that intellectual gold which defies destruction"—but "may be so buried in impurities as not to pay the cost of . . . extraction. The diction, being the vehicle of the thoughts, first presents itself to the intellectual eye; and if the first appearance offends, a further knowledge is not often sought. Whatever professes to benefit by pleasing must please at once. The pleasures of the mind imply something sudden and unexpected; that which elevates must always surprise. What is perceived by slow degrees may gratify us with the consciousness of improvement, but will never strike with the sense of pleasure." *Lives* 1.58-9   1779

19. *Technical terms:* (Dryden's nautical language.) "It is a general rule in poetry that all appropriated terms of art should be sunk in general expressions, because poetry is to speak an universal language." (cf. *supra* 10, *infra* 21.) Especially true of arts not commonly known—e.g., technical navigation. J. confirms this by

an appeal to experience: "I suppose here [*Annus Mirabilis*, stanzas 146-8] is not one term which every reader does not wish away." (The passage quoted contains such terms as *okum, seam, calking-iron, mallet,* etc.) *Lives* 1.433-4   1779

20. The "affluence and comprehension of our language" shown in our poetical translations of ancients. *Lives* 1.421   1779

21. Before time of Dryden "no poetical diction: no system of words at once refined from the grossness of domestick use and free from the harshness of terms appropriated to particular arts. [cf. *supra* 10, 19.] Words too familiar or too remote defeat the purpose of a poet. From those sounds which we hear on small or on coarse occasions, we do not easily receive strong impressions or delightful images; and words to which we are nearly strangers, whenever they occur, draw that attention on themselves which they should transmit to things. Those happy combinations of words which distinguish poetry from prose had been rarely attempted; we had few elegances or flowers of speech. . . ." *Lives* 1.420   1779

22. ". . . the diction of poetry has become more splendid." (Since Dryden's time.) *Lives* 1.453   1779

23. "The sentences [in Oldisworth's life of Smith] are loaded with words of more pomp than use." *Lives* 2.11   1779

24. In Smith's *Phædra and Hippolitus* diction as well as sentiments remote from life: ". . . too luxuriant and splendid for dialogue, and envelopes the thoughts rather than displays them." *Lives* 2.16   1779

25. Command of "colours of language" one of the "qualities that constitute genius." See GENIUS 23   1781

26. *Poetic diction:* Akenside's diction in *The Pleasures of Imagination* "is certainly poetical as it is not prosaick, and elegant as it is not vulgar." [In the first edition,

the sentence reads: "His diction is certainly so far poetical as it is not prosaick, and so far valuable as it is not common."] *Lives* 3.418   1781

27. "Gray thought his language more poetical as it was more remote from common use: finding in Dryden 'honey redolent of Spring,' an expression that reaches the utmost limits of our language, Gray drove it a little more beyond common apprehension, by making 'gales' to be 'redolent of joy and youth.'" *Lives* 3.435. (cf. *supra* 15)   1781

28. In Gray's translations of Northern and Welsh poetry: "the imagery is preserved, perhaps often improved; but the language is unlike the language of other poets." *Lives* 3.441   1781

29. Gray's *Progress of Poesy*, stanza II 3: "sounds big with Delphi, and Egean, and Ilissus, and Meander, and 'hallowed fountain' and 'solemn sound'; but in all Gray's odes there is a kind of cumbrous splendour which we wish away." *Lives* 3.437   1781

30. J. speaks with disapproval of a practice that "has of late arisen . . . of giving to adjectives, derived from substantives, the termination of participles, such as the *cultured* plain, the *daisied* bank; but I was sorry to see, in the lines of a scholar like Gray, 'the *honied* Spring.'" *Lives* 3.434   1781

31. J. criticizes Gray's epithet "buxom health" as "not elegant; he seems not to understand the word." *Lives* 3.435   1781

32. "'Idalia's velvet-green' has something of cant. An epithet or metaphor drawn from Nature ennobles Art; an epithet or metaphor drawn from Art degrades Nature. Gray is too fond of words arbitrarily compounded. 'Many-twinkling' was formerly censured as not analogical; we may say *many-spotted*, but scarcely *many-spotting*." *Lives* 3.436-7   1781

33. Thomson's diction fills the ear more than the mind. See THOMSON 8   1781

34. * Boswell assures us that J. was offended at the license of coining new words or departing from the established meanings of words. (cf. *supra* 10) *Bos.* 1.221   Date?

Diction, Purity of

35. "Barbarous, or impure words and expressions, may be branded with some note of infamy, as they are carefully to be eradicated wherever they are found; and they occur too frequently even in the best writers." (Examples given from Pope, Addison and Dryden.) *Wks.* 9.188   1747

36. "I have laboured [in *The Rambler*] to refine our language to grammatical purity, and to clear it from colloquial barbarisms, licentious idioms, and irregular combinations. Something, perhaps, I have added to the elegance of its construction, and something to the harmony of its cadence. When common words were less pleasing to the ear, or less distinct in their signification, I have familiarised the terms of philosophy, by applying them to popular ideas, but have rarely admitted any word not authorized by former writers; for I believe that whoever knows the *English* tongue in its present extent, will be able to express his thoughts without further help from other nations."[1] *Wks.* 7.395. (*Ram.* 208)   1752

37. J. regards the works of the writers before the Restoration "as *the wells of English undefiled*, as the pure sources of genuine diction." *Wks.* 9.214. (*Pref. Dict.*)   1755

38. Alteration in language through "borrowed terms and exotick expressions" deplored. *Wks.* 9.225-6 (*Pref. Dict.*)   1755

39. J. censures "the folly of naturalizing useless foreigners to the injury of the natives [words]." *Wks.* 9.204. (*Pref. Dict.*)   1755

40. *Translation:* "The great pest of speech." ". . . the

[1] In a letter to Dr. Hawkesworth, written in 1756, Johnson himself uses a Gallicism. *Letters* 1.61

licence of translators, whose idleness and ignorance, if it be suffered to proceed, will reduce us to babble a dialect of *France."* See TRANSLATION 1 1755

41. Gallicisms in *Memoirs of the Court of Augustus* censured. See *supra* 10 1756
42. * See HUME 1, for J.'s censure of Hume's Gallic style. 1763
43. Dryden often used French words from vanity to show rank of company he kept. None of these French words which then crept into conversation has been incorporated or retained in the language. "They continue only where they stood first, perpetual warnings to future innovators." *Lives* 1.463-4 1779
44. J. commends "genuine Anglicism" of Addison's prose style. *Lives* 2.149 Ptd. 1780
45. "In his [Pope's] latter productions the diction is sometimes vitiated by French idioms, with which Bolingbroke had perhaps infected him." *Lives* 3.250. See also *Dict:* "owe"; and "transpire"; and *Bos.* 3.343 1781
46. * "Derange" not an English word. *Wks.* 11.216. (Hawkins's *Apophthegms*) Date?

Dictionaries

1. "As Dictionaries are commodious, they are likewise fallacious: he whose works exhibit an apparent connexion and regular subordination cannot easily conceal his ignorance, or favour his idleness; the completeness of one part will show the deficiency of another: but the writer of a Dictionary may silently omit what he does not know; and his ignorance, if it happens to be discovered, slips away from censure under the name of forgetfulness." A. Macbean's *Dictionary of Ancient Geography*, 1773, *Preface*, p. iv., contributed by J. 1773
2. "He that undertakes to compile a Dictionary, under-

takes that, which, if it comprehends the full extent of his design, he knows himself unable to perform." *Wks.* 14.377. (*Adver. to 4th ed.*, *Dict.*)   1773

3. "Dictionaries are like watches, the worst is better than none, and the best cannot be expected to go quite true." *Letters* 2.415   1784

4. "A perfect performance of any kind is not to be expected, and certainly not a perfect dictionary." *Letters*, 2.426   1784

Didactic Poetry. See also SACRED POETRY

1. *Didactic defined:* "Preceptive; giving precepts: as a *didactick* poem is a poem that gives rules for some art; as the Georgicks." *Dict.*   1755

2. ". . . a long poem of mere sentiments easily becomes tedious; though all the parts are forcible and every line kindles new rapture, the reader, if not relieved by the interposition of something that sooths the fancy, grows weary of admiration, and defers the rest." *Lives* 1.437   1779

3. Blank verse unsuited to didactic poetry. See BLANK VERSE 8   1779

4. ". . . in a didactick poem novelty is to be expected only in the ornaments and illustrations." *Lives* 2.295   Ptd. 1780

5. "To reason in verse is allowed to be difficult; but Blackmore not only reasons in verse, but very often reasons poetically." *Lives* 2.254   Ptd. 1780

6. Pope's *Essay on Man:* "The subject is perhaps not very proper for poetry." *Lives* 3.242   1781

7. Blank verse, from its tendency to over-ornamentation and diffuseness, "will therefore, . . . be too often found . . . in argument loquacious." See BLANK VERSE 20   1781

8. "Almost every poem, consisting of precepts, is so far

arbitrary and immethodical [in construction], that many of the paragraphs may change places with no apparent inconvenience; for of two or more positions, depending upon some remote and general principle, there is seldom any cogent reason why one should precede the other. But for the order in which they stand, whatever it be, a little ingenuity may easily give a reason [as Warburton did for Pope's *Essay on Criticism*]. . . . As the end of method is perspicuity, that series is sufficiently regular that avoids obscurity; and where there is no obscurity it will not be difficult to discover method." *Lives* 3.99   1781

9. Pope's *Essay on Criticism* "exhibits every mode of excellence that can embellish or dignify didactick composition, selection of matter, novelty of arrangement, justness of precept, splendour of illustration, and propriety of digression. . . . In didatick poetry, of which the great purpose is instruction, a simile may be praised which illustrates, though it does not ennoble; in heroicks, that may be admitted which ennobles, though it does not illustrate." *Lives* 3.228-9
1781

Didacticism. See AIM OF WRITING; DIDACTIC POETRY; MORAL ELEMENT

Diligence. See under COMPOSITION

Diversity. See VARIETY

Drama: Actors and Acting

1. Boswell's explanation of J.'s prejudice against players: "The imperfection of his organs," "the cold rejection of his tragedy," "the brilliant success of Garrick . . . whose talents he undoubtedly rated low, compared with his own." Boswell adds that "at all periods of his

life Johnson used to talk contemptuously of players."[1]
Bos. 1.167   Date ?

Drama, Aim of. See also SHAKESPEARE: *Didacticism*.
Compare AIM OF WRITING

1. " 'Tis your's, this night . . .
   To chace the charms of sound, the pomp of show,
   For useful mirth and salutary woe;
   Bid scenic Virtue form the rising age,

---

[1] There is certainly plenty of evidence to support this last assertion: "Whitehead is but a little man to inscribe verses to players." (*Bos.* 1.402); "Now, Sir, to talk of *respect* for a *player!*" (*Bos.* 3.184); Garrick "should no longer subject himself to be hissed by a mob." (*Bos.* 2.438); "Punch has no feelings" (*John. Misc.* 1.457)—these are representative passages to offset which only expressions of esteem for individual players, notably Garrick, can be gleaned. (e.g., *Bos.* 4.243; 3.263; 3.371 n 1; 5.126; 1.326; 1.201; *Letters* 2.345; *John. Misc.* 2.333; *Lives* 2.21; 2.334 and *ib. n* 2; 2.336.) This prejudice, however, along with his other so-called prejudices, was not without substantial foundation. We must keep in mind the general ill-repute of the stage, particularly in the second quarter of the century. Savage, writes Johnson in 1744, "was so much ashamed of having been reduced to appear as a player, that he always blotted out his name from the list when a copy of his tragedy was to be shown to his friends." (*Lives* 2.340.) And Garrick, Johnson is reported to have said, "made his profession respectable." (*Bos.* 3.371 n 1.) Indeed acting, Johnson believed, was essentially undermining to character. It exposed one to "the two powerful corrupters of mankind" praise and money. (*Letters* 2.345.) "To be humane, generous, and candid is a very high degree of merit in any case," he wrote of Wilks, the actor, in 1744, "but those qualities deserve still greater praise when they are found in that condition which makes almost every other man, for whatever reason, contemptuous, insolent, petulant, selfish, and brutal." (*Lives* 2.334.) Perhaps, too, Johnson felt that there was always the tendency for an actor to carry his acting abroad with him into real life.
If Johnson was inclined to over-rate the effect of acting on the players themselves, he certainly under-rated the effect of drama on the audience. It is part of Johnson's greatness that in estimating values, he was ever for getting back to the ultimate realities of human nature and human experience; but in this case he should have considered that he himself was no proper judge of the effect of the acted play upon its audience. His physical limitations of sight and hearing must inevitably have warped his judgement. (e.g., see *John. Misc.* 2.277 and *Bos.* 2.92 n 4.) A person gifted with Johnson's extraordinarily vigorous imagination, but with sight and hearing impaired, might well say "A play read, affects the mind like a play acted," and underestimate the amount of illusion possible on the stage, to the average spectator. (See *Shak. Pref.*, Raleigh, 26-9; and *Bos.* 5.46.) Finally, Johnson clearly had no high opinion of the moral effect of the drama of his day on an audience. The *Idler* essay (47) which portrays the city wit as spoiled by play-going illustrates this. (See also *Bos.* 2.14.)

And Truth diffuse her radiance from the stage."
Wks. 1.198   1747

2. Restoration dramatists "pleas'd their age, and did not aim to mend." See *infra* 40   1747

3. ". . . the design of tragedy is to instruct by moving the passions." See *infra* 44f   1751

4. ". . . the unities of time and place . . . are always to be sacrificed to the nobler beauties of variety and instruction . . . and the greatest graces of a play, are to copy nature and instruct life." See *infra* 47c   1765

Drama: Ballad Opera

5. ". . . a new species of composition, though it be not of the highest kind. We owe to Gay the Ballad Opera; a mode of comedy which at first was supposed to delight only by its novelty, but has now by the experience of half a century been found so well accomodated to the disposition of a popular audience that it is likely to keep long possession of the stage." *Lives* 2.282-3
                                                                         1781

Drama: Battles on the Stage

6. "This passage [*Prologue, Henry V*] shews that Shakespeare was fully sensible of the absurdity of shewing battles on the theatre, which indeed is never done but tragedy becomes farce. Nothing can be represented to the eye but by something like it, and *within a wooden O* nothing very like a battle can be exhibited." *Shak. Pref.*, Raleigh, 126. See also *ib.* 148 for similar note.   1765

Drama: Burlesque. See BURLESQUE

Drama: Characters. See also SHAKESPEARE: *Characters;* DRAMATIC PROPRIETY

7. Greatness or meanness of character in itself not sufficient to distinguish tragedy and comedy. See *infra* 12
                                                                                                     1751

DRAMA 75

8. A hero in tragedy necessary. See *infra* 44f   1751
9. Example of rules "advanced without consulting reason or nature": "that *only three speaking personages should* appear at once upon the stage." See *infra* 44a
    1751
10. Allegorical figures should not become active persons in the drama. See ALLEGORY 4   1779
11. "Dennis objects to the characters [in *Cato*] that they are not natural or reasonable; but as heroes and heroines are not beings that are seen every day, it is hard to find upon what principles their conduct shall be tried." *Lives* 2.135   Ptd. 1780

Drama: Comedy. See also BURLESQUE; DRAMA: *Tragi-Comedy*; *infra* 21; 67; 68; and SHAKESPEARE 25; 26; 27

12. [a] "Comedy has been particularly unpropitious to definers; for though perhaps they might properly have contented themselves, with declaring it to be *such a dramatick representation of human life, as may excite mirth*, they have embarrassed their definition with the means by which the comick writers attain their end, without considering that the various methods of exhilarating their audience, not being limited by nature, cannot be comprised in precept. Thus, some make comedy a representation of mean, and others of bad men; some think that its essence consists in the unimportance, others in the fictitiousness of the transaction. But any man's reflections will inform him, that every dramatick composition which raises mirth, is comick; and that, to raise mirth, it is by no means universally necessary, that the personages should be either mean or corrupt, nor always requisite, that the action should be trivial, nor ever, that it should be fictitious. [b] If the two kinds of dramatick poetry had been defined only by their effects upon the mind, some absurdities might have been prevented, with which the composi-

tions of our greatest poets are disgraced, who, for want of some settled ideas and accurate distinctions, have unhappily confounded tragick with comick sentiments. They seem to have thought, that as the meanness of personages constituted comedy, their greatness was sufficient to form a tragedy; and that nothing was necessary but that they should crowd the scene with monarchs, and generals, and guards; and make them talk, at certain intervals, of the downfal of kingdoms, and the rout of armies. They have not considered, that thoughts or incidents, in themselves ridiculous, grow still more grotesque by the solemnity of such characters; that reason and nature are uniform and inflexible; and that what is despicable and absurd, will not, by any association with splendid titles, become rational or great; that the most important affairs, by an intermixture of an unseasonable levity, may be made contemptible; and that the robes of royalty can give no dignity to nonsense or to folly. 'Comedy,' says *Horace*, 'sometimes raises her voice;' and tragedy may likewise on proper occasions abate her dignity; but as the comick personages can only depart from their familiarity of style, when the more violent passions are put in motion, the heroes and queens of tragedy should never descend to trifle, but in the hours of ease, and intermissions of danger." Examples of such improprieties and absurdities in Dryden's *Don Sebastian* and *Aureng-Zebe. Wks.* 6.345-6. (*Ram.* 125) 1751
13. *Definition of comedy:* "A dramatick representation of the lighter faults of mankind." *Dict.* 1755
14. **Comedy distinguished from farce:* Foote's talent —vice, Johnson calls it—for exhibiting character, "is not comedy, which exhibits the character of a species, as that of a miser gathered from many misers: it is farce, which exhibits individuals." *Bos.* 2.95 1769
15. * ". . . the great end of comedy—making an audience merry." *Bos.* 2.233 1773
16. (Context: Cowley's *Anacreontiques*): "Real mirth

must be always natural, and nature is uniform. Men have been wise in very different modes; but they have always laughed the same way. Levity of thought naturally produced familiarity of language, and the familiar part of language continues long the same: the dialogue of comedy, when it is transcribed from popular manners and real life, is read from age to age with equal pleasure." *Lives* 1.39-40   1779

17. "As the lighter species of dramatick poetry professes the imitation of common life, of real manners, and daily incidents, it apparently presupposes a familiar knowledge of many characters and exact observation of the passing world; the difficulty therefore is to conceive how this knowledge can be obtained by a boy." (Context: Congreve's comedy *The Old Bachelor*.) *Lives* 2.216   Ptd. 1780

Drama, Definition of. See also *infra* 47 for J.'s discussion of the theory of dramatic imitation.

18. "A poem accomodated to action; a poem in which the action is not related, but represented; and in which therefore such rules are to be observed as make the representation probable." *Dict.*   1755

Drama: Dialogue. Compare DIALOGUE. See also SHAKESPEARE: *Dialogue*

19. "Tumour of phrase" and "unvaried equality" in modern tragic dialogue. See *infra* 27   1751
20. The diction of Edmund Smith's *Phædra and Hippolitus* "too luxuriant and splendid for dialogue, and envelopes the thoughts rather than displays them." Too remote from life. *Lives* 2.16   1779
21. The dialogue of comedy of lasting interest when "transscribed from popular manners and real life." See *supra* 16   1779
22. Naturalness desirable. See *infra* 77   Ptd. 1780
23. Success of *Cato* "has introduced or confirmed among

us the use of dialogue too declamatory, of unaffecting elegance, and chill philosophy." *Lives* 2.133
Ptd. 1780

24. Thomson's "diffusive and descriptive style produced declamation rather than dialogue." *Lives* 3.293
1781

Drama: Division into Acts

25. "An act is so much of the drama as passes without intervention of time or change of place. A pause makes a new act. In every real, and therefore in every imitative action, the intervals may be more or fewer, the restriction of five acts being accidental and arbitrary." *Shak. Pref.*, Raleigh, 57   1765

Drama: Endings. See SUICIDAL ENDINGS; DRAMA: *Poetic Justice;* and *infra* 67

Drama: Farce. See BURLESQUE; and *supra* 14

26. *Definition:* "A dramatick representation written without regularity, and stuffed with wild and ludicrous conceits." *Dict.*   1755

Drama, Modern

27. "There is scarce a tragedy of the last century which has not debased its most important incidents, and polluted its most serious interlocutions with buffoonry and meanness; but though perhaps it cannot be pretended that the present age has added much to the force and efficacy of the drama, it has at least been able to escape many faults, which either ignorance had overlooked, or indulgence had licensed. The later tragedies indeed have faults of another kind, perhaps more destructive to delight, though less open to censure. That perpetual tumour of phrase with which every thought is now expressed by every personage, the paucity of adventures which regularity admits, and the unvaried equality of flowing dialogue, has

taken away from our present writers almost all that dominion over the passions which was the boast of their predecessors. Yet they may at least claim this commendation, that they avoid gross faults, and that if they cannot often move terror or pity, they are always careful not to provoke laughter." *Wks.* 6.349-50. (*Ram.* 125) 1751

28. All-importance of love, contrary to nature. See SHAKESPEARE 48. (cf. also DRYDEN 25) 1765

29. Dialogue and characters, except in Shakespearean drama, not true to life. See SHAKESPEARE 22, 30
1765

30. J. prefers modern French and English dramas to tragedies of the Ancients. See ANCIENT WRITERS 20
1779

31. *J. "conjured me [John Hoole] to read and meditate upon the Bible, and not to throw it aside for a play or a novel." *John. Misc.* 2.146. (Hoole) 1784

Drama: Play-Writing. For the dramatic writer's need of knowledge of life, see MILTON 13 and SAVAGE 2

32. Native genius or talent distinguished from experience in play-writing: "The art of the writer, like that of the player, is attained by slow degrees. The power of distinguishing and discriminating comick characters, or of filling tragedy with poetical images, must be the gift of nature, which no instruction nor labour can supply; but the art of dramatick disposition, the contexture of the scenes, the opposition of characters, the involution of the plot, the expedients of suspension, and the stratagems of surprize, are to be learned by practice; and it is cruel to discourage a poet for ever, because he has not from genius what only experience can bestow." *Wks.* 8.98. (*Idl.* 25) 1758

Drama: Poetic Justice

33. J. sides with general public in preferring Tate's happy

ending of *Lear:* "A play in which the wicked prosper, and the virtuous miscarry, may doubtless be good, because it is a just representation of the common events of human life: but since all reasonable beings naturally love justice, I cannot easily be persuaded, that the observation of justice makes a play worse; or, that if other excellencies are equal, the audience will not always rise better pleased from the final triumph of persecuted virtue. . . . I was many years ago [so¹] shocked by *Cordelia's* death, that I know not whether I ever endured to read again the last scenes of the play till I undertook to revise them as an editor." *Shak.*, Raleigh, 161-2   1765

34. "*Angelo's* crimes [in *Measure for Measure*] were such, as must sufficiently justify punishment, whether its end be to secure the innocent from wrong, or to deter guilt by example; and I believe every reader feels some indignation when he finds him spared." *Shak.*, Raleigh, 80   1765

35. "Dryden, petulantly and indecently, denies the heroism of Adam [in *Par. Lost*] because he was overcome; but there is no reason why the hero should not be unfortunate except established practice, since success and virtue do not go necessarily together."² *Lives* 1.176   1779

36. "The rules of tragic art scarcely permit that a perfectly virtuous man should be loaded with misfortunes." See SOPHOCLES 2. (cf. also *ib.* 1)   1779

37. Rowe's *Jane Shore:* "This play, consisting chiefly of domestick scenes and private distress, lays hold upon the heart. The wife is forgiven because she repents, and the husband is honoured because he forgives. This therefore is one of those pieces which we still welcome on the stage." *Lives* 2.69-70   Ptd. 1780

38. "Whatever pleasure there may be in seeing crimes

¹ First edition.
² Addison (*Spec.* No. 297) calls attention to this "imperfection."

punished and virtue rewarded, yet, since wickedness often prospers in real life,[1] the poet is certainly at liberty to give it prosperity on the stage. For if poetry has an imitation of reality, how are its laws broken by exhibiting the world in its true form? The stage may sometimes gratify our wishes; but, if it be truly the *mirror of life*, it ought to shew us sometimes what we are to expect." *Lives* 2.135   Ptd. 1780

39. *J. suggests that a certain character in a projected play should be made to conform to poetical justice. *Bos.* 4.333   1784

Drama, Restoration

40. "The wits of Charles found easier ways to fame,
Nor wish'd for Jonson's art, or Shakespeare's flame.
Themselves they studied; as they felt, they writ:
Intrigue was plot, obscenity was wit.
Vice always found a sympathetic friend;
They pleas'd their age, and did not aim to mend:
Yet bards like these aspir'd to lasting praise,
And proudly hop'd to pimp in future days."
Wks. 1.196-7. (cf. also *supra* 27)   1747

Drama: Rules. See also ARISTOTLE; SHAKESPEARE: "Unities." Compare RULES

41. After the reign of "the wits of Charles":
"Then crush'd by rules, and weaken'd as refin'd,
From bard to bard the frigid caution crept,
Till declamation roar'd, whilst passion slept;
Yet still did Virtue deign the stage to tread,
Philosophy remain'd, though Nature fled."
Wks. 1.197   1747

42. J. implies that his *Irene* does not "depart from Reason's rules." (It would seem from this that J. included

---

[1] cf. Nekayah, in *Rasselas* (ch. XXVII): "But this, at least, may be maintained, that we do not always find visible happiness in proportion to visible virtue," etc. *Wks.* 11.76

at least the three "unities" among "Reason's rules," since *Irene* keeps within them.) See *infra* 57   1749
43. The critic of a manuscript "stores his memory with Taste and Grace, Purity and Delicacy, Manners and Unities, sounds which, having been once uttered by those that understood them, have been since re-echoed without meaning, and kept up to the disturbance of the world, by a constant repercussion from one coxcomb to another." *Wks.* 5.152. (*Ram.* 23)   1750
44. "The accidental prescriptions of authority" not to be confounded with those rules founded on nature and reason. (For amplification of this important statement see RULES 7.) Dramatic rules examined on the basis of this distinction: [a] *Personages:* ". . . that *only three speaking personages should appear at once upon the stage;* a law which, as the variety and intricacy of modern plays has made it impossible to be observed, we now violate without scruple, and, as experience proves, without inconvenience. . . ." [b] *Arbitrary division into five acts:* "is not determined by any necessity arising either from the nature of action or propriety of exhibition. An act is only the representation of such a part of the business of the play as proceeds in an unbroken tenor, or without any intermediate pause. Nothing is more evident than that of every real, and by consequence of every dramatick action, the intervals may be more or fewer than five; and indeed the rule is upon the *English* stage every day broken in effect, without any other mischief than that which arises from an absurd endeavour to observe it in appearance. Whenever the scene is shifted the act ceases, since some time is necessarily supposed to elapse while the personages of the drama change their place." (cf. *supra* 25.) [c] *Unity of Time:* "With no greater right to our obedience have the criticks confined the dramatick action to a certain number of hours. Probability requires that the time of action should approach

somewhat nearly to that of exhibition, and those plays will always be thought most happily conducted which crowd the greatest variety into the least space. But since it will frequently happen that some delusion must be admitted, I know not where the limits of imagination can be fixed. It is rarely observed that minds, not prepossessed by mechanical criticism, feel any offence from the extension of the intervals between the acts; nor can I conceive it absurd or impossible, that he who can multiply three hours into twelve or twenty-four, might image with equal ease a greater number." [d] *Tragi-Comedy* partially defended. (See *infra* 75.) [e] *Unity of Action:* "There are other rules more fixed and obligatory. It is necessary that of every play the chief action should be single; for since a play represents some transaction, through its regular maturation to its final event, two actions equally important must evidently constitute two plays." [f] *The Hero:* "As the design of tragedy is to instruct by moving the passions, it must always have a hero, a personage apparently and incontestably superior to the rest, upon whom the attention may be fixed, and the anxiety suspended. For though of two persons opposing each other with equal abilities and equal virtue, the auditor will inevitably in time choose his favourite, yet as that choice must be without any cogency of conviction, the hopes or fears which it raises will be faint and languid. Of two heroes acting in confederacy against a common enemy, the virtues or dangers will give little emotion, because each claims our concern with the same right, and the heart lies at rest between equal motives." *Wks.* 7.96-100. (*Ram.* 156)   1751

45. ". . . such rules are to be observed as make the representation probable." See *supra* 18   1755

46. Shakespeare's practice of mixing comic and tragic scenes "contrary to the rules of criticism . . . but there is always an appeal open from criticism to

nature." *Shak. Pref.*, Raleigh, 16. (For further defence of this practice, see DRAMA: *Tragi-Comedy*, and SHAKESPEARE: *Tragi-Comedy*)   1765

47. [a] "It is time therefore to tell him [the critic] by the authority of *Shakespeare*, that he assumes, as an unquestionable principle, a position, which, while his breath is forming it into words, his understanding pronounces to be false. It is false, that any representation is mistake[n[1]] for reality; that any dramatick fable in its materiality was ever credible, or, for a single moment, was ever credited. The objection arising from the impossibility of passing the first hour at *Alexandria*, and the next at *Rome*, supposes, that when the play opens, the spectator really imagines himself at *Alexandria*, and believes that his walk to the theatre has been a voyage to *Egypt*, and that he lives in the days of *Antony* and *Cleopatra*. Surely he that imagines this may imagine more. . . . There is no reason why a mind thus wandering in extacy should count the clock, or why an hour should not be a century in that calenture of the brains that can make the stage a field. The truth is, that the spectators are always in their senses, and know, from the first act to the last, that the stage is only a stage, and that the players are only players.[2] They came to hear a certain number of lines recited with just gesture and elegant modulation . . . and where is the absurdity of allowing that space to represent first *Athens*, and then *Sicily*, which was always known to be neither *Sicily* nor *Athens*, but a modern theatre?[3] By supposition, as place is introduced, times may be extended; the time required by the fable elapses for the most part between the acts. . . . The

[1] First edition.
[2] cf. ". . . nobody imagines that he [a player] is the character he represents." *Bos.* 5.46 (1773)
[3] cf. Dryden's "it is an original absurdity for the audience to suppose themselves to be in any other place than in the very theatre in which they sit, which is neither chamber, nor garden, nor yet a public place of any business, but that of the representation." *Wks.* ed. Scott-Saintsbury, 8.375

drama exhibits successive imitations of successive actions; and why may not the second imitation represent an action that happened years after the first, if it be so connected with it, that nothing but time can be supposed to intervene? Time is, of all modes of existence, most obsequious to the imagination; a lapse of years is as easily conceived as a passage of hours. In contemplation we easily contract the time of real actions, and therefore willingly permit it to be contracted when we only see their imitation. [b] It will be asked, how the drama moves, if it is not credited. It is credited with all the credit due to a drama. It is credited, whenever it moves, as a just picture of a real original; as representing to the auditor what he would himself feel, if he were to do or suffer what is there feigned to be suffered or to be done. The reflection that strikes the heart is not, that the evils before us are real evils, but that they are evils to which we ourselves may be exposed. . . . The delight of tragedy proceeds from our consciousness of fiction; if we thought murders and treasons real, they would please no more. Imitations produce pain or pleasure, not because they are mistaken for realities, but because they bring realities to mind. . . . A dramatick exhibition is a book recited with concomitants that encrease or diminish its effect. . . . A play read, affects the mind like a play acted. It is therefore evident, that the action is not supposed to be real; and it follows, that between the acts a longer or shorter time may be allowed to pass, and that no more account of space or duration is to be taken by the auditor of a drama, than by the reader of a narrative, before whom may pass in an hour the life of a hero, or the revolutions of an empire. [c] . . . nothing is essential to the fable, but unity of action. . . . The result of my enquiries, in which it would be ludicrous to boast of impartiality, is, that the unities of time and place are not essential to a just drama, that though they may sometimes conduce to pleasure, they are always to be sacrificed to the nobler beauties of variety and instruction; and that a play, written with nice observation of critical rules, is to be contemplated as an elaborate curiosity, as the product of superfluous and ostentatious art, by which is shewn, rather what is possible, than what is necessary. He that, without diminution of any other excellence, shall preserve all the unities unbroken, deserves the like applause with the architect, who shall display all the orders of architecture in a citadel, without any deduction from its strength; but the principal beauty of a citadel is to exclude the enemy; and the greatest graces of a play, are to copy nature and instruct life." *Shak. Pref.*, Raleigh, 26-30   1765

48. For other evidence that J. did not think a strict preservation of the unities necessary, see SHAKESPEARE 139   1765

49. See *Shak.*, Raleigh, 198-9, in which note J. seems to suggest that the probability of the story is more important than the rules of the drama, in particular, the unity of time.   1765

50. "Had the scene [of *Othello*] opened in *Cyprus*, and the preceding incidents been occasionally related, there had been little wanting to a drama of the most exact and scrupulous regularity." *Shak.*, Raleigh, 201   1765

51. J. refers, apparently with approbation, to the fact that in the *Oedipus Tyrannus* of Sophocles, "the three grand unities . . . are observed with scrupulous exactness." *Poems and Misc. Pieces*, by Thomas Maurice 1779 p. 150 (*Preface* by J.)   1779

52. The rigorous unity of place maintained throughout Addison's *Cato* gives rise to improprieties of scene. *Lives* 2.136   Ptd. 1780

53. "In the construction of his [Rowe's] dramas there is

not much art; he is not a nice observer of the Unities. He extends time and varies place as his convenience requires. To vary the place is not, in my opinion, any violation of Nature, if the change be made between the acts, for it is no less easy for the spectator to suppose himself at Athens in the second act, than at Thebes in the first; but to change the scene, as is done by Rowe in the middle of an act, is to add more acts to the play, since an act is so much of the business as is transacted without interruption. Rowe, by this license, easily extricates himself from difficulties." (The unnaturalness of such license intimated.) *Lives* 2.75-6
Ptd. 1780

Drama, Spanish

54. * "Spanish plays, being wildly and improbably farcical, would please children here, as children are entertained with stories full of prodigies." *Bos.* 4.16. (Langton's *Collection*) Date?

Drama: Tragedy. See also SHAKESPEARE: Tragedies; DRAMA: Tragi-Comedy, Characters and Rules

55. The story of Sir Thomas Overbury "well adapted to the stage, though perhaps not far enough removed from the present age, to admit properly the fictions necessary to complete the plan; for the mind, which naturally loves truth, is always most offended with the violation of those truths of which we are most certain, and we, of course, conceive those facts most certain which approach nearest to our own time." *Lives* 2.338 cf. *infra* 70, 71 and EPIC 9   1744

56. J. appears to accept the current opinion that tragedy should not transgress the bounds of probability. Thus the action should not depend upon enchantment, nor the chief events be produced "by the assistance of supernatural agents." *Wks.* 14.60*ff.* (*Observ. on Macbeth*) See also SHAKESPEARE 149   1745

57. After a recital of various moral sentiments to be learned from *Irene*, the *Prologue* continues:
"If truths like these with pleasing language join;
Ennobled, yet unchang'd, if Nature shine:
If no wild draught depart from Reason's rules,
Nor gods his heroes, nor his lovers fools:
Intriguing wits! his artless plot forgive;
And spare him, beauties! tho' his lovers live.
Be this at least his praise; be this his pride;
To force applause no modern arts are try'd.
. . . .
In Reason, Nature, Truth he dares to trust:
Ye Fops be silent! and ye Wits be just!"
Wks. 11.219   1749

58. ". . . that exaltation above common life, which in tragick or heroick writings often reconciles us to bold flights and daring figures." *Wks.* 5.242-3. (*Ram.* 37)
1750

59. "The imperial tragedy pleases common auditors only by its pomp of ornament, and grandeur of ideas" since it is so far removed from normal human experience. See EXPERIENCE 7   1750

60. Faults of modern tragedies. See *supra* 27   1751

61. *Tragedy and comedy distinguished:* See *supra* 12 a, b
1751

62. Aristotle's rule regarding construction of fable accepted. See FABLE 1   1751

63. Decorum of sentiments in tragedy. See SENTIMENT 1
1751

64. A rule "more fixed and obligatory": "As the design of tragedy is to instruct by moving the passions, it must always have a hero." See *supra* 44f.   1751

65. *Tragedy defined:* "1. A dramatick representation of a serious action." *Dict.*   1755

66. "The delight of tragedy proceeds from our conscious-

ness of fiction; if we thought murders and treasons real, they would please no more." See *supra* 47b 1765

67. *Tragedy and comedy distinguished*: Inexact ideas of those who distinguish between tragedy and comedy according to the nature of the ending. "Tragedy was not in those times [age of Shakespeare] a poem of more general dignity or elevation than comedy; it required only a calamitous conclusion, with which the common criticism of that age was satisfied, whatever lighter pleasure it afforded in its progress." *Shak. Pref.*, Raleigh, 17 1765

68. *Tragedy and comedy distinguished:* "Familiar comedy is often more powerful in the theatre, than on the page; imperial tragedy is always less. The humour of *Petruchio* may be heightened by grimace; but what voice or what gesture can hope to add dignity or force to the soliloquy of *Cato*."[1] *Shak. Pref.*, Raleigh, 28
1765

69. "What is nearest us touches us most. The passions rise higher at domestic than at imperial tragedies." *Letters* 1.162. See also SHAKESPEARE 151 1770

70. J. condemns Edmund Smith's *Phædra and Hippolitus:* "The fable is mythological, a story which we are accustomed to reject as false, and the manners are so distant from our own that we know them not from sympathy, but by study: the ignorant do not understand the action, the learned reject it as a school-boy's tale; *incredulus odi*. What I cannot for a moment believe, I cannot for a moment behold with interest or anxiety. The sentiments thus remote from life are removed yet further by the diction, which is too luxuriant and splendid for dialogue, and envelopes the thoughts rather than displays them." *Lives* 2.16. cf. *supra* 55, *infra* 71 and EPIC 9 1779

71. "*The Royal Convert* [by Rowe] . . . seems to have

[1] For J.'s low opinion of tragic acting, see also *Bos.* 5.38; 2.92; *Wks.* 8.32; and *supra* DRAMA: ACTORS AND ACTING.

a better claim to longevity. The fable is drawn from an obscure and barbarous age, to which fictions are most easily and properly adapted; for when objects are imperfectly seen they easily take forms from imagination." *Lives* 2.68. cf. *supra* 55, 70 and EPIC 9
Ptd. 1780

72. *Domestic tragedy*: "The story [of Rowe's *Fair Penitent*] is domestick, and therefore easily received by the imagination, and assimilated to common life." *Lives* 2.67. (cf. also J.'s admiration of *Jane Shore:* "This play, consisting chiefly of domestick scenes and private distress, lays hold upon the heart." *Lives* 2.69)
Ptd. 1780

73. ". . . the pride of Busiris [in Young's tragedy] is such as no other man can have, and the whole is too remote from known life to raise either grief, terror, or indignation. The *Revenge* approaches much nearer to human practices and manners, and therefore keeps possession of the stage." *Lives* 3.397   1781

Drama: Tragi-Comedy. See SHAKESPEARE: *Tragi-Comedies*

74. "I have, indeed, hitherto avoided the practice of uniting gay and solemn subjects in the same paper [in *The Rambler*], because it seems absurd for an author to counteract himself, to press at once with equal force upon both parts of the intellectual balance, or give medicines, which, like the double poison of *Dryden*, destroy the force of one another. . . . Yet I shall this day publish two letters of very different tendency, which I hope, like tragi-comedy, may chance to please even when they are not critically approved." *Wks.* 6.227. (*Ram.* 107)   1751

75. "I know not whether he that professes to regard no other laws than those of nature, will not be inclined to receive tragi-comedy to his protection, whom, however generally condemned, her own laurels have hitherto

shaded from the fulminations of criticism. For what is there in the mingled drama wnich impartial reason can condemn? The connexion of important with trivial incidents, since it is not only common but perpetual in the world, may surely be allowed upon the stage, which pretends only to be the mirrour of life. The impropriety of suppressing passions before we have raised them to the intended agitation, and of diverting the expectation from an event which we keep suspended only to raise it, may be speciously urged. But will not experience shew this objection to be rather subtle than just? Is it not certain that the tragick and comick affections have been moved alternately with equal force, and that no plays have oftener filled the eye with tears, and the breast with palpitation, than those which are variegated with interludes of mirth? I do not however think it safe to judge of works of genius merely by the event . . . and instead of vindicating tragi-comedy by the success of *Shakespeare*, we ought perhaps to pay new honours to that transcendent and unbounded genius that could preside over the passions in sport; who, to actuate the affections, needed not the slow gradation of common means, but could fill the heart with instantaneous jollity or sorrow, and vary our disposition as he changed his scenes. Perhaps the effects even of *Shakespeare's* poetry might have been yet greater, had he not counteracted himself; and we might have been more interested in the distresses of his heroes, had we not been so frequently diverted by the jokes of his buffoons." *Wks.* 7.98-9. (*Ram.* 156)   1751

76. *Definition of tragi-comedy:* "A drama compounded of merry and serious events." *Dict.*   1755

Drama: Unities. See DRAMA: *Rules*

Drama: Versification

77. ". . . those redundant terminations which the drama

not only admits but requires, as more nearly approaching to real dialogue." *Lives* 2.260   Ptd. 1780

Dramatic Narrative. See under NARRATIVE

Dramatic Propriety

1. Some characters not proper for representation: e.g. leading characters whose good and bad qualities are equally conspicuous. The "splendidly wicked . . . ought no more to be preserved, than the art of murdering without pain." Representation of "the most perfect idea of virtue . . . not angelical, nor above probability . . . but the highest and purest that humanity can reach" advocated in fictional narratives. For amplification of this theory of imitation, see FICTION 1   1750
2. "All ranks of persons" proper to pastoral. See PASTORAL 2   1750
3. Shakespeare's profane expressions unjustified: "There are laws of higher authority than those of criticism." See SHAKESPEARE 142   1765
4. *Characters of nature and characters of manners differentiated. See RICHARDSON 2   1768
5. *". . . a speech on the stage, let it flatter ever so extravagantly, is formular." *Bos.* 2.234   1773
6. Clarke censured Satan's impiety in *Paradise Lost*. J. comments: "For there are thoughts, as he justly remarks, which no observation of character can justify, because no good man would willingly permit them to pass, however transiently, through his own mind." Milton obviates this difficulty by using general expressions. *Lives* 1.173   1779
7. In Dryden are "many passages, which, with all the allowance that can be made for characters and occasions, are such as piety would not have admitted, and such as may vitiate light and unprincipled minds." *Lives* 1.404   1779

Dramatic Propriety 93

8. *"Never fear putting the strongest and best things you can think of into the mouth of your speaker, whatever may be his condition." Crabbe's *Wks*., ed. 1834, 1.91 *ff*. (Quoted in *Letters* 2.287 *n* 2) 1783

Eclogue. See Pastoral

Elegance

1. *Definition of elegance:* "Beauty of art; rather soothing than striking; beauty without grandeur."[1] *Dict.* 1755
2. *Definition of elegant:* "1. Pleasing with minuter beauties. . . . 2. Nice; not coarse; not gross."[2] *Dict.* 1755
3. The early writers "excel in strength and invention, and the latter in elegance and refinement." Imlac in *Rasselas* (ch. X). *Wks.* 11.29-30 1759
4. Defence of Pope's translation of Homer: "Thus it will be found in the progress of learning that in all nations the first writers are simple, and that every age improves in elegance. One refinement always makes way for another, and what was expedient to Virgil was necessary to Pope. . . . Homer doubtless owes to his translator many Ovidian graces not exactly suitable to his character; but to have added can be no great crime if nothing be taken away. Elegance is surely to be desired if it be not gained at the expence of dignity. A hero would wish to be loved as well as to be reverenced." (For rest of passage, see Aim of Writing 25) *Lives* 3.239 1781

Elegy

1. Compared with the epitaph. See Epitaph 1 1740
2. *Definition:* "1. A mournful song . . . 2. A funeral

---

[1] Perhaps the favourite word of eighteenth century reviewers. It is interesting to find Johnson, however, on occasion using the word to express disfavor: e.g., Cowley's letters "shew him to have been above the affectation of unseasonable elegance." (*Lives* 1.8)
[2] e.g., Milton "sometimes descends to the elegant, but his element is the great." (*Lives* 1.177)

song . . . 3. A short poem without point or turns." *Dict.* 1755

3. Referring to Cowley's elegy on Hervey: ". . . When he wishes to make us weep he forgets to weep himself, and diverts his sorrow by imagining how his crown of bays, if he had it, would *crackle* in the *fire*." *Lives* 1.37 1779

4. The insincerity of pastoral and mythological fictions when used in elegy: *Lycidas* "is not to be considered as the effusion of real passion; for passion runs not after remote allusions and obscure opinions. Passion plucks no berries from the myrtle and ivy, nor calls upon Arethuse and Mincius, nor tells of 'rough satyrs and fauns with cloven heel.' 'Where there is leisure for fiction there is little grief.' In this poem there is no nature, for there is no truth; there is no art, for there is nothing new. Its form is that of a pastoral, easy, vulgar, and therefore disgusting: whatever images it can supply are long ago exhausted; and its inherent improbability always forces dissatisfaction on the mind." The lines *We drove a field*, etc., not literally true—"We know that they never drove a field,"—and even if allegorically considered are obscure. "Among the flocks and copses and flowers appear the heathen deities, Jove and Phœbus, Neptune and Æolus, with a long train of mythological imagery, such as a College easily suplies. Nothing can less display knowledge or less exercise invention than to tell how a shepherd has lost his companion and must now feed his flocks alone, without any judge of his skill in piping; and how one god asks another god what is become of Lycidas, and how neither god can tell. He who thus grieves will excite no sympathy; he who thus praises will confer no honour". *Lives* 1.163-4. See also PASTORAL 2; 9; 13 for similar expressions of his distaste for pastoral elegy. 1779

5. For criticism of one of the best English elegies, see SMITH, EDMUND 5   1779
6. For the most sublime and elegant funeral poem in all English literature, see TICKELL 9   Ptd. 1780
7. Elegy "very judiciously and discriminately explained" by Shenstone: "the effusion of a contemplative mind, sometimes plaintive, and always serious, and therefore superior to the glitter of slight ornaments." *Lives* 3.355   1781
8. Shenstone's *Elegies* too much alike in thoughts. "The lines are sometimes, such as elegy requires, smooth and easy." *Lives* 3.355   1781
9. J. does not understand why the quatrain of ten syllables is thought elegiac by some writers: "The character of the elegy is gentleness and tenuity," but Dryden called this measure the most magnificent of all the English measures. *Lives* 2.316   1781
10. ". . . these elegies [by Hammond] have neither passion, nature, nor manners. Where there is fiction, there is no passion; he that describes himself as a shepherd, and his Neæra or Delia as a shepherdess, and talks of goats and lambs, feels no passion. He that courts his mistress with Roman imagery deserves to lose her; for she may with good reason suspect his sincerity. Hammond has few sentiments drawn from nature, and few images from modern life. He produces nothing but frigid pedantry." *Lives* 2.315   1781

Elizabethan Age

1. Survey of its barbarity. *Shak. Pref.*, Raleigh, 31-2. (For its dramatic rudeness—"neither character nor dialogue were yet understood"—see especially *ib.* 36. Throughout J.'s edition of Shakespeare are many similar references to the crudeness of the age. In a review of J. Warton's *Essay on Pope* (*Wks.* 15.476), J. quotes without comment Warton's enumeration of the

five chief periods of literary history: "that of Alexander; of Ptolemy Philadelphus, of Augustus, of Leo the tenth, of Queen Anne." No mention is made of Elizabethan literature.) 1765

Emendation, Textual

1. "Amendments are seldom made without some token of a rent." *Lives* 2.176   Ptd. 1780
2. Thomson's *Liberty* "shortened by Sir George Lyttelton, with a liberty which, as it has a manifest tendency to lessen the confidence of society, and to confound the characters of authors by making one man write by the judgement of another, cannot be justified by any supposed propriety of the alteration or kindness of the friend.—I wish to see it exhibited as its author left it." *Lives* 3.290. (Throughout his edition of Shakespeare, J. keeps reasserting this principle.)   1781

Endings. See SUICIDAL ENDINGS and DRAMA: *Poetic Justice*

English Language. See also DICTION, PURITY OF

1. The Spenserian stanza unsuited to the genius of the English language. See IMITATION 6   1751
2. So much inferior in harmony to the Latin. *Lives* 1.448. cf. MILTON 16; VERSIFICATION 5, 6   1779
3. The "affluence and comprehension of our language" shown in our poetical translations of the Ancients. See TRANSLATION 9   1779
4. The sonnet unsuited to the nature of the English language. See SONNET 2   1779
5. Blank verse unsuited to the nature of the English language. See EPIC 9 and BLANK VERSE 7   1779-81
6. "The time of pronunciation was in the dactylick measures of the learned languages capable of considerable variety . . . but our language having little flexibility

our verses can differ very little in their cadence." See
VERSIFICATION 33   1781
7. Pindaric ode unsuited to the nature of the English
language. See PINDARIC VERSE 8   1781

English Literature. See also FRENCH LITERATURE

1. English writers "equal perhaps always in force and genius, and of late in elegance and accuracy, to those of any other country." *Wks.* 7.69. (*Ram.* 152) 1751
2. England "now justly termed, the capital of literature." *Wks.* 4.626   1761

Enthusiasm. See also PRAISE

1. *Definition:* "1. A vain belief of private revelation; a vain confidence of divine favour or communication[1] ... 2. Heat of imagination; violence of passion; confidence of opinion.[2] 3. Elevation of fancy; exaltation of ideas."[3] *Dict.*   1755
2. ". . . when a man is enthusiastick, he ceases to be reasonable."[4] *Wks.* 10.280   1757
3. "The first part [of Dryden's *To the Pious Memory of ... Mrs. Anne Killigrew*] flows with a torrent of enthusiasm." (J. implies that the first stanza is the finest, and calls the ode "the noblest . . . that our language ever has produced.") *Lives* 1.439   1779
4. "Enthusiasm has its rules." See CONGREVE 3
                                                       Ptd. 1780

---

[1] See *Letters* 2.306 *n* 1 for note on J.'s use of the word in this sense. J. defines *fanaticism* as "Enthusiasm; religious frenzy," and *fanatic:* "An enthusiast; a man mad with wild notions of religion."
[2] e.g., Helmont and Paracelsus are "wild and enthusiastic authors of romantic chymistry" (see *Paracelsus* 1); a "dithyrambick" is "any poem written with wildness and enthusiasm," (*Dict.*); "none is sufficiently enthusiastical to maintain . . ." (*Wks.* 5.401. See also *ib.* 6.149 and *Lives* 2.303)
[3] See *infra* 3 and 5 for illustrations.
[4] cf. Warburton's statement that enthusiasm "makes us give a stronger assent to the *conclusion,* than the evidence of the premises will warrant." *Letters from a Late Eminent Prelate,* ed. 1809, p. 99.

5. "The poet [Thomson, in *The Seasons*] leads us through the appearances of things . . . and imparts to us so much of his own enthusiasm that our thoughts expand with his imagery and kindle with his sentiments." *Lives* 3.299   1781

Epic and Heroic Poetry

1. The established mode of procedure in opening an heroic poem. See OPENING 1   1750
2. ". . . that exaltation above common life, which in tragick or heroick writings often reconciles us to bold flights and daring figures." *Wks.* 5.242-3. (*Ram.* 37)   1750
3. Epic and tragic measures differentiated. See VERSIFICATION 6   1751
4. *Definition of epic:* "Narrative; comprising narrations, not acted but rehearsed. It is usually supposed to be heroick, or to contain one great action atchieved by a hero." *Dict.*   1755
5. Criticism of Cowley's *Davideis* under heads of "plan," "duration of action," "characters," and "fable." *Lives* 1.53-4. See also analysis of *Paradise Lost* along Aristotelian lines: MILTON 43   1779
6. Function of epic poetry "to teach the most important truths by the most pleasing precepts." Knowledge, moral principles, experience in human nature, and technical skill required of the epic poet. First praise of genius should be his: an epic poem "requires an assemblage of all the powers which are singly sufficient for other compositions." See POETRY 22 for whole of this passage.   1779
7. "Bossu is of opinion that the poet's first work is to find a *moral*, which his fable is afterwards to illustrate and establish. This seems to have been the process only of Milton. . . ." *Lives* 1.171   1779
8. J. commends in Dryden's projected epic his supernat-

ural machinery: The "contest between the guardian angels of kingdoms . . . the most reasonable scheme of celestial interposition that ever was formed." Enchantments "afford very striking scenes, and open a vast extent to the imagination; but, as Boileau observes . . . with this incurable defect, that in a contest between heaven and hell" we foresee the outcome. *Lives* 1.385-6   1779

9. *Improper material and metre for epic:* J. criticizes Pope's proposed epic poem, as no great loss to mankind, for, "his hero was Brutus, the Trojan, who, according to a ridiculous fiction, established a colony in Britain. The subject, therefore, was of the fabulous age; the actors were a race upon whom imagination has been exhausted and attention wearied, and to whom the mind will not easily be recalled when it is invited in blank verse, which Pope had adopted with great imprudence, and, I think, without due consideration of the nature of our language. . . . Pope was thoughtless enough to model the names of his heroes with terminations not consistent with the time or country in which he places them." (See *Lives* 3.189 *n* 1 for various readings of this sentence.) *Lives* 3.188-9. cf. DRAMA 55, 70, 71   1781

10. Similes in heroic poetry. See SIMILES 5   1781

Epigram. See also APHORISMS

1. *Definition:* "A short poem terminating in a point." *Dict.*   1755
2. Warton "observes very justly, that the odes [for St. Cecilia's Day] both of Dryden and Pope conclude unsuitably and unnaturally with epigram." *Wks.* 15.473   1756

Epitaph

1. [a] *Definition:* "An *inscription on the tomb.*" Theoretically, therefore, it admits "indiscriminately satire or

praise." In practice, however, it is "an *inscription engraven on a tomb in honour of the person deceased.*" *Purpose:* principally "to perpetuate the examples of virtue. . . . Those EPITAPHS are, therefore, the most perfect, which set virtue in the strongest light, and are best adapted to exalt the reader's ideas and rouse his emulation." [b] *Types of epitaphs:* Lists of achievements of most eminent men unnecessary in epitaphs. "Next in dignity to the bare name is a short character simple and unadorned, without exaggeration, superlatives, or rhetorick." Examples. "But to far the greatest part of mankind a longer encomium is necessary . . . and in the composition of these it is that art is principally required, and precepts therefore may be useful." [c] *Precepts:* The epitaph distinguished from all other compositions by the "particular air of solemnity" required by this situation, which "debars them from the admission of all lighter or gayer ornaments. In this it is that the style of an EPITAPH necessarily differs from that of an ELEGY." Situation in or near churches "makes it proper to exclude . . . all such allusions as are contrary to the doctrines for the propagation of which the churches are erected." Hence the absurdity of copying Roman inscriptions; of allusions to heathen mythology; of expressions of regard "for the senseless remains of a dead man"; e.g., Cowley's epitaph. Impropriety of imitating ancients by addressing the epitaph to the passer-by.[1] Less impropriety in epitaphs in "monkish ages" than in "more enlightened times." Name of the deceased not to be omitted—the first rule for writing epitaphs. Otherwise they cannot inform posterity. Rules for drawing the character of the deceased relate equally to other compositions: "The praise ought not to be general, because the mind is lost in the extent of any indefinite idea, and cannot be affected with what it cannot comprehend." *Truth:* "Though a sepulchral

---

[1] See *Bos.* 4.85 *n* 1: J. breaks his own rule in his epitaph for Mr. Thrale.

inscription is professedly a panegyrick, and, therefore, not confined to historical impartiality, yet it ought always to be written with regard to truth." Though virtues are not to be invented, faults may be omitted, since "the monuments of the dead are not intended to perpetuate the memory of crimes, but to exhibit patterns of virtue. . . . The best subject for EPITAPHS is private virtue; virtue exerted in the same circumstances in which the bulk of mankind are placed, and which, therefore, may admit of many imitators." (cf. BIOGRAPHY 3.) *Wks.* 9.437-44. (*Essay on Epitaphs*) 1740

2. Application of these principles (in 1 a, b, c) to various epitaphs. *Wks.* 9.438-46   1740

3. "To define an epitaph is useless; every one knows that it is an inscription on a tomb. An epitaph, therefore, implies no particular character of writing, but may be composed in verse or prose. It is indeed commonly panegyrical, because we are seldom distinguished with a stone but by our friends; but it has no rule to restrain or modify it, except this, that it ought not to be longer than common beholders may be expected to have leisure and patience to peruse." *Lives* 3.254   1756

4. "The end of an epitaph is to convey some account of the dead; and to what purpose is anything told of him whose name is concealed?" *Lives* 3.257   1756

5. "*Peace to thy shade* is too mythological to be admitted into a Christian temple. . . . Let fiction, at least, cease with life, and let us be serious over the grave." *Lives* 3.261   1756

6. *Pope's Epitaphs*—*No.* 6: "The most valuable of Pope's epitaphs" in that it exalts domestic virtue. *Lives* 3.262   1756

7. *Pope's Epitaphs*—*No.* 7: Gives too general a character: "The difficulty in writing epitaphs is to give a particular and appropriate praise"—though the sub-

ject often makes this difficult, and occasional repetition is pardonable. *Lives* 3.263-4   1756
8. "An epitaph is no easy thing. . . . Thus easy is it to find faults, but it is hard to make an Epitaph." *Letters* 1.186-7   1771
9. *"The writer of an epitaph should not be considered as saying nothing but what is strictly true. Allowance must be made for some degree of exaggerated praise. In lapidary inscriptions a man is not upon oath." *Bos.* 2.407   1775

Epithet

1. *Definition:* "1. An adjective denoting quality good or bad: as the *verdant* grove, the *craggy* mountain's lofty head. . . . 2. It is used by some writers improperly for *title, name.* . . . 3. It is used improperly for *phrase, expression.*" *Dict.*   1755

Essays. Compare PERIODICAL WRITINGS

1. *Periodical essays:* The advantages in this form of writing: its wide circulation, its adaptability to public taste and circumstances, its brevity. *Wks.* 5.6-7. (*Ram.* 1)   1750
2. *Periodical essays:* ". . . a diurnal writer ought to view the world, and . . . he who neglects his cotemporaries, may be, with justice, neglected by them." *Wks.* 5.60. (*Ram.* 10)   1750
3. "A writer of later times has, by the vivacity of his essays, reconciled mankind to the same licentiousness in short dissertations [as in the lyric *q.v.*]; and he therefore who wants skill to form a plan, or diligence to pursue it, needs only entitle his performance an essay, to acquire the right of heaping together the collections of half his life, without order, coherence, or propriety. . . . As vices never promote happiness, though when overpowered by more active and more numerous virtues, they cannot totally destroy it; so

confusion and irregularity produce no beauty, though they cannot always obstruct the brightness of genius and learning. To proceed from one truth to another, and connect distant propositions by regular consequences, is the great prerogative of man. Independent and unconnected sentiments flashing upon the mind in quick succession, may, for a time, delight by their novelty, but they differ from systematical reasoning, as single notes from harmony, as glances of lightning from the radiance of the sun." *Wks.* 7.109-10. (*Ram.* 158)   1751

4. *Periodical essays:* Advantage of the essay writer: no great preliminary study necessary. But a "boundless multiplicity" of subjects from which he is recurrently "obliged to choose, without any principle to regulate his choice." *Wks.* 7.254-5. (*Ram.* 184)   1751

5. *Definition of essay:* "1. Attempt; endeavour. 2. A loose sally of the mind; an irregular indigested piece; not a regular and orderly composition. . . . 3. A trial; an experiment. . . . 4. First taste of anything, first experiment." *Dict.*   1755

6. *Periodical essays:* "For this purpose [of reforming manners by an *arbiter elegantiarum*] nothing is so proper as the frequent publication of short papers, which we read not as study but amusement. If the subject be slight, the treatise likewise is short. The busy may find time, and the idle may find patience." *Lives* 2.93   Ptd. 1780

Exaggeration. See Praise; Enthusiasm; Unnatural, The

Experience. (Contact with the World)

1. Experience, converse with the living world, together with book learning, necessary for the modern writer of fiction. *Wks.* 5.21. (*Ram.* 4)   1750
2. "Among the numerous requisites that most concur to

complete an author, few are of more importance than an early entrance into the living world. . . . Argumentation may be taught in colleges, and theories formed in retirement; but the artifice of embellishment, and the powers of attraction, can be gained only by general converse." *Wks.* 7.167-8. (*Ram.* 168) 1751

3. "To read, write, and converse in due proportions, is, therefore, the business of a man of letters." *Wks.* 9.67 (*Adv.* 85) 1753

4. "To a poet nothing can be useless." See POETRY 14 1759

5. The dramatic writer's need of personal experience. See MILTON 13, and SAVAGE 2 (1744) 1779

6. Pope later "gathered his notions fresh from reality." See POPE 9 1781

Experience. (AS A CRITICAL TEST.) See also under DRAMA: *Rules*; and NATURE

7. *Conformity to general human experience increases interest and sympathy:* "It is not easy for the most artful writer to give us an interest in happiness or misery, which we think ourselves never likely to feel, and with which we have never yet been made acquainted. Histories of the downfal of kingdoms, and revolutions of empires, are read with great tranquillity; the imperial tragedy pleases common auditors only by its pomp of ornament, and grandeur of ideas; and the man whose faculties have been engrossed by business, and whose heart never fluttered but at the rise or fall of the stocks, wonders how the attention can be seized, or the affection agitated, by a tale of love." Hence the superior possibilities in biography for interesting and instructing mankind. (See BIOGRAPHY 3.) "The general and rapid narratives of history, which involve a thousand fortunes in the business of a day, and complicate innumerable incidents in one great transaction, afford few lessons applicable to private life." *Wks.* 5.381-2.

EXPERIENCE 105

(*Ram.* 60) See also DRAMA 69, 72 for similar views.

1750

8. A qualified appeal to experience in examination of tragi-comedy. See DRAMA 75; see also DRAMA: *Rules*

1751

9. History usually remote from common experience. See HISTORY 9

1759

10. J. justifies Shakespeare's method of mingling tragic and comic scenes by an appeal to experience. See SHAKESPEARE 90

1765

11. (Context: Dryden's use of nautical terms.): "Let us then appeal to experience; for by experience at last we learn as well what will please as what will profit." *Lives* 1.433

1779

12. "Judgement is forced upon us by experience. He that reads many books must compare one opinion or one style with another; and when he compares, must necessarily distinguish, reject, and prefer." *Lives* 3.94

1781

13. ". . . the cant of those who judge by principles rather than perception." (J. is arguing that the ear should be the judge of metrical harmony. cf. ANCIENT WRITERS 7.) See VERSIFICATION 30

1781

Fable. (PLOT.) See also STRUCTURE; INVENTION; SUBJECT; SHAKESPEARE: *Plots.* For FABLE (*Fiction, as opposed to Truth*) see FICTION; MYTHOLOGY; compare TRUTH

1. J. accepts Aristotle's rule that a well-constituted fable must have a beginning, a middle and an end. "This precept is to be understood in its rigour only with respect to great and essential events, and cannot be extended in the same force to minuter circumstances and arbitrary decorations, which yet are more happy

as they contribute more to the main design . . . the idea of an ornament admits use, though it seems to exclude necessity." *Samson Agonistes* examined in the light of this rule, *q.v. Wks.* 6.429-36. (*Ram.* 139)   1751

2. *Definition:* "1. A feigned story intended to enforce some moral precept . . . 2. A fiction in general . . . 3. A vitious or foolish fiction . . . 4. The series or contexture of events which constitute a poem epick or dramatick." *Dict.*   1755

3. "It is indeed much more easy to form dialogues than to contrive adventures . . . whether it be that we comprehend but few of the possibilities of life, or that life itself affords little variety, every man who has tried knows how much labour it will cost to form such a combination of circumstances, as shall have at once the grace of novelty and credibility, and delight fancy without violence to reason." *Lives* 1.211   1779

4. *The Fable or Apologue:* Lack of settled notions of authors on a fable. "A Fable or Apologue, such as is now under consideration, seems to be in its genuine state a narrative in which beings irrational, and sometimes inanimate, 'arbores loquuntur, non tantum feræ,' are for the purpose of moral instruction feigned to act and speak with human interests and passions." *Lives* 2.283   1781

Fame, *Literary*. See also CRITICISM, TIME AS AN AID TO; POPULAR JUDGEMENT; NATURE; and OCCASIONAL WORKS

1. Precariousness of literary fame. See AUTHORS 2. 1750
2. Various kinds of "bubbles of artificial fame, which are kept up a while by the breath of fashion, and then break at once, and are annihilated." The precariousness of literary reputation of every sort. "He who has carefully studied human nature, and can well describe

it, may with most reason flatter his ambition. . . . It may, however, satisfy an honest and benevolent mind to have been useful, though less conspicuous." *Wks.* 6.223-6. (*Ram.* 106) 1751

3. "Fame cannot spread wide or endure long that is not rooted in nature, and manured by art." See INVENTION 1 1751

4. *"It is difficult to get literary fame, and it is every day growing more difficult." *Bos.* 2.358 1775

5. An author seldom hurt by criticism. See CRITICISM 13 1780

Familiar Style. See under STYLE

Fancy. See also IMAGINATION

1. Criticism the governess of Fancy. See CRITICISM 26. cf. also *ib.* 28 1750

2. "As it has been my principal design [in *The Rambler*] to inculcate wisdom or piety, I have allotted few papers to the idle sports of imagination," [or rather "fancy" as the context indicates]. *Wks.* 7.396. (*Ram.* 208) 1752

3. *Definition of fancy:* "1. Imagination;[1] the power by which the mind forms to itself images and representations of things, persons, or scenes of being. . . .
2. An opinion loved rather by the imagination than the reason." *Dict.*
Definition of fanciful: "1. Imaginative; rather guided by imagination than reason. . . . 2. Direction by the imagination, not the reason; full of wild images." *Dict.* 1755

4. * ". . . the understanding, when in possession of truth, is satisfied with the simple acquisition; and not, like fancy, inclined to wander after new pleasures, in

---

[1] J., like Addison, does not always discriminate between *fancy* and *imagination;* e.g., see 2 *supra* and IMAGINATION 6. See also *Lives* 3.165-6 and 310 for J.'s use of both terms.

the diversification of objects already known, which, perhaps, may lead to errour." *Wks.* ed. 1825, Oxford, 5.449. (*Pref.* attributed to J., to Payne's *New Tables of Interest*) 1758

5. "The irregular combinations of fanciful invention may delight awhile . . . but the pleasures of sudden wonder are soon exhausted, and the mind can only repose on the stability of truth." See NATURE 31   1765

6. Poems solely of fancy should be short. See SHORT COMPOSITIONS 4   Ptd. 1780

Farce. See DRAMA: *Farce*

Feeling

1. ". . . we can always feel more than we can imagine." See TRUTH 11   1753

2. *Poets who do not share common human feelings:* The metaphysical poets "were not successful in representing or moving the affections. As they were wholly employed on something unexpected and surprising they had no regard to that uniformity of sentiment, which enables us to conceive and to excite the pains and the pleasure of other minds: they never enquired what on any occasion they should have said or done, but wrote rather as beholders than partakers of human nature; as beings looking upon good and evil, impassive and at leisure;" etc. *Lives* 1.20   1779

3. Otway's *The Orphan:* "Its whole power is upon the affections. . . . But if the heart is interested, many other beauties may be wanting, yet not be missed." *Lives* 1.245   1779

4. *Want of feeling:* The success of Addison's *Cato* "has introduced or confirmed among us the use of dialogue too declamatory, of unaffecting elegance, and chill philosophy." *Lives* 2.133   Ptd. 1780

5. * "Of the pathetic in poetry he never liked to speak,

and the only passage I ever heard him applaud as particularly tender in any common book, was Jane Shore's exclamation in the last act, 'Forgive me! *but* forgive me!' " His susceptible heart, however, caused him to burst into tears whenever repeating certain lines from the *Dies iræ. John. Misc.* 1.283-4. (Piozzi)   Date?

6. That work more affecting which represents normal human experience. See EXPERIENCE 7, BIOGRAPHY 3, and DRAMA 69 and 72   Misc. dates

Fiction. See NOVEL, THE; ROMANCE. See also MYTHOLOGY for mythological fictions. Compare TRUTH

1. *Modern fiction:* [a] *Should be true representation of actual life:* "This kind of writing may be termed not improperly the comedy of romance, and is to be conducted nearly by the rules of comick poetry. Its province is to bring about natural events by easy means, and to keep up curiosity without the help of wonder: it is therefore precluded from the machines and expedients of the heroick romance. . . . [b] The task of our present writers . . . requires, together with that learning which is to be gained from books, that experience which can never be attained by solitary diligence, but must arise from general converse and accurate observation of the living world." This makes for greater difficulty. They should strive to be "just copiers of human manners." [c] *Events and characters should be selected with moral end in view:* This their more important concern. "These books are written chiefly to the young, the ignorant, and the idle, to whom they serve as lectures of conduct, and introductions into life." . . . Hence necessity for caution "to secure them from unjust prejudices, perverse opinions, and incongruous combinations of images." The very closeness to real life of such works increases their influence as vehicles of morality. Therefore "care ought to be taken, that, when the choice is unre-

strained, the best examples only should be exhibited; . . . The chief advantage which these fictions have over real life is, that their authors are at liberty, though not to invent, yet to select objects, and to cull from the mass of mankind, those individuals upon which the attention ought most to be employed; as a diamond, though it cannot be made, may be polished by art, and placed in such a situation, as to display that lustre which before was buried among common stones. It is justly considered as the greatest excellency of art, to imitate nature; but it is necessary to distinguish those parts of nature, which are most proper for imitation: greater care is still required in representing life, which is so often discoloured by passion, or deformed by wickedness. If the world be promiscuously described, I cannot see of what use it can be to read the account: or why it may not be as safe to turn the eye immediately upon mankind as upon a mirrour which shows all that presents itself without discrimination. [d] It is therefore not a sufficient vindication of a character, that it is drawn as it appears, for many characters ought never to be drawn; nor of a narrative, that the train of events is agreeable to observation and experience, for that observation which is called knowledge of the world will be found much more frequently to make men cunning than good. The purpose of these writings is surely not only to show mankind, but to provide that they may be seen hereafter with less hazard; to teach the means of avoiding the snares which are laid by TREACHERY for INNOCENCE, without infusing any wish for that superiority with which the betrayer flatters his vanity; to give the power of counteracting fraud, without the temptation to practise it; to initiate youth by mock encounters in the art of necessary defence, and to encrease prudence without impairing virtue." When the good and the bad in characters are given equal prominence, we "are led by degrees to interest ourselves in their favour, we lose the abhorrence of their faults. . . . cf. SHAKESPEARE 145.] There have been men indeed splendidly wicked . . . but . . . their resemblance ought no more to be preserved, than the art of murdering without pain." [e] The fallacy of the "notion, that certain virtues have their correspondent faults, and therefore that to exhibit either apart is to deviate from probability." This maxim "without any relation to practice or to life," neglects the power of the will to choose in accordance with reason. Such fallacies "should be laid open and confuted," as they tend to "confound the colours of right and wrong. . . . In narratives, where historical veracity has no place, I cannot discover why there should not be exhibited the most perfect idea of virtue; of virtue not angelical, nor above probability, for what we cannot credit we shall never imitate, but the highest and purest that humanity can reach, which, exercised in such trials as the various revolutions of things shall bring upon it, may, by conquering some calamities, and enduring others, teach us what we may hope, and what we can perform. Vice, for vice is necessary to be shewn, should always disgust; nor should the graces of gaiety, or the dignity of courage, be so united with it, as to reconcile it to the mind. Wherever it appears, it should raise hatred by the malignity of its practices, and contempt by the meanness of its stratagems; for while it is supported by either parts or spirit, it will be seldom heartily abhorred. . . . It is therefore to be steadily inculcated, that virtue is the highest proof of understanding, and the only solid basis of greatness; and that vice is the natural consequence of narrow thoughts; that it begins in mistake, and ends in ignominy." *Wks.* 5.20-6. (*Ram.* 4) 1750

2. The allegory of Truth, Falsehood, and Fiction: Truth coldly received until robed in Fiction. *Wks.* 6. 162-3. (*Ram.* 96) 1751

3. *Writers of fiction:* These, at least, not subject to the essayist's ever-recurring difficulty of choosing a subject: "Even the relator of feigned adventures, when once the principal characters are established, and the great events regularly connected, finds incidents and episodes crowding upon his mind; every change opens new views, and the latter part of the story grows without labour out of the former." *Wks.* 7.254-5. (*Ram.* 184) 1751

4. ". . . the most artful fiction must give way to truth." See TRUTH 11 1753

5. *Definition of fiction:* "1. The act of feigning or inventing. . . . 2. The thing feigned or invented. . . . 3. A falsehood; a lye." (No other meanings given.) *Dict.* 1755

6. Pope's epitaph on Rowe: "To wish *Peace to thy shade* is too mythological to be admitted into a christian temple. . . . Let fiction, at least, cease with life, and let us be serious over the grave." *Lives* 3.261 1756

7. **Modern fiction:* The plea of writers of fiction "whose business is to furnish that entertainment which fancy perpetually demands," that the beauties of nature are exhausted: re-grouping of familiar images the only source of vanity left. "This plea has been cheerfully admitted; and fancy, led by the hand of a skilful guide, treads over again the flowery path she has often trod before, as much enamoured with every new diversification of the same prospect, as with the first appearance of it." *Wks.* ed. 1825, Oxford, 5.448. (*Pref.* to Payne's *New Tables of Interest*) 1758

8. "Fiction [i.e., that which is not fact] cannot move so much, but that the attention may be easily transferred [from the comic to the tragic and *vice versa*]." See SHAKESPEARE 90b 1765

9. "The delight of tragedy proceeds from our consciousness of fiction; if we thought murders and treasons

real, they would please no more." *Shak. Pref.*, Raleigh,
28   1765

10. *End of fiction:* "Poets, indeed, profess fiction, but the legitimate end of fiction is the conveyance of truth." *Lives* 1.271   1779

11. "Where there is leisure for fiction there is little grief." (Applied to elegy.) See ELEGY 4   1779

12. Concerning the source of Gray's *The Bard:* "The fiction of Horace was to the Romans credible; but its revival disgusts us with apparent and unconquerable falsehood. 'Incredulus odi.' To select a singular event, and swell it to a giant's bulk by fabulous appendages of spectres and predictions, has little difficulty, for he that forsakes the probable may always find the marvellous. And it has little use: we are affected only as we believe; we are improved only as we find something to be imitated or declined. I do not see that *The Bard* promotes any truth, moral or political." *Lives* 3.438   1781

13. * J. "disapproved much of mingling real facts with fiction." *Bos.* 4.187   Date?

14. * J., writes Hawkins, was inclined to favour Richardson's work, "but he seemed not firm in it, and could at any time be talked into a disapprobation of all fictitious relations, of which he would frequently say they took no hold of the mind." *Wks.* 1.217   Date?

First Impressions

1. "It is a rule never to be forgotten, that whatever strikes strongly, should be described while the first impression remains fresh upon the mind." *Bos.* 1.337   1757

2. The importance of first impressions: to please, you must surprise. See DICTION 18   1779

Florid

1. *Definition:* "3. Embellished; splendid; brilliant with

decorations." (No unfavourable implication.) *Dict.*
1755

French Literature. See also under DICTION (for Gallicisms)

1. French letter-writers censured. *Wks.* 7.70. (*Ram.* 152)   1751

2. * J. agrees with Boswell that the French "have the art of accommodating [i.e., "adapting," or "dressing up": see Hill's note on this word] literature." A few of their *Ana* good. "As to original literature, the French have a couple of tragick poets who go round the world, Racine and Corneille, and one comick poet, Molière." Fénelon's "*Telemachus* is pretty well." Voltaire "has not stood his trial yet. And what makes Voltaire chiefly circulate is collection; such as his *Universal History.*" Bossuet not read; Massillon and Bourdaloue do not "go round the world." "In general, however, [adds Boswell] he gave the French much praise for their industry." *Bos.* 5.311. (*Hebrides*, 14 Oct.) 1773

3. * The French have not "les belles lettres." *John. Misc.* 2.289. (Miss Reynolds)   1775

4. * "We are now before the French in literature; but we had it long after them." *Bos.* 3.254   1778

5. J. prefers modern French and English dramas to tragedies of the Ancients. See ANCIENT WRITERS 20 1779

6. English writers less afraid of novelty than the French. *Lives* 1.430   1779

7. "The French . . . were very laudably industrious to enrich their own language with the wisdom of the ancients; but found themselves reduced . . . to turn the Greek and Roman poetry into prose. Whoever could read an author could translate him. From such rivals little can be feared." *Lives* 3.237   1781

8. * J. "admitted that the French, though not the highest, perhaps, in any department of literature, yet in every

French Literature 115

department were very high. . . . Speaking of the French novels compared with Richardson's, he said, they might be pretty baubles, but a wren was not an eagle." (From Maxwell's *Collectanea*, quoted by Bos.) *Bos.* 2.125   Date?

9. * According to a friend of Boswell's, J. "spoke often in praise of French literature. 'The French are excellent in this, (he would say,) they have a book on every subject.'" *Bos.* 4.237   Date?

10. * J. "applauded the number of their books and the graces of their style. 'They have few sentiments (said he), but they express them neatly.'" *John. Misc.* 1.216. (Piozzi)   Date?

11. * "Dr. Johnson was a great reader of French literature." *John. Misc.* 1.334. (Piozzi)   Date ?

12. * J. "thoroughly versed" in French,[1] but "did not understand its pronunciation, nor could he speak it himself with propriety." *John. Misc.* 1.416-7. (Murphy)   Date?

13. * "With French authors he was familiar. He had lately read over the works of Boileau." *John. Misc.* 2.363   Date?

General and the Particular, The. See also under NATURE (GENERAL HUMAN NATURE); SHAKESPEARE: *Truth to Nature*; OCCASIONAL WORKS

1. In epitaphs "the praise ought not to be general, because the mind is lost in the extent of any indefinite idea, and cannot be affected with what it cannot comprehend." *Wks.* 9.443. See also EPITAPH 7   1740

2. Criticism should not be too general. See CRITICISM 25   1748

3. "Poetry cannot dwell upon the minuter distinctions, by which one species differs from another, without de-

---

[1] Johnson's first extensive literary work was a translation from the French—*Lobo's Voyage to Abyssinia*, published in 1735.

parting from that simplicity of grandeur which fills the imagination; nor dissect the latent qualities of things, without losing its general power of gratifying every mind by recalling its conceptions." See PASTORAL 1 c, d, f   1750

4. In biography, particular facts and minute details of daily life often the most revealing and useful. See BIOGRAPHY 3 c, d; 20   1750

5. Though the passions are few, "the alterations which time is always making in the modes of life" are a source of variety. See VARIETY 3   1753

6. "He that writes upon general principles, or delivers universal truths, may hope to be often read, because his work will be equally useful at all times and in every country; but he cannot expect it to be received with eagerness, or to spread with rapidity, because desire can have no particular stimulation; that which is to be loved long must be loved with reason rather than with passion. He that lays out his labours upon temporary subjects, easily finds readers, and quickly loses them; for what should make the book valued when its subject is no more?" Application of this to Butler's *Hudibras*. (See BUTLER 4.) *Wks.* 8.236. (*Idl.* 59)
    1759

7. "The most useful truths are always universal, and unconnected with accidents and customs." *Wks.* 8.264. (*Idl.* 66)   1759

8. "The business of a poet . . . is to examine, not the individual, but the species." See POETRY 14 a, b   1759

9. The Metaphysical Poets could not reach the sublime, "for they never attempted that comprehension and expanse of thought which at once fills the whole mind, and of which the first effect is sudden astonishment, and the second rational admiration. Sublimity is produced by aggregation, and littleness by dispersion. Great thoughts are always general, and consist in posi-

General and Particular 117

tions not limited by exceptions, and in descriptions not descending to minuteness. . . . Those writers who lay on the watch for novelty could have little hope of greatness; for great things cannot have escaped former observation. Their attempts were always analytick: they broke every image into fragments, and could no more represent by their slender conceits and laboured particularities the prospects of nature or the scenes of life, than he who dissects a sun-beam with a prism can exhibit the wide effulgence of a summer noon." *Lives* 1.20-1   1779

10. Cowley "loses the grandeur of generality, for of the greatest things the parts are little; what is little can be but pretty, and by claiming dignity becomes ridiculous. Thus all the power of description is destroyed by a scrupulous enumeration; and the force of metaphors is lost when the mind by the mention of particulars is turned more upon the original than the secondary sense, more upon that from which the illustration is drawn than that to which it is applied." *Lives* 1.45
1779

11. "The same thought is more generally, and therefore more poetically, expressed by Casimir." *Lives* 1.46
1779

12. Cowley's imagery: "what might in general expressions be great and forcible he weakens and makes ridiculous by branching it into small parts." *Lives* 1.53   1779

13. Pedantry and the minute or particular. See PEDANTRY 2   1779

14. Since Dryden's praise of Eleonora, (in elegy *Eleonora*) was inevitably general, as he did not know her, it "fixes no impression on the reader nor excites any tendency to love, nor much desire of imitation. Knowledge of the subject is to the poet what durable materials are to the architect." *Lives*, 1.441-2   1779

15. In the song of Comus "the invitations to pleasure are so general that they excite no distinct images of cor-

rupt enjoyment, and take no dangerous hold on the fancy." *Lives* 1.168   1779

16. In *Paradise Lost*, Satan's "expressions are commonly general, and no otherwise offensive than as they are wicked." See DRAMATIC PROPRIETY 6   1779

17. "I know not that there can be found in his [Rowe's] plays any deep search into nature, any accurate discriminations of kindred qualities, or nice display of passion in its progress; all is general and undefined." *Lives* 2.76   Ptd. 1780

18. "To select a singular event, and swell it to a giant's bulk by fabulous appendages of spectres and predictions, has little difficulty, for he that forsakes the probable may always find the marvellous. And it has little use: we are affected only as we believe. . . ." See FICTION 12   1781

19. "He [Thomson] thinks in a peculiar train, and he thinks always as a man of genius; he looks round on Nature and on Life . . . with a mind that at once comprehends the vast, and attends to the minute." See POETRY 41   1781

20. Gray's *Elegy* "abounds with images which find a mirrour in every mind," etc. See GRAY 17   1781

21. * Mrs. Piozzi "forces" J. to prefer Young's description of night to Dryden's and Shakespeare's "as more forcible, and more general." See YOUNG 6   Date?

Genius. See also under COMPOSITION; INVENTION

1. "The general precept of consulting the genius [see *infra* 6, definition 4] is of little use, unless we are told, how the genius can be known." *Wks.* 5.130. (*Ram.* 19)   1750

2. The "bugbear" "that every kind of knowledge requires a peculiar genius, or mental constitution, framed for the reception of some ideas, and the exclusion of others; and that to him whose genius is not adapted to

the study which he prosecutes, all labour shall be vain and fruitless." Vanity exaggerates this opinion: men of reputation apt to "exalt themselves as endowed by heaven with peculiar powers. . . . To this discouragement it may be possibly answered, that since a genius, whatever it be, is like fire in the flint, only to be produced by collision with a proper subject, it is the business of every man to try whether his faculties may not happily cooperate with his desires. . . ." *Wks.* 5.165-6. (*Ram.* 25) 1750

3. *Rambler* 117, in praise of garrets, ridicules those who claim that genius is affected by environment. *Wks.* 6.292 ff. 1751

4. Critical definitions upset by every new genius. See RULES 5 1751

5. Reliance on the doctrine of "unassisted genius" or intuition attacked: A study of the past the foundation of original creation. (See ANCIENT WRITERS 10.) ". . . though the contemner of books . . . was really born with a genius surpassing the ordinary abilities of mankind; yet surely such gifts of providence may be more properly urged as incitements to labour, than encouragements to negligence. . . . Fame cannot spread wide or endure long that is not rooted in nature, and manured by art." *Wks.* 7.82-7. (*Ram.* 154) 1751

6. *Definition:*[1] "1. The protecting or ruling power of man, places, or things. . . . 2. A man endowed with superior faculties. . . . 3. Mental power or faculties. . . . 4. Disposition of nature by which anyone is qualified for some peculiar employment. . . .[2] 5. Nature; disposition." *Dict.* 1755

7. ". . . the artful introduction of the name [in Pope's *Epitaph, No.* 3], which is inserted with a peculiar

---

[1] For eighteenth century pronouncements on genius, see Hill's note, *Bos.* 2.437 *n* 2, and *Lives* 1.2 *n* 5.
[2] e.g., "he had genius for tragick poetry" (*Wks.* 8.189); see also *ib.* 8.220; and *supra* 1, 2; *infra* 15, 24, 30.

felicity, to which chance must concur with genius, which no man can hope to attain twice, and which cannot be copied but with servile imitation." *Lives* 3.259　　　　　　　　　　　　　　　　　1756

8. ". . . it is cruel to discourage a poet for ever, because he has not from genius what only experience can bestow." *Wks.* 8.98. (*Idl.* 25)　　　　1758

9. "Genius is shewn only by invention." (Not applied specifically to literature.) *Wks.* 8.159. (*Idl.* 40)
　　　　　　　　　　　　　　　　　　　1759

10. Cant phrases of critics satirized: Dick Minim, the fashionable critic, exhorts the aspiring author "to catch those moments when he finds his thoughts expanded and his genius exalted" and "tells him, that every man has his genius, and that *Cicero* could never be a poet." *Wks.* 8.247. (*Idl.* 61.) See also *ib.* 8.329
　　　　　　　　　　　　　　　　　　　1759

11. *"ROBERTSON said, one man had more judgment, another more imagination. JOHNSON. 'No, Sir; it is only, one man has more mind than another. He may direct it differently. . . . I am persuaded that, had Sir Isaac Newton applied to poetry, he would have made a very fine epick poem. I could as easily apply to law as to tragick poetry.' BOSWELL. 'Yet, Sir, you did apply to tragick poetry, not to law.' JOHNSON. 'Because, Sir, I had not money to study law. Sir, the man who has vigour, may walk to the east, just as well as to the west, if he happens to turn his head that way.'" *Bos.* 5.34-5. (*Hebrides*, 15 Aug.)　　　　1773

12. ". . . what genius could be expected in a poet by inheritance?" *Wks.* 10.455. (*Jour. to W.I.*)　　1774

13. ". . . natural deficience cannot be supplied." See PHILIPS, J. 1　　　　　　　　　　　　　　1779

14. "The highest praise of genius is original invention." *Lives* 1.194　　　　　　　　　　　　　　1779

15. Cowley becomes poet by accident: "Such are the acci-

dents, which, sometimes remembered, and perhaps sometimes forgotten, produce that particular designation of mind and propensity for some certain science or employment, which is commonly called Genius. The true Genius is a mind of large general powers, accidentally determined to some particular direction." *Lives* 1. 2   1779

16. "Genius now and then produces a lucky trifle." But the transitoriness of "compositions merely pretty." See MORAL ELEMENT 18   1779

17. ". . . the praise of Marlborough [Addison's *Rosamond*] . . . is, what perhaps every human excellence must be, the product of good-luck improved by genius." *Lives* 2.131   Ptd. 1780

18. Addison's reputation as poet and critic partly the result of his influence and personal character. "But time quickly puts an end to artificial and accidental fame; and Addison is to pass through futurity protected only by his genius." *Lives* 2.126   Ptd. 1780

19. Blackmore never "elevated his views to that ideal perfection which every genius born to excel is condemned always to pursue, and never overtake." *Lives* 2.253
                                                                                    Ptd. 1780

20. J. makes sport of the notion "that every man has his genius, and that the great rule by which all excellence is attained, and all success procured, is, to follow *genius*." *Letters* 2.184. See also *John. Misc.* 1.314
                                                                                     1780

21. "But good sense alone is a sedate and quiescent quality, which . . . preserves safety, but never gains supremacy. Pope had likewise genius; a mind active, ambitious, and adventurous, always investigating, always aspiring; in its widest searches[1] still longing to go forward, in its highest flights still wishing to be higher; always imagining something greater than it knows,

---

[1] J. at first wrote "in its noblest researches." *Bos.* 4.52

always endeavouring more than it can do." *Lives* 3.217
1781

22. "Of genius, that power which constitutes a poet; that quality without which judgement is cold and knowledge is inert; that energy which collects, combines, amplifies, and animates—the superiority must, with some hesitation, be allowed to Dryden [rather than to Pope]." *Lives* 3.222   1781

23. "Pope had, in proportions very nicely adjusted to each other, all the qualities that constitute genius. He had Invention, by which new trains of events are formed and new scenes of imagery displayed, as in *The Rape of the Lock*, and by which extrinsick and adventitious embellishments and illustrations are connected with a known subject, as in the *Essay on Criticism*; he had Imagination, which strongly impresses on the writer's mind and enables him to convey to the reader the various forms of nature, incidents of life, and energies of passion, as in his *Eloisa*, *Windsor Forest*, and the *Ethick Epistles;* he had Judgement, which selects from life or nature what the present purpose requires, and, by separating the essence of things from its concomitants, often makes the representation more powerful than the reality; and he had colours of language always before him ready to decorate his matter with every grace of elegant expression, as when he accommodates his diction to the wonderful multiplicity of Homer's sentiments and descriptions." *Lives* 3.247   1781

24. For J.'s refutation of Pope's favourite theory of the "ruling passion," (a doctrine "pernicious as well as false"), see *Lives* 3.173-5. See also *Wks.* 9.402-3
1781

25. "Those performances, which strike with wonder, are combinations of skilful genius with happy casualty." *Lives* 3.104   1781

26. Thomson "thinks always as a man of genius" and sees with the eye of a poet. See Poetry 41   1781

27. Imitations "may deserve praise, as proofs of great industry and great nicety of observation; but the highest praise, the praise of genius, they cannot claim. The noblest beauties of art are those of which the effect is co-extended with rational nature, or at least with the whole circle of polished life." See NATURE 46   1781

28. "Akenside was one of those poets who have felt very early the motions of genius." *Lives* 3.412   1781

29. * " '. . . there is nothing so little comprehended among mankind as what is genius. They give to it all, when it can be but a part. Genius is nothing more than knowing the use of tools; but there must be tools for it to use: a man who has spent all his life in this room will give a very poor account of what is contained in the next.' [Miss Burney:] 'Certainly, sir; yet there is such a thing as invention? Shakspeare could never have seen a Caliban.' [J.:] 'No; but he had seen a man, and knew, therefore, how to vary him to a monster. A man who would draw a monstrous cow, must first know what a cow commonly is; or how can he tell that to give her an ass's head or an elephant's tusk will make her monstrous? Suppose you show me a man who is a very expert carpenter; another will say he was born to be a carpenter—but what if he had never seen any wood? Let two men, one with genius, the other with none, look at an overturned wagon:—he who has no genius, will think of the waggon only as he sees it, overturned, and walk on; he who has genius, will paint it to himself before it was overturned,—standing still, and moving on, and heavy loaded, and empty; but both must see the waggon, to think of it at all.' " D'Arblay, *Diary and Letters* 2.271-2   1784

30. * "No, Sir, . . . people are not born with a particular genius for particular employments or studies, for it would be like saying that a man could see a great way east, but could not west. It is good sense applied

with diligence to what was at first a mere accident, and which, by great application, grew to be called, by the generality of mankind, a particular genius." *John. Misc.* 2.287. (Miss Reynolds) Date ?

Good Sense.[1] See also REASON; NATURE

1. *Definition of sense:* "5. . . . strength of natural reason." *Dict.* 1755
2. ". . . the dictates of common sense and common honesty, names of greater authority than that of Horace." *Wks.* 10.186 1756
3. "Of his [Pope's] intellectual character the constituent and fundamental principle was Good Sense, a prompt and intuitive perception of consonance and propriety. He saw immediately, of his own conceptions, what was to be chosen, and what to be rejected; and, in the works of others, what was to be shunned, and what was to be copied. But good sense alone is a sedate and quiescent quality, which manages its possessions well, but does not increase them; it collects few materials for its own operations, and preserves safety, but never gains supremacy. Pope had likewise genius; a mind active, ambitious, and adventurous . . ." etc. (For analysis of genius, see GENIUS 21.) *Lives* 3.216-7 1781
4. ". . . by the common sense of readers uncorrupted with literary prejudices, after all the refinements of subtilty and the dogmatism of learning, must be finally decided all claim to poetical honours." *Lives* 3.441
1781

Gothic

1. Not given in J.'s *Dictionary.* As used by J. and his contemporaries the word usually is equivalent to *barbarous,* or *medieval.* Examples: "Gothick romance,"

---

[1] Almost any page of *The Lives of the Poets* will furnish an example of J.'s application of this doctrine of "good sense" to criticism. It is, of course, the dominant critical note of the eighteenth century.

(*Letters* 1.246); "Gothick Fairies," (*Lives* 2.311); "the Gothick ages," (*Lives* 1.283); "*Gothick* swarms," (*Wks.* 10.437). Reynolds refers to "the rudeness of Gothic essays," (*John. Misc.* 2.230 *n*); and of "old Gothic masters," (*ib.* 2.230). Murphy speaks of "the Gothic taste for glittering conceits," (*John. Misc.* 1.478). Miss Reynolds refers to "the gothick dignity of his [J.'s] Aspect . . . when repeating sublime passages," (*John. Misc.* 2.266) which Hill interprets as "the rude dignity." Dennis in 1706, as Hill notes (*Lives* 2.165), attacked the Italian Opera as "barbarous and Gothick." For Addison's use of the word, see *Mod. Philology*, 2.128 *ff*. J. once uses the word in an architectural sense: "The arch . . . is pointed, and therefore *Gothick* or *Saracenical*." (*Wks.* 10.503. *Jour. to W.I.*)

Harsh

1. Perhaps no critical term used by Johnson has done more injury to his reputation as a critic. One reads with something of a shock that in *Lycidas* "the diction is harsh," (*Lives* 1.163); that the songs in *Comus* are "harsh in their diction," (*ib.* 1.169); that Collins and Gray and Prior and Akenside and Shenstone—all are guilty of harshness of style or diction. But a careful examination of Johnson's use of the word, vindicates many of these so-called absurdities. The Johnsonian term "harsh" as a general rule is primarily intellectual in import, rather than musical; it is used commonly in the fourth sense of the word given in the N.E.D.: "Repugnant to the understanding or taste; grating upon the mind or æsthetic faculty; strained, forced . . . ungraceful." "Unpleasing" Johnson himself defines the word, in its fifth meaning. For example, "harsh" is the word normally applied by Johnson to far-fetched interpretations of obscure Shakespearean passages, to words used in a sense not in accordance with common usage, to unnatural constructions, or

strained metaphors, to unfamiliar or antiquated expressions. Among some fifty instances collected from Johnson's edition of Shakespeare, I have not found a single case where harsh is clearly used primarily in the sense of unmelodious. In a large number of cases, there is no auditory significance to the word whatever. Moreover, in the majority of passages where *harsh* occurs in *The Lives of the Poets* there is some reference in the context to the writer's awkwardness or obscurity of style, or departure from the normal, or affectation of the antique, or exotic—*ill-sounding*, the word may imply, but in a very special sense and not necessarily unmusical. Thus, the diction of Collins is "often harsh, unskilfully laboured, and injudiciously selected. He affected the obsolete." (*Lives* 3.341); Akenside "rarely either recalls old phrases or twists his metre into harsh inversions." (*ib.* 3.418); Gray's "language [in *The Bard* and *The Progress of Poesy*] is laboured into harshness. The mind of the writer seems to work with unnatural violence." (*ib.* 3.440); Shenstone's diction is "often harsh, improper, and affected; his words ill-coined or ill-chosen, and his phrase unskilfully inverted," (*ib.* 3.355); and it is significant that a few lines after Johnson has referred to Milton's "Babylonish Dialect in itself harsh and barbarous," he praises the diligence with which Milton "has selected the melodious words," (*ib.* 1.191). When "harsh" and "harshness" are thus viewed historically, Johnson's strictures on the "harsh diction" of Milton's early poems lose much of their absurdity.[1]

Heroic Poetry. See EPIC

Historical Method of Criticism. See under CRITICISM

History. Compare BIOGRAPHY

1. "The Man who knows not the Truth *cannot*, and he who knows it *will not* tell it. . . . Distrust is a nec-

[1] See *Lives* 1.162, 163, 169.

essary Qualification of a Student in History." *Gent. Mag.*, 1742, p. 129   1742

2. J. suggests the marginal notation of important dates in a history of the British Parliament which he projected, as "the proper medium between a journal, which has regard only to time, and a history which ranges facts according to their dependence on each other, and postpones or anticipates according to the convenience of narration. I think the work ought to partake of the spirit of history, which is contrary to minute exactness, and of the regularity of a journal, which is inconsistent with spirit." *Bos.* 1.155

    cir. 1743

3. "The study of *chronology* and *history* seems to be one of the most natural delights of the human mind." *Wks.* 9.411   1748

4. "Histories of the downfal of kingdoms, and revolutions of empires, are read with great tranquillity" since they are so far removed from normal human experience. See EXPERIENCE 7   1750

5. Advantages of the historian over the philosopher or the poet: "But the happy historian has no other labour than of gathering what tradition pours down before him, or records treasure for his use . . . he is not to form, but copy characters. . . . The difficulty of making variety consistent, or uniting probability with surprize, needs not to disturb him; the manners and actions of his personages are already fixed; his materials are provided and put into his hands, and he is at leisure to employ all his powers in arranging and displaying them." Yet few reputations won by writing histories, most of which, "when fashion and novelty have ceased to recommend them, are of no other use than chronological memorials, which necessity may sometimes require to be consulted, but which fright away curiosity, and disgust delicacy." Few English histories of note. The works of Raleigh, Clarendon

and Knolles examined, (the latter a model historian) q.v. Wks. 6.328-32. (*Ram.* 122) 1751

6. Value of the study of history: "To judge rightly of the present we must oppose it to the past. . . . There is no part of history so generally useful as that which relates the progress of the human mind." Imlac, in *Rasselas* (ch. XXIX). Wks. 11.85-6   1759

7. "He that writes the history of his own times, if he adheres steadily to truth, will write that which his own times will not easily endure." Wks. 8.261. (*Idl.* 65)   1759

8. Biography of more practical value than history. See BIOGRAPHY 5   1759

9. The facts of history "rather diversify conversation than regulate life. Few are engaged in such scenes as give them opportunities of growing wiser by the downfal of statesmen or the defeat of generals. . . . Between falsehood and useless truth there is little difference." Wks. 8.339-40. (*Idl.* 84)   1759

10. * " 'Great abilities (said he) are not requisite for an Historian; for in historical composition, all the greatest powers of the human mind are quiescent. He has facts ready to his hand; so there is no exercise of invention. Imagination is not required in any high degree; only about as much as is used in the lower kinds of poetry. Some penetration, accuracy, and colouring will fit a man for the task, if he can give the application which is necessary.' " *Bos.* 1.424-5   1763

11. * "Talking of history, Johnson said, 'We may know historical facts to be true, as we may know facts in common life to be true. Motives are generally unknown. We cannot trust to the characters we find in history, unless when they are drawn by those who knew the persons.' " *Bos.* 2.79   1769

12. *JOHNSON: " 'There is but a shallow stream of thought in history.' BOSWELL. 'But surely, Sir, an

historian has reflection.' JOHNSON. 'Why yes, Sir; and so has a cat when she catches a mouse for her kitten.' "
Bos. 2.195   1772

13. *History of manners most valuable. See BIOGRAPHY 9
                                             1773

14. *J. attacks histories which do not tell the whole truth. *Bos.* 5.255. (*Hebrides*, 24 Sept.)   1773

15. * "All history, so far as it is not supported by contemporary evidence, is romance." *Bos.* 5.403. (*Hebrides*, 20 Nov.)   1773

16. *Conciseness praised: "It is the great excellence of a [historical] writer to put into his book as much as his book will hold." *Bos.* 2.237   1773

17. * "The common remark as to the utility of reading history being made;—JOHNSON. 'We must consider how very little history there is; I mean real authentick history. That certain Kings reigned, and certain battles were fought, we can depend upon as true; but all the colouring, all the philosophy of history is conjecture.' " *Bos.* 2.365-6   1775

18. The ethical and educational value of a study of history. *Lives* 1.100   1779

19. * "Characters should never be given by an historian, unless he knew the people whom he describes, or copies from those who knew them." *Bos.* 3.404   1779

20. Sheffield "had the perspicuity and elegance of an historian, but not the fire and fancy of a poet." *Lives* 2.177   Ptd. 178c

21. *J. does not like to converse upon historical subjects, especially Roman history. *John. Misc.* 1.201-2 and 201 *n* 2. (Piozzi)   Date?

22. * "General history had little of his regard. . . . Sooner than hear of the Punic War, he would be rude to the person that introduced the subject." *John. Misc.* 1.451-2. (Murphy)   Date ?

History, Natural. See also TRAVEL

1. "Natural History is above most other kinds of compositions subject to repetition; every man is fond of the country that he inhabits, and is willing to multiply its products, and celebrate its fertility. But it should also be considered that what has been already compleatly described, it is of no use to describe again, and therefore, in the account of any country, those things should be selected, that are peculiar to it, that are distinguished by some permanent and natural difference from the same species in other places; or that are little known to those in whose language the book is written." *Lit. Mag.*, 1756, p. 176   1756

Human Nature. See under NATURE

Humanist

1. *Definition:* "A philologer; a grammarian." (No other meanings given.) *Dict.*   1755

Humourist

1. *Definition:* "1. One who conducts himself by his own fancy; one who gratifies his own humour. . . .[1] 2. One who has violent and peculiar passions." (No other meanings given.) *Dict.*   1755

Iambic

1. *Definition:* "Verses composed of iambick feat, or a short and long syllable alternately: used originally in satire, therefore taken for satire." *Dict.*   1755

Idyl

1. *Definition:* "A small short poem." *Dict.*   1755

---

[1] e.g., Those who "voluntarily consign themselves to singularity . . . are generally known by the name of *Humourists*," etc. *Wks.* 9.145. (*Adv.* 131)

Imagery

1. *Definition:* "4. Representations in writing; such descriptions as force the image of the thing described upon the mind." *Dict.*   1755

Imagination. See also FANCY. Compare INVENTION; GENIUS; COMPOSITION; RULES

1. "It is ridiculous to oppose judgement to imagination; for it does not appear that men have necessarily less of one as they have more of the other." *Lives* 1.235   1748
2. ". . . in every work of imagination, the disposition of parts, the insertion of incidents, and use of decorations, may be varied a thousand ways with equal propriety." See CRITICISM 69   1750
3. A plea for an original play of the imagination. See IMITATION 5   1751
4. "Imagination, a licentious and vagrant faculty, unsusceptible of limitations, and impatient of restraint, has always endeavoured to baffle the logician, to perplex the confines of distinction, and burst the inclosures of regularity."[1] Hence the difficulty of critical definition. The innovations of genius are perpetually subverting established rules. *Wks.* 6.344-5. (*Ram.* 125)   1751
5. ". . . we can always feel more than we can imagine." See TRUTH 11   1753
6. *Definition:* "1. Fancy; the power of forming ideal pictures; the power of representing things absent to one's self or others."[2] *Dict.*   1755
7. "Imagination selects ideas from the treasures of remembrance, and produces novelty only by varied

---

[1] cf. Dryden: "Imagination in a Poet, is a faculty so wild and lawless, that, like a high-ranging spaniel, it must have clogs tied to it, lest it outrun the Judgement." *Dedicatory Epistle to "The Rival Ladies."*
[2] See note to FANCY 3 for J's indiscriminate use of *fancy* and *imagination.*

combinations." *Wks.* 8.175. (*Idl.* 44)   1759
8. "The Dangerous Prevalence of Imagination."[1] Imlac's discourse in *Rasselas*, (ch. XLIII). *Wks.* 11. 121 ff.   1759
9. Travelling regulates imagination by reality. *Letters* 1.254   1773
10. "Works of imagination excel by their allurement and delight; by their power of attracting and detaining the attention." See AIM OF WRITING 20   1779
11. "Imagination is useless without knowledge." See KNOWLEDGE 2   1779
12. Warburton's "wonderful extent and variety of knowledge, which yet had not oppressed his imagination nor clouded his perspicuity." *Lives* 3.165   1781
13. "Imagination, which strongly impresses on the writer's mind and enables him to convey to the reader the various forms of nature, incidents of life, and energies of passion, as in his [Pope's] *Eloisa, Windsor Forest*, and the *Ethick Epistles.*" One of the qualities that constitute genius. (See GENIUS 23.) *Lives* 3.247   1781
14. "He [Thomson] looks round on Nature and on Life with the eye which Nature bestows only on a poet, the eye that distinguishes in every thing presented to its view whatever there is on which imagination can delight to be detained. . . ." See POETRY 41   1781
15. "The subject [*Pleasures of Imagination*] is well chosen, as it includes all images that can strike or please, and thus comprises every species of poetical delight." *Lives* 3.417   1781
16. * "It is true, Sir, a vivacious quick imagination does sometimes give a confused idea of things, and which do not fix deep, though, at the same time, he has a

---

[1] Among J.'s own resolutions for Sept. 18, 1760, is the resolve "To reclaim imagination" (*John Misc.* 1.25). For the occasion at Forres, where J.'s imagination became "heated," see *Wks.* 10.341.

capacity to fix them in his memory, if he would endeavour at it." *John. Misc.* 2.288. (Miss Reynolds)
Date ?

Imitation. See also PLAGIARISM; PINDARIC VERSE; MYTHOLOGY. Compare ORIGINALITY; and INVENTION. For J.'s position in regard to the doctrine of writing as an imitative art, see DRAMA 47; FICTION 1; and DRAMATIC PROPRIETY

1. *Epitaphs:* The absurdity of copying Roman inscriptions. See EPITAPH 1   1740
2. *Imitation of the Ancients:* Christian writers "by echoing the songs of the ancient bacchanals, and transmitting the maxims of past debauchery . . . not only prove that they want invention, but virtue, and submit to the servility of imitation only to copy that of which the writer, if he was to live now, would often be ashamed." *Wks.* 5.189. (*Ram.* 29)   1750
3. *Pastoral imitations:* ". . . the same images in the same combination." See PASTORAL 1   1750
4. "The imitator treads a beaten walk, and with all his diligence can only hope to find a few flowers or branches untouched by his predecessor, the refuse of contempt, or the omissions of negligence." *Wks.* 6.-90-1. (*Ram.* 86)   1751
5. *A plea for imaginative originality:* ". . . there appears no reason, why imagination should be subject to the same restraint [as science] . . . in the boundless regions of possibility, which fiction claims for her dominion, there are surely a thousand recesses unexplored, a thousand flowers unplucked, a thousand fountains unexhausted, combinations of imagery yet unobserved, and races of ideal inhabitants not hitherto described. Yet, whatever hope may persuade, or reason evince, experience can boast of very few additions to ancient fable. The wars of *Troy*, and the travels of

Ulysses, have furnished almost all succeeding poets with incidents, characters, and sentiments. The *Romans* are confessed to have attempted little more than to display in their own tongue the inventions of the *Greeks*." Even Virgil "seduced by imitation" on occasion.[1] (See VIRGIL 16.) *Wks*. 6.322-4. (*Ram*. 121)

1751

6. *Spenserian imitations:* The present fashion "is the imitation of *Spenser*, which, by the influence of some men of learning and genius, seems likely to gain upon the age. . . . To imitate the fictions and sentiments of *Spenser* can incur no reproach, for allegory is perhaps one of the most pleasing vehicles of instruction. But I am very far from extending the same respect to his diction or his stanza. His style was in his own time allowed to be vicious, so darkened with old words and peculiarities of phrase, and so remote from common use, that *Johnson* boldly pronounces him *to have written no language*. His stanza is at once difficult and unpleasing; tiresome to the ear by its uniformity, and to the attention by its length. It was at first formed in imitation of the *Italian* poets, without due regard to the genius of our language. The *Italians* have little variety of termination, and were forced to contrive such a stanza as might admit the greatest number of similar rhymes; but our words end with so much diversity, that it is seldom convenient for us to bring more than two of the same sound together. If it be justly observed by *Milton*, that rhyme obliges poets to express their thoughts in improper terms, these improprieties must always be multiplied, as the difficulty of rhyme is increased by long concatenations." Spenserian imitators not consistent in disfiguring "their lines with a few obsolete syllables. . . . They ought not only to admit old words, but to avoid new. The laws of imitation are broken by every word introduced

---

[1] For the growing strength of this revolt against servile imitation in the eighteenth century, see an article by R. S. Crane in *Mod. Phil*. 15.201 and *n*.

since the time of *Spenser*. . . . It would indeed be difficult to exclude from a long poem all modern phrases, though it is easy to sprinkle it with gleanings of antiquity. Perhaps, however, the style of *Spenser* might by long labour be justly copied; but life is surely given us for higher purposes than to gather what our ancestors have wisely thrown away, and to learn what is of no value, but because it has been forgotten."[1] *Wks*. 6.325-6. (*Ram*. 121)   1751

7. The relation of imitators to plagiarism. See PLAGIARISM 1   1751

8. "No man ever yet became great by imitation." Invention necessary. See INVENTION 1   1751

9. *Imitation of Ancients:* The ancient writers in possession of nature, "and left us nothing but servile repetition or forced conceits." See ANCIENT WRITERS 13   1751

10. *Definition:* "3. A method of translating looser than paraphrase, in which modern examples and illustrations are used for ancient, or domestick for foreign." *Dict*. See *infra* 19   1755

11. *Epitaphs:* A felicitous turn in Pope's epitaph (No. 3), "which cannot be copied but with servile imitation." See GENIUS 7   1756

12. "I read all the poets of Persia and Arabia. . . . But I soon found that no man was ever great by imitation." Imlac, in *Rasselas* (ch. X). *Wks*. 11.30   1759

13. The danger of seeking nature through imitation of authors. See ANCIENT WRITERS 39   1765

14. *Ballad imitations:* J. treats modern imitations of

---

[1] Dryden, too, found fault with Spenser's "obsolete language, and the ill choice of his stanza," though he admits the harmony of his verses. (*Discourse concerning . . . Satire*, ed. Ker, 2.28-9.) This criticism of the Spenserian stanza can be paralleled also in eighteenth century criticism. Thus in 1756, T. Warton finds the stanza unsuited to the genius of the English language. (*Observations on the Faery Queen*, ed. 1807, 1.157-8) For an interesting review of the eighteenth century attitude toward the Spenserian stanza, see E. P. Morton's article in *Mod. Phil.* 10.365 *ff.*

ancient ballads "with that ridicule which he always displayed when that subject was mentioned." *Bos.* 2.212   1773

15. *Imitations of Spenser, Milton, etc. Warton's antique style censured. See WARTON, T., 3, 4   1777

16. "New arts are long in the world before poets describe them; for they borrow everything from their predecessors, and commonly derive very little from nature or from life." e.g., Boileau the first French author to describe modern war in verse. *Lives* 1.430   1779

17. *Spenserian imitations:* Prior's "imitation of Spenser, which consists principally in *I ween* and *I weet*, without exclusion of later modes of speech, makes his poem neither ancient nor modern." *Lives* 2.204. See also ODE 3 for J.'s censure of the stanza, an adaptation of the Spenserian, which Prior uses for his *Ode to the Queen*   Ptd. 1780

18. Gray's *The Bard* superior in imagery and animation to its original source in Horace. "But to copy is less than to invent, and the copy has been unhappily produced at a wrong time. The fiction of Horace was to the Romans credible; but its revival disgusts us with apparent and unconquerable falsehood. 'Incredulus odi.'" *Lives* 3.438   1781

19. Pope's mode of "imitation" described: "in which the ancients are familiarised by adapting their sentiments to modern topicks, by making Horace say of Shakespeare what he originally said of Ennius . . .", etc. First practised, J. thinks, by Oldham and Rochester. "It is a kind of middle composition between translation and original design, which pleases when the thoughts are unexpectedly applicable and the parallels lucky." Carried further by Pope than by any former poet. *Lives* 3.176   1781

20. "This employment [Pope's *Imitations of Horace*] became his favourite by its facility; the plan was ready to his hand, and nothing was required but to

accomodate as he could the sentiments of an old author to recent facts or familiar images; but what is easy is seldom excellent: such imitations cannot give pleasure to common readers. The man of learning may be sometimes surprised and delighted by an unexpected parallel; but the comparison requires knowledge of the original, which will likewise often detect strained applications. Between Roman images[1] and English manners there will be an irreconcileable dissimilitude, and the work will be generally uncouth and party-coloured; neither original nor translated, neither ancient nor modern." *Lives* 3.246-7 1781

21. *Imitation of the Ancients*, or copying, justifiable at sixteen. (Pope referred to.) *Lives* 3.224 1781

22. *Spenserian imitations:* West's *Imitations of Spenser* successfully performed. "But such compositions are not to be reckoned among the great achievements of intellect, because their effect is local and temporary; they appeal not to reason or passion, but to memory, and presuppose an accidental or artificial state of mind. An Imitation of Spenser is nothing to a reader, however acute, by whom Spenser has never been perused. Works of this kind may deserve praise, as proofs of great industry and great nicety of observation; but the highest praise, the praise of genius, they cannot claim. The noblest beauties of art are those of which the effect is co-extended with rational nature, or at least with the whole circle of polished life; what is less than this can be only pretty, the plaything of fashion and the amusement of a day." *Lives* 3.332-3 1781

23. *Spenserian imitations:* Shenstone's *Schoolmistress* "In Imitation of Spenser" "is surely the most pleasing" of his performances. "The adoption of a particular style in light and short compositions contributes much

---

[1] "In the proof-sheet, 'Roman sentiments.'" G. B. H. *Lives* 3.247 *n* 2.

to the increase of pleasure:[1] we are entertained at once with two imitations, of nature in the sentiments, of the original author in the style, and between them the mind is kept in perpetual employment." *Lives* 3.358-9   1781

24. *Pastoral imitations:* attacked. See PASTORAL 21
   1783

Inspiration. See GENIUS; COMPOSITION

Invention. See also ORIGINALITY; COMPOSITION; IMAGINATION; GENIUS 9, 14

1. "No man ever yet became great by imitation. Whatever hopes for the veneration of mankind must have invention in the design or the execution; either the effect must itself be new, or the means by which it is produced. . . . Fame cannot spread wide or endure long that is not rooted in nature, and manured by art. That which hopes to resist the blast of malignity, and stand firm against the attacks of time, must contain in itself some original principle of growth. The reputation which arises from the detail or transposition of borrowed sentiments, may spread for a while, like ivy on the rind of antiquity, but will be torn away by accident or contempt, and suffered to rot unheeded on the ground." *Wks.* 7.87. (*Ram.* 154)   1751

2. "Among the powers that must conduce to constitute a poet, the first and most valuable is invention, the highest seems to be that which is able to produce a series of events. It is easy when the thread of a story is once drawn, to diversify it with variety of colours; and when a train of action is presented to the mind, a little acquaintance with life will supply circumstances and reflexions, and a little knowledge of books furnish parellels [*sic*] and illustrations. To tell over again a story that has been told already, and to tell it better than the first author, is no rare qualification;

---
[1] *The Schoolmistress* is in burlesque vein.

but to strike out the first hints of a new fable; hence to introduce a set of characters so diversified in their several passions and interests, that from the clashing of this variety may result many necessary incidents; to make these incidents surprizing, and yet natural, so as to delight the imagination without shocking the judgment of a reader; and finally to wind up the whole in a pleasing catastrophe, produced by those very means which seem most likely to oppose and prevent it, is the utmost effort of the human mind. . . . Of all the novels and romances that wit or idleness, vanity or indigence, have pushed into the world, there are very few of which the end cannot be conjectured from the beginning; or where the authors have done more than to transpose the incidents of other tales, or strip the circumstances from one event for the decoration of another. In the examination of a poet's character, it is therefore first to be enquired what degree of invention has been exerted by him . . . Shakespear's excellence is not the fiction of a tale, but the representation of life." (See SHAKESPEARE 50.) *Wks.* 14.477-80. (*Dedication* to *Shakespear Illustrated*, written for Mrs. Lennox.)   1753

3. "Invention, by which new trains of events are formed and new scenes of imagery displayed, as in *The Rape of the Lock*, and by which extrinsick and adventitious embellishments and illustrations are connected with a known subject, as in the *Essay on Criticism*." One of the "qualities that constitute genius." (See GENIUS 23.) *Lives* 3.247   1781

Italian Literature. See also DANTE, PETRARCH, etc.

1. "The names of Redi, Galileo, Caro, Navagero, Fracastoro, Poliziano, Ariosto, Tasso, Petrarca, &c., are unknown to nobody that knows books. Their works are of long standing, therefore they are good, because mankind never unanimously join to praise a bad book

and preserve it from oblivion." Baretti's *Introduction to the Italian Language*, 1755. *Pref.* p. vi. Possibly by J. See Courtney, *Bibliog.*, p. 73   1755

Italian Opera

1. ". . . an exotick and irrational entertainment, which has been always combated [*sic*] and always has prevailed." *Lives* 2.160   1779

Judgement. Compare GOOD SENSE. For the public's judgement, see POPULAR JUDGEMENT

1. Judgement improves with practice, is "hindered by submission to dictatorial decisions." *Shak. Pref.*, Raleigh, 54   1765
2. ". . . judgement in the operations of intellect can hinder faults, but not produce excellence." *Lives* 2.208   Ptd. 1780
3. "Judgement is forced upon us by experience. He that reads many books must compare one opinion or one style with another; and when he compares, must necessarily distinguish, reject, and prefer." *Lives* 3.94
     1781
4. ". . . Judgement, which selects from life or nature what the present purpose requires, and, by separating the essence of things from its concomitants, often makes the representation more powerful than the reality." One of the "qualities that constitute genius." (See GENIUS 23.) *Lives* 3.247   1781

Just

1. *Definition:* "3. Exact; proper; accurate." *Dict.* 1755

Knowledge

1. J.'s Allegory of Wit and Learning, their dissensions and final union, resulting in "a numerous progeny of Arts and Sciences." *Wks.* 5.144-9. (*Ram.* 22)   1750
2. "Imagination is useless without knowledge: nature

Knowledge 141

gives in vain the power of combination, unless study and observation supply materials to be combined." *Lives* 1.212   1779

3. Dryden's elegy too general—he did not know the lady praised. "Knowledge of the subject is to the poet what durable materials are to the architect." *Lives* 1.442
1779

4. Knowledge of one's subject "the first requisite to excellence." *Lives* 2.319. See also AUTHORS 5   1781

5. "The honours due to learning." See TRUTH 24   1781

Labour. See COMPOSITION

Lampoon

1. *Definition:* "A personal satire; abuse; censure written not to reform but to vex." *Dict.*   1755

Latin Poetry, Modern Writers of

1. "Pope had sought for images and sentiments in a region not known to have been explored by many other of the English writers; he had consulted the modern writers of Latin poetry, a class of authors whom Boileau endeavoured to bring into contempt, and who are too generally neglected."[1] *Lives* 3.182
1781

2. * "The pretensions of the English to the reputation of writing Latin founded not so much on the specimens . . . which they have produced, as on the quantity of talent diffused through the country." *Letters* 2.441, App. D. (Windham's *Diary*)   1784

Learning. See KNOWLEDGE

Letter-Writing

1. "The importance of writing letters with propriety . . . since, next to the power of pleasing with his

---

[1] In 1734 J. had published proposals for editing the Latin poems of Politian, to which a history of modern Latin poetry was to be added. *Bos.* 1.90.

presence, every man would wish to be able to give delight at a distance." The necessity for clearness in letters on every-day subjects. *Wks.* 9.408-9   1748

2. [a] ". . . a letter has no peculiarity but its form, and . . . nothing is to be refused admission, which would be proper in any other method of treating the same subject. The qualities of the epistolary style most frequently required are ease and simplicity, an even flow of unlaboured diction, and an artless arrangement of obvious sentiments." But the expression should suit the occasion and matter. "Strict conformity to nature" always required, "because nothing but conformity to nature can make any composition beautiful or just." [b] Letters written for entertainment "are more properly regulated by critical precepts, because the matter and style are equally arbitrary, and rules are more necessary, as there is a larger power of choice. . . . When the subject has no intrinsick dignity, it must necessarily owe its attractions to artificial embellishments, and may catch at all advantages which the art of writing can supply. . . . The purpose for which letters are written when no intelligence is communicated, or business transacted, is to preserve in the minds of the absent either love or esteem; to excite love we must impart pleasure, and to raise esteem we must discover abilities. Pleasure will generally be given, as abilities are displayed by scenes of imagery, points of conceit, unexpected sallies, and artful compliments. Trifles always require exuberance of ornament; the building which has no strength can be valued only for the grace of its decorations. The pebble must be polished with care, which hopes to be valued as a diamond; and words ought surely to be laboured, when they are intended to stand for things." *Wks.* 7.71-4. (*Ram.* 152)   1751

3. French letter-writers censured. *Wks.* 7.70. (*Ram.* 152)   1751

4. *Epistolary endings "in studied varieties of phrase" defended. *Bos.* 5.238-9. (*Hebrides*, 22 Sept.)   1773

5. "Some, when they write to their friends, are all affection; some are wise and sententious; some strain their powers for efforts of gaiety: some write news, and some write secrets; but to make a letter without affection, without wisdom, without gaiety, without news, and without a secret, is, doubtless, the great epistolick art. In a man's letters, you know, Madam, his soul lies naked, his letters are only the mirrour of his breast.[1] . . . Of this great truth; sounded by the knowing to the ignorant, and so echoed by the ignorant to the knowing, what evidence have you now before you!" *Letters* 2.52   1777

6. J. disagrees with Walsh's observations on the epistolary style. *Lives* 1.330   1779

7. Affectation difficult to distinguish from habit. See STYLE 21   1781

8. J. refutes common opinion that "he who writes to his friend lays his heart open before him. . . . There is, indeed, no transaction which offers stronger temptations to fallacy and sophistication than epistolary intercourse." The emotionalism of conversation and business; "but a friendly letter is a calm and deliberate performance in the cool of leisure, in the stillness of solitude, and surely no man sits down to depreciate by design his own character . . . a letter is addressed to a single mind of which the prejudices and partialities are known, and must therefore please, if not by favouring them, by forbearing to oppose them." *Lives* 3.206-7   1781

9. " 'Affectation and ambition' " are "perverters of epistolary integrity." *Lives* 3.208   1781

---

[1] J. is here ridiculing this current opinion. See also *infra* 8; and *John. Misc.* 2.143.

Liberty of the Press

1. For an ironical defence of the Licensers, who had suppressed Brooke's tragedy *Gustavus Vasa*, see *Wks.* 14.38 *ff.* (*Vindication of the Licensers*, etc.)   1739

2. It is human nature to find that "the liberty of the press is a blessing when we are inclined to write against others, and a calamity when we find ourselves overborne by the multitude of our assailants." *Lives* 2.361   1744

3. "The danger of such unbounded liberty and the danger of bounding it have produced a problem in the science of Government, which human understanding seems hitherto unable to solve. If nothing may be published but what civil authority shall have previously approved, power must always be the standard of truth; if every dreamer of innovations may propagate his projects, there can be no settlement; if every murmurer at government may diffuse discontent, there can be no peace; and if every sceptick in theology may teach his follies, there can be no religion. The remedy against these evils is to punish the authors; for it is yet allowed that every society may punish, though not prevent, the publication of opinions, which that society shall think pernicious: but this punishment, though it may crush the author, promotes the book; and it seems not more reasonable to leave the right of printing unrestrained, because writers may be afterwards censured, than it would be to sleep with doors unbolted, because by our laws we can hang a thief."[1] *Lives* 1.107-8   1779

---

[1] cf. "No member of a society has a right to *teach* any doctrine contrary to what the society holds to be true." (*Bos.* 2.249); and "Every man has a right to utter what he thinks truth, and every other man has a right to knock him down for it." (*Bos.* 4.12). See also *Lives* 3.411-2 for Akenside's "unnecessary and outrageous zeal" for liberty.

Licentious

1. *Definition:* "1. Unrestrained by law or morality . . . 2. Presumptuous; unconfined."[1] *Dict.*   1755

Literature

1. *Definition:* "Learning; skill in letters." *Dict.* (e.g., *Bos.* 3.303 *n* 4)   1755

Love. See also AMOROUS VERSES

1. The abuse of love as a dramatic motive. See SHAKESPEARE 48   1765
2. Dryden's *All for Love* "has one fault equal to many, though rather moral than critical, that by admitting the romantick omnipotence of Love, he has recommended as laudable and worthy of imitation that conduct which through all ages the good have censured as vicious, and the bad despised as foolish." *Lives* 1.361   1779
3. *The modern novel and love. See NOVEL 5   Date ?

Low

1. *Definition:* "Not sublime; not exalted in thought or diction." *Dict.*   1755

Lyric Poetry. See also ODE; PINDARIC VERSE

1. "The imagination of the first authors of lyrick poetry was vehement and rapid, and their knowledge various and extensive." Since "the minds of their auditors, not being accustomed to accurate inspection, were easily dazzled by glaring ideas, they applied themselves to instruct, rather by short sentences and strik-

---

[1] Usually there is no moral stigma attached to the word when J. applies it to literature; e.g., Shakespeare's "licentious *English*," (i.e., English which departs from accepted usage. *Shak.* 5.438 *n.*); "Imagination, a licentious and vagrant faculty . . . impatient of restraint," (*Wks.* 6.344-5.) But "a [morally] licentious poem, such as was fashionable in those times." (*Lives* 2.170)

ing thoughts, than by regular argumentation. . . . From this accidental peculiarity of the ancient writers the criticks deduce the rules of lyrick poetry, which they have set free from all the laws by which other compositions are confined, and allow to neglect the niceties of transition, to start into remote digressions, and to wander without restraint from one scene of imagery to another . . . confusion and irregularity produce no beauty, though they cannot always obstruct the brightness of genius and learning." *Wks.* 7.108-9. (*Ram.* 158) 1751

2. *Definition of lyric* (adj.): "Pertaining to an harp, or to odes of poetry sung to an harp; singing to an harp." *Dict.* 1755

3. ". . . quatrains of lines alternately consisting of eight and six syllables make the most soft and pleasing of our lyrick measures." *Lives* 1.467 1779

4. Congreve lacked "the fire requisite for the higher species of lyrick poetry." See CONGREVE 3 Ptd. 1780

5. Akenside's failure as a lyric poet. See ODE 4 1781

Maccaronic Verses

1. "Macaroon . . . a coarse, rude, low fellow; whence *macaronick* poetry, in which the language is purposely corrupted." *Dict.* 1755

2. * "Maccaronick verses are verses made out of a mixture of different languages, that is, of one language with the termination of another." *Bos.* 3.283 1778

Marvellous, The. See also ROMANCES; compare PROBABILITY; NATURE

1. The marvellous in the heroic romance: ease of invention. See ROMANCES 1 1750

2. The marvellous has no place in modern fiction. See FICTION 1 a 1750

3. *Definition:* "3. *The marvellous* is used, in works of

criticism, to express any thing exceeding natural power, opposed to *the probable.*" *Dict.*   1755

4. "There is, undoubtedly, a sense in which all life is miraculous; as it is an union of powers of which we can image no connexion, a succession of motions of which the first cause must be supernatural . . . perhaps, there is no human being, however hid in the crowd from the observation of his fellow-mortals, who, if he has leisure and disposition to recollect his own thoughts and actions, will not conclude his life in some sort a miracle . . ." *Wks.* 4.587   1756

5. Shakespeare "familiarizes the wonderful." See SHAKESPEARE 22   1765

Mask

1. *Definition:* "5. A dramatick performance, written in a tragick stile without attention to rules or probability." *Dict.*   1755

Medieval. See MIDDLE AGES

Memoirs. Compare BIOGRAPHY; DIARIES

1. Truth nowhere "more likely to be found than in private memoirs, which are generally published at a Time when any gross Falsehood may be detected by living Witnesses, and which always contain a thousand incidents, of which the Writer could not but have acquired a certain Knowledge, and which he has no Reason for disguising." *Gent. Mag.* 1742, p. 129   1742

2. *Definition:* "1. An account of transactions familiarly written." *Dict.*   1755

Memory

1. Works which depend upon memory for their appeal, and not upon reason or passion cannot "be reckoned among the great achievements of intellect." See NATURE 46   1781

Metaphors. Compare SIMILES

1. *Definition:* "The application of a word to an use to which in its original import, it cannot be put: as . . . the spring makes the flowers. A metaphor is a simile comprized in a word; the spring putting in action the powers of vegetation, which were torpid in the *winter*, as the powers of a sleeping animal are excited by awaking him." *Dict.* 1755

2. A *"broken metaphor":* In Pope's epitaph *On Sir Godfrey Kneller*, the third couplet "is deformed with a broken metaphor." *Lives* 3.265 1756

3. The "grandeur of generality" praised: ". . . the force of metaphors is lost when the mind by the mention of particulars is turned more upon the original than the secondary sense. . . ." See GENERAL 10 1779

4. A comparison literal on one side and metaphorical on the other is "vicious." *Lives* 1.457; 3.228 1779-81

5. *"Broken metaphors":* examples in Addison and Pope exposed by common sense methods. *Lives* 2.128, 129 Ptd. 1780

6. *A "broken metaphor":* Gray in *The Progress of Poesy*, 1st stanza, "seems . . . to confound the images of 'spreading sound' and 'running water.' A 'stream of musick' may be allowed; but where does Musick, however 'smooth and strong,' after having visited the 'verdant vales,' 'rowl down the steep amain,' so as that 'rocks and nodding groves rebellow to the roar'? If this be said of Musick, it is nonsense; if it be said of Water, it is nothing to the purpose." *Lives* 3.436 1781

7. " 'Idalia's velvet-green' has something of cant. An epithet or metaphor drawn from Nature ennobles Art; an epithet or metaphor drawn from Art degrades Nature." *Lives* 3.436-7 1781

Middle Ages. See CHAUCER; GOWER; GOTHIC; ROMANCES; BLACK LETTER BOOKS

1. "In the monkish ages, however ignorant and unpolished, the EPITAPHS were drawn up with far greater propriety than can be shewn in those which more enlightened times have produced." *Wks.* 9.442   1740
2. Pope's *Temple of Fame* neglected because scene is laid in remote ages and the sentiments mostly "have little relation to general manners or common life." See NATURE 44   1781
3. *The writers of the middle ages "very curious." *Bos.* 4.170   1783

Moderns vs. Ancients. See under ANCIENT WRITERS

Money, Writing for. See COMPOSITION

Moral Element. See also AIM OF WRITING; DIDACTIC POETRY; TRUTH; PRECEPT AND PRACTICE; SHAKESPEARE: *Didacticism*. For licence in the portrayal of vice, see DRAMATIC PROPRIETY. For the value of biography as a guide to conduct, see under BIOGRAPHY; for J.'s belief that all religious verses were unworthy the subject, see under SACRED POETRY; and for romances as unsafe guides to conduct, see under ROMANCES

1. The principal purpose of the epitaph is "to perpetuate the examples of virtue." See EPITAPH 1   1740
2. Epitaphs should not contain expressions inconsistent with the Christian religion. See EPITAPHS 1. cf. J.'s objection to the mingling of the Christian religion and heathen mythology: MYTHOLOGY 11, 12, 13, 14   1740
3. "This must be at least acknowledged, which ought to be thought equivalent to many other excellences, that

this poem [Savage's *Wanderer*] can promote no other purposes than those of virtue, and that it is written with a very strong sense of the efficacy of religion." *Lives* 2.366   1744

4. "This at least must be allowed him [Savage], that he always preserved a strong sense of the dignity, the beauty, and the necessity of virtue, and that he never contributed deliberately to spread corruption amongst mankind. His actions, which were generally precipitate, were often blameable; but his writings, being the productions of study, uniformly tended to the exaltation of the mind, and the propagation of morality and piety." *Lives* 2.380   1744

5. "It is therefore to be steadily inculcated, that virtue is the highest proof of understanding, and the only solid basis of greatness; and that vice is the natural consequence of narrow thoughts; that it begins in mistake, and ends in ignominy." *Wks.* 5.26. (This position underlies the whole of the fourth *Rambler* essay, on fiction. See FICTION 1)   1750

6. Ancient poets "by no means unexceptionable teachers of morality." See ANCIENT WRITERS 3   1750

7. Lack of benefit in pastoral imitations. See PASTORAL 1 b   1750

8. "In pastoral, as in other writings, chastity of sentiment ought doubtless to be observed, and purity of manners to be represented . . . because, having the subject in his own choice, he ought always to consult the interest of virtue." See PASTORAL 2 b   1750

9. Writers censured who "recommend debauchery and lewdness, by associating them with qualities most likely to dazzle the discernment, and attract the affections; and to show innocence and goodness with such attendant weaknesses as necessarily expose them to contempt and derision. . . . What punishment can be adequate to the crime of him . . . who tortures his fancy, and ransacks his memory, only that he

may leave the world less virtuous than he found it. . . ." *Wks.* 6.40-1. (*Ram.* 77)   1750
10. "As it has been my principal design [in *The Rambler*] to inculcate wisdom or piety, I have allotted few papers to the idle sports of imagination. . . . I shall never envy the honours which wit and learning obtain in any other cause, if I can be numbered among the writers who have given ardour to virtue, and confidence to truth." *Wks.* 7.396-7. (*Ram.* 208)   1752
11. "Every art is valued in a joint proportion to its difficulty and usefulness." Wm. Payne's *Intro. to the Game of Draughts. Pref.* by J. rep't'd in *Miscellanies*, by Richard Twiss, 1805, 2.140   1756
12. *"Give nights and days, Sir (said he), to the study of Addison, if you mean either to be a good writer, or what is more worth, an honest man." *John. Misc.* 1.233. (Piozzi)   1765
13. Shakespeare's profane [i.e., irreligious] expressions censured: "There are laws of higher authority than those of criticism." See SHAKESPEARE 142   1765
14. Shakespeare "omits opportunities of instructing or delighting." See SHAKESPEARE 62   1765
15. ". . . the unities of time and place . . . are always to be sacrificed to the nobler beauties of variety and instruction . . . and the greatest graces of a play, are to copy nature and instruct life." See DRAMA 47
1765
16. "Last week I published the lives of the poets, written I hope in such a manner as may tend to the promotion of Piety." *John. Misc.* 1.88. (*Prayers and Med.s*)
1779
17. Dryden defends his immorality on ground of precedent of Ancients, "which is only to say, that he was not the first nor perhaps the greatest offender." *Lives* 1.347   1779
18. "Genius now and then produces a lucky trifle. We

still read the *Dove* of Anacreon and *Sparrow* of Catullus, and a writer naturally pleases himself with a performance which owes nothing to the subject. But compositions merely pretty have the fate of other pretty things, and are quitted in time for something useful: they are flowers fragrant and fair, but of short duration; or they are blossoms to be valued only as they foretell fruits." (Context: Waller's poems.) *Lives* 1.284   1779

19. ". . . one fault equal to many, though rather moral than critical": The false example of "romantick omnipotence of love." See LOVE 2   1779

20. The tendency of amorous verses to misrepresent life. See AMOROUS VERSES 2   1779

21. "From poetry the reader justly expects, and from good poetry always obtains, the enlargement of his comprehension and elevation of his fancy." See POETRY 25   1779

22. ". . . the general tenour and tendency of his [Congreve's] plays must always be condemned. It is acknowledged with universal conviction that the perusal of his works will make no man better; and that their ultimate effect is to represent pleasure in alliance with vice, and to relax those obligations by which life ought to be regulated." *Lives* 2.222   Ptd. 1780

23. Blackmore's prose essays "can be commended only as they are written for the highest and noblest purpose, the promotion of religion."[1] *Lives* 2.246   Ptd. 1780

24. "He [Addison] has restored virtue to its dignity and taught innocence not to be ashamed. This is an elevation of literary character, 'above all Greek, above all Roman fame.' No greater felicity can genius attain

---

[1] "Of the four poets" added to the Collection of *English Poets* at J.'s recommendation "Pomfret and Yalden were clergymen, Watts a Nonconformist minister, and Blackmore a writer of religious poetry. The inclusion of Thomson seems to be due to Johnson." Note by G. B. Hill. *Lives* 3.302 n 1. Thomson was the son of a minister and intended for the ministry.

than that of having purified intellectual pleasure, separated mirth from indecency, and wit from licentiousness; of having taught a succession of writers to bring elegance and gaiety to the aid of goodness," etc. *Lives* 2.125-6 Ptd. 1780

25. J. censures *The Dunciad* for "the grossness of its images." The unnatural delight of Pope and Swift in "ideas physically impure." "But even this fault, offensive as it is, may be forgiven for the excellence of other passages." *Lives* 3.242 1781

26. Gay's *Beggar's Opera* not likely to pervert. See GAY 4
1781

27. "The highest praise which he [Thomson] has received" given by Lord Lyttelton—"that his works contained 'No line which, dying, he could wish to blot.'" *Lives* 3.301 1781

28. ". . . he that forsakes the probable" lessens the moral usefulness of his work. See FICTION 12 1781

29. "Narrations of romantick and impracticable virtue will be read with wonder, but that which is unattainable is recommended in vain: that good may be endeavoured it must be shewn to be possible." *Lives* 3.173 1781

30. J. defends *Rape of the Lock* against Dennis's charge that it lacks a moral. "'The little unguarded follies of the female sex'" at which Pope professes to laugh are with other "small vexations" at the bottom of the misery of man. *Lives* 3.234 1781

31. "I have through my whole progress of authorship honestly endeavoured to teach the right, though I have not been sufficiently diligent to practise it, and have offered mankind my opinion as a rule, but never professed my behaviour as an example." *Letters* 2.234-5
1781

32. "What he [Pope] was upon moral principles ashamed to own, he ought to have suppressed." (*Sober Advice from Horace*, etc.) *Lives* 3.176 1781

33. "Grant, O Lord, that all who shall read my pages, may become more obedient to thy laws." *Letters* 2.378   1784

34. * "Books without the knowledge of life are useless (I have heard him say); for what should books teach but the art of *living?*" *John. Misc.* 1.324. (Piozzi)   Date ?

35. * "And when he talked of authors, his praise went spontaneously to such passages as are sure in his own phrase to leave something behind them useful on common occasions, or observant of common manners." *John. Misc.* 1.282. (Piozzi)   Date ?

36. * "Of a much admired poem, when extolled as beautiful (he replied), 'That it had indeed the beauty of a bubble: the colours are gay (said he), but the substance slight." *John. Misc.* 1.187. (Piozzi)   Date ?

Morality Plays. See MYSTERIES

Mysteries. (MORALITY PLAYS)

1. ". . . one of those wild dramas which were anciently called Mysteries."[1] *Lives* 1.121   1779

Mythology. Compare FICTION

1. The absurdity of "all allusions to the heathen mythology" in an epitaph. See EPITAPH 1   1740

2. "If no wild draught depart from Reason's rules,
   Nor gods his heroes nor his lovers fools:
   Intriguing wits! his artless plot forgive."
   Wks. 11.219. (*Prol.* to *Irene*)   1749

3. ". . . as one absurdity must naturally be expected to make way for another, they [many pastoral writers] have filled their productions with mythological allusions, with incredible fictions," etc. See PASTORAL 2   1750

---

[1] J. is evidently confusing "Mysteries" with "Moralities," as the context shows.

4. Mythological images in Virgil's fifth and sixth Pastorals objected to. See VIRGIL 12 e, f   1753
5. Pope's epitaph for Rowe: "To wish *Peace to thy shade* is too mythological to be admitted into a christian temple: the ancient worship has infected almost all our other compositions, and might therefore be contented to spare our epitaphs. Let fiction, at least, cease with life, and let us be serious over the grave." *Lives* 3.261   1756
6. "Of the ancient poets every reader feels the mythology tedious and oppressive." *Lives* 1.213   1779
7. ". . . the inefficacy and incredibility of a mythological tale." *Lives* 2.17   1779
8. The inappropriateness of mythological fictions in elegy: " 'Where there is leisure for fiction there is little grief.' " See ELEGY 4   1779
9. Mythological fictions make a weak tragic fable: *"incredulus odi."* See DRAMA 70   1779
10. Waller "borrows too many of his sentiments and illustrations from the old mythology, for which it is vain to plead the example of ancient poets: the deities which they introduced so frequently were considered as realities, so far as to be received by the imagination, whatever sober reason might even then determine. But of these images time has tarnished the splendor. A fiction, not only detected but despised, can never afford a solid basis to any position, though sometimes it may furnish a transient allusion, or slight illustration. No modern monarch can be much exalted by hearing that, as Hercules had had his *club*, he has his *navy*."[1] *Lives* 1.295   1779
11. Example of proper use of pagan deities, (i.e., when their falsity pointed out). *Lives* 1.288   1779
12. Dryden's "improper use of mythology." Passage quoted mingles heathen deities and language of religion

---

[1] Addison had argued along these lines in *Spec.* No. 523.

and later "one of the most awful passages of Sacred History." *Lives* 1.427. See also *ib.* 439: Dryden not "serious enough to keep heathen fables out of his religion"; and *ib.* 2.301-2 for similar criticism.   1779
13. Among Dryden's "faults of a less generous and splendid kind": "He makes, like almost all other poets, very frequent use of mythology, and sometimes connects religion and fable too closely without distinction." *Lives* 1.462   1779
14. *Lycidas* "has yet a grosser fault [than the use of pastoral and mythological devices]. With these trifling fictions are mingled the most awful and sacred truths, such as ought never to be polluted with such irreverent combinations. The shepherd likewise is now a feeder of sheep, and afterwards an ecclesiastical pastor, a superintendent of a Christian flock. Such equivocations are always unskilful; but here they are indecent, and at least approach to impiety, of which, however, I believe the writer not to have been conscious." *Lives* 1.165   1779
15. "The mythological allusions [in *Paradise Lost*] have been justly censured, as not being always used with notice of their vanity;[1] but they contribute variety to the narration, and produce an alternate exercise of the memory and the fancy." *Lives* 1.178-9   1779
16. Granville's mythological follies: "He is for ever amusing himself with the puerilities of mythology." *Lives* 2.294   Ptd. 1780
17. ". . . a mythological tragedy, [Granville's *Heroic Love*] upon the love of Agamemnon and Chryseis, and therefore easily sunk into neglect." *Lives* 2.290
Ptd. 1780
18. Rowe's *Ulysses*, "which, with the common fate of mythological stories, is now generally neglected. We have been too early acquainted with the poetical

---

[1] "*Vanity* . . . 4. Falshood; untruth." *Dict.*   1755

heroes to expect any pleasure from their revival: to shew them as they have already been shewn is to disgust by repetition; to give them new qualities or new adventures is to offend by violating received notions." *Lives* 2.68   Ptd. 1780

19. *Kensington Garden* by Tickell: ". . . the fiction unskilfully compounded of Grecian Deities and Gothick Fairies. Neither species of those exploded beings could have done much; and when they are brought together they only make each other contemptible." *Lives* 2.311
                                                                   Ptd. 1780

20. "Despicable" mythological fictions in Prior's love verses. See AMOROUS VERSES 4   Ptd. 1780

21. Prior's "mention of Mars and Bellona [in an *Ode to the Queen*], and his comparison of Marlborough to the Eagle that bears the thunder of Jupiter, are all puerile and unaffecting; and yet more despicable is the long tale told by Lewis in his despair of Brute and Troynovante, and the teeth of Cadmus, with his similes of the raven and eagle, and wolf and lion. By the help of such easy fictions and vulgar topicks, without acquaintance with life and without knowledge of art or nature, a poem of any length, cold and lifeless like this, may be easily written on any subject." *Lives* 2.204   Ptd. 1780

22. Gay's "*The Fan* is one of those mythological fictions which antiquity delivers ready to the hand; but which, like other things that lie open to every one's use, are of little value. The attention naturally retires from a new tale of Venus, Diana, and Minerva." *Lives* 2.283
                                                                           1781

23. ". . . some of his [Gay's] decorations [in *Trivia*] may be justly wished away. An honest blacksmith might have done for Patty what is performed by Vulcan [i.e., the making of a pair of pattens]. The appearance of Cloacina is nauseous and superfluous; a shoeboy could have been produced by the casual

cohabitation of mere mortals. Horace's rule is broken in both cases: there is no 'dignus vindice nodus,' no difficulty that required any supernatural interposition. A patten may be made by the hammer of a mortal, and a bastard may be dropped by a human strumpet. On great occasions and on small the mind is repelled by useless and apparent falsehood." *Lives* 2.284   1781

24. In Gray's *Bard*, third stanza, "we have the puerilities of obsolete mythology [Welsh] . . . attention recoils from the repetition of a tale that, even when it was first heard, was heard with scorn. . . . Theft is always dangerous; Gray has made weavers of his slaughtered bards by a fiction outrageous and incongruous." *Lives* 3.439   1781

25. Gray's "supplication to father Thames, to tell him who drives the hoop or tosses the ball, is useless and puerile. Father Thames has no better means of knowing than himself."[1] (cf. *infra* 31.) *Lives* 3.434-5
     1781

26. "The second stanza [of Gray's *The Progress of Poesy*], exhibiting Mars's car and Jove's eagle, is unworthy of further notice. Criticism disdains to chase a school-boy to his common-places. To the third it may likewise be objected that it is drawn from Mythology, though such as may be more easily assimilated to real life." (The dance of the Loves described.) *Lives* 3.436   1781

27. Stanza III, in Gray's *Progress of Poesy*, "endeavours to tell something, and would have told it had it not been crossed by Hyperion." *Lives* 3.437   1781

28. The mythological birth of Shakespeare in Gray's *Progress of Poesy:* "What is said of that mighty genius is true; but it is not said happily: the real effects of this poetical power are put out of sight by the

---

[1] Johnson makes the Princess in *Rasselas* (ch. xxv), supplicate the Nile. But as G. B. Hill points out, "There is a dignity in Johnson's supplication that is wanting in Gray's." *Lives* 3.435 *n* 2.

pomp of machinery. Where truth is sufficient to fill the mind, fiction is worse than useless; the counterfeit debases the genuine." *Lives* 3.437-8   1781

29. "The next stanzas [in Pope's *Ode on St. Cecilia's Day*] place and detain us in the dark and dismal regions of mythology, where neither hope nor fear, neither joy nor sorrow can be found . . . but what can form avail without better matter?" *Lives* 3.228
1781

30. (J. is eulogizing Pope's new supernatural machinery in *The Rape of the Lock*): "The heathen deities can no longer gain attention: we should have turned away from a contest between Venus and Diana." *Lives* 3.233   1781

31. "But the desire of diversity may be too much indulged: the parts of [Pope's] *Windsor Forest* which deserve least praise are . . . the appearance of Father Thames and the transformation of Lodona. Addison had in his *Campaign* derided the 'Rivers' that 'rise from their oozy beds' to tell stories of heroes, and it is therefore strange that Pope should adopt a fiction not only unnatural but lately censured. The story of Lodona is told with sweetness; but a new metamorphosis is a ready and puerile expedient: nothing is easier than to tell how a flower was once a blooming virgin, or a rock an obdurate tyrant." *Lives* 3.225
1781

32. Thomson's *Agamemnon* "had the fate which most commonly attends mythological stories, and was only endured, but not favoured." *Lives* 3.291   1781

33. J. at one time projected a "*History of the Heathen Mythology, with an explication of the fables, both allegorical and historical, with references to the poets.*" *Wks.* 1.81 n   Date ?

34. * "The machinery of the Pagans is uninteresting to us: when a Goddess appears in Homer or Virgil, we grow weary; still more so in the Grecian tragedies, as in

that kind of composition a nearer approach to Nature is intended. Yet there are good reasons for reading romances; as—the fertility of invention, the beauty of style and expression, the curiosity of seeing with what kind of performances the age and country in which they were written was delighted: for it is to be apprehended, that at the time when very wild improbable tales were well received, the people were in a barbarous state, and so on the footing of children, as has been explained." Pagan deities and mythology now cannot be used; "ministering spirits, the ghosts of the departed, witches, and fairies" alone available as machinery; indeed, the two latter now nearly obsolete. *Bos.* 4.16-17. (Langton's *Collection*) Date?

Narration

1. Simple narration apparently the easiest kind of writing. "Yet we hourly find such an endeavour to entertain or instruct us by recitals, clouding the facts which they intend to illustrate, and losing themselves and their auditors in wilds and mazes, in digression and confusion." *Wks.* 6.328. (*Ram.* 122)   1751
2. Knolles's *History of the Turks*, model of narrative style. See KNOLLES 2   1751
3. "Narration in dramatick poetry is naturally tedious, as it is unanimated and inactive, and obstructs the progress of the action; it should therefore always be rapid, and enlivened by frequent interruption." *Shak. Pref.*, Raleigh, 22   1765
4. "Blank verse will therefore, I fear, be too often found . . . in narration tiresome" from its natural tendency to exuberance and diffuseness. See BLANK VERSE 20
   1781

Nature. (INANIMATE.) See DESCRIPTION

1. The poet should study and observe nature. See POETRY 14   1759

2. Shakespeare relied on direct observation of nature. See
SHAKESPEARE 59   1765
3. Metaphors drawn from nature and from art. See
METAPHORS 7   1781

Nature. (GENERAL HUMAN NATURE AND HUMAN EXPERIENCE.) See also SHAKESPEARE: *Nature;* TRUTH; EXPERIENCE. Compare GENERAL AND THE PARTICULAR, THE; REASON; MARVELLOUS, THE.

4. "Enobled, yet unchang'd, if Nature shine." See
DRAMA 57   1749
5. "It is justly considered as the greatest excellency of art, to imitate nature; but it is necessary to distinguish those parts of nature, which are most proper for imitation: greater care is still required in representing life, which is so often discoloured by passion, or deformed by wickedness." See FICTION 1, for additional extracts from this important essay. ("To imitate nature" seems here to mean the portrayal of that which is conformable to the general fundamental truths of experience, as distinguished from the representation of life, i.e., of actual and particular occurrences or persons. cf. ". . . written with an utter disregard both of life and nature." *Wks.* 5.244)   1750
6. ". . . poetry has to do rather with the passions of men, which are uniform, than their customs, which are changeable." See PASTORAL 1 g   1750
7. "Sentiments like these, as they have no ground in nature, are indeed of little value in any poem;" especially objectionable in pastoral. *Wks.* 5.242. (*Ram.* 37)   1750
8. Pastorals of the occasional type, "written with an utter disregard both of life and nature." (Criticism apparently directed against *Lycidas.*) See PASTORAL 2 c   1750
9. The value of biography arises from its conformity to general human experience. See BIOGRAPHY 3   1750

10. Books which have stood the test of time have proved themselves to be "adequate to our faculties, and agreeable to nature." See CRITICISM 62   1751
11. "He who has carefully studied human nature, and can well describe it, may with most reason flatter his ambition" for lasting fame. *Wks.* 6.226. (*Ram.* 106)
1751
12. ". . . reason and nature are uniform and inflexible." See DRAMA 12 b   1751
13. "Strict conformity to nature" applies to letter writing, "because nothing but conformity to nature can make any composition beautiful or just." See LETTER-WRITING 2 a   1751
14. "No man ever yet became great by imitation. . . . Fame cannot spread wide or endure long that is not rooted in nature, and manured by art." See INVENTION 1   1751
15. "The laws of nature" distinguished from "the accidental prescriptions of authority." See RULES 7. See also *ib.* 8   1751
16. The advantage to the ancient writers of "priority, which put them in possession of the most natural sentiments, and left us nothing but servile repetition or forced conceits." (See also ANCIENT WRITERS 37, 39 for similar views.) *Wks.* 7.171. (*Ram.* 169)
1751
17. "In the pictures of life [in *The Rambler*] I have never been so studious of novelty or surprize, as to depart wholly from all resemblance; a fault which writers deservedly celebrated frequently commit, that they may raise, as the occasion requires, either mirth or abhorrence. Some enlargement may be allowed to declamation, and some exaggeration to burlesque; but as they deviate farther from reality, they become less useful, because their lessons will fail of application. The mind of the reader is carried away from the contemplation of his own manners; he finds in himself no

likeness to the phantom before him; and though he laughs or rages, is not reformed." *Wks.* 7.396. (*Ram.* 208) 1752
18. ". . . human nature is always the same." *Wks.* 9.85. (*Adv.* 99) 1753
19. The poet should aim to make his incidents "surprizing, and yet natural." See INVENTION 2 1753
20. *Definition of Nature:* "10. Sentiments or images adapted to nature, or conformable to truth and reality . . . *Nature* and Homer were he found the same. Pope." *Dict.* 1755
21. "What is meant by 'judge of nature' is not easy to say. Nature is not the object of human judgement; for it is vain to judge where we cannot alter. If by nature is meant, what is commonly called *nature* by the criticks, a just representation of things really existing and actions really performed, nature cannot be properly opposed to *art;* nature being, in this sense, only the best effect of *art.*" *Lives* 3.255 1756
22. "There is not much profundity of criticism [in Joseph Warton's analysis of Pope's *Eloisa*], because the beauties are sentiments of nature, which the learned and the ignorant feel alike." *Wks.* 15.477 1756
23. ". . . all true poetry requires that the sentiments be natural." *Wks.* 8.308. (*Idl.* 77) 1759
24. Imlac in *Rasselas* (ch. X): ". . . the province of poetry is to describe Nature and Passion, which are always the same." *Wks.* 11.29 1759
25. "The business of a poet . . . is to examine, not the individual, but the species; . . . he must disregard present laws and opinions, and rise to general and transcendental truths, which will always be the same." See POETRY 14 1759
26. Collins, "by indulging some peculiar habits of thought was eminently delighted with those flights of imagination which pass the bounds of nature [e.g., his belief in

fairies, giants, etc.]. . . . His poems are the productions of a mind . . . somewhat obstructed in its progress by deviation in quest of mistaken beauties." *Lives* 3.337-8   1763

27. ". . . there is always an appeal open from criticism to nature." *Shak. Pref.*, Raleigh, 16   1765

28. ". . . the power of nature is only the power of using to any certain purpose the materials which diligence procures, or opportunity supplies. Nature gives no man knowledge, and when images are collected by study and experience, can only assist in combining or applying them." *Shak. Pref.*, Raleigh, 37   1765

29. ". . . the greatest graces of a play, are to copy nature and instruct life." *Shak. Pref.*, Raleigh, 30   1765

30. The danger of seeking nature indirectly through imitation of authors. See ANCIENT WRITERS 39   1765

31. "Nothing can please many, and please long, but just representations of general nature. Particular manners can be known to few, and therefore few only can judge how nearly they are copied. The irregular combinations of fanciful invention may delight a-while, by that novelty of which the common satiety of life sends us all in quest; but the pleasures of sudden wonder are soon exhausted, and the mind can only repose on the stability of truth." *Shak. Pref.*, Raleigh, 11   1765

32. Happy ending to *Lear* preferred, since it is more agreeable to human nature. See DRAMA 33   1765

33. *Nature and ballads. See BALLADS 2   1769

34. *An example of "true criticism" based on knowledge of human nature. See BURKE 6   1769

35. Burlesque "unnatural; and from what is unnatural we can derive only the pleasure which novelty produces." See BURLESQUE 4   1779

36. "Of *Hudibras* the manners, being founded on opinions, are temporary and local, and therefore become

every day less intelligible and less striking. What Cicero says of philosophy is true likewise of wit and humour, that 'time effaces the fictions of opinion, and confirms the determinations of Nature.' Such manners as depend upon standing relations and general passions are co-extended with the race of man; but those modifications of life and peculiarities of practice which are the progeny of error and perverseness, or at best of some accidental influence or transient persuasion, must perish with their parents." *Lives* 1.213-4   1779

37. "In all these examples [of the "metaphysical" school of poetry] it is apparent that whatever is improper or vicious is produced by a voluntary deviation from nature in pursuit of something new and strange, and that the writers fail to give delight by their desire of exciting admiration." *Lives* 1.35   1779

38. Dryden's "general [critical] precepts, which depend upon the nature of things and the structure of the human mind," are safer than his "particular positions." *Lives* 1.413   1779

39. "Mixed wit" unnatural and hence soon wearisome. See WIT 8   1779

40. "Real mirth must be always natural, and nature is uniform. Men . . . have always laughed the same way." DRAMA 16   1779

41. Congreve's *Of Pleasing* "is founded on a vulgar but perhaps impracticable principle,
    ["All rules of pleasing in this one unite,
    'Affect not anything in Nature's spite.' "]
and the staleness of the sense is not concealed by any novelty of illustration or elegance of diction." *Lives* 2.233   Ptd. 1780

42. Young, in *Love of Fame*, "plays, indeed, only on the surface of life; he never penetrates the recesses of the mind, and therefore the whole power of his poetry is exhausted by a single perusal: his conceits please only when they surprise." *Lives* 3.394   1781

43. ". . . the cant of those who judge by principles rather than perception." *Lives* 3.248   1781

44. Pope's *The Temple of Fame:* ". . . yet, with all this comprehension of excellence, as its scene is laid in remote ages, and its sentiments, if the concluding paragraph be excepted, have little relation to general manners or common life, it never obtained much notice, but is turned silently over, and seldom quoted or mentioned with either praise or blame." *Lives* 3.226   1781

45. Homer's "positions are general, and his representations natural, with very little dependence on local or temporary customs, on those changeable scenes of artificial life, which, by mingling original with accidental notions, and crowding the mind with images which time effaces, produce ambiguity in diction, and obscurity in books. To this open display of unadulterated nature it must be ascribed, that Homer has fewer passages of doubtful meaning than any other poet either in the learned or in modern languages." *Lives* 3.114   1781

46. "But such compositions [as West's *Imitations of Spenser*] are not to be reckoned among the great achievements of intellect, because their effect is local and temporary; they appeal not to reason or passion, but to memory, and presuppose an accidental or artificial state of mind [i.e., an acquaintance with Spenser] . . . the highest praise, the praise of genius, they cannot claim. The noblest beauties of art are those of which the effect is co-extended with rational nature, or at least with the whole circle of polished life; what is less than this can be only pretty, the plaything of fashion and the amusement of a day." *Lives* 3.332-3   1781

47. Gray's *The Bard* and *The Progress of Poesy:* "The mind of the writer seems to work with unnatural violence. 'Double, double, toil and trouble.' He has a kind

of strutting dignity, and is tall by walking on tiptoe. His art and his struggle are too visible, and there is too little appearance of ease and nature." *Lives* 3.440
                  1781

48. *Extract from Windham's record of Johnson's conversation, Aug. 1784: "Opinion that there were three ways in which writing may be unnatural; by being bombastic and above nature, affected and beside it, fringing every event with ornaments which nature did not afford, or weak and below nature. That neither of the first would please long. That the third might indeed please a good while, or at least many; because imbecility, and consequently a love of imbecility, might be found in many." *Letters* 2.440 (App. D) 1784

Nature. (The "Return to Nature" Movement)

49. The prince in *Rasselas* finds that the sage who tries to explain to him the meaning of the phrase "to live according to nature," was one of those "whom he should understand less as he heard him longer." *Wks.* 11.64-5. (*Ras.* ch. XXII)   1759

50. J. ridicules the "return to nature" movement.[1] See Poetry 39 and Rousseau   1781

Nervous

1. *Definition* (applied to style): ". . . strong, vigorous."[2] *Dict.*   1755

Novel, The. See also Fiction. Compare Romances

1. Other biographers of Savage, "it may be reasonably imagined . . . under the title of *The Life of Savage* . . . will publish only a novel, filled with romantick

---

[1] J. consistently maintains this attitude of scorn toward Rousseauistic believers in "Nature's simple plan." e.g., see *Bos.* 5.125 and note.
[2] e.g., "a style clear, pure, nervous, and expressive," recommended, (*Wks.* 9.121); Shenstone and Hawkins speak approvingly of J's "nervous" style. (*Bos.* 2.452 and *Wks.* 1.196)

adventures, and imaginary amours." *Lives* 2.435. (App. FF) 1743
2. Lack of original invention in novels. See INVENTION 2
1753
3. *Definition:* "1. A small tale, generally of love. [e.g.] Nothing of a foreign nature; like the trifling *novels* which Ariosto inserted in his poems. Dryden.
   Her mangl'd fame in barb'rous pastime lost,
   The coxcomb's *novel* and the drunkard's toast.
Prior." *Dict.* 1755
4. *Hoole: J. "conjured me to read and meditate upon the Bible, and not to throw it aside for a play or a novel." *John. Misc.* 2.146 1784
5. * "It is not . . . because they [modern novels] treat . . . about love, but because they treat of nothing, that they are despicable: we must not ridicule a passion which he who never felt never was happy . . ." etc. *John. Misc.* 1.290. (Piozzi) Date ?

Novelty. Compare ORIGINALITY

1. "Hard is his lot that here by fortune plac'd,
   Must watch the wild vicissitudes of Taste;
   With every meteor of Caprice must play,
   And chace the new-blown bubbles of the day."
   Wks. 1.197. (*Drury-lane Prologue*) 1747
2. "Untainted with the LUST OF INNOVATION." *Irene*, I ii. (*John. Misc.* 1.463) 1749
3. "Both [Wit and Learning] had prejudices, which in some degree hindered their progress towards perfection, and left them open to attacks. Novelty was the darling of WIT" to whom "all that was new was specious." *Wks.* 5.146. (*Ram.* 22) 1750
4. ". . . that power of giving pleasure which novelty supplies." See ANCIENT WRITERS 9 1751
5. A writer should not "violate essential principles by a desire of novelty." *Wks.* 7.100. (*Ram.* 156) 1751

NOVELTY 169

6. Danger of the distortion of reality in search for novelty. See NATURE 17 — 1752
7. The poet should aim to make incidents "surprizing, and yet natural." See INVENTION 2 — 1753
8. Common rhymes condemned, in that thus "half the composition loses the grace of novelty." See VERSIFICATION 17 — 1756
9. "To exact of every man who writes that he should say something new, would be to reduce authors to a small number; to oblige the most fertile genius to say only what is new, would be to contract his volumes to a few pages. Yet, surely, there ought to be some bounds to repetition; libraries ought no more to be heaped for ever with the same thoughts differently expressed, than with the same books differently decorated." *Wks.* 8.345. (*Idl.* 85) — 1759
10. Novelty only a temporary pleasure. See NATURE 31 — 1765
11. * "Nothing odd will do long. *Tristram Shandy* did not last." *Bos.* 2.449 — 1776
12. ". . . novelty is always grateful where it gives no pain. But the merit of such performances [as Philips' *Splendid Shilling*] begins and ends with the first author." *Lives* 1.317 — 1779
13. ". . . the grace of novelty." *Lives* 1.147 — 1779
14. The "metaphysical poets" hindered from moving the affections or attaining to the sublime, by their desire for the "unexpected and surprising. . . . Those writers who lay on the watch for novelty could have little hope of greatness; for great things cannot have escaped former observation." See GENERAL 9. See also NATURE 37 — 1779
15. English writers less afraid of novelty than the French. *Lives* 1.430 — 1779
16. ". . . from what is unnatural we can derive only the pleasure which novelty produces. We admire it awhile

as a strange thing; but, when it is no longer strange, we perceive its deformity. It is a kind of artifice, which by frequent repetition detects itself. . . ." *Lives* 1.218
                 1779

17. An author a poor self-critic because of the pleasing novelty of the act of composition. ". . . novelty is the great source of pleasure." See CRITICISM 5
                Ptd. 1780

18. Penury of thought and want of novelty often concealed by dead language, e.g., "the sonorous magnificence of Roman syllables." *Lives* 2.83 Ptd. 1780

19. Gay's *What d'ye Call it* "was one of the lucky trifles that give pleasure by novelty." *Lives* 2.271 1781

20. ". . . familiar images in laboured language have nothing to recommend them but absurd novelty, which, wanting the attractions of Nature, cannot please long. One excellence of *The Splendid Shilling* is that it is short. Disguise can gratify no longer than it deceives." See BLANK VERSE 17 1781

21. Novel arrangement of rhymes should be avoided in short compositions. See ODE 4 1781

22. * "The floridness of novelty" temporarily aids "infidel writers." See VOLTAIRE 11 1784

23. * "He said to Sir William Scott, 'The age is running mad after innovation; all the business of the world is to be done in a new way; men are to be hanged in a new way; Tyburn itself is not safe from the fury of innovation.' " *Bos.* 4.188. For other testimony to J.'s dislike of "sudden innovation," see *John Misc.* 1.345, 349 Date ?

24. *J. mocks writing in a new manner: "Buckinger had no hands, and he wrote his name with his toes at Charing-cross, for half a crown apiece; that was a new manner of writing!"[1] *John. Misc.* 1.419. (Murphy) For Mrs. Piozzi's version, see *ib.* 1.188 Date ?

---

[1] See *Mod. Lang. Notes*, 26.176 for confirmation of this anecdote.

Numbers

1. *Definition:* "8. Verses; poetry." *Dict.* 1755

Obscurity

1. "One of the most pernicious effects of haste, is obscurity." *Wks.* 7.173. (*Ram.* 169) 1751
2. "Obscurity and clearness are relative terms: to some readers scarce any book is easy, to others not many are difficult." Modern critics censured, who condemn ancient writers for an obscurity which often arises from a modern ignorance of events alluded to. Illustrations from Horace. *Wks.* 9.32-9. (*Adv.* 58) 1753
3. *A defence of "hard words":* "If an author be supposed to involve his thoughts in voluntary obscurity, and to obstruct, by unnecessary difficulties, a mind eager in pursuit of truth . . . he counteracts the first end of writing, and justly suffers the utmost severity of censure, or the more afflictive severity of neglect. But words are only hard to those who do not understand them, and the critick ought always to enquire, whether he is incommoded by the fault of the writer, or by his own. Every author does not write for every reader . . . and many subjects of general use may be treated in a different manner, as the book is intended for the learned or the ignorant. . . . Difference of thoughts will produce difference of language. He that thinks with more extent than another will want words of larger meaning; he that thinks with more subtilty will seek for terms of more nice discrimination. . . . That the vulgar express their thoughts clearly is far from true; and what perspicuity can be found among them proceeds not from the easiness of their language, but the shallowness of their thoughts." A justification of terms of art. *Wks.* 8.279-82. (*Idl.* 70) 1759
4. ". . . every piece ought to contain in itself whatever is necessary to make it intelligible." *Lives* 1.35-6 1779

5. "As the end of method is perspicuity, that series [of truths or precepts, with special reference to didactic poetry] is sufficiently regular that avoids obscurity." See DIDACTIC POETRY 8   1781
6. Homer's "positions are general, and his representations natural, with very little dependence on local or temporary customs, on those changeable scenes of artificial life, which, by mingling original with accidental notions, and crowding the mind with images which time effaces, produce ambiguity in diction, and obscurity in books." Lives 3.114   1781

Occasional Works. See also DEDICATIONS. Compare PRAISE; SATIRE; NATURE; FAME. For attacks on the occasional element in pastoral, see PASTORAL 2c, 12

1. J. blames Queen Caroline in that she tried "to chain down the genius of a writer [Savage] to an annual panegyrick." Lives 2.383   1744
2. Savage must have expected something more than mere increase of reputation when "he prevailed upon himself to attempt a species of writing, of which all the topicks had been long before exhausted, and which was made at once difficult by the multitudes that had failed in it, and those that had succeeded." (Referring to Savage's poem on the death of the king.) Lives 2.344   1744
3. Savage's annual poems to the Queen: ". . . nor can it seem strange that, being confined to the same subject, he should be at some times indolent, and at others unsuccessful; that he should sometimes delay a disagreeable task till it was too late to perform it well; or that he should sometimes repeat the same sentiment on the same occasion, or at others be misled by an attempt after novelty to forced conceptions and farfetched images." Lives 2.384   1744
4. "In proportion as those who write on temporary sub-

jects, are exalted above their merit at first, they are afterwards depressed below it; nor can the brightest elegance of diction, or most artful subtilty of reasoning, hope for much esteem from those whose regard is no longer quickened by curiosity or pride." *Wks.* 6.224-5. (*Ram.* 106)   1751

5. "It often happens, that an author's reputation is endangered in succeeding times, by that which raised the loudest applause among his contemporaries." Examples of obscure contemporary allusions in ancient writers. *Wks.* 9.32-9. (*Adv.* 58)   1753

6. The fate of poems not founded upon general principles or universal truths. See GENERAL 6   1759

7. "To pursue the topic of the day, or to prop a declining party, are generally sure of immediate applause; but in proportion as such poets write to the present world, they must forego their claims to posterity." *Crit. Rev.*, Oct. 1764, p. 170 [270] (Attributed to J. See Courtney, *Bibliog.* 103)   1764

8. *Extravagant flattery permissible when the medium is a dramatic character. Stage praise of royalty is "formular." *Bos.* 2.234   1773

9. *"Panegyrick" compared with biography. See BIOGRAPHY 12   1773

10. *"MUSGRAVE. 'A temporary poem always entertains us.' JOHNSON. 'So does an account of the criminals hanged yesterday entertain us.'" *Bos.* 3.318   1778

11. "Poets, indeed, profess fiction, but the legitimate end of fiction is the conveyance of truth; and he that has flattery ready for all whom the vicissitudes of the world happen to exalt must be scorned as a prostituted mind that may retain the glitter of wit, but has lost the dignity of virtue." *Lives* 1.271   1779

12. "In an occasional performance no height of excellence can be expected from any mind, however fertile in itself, and however stored with acquisitions. He whose

work is general and arbitrary has the choice of his matter, and takes that which his inclination and his studies have best qualified him to display and decorate. He is at liberty to delay his publication, till he has satisfied his friends and himself. . . . The occasional poet is circumscribed by the narrowness of his subject: whatever can happen to man has happened so often that little remains for fancy or invention. We have been all born; we have most of us been married; and so many have died before us that our deaths can supply but few materials for a poet. In the fate of princes the publick has an interest; and what happens to them of good or evil the poets have always considered as business for the Muse. But after so many inauguratory gratulations, nuptial hymns, and funeral dirges, he must be highly favoured by nature or by fortune who says any thing not said before. Even war and conquest, however splendid, suggest no new images; the triumphal chariot of a victorious monarch can be decked only with those ornaments that have graced his predecessors. Not only matter but time is wanting. The poem must not be delayed till the occasion is forgotten. The lucky moments of animated imagination cannot be attended; elegances and illustrations cannot be multiplied by gradual accumulation: the composition must be dispatched while conversation is yet busy and admiration fresh; and haste is to be made lest some other events should lay hold upon mankind. Occasional compositions may however secure to a writer the praise both of learning and facility; for they cannot be the effect of long study, and must be furnished immediately from the treasures of the mind." *Lives* 1.424-5
1779

13. Garth's *Dispensary* intrinsically weak, "and therefore, since it has been no longer supported by accidental and extrinsick popularity, it has been scarcely able to support itself." *Lives* 2.64   1779

14. Prior in his *Carmen Seculare* "retained as much veracity as can be properly exacted from a poet professedly encomiastick." *Lives* 2.185   Ptd. 1780
15. Prior's "occasional poems necessarily lost part of their value, as their occasions, being less remembered, raised less emotion." *Lives* 2.203   Ptd. 1780
16. ". . . occasional poetry must often content itself with occasional praise." *Lives* 2.67   Ptd. 1780
17. Addison's *The Present State of the War:* ". . . which, however judicious, being written on temporary topicks and exhibiting no peculiar powers, laid hold on no attention, and has naturally sunk by its own weight into neglect." *Lives* 2.107   Ptd. 1780
18. "Every thing has its day. Through the reigns of William and Anne no prosperous event passed undignified by poetry. In the last war, when . . . the name of an Englishman was reverenced through Europe, no poet was heard amidst the general acclamation: the fame of our counsellors and heroes was intrusted to the Gazetteer." *Lives* 2.186-7   Ptd. 1780
19. "But what was yet of more importance [than Pope's acquired facility in verse-building], his effusions were always voluntary, and his subjects chosen by himself. His independence secured him from drudging at a task, and labouring upon a barren topick: he never exchanged praise for money, nor opened a shop of condolence or congratulation. His poems, therefore, were scarce ever temporary. He suffered coronations and royal marriages to pass without a song, and derived no opportunities from recent events, nor any popularity from the accidental disposition of his readers. He was never reduced to the necessity of soliciting the sun to shine upon a birth-day, of calling the Graces and Virtues to a wedding, or of saying what multitudes have said before him. When he could produce nothing new, he was at liberty to be silent." Hence his productions never hasty. *Lives* 3.219-20   1781

Oddity. See NOVELTY

Ode. See PINDARIC VERSE; LYRIC POETRY

1. *Definition:* "A poem written to be sung to musick; a lyrick poem; the ode is either of the greater or less kind. The less is characterised by sweetness and ease; the greater by sublimity, rapture, and quickness of transition." *Dict.* 1755
2. "The next ode [by Fenton] is irregular, and therefore defective." *Lives* 2.263   Ptd. 1780
3. Prior's *Ode to the Queen* "is necessarily tedious by the form of the stanza: an uniform mass of ten lines, thirty-five times repeated, inconsequential and slightly connected, must weary both the ear and the understanding." *Lives* 2.204   Ptd. 1780
4. "It is not easy to guess why he [Akenside] addicted himself so diligently to lyric poetry, having neither the ease and airiness of the lighter, nor the vehemence and elevation of the grander ode. . . . Of his odes nothing favourable can be said: the sentiments commonly want force, nature, or novelty; the diction is sometimes harsh and uncouth, the stanzas ill-constructed and unpleasant, and the rhymes dissonant or unskilfully disposed, too distant from each other or arranged with too little regard to established use, and therefore perplexing to the ear, which in a short composition has not time to grow familiar with an innovation." *Lives* 3.419-20   1781

Onomatopæia. See VERSIFICATION: "*Representative Metre*"

Opening of a Work

1. Its difficulty. Established mode of procedure only in heroic poetry. "The rules which the injudicious use of this prerogative suggested to Horace, may indeed be applied to the direction of candidates for inferior

fame; it may be proper for all to remember, that they ought not to raise expectation which it is not in their power to satisfy,[1] and that it is more pleasing to see smoke brightening into flame, than flame sinking into smoke. . . . It may, indeed, be no less dangerous to claim, on certain occasions, too little than too much. There is something captivating in spirit and intrepidity, to which we often yield, as to a resistless power; nor can he reasonably expect the confidence of others, who too apparently distrusts himself . . . the reasons for arrogance and submission . . . nearly equiponderant." *Wks.* 5.2-5. (*Ram.* 1)   1750

2. "It is established at present, that the proemial lines of a poem, in which the general subject is proposed, must be void of glitter and embellishment." Addison has not considered either "precept or example" in pointing out that the lack of adornment of the first lines of *Paradise Lost* conforms "to the example of *Homer*, and the precept of *Horace*." Horace's directions apply to matter, not the manner of expression. Homer, and Virgil open their epics with magnificence and adornment rather than with simplicity. "The intent of the introduction is to raise expectation, and suspend it; something therefore must be discovered, and something concealed; and the poet, while the fertility of his invention is yet unknown, may properly recommend himself by the grace of his language. He that reveals too much, or promises too little; he that never irritates the intellectual appetite, or that immediately satiates it, equally defeats his own purpose. It is necessary to the pleasure of the reader, that the events should not be anticipated, and how then can his attention be invited, but by grandeur of expression?" *Wks.* 7.110-12. (*Ram.* 158)   1751

3. *J. censures the abrupt opening of Gray's *The Bard:* ". . . such arts as these have no merit, unless when

[1] See also *Bos.* 4.154.

they are original. We admire them only once; and this abruptness has nothing new in it. We have had it often before. Nay, we have it in the old song of Johnny Armstrong." *Bos.* 1.403   1763

4. Abrupt beginning of *The Bard* "has been celebrated; but technical beauties can give praise only to the inventor. It is in the power of any man to rush abruptly upon his subject, that has read the ballad of *Johnny Armstrong.*" *Lives* 3.439   1781

Originality. See also INVENTION; NOVELTY. Compare PLAGIARISM; GENIUS

1. "Neither care nor expence has been spared to . . . procure to this book [*The Preceptor*] the merit of an original." *Wks.* 9.405. (*Pref.* to *Preceptor*)   1748

2. ". . . the pleasure of wantoning in common topicks is so tempting to a writer, that he cannot easily resign it; a train of sentiments generally received enables him to shine without labour, and to conquer without a contest." Authors "more inclined to pursue a track so smooth and so flowery, than attentively to consider whether it leads to truth." *Wks.* 5.8-9. (*Ram.* 2)   1750

3. A plea for an original play of the imagination. See IMITATION 5   1751

4. "There are qualities in the products of nature yet undiscovered, and combinations in the powers of art yet untried. It is the duty of every man to endeavour that something may be added by his industry to the hereditary aggregate of knowledge and happiness." *Wks.* 6.375. (*Ram.* 129)   1751

5. ". . . the honour which is always due to an original author." *Wks.* 9.69. (*Adv.* 92)   1753

6. Although "right and wrong are immutable," a moralist has many opportunities for originality in his treatment of a subject. See VARIETY 3   1753

7. "It is, however, not necessary, that a man should forbear to write, till he has discovered some truth unknown before; he may be sufficiently useful, by only diversifying the surface of knowledge, and luring the mind by a new appearance to a second view of those beauties which it had passed over inattentively before. Every writer may find intellects correspondent to his own." *Wks.* 9.154. (*Adv.* 137) 1754

8. "New works may be constructed with old materials, the disposition of the parts may shew contrivance, the ornaments interspersed may discover elegance. It is not always without good effect that men of proper qualifications write in succession on the same subject, even when the latter add nothing to the information given by the former; for the same ideas may be delivered more intelligibly or more delightfully by one than by another, or with attractions that may lure minds of a different form. No writer pleases all, and every writer may please some. But after all, to inherit is not to acquire; to decorate is not to make." *Wks.* 10.186 1756

9. ". . . sentiments, which, though not new, are of great importance, and may be read with pleasure in the thousandth repetition." *Wks.* 10.223 1757

10. "There are truths which, as they are always necessary, do not grow stale by repetition." *Wks.* 10.239 1757

11. *The plea of fiction-writers "that the beauties of nature are now exhausted." See FICTION 7. cf. also ANCIENT WRITERS 9, 13, 16, 37, 39 1758

12. ". . . the uncommon merit of an original design." *Lives* 1.316-7 1779

13. Originality in a didactic poem. See DIDACTIC POETRY 4 Ptd. 1780

14. ". . . the merit of original thought is wanting" in Granville's *Progress of Beauty. Lives* 2.295
Ptd. 1780

15. Originality, "merit of the highest kind." See Congreve 2 Ptd. 1780
16. "Much, however, must be allowed to the author of a new species of composition, though it be not of the highest kind." See GAY 1 1781
17. J. refutes the charge that Pope did not invent supernatural machinery in *The Rape of the Lock*, "a charge which might with more justice have been brought against the author of the *Iliad*, who doubtless adopted the religious system of his country; for what is there but the names of his agents which Pope has not invented? Has he not assigned them characters and operations never heard of before? Has he not, at least, given them their first poetical existence? If this is not sufficient to denominate his work original, nothing original ever can be written. In this work are exhibited in a very high degree the two most engaging powers of an author: new things are made familiar, and familiar things are made new." *Lives* 3.233 1781
18. "As a writer he [Thomson] is entitled to one praise of the highest kind: his mode of thinking and of expressing his thoughts is original." *Lives* 3.298 1781
19. *According to one of J.'s friends, J. "projected . . . a work to shew how small a quantity of REAL FICTION there is in the world; and that the same images, with very little variation, have served all the authours who have ever written." *Bos.* 4.236 Date ?

Ornament

1. ". . . it is an established principle, that all ornaments owe their beauty to their propriety." (Applied to epitaphs.) *Wks.* 9.441-2 1740
2. ". . . the idea of an ornament admits use, though it seems to exclude necessity." See FABLE 1 1751
3. Ornament necessary in letters written for entertainment: "Trifles always require exuberance of ornament." See LETTER-WRITING 2 1751

4. Ornament justified in opening lines of epics. See
 OPENING OF A WORK 2 1751

 5. Ornament in diction: Truth "owes part of her charms
 to her ornaments." See DICTION 2 1751

 6. ". . . he that will not condescend to recommend
 himself by external embellishments, must submit to
 the fate of just sentiment meanly expressed, and be
 ridiculed and forgotten before he is understood." *Wks.*
 7.168. (*Ram.* 168) 1751

 7. Originality placed above decoration of the familiar.
 See ORIGINALITY 8 1756

 8. Ornate writing less difficult than "easy" writing. See
 STYLE 10 1759

 9. *When J. is charged with inconsistency for attacking
 ornamental beauty in architecture or statuary though
 allowing it in writing, he replies: "Why, Sir, all these
 ornaments are useful, because they obtain an easier
 reception for truth; but a building is not at all more
 convenient for being decorated with superfluous carved
 work." *Bos.* 2.439 1776

 10. Ornament and poetry. See POETRY 21 1779

Pamphlets and Small Tracts

 1. Their importance. *Wks.* 9.350-4 (Introd. to the *Harleian Miscellany*). See also *Gent. Mag.*, 1743, *Proposals for Printing . . . The Harleian Miscellany*, at end of volume. 1743-4

Panegyric. See OCCASIONAL WORKS; PRAISE

Particular, The. See GENERAL AND THE PARTICULAR

Passions. See FEELING

Past, The. See ANCIENT WRITERS; ANTIQUE STYLE; GOTHIC

Pastoral. See also VIRGIL; THEOCRITUS, etc. For adverse criticism of pastoral elegy, see ELEGY 4, 10

1. [a] *Popularity:* Scarcely any species of poetry more popular: it represents familiar scenes of the truth of which all are qualified to judge, allures by its picture of an ideal state, and appeals to youth and age. [b] *Pastoral imitators,* "numbers without number . . . after the manner of other imitators," transmit "the same images in the same combination from one to another, till he that reads the title of a poem, may guess at the whole series of the composition; nor will a man, after the perusal of thousands of these performances, find his knowledge enlarged with a single view of nature not produced before, or his imagination amused with any new application of those views to moral purposes." [c] *The narrow range of pastoral:* the "general effects [of nature] on the eye and on the ear are uniform, and incapable of much variety of description. Poetry cannot dwell upon the minuter distinctions, by which one species differs from another, without departing from that simplicity of grandeur which fills the imagination; nor dissect the latent qualities of things, without losing its general power of gratifying every mind by recalling its conceptions. However, as each age makes some discoveries, and those discoveries are by degrees generally known . . . pastoral might receive, from time to time, small augmentations, and exhibit once in a century a scene somewhat varied." [d] *Faulty pastorals:* when nature is drawn from the imagination, with features changed or distorted, to avoid a servile imitation of predecessors. [e] "Not only the images of rural life, but the occasions on which they can be properly produced, are few and general." Little diversity in life of a man living in the country; seldom "such circumstances as attract curiosity. His ambition is without policy, and his love without intrigue. He has no complaints to

make of his rival, but that he is richer than himself; nor any disasters to lament, but a cruel mistress, or a bad harvest." [f] *Piscatory eclogues:* The "piscatory" eclogues of Sannazaro discussed. (See SANNAZARO 1) Two defects in the piscatory eclogue: 1. "The sea . . . has . . . much less variety than the land, and therefore will be sooner exhausted by a descriptive writer." 2. "Another obstacle to the general reception of this kind of poetry, is the ignorance of maritime pleasures, in which the greater part of mankind must always live. . . . They have, therefore, no opportunity of tracing in their own thoughts, the descriptions of winding shores, and calm bays, nor can look on the poem in which they are mentioned, with other sensations than on a sea chart, or the metrical geography of *Dionysius.*" Sannazaro avoids this difficulty by writing in a learned language to a selected public; otherwise "he would soon have discovered how vainly he had endeavoured to make that loved, which was not understood." [g] *Classical pastoral:* Difficult "to improve the pastorals of antiquity, by any great additions or diversifications. Our descriptions may indeed differ from those of Virgil . . . but as nature is in both countries nearly the same, and as poetry has to do rather with the passions of men, which are uniform, than their customs, which are changeable, the varieties, which time or place can furnish, will be inconsiderable." *Wks.* 5.232-8. (*Ram.* 36)   1750

2. [a] *Nature of pastoral:* "a species of composition, in which, above all others, mere nature is to be regarded." J. appeals to ancient pastoral writers, especially Virgil, "from whose opinion it will not appear very safe to depart," against the mistaken notions of modern authors and critics of the pastoral. Definition of pastoral, drawn from Virgil's writings: "*a poem in which any action or passion is represented by its effects upon a country life.* Whatsoever therefore may, according

to the common course of things, happen in the country, may afford a subject for a pastoral poet." [b] *False conceptions of pastoral* tested by this definition: 1. That pastorals should be laid in the golden age, in order to raise the speakers to the level of the sentiments. J.'s answer: "In pastoral, as in other writings, chastity of sentiment ought doubtless to be observed, and purity of manners to be represented; not because the poet is confined to the images of the golden age, but because, having the subject in his own choice, he ought always to consult the interest of virtue." 2. The fallacy "that all refinement should be avoided, and that some slight instances of ignorance should be interspersed." This inconsistent with "golden age" position. 3. "Dorick" language of "obsolete terms and rustick words." This "a mangled dialect, which no human being ever could have spoken" resulting in the inconsistency "of joining elegance of thought with coarseness of diction." Example from Spenser of "studied barbarity" of language and theological sentiments. [c] *True pastoral:* "Pastoral admits of all ranks of persons, because persons of all ranks inhabit the country." Hence "elevation or delicacy of sentiment" permitted; "those ideas only are improper, which, not owing their original to rural objects, are not pastoral." "Pastoral being the *representation of an action or passion, by its effects upon a country life*, has nothing peculiar but its confinement to rural imagery, without which it ceases to be pastoral. This is its true characteristick, and this it cannot lose by any dignity of sentiment, or beauty of diction. . . . It seems necessary to the perfection of this poem, that the occasion which is supposed to produce it, be at least not inconsistent with a country life, or less likely to interest those who have retired into places of solitude and quiet, than the more busy part of mankind. It is therefore improper to give the title of a pastoral to verses, in which the speakers, after the slight mention of their flocks, fall to complaints of errors in the church, and corruptions in the government, or to lamentations of the death of some illustrious person, whom, when once the poet has called a shepherd, he has no longer any labour upon his hands, but can make the clouds weep, and lilies wither, and the sheep hang their heads, without art or learning, genius or study. . . . The facility of treating actions or events in the pastoral style, has incited many writers, from whom more judgment might have been expected, to put the sorrow or the joy which the occasion required into the mouth of Daphne or of Thyrsis, and as one absurdity must naturally be expected to make way for another, they have written with an utter disregard both of life and nature, and filled their productions with mythological allusions, with incredible fictions, and with sentiments which neither passion nor reason could have dictated, since the change which religion has made in the whole system of the world." *Wks.* 5.238-44. (*Ram.* 37) 1750

3. *Ramblers* 42 and 46 contain satire on the ideal rural life portrayed by pastoral writers. *Wks.* 5.272, 296-7. (cf. *supra* 1 e) 1750

4. *Definition:* "A poem in which any action or passion is represented by its effects upon a country life; or according to the common practice in which speakers take upon them the character of shepherds; and idyl; a bucolick. [e.g.] *Pastoral* is an imitation of the action of a shepherd, the form of this imitation is dramatick or narrative, or mixed of both, the fable simple, the manners not too polite nor too rustick. *Pope.*" *Dict.* 1755

5. Pope's projected American pastorals could not have exhibited any "representation of nature or of life." See DESCRIPTION 4 1756

6. Pope's *Pastorals* justly censured, "considered as representations of any kind of life . . . for there is in

them a mixture of Grecian and English, of ancient and modern images. Windsor is coupled with Hybla, and Thames with Pactolus." *Wks.* 15.469   1756

7. Dick Shifter finds rustic simplicity not what pastoral writings had led him to expect. A satire on pastorals. (cf. *supra* 3.) *Wks.* 8.283-8. (*Idl.* 71)   1759

8. "This comedy [Cowley's *Love's Riddle*] is of the pastoral kind, which requires no acquaintance with the living world." *Lives* 1.4   1779

9. Milton's *Epitaphium Damonis* "written with the common but childish imitation of pastoral life." *Lives* 1.97   1779

10. *Lycidas:* "The form is that of a pastoral, easy, vulgar, and therefore disgusting," etc. See ELEGY 4   1779

11. Irreverent mingling of sacred truths and pastoral fictions in *Lycidas*. See MYTHOLOGY 14   1779

12. "Of *Florelio* [by Fenton] it is sufficient to say that it is an occasional pastoral, which implies something neither natural nor artificial, neither comick nor serious." *Lives* 2.263   Ptd. 1780

13. "Congreve testified his gratitude [to the Queen] by a despicable effusion of elegiack pastoral; a composition in which all is unnatural, and yet nothing is new." *Lives* 2.217-8   Ptd. 1780

14. Gay's "*Dione* is a counterpart to *Amynta* and *Pastor Fido*, and other trifles of the same kind, easily imitated, and unworthy of imitation . . . the style of the Italians and of Gay is equally tragical. There is something in the poetical Arcadia so remote from known reality and speculative possibility, that we can never support its representation through a long work. A Pastoral of an hundred lines may be endured; but who will hear of sheep and goats, and myrtle bowers and purling rivulets, through five acts? Such scenes please barbarians in the dawn of literature, and children in the dawn of life; but will be for the most part

thrown away as men grow wise, and nations grow learned." *Lives* 2.284-5   1781

15. "I cannot but regret that it [Shenstone's *Pastoral Ballad*] is pastoral; an intelligent reader acquainted with the scenes of real life sickens at the mention of the *crook*, the *pipe*, the *sheep*, and the *kids*, which it is not necessary to bring forward to notice, for the poet's art is selection, and he ought to shew the beauties without the grossness of the country life." *Lives* 3.356   1781

16. The character of a young man visible in Lyttelton's *Progress of Love:* "The Verses cant of shepherds and flocks, and crooks dressed with flowers. . . ." *Lives* 3.446   1781

17. Of Lyttelton's *Progress of Love* "it is sufficient blame to say that it is pastoral." *Lives* 3.456   1781

18. Pope's *Pastorals:* "It seems natural for a young poet to initiate himself by Pastorals, which, not professing to imitate real life, require no experience, and, exhibiting only the simple operation of unmingled passions, admit no subtle reasoning or deep enquiry." *Lives* 3.224   1781

19. "At the revival of learning in Italy it was soon discovered that a dialogue of imaginary swains might be composed with little difficulty, because the conversation of shepherds excludes profound or refined sentiment; and, for images and descriptions, Satyrs and Fauns, and Naiads and Dryads, were always within call, and woods and meadows, and hills and rivers, supplied variety of matter, which, having a natural power to sooth the mind, did not quickly cloy it." Historical survey of the pastoral from Theocritus to Philips. *Lives* 3.316-8   1781

20. A. Philips's *Pastorals*, in view of *The Guardian's* praise, "cannot surely be despicable. That they exhibit a mode of life which does not exist, nor ever existed,

is not to be objected; the supposition of such a state is
   allowed to Pastoral." *Lives* 3.324   1781
21. J. refers to "Mechanick echoes of the Mantuan song"
   in line contributed, according to Boswell, to Crabbe's
   Village. *Bos*. 4.175 *n* 4   1783

Patriotism, Literary. See CRITICISM 29

Pedantry. See also EXPERIENCE
   1. "Pedantry is the unseasonable ostentation of learning," etc. *Wks*. 7.195. (*Ram*. 173)   1751
   2. "If by pedantry is meant that minute knowledge
   which is derived from particular sciences and studies,
   in opposition to the general notions supplied by a wide
   survey of life and nature. . . ." *Lives* 1.55   1779

Periodical Writings. See also under ESSAYS
   1. Ironic remarks on the stock phrases of periodical writers: *"this occasions great Speculation," "we hear* it is
   wrongly reported," *"it wants Confirmation," "she was
   a Lady of great Beauty, Merit, and Fortune."* Gent.
   Mag., 1740, viii   1740
   2. Of all authors, periodical writers "would be most
   unhappy, if they were much to regard the censures or
   the admonitions of their readers." *Rambler* readers
   insist on conformity to their preconceived opinions.
   But "an author has a rule of choice peculiar to himself;
   and selects those subjects which he is best qualified to
   treat," avoiding those "already treated with too much
   success to invite a competition," and knowing, "that
   he who endeavours to gain many readers must try
   various arts of invitation, essay every avenue of
   pleasure, and make frequent changes in his methods
   of approach." *Wks*. 5.151, 153-5. (*Ram*. 23)   1750
   3. Plea for kindness toward hack writers. *Wks*. 7.30-3.
   (*Ram*. 145)   1751
   4. "He that condemns himself to compose on a stated

day, will often bring to his task an attention dissipated, a memory embarrassed, an imagination overwhelmed, a mind distracted with anxieties, a body languishing with disease: He will labour on a barren topick, till it is too late to change it; or, in the ardour of invention, diffuse his thoughts into wild exuberance, which the pressing hour of publication cannot suffer judgment to examine or reduce." *Wks.* 7.395. (*Ram.* 208) 1752

5. "We have considered that a [periodical] paper should consist of pieces of imagination, pictures of life, and disquisitions of literature." (J. is asking Joseph Warton to contribute to *The Adventurer*.) *Bos.* 1.253
1753

6. Aims of the *London Chronicle:* truth, superior "neatness and purity" of style, avoidance of malignant criticism and the endeavour, "not to pre-occupy judgement by praise or censure, but to gratify curiosity by early intelligence." *Wks.* 9.370-3   1757

7. Difficulty of choosing a title. *Wks.* 8.1. (*Idl.* 1)
1758

8. Novelty increasingly difficult for periodical writers. *Wks.* 8.9. (*Idl.* 3)   1758

9. Historical sketch of the rise of periodical writing. *Lives* 2.94   Ptd. 1780

Pindaric Verse. See also PINDAR. Compare ODE; VERSIFICATION

1. "The verses of Pindar have, as he observes, very little harmony to a modern ear; yet by examining the syllables we perceive them to be regular, and have reason enough for supposing that the ancient audiences were delighted with the sound. The imitator ought therefore to have adopted what he found, and to have added what was wanting: to have preserved a constant return of the same numbers, and to have supplied smoothness

of transition and continuity of thought. It is urged by Dr. Sprat, that the *'irregularity of numbers is the very thing* which makes *that kind of poesy fit for all manner of subjects.'* But he should have remembered that what is fit for every thing can fit nothing well. The great pleasure of verse arises from the known measure of the lines and uniform structure of the stanzas, by which the voice is regulated and the memory relieved. If the Pindarick style be what Cowley thinks it, 'the highest and noblest kind of writing in verse,' it can be adapted only to high and noble subjects; and it will not be easy to reconcile the poet with the critic, or to conceive how that can be the highest kind of writing in verse which, according to Sprat, 'is chiefly to be preferred for its near affinity to prose.' " *Lives* 1.47-8

1779

2. The vogue of Pindarism: its "lax and lawless versification . . . concealed the deficiencies of the barren and flattered the laziness of the idle." *Lives* 1.48

1779

3. Dryden's *Threnodia:* "Its first and obvious defect is the irregularity of its metre, to which the ears of that age however were accustomed." *Lives* 1.438   1779

4. "Some of his [Prior's] poems are written without regularity of measures, for when he commenced poet we had not recovered from our Pindarick infatuation; but he probably lived to be convinced that the essence of verse is order and consonance." *Lives* 2.210

Ptd. 1780

5. Congreve cured "a national error . . . our Pindarick madness." See Congreve 3   Ptd. 1780

6. Pindar uncertain as a precedent for departure from "the stated recurrence of settled numbers . . . as no such lax performances have been transmitted to us, the meaning to that expression ['numeris lege solutis'] cannot be fixed." Bentley's reply to one who relied on authority of Pindar perhaps "might properly

be made to a modern Pindarist . . . 'Pindar was a bold fellow, but thou art an impudent one.' " *Lives* 3.227   1781

7. Some of Watts's odes "deformed by the Pindarick folly then prevailing, and are written with such neglect of all metrical rules as is without example among the ancients." *Lives* 3.303   1781

8. West properly does not confine himself to the versification of his original, (Pindar), "for he saw that the difference of the languages required a different mode of versification." *Lives* 3.331   1781

9. In Gray's *The Bard* the "stanzas are too long, especially his epodes; the ode is finished before the ear has learned its measures, and consequently before it can receive pleasure from their consonance and recurrence." The alliterations " 'ruin,' 'ruthless,' 'helm nor hauberk,' are below the grandeur of a poem that endeavours at sublimity." *Lives* 3.438-9   1781

Plagiarism. See also IMITATION

1. A "general magazine of literature" from which writers are at liberty to draw "thoughts and elegancies," images and methods of composition without being necessarily plagiarists. Definitions and descriptions of the same objects inevitably produce resemblances. "There are other flowers of fiction . . . [which] may be said to have been planted by the ancients in the open road of poetry for the accomodation of their successors, and to be the right of every one that has art to pluck them without injuring their colours or their fragrance.[1] . . . No writer can be fully convicted of imitation, except there is a concurrence of more resemblance than can be imagined to have happened by chance; as where the same ideas are conjoined

---

[1] cf. Fielding: "The ancients may be considered as a rich common, where every person, who has the smallest tenement in Parnassus, has a free right to fatten his Muse." *Tom Jones*, Bk. XII, chap. I.

without any natural series or necessary coherence, or where not only the thought but the words are copied. . . . Conceits, or thoughts not immediately impressed by sensible objects, or necessarily arising from the coalition or comparison of common sentiments, may be with great justice suspected whenever they are found a second time. . . . As not every instance of similitude can be considered as a proof of imitation, so not every imitation ought to be stigmatized as plagiarism. The adoption of a noble sentiment, or the insertion of a borrowed ornament, may sometimes display so much judgment as will almost compensate for invention; and an inferior genius may, without any imputation of servility, pursue the path of the ancients, provided he declines to tread in their footsteps." *Wks.* 7.14-21. (*Ram.* 143) 1751

2. Resemblance between authors inevitable and not necessarily plagiarism: "Writers of all ages have had the same sentiments, because they have in all ages had the same objects of speculation; the interests and passions, the virtues and vices of mankind, have been diversified in different times, only by unessential and casual varieties; and we must, therefore, expect in the works of all those who attempt to describe them, such a likeness as we find in the pictures of the same person drawn in different periods of his life. It is necessary, therefore, that before an author be charged with plagiarism, one of the most reproachful, though, perhaps, not the most atrocious of literary crimes, the subject on which he treats should be carefully considered. . . . Nothing, therefore, can be more unjust, than to charge an author with plagiarism, merely because he assigns to every cause its natural effect; and makes his personages act, as others in like circumstances have always done. There are conceptions in which all men will agree, though each derives them from his own observation." But opportunities in every subject

PLAGIARISM   193

for infinite variety. (See VARIETY 3.) *Wks.* 9.77-83.
(*Adv.* 95)   1753
3. *Definition:* "Theft; literary adoption of the thoughts or works of another." *Dict.*   1755
4. Borrowed lines in one of Pope's epitaphs: "I do not mean to blame these imitations with much harshness; in long performances they are scarcely to be avoided, and in shorter they may be indulged, because the train of the composition may naturally involve them, or the scantiness of the subject allow little choice. However, what is borrowed is not to be enjoyed as our own, and it is the business of critical justice to give every bird of the Muses his proper feather." *Lives* 3.256   1756
5. ". . . how can vanity be gratified by plagiarism, or transcriptions?" *Wks.* 10.222   1757
6. "Theft is always dangerous." Example from Gray's *Bard*. See MYTHOLOGY 24   1781
7. ". . . if he [Watts] owes part of it [his *Logick*] to Le Clerc it must be considered that no man who undertakes merely to methodise or illustrate a system pretends to be its author." *Lives* 3.308   1781

Please, Author Must. See under AIM OF WRITING

Please, Books Which Merely. See under AIM of WRITING

Pleasing, Art of. Compare NOVELTY; ORNAMENT; VARIETY; AIM OF WRITING

1. The pleasure of ornament in letter writing. See LETTER-WRITING 2   1751
2. ". . . the artifice of embellishment, and the powers of attraction, can be gained only by general converse." *Wks.* 7.167. (*Ram.* 168)   1751
3. Arts by which writers are "to attract the notice and favour of mankind." See VARIETY 3   1753
4. New images necessary in order to please. See TRAVEL, BOOKS OF, 3   1760

5. "... upon the whole, all pleasure consists in variety." *Shak. Pref.*, Raleigh, 17   1765
6. An explanation of Dryden's "false magnificence" in his plays: "It was necessary to fix attention; and the mind can be captivated only by recollection or by curiosity; by reviving natural sentiments or impressing new appearances of things: sentences were readier at his call than images; he could more easily fill the ear with some splendid novelty than awaken those ideas that slumber in the heart." *Lives* 1.458-9   1779
7. To please you must surprise, etc. See DICTION 18
   1779
8. Apologies for stage failures useless: "'de gustibus non est disputandum'; men may be convinced, but they cannot be pleased, against their will." *Lives* 2.217   Ptd. 1780
9. "In this work [*Rape of the Lock*] are exhibited in a very high degree the two most engaging powers of an author: new things are made familiar, and familiar things are made new." Illustration of this. *Lives* 3.233-4   1781

𝒫*leasure of Writing.* See under COMPOSITION

𝒫*lot.* See FABLE

𝒫*oet Laureates*
1. Satirical references to. *Wks.* 14.13, 55, 56   1739

𝒫*oetic Justice.* See DRAMA: *Poetic Justice*

𝒫*oetry.* See also AIM OF WRITING; MORAL ELEMENT; VERSIFICATION; DICTION (for poetic diction); GENIUS; NATURE; GENERAL AND THE PARTICULAR; SELECTION. For the ancient poets compared with modern writers, see ANCIENT WRITERS
1. "Painting is so nearly allied to poetry." *Wks.* 9.348. (cf. *infra.* 13, 48)   1742

2. *A new poetical subject:* J. commends Savage for "expatiating . . . upon a kind of beneficence not yet celebrated by any eminent poet, though it now appears more susceptible of embellishments, more adapted to exalt the ideas, and affect the passions, than many of those which have hitherto been thought most worthy of the ornaments of verse. The settlement of colonies in uninhabited countries . . . the appropriation of the waste and luxuriant bounties of nature . . . cannot be considered without giving rise to a great number of pleasing ideas, and bewildering the imagination in delightful prospects; and, therefore, whatever speculations they may produce in those who have confined themselves to political studies, naturally fixed the attention and excited the applause of a poet." The "politician," who sticks to facts and reason, compared with the poet who "is employed in a more pleasing undertaking than that of proposing laws, which, however just or expedient, will never be made, or endeavouring to reduce to rational schemes of government societies which were formed by chance. . . . He guides the unhappy fugitive from want and persecution to plenty, quiet, and security, and seats him in scenes of peaceful solitude and undisturbed repose."
Lives 2.393-4   1744

3. *Text-books of poetry:* J. recommends Bossu and Bouhours, Dryden's *Essays and Prefaces*, the critical papers of Addison, Spence on *Pope's Odyssey* and Trapp's *Prælectiones Poeticæ;* "but a more accurate and philosophical account is expected from a commentary upon *Aristotle's* Art of Poetry, with which the literature of this nation will be in a short time augmented." *Wks.* 9.413. (*Pref.* to the *Preceptor*)
                                                       1748

4. "This kind of writing [modern works of fiction] may be termed not improperly the comedy of romance, and is to be conducted nearly by the rules of comick poetry." See FICTION 1   1750

5. "... poetry has to do rather with the passions of men, which are uniform, than their customs, which are changeable." See PASTORAL 1   1750
6. "The simplicity of grandeur" and the general. See GENERAL 3   1750
7. *Poetry distinguished from prose:* "Yet versification, or the art of modulating his numbers, is indispensably necessary to a poet. Every other power by which the understanding is enlightened, or the imagination enchanted, may be exercised in prose. But the poet has this peculiar superiority, that to all the powers which the perfection of every other composition can require, he adds the faculty of joining musick with reason, and of acting at once upon the senses and the passions." *Wks.* 6.92. (*Ram.* 86)   1751
8. "... without this petty knowledge [of accents and pauses] no man can be a poet." See VERSIFICATION 3   1751
9. *Difficulties of a poet:* "The poet trusts to his invention, and is not only in danger of those inconsistencies, to which every one is exposed by departure from truth; but may be censured as well for deficiencies of matter, as for irregularity of disposition, or impropriety of ornament." See HISTORY 5 for a continuation.   1751
10. "In this passage [*Macbeth* 1. v. 51-5] is exerted all the force of poetry, that force which calls new powers into being, which embodies sentiment, and animates matter." *Wks.* 7.166. (*Ram.* 168)   1751
11. Invention "the first and most valuable" power in a poet. See INVENTION 2   1753
12. *Definition of poet:* "An inventor; an author of fiction; a writer of poems; one who writes in measure." *Definition of poetry:* "Metrical composition; the art or practice of writing poems ... Poems; poetical pieces." *Dict.* See also *infra* 22 for definition of poetry.   1755

13. *Poetry and painting:* ". . . two arts which pursue the same end, by the operation of the same mental faculties, and which differ only as the one represents things by marks permanent and natural, the other by signs accidental and arbitrary. The one therefore is more easily and generally understood, since similitude of form is immediately perceived; the other is capable of conveying more ideas, for men have thought and spoken of many things which they do not see." *Wks.* 8.134-5. (*Idl.* 34.) cf. *supra* 1, *infra* 48   1758

14. [a] *Imlac, in "Rasselas" decides to be a poet:* "I read all the poets of Persia and Arabia. . . . But I soon found that no man was ever great by imitation. My desire of excellence impelled me to transfer my attention to nature and to life. Nature was to be my subject, and men to be my auditors: I could never describe what I had not seen: I could not hope to move those with delight or terrour, whose interests and opinions I did not understand. Being now resolved to be a poet, I saw every thing with a new purpose; my sphere of attention was suddenly magnified: no kind of knowledge was to be overlooked. I ranged mountains and deserts for images and resemblances, and pictured upon my mind every tree of the forest and flower of the valley. I observed with equal care the crags of the rock and the pinnacles of the palace. Sometimes I wandered along the mazes of the rivulet, and sometimes watched the changes of the summer clouds. To a poet nothing can be useless. Whatever is beautiful, and whatever is dreadful, must be familiar to his imagination: he must be conversant with all that is awfully vast or elegantly little. The plants of the garden, the animals of the wood, the minerals of the earth, and meteors of the sky, must all concur to store his mind with inexhaustible variety: for every idea is useful for the enforcement or decoration of moral or religious truth; and he, who knows most, will have

most power of diversifying his scenes, and of gratifying his reader with remote allusions and unexpected instruction. . . . [b] The business of a poet, said Imlac, is to examine, not the individual, but the species; to remark general properties and large appearances; he does not number the streaks of the tulip, or describe the different shades in the verdure of the forest. He is to exhibit in his portraits of nature such prominent and striking features, as recall the original to every mind; and must neglect the minuter discriminations, which one may have remarked, and another have neglected, for those characteristicks which are alike obvious to vigilance and carelessness. But the knowledge of nature is only half the task of a poet; he must be acquainted likewise with all the modes of life. His character requires that he estimate the happiness and misery of every condition; observe the power of all the passions in all their combinations, and trace the changes of the human mind as they are modified by various institutions and accidental influences of climate or custom, from the sprightliness of infancy to the despondence of decrepitude. He must divest himself of the prejudices of his age or country; he must consider right and wrong in their abstracted and invariable state; he must disregard present laws and opinions, and rise to general and transcendental truths, which will always be the same: he must therefore content himself with the slow progress of his name; contemn the applause of his own time, and commit his claims to the justice of posterity. He must write as the interpreter of nature, and the legislator of mankind, and consider himself as presiding over the thoughts and manners of future generations; as a being superior to time and place. [c] His labour is not yet at an end: he must know many languages and many sciences; and, that his style may be worthy of his thoughts, must, by incessant practice, familiarize to himself every delicacy of speech and grace of harmony." Imlac, in *Rasselas* (ch. X). *Wks.* 11.30-32. (cf. ch. VII in which Rasselas is delighted at the poet's knowledge of the world and his skill in painting "the scenes of life".) 1759

15. ". . . the province of poetry is to describe Nature and Passion, which are always the same." *Wks.* 11.29. Imlac, in *Rasselas* (ch. X) 1759

16. ". . . all true poetry requires that the sentiments be natural." *Wks.* 8.308. (*Idl.* 77) 1759

17. ". . . a poet overlooks the casual distinction of country and condition, as a painter, satisfied with the figure, neglects the drapery." See SHAKESPEARE 53 1765

18. *The poetry of St. Kilda, says J., " 'must be very poor, because they have very few images.' BOSWELL. 'There may be a poetical genius shewn in combining these, and in making poetry of them.' JOHNSON. 'Sir, a man cannot make fire but in proportion as he has fuel. He cannot coin guineas but in proportion as he has gold.' " *Bos.* 5.228-9. (*Hebrides*, 19 Sept.) 1773

19. *Boswell tries to justify "middle-rate" poetry. "Johnson repeated the common remark, that, 'as there is no necessity for our having poetry at all, it being merely a luxury, an instrument of pleasure, it can have no value, unless when exquisite in its kind.' " *Bos.* 2.351-2
1775

20. *"BOSWELL. '. . . what is poetry?' JOHNSON. 'Why, Sir, it is much easier to say what it is not. We all *know* what light is; but it is not easy to *tell* what it is.' " *Bos.* 3.38 1776

21. "A work more truly poetical [than *Comus*] is rarely found; allusions, images, and descriptive epithets embellish almost every period with lavish decoration." *Lives* 1.167-8 1779

22. "By the general consent of criticks the first praise of genius is due to the writer of an epick poem, as it requires an assemblage of all the powers which are

singly sufficient for other compositions. Poetry is the art of uniting pleasure with truth, by calling imagination to the help of reason. Epick poetry undertakes to teach the most important truths by the most pleasing precepts, and therefore relates some great event in the most affecting manner." History supplies "narration, which he must improve and exalt by a nobler art, must animate by dramatick energy, and diversify by retrospection and anticipation; morality must teach him the exact bounds and different shades of vice and virtue; from policy and the practice of life he has to learn the discriminations of character and the tendency of the passions, either single or combined; and physiology ["the doctrine of the constitution of the works of nature." *Dict*. See *Lives* 1.100 *n* 1] must supply him with illustrations and images. To put these materials to poetical use is required an imagination capable of painting nature and realizing fiction. Nor is he yet a poet till he has attained the whole extension of his language, distinguished all the delicacies of phrase, and all the colours of words, and learned to adjust their different sounds to all the varieties of metrical modulation." (The above applies primarily to the *epic* poet.) *Lives* 1.170-1   1779

23. "Perhaps no passages are more frequently or more attentively read than those extrinsick paragraphs [in *Par. Lost*, Bks. 3, 7 and 9]; and, since the end of poetry is pleasure, that cannot be unpoetical with which all are pleased." *Lives* 1.175   1779

24. "Pleasure and terrour are indeed the genuine sources of poetry; but poetical pleasure must be such as human imagination can at least conceive, and poetical terrour such as human strength and fortitude may combat." See SACRED POETRY 5   1779

25. "The essence of poetry is invention; such invention as, by producing something unexpected, surprises and delights. . . . Poetry pleases by exhibiting an idea

more grateful to the mind than things themselves afford. This effect proceeds from the display of those parts of nature which attract, and the concealment of those which repel, the imagination. . . . From poetry the reader justly expects, and from good poetry always obtains, the enlargement of his comprehension and elevation of his fancy. . . ." *Lives* 1.291-2

1779

26. The "Metaphysical Poets," "unluckily resolving to shew it [learning] in rhyme, instead of writing poetry they only wrote verses, and very often such verses as stood the trial of the finger better than of the ear; for the modulation was so imperfect that they were only found to be verses by counting the syllables. If the father of criticism has rightly denominated poetry τέχνη μιμητική, *an imitative art*, these writers will without great wrong lose their right to the name of poets, for they cannot be said to have imitated any thing: they neither copied nature nor life; neither painted the forms of matter nor represented the operations of intellect." *Lives* 1.19   1779

27. Poetry's right "to exalt causes into agents, to invest abstract ideas with form, and animate them with activity." See ALLEGORY 4   1779

28. Garth's *Dispensary* "appears . . . to want something of poetical ardour." *Lives* 2.64   1779

29. "The same thought is more generally, and therefore more poetically, expressed by Casimir." *Lives* 1.46

1779

30. *Poetry and prose:* ". . . the first [passage from Dryden], though it may perhaps not be quite clear in prose, is not too obscure for poetry, as the meaning that it has is noble." *Lives* 1.461-2   1779

31. *Poetry and prose:* "Those happy combinations of words which distinguish poetry from prose." See DICTION 21   1779

32. Sheffield "had the perspicuity and elegance of an historian, but not the fire and fancy of a poet." *Lives* 2.177   Ptd. 1780

33. *"The most poetical paragraph"* in all English poetry: J.'s choice is from Congreve's *Mourning Bride*. "He who reads those lines [II i] enjoys for a moment the powers of a poet; he feels what he remembers to have felt before, but he feels it with great increase of sensibility; he recognizes a familiar image, but meets it again amplified and expanded, embellished with beauty, and enlarged with majesty." *Lives* 2.229-30   Ptd. 1780

34. Blackmore "reasons poetically; and finds the art of uniting ornament with strength, and ease with closeness." *Lives* 2.254   Ptd. 1780

35. *Ingredients of a poet:* Experience, intellectual curiosity, good sense, genius, memory, diligence. See POPE 9   1781

36. ". . . genius, that power which constitutes a poet," defined. See GENIUS 22. See also *ib.* 23   1781

37. Pope's *Essay on Man* not merely a prose scheme drawn up by Bolingbroke and transformed from prose to verse by Pope: "The *Essay* plainly appears the fabrick of a poet: what Bolingbroke supplied could be only the first principles; the order, illustration, and embellishments must all be Pope's." *Lives* 3.163   1781

38. "After all this [examination of Pope's versification] it is surely superfluous to answer the question that has once been asked, Whether Pope was a poet? otherwise than by asking in return, If Pope be not a poet, where is poetry to be found? To circumscribe poetry by a definition will only shew the narrowness of the definer,[1] though a definition which shall exclude Pope will not easily be made. Let us look round upon the present

---

[1] In the proof sheet: "is the pedantry of a narrow mind." *Lives* 3.251 n 4.

time, and back upon the past; let us enquire to whom the voice of mankind has decreed the wreath of poetry; let their productions be examined and their claims stated, and the pretensions of Pope will be no more disputed." *Lives* 3.251   1781

39. *Poetry and virtue* (referring to stanza II 2 of Gray's *Progress of Poesy*): Northern caverns and Chili "not the residences of 'Glory' and 'generous Shame.' But that Poetry and Virtue go always together is an opinion so pleasing that I can forgive him who resolves to think it true." *Lives* 3.437   1781

40. *Poetry and virtue* (referring to Gray's *Progress of Poesy*, stanza II 3): "His position is at last false: in the time of Dante and Petrarch, from whom he derives our first school of poetry, Italy was overrun by 'tyrant power' and 'coward vice'; nor was our state much better when we first borrowed the Italian arts." *Lives* 3.437   1781

41. "He [Thomson] thinks in a peculiar train, and he thinks always as a man of genius; he looks round on Nature and on Life with the eye which Nature bestows only on a poet, the eye that distinguishes in every thing presented to its view whatever there is on which imagination can delight to be detained, and with a mind that at once comprehends the vast, and attends to the minute. The reader of *The Seasons* wonders that he never saw before what Thomson shews him, and that he never yet has felt what Thomson impresses." *Lives* 3.298-9   1781

42. "As a poet, had he [Watts] been only a poet, he would probably have stood high among the authors with whom he is now associated. For his judgement was exact, and he noted beauties and faults with very nice discernment; his imagination . . . was vigorous and active, and the stores of knowledge were large by which his fancy was to be supplied. His ear was well-

tuned, and his diction was elegant and copious." *Lives* 3.310   1781

43. "Some passages [in Dyer's *The Ruins of Rome*], however, are conceived with the mind of a poet, as when in the neighbourhood of dilapidating edifices he says,
    'At dead of night
    The hermit oft, 'midst his orisons, hears
    Aghast the voice of Time disparting towers.'"[1]
    Lives 3.345   1781

44. "The subject [*Pleasures of Imagination*] is well chosen, as it includes all images that can strike or please, and thus comprises every species of poetical delight." *Lives* 3.417   1781

45. ". . . the highest praise, the praise of genius, they [imitators of Spenser, etc.] cannot claim. The noblest beauties of art are those of which the effect is coextended with rational nature, or at least with the whole circle of polished life; what is less than this can be only pretty, the plaything of fashion and the amusement of a day." *Lives* 3.333   1781

46. "The poet's art is selection." See PASTORAL 15 for application of this to pastoral poetry.   1781

47. *Poetry and prose:* J. mocks those who think "that not to write prose is certainly to write poetry." See VERSIFICATION 37   1781

48. *Poetry and painting compared:* "Painting, Sir, can illustrate, but cannot inform."[2] *Bos.* 4.321. cf. *supra* 1, 13   Date?

Popular Judgement. Compare CRITICISM; PREJUDICE

1. "This criticism [of Savage's *The Wanderer*] is universal [i.e., universally held], and therefore it is reason-

---

[1] Wordsworth, as Hill points out (*ib. n* 4), calls this same passage "a beautiful instance of the modifying and *investive* power of imagination."
[2] For J.'s scorn of painting, see *John. Misc.* 1.214

able to believe it at least in a great degree just. . . ."
Lives 2.365   1744

2. "It must be however allowed, in justification of the publick [for their neglect of Savage's poem *Of Public Spirit*], that this performance is not the most excellent of Mr. Savage's works," etc. *Lives* 2.397   1744

3. "Men willingly pay to fortune that regard which they owe to merit, and are pleased when they have an opportunity at once of gratifying their vanity and practising their duty." *Lives* 2.358   1744

4. ". . . as the greatest part of mankind have no other reason for their opinions than that they are in fashion . . ." *Wks.* 14.63   1745

5. "Ah! let not censure term our fate our choice,
The stage but echoes back the public voice;
The drama's laws the drama's patrons give,
For we that live to please, must please to live. . . .
'Tis your's, this night, to bid the reign commence
Of rescu'd Nature, and reviving Sense."[1]
Wks. 1.198. (Drury-lane *Prologue*)   1747

6. "He that endeavours after fame by writing, solicits the regard of a multitude fluctuating in measures, or immersed in business, without time for intellectual amusements; he appeals to judges preposessed by passions, or corrupted by prejudices, which preclude their approbation of any new performance. Some are too indolent to read any thing, till its reputation is established; others too envious to promote that fame which gives them pain by its increase." Opposition to the new and to the known. The learned fear to hazard their reputation; the ignorant apt to refuse to be pleased. Reputation not in proportion to industry, learning or wit. *Wks.* 5.13. (*Ram.* 2)   1750

7. The precariousness of literary fame in J.'s time: subject to the caprice of the public. *Wks.* 5.140. (*Ram.* 21)
                                                                                1750

---

[1] cf. *infra* 28, and note.

8. ". . . there always lies an appeal from domestick criticism to a higher judicature, and the publick, which is never corrupted, nor often deceived, is to pass the last sentence upon literary claims." *Wks.* 5.153. (*Ram.* 23) For context, see CRITICISM 69   1750

9. ". . . I have found reason to pay great regard to the voice of the people, in cases where knowledge has been forced upon them by experience . . ."[1] *Wks.* 5.162. (*Ram.* 25)   1750

10. ". . . the common voice of the multitude uninstructed by precept, and unprejudiced by authority, which, in questions that relate to the heart of man, is, in my opinion, more decisive than the learning of Lipsius."[2] *Wks.* 5.332-3. (*Ram.* 52)   1750

11. "To deny praise to a performance which so many thousands have laboured to imitate [Virgil's fifth pastoral], would be to judge with too little deference for the opinion of mankind." (J. however continues by attacking this pastoral.) *Wks.* 9.71. (*Adv.* 92)   1753

12. The test of public opinion "the only trial that can stamp its [a work's] value. From the publick, and only from the publick, is he [an author] to await a confirmation of his claim, and a final justification of self-esteem; but the publick is not easily persuaded to favour an author. If mankind were left to judge for themselves, it is reasonable to imagine, that of such writings, at least, as describe the movements of the human passions, and of which every man carries the archetype within him, a just opinion would be formed;"[2] but the fate of books not governed by "general consent arising from general conviction. . . . A

---

[1] Johnson had no use for *mob* opinion, however. In his epitaph for Mr. Thrale, for instance, he commends his friend as "a spirited contemner of the clamorous multitude." J.'s *Poetical Wks.*, ed. Kearsley, 1789, p. 210.

[2] cf. Dryden: Ovid needs no other judges of the passions than the generality of his readers, "for, all passions being inborn with us, we are almost equally judges when we are concerned in the representation of them." *Pref. to Ovid's Epistles*, "Essays of John Dryden," ed. Ker, 1.233.

few, a very few, commonly constitute the taste of the time; the judgment which they have once pronounced, some are too lazy to discuss, and some too timorous to contradict: it may however be, I think, observed, that their power is greater to depress than exalt, as mankind are more credulous of censure than of praise." *Wks.* 9.160-1. (*Adv.* 138)   1753

13. "Their [certain Italian writers'] works are of long standing, therefore they are good, because mankind never unanimously join to praise a bad book and preserve it from oblivion."[1] See ITALIAN LITERATURE 1   1755

14. The poet must "content himself with the slow progress of his name; contemn the applause of his own time, and commit his claims to the justice of posterity." Imlac in *Rasselas*, (ch. X). *Wks.* 11.32. For context, see POETRY 14   1759

15. "The bard may supplicate, but cannot bribe.
    Yet judg'd by those whose voices ne'er were sold,
    He feels no want of ill persuading gold;
    But confident of praise, if praise be due,
    Trusts without fear to merit and to you."
    Wks. 11.348   1768

16. * "It is laudable in a man to wish to live by his labours; but he should write so as he may *live* by them, not so as he may be knocked on the head." *Bos.* 2.221   1773

17. **Pilgrim's Progress* "has had the best evidence of its merit, the general and continued approbation of mankind." *Bos.* 2.238   1773

18. * "*Thomas à Kempis* (he observed) must be a good book, as the world has opened its arms to receive it." *Bos.* 3.226   1778

19. *Speaking of Tillotson's style: "I should be cautious of objecting to what has been applauded by so many suffrages." *Bos.* 3.247-8   1778

---

[1] Authenticity doubtful.

20. ". . . that cannot be unpoetical with which all are pleased." See POETRY 23   1779

21. "The authority of Addison is great; yet the voice of the people, when to please the people is the purpose, deserves regard. In this question [concerning the public's neglect of Smith's tragedy, *Phædra and Hippolitus*], I cannot but think the people in the right." *Lives* 2.16. See also AIM OF WRITING 19   1779

22. ". . . when the end is to please the multitude, no man perhaps has a right, in things admitting of gradation and comparison, to throw the whole blame upon his judges, and totally to exclude diffidence and shame by a haughty consciousness of his own excellence." *Lives* 1.14   1779

23. Dryden "determines very justly that of the plan and disposition, and all that can be reduced to principles of science, the author may depend upon his own opinion; but that in those parts where fancy predominates self-love may easily deceive. He might have observed, that what is good only because it pleases cannot be pronounced good till it has been found to please." *Lives* 1.340   1779

24. "But let it be remembered, that minds are not levelled in their powers but when they are first levelled in their desires. Dryden and Settle had both placed their happiness in the claps of multitudes." *Lives* 1.346   1779

25. ". . . he who pleases many must have some species of merit." *Lives* 1.302   1779

26. "About things on which the public thinks long it commonly attains to think right." *Lives* 2.132. See also CRITICISM 62, 63   Ptd. 1780

27. "Writers commonly derive their reputation from their works; but there are works which owe their reputation to the character of the writer. The publick sometimes has its favourites, whom it rewards for one species of excellence with the honours due to another. From him

whom we reverence for his beneficence we do not willingly withhold the praise of genius: a man of exalted merit becomes at once an accomplished writer, as a beauty finds no great difficulty in passing for a wit." *Lives* 2.293-4 Ptd. 1780

28. "That it [*The Drummer*] should have been ill received would raise wonder did we not daily see the capricious distribution of theatrical praise."[1] *Lives* 2.106 Ptd. 1780

29. "These apologies are always useless, 'de gustibus non est disputandum'; men may be convinced, but they cannot be pleased, against their will. But though taste is obstinate it is very variable, and time often prevails when arguments have failed." *Lives* 2.217 Ptd. 1780

30. "Of his [Gay's] little poems the publick judgement seems to be right. . . ." *Lives* 2.284. See also, for J.'s agreement with the public's judgement, OTWAY 5 and CRITICISM 7 1781

31. ". . . I am not writing only to poets and philosophers." (J. decides not to give more examples of Pope's corrections of his *Iliad*.) *Lives* 3.126 1781

32. Pope's professed contempt of the world "apparently counterfeited. How could he despise those whom he lived by pleasing, and on whose approbation his esteem of himself was superstructed? Why should he hate those to whose favour he owed his honour and his ease? Of things that terminate in human life the world is the proper judge: to despise its sentence, if it were possible, is not just; and if it were just is not possible." *Lives* 3.210 1781

33. "But Wit can stand its ground against Truth only a little while. The honours due to learning have been justly distributed by the decision of posterity." *Lives* 3.11 1781

34. J. censures Dryden because he wrote "merely for the

[1] cf. ". . . he [Garrick] should no longer subject himself to be hissed by a mob," etc. *Bos.* 2.438. See also *supra* 5.

people; and when he pleased others, he contented himself." See POPE 3   1781

35. Gray's *The Progress of Poesy* and *The Bard:* "Though either vulgar ignorance or common sense at first universally rejected them, many have been since persuaded to think themselves delighted." *Lives* 3.436
1781

36. "In the character of his [Gray's] *Elegy* I rejoice to concur with the common reader; for by the common sense of readers uncorrupted with literary prejudices, after all the refinements of subtilty and the dogmatism of learning, must be finally decided all claim to poetical honours." *Lives* 3.441   1781

37. *J. "held all authors very cheap, that were not satisfied with the opinion of the publick about them. He used to say, that every man who writes, thinks he can amuse or inform mankind, and they must be the best judges of his pretensions." *John. Misc.* 2.7. (Hawkins's *Apophthegms*)   Date?

38. *"He had, indeed, upon all occasions, a great deference for the general opinion: 'A man (said he) who writes a book, thinks himself wiser or wittier than the rest of mankind; he supposes that he can instruct or amuse them, and the publick to whom he appeals, must, after all, be the judges of his pretensions.'" *Bos.* 1.200   Date?

39. *"Of authors he [J.] used to say, that as they think themselves wiser or wittier than the rest of the world, the world, after all, must be the judge of their pretensions to superiority over them." *John. Misc.* 2.19. (Hawkins's *Apophthegms*)   Date?

Posthumous Compositions
 1. Their common fate. *Wks.* 8.260-2. (*Idl.* 65)   1759

Practice. See also PRECEPT AND PRACTICE
 1. "In every art, practice is much; in arts manual, practice is almost the whole." *Wks.* 4.623   1761

Praise. Compare also DEDICATIONS; ENTHUSIASM; OCCASIONAL WORKS

1. "Poets are sometimes in too much haste to praise." *Lives* 2.289   Ptd. 1780
2. *J. to Mrs. Thrale: "I know nobody who blasts by praise as you do: for whenever there is exaggerated praise, every body is set against a character." *Bos.* 4.81-2   1781
3. *". . . he who praises everybody, praises nobody. When both scales are equally loaded, neither can preponderate." *John. Misc.* 2.327. (*Anecdotes* by Steevens. Repeated by Hawkins. *Wks.* 11.216)   Date?
4. *J.'s "obstinate silence, whilst all the company were in raptures." *John. Misc.* 2.224. (Reynolds)   Date?
5. *Boswell quotes Mrs. Thrale as saying: "I do not know for certain what will please Dr. Johnson: but I know for certain that it will displease him to praise anything, even what he likes, extravagantly."[1] *Bos.* 3.225   Date?

[1] But Johnson himself praised extravagantly on a few occasions. Even Mrs. Thrale hardly went to such lengths as did Johnson when the topic was Fanny Burney's *Evelina*. It is interesting to note some of the productions which he lauded in superlative terms: Savage's *Volunteer Laureate* "may be justly ranked among the best pieces that the death of princes has produced." Its original combination of images. "The beauty of this peculiar combination of images is so masterly, that it is sufficient to set this poem above censure" (*Lives* 2.407); in the same writer's *The Author to be Let*, the "exact observations on human life . . . would do honour to the greatest names" (*ib.* 2.358-9); *The Rape of the Lock* is justly praised as "the most exquisite example of ludicrous poetry" (*ib.* 3.104); Pope's "*Epistle of Eloise to Abelard* is one of the most happy productions of human wit" (*ib.* 3.235); Pope's *Letter on Pastorals* "an unexampled and unequalled artifice of irony" (*ib.* 3.319); Tickell's *Elegy* prefixed to his edition of Addison's works is eulogized: ". . . nor is a more sublime or more elegant funeral poem to be found in the whole compass of English literature" (*ib.* 2.310); and the description of the temple, in Congreve's *Mourning Bride*, Johnson called "the finest poetical passage he had ever read; he recollected none in Shakespeare equal to it" (*Bos.* 2.85). Of translations, Pope's *Iliad* is ". . . the noblest version [i.e., "translation." See VERSION.] of poetry which the world has ever seen" (see POPE 41); and the same is called "a performance which no age or nation can pretend to equal" (*Lives* 3.236); Rowe's translation of *Lucan* is "one of the greatest productions of English poetry" (see TRANSLATION 14). Johnson's oft-expressed admiration for Shakespeare and Milton's *Paradise Lost* should also be remembered.

Precedents. See ANCIENT WRITERS; and RULES

Precept and Practice. See also MORAL ELEMENT

1. Savage's "writings may improve mankind when his failings shall be forgotten," etc. See SAVAGE 2   1744
2. Frequently a "striking contrariety between the life of an author and his writings." This unfortunate as it lessens his authority. Reasons why "a man writes much better than he lives." Such a man not necessarily a hypocrite. (cf. *Bos.* 5.359-60.) "Thus much at least may be required of him, that he shall not act worse than others because he writes better, nor imagine that, by the merit of his genius, he may claim indulgence beyond mortals of the lower classes, and be excused for want of prudence, or neglect of virtue." An author's "graces of writing" and his conversation often at variance. (See CONVERSATION 2.) *Wks.* 5.88-94. (*Ram.* 14)   1750
3. "He, by whose writings the heart is rectified, the appetites counteracted, and the passions repressed, may be considered as not unprofitable to the great republic of humanity, even though his behaviour should not always exemplify his rules." *Wks.* 6.38-9. (*Ram.* 77)   1750
4. *That an author does not practise what he teaches "does not make his book the worse. People are influenced more by what a man says, if his practice is suitable to it,—because they are blockheads. The more intellectual people are, the readier will they attend to what a man tells them. If it is just, they will follow it, be his practice what it will. No man practises so well as he writes."[1] *Bos.* 5.210. (*Hebrides*, 14 Sept.)   1773
5. ". . . to write and to live are very different" the

---

[1] But cf., ". . . no fraud is innocent; for the confidence which makes the happiness of society is in some degree diminished by every man, whose practice is at variance with his words." *Wks.* 4.584.

world shows us. Addison an exception.¹ *Lives* 2.125
Ptd. 1780
6. *". . . the best part of an author will always be found in his writings." *Wks.* 1.410. (Hawkins's *Life.*) See also *John. Misc.* 2.310   Date?

Prefaces

1. ". . . the author of almost every book retards his instructions by a preface." *Wks.* 9.369. (*Prelim. Discourse to the London Chronicle*)   1757

Prejudice. Compare CRITICISM; REASON

1. The poet " 'must divest himself of the prejudices of his age or country.' " See POETRY 14   1759
2. "To be prejudiced is always to be weak." Yet some prejudices "near to laudable," e.g., blind patriotism. *Wks.* 10.94   1775
3. ". . . the power of prejudice every day observed." *Lives* 1.373   1779
4. The best criticism comes from "the common sense of readers uncorrupted with literary prejudices." See POPULAR JUDGEMENT 36   1781

Probability. See also NATURE; TRUTH; FICTION; MARVELLOUS, THE; and for the degree of credibility necessary to drama, see under DRAMA: *Tragedy*, and DRAMA 4, 44c. For probability and the burlesque, see BURLESQUE

1. ". . . he who tells nothing exceeding the bounds of probability, has a right to demand that they should believe him who cannot contradict him." *Wks.* 9.431. (*Pref. to Lobo*)   1735
2. *"Nothing is good but what is consistent with truth

---

¹ cf. "good principles and an irregular life . . . consistent with each other" (*Wks.* 1.410); and see *Ram.* 14; *Letters* 2.234-5.

or probability." *Bos.* 5.361. (*Hebrides*, 26 Oct.)
                                                          1773
3. "He that forsakes the probable" decreases the moral usefulness of his work. See FICTION 12   1781

Propriety. See DECORUM

Prose. For the distinction between poetry and prose see under POETRY. For the danger of blank verse lapsing into "crippled prose," see BLANK VERSE 8, 17, 22

1. *Temple's prose. See TEMPLE 1   1778
2. "Sublime and solemn prose gains little by a change to blank verse." *Lives* 2.264   Ptd. 1780

Prosody. See VERSIFICATION

Puns and Verbal Conceits. See also under SHAKESPEARE: Style

1. "But of all meanness that has least to plead which is produced by mere verbal conceits, which depending only upon sounds, lose their existence by the change of a syllable." Examples from *Samson Agonistes*.[1] *Wks.* 6.439-40. (*Ram.* 140)   1751
2. Milton's play on words censured. See MILTON 43
                                                          1779

Quaint

1. *Definition:* "1. Nice; scrupulously, minutely, superfluously exact; having petty elegance." *Dict.*   1755

Quotation

1. *Burton's *Anatomy of Melancholy* "is, perhaps, overloaded with quotation." *Bos.* 2.440   1776
2. *Not pedantry, but "a good thing; there is a commun-

---

[1] Boswell testifies to J.'s contempt for puns: e.g., *Bos.* 2.241; 4.316; 5.32 and *n* 3. "Punster" is defined in his *Dictionary* as "a low wit, who endeavours at reputation by double meaning." But for occasions on which J. himself punned, see *Bos.* 3.325; 4.73, 81.

ity of mind in it. Classical quotation is the *parole* of literary men all over the world." *Bos.* 4.102   1781
3. *J. agrees with Hannah More that the greatest compliment to an author is to quote him. *John. Misc.* 2.207. (H. More)   Date?

Race

1. *Definition:* "6. A particular strength or taste of wine, applied by *Temple* to any extraordinary natural force of intellect." *Dict.*   1755
2. Thomson's *Seasons* "improved in general [by the author's revisions]; yet I know not whether they have not lost part of what Temple calls their *race*, a word which, applied to wines, in its primitive sense, means the flavour of the soil." *Lives* 3.300-1   1781

Reading

1. *"A man ought to read just as inclination leads him; for what he reads as a task will do him little good. A young man should read five hours in a day, and so may acquire a great deal of knowledge." *Bos.* 1.428   1763
2. J.'s advice to an Oxford student (Strahan): "Do not omit to mingle some lighter books with those of more importance; that which is read *remisso animo* is often of great use, and takes great hold of the remembrance." *Letters* 1.118   1765
3. *J. offended at being asked if he had read a certain book through: "No, Sir, do *you* read books *through?*" *Bos.* 2.226   1773
4. Value of reading as an aid to judgement. See JUDGEMENT 3   1781
5. *J. objects to the theory that a book should be read through: "This is surely strange advice; you may as well resolve that whatever men you happen to get acquainted with, you are to keep to them for life. A book may be good for nothing; or there may be only one thing in it worth knowing; are we to read it all through?" etc. *Bos.* 4.308   1784

6. *Lady Mary Wortley Montagu's *Letters* the only book he ever read through from choice. *John. Misc.* 1.319. (Piozzi.) See also *Letters* 1.60; *John. Misc.* 286 *n* 2; *Bos.* 1.71 and *n* 1   Date?

Realism. Compare SELECTION

1. "If the world be promiscuously described, I cannot see of what use it can be to read the account: or why it may not be as safe to turn the eye immediately upon mankind as upon a mirrour which shows all that presents itself without discrimination . . . for many characters ought never to be drawn." e.g., the "splendidly wicked." For amplification of this, see FICTION 1   1750
2. "To paint things as they are requires a minute attention, and employs the memory rather than the fancy." *Lives* 1.177   1779

Reason. Compare GOOD SENSE; NATURE; PREJUDICE

1. "In Reason, Nature, Truth he dares to trust." *Wks.* 11.219. (J.'s prologue to *Irene*)   1749
2. ". . . reason and nature are uniform and inflexible." See DRAMA 12b   1751
3. ". . . reason wants not Horace to support it." *Lives* 1.423   1779
4. ". . . such readers as draw their principles of judgement rather from books than from reason." See CRITICISM 49   1779
5. Works which depend upon memory for their appeal, and not upon reason or passion cannot "be reckoned among the great achievements of intellect."[1] See NATURE 46   1781

[1] For reason as a guide to conduct, however, compare the account in *Rasselas* (ch. XVIII) of the philosopher who discoursed eloquently of reason, but did not find it adequate to meet the sorrows of life; and Nekayah's remark (ch. XXVIII): "There are a thousand familiar disputes which reason never can decide; questions that elude investigation, and make logick ridiculous; cases where something must be done, and where little can be said."

Religious Poetry. See SACRED POETRY

Renaissance, The
1. "Next to the ancients, those writers deserve to be mentioned, who, at the restoration of literature, imitated their language and their style with so great success, or who laboured with so much industry to make them understood: such were *Philelphus* and *Politian, Scaliger* and *Buchanan*, and the poets of the age of *Leo the Tenth.*" *Wks.* 9.347   1742
2. "Learning was then rising on the world; but ages so long accustomed to darkness, were too much dazzled with its light to see any thing distinctly. The first race of scholars in the fifteenth century, and some time after, were, for the most part, learning to speak, rather than to think, and were therefore more studious of elegance than of truth. The contemporaries of *Boethius* thought it sufficient to know what the ancients had delivered. The examination of tenets and of facts was reserved for another generation." *Wks.* 10.329. (*Jour. to W.I.*)   Composed 1774

"Representative Metre." (ONOMATOPŒIA.) See under VERSIFICATION

Review
1. *Definition* (vb.): "4. To survey; to overlook; to examine."[1] *Dict.*   1755

Reviewers. See under CRITICISM

Rhetoric
1. The epitaph of greatest dignity excludes rhetoric. See EPITAPH 1   1740
2. "*Rhetorick* and *poetry* supply life with its highest intellectual pleasures; and in the hands of virtue are of

---

[1] See G. B. Hill's note on this word, *Letters* 2.235 *n* 4.

great use for the impression of just sentiments, and recommendations of illustrious examples." Suggestions for teaching "these great arts." *Wks.* 9.413   1748

Rhyme. See under VERSIFICATION; and BLANK VERSE AND RHYME

Romances. Compare FICTION; NOVEL, THE; PROBABILITY; MARVELLOUS, THE; etc.

1. *The "heroick romance"* compared with modern fiction: ". . . almost all the fictions of the last age will vanish, if you deprive them of a hermit and a wood, a battle and a shipwreck. Why this wild strain of imagination found reception so long, in polite and learned ages, it is not easy to conceive; but we cannot wonder that while readers could be procured, the authors were willing to continue it; for when a man had by practice gained some fluency of language, he had no further care than to retire to his closet, let loose his invention, and heat his mind with incredibilities; a book was thus produced without fear of criticism, without the toil of study, without knowledge of nature, or acquaintance with life." *Wks.* 5.20-1. (*Ram.* 4)   1750
2. Romances of little influence on conduct, because of their unreality. The reader "amused himself with heroes and with traitors, deliverers and persecutors, as with beings of another species." *Wks.* 5.22. (*Ram.* 4)   1750
3. *Imperia,* "having spent the early part of her life in the perusal of romances, brought with her into the gay world all the pride of *Cleopatra;* expected nothing less than vows, altars, and sacrifices." Thus her mind was "vitiated . . . by false representations." *Wks.* 6.283-4. (*Ram.* 115)   1751
4. Lack of original invention in romances. See INVENTION 2   1753
5. *Definition of romance:* "1. A military fable of the

middle ages; a tale of wild adventures in war and love." *Dict.*   1755

6. ". . . from the time of life when fancy begins to be over-ruled by reason and corrected by experience, the most artful tale raises little curiosity when it is known to be false; though it may, perhaps, be sometimes read as a model of a neat or elegant style, not for the sake of knowing what it contains, but how it is written; or those that are weary of themselves, may have recourse to it as a pleasing dream, of which, when they awake, they voluntarily dismiss the images from their minds." *Wks.* 8.339. (*Idl.* 84)   1759

7. Unsafe guides to conduct. See SHAKESPEARE 22
     1765

8. J. laments: "But this is the age . . . in which the giants of antiquated romance have been exhibited as realities." *Wks.* 1.490. (Hawkins's *Life*)   1774

9. "I sat down on a bank, such as a writer of romance might have delighted to feign. I had indeed no trees to whisper over my head, but a clear rivulet streamed at my feet. The day was calm, the air soft, and all was rudeness, silence, and solitude," etc. *Wks.* 10.361. (*Jour. to W.I.*)   Composed 1774

10. "Romance does not often exhibit a scene that strikes the imagination more than this little desert in these depths of western obscurity, occupied not by a gross herdsman . . . but by a gentleman and two ladies, of high birth." *Wks.* 10.494. (*Jour to W.I.*)
     Composed 1774

11. "The fictions of the *Gothick* romances were not so remote from credibility as they are now thought. . . . Whatever is imaged in the wildest tale, if giants, dragons, and enchantment be excepted, would be felt by him, who, wandering in the mountains without a guide, or upon the sea without a pilot, should be carried amidst his terror and uncertainty, to the hospi-

tality and elegance of *Raasay* or *Dunvegan*." *Wks.* 10.408-9. (*Jour. to W.I.*)   Composed 1774

12. "These castles [in the Hebrides] afford another evidence that the fictions of romantick chivalry had for their basis the real manners of the feudal times," etc. *Wks.* 10.511. (*Jour. to W.I.*)   Composed 1774

13. *"Johnson had with him upon this jaunt, '*Il Palmerino d'Inghilterra*,' . . . but did not like it much. He said, he read it for the language." *Bos.* 3.2   1776

14. *According to Bishop Percy, "when a boy he [J.] was immoderately fond of reading romances of chivalry, and he retained his fondness for them through life; so that . . . spending part of a summer [1764] at my parsonage-house in the country, he chose for his regular reading the old Spanish romance of *Felixmarte of Hircania*, in folio, which he read quite through. Yet I have heard him attribute to these extravagant fictions that unsettled turn of mind which prevented his ever fixing in any profession." *Bos.* 1.49. (See also *Quellen und Forschungen* 103.9 for similar testimony from Percy)   Date?

15. *A justification of romances. See MYTHOLOGY 34, and *Bos.* 4.8 *n* 3   Date?

Romantic

1. *Definition:* "1. Resembling the tales of romances; wild. . . . 2. Improbable; false. 3. Fanciful; full of wild scenery. [e.g.] The dun umbrage, o'er the falling stream, *Romantick* hangs. *Thomson's Spring*." *Dict.* Examples: "Romantick absurdities or incredible fictions" (*Wks.* 9.431. 1735); "A voyage to the moon, however romantic and absurd the scheme may now appear" (*Wks.* 9.14. 1753); "When night overshadows a romantick scene, all is stillness, silence, and quiet," etc. (*Wks.* 9.104. 1753); "wild and enthusiastic authors of romantic chymistry" (see PARACELSUS 1. 1756); "The enterprize was considered as

romantic," i.e., wild, foolhardy (*Wks.* 4.562. 1756); "The sentiment of *Shakespeare* is partly just, and partly romantick" (*Shak.* 8.256 *n* 6. 1765); Dryden's *All for Love* censured for showing "the romantick omnipotence of love" (*Lives* 1.361. 1779); ". . . no romantick or incredible act of generosity" (*ib.* 1.384. 1779); ". . . a ridiculous and romantick complaint" (*ib.* 3.144. 1781); ". . . romantick and impracticable virtue" (*ib.* 3.173. 1781)   1755, etc.

Romantic Movement. Although J. nowhere uses this term, various stirrings of Romanticism are criticized (generally adversely) under GENIUS; BALLADS; COMPOSITION; NATURE; GENERAL AND THE PARTICULAR; etc.

Rules. See DRAMA: *Rules*; SHAKESPEARE: *"Unities"*; ANCIENT WRITERS; CRITICISM; ARISTOTLE

1. "Criticism has been cultivated in every age of learning . . . till the rules of writing are become rather burthensome than instructive to the mind." *Wks.* 9.436
1740

2. ". . . the rules of stile, like those of law, arise from precedents often repeated." *Wks.* 9.185. (*Plan of Dict.*)   1747

3. When Criticism is convinced "that the laws of just writing had been observed," she consigns the work examined over to immortality. (For sins against these laws, see CRITICISM 26.) *Wks.* 5.17. (*Ram.* 3. Allegory on Criticism)   1750

4. "I know not whether, for the same reason [to avoid the distraction of conflicting advice], it is not necessary for an author to place some confidence in his own skill, and to satisfy himself in the knowledge that he has not deviated from the established laws of composition. . . ." *Wks.* 5. 150. (*Ram.* 23)   1750

5. "Definitions have been no less difficult or uncertain in criticisms than in law. Imagination, a licentious and vagrant faculty, unsusceptible of limitations, and impatient of restraint, has always endeavoured to baffle the logician, to perplex the confines of distinction, and burst the inclosures of regularity. There is therefore scarcely any species of writing, of which we can tell what is its essence, and what are its constituents; every new genius produces some innovation, which, when invented and approved, subverts the rules which the practice of foregoing authors had established." *Wks.* 6.344-5. (*Ram.* 125) 1751

6. ". . . rules are more necessary, as there is a larger power of choice." See LETTER-WRITING 2 b. For epistolary rules, see LETTER-WRITING 1751

7. "The accidental prescriptions of authority, when time has procured them veneration, are often confounded with the laws of nature, and those rules are supposed coeval with reason, of which the first rise cannot be discovered." All the received laws of criticism "had not the same original right to our regard. Some are to be considered as fundamental and indispensable, others only as useful and convenient; some as dictated by reason and necessity, others as enacted by despotick antiquity; some as invincibly supported by their conformity to the order of nature and operations of the intellect; others as formed by accident, or instituted by example, and therefore always liable to dispute and alteration." Examination of dramatic rules on the basis of this distinction: limitation of number of personages on stage at one time to three, of number of acts to five, attacked; unity of time declared unnecessary, of action, necessary; tragi-comedy partially defended; a single hero necessary. (See DRAMA 44.) "It ought to be the first endeavour of a writer to distinguish nature from custom; or that which is established because it is right, from that which is right only be-

cause it is established; that he may neither violate essential principles by a desire of novelty, nor debar himself from the attainment of beauties within his view, by a needless fear of breaking rules which no literary dictator had authority to enact." *Wks.* 7.96-100. (*Ram.* 156)   1751

8. "Criticism . . . has not yet attained the certainty and stability of science. The rules hitherto received, are seldom drawn from any settled principle or self-evident postulate, or adapted to the natural and invariable constitution of things; but will be found upon examination the arbitrary edicts of legislators, authorised only by themselves, who, out of various means by which the same end may be attained, selected such as happened to occur to their own reflexion, and then, by a law which idleness and timidity were too willing to obey, prohibited new experiments of wit, restrained fancy from the indulgence of her innate inclination to hazard and adventure, and condemned all future flights of genius to pursue the path of the *Meonian* eagle. This authority may be more justly opposed, as it is apparently derived from them whom they endeavour to controul . . . practice has introduced rules, rather than rules have directed practice. For this reason the laws of every species of writing have been settled by the ideas of him who first raised it to reputation, without enquiry whether his performances were not yet susceptible of improvement. The excellencies and faults of celebrated writers have been equally recommended to posterity; and so far has blind reverence prevailed, that even the number of their books has been thought worthy of imitation. . . . When rules are thus drawn, rather from precedents than reason, there is danger not only from the faults of an author, but from the errors of those who criticise his works; since they may often mislead their pupils by false representations, as the *Ciceronians* of the six-

teenth century were betrayed into barbarisms by corrupt copies of their darling writer." *Wks.* 7.107-10. (*Ram.* 158.) See LYRIC POETRY 1; ESSAYS 3; OPENING OF A WORK 2, for application of above. 1751

9. ". . . rules are the instruments of mental vision, which may indeed assist our faculties when properly used, but produce confusion and obscurity by unskilful application." See CRITICISM 33 1751

10. Virgil's *Pastorals* examined "without any inquiry how far my sentiments deviate from established rules or common opinions." *Wks.* 9.68. (*Adv.* 92) 1753

11. "All violation of established practice implies in its own nature a rejection of the common opinion, a defiance of common censure, and an appeal from general laws to private judgment: he, therefore, who differs from others without apparent advantage, ought not to be angry if his arrogance is punished with ridicule. . . . In moral and religious questions only, a wise man will hold no consultations with fashion, because these duties are constant and immutable. . . ." (These remarks not applied specifically to literature.) *Wks.* 9.146-7. (*Adv.* 131) 1754

12. "Prudence operates on life in the same manner as rules on composition; it produces vigilance rather than elevation, rather prevents loss than procures advantage; and often escapes miscarriages, but seldom reaches either power or honour. . . . Rules may obviate faults, but can never confer beauties; and prudence keeps life safe, but does not often make it happy. The world is not amazed with prodigies of excellence, but when wit tramples upon rules, and magnanimity breaks the chains of prudence." *Wks.* 8.228. (*Idl.* 57) 1759

13. "With critical writings we [the English] abound sufficiently to enable pedantry to impose rules which can seldom be observed. . . ." *Wks.* 8. 366. (*Idl.* 91) 1760

14. "Dryden, petulantly and indecently, denies the heroism of Adam [in *Paradise Lost*] because he was overcome; but there is no reason why the hero should not be unfortunate except established practice, since success and virtue do not go necessarily together." *Lives* 1.176   1779
15. "But one language cannot communicate its rules to another." (Versification is under discussion.) See Blank Verse 7   1779
16. *". . . ever despise those opinions that are formed by the rules." See Criticism 81   1779
17. *J. to Fanny Burney, when she tells him that Murphy has given her rules to follow in writing her new comedy: "Never mind, my dear,—ah! you'll do without,—you want no rules." D'Arblay, *Diary and Letters*, 1.210   1779
18. Shakespeare, "the greatest [English] dramatist, wrote without rules, conducted through life and nature by a genius that rarely misled, and rarely deserted him." *Lives* 1.410   1779
19. Truth superior to rule. See Truth 23   1779
20. Congreve "has shewn us that enthusiasm has its rules, and that in mere confusion there is neither grace nor greatness." See Congreve 3   Ptd. 1780
21. The "dogmatism of learning" *vs.* common sense in criticism. See Popular Judgement 36   1781
22. "Dryden [as a prose writer] obeys the motions of his own mind, Pope constrains his mind to his own rules of composition." But both excelled in prose. See Pope 3   1781
23. J. appeals to Horace's rule on supernatural machinery. See Mythology 23. (J. also applies this rule to *Paradise Lost*. See *Lives* 1.175. cf. also Opening of a Work 1)   1781
24. ". . . the cant of those who judge by principles rather than perception." See Versification 30   1781

25.*J. used to remark that lines 67-8 in Pope's *Epistle to Jervas:*
"Led by some rule that guides, but not constrains,
And finish'd more through happiness than pains"—
was "a union that constituted the ultimate degree of excellence in the fine arts." *John Misc.* 2.254. (Miss Reynolds) Date?

Sacred Poetry

1. "To speak not inadequately of things really and naturally great, is a task not only difficult but disagreeable; because the writer is degraded in his own eyes by standing in comparison with his subject, to which he can hope to add nothing from his imagination." *Wks.* 4.594. (Not specifically applied to sacred poetry)
1756

2. Neglect of Cowley's *Davideis* partly attributable to its subject: "indisposed to the reception of poetical embellishments." "All amplification [of 'Sacred History'] is frivolous and vain . . . in some degree profane. Such events as were produced by the visible interposition of Divine Power are above the power of human genius to dignify." The Bible portrays an age so remote from the present, "a distinct species of mankind, that lived and acted with manners uncommunicable," that their joys and griefs lose in interest. *Lives* 1.49-51
1779

3. ". . . in sacred poetry who has succeeded?" *Lives* 1.75
1779

4. [a] "Let no pious ear be offended if I advance, in opposition to many authorities, that poetical devotion cannot often please. The doctrines of religion may indeed be defended in a didactick poem, and he who has the happy power of arguing in verse will not lose it because his subject is sacred. A poet may describe the beauty and the grandeur of Nature, the flowers of the Spring, and the harvests of Autumn, the vicissitudes of

the Tide, and the revolutions of the Sky, and praise the Maker for his works in lines which no reader shall lay aside. The subject of the disputation is not piety, but the motives to piety; that of the description is not God, but the works of God. Contemplative piety, or the intercourse between God and the human soul, cannot be poetical. Man admitted to implore the mercy of his Creator and plead the merits of his Redeemer is already in a higher state than poetry can confer." [b] *Sacred poetry cannot surprise:* "The essence of poetry is invention; such invention as, by producing something unexpected, surprises and delights." But there are few possible devotional topics, and these are universally known: "they can receive no grace from novelty of sentiment, and very little from novelty of expression. Poetry pleases by exhibiting an idea more grateful to the mind than things themselves afford." This achieved by selection. ". . . but religion must be shewn as it is; suppression and addition equally corrupt it, and such as it is, it is known already." [c] Sacred poetry rarely enlarges the reader's comprehension or elevates the fancy as all poetry should. But "Omnipotence cannot be exalted; Infinity cannot be amplified; Perfection cannot be improved." Faith, Thanksgiving, Repentance and Supplication are above poetical embellishments. Simplicity the key to religious sublimity. "All that pious verse can do is to help the memory and delight the ear, and for these purposes it may be very useful; but it supplies nothing to the mind. The ideas of Christian Theology are too simple for eloquence, too sacred for fiction, and too majestick for ornament; to recommend them by tropes and figures is to magnify by a concave mirror the sidereal hemisphere." *Lives* 1.291-3 1779

5. Some ideas in *Paradise Lost* too sacred or awful: "Such images rather obstruct the career of fancy than incite it. Pleasure and terrour are indeed the genuine sources

of poetry; but poetical pleasure must be such as human imagination can at least conceive, and poetical terrour such as human strength and fortitude may combat. The good and evil of Eternity are too ponderous for the wings of wit; the mind sinks under them in passive helplessness, content with calm belief and humble adoration." *Lives* 1.182   1779

6. "As the sentiments [of an ode by Fenton] are pious they cannot easily be new, for what can be added to topicks on which successive ages have been employed!" *Lives* 2.263-4   Ptd. 1780

7. Burlesquing the Scriptures condemned by J. *Lives* 2.247 and *ib.* 3.215   1780-1

8. "That [Pope's] *The Messiah* excells the *Pollio* is no great praise, if it be considered from what original [Isaiah] the improvements are derived." *Lives* 3.226   1781

9. "But his [Watts's] devotional poetry is, like that of others, unsatisfactory. The paucity of its topicks enforces perpetual repetition, and the sanctity of the matter rejects the ornaments of figurative diction. It is sufficient for Watts to have done better than others what no man has done well." *Lives* 3.310   1781

10. ". . . the great reason why the reader [of Young's *The Last Day*] is disappointed is that the thought of the LAST DAY makes every man more than poetical by spreading over his mind a general obscurity of sacred horror, that oppresses distinction and disdains expression." *Lives* 3.393-4   1781

11. *When J. "would try to repeat the . . . *Dies iræ, Dies illa,* he could never pass the stanza ending thus, *Tantus labor non sit cassus,* without bursting into a flood of tears; which sensibility I used to quote against him when he would inveigh against devotional poetry, and protest that all religious verses were cold and feeble, and unworthy the subject, which ought to be treated with higher reverence, he said, than either

poets or painters could presume to excite or bestow." *John. Misc.* 1.284. (Piozzi) Date?

12. *J. "often expressed his dislike of religious poetry. *Wks.* 1.46 *n.* (Hawkins's *Life*) Date?

Satire. Compare OCCASIONAL WORKS

1. "WIT, cohabiting with MALICE, had a son named SATYR, who followed him, carrying a quiver filled with poisoned arrows, which, where they once drew blood, could by no skill ever be extracted. These arrows he frequently shot at LEARNING, when she was most earnestly or usefully employed. . . . Minerva therefore deputed CRITICISM to her aid, who generally broke the point of SATYR's arrows, turned them aside, or retorted them on himself." *Wks.* 5.147-8. (*Ram.* 22; Allegory of Wit and Learning) 1750
2. *Definition:* "A poem in which wickedness or folly is censured. Proper *satire* is distinguished, by the generality of the reflections, from a *lampoon* which is aimed against a particular person; but they are too frequently confounded." *Dict.* 1755
3. The tendency of general lampooners of mankind is to "exhaust their virulence upon imaginary crimes, which, as they never existed, can never be amended." *Wks.* 8.178. (*Idl.* 45) 1759
4. "It is of the nature of personal invectives to be soon unintelligible; and the authour that gratifies private malice, *animam in volnere ponit*, destroys the future efficacy of his own writings, and sacrifices the esteem of succeeding times to the laughter of a day." *Shak.*, Raleigh, 87 1765
5. "Personal resentment, though no laudable motive to satire, can add great force to general principles. Self-love is a busy prompter." *Lives* 1.437 1779
6. J. defends poems such as the *Dunciad:* "Dulness or deformity are not culpable in themselves, but may be very justly reproached when they pretend to the hon-

our of wit or the influence of beauty. If bad writers were to pass without reprehension what should restrain them? . . . and upon bad writers only will censure have much effect. . . . All truth is valuable, and satirical criticism may be considered as useful when it rectifies error and improves judgement: he that refines the publick taste is a publick benefactor." *Lives* 3. 241-2   1781

7. *"He did not . . . encourage general satire, and for the most part professed himself to feel directly contrary to Dr. Swift; 'who (says he) hates the world, though he loves John and Robert, and certain individuals.' " *John. Misc.* 1.327. (Piozzi; cf. her similar testimony, *ib.* 223: ". . . nobody had a more just aversion to general satire.")   Date?

Scotch Writers.[1] See BEATTIE; BLAIR; BOETHIUS; BUCHANAN; HUME; JOHNSTON, ARTHUR; KAMES; MACPHERSON; ROBERTSON; SMITH; SMOLLETT, etc.

1. *"His prejudice against Scotland appeared remarkably strong at this time. When I talked of our advancement in literature, 'Sir, (said he,) you have learnt a little from us, and you think yourselves very great men. Hume would never have written History, had not Voltaire written it before him. He is an echo of Voltaire.' BOSWELL. 'But, Sir, we have Lord Kames.' JOHNSON. 'You *have* Lord Kames. Keep him; ha, ha, ha! We don't envy you him.' " When pressed for an opinion on Robertson, J. replied: " 'Sir, I love Robertson, and I won't talk of his book [*History of Scotland*].' " Boswell adds, however, that in spite of this

[1] A great deal too much has been made of Johnson's prejudice against the Scotch. We must constantly take into account his humorous exaggeration for conversational purposes. The theme, to Johnson and his circle, was frequently but a tilting yard, where the doctor held himself ever ready to splinter a lance of pleasantry with his challengers. As Bardolph's nose to Falstaff, so Boswell and his fellow-Scotchmen were to Johnson, a sure refuge from the importunate "Black Dog." See *John. Misc.* 2.49, 216; *Bos.* 2.77, etc.

sally, J. "had too good taste not to be fully sensible of the merits of that admirable work." *Bos.* 2.53   1768
2. "The *Latin* poetry of *Deliciæ Poëtarum Scotorum* would have done honour to any nation." *Wks.* 10.344. (*Jour. to W.I.*)   Composed 1774
3. *"But the test he [J.] offered to prove that Scotland . . . had not sufficient [learning] for the dignity of literature, was, that he defied any one to produce a classical book, written in Scotland since Buchanan. Robertson, he said, used pretty words, but he liked Hume better, and neither of them would he allow to be more to Clarendon, than a rat to a cat." *John. Misc.* 2.48. (Campbell)   1775
4. *The Scotch: "It is with their learning as with provisions in a besieged town, every one has a mouthful, and no one a bellyfull." *John. Misc.* 2.5. (Hawkins's *Apophthegms.*) See also *Bos.* 2.363 for this anecdote.   Date?
5. *"When a Scotsman was talking against Warburton, Johnson said he had more literature than had been imported from Scotland since the days of Buchanan. Upon his mentioning other eminent writers of the Scots,—'These will not do,' said Johnson, 'let us have some more of your northern lights, these are mere farthing candles.' " *John. Misc.* 2.15. (Hawkins's *Apophthegms*)   Date?
6. *J. bowls down Scotch authors like nine-pins. *John. Misc.* 1.188. (Piozzi)   Date?
7. *"We have taught that nation to write, and do they pretend to be our teachers? let me hear no more of the tinsel of Robertson, and the foppery of Dalrymple." *John. Misc.* 2.10. cf. *Bos.* 2.236 for similar remark.
                                                                      Date?

Selection

1. The writer of modern fiction should select events and characters with moral end in view. "It is justly con-

sidered as the greatest excellency of art, to imitate nature; but it is necessary to distinguish those parts of nature, which are most proper for imitation: greater care is still required in representing life." See FICTION 1 c, d, e   1750

2. "Against this objection [to the marine pastorals of Sannazaro, that the sea is an object of terror, and hence unsuitable for pastoral] he might be defended by the established maxim, that the poet has a right to select his images, and is no more obliged to shew the sea in a storm, than the land under an inundation; but may display all the pleasures, and conceal the dangers of the water, as he may lay his shepherd under a shady beach, without giving him an ague, or letting a wild beast loose upon him." *Wks.* 5.236. (*Ram.* 36)   1750

3. "The poet . . . having the subject in his own choice, . . . ought always to consult the interest of virtue." See PASTORAL 2   1750

4. Shakespeare's indelicacy in common scenes perhaps faithful to the manners of the age. "There must, however, have been always some modes of gayety preferable to others, and a writer ought to chuse the best." *Shak. Pref.*, Raleigh, 22   1765

5. ". . . the poet's art is selection." See PASTORAL 15   1781

Sense. See GOOD SENSE

Senses (AS A BASIS OF CRITICISM). See EXPERIENCE

Sensibility. See FEELING

1. *Definition:* "1. Quickness of sensation.[1] . . . 2. Quickness of perception." *Dict.*   1755

---

[1] cf. "*Feeling* for *tenderness* or *sensibility* is a word merely colloquial, of late introduction, not yet sure enough of its own existence to claim a place upon a stone." (Hogarth's epitaph is under discussion.) "Sensibility; tenderness" is, however, the second meaning of *feeling* in J.'s *Dict.* See *Letters* 1.187 and *n* 1.

Sentences

1. "Pointed or epigrammatical expressions" unsuited to tragedy. See SENTIMENT 2   1751
2. *Definition of sentence:* "3. A maxim; an axiom, generally moral."[1] *Dict.*   1755
3. "In all pointed sentences, some degree of accuracy must be sacrificed to conciseness." *Wks.* 10.286.
1767

Sentiment

1. "Sentiments are proper and improper as they consist more or less with the character and circumstances of the person to whom they are attributed, with the rules of the composition in which they are found, or with the settled and unalterable nature of things." Anachronisms censured. "Another species of impropriety, is the unsuitableness of thoughts to the general character of the poem. The seriousness and solemnity of tragedy necessarily rejects all pointed or epigrammatical expressions, all remote conceits and opposition of ideas. . . . All allusions to low and trivial objects, with which contempt is usually associated, are doubtless unsuitable to a species of composition [tragedy] which ought to be always awful, though not always magnificent. . . . But of all meanness that has least to plead which is produced by mere verbal conceits, which depending only upon sounds, lose their existence by the change of a syllable." Illustrations of the violation of each of these principles in Milton's *Samson Agonistes. Wks.* 6.437-40. (*Ram.* 140)
1751
2. *Definition:* "1. Thought; notion; opinion. . . . 2. The

[1] This is the most frequent meaning of the word in J.'s criticism; e.g., "The sentences are keenly pointed" (referring to Greville's *Maxims. Letters* 1.61); Phocylydes "a writer of moral sentences in verse" (T. Browne, *Wks.*, ed. Wilkins, 1835, 4.107 *n* 3); rhyme makes "sentences stand more independent on each other" (*Lives* 1.436); "sentences were readier at his call than images." (*ib.* 1.459).

sense considered distinctly from the language or things; a striking sentence in a composition."¹ *Dict.*   1755

Sermons

1. See COMPOSITION 26 for advice on sermon writing.
1780
2. *". . . sermons make a considerable branch of English literature; so that a library must be very imperfect if it has not a numerous collection of sermons." *Bos.* 4.105   1781

Short Compositions. See also AMOROUS VERSES

1. "It was unsuitable to the nicety required in short compositions to close his verse with the word *too*." See VERSIFICATION 16   1756
2. Borrowed lines "may be indulged" in short compositions. See PLAGIARISM 4   1756
3. "All that short compositions can commonly attain is neatness and elegance." *Lives* 1.163   1779
4. "No poem should be long of which the purpose is only to strike the fancy, without enlightening the understanding by precept, ratiocination, or narrative. A blaze first pleases, and then tires the sight." *Lives* 2.263   Ptd. 1780
5. J. praises the under-rated *"Namby Pamby"* pieces by A. Philips: "little things are not valued but when they are done by those who can do greater." *Lives* 3.324
1781
6. "The adoption of a particular style [in imitation of an author] in light and short compositions contributes much to the increase of pleasure." See IMITATION 23
1781

---

¹ No other meaning given. "Feeling" or "emotional sensitiveness" was commonly expressed by the word "sensibility," *q.v.* "Sentimental" is not defined in J.'s *Dictionary*. In 1773, Beattie calls it "a new word, which has become very common of late." (*Essays,* ed. 1779, p. 303).

7. Avoid distant rhymes and unfamiliar metrical arrangement in short compositions. See ODE 4   1781

Similes. Compare METAPHORS

1. *"I told him [Cibber] that when the ancients made a simile, they always made it like something real." *Bos.* 3.73   *cir.* 1754?
2. *Definition of simile:* "A comparison by which any thing is illustrated or aggrandized." *Dict.*   1755
3. The "Alps" simile in Pope's *Essay on Criticism* "is perhaps the best simile in our language." For analysis, see POPE 25   1756
4. "A poetical simile is the discovery of likeness between two actions in their general nature dissimilar, or of causes terminating by different operations in some resemblance of effect. But the mention of another like consequence from a like cause, or of a like performance by a like agency, is not a simile, but an exemplification." Illustration. "A simile may be compared to lines converging at a point and is more excellent as the lines approach from greater distance: and exemplification may be considered as two parallel lines which run on together without approximation, never far separated, and never joined." *Lives* 2.129-30   Ptd. 1780
5. The "Alps" simile in Pope's *Essay on Criticism* [ll. 219*ff.*] "perhaps the best that English poetry can shew. A simile, to be perfect, must both illustrate and ennoble the subject; must shew it to the understanding in a clearer view, and display it to the fancy with greater dignity: but either of these qualities may be sufficient to recommend it. In didactick poetry, of which the great purpose is instruction, a simile may be praised which illustrates, though it does not ennoble; in heroicks, that may be admitted which ennobles, though it does not illustrate. That it may be complete it is required to exhibit, independently of its references, a pleasing image; for a simile is said to be a short epi-

sode." But sometimes antiquity over-attentive to this. "In their similes the greatest writers have sometimes failed: the ship-race, compared with the chariot-race [*Aeneid* V. 144], is neither illustrated nor aggrandised," etc. "The simile of the Alps has no useless parts, yet affords a striking picture by itself: . . . it assists the apprehension, and elevates the fancy." *Lives* 3.229-30   1781

Sonnet

1. *Definition:* "1. A short poem consisting of fourteen lines, of which the rhymes are adjusted by a particular rule. It is not very suitable to the English language, and has not been used by any man of eminence since *Milton.*" Milton's sonnet, "A book was writ of late called *Tetrachordon*," quoted in full. "2. A small poem."[1] *Dict.*   1755
2. "The fabrick of a sonnet, however adapted to the Italian language, has never succeeded in ours, which, having greater variety of termination, requires the rhymes to be often changed." *Lives.* 1.169-70   1779

Spanish Literature. See Drama, Spanish; Cervantes; etc.

Spenserian Imitations. See under Imitation

Structure. See also under Fable; Shakespeare: *Plots*; Drama; Pindaric Verse

1. Lack of restraint and order in lyric poetry and in "essays" censured: "To proceed from one truth to another, and connect distant propositions by regular consequences, is the great prerogative of man," etc. See Essays 3; Lyric Poetry 1   1751

---

[1] A "sonnetteer," J. defines: "A small poet, in contempt." *Ib.*

2. Arbitrary structural order of a poem "consisting of precepts." See DIDACTIC POETRY 8   1781
3. Inevitable lack of a plan other than arbitrary, of "a regular subordination of parts terminating in the principal and original design," in descriptive poetry. See DESCRIPTION 7, 8   1781

Style. See also ANTIQUE STYLE; DICTION; VERSIFICATION; ORNAMENT; LETTER-WRITING; etc.

1. "The greatest and most necessary task [for a young student] still remains, to attain a habit of expression, without which knowledge is of little use. This is necessary in Latin, and more necessary in English; and can only be acquired by a daily imitation of the best and correctest authours." *Bos.* 1.100   *cir.* 1736
2. ". . . the rules of stile, like those of law, arise from precedents often repeated." *Wks.* 9.185. (*Plan of Dict.*)   1747
3. ". . . there are in general three forms of style, each of which demands its particular mode of elocution: the *familiar*, the *solemn*, and the *pathetick*." Directions for vocal interpretation of each. *Wks.* 9.408   1748
4. "The grossness of vulgar habits obstructs the efficacy of virtue, as impurity and harshness of style impair the force of reason, and rugged numbers turn off the mind from artifice of disposition, and fertility of invention." *Wks.* 7.154. (*Ram.* 166)   1751
5. The importance of style; how to achieve a good style. See AUTHORS 5   1753
6. Jonas Hanway's bad grammar; "but with us to mean well is a degree of merit which overbalances much greater errors than impurity of style." *Wks.* 10.260   1757
7. *Types of style:* "It is difficult to enumerate every species of authors whose labours counteract themselves;

the man of exuberance and copiousness, who diffuses every thought through so many diversities of expression, that it is lost like water in a mist; the ponderous dictator of sentences, whose notions are delivered in the lump, and are, like uncoined bullion, of more weight than use; the liberal illustrator, who shews by examples and comparisons what was clearly seen when it was first proposed; and the stately son of demonstration, who proves with mathematical formality what no man has yet pretended to doubt. There is a mode of style for which I know not that the masters of oratory have yet found a name, a style by which the most evident truths are so obscured, that they can no longer be perceived, and the most familiar propositions so disguised that they cannot be known. . . . This style may be called the *terrifick*, for its chief intention is to terrify and amaze; it may be termed the *repulsive*, for its natural effect is to drive away the reader; or it may be distinguished, in plain *English*, by the denomination of the *bugbear style*, for it has more terror than danger, and will appear less formidable as it is more nearly approached." Example of the "terrifick style." *Wks.* 8.143-5. (*Idl.* 36)   1758

8. The poet should cultivate style. See POETRY 14 c

                                                               1759

9. "Language proceeds, like every thing else, through improvement to degeneracy. . . . Then begin . . . the regulation of figures, the selection of words, the modulation of periods, the graces of transition, the complication of clauses, and all the delicacies of style and subtilties of composition, useful while they advance perspicuity, and laudable while they increase pleasure, but easy to be refined by needless scrupulosity till they shall more embarrass the writer than assist the reader or delight him. . . . From the time of *Gower* and *Chaucer*, the *English* writers have studied elegance, and advanced their language, by successive improve-

ments, to as much harmony as it can easily receive, and as much copiousness as human knowledge has hitherto required ... every man now endeavours to excel others in accuracy, or outshine them in splendour of style, and the danger is, lest care should too soon pass to affectation." *Wks.* 8.253-5. (*Idl.* 63)   1759

10. *The "familiar" or "easy style":* "Easy poetry is that in which natural thoughts are expressed without violence to the language. The discriminating character of ease consists principally in the diction, for all true poetry requires that the sentiments be natural. Language suffers violence by harsh or by daring figures, by transposition, by unusual acceptations of words, and by any licence, which would be avoided by a writer of prose. Where any artifice appears in the construction of the verse, that verse is no longer easy. Any epithet which can be ejected without diminution of the sense, any curious iteration of the same word, and all unusual, though not ungrammatical structure of speech, destroy the grace of easy poetry." False conceptions of easy poetry: "Affectation ... sometimes mistaken for it; and those who aspire to gentle elegance, collect female phrases and fashionable barbarisms, and imagine that style to be easy which custom has made familiar." Easy poetry "understood as long as the language lasts;" the modish follies of speech perishable. Ease excludes pomp but admits greatness and wit. "It is less difficult to write a volume of lines swelled with epithets, brightened by figures, and stiffened by transpositions, than to produce a few couplets graced only by naked elegance and simple purity, which require so much care and skill, that I doubt whether any of our authors has yet been able, for twenty lines together, nicely to observe the true definition of easy poetry." *Wks.* 8.308-11. (*Idl.* 77)   1759

11. *Whitehead's familiar style censured: "Grand* nonsense is insupportable." *Bos.* 1.402   1763

12. "If there be, what I believe there is, in every nation, a stile which never becomes obsolete, a certain mode of phraseology so consonant and congenial to the analogy and principles of its respective language as to remain settled and unaltered; this style is probably to be sought in the common intercourse of life, among those who speak only to be understood, without ambition of elegance. The polite are always catching modish innovations, and the learned depart from established forms of speech, in hope of finding or making better . . . but there is a conversation above grossness and below refinement, where propriety resides, and where this poet [Shakespeare] seems to have gathered his comick dialogue." *Shak. Pref.*, Raleigh, 19-20 1765

13. *"Sir, you must first define what you mean by style, before you can judge who has a good taste in style, and who has a bad. The two classes of persons whom you have mentioned [those who prefer Swift's style and those who prefer a fuller and grander] don't differ as to good and bad. They both agree that Swift has a good neat style; but one loves a neat style, another loves a style of more splendour. In like manner, one loves a plain coat, another loves a laced coat; but neither will deny that each is good in its kind." *Bos.* 2.191-2
   1772

14. *Conciseness of style praised: ". . . is it the great excellence of a [?historical] writer to put into his book as much as his book will hold." *Bos.* 2.237   1773

15. *J. defends his own style. See JOHNSON 2   1777

16. *J. believes every man has a style peculiar to himself. *Bos.* 3.280   1778

17. *The "familiar style"*: "Cowley, whatever was his subject, seems to have been carried by a kind of destiny to the light and the familiar, or to conceits which require still more ignoble epithets." *Lives* 1.46   1779

18. Addison's prose "the model of the middle style." See ADDISON 12   Ptd. 1780

19. The excessive luxuriance of expression in Akenside's *Pleasures of Imagination* clouds the sense: "attention deserts the mind and settles in the ear." *Lives* 3.417
   1781
20. *Best didactic style:* A simple, unadorned style with "easy and safe conveyance of meaning" like Swift's, the best "for purposes merely didactick, when something is to be told that was not known before . . . but against that inattention by which known truths are suffered to lie neglected it makes no provision; it instructs, but does not persuade." (But see SWIFT 7: the tremendous effects of his style.) *Lives* 3.52   1781
21. (Context: letter-writing): "It is indeed not easy to distinguish affectation from habit; he that has once studiously formed a style rarely writes afterwards with complete ease." *Lives* 3.160   1781
22. *J. disapproves of parentheses and of the phrases *the former* and *the latter*. *Bos.* 4.190. (See also *ib. n* 2)
   Date?

Subjects. See also SACRED POETRY; OCCASIONAL WORKS. For proper tragic subjects, see under DRAMA: *Tragedy*

1. A new source of poetic pleasure in pioneer life. See POETRY 2   1744
2. The unfortunate author who cannot choose his own subject. *Wks.* 5.141. (*Ram.* 21)   1750
3. A periodical writer's "rule of choice peculiar to himself." See PERIODICAL WRITINGS 2   1750
4. Private life a proper subject for biography. See BIOGRAPHY 3 c, d   1750
5. The essay writer's difficulty in choosing from a "boundless multiplicity" of subjects. See ESSAYS 4   1751
6. Choice of the same subject by authors not wholly without advantage: each treatment has its own particular appeal. The changing fashions in composition redeem from staleness. See VARIETY 3   1753

7. Trite subjects which nevertheless bear repetition while human nature remains the same. e.g., spring, night, a poetical grove. *Wks.* 9.103-4. (*Adv.* 108)   1753

8. "Some of the most pleasing performances have been produced by learning and genius exercised upon subjects of little importance. It seems to have been in all ages the pride of wit, to shew how it could exalt the low, and amplify the little. To speak not inadequately of things really and naturally great, is a task not only difficult but disagreeable." The author's imagination cannot hope to add to his subject; "but it is a perpetual triumph of fancy to expand a scanty theme, to raise glittering ideas from obscure properties, and to produce to the world an object of wonder to which nature had contributed little." Illustrations of this. *Wks.* 4.594-5   1756

9. The perishability of temporary subjects. See GENERAL 6   1759

10. The struggle between pleasure and virtue not "a trite or exhausted subject, for the truth is, that there is no other to be chosen . . . nor can history or poetry exhibit more than pleasure triumphing over virtue, and virtue subjugating pleasure." *Critical Review*, Apr. 1763, p. 314. (Review of Graham's *Telemachus*)   1763

11. ". . . not even *Shakespeare* can write well without a proper subject. It is a vain endeavour for the most skilful hand to cultivate barrenness, or to paint upon vacuity." *Shak.*, Raleigh, 133   1765

12. "To reason in verse is allowed to be difficult. . . ." *Lives* 2.254   Ptd. 1780

13. "History will always take stronger hold of the attention than fable." See POPE 58   1781

14. The "fabulous age," an improper subject. See EPIC 9   1781

15. (Context: Pope's *Eloisa to Abelard*): ". . . the sub-

ject is so judiciously chosen that it would be difficult, in turning over the annals of the world, to find another which so many circumstances concur to recommend." Abelard and Eloisa deserve our notice, and hence attract our interest. Their story undisputed history. ("The heart naturally loves truth.") "Their fate does not leave the mind in hopeless dejection; for they both found quiet and consolation in retirement and piety. So new and so affecting is their story that it supersedes invention, and imagination ranges at full liberty without straggling into scenes of fable." *Lives* 3.235
                 1781

16. "The subject [of the *Essay on Man*] is perhaps not very proper for poetry. . . ." *Lives* 3.242 1781
17. "The subject [*Pleasures of Imagination*] is well chosen, as it includes all images that can strike or please, and thus comprises every species of poetical delight." *Lives* 3.417 1781
18. The meanness of Dyer's subject "and the irreverence habitually annexed to trade and manufacture, sink him under insuperable oppression" in *The Fleece*, in spite of "all the writer's arts of delusion." *Lives* 3.346
                 1781
19. The subject of the *Dunciad* "had nothing generally interesting." *Lives* 3.146 1781
20. Somerville's injudicious choice of subject: *The Chace*. His great knowledge of his theme: "the first requisite to excellence"; but "it is impossible to interest the common readers of verse in the dangers or pleasures of the chase." *Lives* 2.319. cf. GRAINGER 3 1781

Sublime, The. See also SACRED POETRY

1. The sublime and the general. See GENERAL 9 1779
2. Waller "not so liberally supplied with grand as with soft images; for beauty is more easily found than magnanimity." *Lives* 1.283 1779

Suicidal Endings
1. ". . . a method by which, as Dryden remarked, a [dramatic] poet easily rids his scene of persons whom he wants not to keep alive." *Lives* 3.396-7   1781
2. Gray's *The Bard* "might have been concluded with an action of better example: but suicide is always to be had without expence of thought." *Lives* 3.440   1781

Sympathy. See FEELING

Tales.[1]
1. ". . . the merit of such stories is the art of telling them," not their originality. *Lives* 2.201   Ptd. 1780

Taste. Cf. CRITICISM: *Rules;* POPULAR JUDGEMENT
1. *"Talking on the subject of taste in the arts, he [J.] said, that difference of taste was, in truth, difference of skill." Taste in style discussed. *Bos.* 2.191   1772
2. *Criticism by "natural taste and feelings." See CRITICISM 81   1779
3. "These apologies are always useless, 'de gustibus non est disputandum'; men may be convinced, but they cannot be pleased, against their will. But though taste is obstinate it is very variable, and time often prevails when arguments have failed." *Lives* 2.217
                                                                       Ptd. 1780

Tediousness. For the "most fatal of all faults," see under AIM OF WRITING
1. It is difficult for an author to detect his own tediousness. See CRITICISM 5   Ptd. 1780

Temporary Poems. See OCCASIONAL POEMS. See also under GENERAL

Terse
1. *Definition:* "1. Smooth. . . . 2. Cleanly written; neat; elegant without pompousness." *Dict.*   1755

---

[1] By *Tales* J. refers to the popular short story in verse which was long a literary staple.

Time. SEE CRITICISM, TIME AS AN AID TO

Tragedy. See under DRAMA: *Tragedy*

Translation

1. "The great pest of speech is frequency of translation. No book was ever turned from one language into another, without imparting something of its native idiom; this is the most mischievous and comprehensive innovation . . . new phraseology . . . alters not the single stones of the building, but the order of the columns. If an academy should be established for the cultivation of our style, which I, who can never wish to see dependence multiplied, hope the spirit of *English* liberty will hinder or destroy, let them, instead of compiling grammars and dictionaries, endeavour . . . to stop the licence of translators, whose idleness and ignorance, if it be suffered to proceed, will reduce us to babble a dialect of *France.*" *Wks.* 9.226. (*Pref. Dict.*)
1755

2. ". . . undoubtedly, translations into the prose of a living language must be laid aside, whenever the language changes, because the matter being always to be found in the original, contributes nothing to the preservation of the form superinduced by the translator. . . . The great difficulty of a translator is to preserve the native form of his language, and the unconstrained manner of an original writer." *Wks.* ed. 1825, Oxford, 6.77-8
1756

3. The great success of moderns at translation. A historical review of translation: its "servile closeness" until the Restoration. "There is undoubtedly a mean to be observed. *Dryden* saw very early that closeness best preserved an author's sense, and that freedom best exhibited his spirit; he therefore will deserve the highest praise, who can give a representation at once faithful and pleasing, who can convey the same thoughts with

the same graces, and who when he translates changes nothing but the language." *Wks.* 8.272-8. (*Idl.* 68, 69) 1759
4. *Books of science and history (when not embellished with oratory) may be translated exactly. But "poetry, indeed, cannot be translated; and, therefore, it is the poets that preserve languages; for we would not be at the trouble to learn a language, if we could have all that is written in it just as well in a translation." *Bos.* 3.36 1776
5. *"We must try its effect as an English poem; that is the way to judge of the merit of a translation. Translations are, in general, for people who cannot read the original." *Bos.* 3.256 1778
6. A free translation is to be "distinguished from that which is wild and licentious." Reproduce sense and preserve the spirit of the original, here seems to be J.'s ideal. *Poems and Miscellaneous Pieces* by Thomas Maurice, 1779, p. 152. (Preface by J. unsigned, to Maurice's translation of *Oedipus Tyrannus*) 1779
7. Denham's "judicious character of a good translator" quoted: servile word-by-word translators condemned—
"They but preserve the ashes, thou the flame,
True to his sense, but truer to his fame."
Lives 1.77 1779
8. ". . . the shackles of verbal interpretation, which must for ever debar it from elegance. . . ." *Lives* 1.373 1779
9. "The affluence and comprehension of our language is very illustriously displayed in our poetical translations of ancient writers: a work which the French seem to relinquish in despair." The development of the art of translation traced from early servile imitation, to Cowley, who "left his authors." Dryden fixed "the limits of poetical liberty" and gave us "just rules and examples of translation. When languages are formed upon different principles, it is impossible that the same modes of expression should always be elegant in both.

While they run on together the closest translation may be considered as the best; but when they divaricate each must take its natural course. Where correspondence cannot be obtained it is necessary to be content with something equivalent. 'Translation therefore,' says Dryden, 'is not so loose as paraphrase, nor so close as metaphrase.' All polished languages have different styles: the concise, the diffuse, the lofty, and the humble. In the proper choice of style consists the resemblance which Dryden principally exacts from the translator. He is to exhibit his author's thoughts in such a dress of diction as the author would have given them, had his language been English. . . . A translator is to be like his author: it is not his business to excel him." The reasonableness of these rules. Seldom opposed. *Lives* 1.421-3   1779

10. The translation by Hughes of Fontenelle's *Dialogues of the Dead* now neglected; "for by a book not necessary, and owing its reputation wholly to its turn of diction, little notice can be gained but from those who can enjoy the graces of the original." *Lives* 2.160
         1779
11. Thoughts more easy to preserve in translation than diction. "The author, having the choice of his own images, selects those which he can best adorn; the translator must at all hazards follow his original, and express thoughts which perhaps he would not have chosen." *Lives* 1.448   1779
12. Stepney, "a very licentious translator, and does not recompense his neglect of the author by beauties of his own." *Lives* 1.311   1779
13. Denham "appears to have been one of the first that understood the necessity of emancipating translation from the drudgery of counting lines and interpreting single words. How much this servile practice obscured the clearest and deformed the most beautiful parts of the ancient authors may be discovered by a perusal of our earlier versions; some of them the works of men

well qualified, not only by critical knowledge, but by poetical genius, who yet by a mistaken ambition of exactness degraded at once their originals and themselves." *Lives* 1.79   1779
14. Rowe's *Translation of Lucan* "one of the greatest productions of English poetry; for there is perhaps none that so completely exhibits the genius and spirit of the original. . . . His author's sense is sometimes a little diluted by additional infusions, and sometimes weakened by too much expansion. But such faults are to be expected in all translations, from the constraint of measures and dissimilitude of languages." *Lives* 2.77   Ptd. 1780
15. Addison's translations are "too licentiously paraphrastical," but, "what is the first excellence of a translator, such as may be read with pleasure by those who do not know the originals." *Lives* 2.145   Ptd. 1780
16. Brief review of the history of translation among Greeks, Romans, Italians and French. *Lives* 3.236-7   1781
17. J. defends Pope's *Iliad* for being "not Homerical": "Pope wrote for his own age and his own nation," etc. See POPE 41   1781
18. "Minute enquiries into the force of words are less necessary in translating Homer than other poets, because his positions are general, and his representations natural," etc. (See NATURE 45.) *Lives* 3.114   1781
19. West properly does not confine himself to versification of his original. See PINDARIC VERSE 8   1781

Travel, Books of. See also HISTORY, NATURAL. Compare DESCRIPTION
1. The lack of veracity in most travellers' "Relations." Many excusable reasons for such errors. *Gent. Mag.*, 1742, p. 320   1742
2. J. cannot recommend Dr. Edward Browne's book of his travels "as likely to give much pleasure to common readers; for . . . a great part of his book seems to contain very unimportant accounts of his passage from

one place where he saw little, to another where he saw no more." *Wks.* 4.603   1756

3. "Every writer of travels should consider, that, like all other authors, he undertakes either to instruct or please, or to mingle pleasure with instruction. He that instructs must offer to the mind something to be imitated, or something to be avoided; he that pleases must offer new images to his reader, and enable him to form a tacit comparison of his own state with that of others." The usual writer of travels "conducts his reader through wet and dry, over rough and smooth, without incidents, without reflection; and, if he obtains his company for another day, will dismiss him again at night, equally fatigued with a like succession of rocks and streams, mountains and ruins. . . . He that would travel for the entertainment of others, should remember that the great object of remark is human life. Every nation has something particular in its manufactures, its works of genius, its medicines, its agriculture, its customs, and its policy. He only is a useful traveller, who brings home something by which his country may be benefited; who procures some supply of want or some mitigation of evil, which may enable his readers to compare their condition with that of others, to improve it whenever it is worse, and whenever it is better to enjoy it." *Wks.* 8.386-9. (*Idl.* 97)   1760

4. *Barretti, in the *Preface* to his *Journey from London to Genoa*, says: "I have spared no pains to carry my reader in some measure along with me; to make him see what I saw, hear what I heard, feel what I felt, and even think and fancy whatever I thought and fancied myself." Barretti adds that J. suggested this method to him. "It was he that exhorted me to write daily, and with all possible minuteness." Quoted in J.'s *Letters* 1.165 *n* 4 and *Bos.* 1.365 *n* 2   *cir.* 1760

5. "Those whose lot it is to ramble can seldom write, and those who know how to write very seldom ramble." *Letters* 1.166   1770

6. *J. mocks travellers' relations which convey false impressions. *Bos.* 5.55-6. (*Hebrides*, 18 Aug.) 1773
7. "These diminutive observations [on the ventilation of Scotch houses] seem to take away something from the dignity of writing, and therefore are never communicated but with hesitation. . . ." But justified by the importance of trifles in daily life. *Wks.* 10.338. (*Jour. to W.I.*) Composed 1774
8. "Dilatory notation" a cause of the false relations of travellers. *Wks.* 10.499-500. (*Jour. to W.I.*) Composed 1774
9. *J. remarks that writers of travels "were more defective than any other writers." *Bos.* 2.377 1775
10. *". . . books of travel will be good in proportion to what a man has previously in his mind; his knowing what to observe; his power of contrasting one mode of life with another." *Bos.* 3.301-2 1778
11. J. calls Gray's account of his journey to Scotland (in his *Letters*) "very curious and elegant; for as his comprehension was ample his curiosity extended to all the works of art, all the appearances of nature, and all the monuments of past events." *Lives* 3.427 1781
12. Description falls short of reality. See DESCRIPTION 11, 12 1783
13. *"He censured a writer of entertaining Travels for assuming a feigned character, saying . . . 'He carries out one lye; we know not how many he brings back.' " *Bos.* 4.320 Date?

Truth. See also NATURE; AIM OF WRITING; TRAVEL. Compare FICTION; PROBABILITY; MYTHOLOGY; etc. For the unreality of pastoral poetry, see PASTORAL; and for love poetry's misrepresentation of life, see under AMOROUS VERSES

1. Epitaphs "ought always to be written with regard to truth." See EPITAPH 1 1740

2. "... preserve an unvaried regard to truth." See CHANGE OF OPINIONS 1   1744
3. "... the mind ... naturally loves truth." See DRAMA 55   1744
4. "... his [Savage's] friend had too much tenderness to reply that next to the crime of writing contrary to what he thought, was that of writing without thinking." *Lives* 2.361   1744
5. "In Reason, Nature, Truth he dares to trust." (Referring to *Irene*.) See DRAMA 57   1749
6. Criticism, the daughter of Labour and of Truth, carries a torch, lighted by Truth, which shows everything in its true form. See CRITICISM 26   1750
7. In biography, "if we owe regard to the memory of the dead, there is yet more respect to be paid to knowledge, to virtue, and to truth." *Wks.* 5.386. (*Ram.* 60.) (For further discussion of whether the biographer should tell the whole truth, see BIOGRAPHY 2, 10, 14, 15, 19, 20)   1750
8. "... the duty of criticism is ... to promulgate the determinations of truth, whatever she shall dictate." See CRITICISM 29   1751
9. Truth, Falsehood and Fiction—an allegory. See FICTION 2   1751
10. J.'s critical principles in *The Rambler* based "on unalterable and evident truth." *Wks.* 7.396. (*Ram.* 208)   1752
11. The fact that Virgil's two best pastorals (first and tenth) were produced by actual occurrences "may ... be of use to prove, that we can always feel more than we can imagine, and that the most artful fiction must give way to truth." *Wks.* 9.76. (*Adv.* 92)   1753
12. "There is no crime more infamous than the violation of truth." (Not specifically applied to literature.) *Wks.* 8.75. (*Idl.* 20)   1758
13. Greater truth to be expected in autobiography than in

biography. See BIOGRAPHY 5. (Compare MEMOIRS 1)
1759

14. "Between falsehood and useless truth there is little difference." See HISTORY 9   1759

15. ". . . the mind can only repose on the stability of truth." See NATURE 31   1765

16. *J. implies that the true critic "shews all beauty to depend on truth." Bos. 2.90. For context, see BURKE 6   1769

17. *"Nothing is good but what is consistent with truth or probability." Bos. 5.361. (Hebrides, 26 Oct.)   1773

18. Tragedy based on truth desirable. See DRAMA 70
1779

19. "Poets, indeed, profess fiction, but the legitimate end of fiction is the conveyance of truth." Lives 1.271
1779

20. "But the basis of all excellence is truth." This principle applied to love poems. See AMOROUS VERSES 3
1779

21. "Truth indeed is always truth, and reason is always reason; they have an intrinsick and unalterable value; and constitute that intellectual gold which defies destruction," but it "may be so buried in impurities as not to pay the cost of . . . extraction." (DICTION 18. Compare DICTION 2: Truth "owes part of her charms to her ornaments.") Lives 1.59   1779

22. ". . . subtilty and harmony united are still feeble, when opposed to truth." Lives 1.380   1779

23. "The substance of the narrative [of *Paradise Lost*] is truth; and as truth allows no choice, it is, like necessity, superior to rule." Lives 1.174   1779

24. "But Wit can stand its ground against Truth only a little while. The honours due to learning have been justly distributed by the decision of posterity." Lives 3.11   1781

25. Reality more arresting than fiction. See POPE 58
 1781
26. Among J.'s reasons why *Eloisa to Abelard* is one of the best subjects possible, is its truth. "The heart naturally loves truth. The adventures and misfortunes of this illustrious pair are known from undisputed history. . . . So new and so affecting is their story that it supersedes invention, and imagination ranges at full liberty without straggling into scenes of fable." *Lives* 3.235 1781
27. "Where truth is sufficient to fill the mind, fiction is worse than useless; the counterfeit debases the genuine." See MYTHOLOGY 28 1781
28. "I do not see that *The Bard* [Gray] promotes any truth, moral or political." *Lives* 3.438. See also FICTION 12 1781
29. "All truth is valuable, and satirical criticism may be considered as useful when it rectifies error and improves judgement: he that refines the publick taste is a publick benefactor." *Lives* 3.242 1781
30. Writers cautioned against even little violations of truth. *Bos.* 4.361 1784

Unity. See under DRAMA: *Rules* for "the unities"
 1. *Definition:* "4. Principle of dramatick writing, by which the tenour of the story, and propriety of representation is preserved. [e.g.] The *unities* of time, place, and action, are exactly observed. *Dryden's Pref. to All for Love.*" *Dict.* 1755

Unnatural, The. See NATURE; FICTION; MYTHOLOGY; MARVELLOUS, THE; etc.

Variety. For variety in versification, see VERSIFICATION 2, 7, 17, 26, 30. For the slight opportunity for variety in pastoral poetry, see PASTORAL 1
 1. Little sagacity needed if the critic is determined to find

faults: "for, in every work of imagination, the disposition of parts, the insertion of incidents, and use of decorations, may be varied a thousand ways with equal propriety." See CRITICISM 69   1750

2. The periodical writer "who endeavours to gain many readers must try various arts of invitation, essay every avenue of pleasure, and make frequent changes in his methods of approach." *Wks.* 5.155. (*Ram.* 23) 1750

3. Though "right and wrong are immutable," the moralist has many modes of composition from which to choose. Though the passions are few, "the alterations which time is always making in the modes of life" are a source of variety "to attract the notice and favour of mankind." "Thus love is uniform, but courtship is perpetually varying," etc. . . . "The complaint, therefore, that all topicks are preoccupied, is nothing more than the murmur of ignorance or idleness, by which some discourage others and some themselves: the mutability of mankind will always furnish writers with new images, and the luxuriance of fancy may always embellish them with new decorations." *Wks.* 9.78-83. (*Adv.* 95)   1753

4. ". . . upon the whole, all pleasure consists in variety." *Shak. Pref.*, Raleigh, 17   1765

5. The unities of time and place "by circumscribing the extent of the drama, lessen its variety" and "are always to be sacrificed to the nobler beauties of variety and instruction." *Shak. Pref.*, Raleigh, 29-30   1765

6. The mind gratified by the "endless diversity" of Shakespeare. See SHAKESPEARE 76   1765

7. "The great source of pleasure is variety. Uniformity must tire at last, though it be uniformity of excellence. We love to expect; and, when expectation is disappointed or gratified, we want to be again expecting. For this impatience of the present, whoever would please must make provision. The skilful writer *irritat, mulcet*; makes a due distribution of the still and ani-

mated parts. It is for want of this artful intertexture and those necessary changes that the whole of a book may be tedious, though all the parts are praised." *Lives* 1.212   1779

8. Shenstone's *Elegies* too much alike: ". . . his thoughts are pure and simple, but wanting combination they want variety. . . . That of which the essence is uniformity will be soon described." *Lives* 3.355   1781

9. Diversity necessary in descriptive poetry. See DESCRIPTION 7   1781

Versification. See also BLANK VERSE AND RHYME; DRAMA: *Versification*; ODE; PINDARIC VERSE; SONNET

1. *Its importance:* Versification, "or the art of modulating his numbers, is indispensably necessary to a poet. . . . [See POETRY 7.] I suppose there are few who do not feel themselves touched by poetical melody, and who will not confess that they are more or less moved by the same thoughts, as they are conveyed by different sounds, and more affected by the same words in one order than in another. The perception of harmony is indeed conferred upon men in degrees very unequal, but there are none who do not perceive it, or to whom a regular series of proportionate sounds cannot give delight." *Wks.* 6.92. (*Ram.* 86)   1751

2. *Heroic measure:* "The heroick measure of the *English* language may be properly considered as pure or mixed. It is pure when the accent rests upon every second syllable through the whole line. . . . The repetition of this sound or percussion at equal times, is the most complete harmony of which a single verse is capable, and should therefore be exactly kept in distichs, and generally in the last line of a paragraph, that the ear may rest without any sense of imperfection. But, to preserve the series of sounds untransposed in a long composition, is not only very difficult but tiresome and

disgusting; for we are soon wearied with the perpetual recurrence of the same cadence. Necessity has therefore enforced the mixed measure, in which some variation of the accents is allowed; this, though it always injures the harmony of the line considered by itself, yet compensates the loss by relieving us from the continual tyranny of the same sound, and makes us more sensible of the harmony of the pure measure. . . . In the first pair of syllables the accent may deviate from the rigour of exactness, without any unpleasing diminution of harmony. . . . But, excepting in the first pair of syllables, which may be considered as arbitrary, a poet who, not having the invention or knowledge of *Milton*, has more need to allure his audience by musical cadences, should seldom suffer more than one aberration from the rule in any single verse. . . . The detriment which the measure suffers by this inversion of the accents is sometimes less perceptible, when the verses are carried one into another, but is remarkably striking in this place, where the vicious verse concludes a period; and is yet more offensive in rhyme, when we regularly attend to the flow of every single line." The ancients did not confound the iambic and the trochaic: "established practice" is against it. "But where the senses are to judge, authority is not necessary, the ear is sufficient to detect dissonance, nor should I have sought auxiliaries on such an occasion against any name but that of *Milton*." *Wks.* 6.92-6. (*Ram.* 86)
  1751

3. *Its importance:* ". . . it is certain that without this petty knowledge [of accents and pauses] no man can be a poet; and that from the proper disposition of single sounds results that harmony that adds force to reason, and gives grace to sublimity; that shackles attention, and governs passions." *Wks.* 6.103-4. (*Ram.* 88)
  1751

4. *Consonants:* "That verse may be melodious and pleas-

ing, it is necessary, not only that the words be so ranged as that the accent may fall on its proper place, but that the syllables themselves be so chosen as to flow smoothly into one another. This is to be effected by a proportionate mixture of vowels and consonants, and by tempering the mute consonants with liquids and semivowels. The *Hebrew* grammarians have observed, that it is impossible to pronounce two consonants without the intervention of a vowel, or without some emission of the breath between one and the other; this is longer and more perceptible, as the sounds of the consonants are less harmonically conjoined, and, by consequence, the flow of the verse is longer interrupted." A line of monosyllables in English almost always harsh, because "being of *Teutonick* original, or formed by contraction" they "commonly begin and end with consonants." *Wks.* 6.104. (*Ram.* 88) 1751

5. *Elision of vowels:* Milton "has indeed been more attentive to his syllables than to his accents, and does not often offend by collisions of consonants, or openings of vowels upon each other, at least not more often than other writers who have had less important or complicated subjects to take off their care from the cadence of their lines. The great peculiarity of *Milton's* versification, compared with that of later poets, is the elision of one vowel before another, or the suppression of the last syllable of a word ending with a vowel, when a vowel begins the following word." This licence practised in other languages, but unsuited "to the genius of the *English* tongue," which is already "overstocked with consonants" because of the gradual detruncation of our syllables through non-pronunciation of final *e* and of other vowels. "*Milton* therefore seems to have somewhat mistaken the nature of our language, of which the chief defect is ruggedness and asperity, and has left our harsh cadences yet harsher. But his elisions are not all equally to be censured; in

some syllables they may be allowed, and perhaps in a few may be safely imitated. The abscission of a vowel is undoubtedly vicious when it is strongly sounded, and makes, with its associate consonant, a full and audible syllable." Elision more justifiable when the vowel "is so faintly pronounced in common speech, that the loss of it in poetry is scarcely perceived. . . . Yet even these contractions encrease the roughness of a language too rough already; and though in long poems they may be sometimes suffered, it never can be faulty to forbear them." (cf. *infra* 14) *Wks.* 6.106-8. (*Ram.* 88) 1751

6. *Epic and tragic measure differentiated:* Milton's frequent use of "the hypermetrical or redundant line of eleven syllables . . . but though they [such verses] are not unpleasing or dissonant, they ought not to be admitted into heroick poetry, since the narrow limits of our language allow us no other distinction of epick and tragick measures, than is afforded by the liberty of changing at will the terminations of the dramatick lines, and bringing them by that relaxation of metrical rigour nearer to prose." *Wks.* 6.108-9. (*Ram.* 88) 1751

7. *Pauses:* "As harmony is the end of poetical measures, no part of a verse ought to be so separated from the rest as not to remain still more harmonious than prose, or to shew, by the disposition of the tones, that it is part of a verse." Proceeding from this fundamental position, J. eliminates all but the five middle pauses in the English heroic line as unharmonious on the ground that "the order and regularity of accents cannot well be perceived in a succession of fewer than three syllables." This general rule not unalterable however: "something may be allowed to variety, and something to the adaptation of the numbers to the subject; but it will be found generally necessary, and the ear will seldom fail to suffer by its neglect. . . . When the

pause falls upon the third syllable or the seventh, the harmony is better preserved; but as the third and seventh are weak syllables, the period leaves the ear unsatisfied, and in expectation of the remaining part of the verse. . . . It may be, I think, established as a rule, that a pause which concludes a period should be made for the most part upon a strong syllable, as the fourth and sixth; but those pauses which only suspend the sense may be placed upon the weaker." As the fifth syllable, like the third and seventh, is weak, it follows by the process of elimination that: "The noblest and most majestick pauses which our versification admits, are upon the fourth and sixth syllables, which are both strongly sounded in a pure and regular verse, and at either of which the line is so divided, that both members participate of harmony. . . . But far above all others, if I can give any credit to my own ear, is the rest upon the sixth syllable, which taking in a complete compass of sound, such as is sufficient to constitute one of our lyrick measures, makes a full and solemn close. Some passages which conclude at this stop, I could never read without some strong emotions of delight or admiration." *Wks.* 6.117-20. (*Ram.* 90) 1751

8. *"Representative metre"*: "There is nothing in the art of versifying so much exposed to the power of imagination as the accommodation of the sound to the sense, or the representation of particular images, by the flow of the verse in which they are expressed. Every student has innumerable passages, in which he, and perhaps he alone, discovers such resemblances." Homer's conscious use of a "representative metre" greatly exaggerated by the imagination of Dionysius of Halicarnassus. Virgil, however, not "less happy in this than in the other graces of versification." Pope's celebrated attempt at "representative metre" (*Essay on Crit.* Pt. II, ll. 366-73), though "laboured with great attention," far from successful. (See POPE 11 for analysis of this

passage. cf. also *infra* 9, 18, 22, 33.) *Wks.* 6.129-37.
(*Ram.* 92) 1751

9. *"Representative metre"*: Every good poet will unconsciously suit his measure to his thought in a general way. But: "It is scarcely to be doubted, that on many occasions we make the musick which we imagine ourselves to hear; that we modulate the poem by our own disposition, and ascribe to the numbers the effects of the sense." Undeniably, Homer, Virgil and Milton consciously used "representative metre" to convey "particular and distinct images." But the effect is often casual, "to be attributed rather to fortune than skill," since "every language has many words formed in imitation of the noises which they signify. . . . But many beauties of this kind, which the moderns, and perhaps the ancients, have observed, seem to be the product of blind reverence acting upon fancy. . . . The representative power of poetick harmony consists of sound and measure; of the force of the syllables singly considered, and of the time in which they are pronounced. Sound can resemble nothing but sound, and time can measure nothing but motion and duration. The criticks, however, have struck out other similitudes; nor is there any irregularity of numbers which credulous admiration cannot discover to be eminently beautiful. . . . We may, however, without giving way to enthusiasm, admit that some beauties of this kind may be produced. A sudden stop at an unusual syllable may image the cessation of action, or the pause of discourse. . . . The measure or time in pronouncing may be varied so as very strongly to represent, not only the modes of external motion, but the quick or slow succession of ideas, and consequently the passions of the mind. This at least was the power of the spondaick and dactylick harmony, but our language can reach no eminent diversities of sound. We can indeed sometimes, by encumbering and retarding the line, shew the difficulty of a progress made by

strong efforts and with frequent interruptions, or mark a slow and heavy motion. . . . It is not indeed to be expected, that the sound should always assist the meaning, but it ought never to counteract it." True and false examples of "representative metre" in Milton. (See MILTON 20. cf. also *supra* 8 and *infra* 18, 22, 33) *Wks.* 6.143-51. (*Ram.* 94)   1751

10. *The Spenserian stanza:* ". . . is at once difficult and unpleasing; tiresome to the ear by its uniformity, and to the attention by its length." See IMITATION 6
        1751

11. *Versification:* "is the arrangement of a certain number of syllables according to certain laws." *Gram. of the Eng. Tongue, Dict.*   1755

12. In iambic measures "the accents are to be placed on even syllables; and every line considered by itself is more harmonious, as this rule is more strictly observed." *Gram. of the Eng. Tongue, Dict.*   1755

13. *Alexandrines:* "The pause in the Alexandrine must be at the sixth syllable." *Gram. of the Eng. Tongue, Dict.* (cf. *supra* 7)   1755

14. "Our versification admits of few licences," a few elisions excepted. *Gram. of the Eng. Tongue, Dict.* (cf. *supra* 5)   1755

15. *Metrical limitations:* ". . . poetical measures have not in any language been so far refined as to provide for the subdivisions of passion. They can only be adapted to general purposes; but the particular and minuter propriety must be sought only in the sentiment and language." For application of this, see POPE 57. *Wks.* 15.472   1756

16. *Rhyme words:* J. objects to close of verse with *too* in a short composition: "every rhyme should be a word of emphasis, nor can this rule be safely neglected, except where the length of the poem makes slight inaccuracies excusable, or allows room for beauties

sufficient to overpower the effects of petty faults."
Lives 3.258. cf. *infra* 17, 19, 20, 34   1756

17. *Common rhymes:* "Unvaried rhymes, says this writer [J. Warton in *Essay on Pope*], highly disgust readers of a good ear. It is surely not the ear but the mind that is offended. The fault rising from the use of common rhymes is, that by reading the past line the second may be guessed, and half the composition loses the grace of novelty." (cf. *supra* 16; *infra* 19, 20, 34.) *Wks.* 15.475. (Review of J. Warton's *Essay on Pope*)
     1756

18. *"Representative metre"* satirized: Dick Minim's discovery of such beauties in *Hudibras* and *Paradise Lost. Wks.* 8.242-3, 246. (*Idl.* 60, 61)   1759

19. "Rhyme . . . has this convenience, that sentences stand more independent on each other, and striking passages are therefore easily selected and retained." *Lives* 1.436   1779

20. Waller's faults of versification: frequent use of the expletive *do* (cf. *infra* 27); "his rhymes are sometimes weak words": e.g., *so*; double rhymes in heroic verse (cf. *supra* 16, 17, 19; *infra* 34); obsolete terminations of verbs, e.g. *waxeth*; the final syllable of the preterite sometimes retained, e.g., *amazed*, "of which I know not whether it is not to the detriment of our language that we have totally rejected them"; an occasional triplet. *Lives* 1.293-4   1779

21. "The great pleasure of verse arises from the known measure of the lines and uniform structure of the stanzas, by which the voice is regulated and the memory relieved." See PINDARIC VERSE 1   1779

22. *"Representative metre":* J. questions Cowley's success in adapting sound to sense, (with one notable exception). "Verse can imitate only sound and motion." *Lives* 1.62-3   1779

23. *Hemistichs:* ". . . all that can be done by a broken

verse, a line intersected by a *cæsura* and a full stop will equally effect." *Lives* 1.63   1779
24. *Closed couplets:* ". . . the art of concluding their sense in couplets; which has perhaps been with rather too much constancy pursued." *Lives* 1.81   1779
25. ". . . quatrains of lines alternately consisting of eight and six syllables make the most soft and pleasing of our lyrick measures." *Lives* 1.467. cf. *infra* 35   1779
26. *The triplet and the alexandrine:* ". . . are not universally approved. . . . In examining their propriety it is to be considered that the essence of verse is regularity, and its ornament is variety. To write verse is to dispose syllables and sounds harmonically by some known and settled rule—a rule however lax enough to substitute similitude for identity, to admit change without breach of order, and to relieve the ear without disappointing it. Thus a Latin hexameter is formed from dactyls and spondees differently combined; the English heroick admits of acute or grave syllables variously disposed. The Latin never deviates into seven feet, or exceeds the number of seventeen syllables; but the English alexandrine breaks the lawful bounds, and surprises the reader with two syllables more than he expected. The effect of the triplet is the same: the ear has been accustomed to expect a new rhyme in every couplet; but is on a sudden surprised with three rhymes together, to which the reader could not accommodate his voice did he not obtain notice of the change from the braces of the margins. Surely there is something unskilful in the necessity of such mechanical direction. Considering the metrical art simply as a science, and consequently excluding all casualty, we must allow that triplets and alexandrines inserted by caprice are interruptions of that constancy to which science aspires. And though the variety which they produce may very justly be desired, yet to make our poetry exact there ought to be some stated mode of admitting them.

But till some such regulation can be formed, I wish them still to be retained in their present state. They are sometimes grateful to the reader, and sometimes convenient to the poet." *Lives* 1.467-8   1779

27. Lines "weakened with expletives." *Lives* 2.233. See also *ib.* 2.131. cf. *supra* 20   Ptd. 1780

28. When Prior "commenced poet we had not recovered from our Pindarick infatuation; but he probably lived to be convinced that the essence of verse is order and consonance." *Lives* 2.210   Ptd. 1780

29. *Metrical regularity:* "Both the odes [Dryden's and Pope's *Odes for St. Cecilia's Day*] want the essential constituent of metrical compositions, the stated recurrence of settled numbers." *Lives* 3.227   1781

30. *"The most perfect fabrick of English verse":* "Poetical expression includes sound as well as meaning. 'Musick,' says Dryden, 'is inarticulate poetry'; among the excellences of Pope, therefore, must be mentioned the melody of his metre. By perusing the works of Dryden he discovered the most perfect fabrick of English verse . . . his poetry has been censured as too uniformly musical, and as glutting the ear with unvaried sweetness. I suspect this objection to be the cant of those who judge by principles rather than perception; and who would even themselves have less pleasure in his works if he had tried to relieve attention by studied discords, or affected to break his lines and vary his pauses." *Lives* 3.248   1781

31. *Over-refinement:* "But though he [Pope] was thus careful of his versification he did not oppress his powers with superfluous rigour. He seems to have thought with Boileau that the practice of writing might be refined till the difficulty should overbalance the advantage." *Lives* 3.249   1781

32. *Over-refinement:* "New sentiments and new images others may produce, but to attempt any further improvement of versification [over Pope's] will be dan-

gerous. Art and diligence have now done their best, and what shall be added will be the effort of tedious toil and needless curiosity." *Lives* 3.251. See *supra* 31
    1781

33. *"Representative metre"*: "This notion of representative metre [Pope's "the sound must seem an echo to the sense"], and the desire of discovering frequent adaptations of the sound to the sense, have produced, in my opinion, many wild conceits and imaginary beauties. All that can furnish this representation are the sounds of the words considered singly, and the time in which they are pronounced." Sound words comparatively few; the time of pronunciation more varied "in the dactylick measures of the learned languages, . . . but, our language having little flexibility, our verses can differ very little in their cadence. . . . Motion, however, may be in some sort exemplified; and yet it may be suspected that even in such resemblances the mind often governs the ear, and the sounds are estimated by their meaning." J. illustrates this by parody of four lines from Broome's translation of the *Odyssey*; and by comparison of two passages from Pope. (See POPE: VERSIFICATION 13.) "Beauties of this kind are commonly fancied; and when real are technical and nugatory, not to be rejected and not to be solicited." *Lives* 3.230-2
    1781

34. *Rhymes* should not be too distant nor "arranged with too little regard to established use" in short compositions. See ODE 4. See also *Lives* 1.440. cf. *supra* 16, 17, 19, 20
    1781

35. The quatrain of ten syllables not particularly suited to elegy. See ELEGY 9. cf. *supra* 25
    1781

36. Watts "writes too often without regular measures, and too often in blank verse; the rhymes are not always sufficiently correspondent." *Lives* 3.311
    1781

37. Collins "puts his words out of the common order, seeming to think, with some later candidates for fame, that

not to write prose is certainly to write poetry. His lines commonly are of slow motion, clogged and impeded with clusters of consonants." *Lives* 3.341
1781

Version

1. *Definition:* "3. Translation. . . . 4. The act of translating." *Dict.*[1]   1755

Vulgar

1. *Definition of vulgar* (adj.) : "1. Plebian; suiting to the common people. . . . 2. Mean, low; being of the common rate. . . . 3. Publick; commonly bruited." *Dict.*[2]   1755
2. *Definition of vulgar* (noun): "The common people." *Dict.*   1755

Wit

1. Allegory of Wit and Learning: their dissensions and final union, resulting in "a numerous progeny of ARTS and SCIENCES." *Wks.* 5.144-9. (*Ram.* 22)   1750
2. "A wit, Mr. *Rambler*, in the dialect of ladies, is not always a man, who, by the action of a vigorous fancy upon comprehensive knowledge, brings distant ideas unexpectedly together, who by some peculiar acuteness discovers resemblance in objects dissimilar to common eyes, or by mixing heterogeneous notions dazzles the attention with sudden scintillations of conceit. A lady's wit is a man who can make ladies laugh. . . ." *Wks.* 7.4. (*Ram.* 141)   1751
3. "Eumathes" in *The Rambler* (194), defines wit as

---

[1] e.g., Pope's *Iliad* "the noblest version of poetry which the world has ever seen." *Lives* 3.119. The only other meanings given are "change, transformation"; and "change of direction."

[2] *Lycidas:* "Its form is that of a pastoral, easy, vulgar, and therefore disgusting," (*Lives* 1.163); Akenside's "diction is certainly . . . elegant as it is not vulgar," (*ib.* 3.418. In the 1st ed., "valuable as it is not common.")

"the unexpected copulation of ideas, the discovery of some occult relation between images in appearance remote from each other; an effusion of wit, therefore, presupposes an accumulation of knowledge; a memory stored with notions, which the imagination may cull out to compose new assemblages." *Wks.* 7.314   1752

4. *Definition:* "1. The powers of the mind; the mental faculties; the intellects. . . . 2. Imagination; quickness of fancy. . . . 3. Sentiments produced by quickness of fancy. . . . 4. A man of fancy. . . . 5. A man of genius. . . . 6. Sense; judgment. . . . 7. In the plural. Sound mind; intellect not crazed. . . . 8. Contrivance; stratagem; power of expedients. . . ." *Dict.*   1755

5. Floretta drinks magic draught, which bestows wit upon her: "As she returned she felt new successions of imagery rise in her mind, and whatever her memory offered to her imagination, assumed a new form, and connected itself with things to which it seemed before to have no relation." Wit enables her to detect and expose defects, until she becomes shunned and hated. *Wks.* 14.372 *ff.* (*The Fountains: a Fairy Tale*)   1766

6. *"Wit is wit, by whatever means it is produced; and, if good, will appear so at all times." *Bos.* 3.41   1776

7. ". . . Pope's account of wit is undoubtedly erroneous; he depresses it below its natural dignity, and reduces it from strength of thought to happiness of language. If by a more noble and more adequate conception that be considered as Wit which is at once natural and new, that which though not obvious is, upon its first production, acknowledged to be just; if it be that, which he that never found it, wonders how he missed; to wit of this kind the metaphysical poets have seldom risen. . . . But Wit, abstracted from its effects upon the hearer, may be more rigorously and philosophically considered as a kind of *discordia concors*; a combination of dissimilar images, or discovery

of occult resemblances in things apparently unlike. Of wit, thus defined, they have more than enough." etc. *Lives* 1.19-20   1779

8. "These conceits Addison calls mixed wit, that is, wit which consists of thoughts true in one sense of the expression, and false in the other. Addison's representation is sufficiently indulgent: that confusion of images may entertain for a moment, but being unnatural it soon grows wearisome." *Lives* 1.41   1779

9. "If inexhaustible wit could give perpetual pleasure no eye would ever leave half-read the work of Butler; for what poet has ever brought so many remote images so happily together?" *Lives* 1.212   1779

10. "But Wit can stand its ground against Truth only a little while." See TRUTH 24   1781

11. *Pope's definition of "true wit" both "false and foolish." See POPE 27   1782

PART TWO
Authors and Works

PART TWO
Authors and Works

Addison, Joseph. (GENERAL CRITICISM)
1. Example of barbarous diction. *Wks.* 9.188   1747
2. Critical papers of A. recommended, for teaching the art of poetry. See POETRY 3   1748
3. Roscommon is "perhaps the only correct writer in verse before Addison." *Lives* 1.235   1748
4. An example in A. of a false interpretation of the ancients. See OPENING OF A WORK 2   1751
5. J. drew 4.3% of the literary illustrations in his *Dictionary* from Addison, from Shakespeare 15.6%, Dryden 9.2%, Milton 7.8%, Pope 3.5% Spenser 2.9%. See J. W. Good's *Studies in the Milton Tradition*, 198 n 112   1755
6. *"Mr. Addison was, to be sure, a great man; his learning was not profound; but his morality, his humour, and his elegance of writing, set him very high." *Bos.* 1.425   1763
7. *Mrs. Piozzi recalls J. "earnestly recommending Addison's works to Mr. Woodhouse as a model for imitation. 'Give nights and days, Sir (said he), to the study of Addison, if you mean either to be a good writer, or what is more worth, an honest man.'" *John. Misc.* 1.233   1765
8. *A. did not go deeply into Italian literature. "He shews a great deal of French learning." *Bos.* 5.310. (*Hebrides*, 14 Oct.)   1773
9. *Swift inferior to Addison in delicate humour. See SWIFT 5   1773

10. "The authority of Addison is great; yet the voice of the people, when to please the people is the purpose, deserves regard." J. sides with the people against Edmund Smith's *Phædra and Hippolitus*, praised by A. *Lives* 2.16   1779

11. *As poet:* (*Lives* 2) His poetry "has not often those felicities of diction which give lustre to sentiments, or that vigour of sentiment that animates diction: there is little of ardour, vehemence, or transport; there is very rarely the awfulness of grandeur, and not very often the splendour of elegance. He thinks justly; but he thinks faintly. . . . Yet, if he seldom reaches supreme excellence, he rarely sinks into dulness" or absurdity. Calmness and equability; "sometimes with little that delights, but seldom with any thing that offends." (127) "His poetry is polished and pure: the product of a mind too judicious to commit faults, but not sufficiently vigorous to attain excellence. He has sometimes a striking line, or a shining paragraph; but in the whole he is warm rather than fervid, and shews more dexterity than strength." However, "one of our earliest examples of correctness." *Versification:* learned from Dryden; he debased rather than refined it. Dissonant rhymes; broken lines in his *Georgick*; uses both triplets and alexandrines. Careless of "mere structure of verses." "But his lines are very smooth in *Rosamond*, and too smooth in *Cato*." (145)   Ptd. 1780

12. *As prose writer:* (*Lives* 2) "His prose is the model of the middle style; on grave subjects not formal, on light occasions not groveling; pure without scrupulosity, and exact without apparent elaboration; always equable, and always easy, without glowing words or polished sentences." No ambitious ornaments turn him aside; no "hazardous innovations. His page is always luminous, but never blazes in unexpected splendour." Avoidance of harshness and severity of diction—hence sometimes verbose, "sometimes descends too much to

the language of conversation": yet his idiomatical language contributes to his genuine Anglicism. "What he attempted, he performed; he is never feeble, and he did not wish to be energetick; he is never rapid, and he never stagnates. His sentences have neither studied amplitude, nor affected brevity; his periods, though not diligently rounded, are voluble and easy. Whoever wishes to attain an English style, familiar but not coarse, and elegant but not ostentatious, must give his days and nights to the volumes of Addison." (149-50)
Ptd. 1780

13. *As critic:* (*Lives* 2) ". . . a name which the present generation is scarcely willing to allow him." (145). But J. defends A.—just the type of criticism his age needed. "His purpose was to infuse literary curiosity by gentle and unsuspected conveyance into the gay, the idle, and the wealthy. . . . His attempts succeeded; enquiry was awakened, and comprehension expanded . . . by the blandishments of gentleness and facility he has made Milton an universal favourite." (146-7.) His "lower disquisitions": his serious criticism of *Chevy Chase* exposed him to ridicule. (147.) *Remarks on Ovid* contains "specimens of criticism sufficiently subtle and refined; let them peruse likewise his *Essays on Wit* and on *The Pleasures of Imagination*, in which he founds art on the base of nature, and draws the principles of invention from dispositions inherent in the mind of man with skill and elegance, such as his contemners will not easily attain." (148) Ptd. 1780

14. *As moralist:* (*Lives* 2) A. "employed wit on the side of virtue and religion. He not only made the proper use of wit himself, but taught it to others; and from his time it has been generally subservient to the cause of reason and of truth. . . . He has restored virtue to its dignity, and taught innocence not to be ashamed. This is an elevation of literary character, 'above all

Greek, above all Roman fame.'" (125-6.) A safe teacher of wisdom. (148.) Truth "wears a thousand dresses, and in all is pleasing." (149.)   Ptd. 1780

15. *As student of human nature:* (*Lives* 2) "He had read with critical eyes the important volume of human life, and knew the heart of man from the depths of stratagem to the surface of affectation." (121; see also *ib.* 2.124.) "As a describer of life and manners . . . perhaps the first of the first rank." (148)   Ptd. 1780

16. *As humourist:* (*Lives* 2) His humour, peculiar to himself; "so happily diffused as to give the grace of novelty to domestick scenes and daily occurrences. He never 'outsteps the modesty of nature,' nor raises merriment or wonder by the violation of truth. His figures neither divert by distortion, nor amaze by aggravation. He copies life with so much fidelity that he can be hardly said to invent." Yet air of originality over all. (148)   Ptd. 1780

17. *J., in his conversation as in his writings, extols A.'s prose. Mrs. Piozzi, however, adds that she fancied J. "did never like, though he always thought fit to praise it" like a man who praises elegant porcelain, but prefers to "eat off *plate*." John. Misc. 1.283   Date?

18. *"*He is the Raphael of Essay Writers.*" John. Misc. 1.466-7.(Murphy)   Date?

Addison. (WORKS)

19. *Campaign, The.* J. thinks J. Warton's criticism (A "Gazette in Rhyme") too severe. Who has described war more justly or forcefully? A. "not blinded by the dust of learning: his images are not borrowed merely from books." Shows a "rejection and contempt of fiction . . . rational and manly" by endowing his hero not with personal prowess and "'mighty bone'" but with self-command. (See *Lives* 1.317.) Simile of the angel not strictly a simile but an exemplification. (See SIMILES 4.) "Just and noble; but the simile gives almost the

same images a second time." *Lives* 2.128-31 Ptd. 1780
20. *Cato.* J. Warton, in *Essay on Pope*, "justly censures Cato for want of action and of characters; but scarcely does justice to the sublimity of some speeches and the philosophical exactness in the sentiments." The simile of mount Atlas "is indeed common." *Wks.* 15.476-7. (Review of Warton's *Essay*) 1756
21. *Cato.* "Many lines in *Cato's* soliloquy are at once easy and sublime." *Wks.* 8.310. (*Idl.* 77) 1759
22. *Cato.* "*Addison* speaks the language of poets, and *Shakespeare* of men. We find in *Cato* innumerable beauties which enamour us of its authour, but we see nothing that acquaints us with human sentiments or human actions; we place it with the fairest and the noblest progeny which judgment propagates by conjunction with learning, but *Othello* is the vigorous and vivacious offspring of observation impregnated by genius. *Cato* affords a splendid exhibition of artificial and fictitious manners, and delivers just and noble sentiments, in diction easy, elevated and harmonious, but its hopes and fears communicate no vibration to the heart; the composition refers us only to the writer; we pronounce the name of *Cato*, but we think on *Addison.*" *Shak. Pref.*, Raleigh, 33-4 1765
23. *Cato.* (*Lives* 2) The play's greatest weakness is in the scenes of love. J. thinks that these are not added, as Pope said, for "the love is so intimately mingled with the whole action that it cannot easily be thought extrinsick and adventitious"—if taken away, what left? (103.) J. criticizes last six lines: examples of tautology, redundancy, copying from Dryden, and absurdity: "*Discord* is made to produce *Strife*." (121-2.) "Unquestionably the noblest production of Addison's genius." The popular judgement on the whole right: "a poem in dialogue rather than a drama, rather a succession of just sentiments in elegant language than a representation of natural affections, or of any state prob-

able or possible in human life. Nothing here 'excites or assuages emotion'; here is 'no magical power of raising phantastick terror or wild anxiety.' The events are expected without solicitate, and are remembered without joy or sorrow. Of the agents we have no care: we consider not what they are doing, or what they are suffering; we wish only to know what they have to say." We leave Cato to the Gods—above our care. Not one of the other characters "strongly attracts either affection or esteem. But they are made the vehicles of such sentiments and such expression that there is scarcely a scene in the play which the reader does not wish to impress upon his memory." (132-3)   Ptd. 1780

24. *Cato.* J. defends A.'s neglect of poetic justice. J. partly agrees with Dennis that characters are unnatural, e.g., Cato. But upon what principles shall we judge heroes and heroines, beings not seen every day? (See DRAMA 11.) Probability of the action and reasonableness of the plan: Dennis most formidable when attacking these, for A.'s rigorous attention to the "unities" leads to impropriety of scene. *Lives* 2.135-6   Ptd. 1780

25. *Cato.* *"He thought *Cato* the best model of tragedy we had; yet he used to say, of all things, the most ridiculous would be, to see a girl cry at the representation of it." *John. Misc.* 2.13. (*Hawkins's Apophthegms*)   Date?

26. *Dialogues on Medals.* These "shew that he had perused the works [of Latin poets] with great diligence and skill." *Lives* 2.121   Ptd. 1780

27. *Drummer, The.* J. thinks it is by A.: "the characters are such as Addison would have delineated and the tendency such as Addison would have promoted." J. surprised at its ill reception. *Lives* 2.106   Ptd. 1780

28. *Epilogue* to A. Philips's *Distrest Mother.* Ascribed to Addison. "The most successful Epilogue that was ever yet spoken on the English theatre." Rivalry with Prior's *Epilogue* to *Phædra. Lives* 3.315   1781

29. *Essay on the Georgicks.* "Juvenile, superficial, and uninstructive, without much either of the scholar's learning or the critick's penetration." *Lives* 2.83
    Ptd. 1780
30. *Freeholder, The.* "In argument he [A.] had many equals; but his humour was singular and matchless. Bigotry itself must be delighted with the Tory Foxhunter." "Some strokes less elegant and less decent." *Lives* 2.109   Ptd. 1780
31. *Guardian.* (See also *infra.*) "The character of 'Guardian' was too narrow and too serious: it might properly enough admit both the duties and the decencies of life, but seemed not to include literary speculations, and was in some degree violated by merriment and burlesque . . . it was a continuation of *The Spectator*, with the same elegance and the same variety, till some unlucky sparkle from a Tory paper set Steele's politicks on fire. . . ." *Lives* 2.104-5   Ptd. 1780
32. *Guardian.* "Many of these papers [A.'s *Spectator* and *Guardian* essays] were written with powers truly comick, with nice discrimination of characters, and accurate observation of natural or accidental deviations from propriety." *Lives* 2.106   Ptd. 1780
33. *Latin Compositions.* "Indeed entitled to particular praise." *Lives* 2.82-5   Ptd. 1780
34. *Letter from Italy.* (*Lives* 2) "Justly considered as the most elegant, if not the most sublime, of his poetical productions." (86.) Never over-praised though always praised. "More correct, with less appearance of labour, and more elegant, with less ambition of ornament, than any other of his poems." (128)   Ptd. 1780
35. *Minor English Poems.* (*Lives* 2) "They have little that can employ or require a critick." In Addison's *Verses to Kneller*, the parallel of the Princes and Gods often happy. (144.) His poems addressed to Dryden, to Somers, and to the king, typical of the calmness, cautiousness and unoffending mediocrity of his com-

positions. (127.) *Ode for St. Cecilia's Day.* "Has something in it of Dryden's vigour." (127.) *Account of the . . . English Poets.* "Not worse than his usual strain." (128.) Contains "a very confident and discriminative character of Spenser, whose work he had then never read. So little sometimes is criticism the effect of judgement." (84) Ptd. 1780

36. *Present State of the War.* Exhibits no peculiar powers. *Lives* 2.107 Ptd. 1780

37. *Remarks on . . . Italy.* *"It is a tedious book; and, if it were not attached to Addison's previous reputation, one would not think much of it. Had he written nothing else, his name would not have lived." *Bos.* 5.310. (*Hebrides*, 14 Oct.) 1773

38. *Remarks on . . . Italy.* Observations "such as might be supplied by a hasty view." Most amusing passage —account of San Marino. Of many parts "it is not a very severe censure to say that they might have been written at home. His elegance of language and variegation of prose and verse, however, gain upon the reader." *Lives* 2.87 Ptd. 1780

39. *Rosamond.* J. justifies Addison's choice of "measure" in scene between Grideline and Sir Trusty. See POPE 57 1756

40. *Rosamond.* "Though it is seldom mentioned, [it] is one of the first of Addison's compositions. The subject is well chosen, the fiction is pleasing, and the praise of Marlborough, for which the scene gives an opportunity, is, what perhaps every human excellence must be, the product of good-luck improved by genius." The thoughts, "sometimes great, and sometimes tender." Versification, "easy and gay." Dialogue, "seems commonly better than the songs." Sir Trusty and Grideline (comic characters), "though of no great value, are yet such as the poet intended." "Sir Trusty's account of the death of Rosamond is, I think, too grossly absurd. The whole drama is airy and elegant; engaging in its

process, and pleasing in its conclusion." Addison would probably have excelled in the lighter parts of poetry. *Lives* 2.131-2   Ptd. 1780

41. *Spectator.* See under SPECTATOR.
42. *Tatler.* See under TATLER.
43. *Translations.* "Want the exactness of a scholar." "Too licentiously paraphrastical." "For the most part smooth and easy, and, what is the first excellence of a translator, such as may be read with pleasure by those who do not know the originals." *Lives* 2.145   Ptd. 1780
44. *Whig Examiner.* "In which is employed all the force of gay malevolence and humorous satire. . . . Every reader of every party . . . must wish for more . . . for on no occasion was the genius of Addison more vigorously exerted, and on none did the superiority of his powers more evidently appear." *Lives* 2.107   Ptd. 1780

Aeschylus. See also GREEK DRAMATISTS

1. *Prometheus.* The absurdity of making allegorical figures active persons in *Prometheus.* See ALLEGORY 4
                                                                         1779

Akenside, Mark

1. *"A superior poet both to Gray and Mason." *Bos.* 3.32   1776
2. J. quotes A.'s commendation of Dyer's *The Fleece,* though disagreeing, for A. "upon a poetical question has a right to be heard." *Lives* 3.346-7   1781
3. His early stirrings of genius. *Lives* 3.412   1781
4. *Odes.* *"I see they have published a splendid edition of Akenside's works. One bad ode may be suffered; but a number of them together makes one sick." *Bos.* 2.164   1772
5. *Odes.* (*Lives* 3) "It is not easy to guess why he addicted himself so diligently to lyrick poetry, having

neither the ease and airiness of the lighter, nor the vehemence and elevation of the grander ode. When he lays his ill-fated hand upon his harp his former powers seem to desert him: he has no longer his luxuriance of expression nor variety of images. His thoughts are cold and his words inelegant." (419.) "Of his odes nothing favourable can be said: the sentiments commonly want force, nature, or novelty; the diction is sometimes harsh and uncouth, the stanzas ill-constructed and unpleasant, and the rhymes dissonant or unskilfully disposed, too distant from each other or arranged with too little regard to established use, and therefore perplexing to the ear, which in a short composition has not time to grow familiar with an innovation." Not necessary to examine such compositions singly: they are generally dull, and so not read. (419-20.) *Epistle to Curio.* Originally "written with great vigour and poignancy" but later transformed "into an ode disgraceful only to its author." (419)   1781

6. *Pleasures of Imagination.* *"Sir, I could not read it through." Bos. 2.164   1772

7. *Pleasures of Imagination.* (*Lives* 3) "His greatest work." (412.) "His great work." "Raised expectations . . . not . . . very amply satisfied. It has undoubtedly a just claim to very particular notice as an example of great felicity of genius and uncommon amplitude of acquisitions, of a young mind stored with images, and much exercised in combining and comparing them." J. concerned with his poetry not with his "philosophical or religious tenets." Subject well chosen: "it includes all images that can strike or please, and thus comprises every species of poetical delight." Difficulty in "choice of examples and illustrations, and it is not easy in such exuberance of matter to find the middle point between penury and satiety. The parts seem artificially disposed, with sufficient coherence, so as that they cannot change their places without injury

to the general design." Images "displayed with such luxuriance of expression that they are hidden . . . by a 'Veil of Light'; they are forms fantastically lost under superfluity of dress . . . attention deserts the mind and settles in the ear. The reader wanders through the gay diffusion, sometimes amazed and sometimes delighted; but after many turnings in the flowery labyrinth comes out as he went in. He remarked little, and laid hold on nothing." (416-7.) *Versification:* "Justice requires that praise should not be denied. In the general fabrication of his lines he is perhaps superior to any other writer of blank verse." (417. See BLANK VERSE 20.) "He is to be commended as having fewer artifices of disgust than most of his brethren of the blank song. He rarely either recalls old phrases or twists his metre into harsh inversions. The sense, however, of his words is strained." (418.) *Diction:* "His diction is certainly poetical as it is not prosaick, and elegant as it is not vulgar."[1] (418.) *Revised version:* "He seems to have somewhat contracted his diffusion; but I know not whether he has gained in closeness what he has lost in splendour. In the additional book *The Tale of Solon* is too long." (418.) "One great defect" —his picture of man unfinished—immortality of the soul "scarcely once hinted."[2] (418-9) 1781

Alabaster

1. *Roxana.* "If we produced anything [in Latin verse] worthy of notice before the elegies of Milton it was perhaps Alabaster's *Roxana.*" *Lives* 1.87-8   1779

Anacreon

1. "The gentle Anacreon." *Lives* 1.59   1779
2. *Anacreon's Dove.* "As I never was struck with any

---

[1] In 1st ed.: "His diction is certainly so far poetical as it is not prosaick, and so far valuable as it is not common."
[2] This point first appears in the 1783 ed.

thing in the Greek language till I read *that*, so I never read any thing in the same language since, that pleased me as much." *John. Misc.* 1.176. (Piozzi)   Date?

Arbuthnot, John

1. *"Talking of the eminent writers in Queen Anne's reign, he observed, 'I think Dr. Arbuthnot the first man among them. He was the most universal genius, being an excellent physician, a man of deep learning, and a man of much humour.'" *Bos.* 1.425   1763
2. *Swift inferior to Arbuthnot in coarse humour. See SWIFT 5   1773
3. J. praises his character. "A man estimable for his learning . . . of great comprehension . . . acquainted with ancient literature, and able to animate his mass of knowledge by a bright and active imagination; a scholar with great brilliancy of wit; a wit, who, in the crowd of life, retained and discovered a noble ardour of religious zeal." *Lives* 3.177   1781
4. **Tale of a Tub* attributed to Arbuthnot. See SWIFT 32   Date?
5. *Letters* (included in Pope's Letters): Pope, Swift, and A. compared in this volume. "Arbuthnot [writes] like one who lets thoughts drop from his pen as they rise into his mind." *Lives* 3.160   1781
6. *Memoirs of Scriblerus.* See POPE 46   1781

Ariosto

1. Works commended.[1] See ITALIAN LITERATURE 1   1755
2. His "pravity." "Though the *Deliverance of Jerusalem* may be considered as a sacred subject, the poet has been very sparing of moral instruction." *Lives* 1.179   1779

---

[1] Authenticity of this passage doubtful.

3. "The darling and the pride of Italy" by his power of pleasing. *Lives* 1.454   1779
4. Pope borrows for his own epitaph from "the following tuneless lines" of Ariosto. *Lives* 3.271-2   1781

Aristotle

1. J. accepts Aristotelian law of construction ("a beginning, a middle, and an end"), and bases an examination of *Samson Agonistes* on this "rule laid down by this great critick." See MILTON 49. (See also SHAKESPEARE 91 for justification of Shakespeare's action by Aristotle's rule)   1751
2. *J. explains Aristotle's doctrine of the purging of the passions. *Bos.* 3.39   1776
3. In his examination of the *Oedipus Tyrannus* of Sophocles, J. follows Aristotle's "rules of tragic art." "To pity and to condemn. . . . This is the doctrine of Aristotle and of nature." See SOPHOCLES 2   1779
4. J. examines Cowley's *Davideis* and Milton's *Paradise Lost* along Aristotelian lines. See COWLEY 14 and MILTON 43   1779
5. "Metaphysical" poetry judged by "the father of criticism's" definition. *Lives* 1.19   1779

Ascham, Roger

1. *According to Hawkins, J. formed his style through study of Ascham and others. *Wks.* 1.97   *cir.* 1741
2. "An author undeservedly neglected." *Wks.* 14.487
   1761
3. *Style*, etc. (*Wks.* 4) "The elegance of his [Latin] style." (622.) Gives "an example of diction more natural and more truly English than was used by the common writers of that age." (623.) "*Report and discourse of the affairs in Germany*": written in "a style which to the ears of that age was undoubtedly mellifluous, and which is now a very valuable specimen of

genuine English." (630.) "His usual elegance" in letter-writing. (631.) *Scholemaster:* "Conceived with great vigour, and finished with great accuracy; and perhaps contains the best advice that was ever given for the study of languages." (634.) Unjustified neglect of his works; "his knowledge and his eloquence." (637)   1761

4. "Haddon and Ascham, the pride of Elizabeth's reign, however they may have succeeded in prose, no sooner attempt [Latin] verses than they provoke derision." *Lives* 1.87   1779

Bacon, Francis

1. "Bacon attained to degrees of knowledge scarcely ever reached by any other man." *Wks.* 9.61. (*Adv.* 85)   1753

2. B. "perhaps the only man of later ages, who has any pretensions to dispute with him [Newton] the palm of genius or science." His knowledge of human nature, contrasted with his personal failings. *Wks.* 9.142-3. (*Adv.* 131)   1754

3.*"He [J.] told me [Bos.] that Bacon was a favourite authour with him; but he had never read his works till he was compiling the English Dictionary." *Bos.* 3.194   1777

4. *"Dr. Johnson said that he should be much pleased to write the Life of that man [Bacon], from whose writings alone a Dictionary of the English Language might be compiled."[1] *John. Misc.* 2.302. (Seward)   Date?

5. *Essays*. "Bacon . . . seems to have pleased himself chiefly with his Essays, *which come home to men's business and bosoms*, and of which, therefore, he declares his expectation, that they will live as long as books last." *Wks.* 6.226. (*Ram.* 106)   1751

6. *Essays*. *"Their excellence and their value consisted

---

[1] See Hill's note on this. *Bos.* 3.194 *n* 2

in being the observations of a strong mind operating upon life; and in consequence you find there what you seldom find in other books." *John. Misc.* 2.229. (Reynolds) Date?

Baretti, Giuseppe

1. *Account of the Manners and Customs of Italy.* *"His account of Italy is a very entertaining book . . . and, Sir, I know no man who carries his head higher in conversation than Baretti. There are strong powers in his mind. He has not, indeed, many hooks; but with what hooks he has, he grapples very forcibly." *Bos.* 2.57
1768
2. *Dialogues.* *J. joins Boswell in censuring them: "Nothing odd will do long." *Bos.* 2.449   1776
3. *Journey from London to Genoa.* J. to Mrs. Thrale: "That Baretti's book would please you all I made no doubt. I know not whether the world has ever seen such Travels before. Those whose lot it is to ramble can seldom write, and those who know how to write very seldom ramble." *Letters* 1.165-6   1770

Barnes, Joshua

1. Dedication of a Greek anacreontic to the Duke [of Marlborough] the worst instance of "servile absurdity." *Lives* 2.89. (J. also quotes Barnes, *ib.* 3.81)
Ptd. 1780

Beattie, James

1. *Essay on Truth.* "Beattie's book is, I believe, every day more liked; at least, I like it more, as I look more upon it." *Bos.* 2.201-2   1772
2. *Essay on Truth.* *"Sir, he has written like a man conscious of the truth, and feeling his own strength." *Bos.* 5.29. (*Hebrides*, 15 Aug.)   1773
3. *Essay on Truth.* *"Beattie has confuted him [Hume]" in this essay. *Bos.* 5.274. (*Hebrides*, 1 Oct.)   1773

4. *Essay on Truth.* *A subject of his constant praise. *John. Misc.* 1.429-30. (Murphy)   Date?

5. *Hermit.* *"Such was his [J.'s] sensibility, and so much was he affected by pathetick poetry, that, when he was reading Dr. Beattie's *Hermit* in my presence, it brought tears into his eyes." *Bos.* 4.186   *cir.* 1783?

6. *Ode on the Birth of Lord Hay.* *J. did not admire it, but when asked his opinion "got off very well, by . . . reading the second and third stanzas of it with much melody." *Bos.* 5.105. (*Hebrides*, 25 Aug.)   1773

Behn, Afra

1. Unequalled in "hyperbolical adulation." *Lives* 1.399
1779

Bentley, Richard

1. "May the shade, at least, of one great English critick [probably Bentley. See *Bos.* 1.153 *n.* 7] rest without disturbance; and may no man presume to insult his memory, who wants his learning, his reason, or his wit." *Wks.* ed. Oxford, 1825, 5.182   1742

2. J. exposes misinterpretation by "the learned Dr. Bentley" of passage in *Paradise Lost. Wks.* 9.186   1747

3. "Perhaps better skilled in grammar than in poetry." *Lives* 1.181   1779

4. *J. praises highly and recites B.'s verses in Dodsley's *Collection:* "They are the forcible verses of a man of strong mind,[1] but not accustomed to write verse; for there is some uncouthness in the expression." *Bos.* 4.24. (Langton's *Collection*)   Date?

5. *For complaint as to his scholarship, see *John. Misc.* 2.142   Date?

---

[1] In Boswell's *Diary*, which is the basis of this passage, the reading is: "Yes Sir they are very well but they are well in the manner of a man of a strong mind," etc. See *Catalogue of the Johnsonian Collection of R. B. Adam.*

Birch, Thomas

1. His *History of the Royal Society of London* briefly reviewed by J. in *The Literary Magazine*, 1756. Rp't. in *Wks.*, ed. Oxford, 1825, 6.76-7   1756
2. *"A pen is to Tom a torpedo, the touch of it benumbs his hand and his brain: Tom can talk; but he is no writer." *Wks.* 1.209. (Hawkins's *Life*. See also *Bos.* 1.159-60 for Boswell's claim that J. "had no mean opinion of Birch." For J.'s Greek epigram on Birch, see *Wks.* 11.397)   Date?

Blacklock, Thomas

1. *The poetry of this blind writer: "We may be absolutely sure that such passages [describing visible objects] are combinations of what he has remembered of the works of other writers who could see." *Bos.* 1.466   1763
2. "I looked on him with reverence." *Letters* 1.230   1773

Blackmore, Sir Richard[1]

1. (*Lives* 2) B. "has been exposed to worse treatment than he deserved." (252.) "As an author he may justly claim the honours of magnanimity." (253.) "His literature [reading] was, I think, but small . . . but though he could not boast of much critical knowledge his mind was stored with general principles." (253.) "Having formed a magnificent design he was careless of particular and subordinate elegances; he studied no niceties of versification; he waited for no felicities of fancy"—first thoughts in first words. No aspiration for ideal perfection. Few lines stand out from rest in excellence.[2] (253-4)   Ptd. 1780

---

[1] Added to *English Poets* at J.'s recommendation. (*Lives* 3.302. See also *ib.* 2.242, and *Letters* 2.275 *n* 4)
[2] This statement not in first ed.

2. *Alfred.* B. "dignified Alfred . . . with twelve books." Public indifferent. *Lives* 2.249   Ptd. 1780

3. *Creation.* *"He said, the criticks had done too much honour to Sir Richard Blackmore, by writing so much against him." His *Creation* patched together with the aid of various wits. *Bos.* 2.107-8   1769

4. *Creation.* (*Lives* 2) Should not be judged by his other works. (242.) Surpassed himself. (243.) Inserted in *Eng. Poets* at J.'s recommendation. (242.) Though corrected by his friends, the general design and poetical spirit is B's. "This poem, if he had written nothing else, would have transmitted him to posterity among the first favorites of the English muse." (244.) Appears to be more carefully done than B.'s other work: "it wants neither harmony of numbers, accuracy of thought, nor elegance of diction." Its two constituent parts, "ratiocination and description." B. "not only reasons in verse, but very often reasons poetically; and finds the art of uniting ornament with strength, and ease with closeness. . . . In his descriptions both of life and nature the poet and the philosopher happily co-operate; truth is recommended by elegance, and elegance sustained by truth. In the structure and order of the poem not only the greater parts are properly consecutive, but the didactick and illustrative paragraphs are so happily mingled that labour is relieved by pleasure, and the attention is led on through a long succession of varied excellence to the original position, the fundamental principle of wisdom and of virtue." (254-5)   Ptd. 1780

5. *Eliza.* Still-born. J. had never seen it till borrowed for his *Lives*. *Lives* 2.242   Ptd. 1780

6. *Essays upon Several Subjects.* (*Lives* 2) "Can be commended only as they are written for the highest and noblest purpose, the promotion of religion." "Blackmore's prose is not the prose of a poet; for it is languid, sluggish, and lifeless: his diction is neither daring nor

exact, his flow neither rapid nor easy, and his periods neither smooth nor strong." Little clarity of thought or expression. (246.) *Essay on the Spleen* commended. (248) Ptd. 1780
7. *Lay Monastery, The.* (Periodical.) The central figure, Mr. Johnson, ridiculed. *Lives* 2.244, 246   Ptd. 1780
8. *Medical Treatises.* J. observes there "an affected contempt of the Ancients, and a supercilious derision of transmitted knowledge." "Of this indecent arrogance" J. quotes a specimen. *Lives* 2.250-1   Ptd. 1780
9. *New Version of the Psalms.* "Blackmore's name must be added to those of many others who, by the same attempt, have obtained only the praise of meaning well." *Lives* 2.249   Ptd. 1780
10. *Satire against Wit.* Degraded himself by praise of men of high rank. He cannot keep his poetry free from trade: his "Bank for Wit." *Lives* 2.241   Ptd. 1780

Blackwell, Thomas

1. *Memoirs of the Court of Augustus. Faults:* Author's vanity disgusts. His magnificent promises unfulfilled. Little new. Affectations: over-luxuriant style, anachronistic modern terms, "a furious and unnecessary zeal for liberty." Some just sentiments. Author's overheated imagination and misplaced enthusiasm. Use of Gallicisms and technical terms, and of words, "appropriated to jocularity and levity" condemned. Grand and burlesque expressions sometimes mixed together. Coined words and phrases. Gaudy or hyperbolical epithets. Sonority which draws attention from the meaning. *Merits:* "The work of a man of letters"; its accuracy; vivacity. "Sufficiently entertaining to invite readers." *Wks.* 10.185-193   1756

Blair, Hugh

1. *Grave, The.* *J. "did not like it much." *Bos.* 3.47
1748

Bocage, Mme. Du
1. *Columbiade, The.* *See SEWARD 2   1784

Boccaccio
1. His authority. See DANTE 1   1755
2. Celebrity of the tales paraphrased by Dryden. See DRYDEN 41   1779

Boethius, Hector
1. "May be justly reverenced as one of the revivers of elegant learning. . . . The style of *Boethius*, though, perhaps, not always rigorously pure, is formed with great diligence upon ancient models, and wholly uninfected with monastick barbarity. His history is written with elegance and vigour, but his fabulousness and credulity are justly blamed." His credulity excusable "in an age when all men were credulous." *Wks.* 10.329. (*Jour. to W.I.*)   Composed 1774

Boileau-Despréaux, N.[1]
1. B.'s remarks on low diction examined. *Wks.* 7.164. (*Ram.* 168)   1751
2. "As Boileau observes, and Boileau will be seldom found mistaken." *Lives* 1.385   1779
3. B.'s "injudicious and peevish contempt of modern Latin [verse]." *Lives* 2.82. (See also *ib.* 3.182)   Ptd. 1780
4. J. implies that he agrees with Boileau and Pope "that the practice of writing might be refined till the difficulty should overbalance the advantage." *Lives* 3.249   1781
5. *J. "a professed admirer of Boileau." *John. Misc.* 1. 416. (Murphy)   Date?

---

[1] Percy H. Houston devotes a chapter to "Johnson and Boileau" in his interesting work, *Doctor Johnson: A Study in Eighteenth Century Humanism*, Harvard University Press, 1923.

6. *J. "took no critic from the shelf, neither Aristotle, Bossu, nor Boileau." *John. Misc.* 2.372. (Tyers)
   Date?

7. *"With French authors he was familiar. He had lately read over the works of Boileau." *John. Misc.* 2.363. (Tyers)   Date?

8. *J. "delighted exceedingly in Boileau's works." *John. Misc.* 1.334. (Piozzi)   Date?

9. *Le Lutrin.* J. defends *Rape of the Lock* from Dennis's charge that this poem is inferior to B.'s *Lutrin* because of its want of a moral. See POPE 65   1781

10. *Satire sur les Femmes.* Pope's *Characters of Women* compared with Boileau's *Satire* [X], which J. declares inferior, though "he surely is no mean writer to whom Boileau shall be found inferior." *Lives* 3.245
    1781

Bolingbroke, Henry St. John, First Viscount

1. *J. to Dr. Burney: "No, Sir, I have never read Bolingbroke's impiety, and therefore am not interested about its confutation." *Bos.* 1.330. (Dr. Burney)   cir. 1758

2. Pope's collection of *Letters:* "I know not whether there does not appear something more studied and artificial in his productions than the rest, except one long letter by Bolingbroke, composed with all the skill and industry of a professed author." *Lives* 3.159
   1781

3. "None of his [Pope's] noble friends were such as that a good man would wish to have his intimacy with them known to posterity: he can derive little honour from the notice of Cobham, Burlington, or Bolingbroke." *Lives* 3.205-6   1781

4. For Bolingbroke's use of French idioms, see DICTION 45   1781

Borrichius. See Rapin 1

Bossu, René Le
1. Recommended in teaching the art of poetry. See Poetry 3   1748
2. His opinion quoted. *Lives* 1.171   1779

Bossuet, J.B.
1. *"Nobody reads him." See French Literature 2   1773

Boswell, James
1. *Account of Corsica.* J. in letter to Boswell: "Your History is like other histories, but your Journal is in a very high degree curious and delightful. There is between the History and the Journal that difference which there will always be found between notions borrowed from without, and notions generated within. Your History was copied from books; your Journal rose out of your own experience and observation. You express images which operated strongly upon yourself, and you have impressed them with great force upon your readers. I know not whether I could name any narrative by which curiosity is better excited, or better gratified." *Bos.* 2.70. (See also *ib.* 2.11)   1769
2. *Journal of a Tour to the Hebrides.* *J. often takes "great delight" in reading B.'s manuscript Journal. "It is not written in a slovenly manner. It might be printed, were the subject fit for printing." *Bos.* 5.226-7. (*Hebrides*, 19 Sept.)   1773
3. *Journal of a Tour to the Hebrides.* *"The more I read of this [B.'s MS. Journal], I think the more highly of you." *Bos.* 5.262. (*Hebrides*, 27 Sept.)   1773
4. *Journal of a Tour to the Hebrides.* *"Dr. Johnson said it [B.'s MS. Journal] was a very exact picture of a portion of his life." *Bos.* 5.279. (*Hebrides*, 3 Oct.)   1773

5. *Journal of a Tour to the Hebrides.* *"He [J.] read this day a good deal of my [MS.] *Journal* . . . and was pleased, for he said, 'I wish thy books were twice as big.' "[1] *Bos.* 5.307. (*Hebrides*, 12 Oct.)   1773
6. *Journal of a Tour to the Hebrides.* J. to Mrs. Thrale: "I am not sorry that you read Boswel's journal [in MS.]. Is it not a merry piece?" *Letters* 1.320   1775
7. *Matrimonial Thought, A.* *"It is very well, Sir; but you should not swear." *Bos.* 2.111   1769

Bouhours, Father Dominic

1. Recommended in teaching the art of poetry. See POETRY 3   1748
2. *J. implies that he is a true critic, "who shews all beauty to depend on truth." See BURKE 6   1769

Bourdaloue, L.

1. *Did not "go round the world." See FRENCH LITERATURE 2   1773

Broome, William

1. "Though it cannot be said that he was a great poet, it would be unjust to deny that he was an excellent versifyer; his lines are smooth and sonorous, and his diction is select and elegant. His rhymes are sometimes unsuitable: in his *Melancholy* he makes *breath* rhyme to *birth* in one place, and to *earth* in another. Those faults occur but seldom; and he had such power of words and numbers as fitted him for translation, but, in his original works, recollection seems to have been his business more than invention." His frequent—often open—imitation of other writers. "To detect his imitations were tedious and useless. What he takes he seldom makes worse; and he cannot be justly thought a mean man whom Pope chose for an associate . . ." etc. *Lives* 3.80-1   1781

---

[1] See Hill's note on "big." *Bos.* 5.425. (App. C)

2. *Translations:* (*Lives* 3) *Iliad*, (in collaboration with Ozell and Oldisworth). "It has long since vanished, and is now in no danger from the criticks." (76.) *Odyssey*, (with Pope and Fenton). "This translation is a very important event in poetical history." (77.) Spence's criticism of this "commonly just." (143.) J. parodies B.'s four lines on the labour of Sisyphus, "one of the most successful attempts"—at adapting the sound to the sense, in order to show that "the mind often governs the ear, and the sounds are estimated by their meaning." (231. See VERSIFICATION 33)   1781
3. *Odyssey, Notes to.* "Broome . . . endeavoured not unsuccessfully to imitate his master [Pope]." *Lives* 3.241   1781

Brown, Thomas

1. "The facetious Thomas Brown . . . a man not deficient in literature nor destitute of fancy;" but his highest aim "to be a *merry fellow*." Small jests or gross buffoonery the result; hence little intrinsic value in his works. Read only while novelty lasted. *Lives* 1.381   1779
2. *Dialogues.* "Like his other works: what sense or knowledge they contain is disgraced by the garb in which it is exhibited. . . . The whole animation of these compositions arises from a profusion of ludicrous and affected comparisons." *Lives* 1.381-2   1779

Browne, Sir Thomas

1. (*Wks.* 4) His "imagination vigorous and fertile." (587.) "His exuberance of knowledge, and plenitude of ideas, sometimes obstruct the tendency of his reasoning, and the clearness of his decisions." Superfluity of images; "always starting into collateral considerations: but the spirit and vigour of his pursuit always gives delight; and the reader follows him, without reluctance, through his mazes, in themselves flowery

and pleasing, and ending at the point originally in view." Great excellences and great faults in his style: "It is vigorous, but rugged; it is learned, but pedantick; it is deep, but obscure; it strikes, but does not please; it commands, but does not allure: his tropes are harsh, and his combinations uncouth." The general linguistic instability of the age. "Browne, though he gave less disturbance to our structures in phraseology [than Milton], yet poured in a multitude of exotick words; many, indeed, useful and significant . . . but many superfluous . . . and some so obscure, that they conceal his meaning rather than explain it. . . . His style is, indeed, a tissue of many languages; a mixture of heterogeneous words." Terms misapplied. Augmented our philosophical diction, however. Uncommon words and phrases the result of uncommon sentiments. Sought compactness of expression. (611-2.) "But his innovations are sometimes pleasing, and his temerities happy: he has many *verba ardentia*, forcible expressions, which he would never have found, but by venturing to the utmost verge of propriety; and flights which would never have been reached, but by one who had very little fear of the shame of falling."[1] (612-3) 1756

2. *J. admired him "for his penetration," says Hawkins. *Wks.* 1.271 Date?

3. *Garden of Cyrus, The.* Defects in method. "This sport of fancy." *Wks.* 4.594-5. See also SUBJECT 8 1756

4. *Hydriotaphia; Urn Burial.* "There is, perhaps, none of his works which better exemplifies his reading or memory." "Rather for curiosity than use." *Wks.* 4. 592 1756

5. *Miscellaneous Tracts.* (*Wks.* 4) Have "the merit of giving to mankind what was too valuable to be suppressed. (596.) *Observations upon Several Plants.*

[1] For the alleged influence of Browne on J.'s style, see *John. Misc.* 2.351 and *n* 11

"Often shew some propriety of description, or elegance of allusion, utterly undiscoverable to readers not skilled in Oriental botany." (596-7.) *Of Garlands.* "A subject merely of learned curiosity." (597.) *Repertorium.* "There is not matter proportionate to the skill of the antiquary." (600)   1756

6. *Pseudodoxia Epidemica: Enquiries into Vulgar Errors.* "Arose not from fancy and invention, but from observation and books." Its lack of coherence. J. wishes he had delayed publication and enlarged it with later observations. *Wks.* 4.590   1756

7. *Religio Medici.* (*Wks.* 4) "Excited the attention of the publick, by the novelty of paradoxes, the dignity of sentiment, the quick succession of images, the multitude of abstruse allusions, the subtlety of disquisition, and the strength of language." (585.) Examples of "liberty of thought and expression." (586.) "The peculiarities of this book." (588)   1756

Buchanan, George

1. See RENAISSANCE 1   1742
2. *"Buchanan, he said, was a very fine poet; and observed, that he was the first who complimented a lady, by ascribing to her the different perfections of the heathen goddesses; but that Johnston improved upon this, by making his lady, at the same time, free from their defects. He dwelt upon Buchanan's elegant verses to Mary Queen of Scots, *Nympha Caledoniæ*, &c." *Bos.* 1.460   1763
3. *"Buchanan . . . has fewer *centos*[1] than any modern Latin poet. He not only had great knowledge of the Latin language, but was a great poetical genius. Both the Scaligers praise him." *Bos.* 2.96   1769

---

[1] "A composition formed by joining scrapes [scraps] from other authours." *Dict.* 1755

4. Praises his Latin poems. *Bos.* 5.398. (*Hebrides*, 11-20 Nov.) 1773

5. B., "whose name has as fair a claim to immortality as can be conferred by modern latinity, and perhaps a fairer than the instability of vernacular languages admits." *Wks.* 10.317. (*Jour. to W.I.*)
Composed 1774

6. "The elegant Buchanan." See JOHNSTON 2
Composed 1774

7. *J. "defied any one to produce a classical book, written in Scotland since Buchanan." See SCOTCH WRITERS 3
1775

8. *"He uniformly gave liberal praise to George Buchanan, as a writer." *Bos.* 4.185 cir. 1783?

9. *"The only man of genius his country ever produced." *Bos.* 4.186 cir. 1783?

Buckingham, George Villiers, Second Duke of

1. *The Rehearsal.* *"Colman mannte den *Rehearsal* als ein ehmals bewundertes meisterstück, das man nicht mehr zu lesen im Stande sey: *There was to little salt in too keep it sweet* [*sic*], sagte Johnson." *Mod. Lang. Notes* 26.176-7. (Letter of H. P. Sturz, who met J. when the King of Denmark visited England in 1768)
1768

2. *The Rehearsal.* *" 'Bayes, in *The Rehearsal*, is a mighty silly character. If it was intended to be like a particular man, it could only be diverting while that man was remembered. But I question whether it was meant for Dryden.' . . . I [Boswell] maintained that it had merit as a general satire on the self-importance of dramatick authours. But even in this light he held it very cheap." *Bos.* 2.168 1772

3. *The Rehearsal.* "Though by some artifice of action it yet keeps possession of the stage, it is not possible now to find anything that might not have been written

without so long delay, or a confederacy so numerous. . . . Much of the personal satire . . . is now lost or obscured." *Lives* 1.368-9   1779

4. *The Rehearsal.* *"It has not wit enough to keep it sweet. . . . It has not vitality enough to preserve it from putrefaction." *Bos.* 4.320   Date?

5. *The Rehearsal.* *"The greatness of Dryden's reputation is now the only principle of vitality which keeps the Duke of Buckingham's play from putrefaction." *John. Misc.* 1.185. (Piozzi)   Date?

Buckingham, John Sheffield, Duke of. See SHEFFIELD

Bunyan, John[1]

1. *"Johnson praised John Bunyan highly. 'His *Pilgrim's Progress* has great merit, both for invention, imagination, and the conduct of the story; and it has had the best evidence of its merit, the general and continued approbation of mankind. . . . It is remarkable, that it begins very much like the poem of Dante; yet there was no translation of Dante when Bunyan wrote. There is reason to think that he had read Spenser.' " *Bos.* 2.238   1773

2. *One of only three works not long enough. See CERVANTES 2   Date?

3. *When J. learns Percy's child has not read *Pilgrim's Progress*, he replies, " 'then I would not give one farthing for you;' and he set her down and took no further notice of her." *John. Misc.* 2.406   Date?

Burke, Edmund

1. *The particular excellence of Burke's eloquence is "copiousness and fertility of allusion; a power of diversifying his matter, by placing it in various relations. Burke has great information, and great command of

---

[1] For the eighteenth century's estimate of Bunyan, see *John. Misc.* 1.332 *n* 4

language; though, in my opinion, it has not in every respect the highest elegance." *Bos.* 5.213. (*Hebrides*, 15 Sept.) 1773

2. *"He said that he looked upon Burke to be the author of Junius, and that though he would not take him *contra mundum*, yet he would take him against any man." *John. Misc.* 2.41 1775

3. *"Yes; Burke *is* an extraordinary man. His stream of mind is perpetual."¹ *Bos.* 2.450 1776

4. *"I should have believed Burke to be Junius, because I know no man but Burke who is capable of writing these letters; but Burke spontaneously denied it to me." *Bos.* 3.376 1779

5. *Letter to the Sheriffs of Bristol.* *J. "censured the composition much." *Bos.* 3.186-7 1777

6. . . . *Of the Sublime and the Beautiful.* *"We have an example of true criticism in Burke's *Essay on the Sublime and Beautiful*; and, if I recollect, there is also Du Bos; and Bouhours, who shews all beauty to depend on truth. There is no great merit in telling how many plays have ghosts in them, and how this Ghost is better than that. You must shew how terrour is impressed on the human heart. In the description of night in *Macbeth* [III. ii], the beetle and the bat detract from the general idea of darkness,—inspissated gloom". *Bos.* 2.90 1769

Burman, Peter

1. "His style is lively and masculine, but not without harshness and constraint, nor, perhaps, always polished to that purity which some writers have attained." *Wks.* 4.490 1742

Burnet, Gilbert

1. Unreliability of his narrations. *Lives* 1.128 1779
2. *History of my own Times.* *"The first part of it [in

¹ J. frequently eulogizes Burke's powers in *Bos.*: e.g., see 2.16, 450; 5.269

so far as Burnet himself was a participant] is one of the most entertaining books in the English language; it is quite dramatick." *Bos.* 5.285. (*Hebrides*, 4 Oct.)   1773

3. *History of my own Times.* *"Very entertaining. The style, indeed, is mere chit-chat." Burnet prejudiced. *Bos.* 2.213   1773

4. *Life and Death of Rochester.* "Which the critick ought to read for its elegance, the philosopher for its arguments, and the saint for its piety." *Lives* 1.222   1779

Burney, Dr. Charles

1. *The Present State of Music in France and Italy.* . . . *" 'You are my model, Sir', said he [J.] to Dr. Burney, soon after he published his *Tour to the Hebrides.* 'I had that clever dog Burney's Musical Tour in my eye. . . .' " *John. Misc.* 2.303. (See also *Bos.* 4.186 for similar statement)   *cir.* 1775

Burney, Frances. (Mme. D'Arblay)

1. *Cecilia.* *J. likes the character Mr. Albany: "He is one of my first favourites. Very fine indeed are the things he says." D'Arblay, *Diary and Letters*, 2.127   1782

2. *Cecilia.* *" 'Dr. Johnson made me read it, ma'am.' . . . '*Made* you, sir?' said the Doctor; 'you give an ill account of your own taste or understanding, if you wanted any *making* to read such a book as *Cecilia.*' " D'Arblay, *Diary and Letters* 2.156-7   1782

3. *Cecilia.* *"Johnson. (with an air of animated satisfaction) 'Sir, if you talk of *Cecilia*, talk on.' " *Bos.* 4.223   1783

4. *Evelina.* *J. laughs heartily at some of the comic parts. D'Arblay, *Diary and Letters* 1.46   1778

5. *Evelina.* *Mrs. Thrale to Dr. Burney: "Mr. Johnson returned home, full of the praises of the *Book* [*Eve-*

lina] I had lent him, and protesting there were passages in it which might do *honour* to Richardson. We talk of it for ever, and he feels ardent after the *dénouement*; he could not get *rid* of the Rogue, he said!" D'Arblay, *Diary and Letters*, 1.48   1778

6. *Evelina.* *"Mrs. Thrale told him [Dr. Burney], that when he [J.] gave her the first volume of *Evelina*, which she had lent him, he said, 'Why, madam, why, what a charming book you lent me!' and eagerly inquired for the rest. He was particularly pleased with the Snow-hill scenes, and said that Mr. Smith's vulgar gentility was admirably portrayed; and when Sir Clement joins them, he said there was a shade of character prodigiously well marked." D'Arblay, *Diary and Letters* 1.49   1778

7. *Evelina.* *Mrs. Thrale tells Mrs. Burney that "Dr. Johnson's favourite [character in *Evelina*] is Mr. Smith. He declares the fine gentleman *manqué* was never better drawn; and he acted him all the evening, saying he was 'all for the ladies!' He repeated whole scenes by heart. . . . Oh you can't imagine how much he is pleased with the book; he 'could not get rid of the rogue' he told me." D'Arblay, *Diary and Letters*, 1.54-5   1778

8. *Evelina.* *J. to Miss Burney: " 'Oh, you are a sly little rogue!—what a Holborn beau have you drawn!' 'Ay, Miss Burney,' said Mrs. Thrale, 'the Holborn beau is Dr. Johnson's favourite; and we have all your characters by heart, from Mr. Smith up to Lady Louisa.' 'Oh, Mr. Smith, Mr. Smith is the man!' cried he, laughing violently. 'Harry Fielding never drew so good a character!—such a fine varnish of low politeness!—such a struggle to appear a gentleman! Madam, there is no character better drawn anywhere—in any book or by any author.' " D'Arblay, *Diary and Letters* 1.71-2   1778

9. *Evelina.* *J. at first unwilling to read it, says Mrs.

Thrale, "but when he was going to town, I put the first volume into the coach with him; and then, when he came home, the very first words he said to me were 'Why, Madam, this *Evelina* is a charming creature!' —and then he teased me to know who she married, and what became of her,—and I gave him the rest." D'Arblay, *Diary and Letters* 1.74   1778

10. *Evelina.* *"There is nothing so delicately finished in all Harry Fielding's works as in *Evelina*." D'Arblay, *Diary and Letters*, 1.90   1778

11. *Evelina.* *J. calls Miss Burney an extraordinary proof of woman's increasing importance in literature: "So extraordinary . . . that I know none like her,—nor do I believe there is, or there ever was, a man who could write such a book so young . . . [Pope's] *Windsor Forest* . . . though so delightful a poem, by no means required the knowledge of life and manners, nor the accuracy of observation, nor the skill of penetration, necessary for composing such a work as *Evelina:* he who could ever write *Windsor Forest*, might as well write it young as old. Poetical abilities require not age to mature them; but *Evelina* seems a work that should result from long experience, and deep and intimate knowledge of the world; yet it has been written without either. Miss Burney is a real wonder. What she is, she is intuitively." D'Arblay, *Diary and Letters* 1.246-7   1779

12. *Evelina.* *"Johnson says nothing like it has appeared for years!" Mrs. Thrale in Mme. D'Arblay's *Diary* 1.291   1779

13. *Evelina.* J. recommends it. *Letters* 2.137   1780

Burton, Robert

1. *Anatomy of Melancholy.* *"A valuable work. It is, perhaps, overloaded with quotation. But there is great spirit and great power in what Burton says, when he writes from his own mind." *Bos.* 2.440   1776

2. *Anatomy of Melancholy.* *"The only book that ever took him out of bed two hours sooner than he wished to rise." *Bos.* 2.121. (Maxwell's *Collectanea*) Date?
3. *Anatomy of Melancholy.* *"Burton on melancholy was a book that he frequently resorted to for the purpose of exhilaration." *Wks.* 1.40. (Hawkins's *Life.* See also *Wks.* 2.151 note, for similar testimony, from Hawkins) Date?

Butler, Samuel

1. *"There is more thinking in him [Milton] and in Butler, than in any of our poets." *Bos.* 2.239.   1773
2. "A man whose name can only perish with his language." *Lives* 1.209   1779
3. Prior [in *Alma*] "had not Butler's exuberance of matter and variety of illustration . . . he wanted the bullion of his master. Butler pours out a negligent profusion, certain of the weight, but careless of the stamp." *Lives* 2.205   Ptd. 1780
4. *Hudibras.* "These observations [See GENERAL 6] will shew the reason why the poem of *Hudibras* is almost forgotten, however embellished with sentiments and diversified with allusions, however bright with wit, and however solid with truth. The hypocrisy which it detected, and the folly which it ridiculed, have long vanished from publick notice . . . the book which was once quoted by princes, and which supplied conversation to all the assemblies of the gay and witty, is now seldom mentioned, and even by those that affect to mention it, is seldom read. So vainly is wit lavished upon fugitive topicks, so little can architecture secure duration when the ground is false." *Wks.* 8.237. (*Idl.* 59)   1759
5. *Hudibras.* *"There is in *Hudibras* a great deal of bullion which will always last. But to be sure the brightest strokes of his wit owed their force to the impression of the characters, which was upon men's minds at the time." *Bos.* 2.369-70   1775

6. *Hudibras.* *"Hudibras has a profusion of these [wit and humour]; yet it is not to be reckoned a poem." Bos. 3.38   1776
7. *Hudibras.* (*Lives* 1) "One of those compositions of which a nation may justly boast, as the images which it exhibits are domestick, the sentiments unborrowed and unexpected, and the strain of diction original and peculiar." (209.) *The action*—unfinished, yet it hardly could have been one. Paucity of events—more said than done. "The scenes are too seldom changed, and the attention is tired with long conversation." (211.) The action possesses "such probability as burlesque requires." One violation: the whipping scene. (216.) *Dialogue*, needs to be enlivened, and varied. Too much uniformity. Its inexhaustible wit—"for what poet has ever brought so many remote images so happily together?"—palls from super-abundance. We tire of wondering. *B.'s knowledge*—can expand and illustrate every topic with "all the accessories that books can furnish." Travelled the bypaths of literature as well. "If the French boast the learning of Rabelais, we need not be afraid of confronting them with Butler." (212.) *Experience*—contributed "the most valuable parts of his performance." From his observation of human nature came quotable distichs. (213.) *The "manners"*—local, "founded on opinions" and hence perishable. Much humour lost by this. (See NATURE 36.) *Diction*—grossly familiar. (217.) *"Numbers"*—"purposely neglected, except in a few places. . . . The measure is quick, spritely, and colloquial, suitable to the vulgarity of the words and the levity of the sentiments." But lifted by vigour of fancy, and knowledge and novelty. (217-8)   1779

Callimachus

1. *"A writer of little excellence." Bos. 4.2. (Langton's Collection)   Date?

Calpurnius. See NEMESIANUS

Camoens, Luis

1. *Lusiad.* *J. speaks highly of its merit. *Bos.* 4.251
1772

Capell, Edward

1. *Preface to Shakespeare.* *"If the man would have come to me, I would have endeavoured to endow his purposes with words; for, as it is, he doth gabble monstrously." *Bos.* 4.5. (Langton's *Collection*)
Date?
2. *His abilities "just sufficient, Sir, to enable him to select the black hairs from the white ones, for the use of the periwig-makers. Were he and I to count the grains in a bushel of wheat for a wager, he would certainly prove the winner."[1] *John. Misc.* 2.316. (Steevens)
Date?

Carleton, George

1. *Memoirs.* *J. "so much pleased with it, that he sat up till he had read it through, and found in it such an air of truth, that he could not doubt of its authenticity." *Bos.* 4.334
1784

Carlisle, Fifth Earl of

1. *Poems.* *J. praises them. *Bos.* 4.113
1781
2. *The Father's Revenge.* Construction "not completely regular; the stage is too often vacant, and the scenes are not sufficiently connected. This, however, would be called by Dryden only a mechanical defect; which takes away little from the power of the poem." Petty imperfections of diction. Dialogue "seems to want that quickness of reciprocation which characterises the

---

[1] Anecdotes by Steevens are not always trustworthy. The fact that Steevens had criticized scornfully Capell's Shakespearean labours, (see *D. N. B.*) does not help matters.

English drama." The sentiments praised. The imagery includes a comparison which "seems to have all that can be desired to make it please. It is new, just, and delightful." With the characters, J. has no fault to find. The catastrophe affecting. *Bos.* 4.247-8   1783

Caro

1. Included in list of important Italian authors. See ITALIAN LITERATURE 1   1755

Carte, Thomas

1. *Life of . . . Ormond.* *"Ill-written. The matter is diffused in too many words; there is no animation, no compression, no vigour." *Bos.* 5.296. (*Hebrides*, 8 Oct.)   1773

Carter, Mrs. Elizabeth[1]

1. *J. esteemed her contributions to *The Rambler*, (Nos. 44 and 100). *John. Misc.* 1.180. (Piozzi)   Date?

Casimir

1. "A writer who has many of the beauties and faults of Cowley." *Lives* 1.46   1779

Castiglione

1. *Il Corteggiano.* * "The best book that ever was written upon good breeding." *Bos.* 5.265. (*Hebrides*, 2 Oct.)   1773

2. *Il Corteggiano.* His *Courtier* and Casa's book of *Manners*, forerunners of *Spectator*. Commended. *Lives* 2.92-3   Ptd. 1780

Cave, Edward

1. J.'s Latin tribute to Cave's *Gentleman's Magazine*. *Wks.* 1.90. (Hawkins's *Life*)   1738

---

[1] Her learning won even J.'s respect and praise. e.g., see *Bos.* 1.122-3 and *n* 4

Cervantes

1. *Don Quixote.* "A book to which a mind of the greatest powers may be indebted without disgrace." *Lives* 1.209   1779
2. *Don Quixote.* *"Was there ever yet any thing written by mere man that was wished longer by its readers, excepting Don Quixote, Robinson Crusoe, and the Pilgrim's Progress?" *John. Misc.* 1.332. (Piozzi)
                                                                                                     Date?
3. *Don Quixote.* * "After Homer's *Iliad*, Mr. Johnson confessed that the work of Cervantes was the greatest in the world, speaking of it . . . as a book of entertainment." *John. Misc.* 1.332-3. (Piozzi)   Date?

Chambers, Ephraim

1. J.'s style founded upon Chambers' *Proposal* for his *Dictionary*. See TEMPLE 2 and JOHNSON 1,5
                                                                                         Misc. dates

Chapman, George

1. *Translation of Homer.* "Though now totally neglected, seems to have been popular almost to the end of the last century." Consulted frequently by Pope. *Lives* 3.115   1781

Chapone, Mrs. See MULSO

Chatterton, Thomas

1. *"This is the most extraordinary young man that has encountered my knowledge. It is wonderful how the whelp has written such things." *Bos.* 3.51   1776
2. *J. convinced that the Chatterton poems are forgeries. *Bos.* 3.50. (See also *ib.* 3.50 *n* 5; 4.141 and *Letters* 1.398)   1776
3. *J. laments that Hannah More "had not married Chatterton, that posterity might have seen a propa-

gation of poets." *John. Misc.* 2.197. (H. More)
                                              1782
4. *The Chatterton controversy:* *"It is a sword that cuts both ways. It is as wonderful to suppose that a boy of sixteen years old had stored his mind with such a train of images and ideas as he had acquired, as to suppose the poems, with their ease of versification and elegance of language, to have been written by Rowlie in the time of Edward the Fourth." *John. Misc.* 2.15. (Hawkins's *Apophthegms*)   Date?

Chaucer, Geoffrey[1]

1. Gower, rather than Chaucer, "the father of our poetry." See GOWER 1, 2   1755-9
2. *Boethius, Translation of.* Chaucer censured for his literalness in translating Boethius. *Wks.* 8.275. (*Idl.* 69)   1759
3. Except Chaucer, "there were no writers in *English* [before Shakespeare], and perhaps not many in other modern languages, which shewed life in its native colours." *Shak. Pref.*, Raleigh, 37   1765
4. *Canterbury Tales.* "The tale of *The Cock* seems hardly worth revival [by Dryden]; and the story of *Palamon and Arcite*, containing an action unsuitable to the times in which it is placed" received "hyperbolical commendation" by Dryden in Preface. *Lives* 1.455
                                              1779
5. *House of Fame.* "The original vision of Chaucer was never denied to be much improved [in Pope's *Temple of Fame*]." *Lives* 3.226   1781

Chesterfield, Fourth Earl of

1. *His *Letters* "teach the morals of a whore, and the manners of a dancing master." *Bos.* 1.266   *cir.* 1774
2. *Letters.* *"Johnson took his revenge, [for being called

---

[1] At one time, J. proposed to edit Chaucer. See *Wks.* 1.82 n

"a respectable Hottentot"[1]] by saying of it, 'that the instructions to his son inculcated the manners of a dancing master, and the morals of a prostitute.' Within this year or two he observed (for anger is a short-lived passion), that, bating some improprieties, it contained good directions, and was not a bad system of education." *John. Misc.* 2.348. (Tyers)   *cir.* 1774-84

3. *Letters.* *"Lord Chesterfield's *Letters to his Son*, I think, might be made a very pretty book. Take out the immorality, and it should be put into the hands of every young gentleman." *Bos.* 3.53   1776

Chevy Chase. See BALLADS 4, 6

Chillingworth, William

1. *According to Hawkins, J. formed his style by study of C. among others. *Wks.* 1.97   *cir.* 1741

Churchill, Charles

1. *"He [J.] talked very contemptuously of Churchill's poetry, observing, that 'it had a temporary currency, only from its audacity of abuse, and being filled with living names, and that it would sink into oblivion.' I ventured to hint that he was not quite a fair judge, as Churchill had attacked him violently. JOHNSON. 'Nay, Sir, I am a very fair judge. He did not attack me violently till he found I did not like his poetry; and his attack on me shall not prevent me from continuing to say what I think of him, from an apprehension that it may be ascribed to resentment. No, Sir, I called the fellow a blockhead at first, and I will call him a blockhead still. However, I will acknowledge that I have a better opinion of him now, than I once had; for he has shewn more fertility than I expected. To be sure, he is a tree that cannot produce good fruit: he only bears crabs. But, Sir, a tree that produces a great many crabs

---

[1] But Hill has shown that Chesterfield's "Hottentot" was not J. See *Bos.* 1.267 *n* 2

is better than a tree which produces only a few.' " *Bos.* 1.418-9. (cf. *John. Misc.* 2.9, where J., according to Hawkins, called C. "a shallow fellow.")   1763

Cibber, Colley. See also VANBRUGH: *The Provok'd Husband*

1. "Great George's acts let tuneful Cibber sing; For Nature form'd the Poet for the King." *Bos.* 1.149   1741?
2. Savage forced to submit to emendations of C. (The inferiority of C. as critic implied.) *Lives* 2.339   1744
3. The "rays of genius . . . that glimmered through all the mists which poverty and Cibber had been able to spread over it [Savage's *Tragedy of Sir Thomas Overbury*]." *Lives* 2.341   1744
4. *"Colley Cibber, Sir, was by no means a blockhead; but by arrogating to himself too much, he was in danger of losing that degree of estimation to which he was entitled." His birthday *Odes* not intentionally bad, as some have claimed. "Cibber's familiar style, however, was better than that which Whitehead has assumed. *Grand* nonsense is insupportable." *Bos.* 1. 401-2   1763
5. *"BOSWELL. 'You have read his apology, Sir?' JOHNSON. 'Yes, it is very entertaining.' " But Cibber himself " 'a poor creature. I remember when he brought me one of his Odes to have my opinion of it; I could not bear such nonsense, and would not let him read it to the end; so little respect had I for *that great man!* (laughing.)' " *Bos.* 2.92-3   1769
6. *"Dr. Johnson, as usual, spoke contemptuously of Colley Cibber.[1] . . . He, however, allowed consider-

---

[1] cf. Hussey's marginal MS. note on a copy of Boswell's *Johnson*, first ed.: "I have heard Johnson speak respectfully and with kindness of Colley Cibber." See *Lives* 2.341 *n* 2. But C.'s "impenetrable impudence" is referred to, *ib.* 3.187

able merit to some of his comedies, and said there was no reason to believe that the *Careless Husband* was not written by himself." *Bos.* 2.340   1775
7. *Apology.* *J. allows it to be "very well done, to be sure, Sir. That book is a striking proof of the justice of Pope's remark:
   'Each might his several province well command,
   Would all but stoop to what they understand.'"
   Bos. 3.72   1776
8. *Plays.* *"Boswell. 'And his plays are good.' Johnson. 'Yes; but that was his trade; *l'esprit du corps*; he had been all his life among players and playwriters.'" *Bos.* 3.72   1776
9. "In *The Dunciad,* among other worthless scribblers, he [Pope] had mentioned Cibber." *Lives* 3.184   1781
10. *A Letter to Mr. Pope.* "Written with little power of thought or language." Would soon have been forgotten if let alone. *Lives* 3.185-6   1781
11. Referring to the Pope-Cibber quarrel, J. comments: "The dishonour of being shewn as Cibber's antagonist could never be compensated by the victory." *Lives* 3.186   1781
12. *An absurd couplet in one of his *Odes.* *Bos.* 3.72-3. (See also *ib.* 1.402 and 3.183-4)   *cir.* 1781?

Cicero

1. Cicero's "usual elegance and magnificence of language . . . in his relation of the dream of *Scipio.*" *Wks.* 6.300. (*Ram.* 118)   1751

Clarendon, First Earl of

1. Clarendon's *History* compared with the *Account of the Duchess of Marlborough.* See Hooke, Nathaniel   1742
2. Clarendon's historical writings: diction inexact and not suited to the purposes of history. "It is the effusion

of a mind crowded with ideas, and desirous of imparting them; and therefore always accumulating words, and involving one clause and sentence in another. But there is in his negligence a rude inartificial majesty, which, without the nicety of laboured elegance, swells the mind by its plenitude and diffusion. His narration is not perhaps sufficiently rapid, being stopped too frequently by particularities, which, though they might strike the author who was present at the transactions, will not equally detain the attention of posterity. But his ignorance or carelessness of the art of writing are amply compensated by his knowledge of nature and of policy; the wisdom of his maxims, the justness of his reasonings, and the variety, distinctness, and strength of his characters." *Wks.* 6.330-1. (*Ram.* 122)   1751

3. *History of the Rebellion (Supplement.)* "The sequel of *Clarendon's* history, at last happily published, is an accession to *English* literature equally agreeable to the admirers of elegance and the lovers of truth." *Wks.* 8.259. (*Idl.* 65)   1759

4. *His historical characters trustworthy because he personally knew them. *Bos.* 2.79   1769

5. *J. prefers Clarendon to the Scotch historians. See SCOTCH WRITERS 3   1775

6. *Clarendon's faulty style "supported by his matter. It is, indeed, owing to a plethory of matter that his style is so faulty." *Bos.* 3.258   1778

Collier, Jeremy

1. *A Short View of . . . the English Stage.* J. believes him sincere in his religious zeal. Pays tribute to his controversial skill. *Lives* 2.220-1   Ptd. 1780

Collins, John

1. *"I regard Collins's performance [a pamphlet against Steevens] . . . as a great gun without powder or shot." *John. Misc.* 2.316-7. (Steevens)   cir. 1777?

Collins, William

1. Referring to his insanity: "I knew him a few years ago full of hopes and full of projects, versed in many languages, high in fancy, and strong in retention. This busy and forcible mind is now . . .," etc. *Letters* 1.36   1754
2. "That man is no common loss." *Letters* 1.63   1756
3. "A man of extensive literature, and of vigorous faculties. . . . He had employed his mind chiefly upon works of fiction and subjects of fancy, and by indulging some peculiar habits of thought was eminently delighted with those flights of imagination which pass the bounds of nature, and to which the mind is reconciled only by a passive acquiescence in popular traditions. He loved fairies, genii, giants, and monsters"; etc. "This was, however, the character rather of his inclination than his genius; the grandeur of wildness and the novelty of extravagance were always desired by him, but were not always attained. Yet as diligence is never wholly lost, if his efforts sometimes caused harshness and obscurity, they likewise produced in happier moments sublimity and splendour. This idea which he had formed of excellence led him to oriental fictions and allegorical imagery, and perhaps, while he was intent upon description, he did not sufficiently cultivate sentiment. His poems are the productions of a mind not deficient in fire, nor unfurnished with knowledge either of books or life, but somewhat obstructed in its progress by deviation in quest of mistaken beauties." *Lives* 3.337-8   1763
4. "A man of uncommon learning and abilities." *Shak.*, Raleigh, 182   1765
5. *Diction and versification.* "His diction was often harsh, unskilfully laboured, and injudiciously selected. He affected the obsolete when it was not worthy of revival; and he puts his words out of the common order, seeming to think, with some later candidates for

fame, that not to write prose is certainly to write poetry. His lines commonly are of slow motion, clogged and impeded with clusters of consonants. As men are often esteemed who cannot be loved, so the poetry of Collins may sometimes extort praise when it gives little pleasure." *Lives* 3.341   1781

6. *College Exercises.* "His English exercises [at College] were better than his Latin." *Lives* 3.334   1781

Colman, George, the Elder

1. *The Jealous Wife.* Successful, "though not written with much genius." *Bos.* 1.364   1761
2. *Odes to Obscurity and Oblivion.* *"They are Colman's best things. . . . The first of these Odes is the best: but they are both good. They exposed a very bad kind of writing." (They ridiculed Mason and Gray.) *Bos.* 2.334-5   1775
3. "Two odes [by Colman] on *Oblivion and Obscurity*, in which his [Gray's] Lyrick performances were ridiculed with much contempt and much ingenuity." *Lives* 3.427   1781
4. *Ode to Obscurity.* *"Colman never produced a luckier thing than his first Ode in ridicule of Gray; a considerable part of it may be numbered among those felicities which no man has twice attained." *Wks.* 11.214. (Hawkins's *Apophthegms.* Also repeated by Steevens. See *John. Misc.* 2.320)   Date?

Commonsense Journal

1. J. attacks author of this journal: his "Scurrility and false grammar," and his "barbarous and indecent" style. *Gent. Mag.*, 1738, iv. (*To the Reader*)   1738

Congreve, William

1. *As playwright.* Example of repetition in Congreve's comic plots. *Shak. Pref.*, Raleigh, 41   1765
2. *As playwright.* (*Lives* 2) The immorality of his plays

condemned. (See MORAL ELEMENT 22, and *Lives* 3. 205.) "Has merit of the highest kind: he is an original writer, who borrowed neither the models of his plot nor the manner of his dialogue." J. "cannot speak distinctly" of his plays: long since read. Characters "commonly fictitious and artificial, with very little of nature and not much of life." "Peculiar idea of comick excellence, which he supposed to consist in gay remarks and unexpected answers; but that which he endeavoured, he seldom failed of performing. His scenes exhibit not much of humour, imagery, or passion; his personages are a kind of intellectual gladiators . . . the contest of smartness is never intermitted; his wit is a meteor playing to and fro with alternate coruscations. His comedies have therefore, in some degree, the operation of tragedies: they surprise rather than divert, and raise admiration oftener than merriment. But they are the works of a mind replete with images, and quick in combination." (228.) "While comedy or while tragedy is regarded his plays are likely to be read." 234. For individual plays, see *infra*) Ptd. 1780

3. *As a poet.* (*Lives* 2) C. exhibits "nothing but impotence and poverty. He has in these little pieces neither elevation of fancy, selection of language, nor skill in versification." (229. But see *infra, Mourning Bride.*) *The Mourning Muse of Alexis* "a despicable effusion of elegiack pastoral; a composition in which all is unnatural, and yet nothing is new." (217-8.) J. quotes from this to show how bad C. could be. (230.) His elegiac poems censured. (230-1.) *The Birth of the Muse* "a miserable fiction." (232.) "Of his irregular poems that to Mrs. Arabella Hunt seems to be the best." (232.) "His petty poems are seldom worth the cost of criticism." (Several briefly commented upon.) "This tissue of poetry, from which he seems to have hoped a lasting name, is totally neglected, and known only as it is appended to his plays . . . except what

relates to the stage, I know not that he has ever written a stanza that is sung or a couplet that is quoted. The general character of his *Miscellanies* is that they shew little wit and little virtue."[1] Yet C. cured our "Pindarick madness" and corrected "a national error." "He first taught the English writer that Pindar's odes were regular." Though lacking the necessary lyric fire, "he has shewn us that enthusiasm has its rules, and that in mere confusion there is neither grace nor greatness." 233-4) Ptd. 1780

4. *As translator.* In all, strength and sprightliness wanting. His imitations of Horace, "feebly paraphrastical"; his version of Juvenal wants "the massiness and vigour of the original," but excusable as a juvenile production. *Hymn to Venus* from Homer, perhaps the best of his translations. "His lines are weakened with expletives, and his rhymes are frequently imperfect." *Lives* 2.233 Ptd. 1780

5. *Double Dealer, The.* His apology for its stage failure useless, as such always are: "men may be convinced, but they cannot be pleased, against their will." *Lives* 2.217 Ptd. 1780

6. *Incognita.* A novel of his youth. Preface uncommonly judicious considering his age. "I would rather praise it [the novel] than read it." *Lives* 2.214 Ptd. 1780

7. *Love for Love.* "A comedy of nearer alliance to life, and exhibiting more real manners" than *The Double Dealer* or *The Old Batchelor. Lives* 2.218. Ptd. 1780

8. *Mourning Bride, The.* *"Johnson said, that the description of the temple, in the *Mourning Bride*,[2] was the finest poetical passage he had ever read; he recollected none in Shakespeare equal to it. . . . 'Congreve has *nature*;' (smiling on the tragick eagerness of Garrick;) but composing himself, he added, 'Sir, this is not comparing Congreve on the whole, with Shakespeare on the whole; but only maintaining that

---

[1] J. at first wrote "no virtue." See *Bos.* 4.56
[2] See note, p. 315

Congreve has one finer passage than any that can be found in Shakespeare. Sir, a man may have no more than ten guineas in the world, but he may have those ten guineas in one piece; and so may have a finer piece than a man who has ten thousand pounds: but then he has only one ten-guinea piece. What I mean is, that you can shew me no passage where there is simply a description of material objects, without any intermixture of moral notions, which produces such an effect.' " *Bos.* 2.85-6   1769
9. *Mourning Bride, The* *"He again talked of the passage in *Congreve*[1] with high commendation, and said, 'Shakespeare never has six lines together without a fault. Perhaps you may find seven, but this does not refute my general assertion.' " *Bos.* 2.96   1769
10. *Mourning Bride, The.* (*Lives* 2) "A tragedy so written as to shew him sufficiently qualified for either kind of dramatick poetry." More bustle than sentiment. Plot busy and intricate and events hold attention but usually "we are rather amused with noise and perplexed with stratagem than entertained with any true delineation of natural characters." (218-9.) C. no poet, yet J. thinks that the most poetical paragraph in whole mass of English poetry is, perhaps, from *The Mourning Bride:*[1] "He who reads those lines enjoys for

[1] *Almeria.* It was a fancy'd noise; for all is hush'd.
Leonora. It bore the accent of a human voice.
Almeria. It was thy fear, or else some transient wind
Whistling thro' hollows of this vaulted aisle;
We'll listen—
Leonora. Hark!
Almeria. No, all is hush'd and still as death,—'Tis dreadful!
How reverend is the face of this tall pile,
Whose ancient pillars rear their marble heads,
To bear aloft its arch'd and ponderous roof,
By its own weight made stedfast and immoveable,
Looking tranquillity! It strikes an awe
And terror on my aching sight; the tombs
And monumental caves of death look cold,
And shoot a chillness to my trembling heart.
Give me thy hand, and let me hear thy voice;
Nay, quickly speak to me, and let me hear
Thy voice—my own affrights me with its echoes.   (Act II, Sc. i)

a moment the powers of a poet: he feels what he remembers to have felt before, but he feels it with great increase of sensibility; he recognises a familiar image, but meets it again amplified and expanded, embellished with beauty, and enlarged with majesty." (229-30.) *Double Dealer, Love for Love, Mourning Bride* and *Old Batchelor* give an unsurpassed example of early genius. (219)   Ptd. 1780

11. *Mourning Bride, The.* *Mrs. Piozzi says that "he told me, how he used to teize Garrick by commendations of the tomb scene . . . protesting that Shakespeare had in the same line of excellence nothing as good: 'All which is strictly *true* (said he); but that is no reason for supposing Congreve is to stand in competition with Shakespeare: these fellows know not how to blame, nor how to commend.'" *John. Misc.* 1.186   Date?

12. *Old Batchelor, The.* (*Lives* 2) "Apparently composed with great elaborateness of dialogue, and incessant ambition of wit . . . a very wonderful performance" considering writer's age. (214.) *Comic characters* from his reading, not from life. "The *dialogue* is one constant reciprocation of conceits, ["similes" J. wrote at first. See *Bos.* 4.56] or clash of wit, in which nothing flows necessarily from the occasion, or is dictated by nature. The characters . . . are either fictitious and artificial, as those of Heartwell and the Ladies; or easy and common . . . and the catastrophe arises from a mistake not very probably produced, by marrying a woman in a mask. Yet this gay comedy . . . will still remain the work of very powerful and fertile faculties; the dialogue is quick and sparkling, the incidents such as seize the attention, and the wit so exuberant that it 'o'er-informs its tenement.'" (216-7)   Ptd. 1780

Connoisseur, The

1. *"He said it wanted matter." *Bos.* 1.420   1763

Corneille, Pierre

1. *Corneille and Racine, the two French "tragick poets who go round the world." See FRENCH LITERATURE 2   1773
2. *"Corneille is to Shakespeare . . . as a clipped hedge is to a forest." *John. Misc.* 1.187. (Piozzi)   Date?

Cowley, Abraham. See also METAPHYSICAL POETS

1. "A man, whose learning and poetry were his lowest merits." *Wks.* 9.441   1740
2. The genius of C. referred to. *Wks.* 5.36, 37. (*Ram.* 6)   1750
3. "An author not sufficiently studious of harmony." Example of an offensive inversion of accent. *Wks.* 6.95. (*Ram.* 86)   1751
4. His misuse of the term "poverty" in his poetry. *Wks.* 7.360. (*Ram.* 202)   1752
5. An example from Cowley of ease joined to wit. "Cowley seems to have possessed the power of writing easily beyond any other of our poets, yet his pursuit of remote thoughts led him often into harshness of expression." *Wks.* 8.311. (*Idl.* 77)   1759
6. *Excelled in the art of condensation. See POPE 12   1773
7. (*Lives* 1) "Cowley, like other poets who have written with narrow views and, instead of tracing intellectual pleasure to its natural sources in the mind of man, paid their court to temporary prejudices, has been at one time too much praised and too much neglected at another." (18.) C. excels his predecessors in "metaphysical" style, "having as much sentiment and more musick." (22.) C. "almost the last of that [metaphysical] race and undoubtedly the best." (35.) "The power of Cowley is not so much to move the affections, as to exercise the understanding." (37.) His "critical

abilities have not been sufficiently observed." (38.) A good critic of his own works. (39.) Power seems to have been naturally greatest "in the familiar and the festive." (40.) His lasciviousness but not "profaneness." (42.) Fault of C. "is that of pursuing his thoughts to their last ramifications, by which he loses the grandeur of generality." (45. See GENERAL 10.) Tends, whatever his subject [in Pindaric Odes?] "to the light and the familiar, or to conceits which require still more ignoble epithets." (46.) "He wrote with abundant fertility, but negligent or unskilful selection; with much thought, but with little imagery; . . . he is never pathetick, and rarely sublime, but always either ingenious or learned, either acute or profound. . . . He read much, and yet borrowed little." Perhaps most original of poets, in that respect. (55-6.) His "metaphysical" manner the result of the prevailing style; his sentiments his own. (56-7.) Did not sufficiently inquire "by what means the ancients have continued to delight through all the changes of human manners" and hence "contented himself with a deciduous laurel," which time has been "stealing from his brows." (56.) May have learned from Donne "that light allusion to sacred things" offensive to present age. (58.) *Diction.* He seeks no "neatness of phrase . . . no elegances either lucky or elaborate"; "few epithets, and those scattered without peculiar propriety or nice adaptation. . . . He has given . . . the same diction, to the gentle Anacreon and the tempestuous Pindar." (59.) *Versification.* His numbers "commonly harsh to modern ears" though "many noble lines" and occasional grandeur. In general, carelessness, meanness and asperity. Contractions, "often rugged and harsh." Rhymes often "pronouns or particles, or the like unimportant words, which disappoint the ear and destroy the energy of the line. His combination of different measures is sometimes dissonant and unpleasing; he joins verses together, of which the former does not slide easily into the latter." *Do* and *did*, now censured, but then permissible. (59-60.) "His heroick lines are often formed of monosyllables, but yet they are sometimes sweet and sonorous." (61.) "Representative" versification—one supreme example. (62-3.) Hemistichs—useless and unauthorized by Virgil. Triplets—used in one poem "with great happiness." (63.) "If Cowley had sometimes a finished line he had it by chance." (466.) *Prose Essays*. The reverse of his poetry. Thoughts natural; style "has a smooth and placid equability" insufficiently recognised. "Nothing is far-sought, or hard-laboured; but all is easy without feebleness, and familiar without grossness." (64.) *Summary*. "He brought to his poetick labours a mind replete with learning." His pages embellished with book ornaments. "The first who imparted to English numbers the enthusiasm of the greater ode, and the gaiety of the less; . . . he was equally qualified for spritely sallies and for lofty flights; . . . he was among those who freed translation from servility, and instead of following his author at a distance, walked by his side; and . . . if he left versification yet improvable, he left likewise from time to time such specimens of excellence as enabled succeeding poets to improve it." (64-5) 1779

8. Prior's "Amorous Effusions . . . have the coldness of Cowley without his wit." *Lives* 2.202   Ptd. 1780

9. *J. admired C. "for the ease and unaffected structure of his periods." *Wks*. 1.271. (Hawkins's *Life*)
   Date?

10. *Anacreontiques*. Pleasing, rather than faithful. Most finished of C.'s poems. Diction and sentiments show "nothing of the mould of time." (Real mirth always the same—popular language changes less. See DRAMA 16) 1779

11. *Chronicle, The*. "A composition unrivalled and alone:

such gaiety of fancy, such facility of expression, such varied similitude, such a succession of images, and such a dance of words, it is vain to expect except from Cowley. His strength always appears in his agility; his volatility is not the flutter of a light, but the bound of an elastick mind. His levity never leaves his learning behind it; the moralist, the politician, and the critick, mingle their influence even in this airy frolick of genius." *Lives* 1.37 1779

12. *Cutter of Colman Street, The.* A play which "has, in a very great degree, the power of fixing attention and exciting merriment." *Lives* 1.14 1779

13. *Cutter of Colman Street, The.* *"Its merit, in the opinion of Dr. Johnson, consisted greatly in an exact discrimination of a variety of new characters, and in the pointed ridicule of puritanical manners therein displayed. I have heard him, with great delight, refer to the following dialogue of Cutter and Mrs. Tabitha." Note by Hawkins. *Wks.* 2.18 Date?

14. *Davideis.* (*Lives* 1) Subject unsuited to poetical embellishment. (49-51. See SACRED POETRY 2.) "Nothing can be more disgusting than a narrative spangled with conceits, and conceits are all that the *Davideis* supplies. One of the great sources of poetical delight is description, or the power of presenting pictures to the mind. Cowley gives inferences instead of images, and shews not what may be supposed to have been seen, but what thoughts the sight might have suggested." (51.) Lack of fitness: allusions or expression too "vulgar" or too exaggerated for context. (52-3.) Images weakened by profusion of detail. Tedious digressions. (53.) The action, though unfinished, examined along Aristotelian lines. (53-4.) Characters, "depraved like every other part by improper decorations;" otherwise, deserve "uncommon praise." (54.) More pedantry than in Tasso. (55.) In this, as in all C.'s works, "we find wit and learning unprofitably

squandered. Attention has no relief; the affections are never moved; we are sometimes surprised, but never delighted, and find much to admire, but little to approve. Still, however, it is the work of Cowley, of a mind capacious by nature, and replenished by study." (55)   1779

15. *Juvenilia.* His precocity as a youthful poet and dramatist illustrated. His "learned puerilities." *Lives* 1.3-4
  1779
16. *Latin compositions.* C. superior to Milton; inferior to May. *Lives* 1.12-13. (See also *ib.* 1.4)   1779
17. *Miscellanies.* "Such an assemblage of diversified excellence no other poet has hitherto afforded." "Great variety of style and sentiment." Brief examination of a number of minor pieces. *Lives* 1.35-9. See also *supra* 11   1779
18. *Mistress, The.* (*Lives* 1) Love poems without sincere emotion. (6-8. See AMOROUS VERSES 3.) "Written with exuberance of wit, and with copiousness of learning . . . so that the reader is commonly surprised into some improvement." But as love verses, they do not express love or incite it. Hyperbole: "every stanza is crouded with darts and flames, with wounds and death, with mingled souls, and with broken hearts." Full of "mixed wit," momentarily entertaining, "but being unnatural it soon grows wearisome. [See WIT 8.] . . . Cowley's *Mistress* has no power of seduction; she 'plays round the head, but comes not at [to] the heart'. . . . The compositions are such as might have been written for penance by a hermit, or for hire by a philosophical rhymer who had only heard of another sex; for they turn the mind only on the writer, whom, without thinking on a woman but as the subject for his talk, we sometimes esteem as learned and sometimes despise as trifling, always admire as ingenious, and always condemn as unnatural." (40-2.) "What Cowley has written upon Hope [*Against Hope*] shews

an unequalled fertility of invention." (33) 1779
19. *Pindaric Odes.* (*Lives* 1) C.'s "bold and vigorous attempt to recover" this form of writing. Not always true to spirit of Pindar. An example of "rhyming prose," of feeble diction, etc. (43-5.) *The Muse.* C. pursues "thoughts to their last ramifications . . . by which he loses the grandeur of generality." (45. See GENERAL 10.) "To the disproportion and incongruity of Cowley's sentiments must be added the uncertainty and looseness of his measures." This not Pindaric. (47. See PINDARIC VERSE 1.) "Though the mode of their composition be erroneous, yet many parts deserve at least that admiration which is due to great comprehension of knowledge and great fertility of fancy." Thoughts often new and striking; mingled greatness and littleness; "total negligence of language." (48)
1779

Crabbe, George

1. J. to Reynolds: "I have sent you back Mr. Crabbe's poem [*The Village*], which I read with great delight. It is original, vigorous, and elegant. . . . I do not doubt of Mr. Crabbe's success."[1] *Letters* 2.287-8. (See also Letter 831, *ib.* 2.288) 1783

Creech, Thomas

1. Only one of Juvenal's translators who tried to imitate his grandeur. *Lives* 1.447 1779

Critical Review

1. *J. tells the king that "the *Monthly Review* was done with most care, the *Critical* upon the best principles." *Bos.* 2.40 1767
2. *"The Critical Reviewers, I believe, often review

---

[1] See *Bos.* 4.175 and *n* 4 for J.'s revision of *The Village.*

without reading the books through; but lay hold of a topick, and write chiefly from their own minds." *Bos.* 3.32   1776

Crousaz

1. *Controversy with Warburton on Pope's "Essay on Man."* J. thinks that Crousaz "is far from deserving either indignation or contempt; that his notions are just, though they are sometimes introduced without necessity, and defended when they are not opposed; and that his abilities and parts are such as may entitle him to reverence from those who think his criticisms superfluous." *Wks.* 9.365. (See also WARBURTON 1; *Lives* 3.165; *Bos.* 5.80)   1743

Cumberland, Richard

1. *Odes.* *"Why, Sir, they would have been thought as good as Odes commonly are, if Cumberland had not put his name to them; but a name immediately draws censure, unless it be a name that bears down everything before it . . . he has not only loaded them with a name, but has made them carry double." *Bos.* 3.43-4   1776

Dalrymple, Sir John

1. *Memoirs of Great-Britain and Ireland.* *The author fair and impartial. "But nothing can be poorer than his mode of writing, it is the mere bouncing of a schoolboy. Great He but greater She! and such stuff." *Bos.* 2.210   1773
2. *J. parodies his style. *Bos.* 5.403. (*Hebrides*, 20 Nov.)   1773
3. *"The foppery of Dalrymple." *John. Misc.* 2.10. (Hawkins's *Apophthegms*.) J. uses the same phrase in *Bos.* 2.236-7   Date?

Dante[1]

1. "The Florentine dialect prevailed, and every one subscribed to the authority of Dante, Petrarca, and Bocaccio."[2] Baretti's *Intro. to the Ital. Language.* 1755. Preface, possibly by J. See Courtney, *Bibliography*, p. 73   1755
2. **The Pilgrim's Progress* "begins very much like the poem of Dante." See BUNYAN 1   1773
3. For the age of Dante and Petrarch, see POETRY 40
                                                                                                      1781

D'Arblay, Mme. See BURNEY, FRANCES

Davies, Sir John

1. *Nosce Teipsum.* Waller "might have studied with advantage the poem of Davi[e]s, which, though merely philosophical, yet seldom leaves the ear ungratified." *Lives* 1.293   1779

---

[1] The scanty and inadequate references to Dante which follow betray no unusual ignorance. Boswell, who had been in Italy, quoted on the authority of Rhedi, three lines by an "Italian writer" apparently without realizing that they were from Dante's *Inferno*. (*Notes and Queries*, 7th series, 5.85.) The Earl of Chesterfield wrote to his son that he was "fully convinced that Dante was not worth the pains necessary to understand him." (Letter to Philip Stanhope of 8 Feb. O.S., 1750.) And Horace Walpole, as might be expected, found him "extravagant, absurd, disgusting, in short a Methodist parson in Bedlam." (Letter to William Mason, 1782.) Thomas Warton in his *History of English Poetry* thought it necessary to devote some thirteen pages to a résumé of the *Divine Comedy*. On the whole he is appreciative, but even he speaks of "the childish or ludicrous excesses of these bold inventions" and of Dante's "disgusting fooleries." (*Hist. of Eng. Poetry*, ed. Price, 1830, 3.205*ff*.) Among the few who "discovered" Dante in the eighteenth century is Thomas Warton's brother, Joseph, who frequently eulogized him. (e.g., *Essay on . . . Pope*, ed. 1806, 1.182-3, 252, etc.; *Adventurer*, Nos. 59, 87.) An even finer and little known appreciation of Dante came from Johnson's friend, Charles Burney. (*A General History of Music*, 1782, 2.319-20.) The lack of a translation in English is at once a cause of the age's ignorance and an indication of the public's indifference. The first complete translation in English of the *Commedia* did not appear until 1782. (See Toynbee, *Britain's Tribute to Dante*, p. 33.)

[2] Earlier in this preface, however, in a list of nine Italian authors whose names "are unknown to nobody that knows books," Dante does not appear. See ITALIAN LITERATURE 1

Defoe, Daniel

1. *J. enumerates most of his works, "allowing a considerable share of merit to a man, who, bred a tradesman, had written so variously and so well. Indeed, his *Robinson Crusoe* is enough of itself to establish his reputation." *Bos.* 3.267-8   1778
2. *Robinson Crusoe.* *One of only three works long enough. See CERVANTES 2   Date?

Delany, Patrick

1. *"I have seen an introductory preface to a second edition of one of his books, which was the finest thing I ever read in the declamatory way." *John. Misc.* 2.54. (Campbell)   1775

Denham, Sir John

1. (*Lives* 1) "Deservedly considered as one of the fathers of English poetry." (75.) "Nothing is less exhilarating than the ludicrousness of Denham . . . he is familiar, he is gross; but he is never merry." A possible exception. D. well qualified to write grave burlesque. (76.) The strength of D.'s style and its compactness illustrated. (79-80.) *Versification.* Gradually improved from "concatenated metre" to closed couplets. (80-1.) Rhymes, "such as seem found without difficulty by following the sense." Usually exact, sometimes upon a word too feeble to sustain it. (81-2.) Rhymes sometimes repeated too closely. *Summary.* "He is one of the writers that improved our taste and advanced our language," though he left much to be done. (82. See also *Lives* 1.419)   1779
2. *Minor Poems.* Briefly criticized. That on the death of Cowley the best: "the numbers are musical, and the thoughts are just." *Lives* 1.76-7   1779
3. *Translations.* D. "One of the first that understood the necessity of emancipating translation from the drudg-

ery of counting lines and interpreting single words. . . . Denham saw the better way, but has not pursued it with great success." *Lives* 1.79   1779
4. *Cooper's Hill.* (*Lives* 1) Confers rank of original author. D. apparently the originator of English "local poetry." (77.) "The digressions are too long, the morality too frequent, and the sentiments sometimes such as will not bear a rigorous enquiry." The deservedly celebrated quatrain, "O could I flow like thee," etc., analyzed. "It has beauty peculiar to itself, and must be numbered among those felicities which cannot be produced at will by wit and labour, but must arise unexpectedly in some hour propitious to poetry." (78-9)   1779
5. *Cooper's Hill.* Excelled by Pope. *Lives* 3.225   1781

Dennis, John

1. Shakespearean criticisms of Dennis, Rymer and Voltaire refuted: "These are the petty cavils of petty minds." Their judgements formed upon narrower principles than "adherence to general nature." *Shak. Pref.*, Raleigh, 14-15. (See also *ib.* 39-40)   1765
2. *J. wishes to see his *Critical Works* collected, and believes that they would sell. *Bos.* 3.40   1776
3. *Attacks on Addison's "Cato".* (*Lives* 2) Upon publication, *Cato* "attacked by the acute malignity of Dennis, with all the violence of angry criticism." (102.) His criticism, "though sometimes intemperate, was often irrefragable." (104.) D's dislike of *Cato* "not merely capricious. He found and shewed many faults: he shewed them indeed with anger, but he found them with acuteness, such as ought to rescue his criticism from oblivion; though, at last, it will have no other life than it derives from the work which it endeavours to oppress." (133.) D.'s attack on Addison's use of unities most effective: "the objections are skilfully formed and vigorously urged." (136.) "There is, as

Dryden expresses it, perhaps 'too much horse-play in his raillery'; but if his jests are coarse, his arguments are strong. Yet as we love better to be pleased than to be taught, *Cato* is read, and the critick is neglected." When D. attacked sentiments of Cato "he then amused himself with petty cavils, and minute objections." (144) Ptd. 1780

4. D. attacked Blackmore's *Prince Arthur*, "by a formal criticism, more tedious and disgusting than the work which he condemns." *Lives* 2.238 Ptd. 1780

5. *Reflections Critical and Satyrical upon a Late Rhapsody; Call'd An Essay upon Criticism.* "The pamphlet is such as rage might be expected to dictate." Some just criticism, however. *Lives* 3.96-7. (For other comments, mostly caustic, on Dennis's attacks on Pope, see *ib.* 3.105, 136, 225; and POPE 65) 1781

Derrick, Samuel

1. *J. confirms Boswell's opinion that Derrick is "but a poor writer." *Bos.* 1.455 1763
2. *"Sir, I have often said, that if Derrick's letters had been written by one of a more established name, they would have been thought very pretty letters." *Bos.* 1.456. (Repeated, *Bos.* 5.117) 1773?
3. *"Johnson, for sport perhaps, or from the spirit of contradiction, eagerly maintained that Derrick had merit as a writer." J., asked whether Derrick or Smart was the better poet, replies: "Sir, there is no settling the point of precedency between a louse and a flea."[1] *Bos.* 4.192-3 Date?

Digby, Sir Kenelm

1. His criticism of Browne's *Religio Medici*, "in which, though mingled with some positions fabulous and uncertain, there are acute remarks, just censures, and

---

[1] A writer in the *European Magazine*, 30.160, claims that the question of precedence concerned Derrick and Boyce—not Smart. See *Bos.* 4.192 *n* 2

profound speculations; yet its principal claim to admiration is, that it was written in twenty-four hours." *Wks.* 4.585   1756

Dionysius of Halicarnassus

1. Exaggerates Homer's use of "representative metre." See VERSIFICATION 8. (See also *Wks.* 6.147-8)   1751

Doddridge, Philip

1. *"Author of one of the finest epigrams in the English language." *Bos.* 5.271. (*Hebrides*, 30 Sept.)   1773

Dodsley, Robert

1. *Cleone.* *Is read aloud to J. At the end of an act: "'Come let's have some more, let's go into the slaughter-house again, Lanky. But I am afraid there is more blood than brains.' Yet he afterwards said, 'When I heard you read it, I thought higher of its power of language: when I read it myself, I was more sensible of its pathetick effect . . . if Otway had written this play, no other of his pieces would have been remembered.'" *Bos.* 4.20-1. (Langton's *Collection*)   cir. 1758

2. *Public Virtue.* *"He said, 'It was fine *blank* (meaning to express his usual contempt for blank verse); however, this miserable poem did not sell.'" *Bos.* 4.20. (Langton's *Collection*)   Date?

Donne, John. See also METAPHYSICAL POETS

1. J. quotes from D., to illustrate the conceits, absurdities and indelicacies of the "metaphysical" poets. *Lives* 1.23-34   1779

2. "From Donne he [Cowley] may have learned that familiarity with religious images, and that light allusion to sacred things . . . which would not be borne in the present age." *Lives* 1.58   1779

3. Jonson's "manner resembled that of Donne more in

the ruggedness of his lines than in the cast of his sentiments." *Lives* 1.22. (See also *ib.* 1.426.)   1779

Dorset, Charles Sackville, Sixth Earl of

1. (*Lives* 1) "A man whose elegance and judgement were universally confessed." (306.) J. ridicules Dryden for saying that Dorset rivals antiquity in satire: "of this rival to antiquity, all the satires were little personal invectives, and . . . his longest composition was a song of eleven stanzas." (307.) His performances, "the effusions of a man of wit, gay, vigorous, and airy. His verses to Howard shew great fertility of mind." (308)   1779

Drayton, Michael

1. *Poly-Olbion*. The combat between the giant Colbrand and Guy of Warwick "very pompously described." *Shak.*, Raleigh, 104. (See also *ib.* 151 for similar note)   1765

Dryden, John. (GENERAL CRITICISM.) For a comparison of Dryden with Pope, see POPE. (COMPARED WITH DRYDEN)

1. *Diction*. Example of impurity of diction. *Wks.* 9.188   1747
2. *Essays and Prefaces* recommended by J. for teaching the art of poetry. See POETRY 3   1748
3. "Dryden, whose warmth of fancy, and haste of composition, very frequently hurried him into inaccuracies," is ridiculed for line: "I follow fate, which does too fast pursue." Ambiguity of the line exposed. *Wks.* 5.201-2. (*Ram.* 31)   1750
4. "He sometimes slipped into errors by the tumult of his imagination, and the multitude of his ideas." *Wks.* 5.202-3 (*Ram.* 31)   1750
5. *His criticism*. Most of it written "to recommend the

work upon which he then happened to be employed." *Wks.* 6.140. (*Ram.* 93) 1751
6. J. drew 9.2% of the literary illustrations in his *Dictionary* from Dryden. See ADDISON 5 1755
7. "Some of his [Mercutio's] sallies are perhaps out of the reach of *Dryden*; whose genius was not very fertile of merriment, nor ductile to humour, but acute, argumentative, comprehensive, and sublime." *Shak.*, Raleigh, 188 1765
8. *Style. Its "eminent excellence." *Bos.* 3.280 1778
9. *Versification.* Improved by D. *Lives* 1.318 1779
10. (*Lives* 1) "Of the great poet . . . the curiosity which his reputation must excite will require a display more ample than can now be given." (331.) His extraordinary facility of composition. (367.) "As Dryden's genius was commonly excited by some personal regard he rarely writes upon a general topick." (376.) "To reason in verse was, indeed, one of his powers; but subtilty and harmony united are still feeble, when opposed to truth." (With particular reference to D.'s *Hind and the Panther*.) (380.) "His works afford too many examples of dissolute licentiousness and abject adulation. . . . Such degradation of the dignity of genius, such abuse of superlative abilities, cannot be contemplated but with grief and indignation." (398-9.) Unequalled since Roman emperors in "the meanness and servility of hyperbolical adulation," unless by Afra Behn. (399.) *D.'s learning.* D. no scholar; kept to beaten track in reading. "Yet it cannot be said that his genius is ever unprovided of matter, or that his fancy languishes in penury of ideas. His works abound with knowledge, and sparkle with illustrations . . . every page discovers a mind very widely acquainted both with art and nature, and in full possession of great stores of intellectual wealth." Probably haphazard acquisitions, picked up from experience, rather than from books.

DRYDEN (GENERAL CRITICISM) 331

(416-7.) *D.'s comprehensive mind.* "His compositions are the effects of a vigorous genius operating upon large materials." (457.) Strong reason, rather than quick sensibility, predominated; "he studied rather than felt, and produced sentiments not such as Nature enforces, but meditation supplies." (457.) The "simple and elemental passions" seldom presented. (See also 459.) He hardly conceives of love but in its turbulent aspects; hence seldom pathetic. No pleasure in simplicity. (457-8.) Perhaps, not the public taste, but his "difficulty . . . in exhibiting the genuine operations of the heart" the real cause of the "false magnificence" in his plays. (458.) Ratiocination, the favourite exercise of his mind: sometimes his learning out of place. (459.) "Next to argument, his delight was in wild and daring sallies of sentiment, in the irregular and excentrick violence of wit." Hence often nonsense and absurdity. (460.) *Comedy.* D.'s mirth arises not so much "from any original humour or peculiarity of character . . . as from incidents and circumstances, artifices and surprises; from jests of action rather than of sentiment. What he had of humourous or passionate, he seems to have had not from nature, but from other poets; if not always as a plagiary, at least as an imitator." (459-60.) *Poverty.* Its influence on D.'s writings perhaps exaggerated. If excellence of his works lessened, their number increased. (423.) *Images.* Many either just or splendid. Bursts of extravagance. (461-2.) *Improper use of mythology.* "He had sometimes faults of a less generous and splendid kind. He makes, like almost all other poets, very frequent use of mythology, and sometimes connects religion and fable too closely without distinction." (462. See also *infra, Astraea Redux.*) "Faults of affectation." Pedantic show of knowledge: technical terms, e.g., nautical. Unexpectedly "mean" sometimes. French words often used from vanity to show rank of his company. D. could never "resist the temptation of a jest." (462-3)   1779

11. *As a critic.* "To the critical sentence of Dryden the highest reverence would be due, were not his decisions often precipitate and his opinions immature." *Lives* 1.217   1779

12. *As a critic.* (See also *infra* 34.) (*Lives* 1) Criticism then almost new. D. "had considered with great accuracy the principles of writing. . . . By these dissertations the publick judgement must have been much improved." (366.) J. defends D. as literary dictator: "he who excels has a right to teach, and he whose judgement is incontestable may . . . examine and decide." (396.) "A man, whom every English generation must mention with reverence as a critick and a poet." (410.) D. "may be properly considered as the father of English criticism, as the writer who first taught us to determine upon principles the merit of composition." (410.) In *Essay of Dramatic Poesy* "and in all his other essays on the same subject, the criticism of Dryden is the criticism of a poet; not a dull collection of theorems, nor a rude detection of faults . . . but a gay and vigorous dissertation, where delight is mingled with instruction, and where the author proves his right of judgement by his power of performance." His manner of criticizing superior to Rymer's. D.'s graces of elegance. "Dryden's criticism has the majesty of a queen; Rymer's has the ferocity of a tyrant." (412-3.) D. "enlarged or rectified his notions by experience"; hence "his mind stored with principles and observations." (413.) "His general precepts, which depend upon the nature of things and the structure of the human mind," safe to recommend. His "occasional and particular positions were sometimes interested, sometimes negligent, and sometimes capricious." (413.) A changeable critic—e.g., his defence and desertion of dramatic rhyme. (414.) "His remarks on

ancient or modern writers are not always to be trusted." (415.) *Translation.* Reasonableness of D.'s rules. (423. See TRANSLATION 9) 1779

13. *Versification and style.* (*Lives* 1) His prose has not "the formality of a settled style, in which the first half of the sentence betrays the other. The clauses are never balanced, nor the periods modelled; every word seems to drop by chance, though it falls into its proper place. Nothing is cold or languid; the whole is airy, animated, and vigorous: what is little is gay; what is great is splendid . . . every thing is excused by the play of images and the spriteliness of expression. Though all is easy, nothing is feeble; though all seems careless, there is nothing harsh."[1] Nothing obsolete to-day. A style "expressing with clearness what he thinks with vigour." Not settled enough to be easily imitated. (418.) But first praise due him "as he refined the language, improved the sentiments, and tuned the numbers of English poetry." (419.) *Diction.* Before time of Dryden no poetical diction. (See DICTION 21.) "The new versification, as it was called, may be considered as owing its establishment to Dryden." Henceforth, no relapse to former savageness. (420-1.) By writing tragedies in rhyme, "he soon obtained the full effect of diligence, and added facility to exactness." (436.) "Whatever subjects employed his pen he was still improving our measures and embellishing our language." (455.) "Faults of negligence . . . beyond recital." Unevenness of work such that "ten lines are seldom found together without something of which the reader is ashamed." (464.) Did not aim at perfection. "More musick than Waller, more vigour than Denham, and more nature than Cowley." Above his contemporaries with no incentive to effort. (464-5.) Was no lover of labour. (465; 413.) Or of finish. (413.) D.'s versification summed up in Pope's triplet:

[1] See note on this word.

"Dryden taught to join
The varying verse, the full-resounding line,
The long majestick march, and energy divine." (465.)
"Dryden knew how to chuse the flowing and the sonorous words; to vary the pauses and adjust the accents; to diversify the cadence, and yet preserve the smoothness of his metre." (466.) Established use of triplets and alexandrines. (466. See VERSIFICATION 26.) His rhymes commonly just. But he often ends first line with a weak syllable, not second, as is commonly done. Sometimes D. breaks couplet by a new paragraph or sentence. D. sometimes neglects rule that the alexandrine should break at sixth syllable. (468-9.) *Summary.* "Perhaps no nation ever produced a writer that enriched his language with such variety of models. To him we owe the improvement, perhaps the completion of our metre, the refinement of our language, and much of the correctness of our sentiments. By him we were taught 'sapere et fari,' to think naturally and express forcibly." D. perhaps "the first who joined argument with poetry. He shewed us the true bounds of a translator's liberty." "He found it [English poetry] brick, and he left it marble." (469) 1779

14. *Versification.* Hammond's elegiac stanza. J. appeals to D., "whose knowledge of English metre was not inconsiderable." *Lives* 2.316   1781

15. Pope's indebtedness to Dryden for his discovery of "the most perfect fabrick of English verse." See POPE 14   1781

16. *Diction.* Dryden's epithet "'honey redolent of Spring,' an expression that reaches the utmost limits of our language." *Lives* 3.435   1781

17. J. suspects himself "of some partial fondness for the memory of Dryden"—perhaps not without good reason, however. *Lives* 3.223   1781

18. *J. had the highest opinion of Pope's writings. "His superior reverence of Dryden notwithstanding still ap-

peared in his talk as in his writings." *John. Misc.* 1. 184-5. (Piozzi) Date?
19. *J. (in disgust at Garrick's rapturous praise of D.) "suddenly challenged him to produce twenty lines in a series that would not disgrace the poet and his admirer." J. points out sixteen faults in a passage he had once commended. *John. Misc.* 1.185 (Piozzi)
Date?

Dryden. (WORKS)

20. *Absalom and Achitophel.* *J. "gave great applause to the character of Zimri." *Bos.* 2.85   1769
21. *Absalom and Achitophel.* (*Lives* 1) "The memorable satire." (373.) Its contemporary popularity: "to all the attractions of wit, elegance, and harmony [were] added the co-operation of all the factious passions." (374.) Considered as a poem political and controversial, it comprises "all the excellences of which the subject is susceptible: acrimony of censure, elegance of praise, artful delineation of characters, variety and vigour of sentiment, happy turns of language, and pleasing harmony of numbers; and all these raised to such a height as can scarcely be found in any other English composition." (436.) *Faults:* "Some lines are inelegant or improper, and too many are irreligiously licentious." Original structure defective: "allegories drawn to great length will always break." "Another inconvenience: it admitted little imagery or description, and a long poem of mere sentiments easily becomes tedious." (See DIDACTIC POETRY 2.) Action and catastrophe lack probability:—like enchanted castle vanishing. Dryden's insertion in Tate's second part, "for poignancy of satire exceeds any part of the former." (436-7)   1779
22. *Alexander's Feast.* (Second *Ode for St. Cecilia's Day.*) Unsuitable and unnatural epigrammatic conclusion. *Wks.* 15.473. (Review of J. Warton's *Essay on . . . Pope.*)   1756

23. *Alexander's Feast.* (*Lives* 1) "Has been always considered as exhibiting the highest flight of fancy and the exactest nicety of art. . . . If indeed there is any excellence beyond it in some other of Dryden's works that excellence must be found." Perhaps superior on the whole to *Ode on Killigrew*, "but without any single part equal to the first stanza of the other." Negligences illustrated. (456-7.) "Vicious conclusion": mixed metaphor. (457)   1779
24. *Alexander's Feast.* Dryden's ode superior to Pope's. See POPE 57, 58   1756, 1781
25. *All for Love.* Universally accounted to have "fewest improprieties of style or character." But one fault equal to many, "though rather moral than critical": it admits "the romantick omnipotence of Love"—a false example to set. See LOVE 2   1779
26. *Almanzor and Almahide, or the Conquest of Grenada.* (*Two parts.*) Improbability: "written with a seeming determination to glut the publick with dramatick wonders; to exhibit in its highest elevation a theatrical meteor of incredible love and impossible valour, and to leave no room for a wilder flight to the extravagance of posterity. All the rays of romantick heat . . . glow in Almanzor. . . . He is above all laws; he is exempt from all restraints. . . . Yet the scenes are, for the most part, delightful; they exhibit a kind of illustrious depravity and majestick madness: such as, if it is sometimes despised, is often reverenced, and in which the ridiculous is mingled with the astonishing." *Lives* 1.348-9   1779
27. *Annus Mirabilis.* *J. quotes a nonsensical stanza [st. 164] from Dryden's *Annus Mirabilis.* Bos. 2.241   1773
28. *Annus Mirabilis.* (*Lives* 1) "One of his most elaborate works." (338.) "One of his greatest attempts." (430.) "Written with great diligence," yet not equal to subject: disappointing. General fault: "he affords

more sentiment than description, and does not so much impress scenes upon the fancy as deduce consequences and make comparisons." (430-1) Analyzed (431-5): Examples of "indecent" hyperbole; of "the sublime . . . mingled with the ridiculous"; "images too domestick to mingle properly with the horrors of war"; unfortunate nautical language (see DICTION 19); an artful digression; etc. 1779

29. *Astraea Redux.* (*Lives* 1) "Ambition of forced conceits" illustrated. An example of "such a cluster of thoughts unallied to one another as will not elsewhere be easily found." (426.) "He had not yet learned, indeed he never learned well, to forbear the improper use of mythology": (Heathen and Christian religions mingled in passage quoted. See also *supra* 11) (427.) "How far he was yet from thinking it necessary to found his sentiments on Nature appears from the extravagance of his fictions and hyperboles." (427) 1779

30. *Aureng-Zebe.* Indamora employs Arimant to carry a message to his rival for her love: a scene in which "every circumstance concurs to turn tragedy to farce." "Sufficient to awaken the most torpid risibility." *Wks.* 6.347-9. (*Ram.* 125) 1751

31. *Aureng-Zebe.* "Has the appearance of being the most elaborate of all the dramas. The personages are imperial; but the dialogue is often domestick, and therefore susceptible of sentiments accomodated to familiar incidents. The complaint of life is celebrated,[1] and there are many other passages that may be read with pleasure." *Lives* 1.360-1 1779

32. *Britannia Rediviva.* Its "exorbitant adulation." *Lives* 1.446 1779

33. *Cleomenes.* Unimportant. *Lives* 1.363 1779

34. *Critical writings.* (See also *supra*, D. *as a critic*, and

---

[1] Bos. quotes it (*Bos.* 4.303), and, according to Maxwell, J. would frequently quote a couplet from this passage. (*Bos.* 2.124)

2.) (*Lives* 1) Preface to *Annus Mirabilis*. "Many critical observations, of which some are common, and some perhaps ventured without much consideration." (338.) *Notes and Observations on the Empress of Morocco*. "Such criticism as malignant impatience could pour out in haste." (342.) Preface to *An Evening's Love*. (*The Mock Astrologer*.) "Seems very elaborately written, and contains many just remarks on the Fathers of the English drama. . . . His criticisms upon tragedy, comedy, and farce are judicious and profound." (347.) *All for Love*. "The prologue and the epilogue, though written upon the common topicks of malicious and ignorant criticism . . . are deservedly celebrated for their elegance and spriteliness." (362.) *Preface* to D.'s translation of *Fresnoy's* "*Art of Painting*" "exhibits a parallel of poetry and painting, with a miscellaneous collection of critical remarks, such as cost a mind stored like his no labour to produce them." (387.) *Essay of Dramatic Poesy*. "An elegant and instructive dialogue." (340.) "The first regular and valuable treatise on the art of writing." (411.) "It will not be easy to find in all the opulence of our language a treatise so artfully variegated with successive representations of opposite probabilities, so enlivened with imagery, so brightened with illustrations. His portraits of the English dramatists are wrought with great spirit and diligence. The account of Shakespeare . . . a perpetual model of encomiastick criticism; exact without minuteness, and lofty without exaggeration," etc. (412) 1779

35. *Dedications*. (*Lives* 1) Elegant, though too flattering. (355, 364, 366.) *State of Innocence*. "Addressed . . . in a strain of flattery which disgraces genius, and which it was wonderful that any man that knew the meaning of his own words could use without self-detestation. It is an attempt to mingle earth and heaven, by praising human excellence in the language of religion." (359) 1779

36. *Don Sebastian.* Impropriety of dialogue. See DRAMA
    12*b*   1751
37. *Don Sebastian.* Commonly esteemed first or second of D.'s plays. "Not without sallies of frantick dignity, and more noise than meaning, yet as it makes approaches to the possibilities of real life, and has some sentiments which leave a strong impression," it long attracted attention. Several comic scenes which this age would not endure. "Passages of excellence universally acknowledged." *Lives* 1.362-3   1779
38. *Duke of Guise.* "Seems to deserve notice only for the offence which it gave." *Lives* 1.357   1779
39. *Eleonora.* (*Lives* 1) Analyzed. (440-1.) The praise, being inevitably general, (D. did not know the lady), is thereby weakened. "Knowledge of the subject is to the poet what durable materials are to the architect." (441-2)   1779
40. *Epic:* D.'s projected epic on Arthur or the Black Prince. J. commended his intended supernatural machinery—a contest between the guardian angels of kingdoms—as "the most reasonable scheme of celestial interposition that ever was formed." *Lives* 1.385
    1779
41. *Fables.* (*Lives* 1) The first English example of a new style: "a renovation of ancient writers, by modernizing their language." (454.) "The tale of *The Cock* [Chaucer] seems hardly worth revival." (455.) *Palamon and Arcite.* J. censures D.'s "hyperbolical commendation" of the story. (455.) *Sigismonda* (from Boccaccio) "may be defended by the celebrity of the story." "*Theodore and Honoria,* though it contains not much moral, yet afforded opportunities of striking description." (455)   1779
42. *Heroick Stanzas* (on the death of Cromwell). "His heroick stanzas have beauties and defects; the thoughts are vigorous, and though not always proper shew a mind replete with ideas; the numbers are smooth, and

the diction, if not altogether correct, is elegant and easy." *Lives* 1.425   1779

43. *Hind and the Panther.* (*Lives* 1) "A fable which exhibits two beasts talking Theology appears at once full of absurdity." (380. See also *supra* 10.) "The scheme of the work is injudicious and incommodious: for what can be more absurd than that one beast should counsel another to rest her faith upon a pope and council?" Exhibits, "negligence excepted, his deliberate and ultimate scheme of metre." J. approves a departure from the normal closed couplet: Dryden here pleases by variety rather than offends by ruggedness. (442-4.) Style has not always heroic dignity. (444-5.) "The original incongruity runs through the whole: the king is now Caesar, and now the Lyon; and the name Pan is given to a Supreme Being." (445.) But "great smoothness of metre," wide knowledge, multiplicity of images, "embellished with pointed sentences, diversified by illustrations, and enlivened by sallies of invective." "Few negligences in the subordinate parts." (446)   1779

44. *Indian Emperor.* Passages on night by "two great poets," (Dryden and Shakespeare), compared. See SHAKESPEARE 130   1745

45. *Indian Emperor.* *J. "forced . . . to prefer Young's description of Night" to those of Dryden and Shakespeare. See YOUNG 6   Date?

46. *Juvenile compositions. Lives* 1.332-3   1779

47. *Killigrew, To the Pious Memory of* . . . *Mrs. Anne.* (*Lives* 1) "Undoubtedly the noblest ode that our language ever has produced. The first part flows with a torrent of enthusiasm. 'Fervet immensusque ruit.'" Stanzas of unequal merit—inevitable. (439.) Compared with *Alexander's Feast, q.v.* (456)   1779

48. *Mac Flecknoe.* "A poem exquisitely satirical." *Lives* 1.383   1779

49. *Medal, The.* On narrower plan than *Absalom* and

"gives less pleasure, though it discovers equal abilities
... the superstructure cannot extend beyond the
foundation; a single character or incident cannot furnish as many ideas as a series of events or multiplicity
of agents." Yet it abounds in humorous and serious
satire. *Lives* 1.438   1779

50. *Miscellaneous original poems* (included in D.'s volume of *Fables*). "Which, with his prologues, epilogues,
and songs, may be comprised in Congreve's remark,
that even those, if he had written nothing else, would
have entitled him to the praise of excellence in his
kind." *Lives* 1.456   1779

51. *Prologues*. (See also *supra* under *Critical Writings*.)
*His prologues compared with Garrick's. See GARRICK 3   1775

52. *Religio Laici*. Subject argumentative rather than poetical. But "of great excellence in its kind." Happy
example of "middle kind of writing." In parts, "rises
to high poetry." *Lives* 1.442   1779

53. *Song for St. Cecilia's Day*. (1687) (*Lives* 1) "Lost
in the splendor of the second [*Alexander's Feast*]."
Contains "passages which would have dignified any
other poet." First stanza "vigorous and elegant" but
marred by a too technical word ("diapason") and too
remote rhymes. Conclusion "striking, but it includes
an image [of the Judgement Day] so awful in itself
that it can owe little to poetry." (439-40.) Compared
with *Killigrew* ode. (456. See *supra* 47)   1779

54. *Spanish Friar, The*. His skill in connecting the two
plots excelled by Shakespeare in *The Merchant of
Venice*. Shak., Raleigh, 82   1765

55. *Spanish Friar, The*. "A tragi-comedy, eminent for the
happy coincidence and coalition of the two plots ...
the real power both of the serious and risible parts."
Lives 1.356-7   1779

56. *State of Innocence*. "Rather a tragedy in heroick

rhyme [than an opera], but of which the personages [e.g. Satan and Raphael] are such as cannot decently be exhibited on the stage." *Lives* 1.359   1779
57. *Threnodia Augustalis.* Not his happiest. "Its first and obvious defect is the irregularity of its metre, to which the ears of that age however were accustomed. What is worse, it has neither tenderness nor dignity, it is neither magnificent nor pathetick." Its lack of images; those he has, distorted. Unseasonable merriment, "nor was he serious enough to keep heathen fables out of his religion." Conclusion insincere. *Lives* 1.438-9   1779
58. *To my Lord Chancellor.* (*Lives* 1) Analyzed. (428-30.) D.'s "subtle and comprehensive" mind, and "penetrating remarks on human nature, for which he seems to have been peculiarly formed," illustrated. (428-9.) "Into this poem he seems to have collected all his powers, and after this he did not often bring upon his anvil such stubborn and unmalleable thoughts." (429)   1779
59. *To his Sacred Majesty . . . on his Coronation.* "Has a more even tenour of thought." *Lives* 1.428   1779
60. *Translations.* (*Lives* 1) *Homer:* translation from *Iliad.* "The reader cannot but rejoice that this project went no further" considering Pope's translation. (389.) Of *Juvenal.* Preserves wit, but wants dignity of its original. Some passages will never be excelled. (447.) Of *Persius.* "Shining parts" but seems "written merely for wages, in an uniform mediocrity." (447.) Of *Virgil. Pollio* commended. (447.) *Aeneid.* "Certainly excelled whatever had appeared in English." (449. For comparison with Pitt's version, see Pitt 2.) "When admiration had subsided the translation was . . . found like all others to be sometimes erroneous and sometimes licentious." (453)   1779
61. *Tyrannic Love.* "Conspicuous for many passages of strength and elegance and many of empty noise and ridiculous turbulence." *Lives* 1.348   1779

62. *Wild Gallant.* "The form in which it now appears . . . is yet sufficiently defective to vindicate the criticks." *Lives* 1.336   1779

Du Bos, Abbé

1. *J. intimates that he is a true critic "who shews all beauty to depend on truth." See BURKE 6   1769

Du Halde, J. B.

1. *History of China,* Letter on. (*Wks.* 14.552.) Favourably reviewed. (*Gent. Mag.* 1742, pp. 320-3, 353-7, 484-6.) J. advises B. to "consult" it. (*Bos.* 2.55)
    Misc. dates

Duke, Richard

1. "Appears from his writing to have been not ill qualified for poetical compositions." Some vigorous lines in his *Review.* "His poems are not below mediocrity; nor have I found much in them to be praised." Had both the wit of the times and its dissoluteness. *Lives* 2.24   1779

Dyer, John

1. *The Fleece.* *"He spoke slightingly of Dyer's *Fleece.*—'The subject, Sir, cannot be made poetical. How can a man write poetically of serges and druggets? Yet you will hear many people talk to you gravely of that *excellent* poem, *The Fleece.*'" *Bos.* 2.453   1776

2. *The Fleece.* (*Lives* 3) "His greatest [most extensive. See YOUNG 11 *n*] poetical work." (344.) Never popular; "now universally neglected." J. "can say little that is likely to recall it to attention. The woolcomber and the poet appear to me such discordant natures, that an attempt to bring them together is to 'couple the serpent with the fowl.'" Rural imagery, digressions, small images in great words, and "all the writer's arts of delusion" cannot save the meanness of the subject. The

disgust of blank verse further repels the reader. (345-6) 1781
3. (*Lives* 3) "Is not a poet of bulk or dignity sufficient to require an elaborate criticism." (345.) His "mind was not unpoetical." (346) 1781
4. *Grongar Hill.* "The happiest of his productions; it is not indeed very accurately written, but the scenes which it displays are so pleasing, the images which they raise so welcome to the mind, and the reflections of the writer so consonant to the general sense or experience of mankind, that when it is once read it will be read again." *Lives* 3.345 1781
5. *Ruins of Rome.* The idea "strikes more but pleases less [than that of *Grongar Hill*], and the title raises greater expectation than the performance gratifies. Some passages, however, are conceived with the mind of a poet." *Lives* 3.345 1781

Edwards, Thomas

1. Warburton's superiority to Edwards as a critic. See WARBURTON 4 *cir.* 1747

Erasmus

1. "Compelled by want to attendance and solicitation, and so much versed in common life, that he has transmitted to us the most perfect delineation of the manners of his age, he joined to his knowledge of the world, such application to books, that he will stand for ever in the first rank of literary heroes." *Wks.* 6. 237. (*Ram.* 108) 1751
2. *Ciceronianus.* "My affection and understanding went along with Erasmus, except that once or twice he somewhat unskilfully entangles Cicero's civil or moral, with his rhetorical character." *Bos.* 4.353 1784
3. "Erasmus on the New Testament" comforts and calms J. in his last illness. *Wks.* 1.577 1784

Euripides. See also GREEK DRAMATISTS
1. The absurdity of making allegorical figures persons in the *Alcestis.* See ALLEGORY 4   1779

Evans, Lewis
1. *Map and Account of the Middle Colonies in America.* "Written with such elegance as the subject admits, though not without some mixture of the American dialect; a tract of corruption to which every language widely diffused must always be exposed." *Wks.* 15.455   1756

Farquhar, George
1. *"I think Farquhar a man whose writings have considerable merit." *Bos.* 4.7. (Langton's *Collection*)   Date?

Fénelon, Archbishop
1. *Telemachus.* *"Is pretty well." See FRENCH LITERATURE 2   1773

Fenton, Elijah
1. Fenton's character of Roscommon, as a writer "too general to be critically just." *Wks.* 14.417 *n.* (*Life of Roscommon*)   1748
2. "If he did not stand in the first rank of genius he may claim a place in the second; and, whatever criticism may object to his writings, censure could find very little to blame in his life." *Lives* 3.267   1756
3. (*Lives* 2) "The elegance of his poetry." (259.) "Fenton may be justly styled an excellent versifier and a good poet." (264)   Ptd. 1780
4. *Florelio.* "It is sufficient to say that it is an occasional pastoral, which implies something neither natural nor artificial, neither comick nor serious." *Wks.* 2.263   Ptd. 1780
5. *Isaiah, Paraphrase on.* Of this, "nothing very favour-

able can be said. Sublime and solemn prose gains little by a change to blank verse; and the paraphrast has deserted his original by admitting images not Asiatick, at least not Judaical": e.g., "peace," "dove-eyed." *Lives* 2.264   1780

6. *Mariamne.* Its "peculiar system of versification." Lines of ten syllables with few redundant terminations which drama requires for naturalness. Difficult to discover his principle of construction. *Lives* 2.260-1
Ptd. 1780

7. *Milton.* "A short and elegant account of Milton's life, written at once with tenderness and integrity," prefixed to his edition of Milton. *Lives* 2.261
Ptd. 1780

8. *Minor poems.* Briefly analyzed. "Some are very trifling, without any thing to be praised either in the thought or expression." *Lives* 2.264   Ptd. 1780

9. *Ode, An.* "The next ode is irregular, and therefore defective. As the sentiments are pious they cannot easily be new, for what can be added to topicks on which successive ages have been employed!" *Lives* 2.263-4   Ptd. 1780

10. *Ode to the Sun.* "A common plan without uncommon sentiments; but its greatest fault is its length." (See SHORT COMPOSITIONS 4)   Ptd. 1780

11. *Odyssey.* (*Lives* 2) "Readers of poetry . . . have never been able to distinguish their [Fenton's and Broome's] books from those of Pope." (260. See also *ib.* 3.77.) Fenton's blank verse translation from *Odyssey* "will find few readers while another can be had in rhyme." (264)   Ptd. 1780

12. *Waller.* Published "a very splendid edition of Waller." *Lives* 2.261   Ptd. 1780

Fielding, Henry

1. *Compared with Richardson. See RICHARDSON 2
1768

2. *"Fielding being mentioned, Johnson exclaimed, 'he was a blockhead;' and upon my expressing my astonishment at so strange an assertion, he said, 'What I mean by his being a blockhead is that he was a barren rascal.' BOSWELL. 'Will you not allow, Sir, that he draws very natural pictures of human life?' JOHNSON. 'Why, Sir, it is of very low life. Richardson used to say, that had he not known who Fielding was, he should have believed he was an ostler. Sir, there is more knowledge of the heart in one letter of Richardson's, than in all *Tom Jones*. I, indeed, never read *Joseph Andrews.*' " Bos. 2.173-4   1772

3. *Amelia.* *"He told us, he read Fielding's *Amelia* through without stopping." (Johnson had just made the remark that "what we read with inclination makes a much stronger impression.") Bos. 3.43   1776

4. *Amelia.* *"Fielding's Amelia was the most pleasing heroine of all the romances (he said); but that vile broken nose never cured, ruined the sale of perhaps the only book, which being printed off betimes one morning, a new edition was called for before night." John. Misc. 1.297. (Piozzi)   Date?

5. *Fielding's works compared with *Evelina*. See BURNEY, F. 8   1778

6. *The superiour moral qualities of Richardson's writings. See RICHARDSON 13   Date?

7. *Tom Jones.* *Hannah More wrote in 1780: "I never saw Johnson really angry with me but once. . . . I alluded rather flippantly, I fear, to some witty passage in *Tom Jones:* he replied, 'I am shocked to hear you quote from so vicious a book. I am sorry to hear you have read it: a confession which no modest lady should ever make. I scarcely know a more corrupt work.' . . . He went so far as to refuse to Fielding the great talents which are ascribed to him, and broke out into a noble panegyric on his competitor, Richardson; who, he said, was as superior to him in talents as in virtue." John. Misc. 2.189-90   Date?

8. *"Johnson used to quote with approbation a saying of Richardson's, 'that the virtues of Fielding's heroes were the vices of a truly good man.'" *Bos.* 2.49
Date?

Fracastorio

1. Works commended. See ITALIAN LITERATURE 1
1755

Francis, Philip

1. *Francis the best translator of "the lyrical part of Horace." *Bos.* 3.356   1778

Frederick the Great

1. "His letters have an air of familiar elegance." *Wks.* 4.537   1756
2. *"As to his being an authour, I have not looked at his poetry; but his prose is poor stuff. He writes just as you might suppose Voltaire's footboy to do, who has been his amanuensis. He has such parts as the valet might have, and about as much of the colouring of the style as might be got by transcribing his works." *Bos.* 1.434   1763

Galileo

1. Works commended. See ITALIAN LITERATURE 1   1755

Garrick, David

1. *Mrs. Thrale defends the line from G.'s song in *Florizel and Perdita* [*The Winter's Tale*]: "They smile with the simple, and feed with the poor" (misquoted by Mrs. Thrale or by Boswell). "JOHNSON. 'Nay, my dear lady, this will never do. Poor David! Smile with the simple;— What folly is that? And who would feed with the poor that can help it? No, no; let me smile with the wise, and feed with the rich.'" *Bos.* 2.78-9   1769

2. *Epitaph for Hogarth.* Analyzed by J. *Letters* 1.187
1771
3. *Prologues.* *"Dryden has written prologues superiour to any that David Garrick has written; but David Garrick has written more good prologues than Dryden has done. It is wonderful that he has been able to write such variety of them." *Bos.* 2.325   1775
4. *Of his fable of the blackbird and the eagle, J. remarks that it has not "much of the spirit of fabulosity," since it is not true to animal nature. *Early Diary of Frances Burney*, ed. Ellis, 1907, 2.157   1777
5. *Prologues and Epilogues. Prologue to Bonduca.* *"I got through half a dozen lines [of G.'s *Prologue to Bonduca*], but I could observe no other subject than eternal dulness. I don't know what is the matter with David; I am afraid he is grown superannuated, for his prologues and epilogues used to be incomparable." D'Arblay, *Diary and Letters*, 1.57   1778
6. *J. agrees with Boswell that Garrick "is a very sprightly writer." *Bos.* 3.263   1778

Garth, Samuel

1. His unfitness as a critic. *Wks.* 5.160. (*Ram.* 24)
1750
2. Garth "is mentioned perhaps with too much honour" as comic forerunner of Pope. *Wks.* 15.476   1756
3. "His poetry has been praised at least equally to its merit." *Lives* 2.63   1779
4. *Dispensary, The.* "There is a strain of smooth and free versification; but few lines are eminently elegant. No passages fall below mediocrity, and few rise much above it. The plan seems formed without just proportion to the subject; the means and end have no necessary connection." General design open to criticism, but little inaccuracy or negligence. Vigour; finish. "It appears, however, to want something of poetical ardour, and something of general delectation; and there-

fore, since it has been no longer supported by accidental and extrinsick popularity, it has been scarcely able to support itself." *Lives* 2.63-4   1779

5. *Preface to Ovid's Metamorphoses.* "Written with more ostentation than ability: his notions are half-formed, and his materials immethodically confused." *Lives* 2.62   1779

Gay, John

1. "As a poet he cannot be rated very high. He was, as I once heard a female critick remark, 'of a lower order.' He had not in any great degree the *mens divinior*, the dignity of genius. Much, however, must be allowed to the author of a new species of composition, though it be not of the highest kind. We owe to Gay the Ballad Opera." A mode of comedy likely to last—suited to the popular taste. "There are many writers read with more reverence to whom such merit of originality cannot be attributed." *Lives* 2.282-3   1781

2. *Beggar's Opera.* (See also *supra* 1.) *Its influence overestimated: " 'I do not believe that any man was ever made a rogue by being present at its representation. At the same time I do not deny that it may have some influence, by making the character of a rogue familiar, and in some degree pleasing.' Then collecting himself as it were, to give a heavy stroke: 'There is in it such a *labefactation* of all principles, as may be injurious to morality.' " *Bos.* 2.367   1775

3. *Beggar's Opera.* *"I should have thought it would succeed, not from any great excellence in the writing, but from the novelty, and the general spirit and gaiety of the piece, which keeps the audience always attentive, and dismisses them in good humour." *Bos.* 3.321   1778

4. *Beggar's Opera.* "The play, like many others, was plainly written only to divert, without any moral purpose, and is therefore not likely to do good; nor

can it be conceived, without more speculation than life requires or admits, to be productive of much evil. Highwaymen and housebreakers seldom frequent the play-house or mingle in any elegant diversion; nor is it possible for any one to imagine that he may rob with safety because he sees Macheath reprieved upon the stage." *Lives* 2.278 1781
5. *Dione.* "*Dione* is a counterpart to *Amynta* and *Pastor Fido*, and other trifles of the same kind, easily imitated, and unworthy of imitation." See PASTORAL 14
1781
6. *Fables.* G.'s fables do not always conform to J.'s definition (see FABLE 4)—"for a Fable he gives now and then a Tale or an abstracted Allegory[1];" and some do not convey a moral. "They are, however, told with liveliness: the versification is smooth, and the diction, though now and then a little constrained by the measure or the rhyme, is generally happy." *Lives* 2.283
1781
7. *Fan, The.* A mythological fiction of little value. See MYTHOLOGY 22 1781
8. "*Little Poems.*" "Of his little poems the publick judgement seems to be right; they are neither much esteemed, nor totally despised." The least pleasing are those echoes of *Gulliver.* See SWIFT 17 1781
9. *Rural Sports.* "Such as was easily planned and executed: it is never contemptible, nor ever excellent." *Lives* 2.283 1781
10. *Shepherd's Week, The.* "But the effect of reality and truth became conspicuous, even when the intention was to shew them groveling and degraded."[2] Their popularity from "just representations of rural manners." The *Proeme* to this in antique language, and hence in a style "never spoken nor written in any age or in any place." *Lives* 2.269 1781

[1] ". . . or an Allegory," in first ed.
[2] Gay intended to ridicule the artificial pastoral of the day by exhibiting the true grossness and ignorance of country life.

11. *Three Hours after Marriage.* "It has the fate which such outrages deserve."¹ *Lives* 2.272   1781

12. *Trivia.* "To *Trivia* may be allowed all that it claims: it is spritely, various, and pleasant. The subject is of that kind which Gay was by nature qualified to adorn; yet some of his [mythological] decorations may be justly wished away." See MYTHOLOGY 23   1781

13. *What d'ye call it.* "Of this performance the value certainly is but little; but it was one of the lucky trifles that give pleasure by novelty." Its success. *Lives* 2.271
        1781

Gentleman's Magazine. See also CAVE

1. Its wide reputation and success. *Wks.* 4.525-6. See also *Gent. Mag.*, 1741, p. iii (Preface)   1754

Glover, Richard

1. *Leonidas.* *The good passages must be *sought* for. *Bos.* 5.116. (*Hebrides*, 27 Aug.)   1773

Goldsmith, Oliver

1. *"One of the first men we now have as an authour." *Bos.* 1.408   1763

2. *"His genius is great, but his knowledge is small." (Applied to G.'s conversation.) *Bos.* 2.196   1772

3. *"Sir, he knows nothing; he has made up his mind about nothing." *Bos.* 2.215   1773

4. *J. does not think G. one of his imitators, and says he "had great merit." *Bos.* 2.216   1773

5. *"It is amazing how little Goldsmith knows. He seldom comes where he is not more ignorant than any one else." His company liked: "When people find a man of the most distinguished abilities as a writer, their inferiour while he is with them, it must be highly

---

¹ It attacked, with considerable grossness, Dr. Woodward, the fossilist. Pope and Arbuthnot undoubtedly had a hand in it.

gratifying to them . . . he is master of a subject in his study, and can write well upon it; but when he comes into company, grows confused, and unable to talk. Take him as a poet, his *Traveller* is a very fine performance; ay, and so is his *Deserted Village*, were it not sometimes too much the echo of his *Traveller*. Whether, indeed, we take him as a poet,—as a comick writer,—or as an historian, he stands in the first class." *Bos.* 2.235-6   1773

6. *As a possible biographer of J.: "The dog would write it best to be sure . . . but his particular malice towards me, and general disregard for truth, would make the book useless to all, and injurious to my character." *John. Misc.* 1.166. (Piozzi)   1773

7. *"You will find ten thousand fit to do what they [military officers] did, before you find one who does what Goldsmith has done." *Bos.* 5.137. (*Hebrides*, 31 Aug.)   1773

8. "But let not his frailties be remembered; he was a very great man." *Bos.* 2.281   1774

9. J.'s Greek "tetastrick" on the death of Goldsmith. *Bos.* 2.282   1774

10. *"If nobody was suffered to abuse poor Goldy, but those who could write as well, he would have few censors." Northcote's *Reynolds*, 1.327   *cir.* 1774

11. *J. declares "that Goldsmith was the best writer he ever knew, upon every subject he wrote upon." *John. Misc.* 2.49-50. (Campbell)   1775

12. "Qui nullum fere scribendi genus
        Non tetigit
   Nullum quod tetigit non ornavit:
     Sive risus essent movendi,
       Sive lacrimæ,
   Affectuum potens at lenis dominator:
   Ingenio sublimis, vividus, versatilis,
   Oratione grandis, nitidus, venustus:
   Hoc monumento memoriam coluit

Sodalium amor,
Amicorum fides,
Lectorum veneratio."

Wks. 14.543-4. (For J.'s translation of this epitaph, see Kearsley's ed. of J.'s *Poetical Works*, 1789, pp. 207-8. For its history, see *Bos.* 3.81-5) 1776

13. *"Goldsmith, however, was a man, who, whatever he wrote, did it better than any other man could do. He deserved a place in Westminster-Abbey, and every year he lived, would have deserved it better. He had, indeed, been at no pains to fill his mind with knowledge. He transplanted it from one place to another; and it did not settle in his mind; so he could not tell what was in his own books." *Bos.* 3.253 1778

14. *"Goldsmith had no settled notions upon any subject; so he talked always at random." *Bos.* 3.252 1778

15. *" 'See, madam,' said Dr. Johnson, laughing, 'what it is to have the favour of a literary man! I think I have had no hero a great while; Dr. Goldsmith was my last; but I have had none since his time till my little Burney came!' " D'Arblay, *Diary and Letters*, 1.132 1778

16. *Referring to the charge that Goldsmith had stolen the character of Croaker in *The Good-natured Man* from Johnson's Suspirius in the *Rambler:* " 'Ah, madam!' cried he, 'Goldsmith was not scrupulous; but he would have been a great man had he known the real value of his own internal resources.' " D'Arblay, *Diary and Letters*, 1.77 1778

17. G., "a man of such variety of powers and such felicity of performance that he always seemed to do best that which he was doing; a man who had the art of being minute without tediousness, and general without confusion; whose language was copious without exuberance, exact without constraint, and easy without weakness." *Lives* 2.49 1781

18. *"Is there a man, Sir, now who can pen an essay with

such ease and elegance as Goldsmith?" *Letters*, 2.326 *n* 2 1783?
19. *"No man was more foolish when he had not a pen in his hand, or more wise when he had." *Bos.* 4.29. (Langton's *Collection*) Date?
20. *Deserted Village.* *Praised. See *supra* 5   1773
21. *Good-natured Man.* *"He praised Goldsmith's *Good-natured Man*; said, it was the best comedy that had appeared since *The Provoked Husband*, and that there had not been of late any such character exhibited on the stage as that of Croaker." *Bos.* 2.48. (See also *supra* 16)   1768
22. *History of . . . Animated Nature.* *"He is now writing a Natural History and will make it as entertaining as a Persian Tale." *Bos.* 2.237   1773
23. *History of . . . Animated Nature.* *"Goldsmith, Sir, will give us a very fine book upon the subject; but if he can distinguish a cow from a horse, that, I believe, may be the extent of his knowledge of natural history." *Bos.* 3.84 *n* 2 by Boswell.   *cir.* 1773?
24. *History of Rome.* *J. places G. above the other historians of his age. "It is the great excellence of a writer to put into his book as much as his book will hold. Goldsmith has done this in his *History [of Rome]*. . . . Goldsmith tells you shortly all you want to know. . . . Goldsmith's plain narrative will please again and again. . . . Sir, he has the art of compiling, and of saying every thing he has to say in a pleasing manner." *Bos.* 2.236-7   1773
25. *Life of Thomas Parnell.* *J. thinks it poor: "not that it is poorly written, but that he had poor materials; for nobody can write the life of a man, but those who have eat and drunk and lived in social intercourse with him." *Bos.* 2.166. (See also *Lives* 2.49)   1772
26. *Life of Thomas Parnell.* "His criticism it is seldom safe to contradict." (J. is discussing G.'s critical remarks in his *Life of Thomas Parnell.*) *Lives* 2.52   1781

27. *She Stoops to Conquer.* "The manager predicts ill success. I hope he will be mistaken. I think it deserves a very kind reception." *Bos.* 2.208   1773
28. *She Stoops to Conquer.* "The chief diversion arises from a stratagem by which a lover is made to mistake his future father-in-law's house for an inn. This, you see, borders upon farce. The dialogue is quick and gay, and the incidents are so prepared as not to seem improbable." *Bos.* 2.205-6   1773
29. *She Stoops to Conquer.* *"I know of no comedy for many years that has so much exhilarated an audience, that has answered so much the great end of comedy— making an audience merry." *Bos.* 2.233   1773
30. *Traveller.* Its "elegant" dedication. "The author already [in passage quoted by J.] appears, by his numbers, to be a versifier; and by his scenery, to be a poet; it therefore only remains that his sentiments discover him to be a just estimator of comparative happiness. . . . Such is the poem, on which we now congratulate the public, as on a production to which, since the death of Pope, it will not be easy to find anything equal." *The Critical Review,* Dec., 1764, pp. 458-62. (Review by J.)   1764
31. *Traveller.* *"There has not been so fine a poem since Pope's time." *Bos.* 2.5. (See also *Wks.* 1.420 for confirmation by Hawkins)   1766
32. *Traveller.* *Praised. See *supra* 5   1773
33. *Traveller.* *J. speaks highly of this poem and repeats "from it the character of the British nation . . . with such energy that the tear started into his eye." *Bos.* 5.344. (*Hebrides,* 23 Oct.)   1773
34. *Traveller.* *"The merit of *The Traveller* is so well established, that Mr. Fox's praise cannot augment it, nor his censure diminish it." *Bos.* 3.252   1778
35. *Traveller.* *J. "was seen to weep whilst he repeated Goldsmith's character of the English in his *Traveller.*" *John. Misc.* 2.6. (Hawkins's *Apophthegms*)   Date?

36. *Traveller.* *"Of Goldsmith's *Traveller* he used to speak in terms of the highest commendation." *John. Misc.* 2.268. (Miss Reynolds)　　　Date?
37. *Vicar of Wakefield.* *J. "saw its merit" according to Boswell, when he sold the manuscript for Goldsmith. *Bos.* 1.416　　　1762
38. *Vicar of Wakefield.* *"His *Vicar of Wakefield* I myself did not think would have had much success." *Bos.* 3.321　　　1778
39. *Vicar of Wakefield.* *Mrs. Thrale to J.:—"Don't you like it, sir?" "No, madam, it is very faulty; there is nothing of real life in it, and very little of nature. It is a mere fanciful performance." D'Arblay, *Diary and Letters*, 1.77　　　1778
40. *Vicar of Wakefield.* *Two fine passages foolishly struck out by G. *Bos.* 3.376　　　1779

Gower, John

1. "The father of our poetry . . . he that reads the works of *Gower* will find smooth numbers and easy rhymes, of which *Chaucer* is supposed to have been the inventor, and the *French* words, whether good or bad, of which *Chaucer* is charged as the importer." His diction "in general like that of his contemporaries: and some improvements he undoubtedly made by the various dispositions of his rhymes, and by the mixture of different numbers, in which he seems to have been happy and judicious." *Hist. of the Eng. Lang.*, *Dict.* ed. 1755　　　1755
2. "Who, however obscured by his scholar's [Chaucer's] popularity, seems justly to claim the honour which has been hitherto denied him, of shewing his countrymen that something more was to be desired, and that *English* verse might be exalted into poetry." *Wks.* 8.254. (*Idl.* 63)　　　1759

Graham, Rev. George

1. *Telemachus. A mask.* "We recommend the fertility of

imagination, the depth of sentiment, and the knowledge of passion, which are occasionally displayed, to the observation of those readers who have skill to discern, and delicacy to taste them." *Critical Review,* Apr. 1763, p. 318. (Review by J.)   1763

Grainger, James

1. *The Sugar Cane.* "The qualifications of an American traveller are knowledge of Nature and copiousness of language, acuteness of observation, and facility of description. It is therefore with that pleasure which every rational mind finds in the hope of enlarging the empire of science, that we see these enlightened regions visited by a man who examines them as a philosopher, and describes them as a poet." A "fine personification," which opens the fourth book, quoted. *London Chronicle,* 1764, p. xvi. (Review by J. of *The Sugar Cane*) 1764

2. *The Sugar Cane.* "The reader must not be deterred by the title-page, since the most languid will here find his passions excited, and the imagination indulged to the highest pitch of luxury. A new creation is offered, of which an European has scarce any conception. . . . It is, indeed, a little extraordinary how regions so poetically striking, and so well known to the merchant, have been so little visited by the muse: and that . . . we have been destitute till now of an American poet, that could bear any degree of competition." J. refers to "this original performance." The author, imitating Virgil, has "happily effected" the difficult task of reconciling "the wild imagery of an Indian picture to the strict rules of critical exactness . . . and although he treads upon unclassic ground, yet maintains a classical regularity. . . . The character of a good planter is beautifully described." Interest increases throughout the poem. In "extending the bounds of natural history, while he seems only to address the imagination

... doctor Grainger has the advantage of many poets." His celebration of Rum: he has "maintained his description without sinking, and the poet has elegantly described a liquor which yet he seems ashamed to name." His "striking invocation to the genius of Africa." In directions for slave-buying the "tenderness and humanity, with which the former part of the poem seems replete, is, in some measure, forgotten. . . . The poet had an untrodden country to clear; and, though he may not have entirely subdued the native rudeness of the soil, yet he certainly has opened a delightful tract for future cultivation." *Critical Review*, Oct. 1764, pp. 170 [270]-277. (Review by J.) 1764

3. *The Sugar Cane.**"*The Sugar-Cane*, a poem, did not please him; for, he exclaimed, 'What could he make of a sugar-cane? One might as well write the 'Parsley-bed, a Poem;' or 'The Cabbage-garden, a Poem.'" *Bos.* 2.454   1776

4. *Ode on Solitude.* *J. praises this *Ode*, and repeats the passage "O Solitude, romantick maid," etc., observing, "This, Sir, is very noble." *Bos.* 3.197. (According to Mrs. Piozzi, J. often quoted and expressed admiration for this passage. See *John. Misc.* 2.266)   1777

Granville, George, Baron Lansdowne

1. The "*Granvilles, Montagues, Stepneys*, and *Sheffields* of their time," i.e., writers of "bubbles of artificial fame," soon annihilated. *Wks.* 6.223. (*Ram.* 106)
1751

2. G.'s contemporary reputation as a poet influenced by his character, manners, party loyalty, etc. "With those advantages, having learned the art of versifying, he declared himself a poet; and his claim to the laurel was allowed. But by a critick of a later generation who takes up his book without any favourable prejudices, the praise already received will be thought sufficient; for his works do not shew him to have had much com-

prehension from nature, or illumination from learning." Apparently "no ambition above the imitation of Waller, of whom he has copied the faults, and very little more. He is for ever amusing himself with the puerilities of mythology." *Lives* 2.294   Ptd. 1780

3. *Plays*. (*Lives* 2) G. "could not admire without bigotry; he copied the wrong as well as the right from his masters, and may be supposed to have learned obscenity from Wycherley as he learned mythology from Waller." (290.) *Jew of Venice*. "As Rowe remarks, the character of *Shylock* is made comick, and we are prompted to laughter instead of detestation." (290.) *Peleus and Thetis*. (Masque.) "Here and there a pretty line; but it is not always melodious, and the conclusion is wretched." (296.) *British Enchanters*. Its bad anachronism. "But the dialogue has often the air of Dryden's rhyming plays, and the songs are lively, though not very correct. This is, I think, far the best of his works; for if it has many faults it has likewise passages which are at least pretty, though they do not rise to any high degree of excellence."[1] (296)
                                          Ptd. 1780

4. *Poems*. (*Lives* 2) *Juvenilia*. (286-7.) *Several Orations of Demosthenes*, etc. (G. co-translator of. 291.) *Beauty and Law*, "after having rattled a while with Juno and Pallas . . . at last concludes its folly with profaneness." (294.) *Verses to Mira*. "Have little in them of either art or nature, of the sentiments of a lover, or the language of a poet: there may be found now and then a happier effort, but they are commonly feeble and unaffecting, or forced and extravagant." (295.) "*Little Pieces*." "Seldom either spritely or elegant, either keen or weighty. They are trifles written by idleness, and published by vanity."[2] (295.)

---

[1] J. tells Nichols to add the preface to the *British Enchanters* to the life. *Letters* 2.131

[2] But J. repeats two verses (with variations) of Granville's on a certain tavern occasion. *Bos.* 1.251

The Progress of Beauty. "Not deficient in splendour and gaiety; but the merit of original thought is wanting." (295.) *Essay upon unnatural Flights in Poetry.* "Not inelegant nor injudicious, and has something of vigour beyond most of his other performances: his precepts are just, and his cautions proper," etc. (295)
                                                                Ptd. 1780

5. *Prologues and Epilogues.* "Have a just claim to praise." *Lives* 2.295   Ptd. 1780

Gray, Thomas

1. *"Sir, I do not think Gray a first-rate poet. He has not a bold imagination, nor much command of words. The obscurity in which he has involved himself will not persuade us that he is sublime. His *Elegy in a Church-yard* has a happy selection of images, but I don't like what are called his great things." (See *The Bard* for criticism of this ode which follows.) *Bos.* 1.402-3   1763

2. *Boswell. "I mentioned that we were to have the remains of Mr. Gray, in prose and verse, published by Mr. Mason. Johnson. 'I think we have had enough of Gray.'" *Bos.* 2.164   1772

3. *"Boswell. . . . 'Surely he [Gray] was not dull in poetry.' Johnson. 'Sir, he was dull in company, dull in his closet, dull every where. He was dull in a new way, and that made many people think him GREAT. He was a mechanical poet.' He then repeated some ludicrous lines . . . and said, 'Is not that GREAT, like his Odes?'" *Bos.* 2.327   1775

4. *Inferior as a poet to Akenside. *Bos.* 3.32   1776

5. *"Boswell. 'Does not Gray's poetry, Sir, tower above the common mark?' Johnson. 'Yes, Sir; but we must attend to the difference between what men in general cannot do if they would, and what every man may do if he would. Sixteen-string Jack towered above the common mark.'" *Bos.* 3.38   1776

6. *G.'s poetry.* (*Lives* 3) "I hope not to be looked on as an enemy to his name if I confess that I contemplate it with less pleasure than his life." (433.) *Manner of composition.* Every line "laboured"; G. subject to certain favourable times, and happy moments for composition. J. calls this "a fantastick foppery." (433)
                                                                1781
7. *"Gray was the very Torré of poetry;[1] he played his coruscations so speciously, that his steel dust is mistaken by many for a shower of gold." *Wks.* 11.214-5. (Hawkins's *Apophthegms.* Perhaps taken from Steevens. See *John. Misc.* 2.321)   Date?
8. *J. parodies Gray. *John. Misc.* 1.191. (Piozzi)
                                                                Date?
9. *"Of Gray he always spoke as he wrote, and called his poetry artificial." J. did not like his odes. *John. Misc.* 2.372. (Tyers)   Date?
10. *Agrippina.* "The judgement of every reader will confirm" R. West's adverse opinion of this tragedy. "It was certainly no loss to the English stage that *Agrippina* was never finished." *Lives* 3.423   1781
11. *Alliance of Education and Government.* Of more importance than *Ode on the Death of a Favourite Cat.* "Many excellent lines." *Lives* 3.424   1781
12. *Bard, The.* (See also *infra, Odes.*) *J. does not like "what are called his great things." The abrupt opening of *The Bard* censured: "such arts as these have no merit, unless when they are original. We admire them only once; and this abruptness has nothing new in it. We have had it often before. Nay, we have it in the old song of Johnny Armstrong. . . . The two next lines [ll. 3-4] in that Ode [*The Bard*] are, I think, very good." *Bos.* 1.403   1763
13. *Bard, The.* (*Lives* 3) J. agrees with Algarotti that it is superior to its original, except that it is a copy: "There is in *The Bard* more force, more thought, and

---

[1] For Torré's fireworks, see *Bos.* 4.324

more variety. But to copy is less than to invent, and the copy has been unhappily produced at a wrong time." (438.) The revival of Horace's fiction disgusts to-day because not believed. "He that forsakes the probable" lessens the moral usefulness of his work. (See FICTION 12 for the whole of this important critical statement.) *Versification:* Stanzas "too long, especially his epodes." (See PINDARIC VERSE 9.) Alliterations—" 'ruin,' 'ruthless,' 'helm nor hauberk,' are below the grandeur of a poem that endeavours at sublimity." Abrupt beginning celebrated, "but technical beauties can give praise only to the inventor." (438-9.) Analysis of individual stanzas: "puerilities of obsolete mythology," indistinct personification, suicidal ending, etc., censured. (439-40) 1781

14. *Elegy Written in a Country Church-Yard.* *"Has a happy selection of images." *Bos.* 1.403 1763

15. *Elegy Written in a Country Church-Yard.* *"No, Sir, there are but two good stanzas in Gray's poetry, which are in his *Elegy in a Country Church-yard.*' He then repeated the stanza, 'For who to dumb forgetfulness a prey,' &c. mistaking one word; for instead of *precincts* he said *confines.* He added, 'The other stanza I forget.' " *Bos.* 2.328. (Repeated in *John. Misc.* 2.52) 1775

16. *Elegy Written in a Country Church-Yard.* "Gray has the advantage [in his *Elegy* over Parnell's *Night Piece*] in dignity, variety, and originality of sentiment." *Lives* 2.53 1781

17. *Elegy Written in a Country Church-Yard.* J. agrees with the favourable verdict of the common reader. (See POPULAR JUDGEMENT 36.) "The *Church-yard* abounds with images which find a mirrour in every mind, and with sentiments to which every bosom returns an echo. The four stanzas beginning 'Yet even these bones' are to me original: I have never seen the notions in any other place; yet he that reads them here persuades himself that he has always felt them. Had Gray written

often thus it had been vain to blame, and useless to praise him." *Lives* 3.441-2   1781

18. *Hymn to Adversity.* (See also *infra*, *Odes.*) Founded on hint from Horace, "but Gray has excelled his original by the variety of his sentiments and by their moral application. Of this piece, at once poetical and rational, I will not by slight objections violate the dignity." *Lives* 3.435-6   1781

19. *Latin Poems.* J. wishes Gray had kept on with them: in spite of "embarrassment in his phrase, and some harshness in his Lyrick numbers, his copiousness of language is such as very few possess, and his lines, even when imperfect, discover a writer whom practice would quickly have made skilful." *Lives* 3.424   1781

20. *Letters* (ed. Mason). *Boswell wrote to Temple, May 10, 1775:—"Dr. Johnson does not like the book. He however says that one should consider that these letters were written and received in a long series of years, and so might do very well at the time; whereas now we must read them as one mass, which makes a great difference." *Letters of Boswell*, ed. C. B. Tinker, 1.222-3   1775

21. *Letters* (ed. Mason). "The book which is now most read, but which, as far as I have gone, is but dull, is Gray's letters, prefixed by Mr. Mason to his poems. . . . I can hardly recommend the purchase." (J. to Mrs. Thrale.) *Letters*, 1.317   1775

22. *Letters.* (*Lives* 3) "Contain a very pleasing account" of his journey on Continent. (422.) His account of journey to Scotland "very curious and elegant": his curiosity towards art, nature and antiquity. (427.) "He that reads his epistolary narration [of his visit to Westmoreland and Cumberland] wishes that to travel, and to tell his travels, had been more of his employment." (428.)   1781

23. *Long Story, A.* "An odd composition . . . which adds little to Gray's character."[1] *Lives* 3.425   1781

[1] In first ed.: "which, though perhaps it adds little to Gray's character, I am not pleased to find wanting in this Collection. It will therefore be added to this Preface."

24. *Ode on a Distant Prospect of Eton College.* (See also *infra, Odes.*) "Suggests nothing to Gray which every beholder does not equally think and feel." Supplication to Father Thames "useless and puerile." "Epithet 'buxom health' is not elegant; he seems not to understand the word." Gales "redolent of joy and youth": distortion of the language, even more beyond common comprehension than Dryden's similar phrase. *Lives* 3.434-5   1781
25. *Ode on the Death of a Favourite Cat.* "Was doubtless by its author considered as a trifle, but it is not a happy trifle." "Nymph" applied to cat "with some violence both to language and sense; but there is good use made of it when it is done." "The sixth stanza contains a melancholy truth, that 'a favourite has no friend,' but the last ends in a pointed sentence of no relation to the purpose; if what glistered had been 'gold,' the cat would not have gone into the water; and, if she had, would not less have been drowned." *Lives* 3.434

    1781
26. *Ode on the Spring.* (See also *infra, Odes.*) "Has something poetical, both in the language and the thought; but the language is too luxuriant, and the thoughts have nothing new." Condemns "*honied* Spring." (See DICTION 30.) "The morality is natural, but too stale; the conclusion is pretty." *Lives* 3.434   1781
27. *Odes.* (See also individual odes, *infra* and *supra.*) *J. ridicules G.'s *Odes.* (See *supra* 3.) "Mrs. Thrale maintained that his Odes were melodious; upon which he exclaimed,
    'Weave the warp, and weave the woof;'—
I added, in a solemn tone,
    'The winding-sheet of Edward's race.'
'*There* is a good line.' 'Ay, (said he), and the next line is a good one,' (pronouncing it contemptuously;)
    'Give ample verge and room enough.' "[1]
Bos. 2.327   1775

[1] Should read "Give ample room and verge enough."

28. *Odes.* *"A very bad kind of writing" exposed. See
    MASON 1   1775
29. *Odes: The Progress of Poesy* and *The Bard.* (*Lives* 3)
    At first received with "mute amazement. . . . Some
    hardy champions undertook to rescue them from neg-
    lect, and in a short time many were content to be shewn
    beauties which they could not see." (426.) "The 'Won-
    derful Wonder of Wonders,' the two Sister Odes; by
    which, though either vulgar ignorance or common sense
    at first universally rejected them, many have been
    since persuaded to think themselves delighted." (436.)
    "These odes are marked by glittering accumulations of
    ungraceful ornaments: they strike, rather than please;
    the images are magnified by affectation; the language
    is laboured into harshness.[1] The mind of the writer
    seems to work with unnatural violence. 'Double,
    double, toil and trouble.' He has a kind of strutting
    dignity, and is tall by walking on tiptoe. His art and
    his struggle are too visible, and there is too little ap-
    pearance of ease and nature. To say that he has no
    beauties would be unjust: a man like him, of great
    learning and great industry, could not but produce
    something valuable. When he pleases least, it can only
    be said that a good design was ill directed." (440-1)
                                                      1781
30. *Odes.* *"They are forced plants raised in a hot-bed;
    and they are poor plants; they are but cucumbers after
    all." *Bos.* 4.13. (Langton's *Collection*)   Date?
31. *Progress of Poesy.* (See also *supra*, *Odes*.) Detailed
    analysis: Its obscurity, mythological conventions, un-
    natural diction, cumbrous splendour, etc., censured.
    Lives 3.436-8   1781
32. *Translations.* "His translations of Northern and Welsh
    Poetry deserve praise: the imagery is preserved, per-
    haps often improved; but the language is unlike the
    language of other poets." *Lives* 3.441   1781

[1] See HARSH for J.'s use of this word.

Greek Dramatists. See also individual Greek dramatists.

1. *J. "acknowledged that his studies had not lain amongst them."[1] *John. Misc.* 2.78. (Cumberland) Date?
2. *The machinery of the Grecian tragedies wearisome. See MYTHOLOGY 34 Date?

Green, Matthew

1. *The Spleen "not poetry." *Bos.* 3.38   1776

Greville, Richard Fulke

1. *Maxims, Characters and Reflections.* "Written with uncommon knowledge of mankind, which is the chief excellence of such a book. The sentences are keenly pointed, and vigorously pushed, which is their second excellence. But it is too Gallick, and the proper names are often ill-formed or ill-chosen. To use a French phrase, I think the good *carries it over* the bad. The good is in the constituent, the bad in the accidental parts." *Letters* 1.60-1   1756

Grey, Dr. Zachary

1. Criticized as editor of Shakespeare. *Shak. Pref.*, Raleigh, 50-1   1765

Grotius, Hugo

1. J. seeks aid for the nephew of Grotius, "from whom perhaps every man of learning has learnt something." *Bos.* 3.125   1777
2. "The noble epigram of Grotius upon the death of Scaliger." *Lives* 1.57   1779

---

[1] Joseph Warton's remark in 1756 gives historical perspective to this confession: "It was not fashionable in POPE's time, nor among his acquaintance, attentively to study these poets [Sophocles, Euripides, etc.]. By a strange fatality, they have not in this kingdom obtained the rank they deserve amongst classic writers ... hardly a critic among us, has professedly pointed out their excellencies." (*Essay on ... Pope*, ed. 1806, 1.361)

Grove, Henry. See SPECTATOR 2

Grub-Street Journal
1. "That enemy to all Works of Merit." *Gent. Mag.*, 1738, iii *n.* (*To the Reader*)   1738

Guarini
1. *Amynta* and *Pastor Fido*, "trifles . . . easily imitated, and unworthy of imitation." See PASTORAL 14   1781

Halifax, Charles Montagu, Earl of. For his collaboration with Prior, see PRIOR 6
1. The "Montagues . . . of their time." See GRANVILLE 1   1751
2. "His poetry, of which a short time has withered the beauties. It would now be esteemed no honour, by a contributor to the monthly bundles of verses, to be told that, in strains either familiar or solemn, he sings like Montague." *Lives* 2.47   1779
3. "Halifax, who, by having been first a poet, and then a patron of poetry, had acquired the right of being a judge." *Lives* 3.126   1781

Hamilton, William. (Of Bangour)
1. *J. ridicules his verses:—"no power of thinking . . . nothing that strikes one," etc. *Bos.* 3.150-1   1777

Hammond, James
1. (*Lives* 2) Hard to find three stanzas that deserve to be remembered. (315.) "His verses are not rugged, but they have no sweetness: they never glide in a stream of melody." (315-6.) J. questions his use of "quatrain of ten syllables" in elegy. See ELEGY 9   1781
2. *Love Elegies.* *J. calls them "poor things." *Bos.* 5.268. (*Hebrides*, 29 Sept.)   1773

3. *Love Elegies.* "The truth is these elegies have neither passion, nature, nor manners [See ELEGY 10]. . . . He produces nothing but frigid pedantry." *Lives* 2.315   1781
4. *Love Elegies.* *A "hag or witch" introduced (in *Elegy* V) "where the effect is unmeaning and disgusting." *Bos.* 4.17. (Langton's *Collection*)   Date?

Hampton, James

1. *Translation of Polybius.* Highly commended in a brief review by J. in *The Literary Magazine* 1756: "This appears to be one of the books, which will long do honour to the present age . . . and there is reason to believe that this [translation] will grow in reputation, while the English tongue continues in its present state. . . . His book has the dignity of antiquity, and the easy flow of a modern composition." *Wks.* ed. 1825, Oxford, 6.77-8   1756

Hanmer, Sir Thomas

1. Censured as Shakespearean editor. Shirks obscure passages. Few important original emendations. The pomp of this edition "recommends it more than its accuracy. There is no distinction made between the ancient reading, and the innovations of the editor; there is no reason given for any of the alterations which are made; the emendations of former critics are adopted without any acknowledgment, and few of the difficulties are removed which have hitherto embarrassed the readers of *Shakespeare.*" *Wks.* 14.111-3. (*Observ. on Macb.*)   1745
2. Possessed the intuition necessary to emendatory criticism. His edition praised—with reservations. *Shak. Pref.*, Raleigh, 46-7   1765

Hannes, Dr. Edward

1. The Latin *Ode to St. John* by J. Philips "seems better turned than the odes of Hannes." *Lives* 1.318   1779

Hanway, Jonas

1. *"Jonas . . . acquired some reputation by travelling abroad, but lost it all by travelling at home." *Bos.* 2.122. (Maxwell's *Collectanea*)   Date?

Harris, James

1. *"A coxcomb . . . not as a man, but as an authour." *Bos.* 5.377-8. (*Hebrides*, 3 Nov.) See also *John. Misc.* 1.187; 2.70-1, 344; *Wks.* 1.255; *Bos.* 3.245   1773

Hawkesworth, Dr. John

1. *J. approves "very highly" of H.'s *Ode on Life*. *John. Misc.* 2.167   ante 1747
2. His writings show "a very powerful mind." *Letters* 2.8   1777
3. J. praises the *Life of Swift* by H., "a man capable of dignifying his narration with so much elegance of language and force of sentiment." *Lives* 3.1   1781

Hayley, William

1. *J. prevailed upon "to read *The Triumphs of Temper*, when it was in its zenith, . . . but never got beyond the two first pages." *John. Misc.* 2.420-1. (Mrs. Rose)   cir. 1781

Hervey, Rev. James

1. *J. burlesques his *Meditations on a Flower-garden* and other subjects, by extemporaneous reflections on a pudding. *Wks.* 1.388. (See also *Bos.* 5.351-2 for this anecdote)   Date?

Hill, Aaron

1. Savage "had indeed in Mr. Hill another critick of a very different class [from Cibber]." *Lives* 2.339
    1744

2. "Remarkable for singularity of sentiment and bold experiments in language." *Lives* 2.339-40   1744
3. His "affecting lines" on Savage in *The Plain Dealer*. *Lives* 2.341. (See also *ib. n* 7 for this publication)
    1744
4. Writes *Prologue* and *Epilogue* for Mallet's *Eurydice*, "neither of which can be much commended." *Lives* 3.402   1781

Holyday, Barten

1. His translations. See MAY 1; and *John. Misc.* 2.387. *Lives* 1.422, 446   Misc. dates

Home, Henry. See KAMES

Home, John

1. *Douglas.* *J. reiterates a former statement "that there were not ten good lines in the whole play." Upon Boswell's quoting a passage (I.i), J. exclaims:—"That will not do, Sir. Nothing is good but what is consistent with truth or probability, which this is not . . . [J. then quotes passage from Juvenal on virtue.] And, after this, comes Johnny Home, with his *earth gaping*, and his *destruction crying:*—Pooh!" *Bos.* 5.360-2. (*Hebrides*, 26 Oct.)   1773
2. *Douglas.* *"That foolish play." *Bos.* 2.320   Date?

Homer. See also ANCIENT WRITERS. For comparison with Virgil, see under VIRGIL. See also MILTON 43a for an implied comparison of the *Iliad* with *Paradise Lost*

1. "The father of all poetical beauty." *Wks.* 6.130. (*Ram.* 92)   1751
2. Homer's deliberate use of a "representative" metre greatly exaggerated by the imagination of Dionysius of Halicarnassus. Probably "the veneration with

which *Homer* was read, produced many supposititious beauties." See VERSIFICATION 8   1751

3. True and false examples of "representative" verse in Homer. Blind reverence sometimes imagined such beauties. See VERSIFICATION 9   1751

4. *Odyssey*. An example of Homer's truth to human nature unsuccessfully imitated by Virgil. See VIRGIL 15   1751

5. Homer's epic openings: their splendour and ornaments. See OPENING OF A WORK 2   1751

6. "We see how little the united experience of mankind have been able to add to the heroick characters displayed by *Homer*, and how few incidents the fertile imagination of modern *Italy* has yet produced, which may not be found in the *Iliad* and *Odyssey*." *Wks.* 8.265. (*Idl.* 66)   1759

7. "Perhaps it would not be easy to find any authour, except *Homer*, who invented so much as *Shakespeare*." *Shak. Pref.*, Raleigh, 39   1765

8. "The poems of *Homer* we yet know not to transcend the common limits of human intelligence, but by remarking, that nation after nation, and century after century, has been able to do little more than transpose his incidents, new-name his characters, and paraphrase his sentiments." *Wks.* 9.241. (*Shak. Pref.*) See also ANCIENT WRITERS 9   1765

9. Homer supreme in interest. See SHAKESPEARE 64   1765

10. *J. praises Homer: his learning; his writings portray the varied life of the age. " 'And there are in Homer such characters of heroes, and combinations of qualities of heroes, that the united powers of mankind ever since have not produced any but what are to be found there.' MONBODDO. 'Yet no character is described.' JOHNSON. 'No; they all develope themselves.' " *Bos.* 5.78-9. (*Hebrides*, 21 Aug.)   1773

11. *His ability "to appropriate to particular persons qualities which are common to all mankind." *Bos.* 3.74-5   1776
12. *Iliad.* *"RAMSAY. . . . 'I should like to see a translation of it in poetical prose. . . . JOHNSON. 'Sir, you could not read it without the pleasure of verse.'" *Bos.* 3.333   1778
13. "Minute enquiries into the force of words are less necessary in translating Homer than other poets, because his positions are general, and his representations natural, with very little dependence on local or temporary customs [see NATURE 45] . . . among the readers of Homer the number is very small of those who find much in the Greek more than in the Latin, except the musick of the numbers." *Lives* 3.114   1781
14. Translation "was totally unknown to the inhabitants of Greece. They had no recourse to the Barbarians for poetical beauties, but sought for every thing in Homer, where, indeed, there is but little which they might not find." *Lives* 3.236-7   1781
15. That Pope's translation of *Iliad* wants Homer's "awful simplicity, his artless grandeur, his unaffected majesty . . . cannot be totally denied." *Lives* 3.238   1781
16. "The wonderful multiplicity of Homer's sentiments and descriptions." *Lives* 3.247   1781
17. *Odyssey.* *The story preferred to that of the *Aeneid.* See VIRGIL 18   1783
18. *"The source of every thing, in or out of nature, that can serve the purpose of poetry, is to be found in Homer;—every species of distress, every modification of heroic character, battles, storms, ghosts, incantations, &c. Dr. Johnson said he had never read through the Odyssey completely in the original." *Letters* 2.440. (App. D. From Windham's *Diary*)   1784

19. *Iliad.* Greatest work "of entertainment" in the world.
John. Misc. 1.332-3. (Piozzi) Date?

Hooke, Nathaniel

1. *Account of Conduct of the Dowager Duchess of Marlborough.* (*Gent. Mag.*, 1742.) Entertaining and instructive for its revelation of character, and of "the secret Causes of important Events"; and "the polite Writer may learn an unaffected Dignity of Stile, and an artful Simplicity of Narration." Quotation of source letters commended. The letters of Queen Anne "written with great Purity and Correctness, without any forced Expressions, affected Phrases, or unnatural Sentiments." (129-30.) "This Account I think as *entertaining,* and perhaps as edifying as any Memoirs I have met with. . . . The *Spirit, Humour,* and *Language* of this extraordinary Piece proclaim it genuine. All that Vivacity and Contempt of Dignities, which distinguish her from all other Ladies, shine with such Lustre in the Book as to set it beyond Comparison, except with Lord *Clarendon's* History, which I conceive to be like it." (204) 1742

Hoole, John

1. *Cleonice.* "The plot is so well framed, the intricacy so artful, and the disentanglement so easy, the suspense so affecting, and the passionate parts so properly interposed, that I have no doubt of its success."[1] *Bos.* 2.289. (Letter to Hoole) 1774

Horace

1. J. commends Horace's rules for beginning a work. See OPENING OF A WORK 1 1750
2. Energy of a passage. *Wks.* 7.17. (*Ram.* 143) 1751
3. Examples of obscure passages or apparent improprieties in Horace which a knowledge of contemporary

---

[1] It was a failure.

events would probably illuminate. *Wks.* 9.34-8.
(*Adv.* 58) 1753

4. "Mr. *Blackwell* knows well the opinion of *Horace*, concerning those that open their undertakings with magnificent promises; and he knows likewise the dictates of common sense and common honesty, names of greater authority than that of *Horace*, who direct that no man should promise what he cannot perform." *Wks.* 10.186 1756

5. *J. told Boswell "that Horace's Odes were the compositions in which he took most delight, and it was long before he liked his Epistles and Satires." *Bos.* 1.70 1777

6. *"He said, 'the lyrical part of Horace never can be perfectly translated; so much of the excellence is in the numbers and the expression. Francis has done it best.'" *Bos.* 3.356 1778

7. Gray's *Bard* compared with Horace, *Odes*, I.15. *Lives* 3.438 1781

8. Young in *Love of Fame, the Universal Passion,* "has the gaiety of Horace without his laxity of numbers." *Lives* 3.394 1781

Hughes, John

1. J. quotes Swift and Pope on the character of his genius: "Too grave a poet . . . and I think among the *mediocrists*, in prose as well as verse." (Swift) "What he wanted in genius, he made up as an honest man; but he was of the class you think him." (Pope to Swift.) *Lives* 2.164-5 1779

2. *Minor pieces. Lives* 2.159-61 1779

3. *Siege of Damascus.* "It is unnecessary to add a private voice to such continuance of approbation." Unreasonable as at present acted: not according to original draft. *Lives* 2.163 1779

4. *Spenser, Edition of.* "A work for which he was well

qualified as a judge of the beauties of writing," but poor antiquarian. *Lives* 2.162. See also *Bos.* 1.270

1779

Hume, David

1. *"Why, Sir, his style is not English; the structure of his sentences is French. Now the French structure and the English structure may, in the nature of things, be equally good. But if you allow that the English language is established, he is wrong. My name might originally have been Nicholson, as well as Johnson; but were you to call me Nicholson now, you would call me very absurdly." *Bos.* 1.439   1763
2. *"He is an echo of Voltaire." For context, see SCOTCH WRITERS 1   1768
3. *Referring to Hume's historical writings: "I have not read Hume." *Bos.* 2.236   1773
4. *His pernicious philosophy. *Bos.* 5.29. (*Hebrides*, 15 Aug.)   1773
5. *Not more, compared to Clarendon, "than a rat to a cat." See SCOTCH WRITERS 3   1775
6. *"All infidel writers drop into oblivion." See VOLTAIRE 11   1784
7. *"Hume has taken his style from Voltaire. He would never hear Hume mentioned with any temper:—'A man,' said he, 'who endeavoured to persuade his friend who had the stone to shoot himself.' "[1] *John. Misc.* 2.10. (Hawkins's *Apophthegms*)   Date?

Hurd, Richard

1. *"Comes off badly." See SHENSTONE 1. See also *Lives* 2.145 for J.'s critical disagreement with H.   *cir.* 1765

Il Palmerin de Inglaterra

1.*J. takes this romance with him on one of his trips to

---

[1] See also *ib.* 2.437; *Bos.* 5.29; 2.443, for attacks on Hume's pernicious philosophy.

Lichfield, but, says Boswell, "did not like it much. He said, he read it for the language." *Bos.* 3.2. cf. *Bos.* 1.49   1776

Jack the Giant-Killer

1. "This little dog [J. himself] does nothing, but I hope he will mend; he is now reading Jack the Giant-killer. Perhaps so noble a narrative may rouse in him the soul of enterprise." *Letters* 1.134-5. (For a defence of this as a book for children, see *Bos.* 4.8 *n* 3)   1768

Jeffreys, George

1. Wrote best "encomiastick verses" on *Cato*. *Lives* 2. 103   Ptd. 1780

Jenyns, Soame

1. *A Free Enquiry into the Nature and Origin of Evil.* Reviewed by J. *Wks.* 10.220 *ff*.   1757

Jephson, Robert

1. *Braganza.* *"Dr. Johnson calls the act in *Braganza* with the monk, paralytick on one side; *i.e.* the monk is introduced without any notification of his character, so that any monk, or any other person might as well be introduced in the same place, and for the same purpose." *John. Misc.* 2.46. (Campbell)   1775

Johnson, Samuel. For J.'s habit of rapid composition, see under COMPOSITION

1. *"It was at this time [*c.* 1747], he said, he aimed at elegance of writing, and set for his emulation the Preface of Chambers to his *Cyclopedia.*" *John. Misc.* 2. 347-8. (Tyers)   *cir.* 1747
2. *Lord Monboddo, referring to the *Journey to the Western Islands*, disapproves "of the richness of Johnson's language, and of his frequent use of metaphorical expressions. JOHNSON. 'Why, Sir, this criticism would

be just, if in my style, superfluous words, or words too big for the thoughts, could be pointed out; but this I do not believe can be done.' " J. defends his use of the word *illustrious*. " 'And, Sir, as to metaphorical expression, that is a great excellence in style, when it is used with propriety, for it gives you two ideas for one; —conveys the meaning more luminously, and generally with a perception of delight.' " *Bos.* 3.173-4

1777

3. *J. as critic.* *Hannah More writes: "I told him [J.] I was delighted at his approbation [of her poem, *Le Bas Bleu*]; he answered quite characteristically, 'And so you may, for I give you the opinion of a man who does not rate his judgment in these things very low, I can tell you.' " *Memoirs of . . . Hannah More*, ed. Roberts, 1835, 1.183   1784

4. *His style.* *"Sir, if Robertson's style be faulty, he owes it to me; that is, having too many words, and those too big ones." *Bos.* 3.173   Date?

5. *J. once told Boswell "that he had formed his style upon that of Sir William Temple, and upon Chambers's Proposal for his *Dictionary*." But Boswell thinks J.'s style unlike Temple's. *Bos.* 1.218-9   Date?

6. *As biographer.* *"Mr. Fowke once observed to Dr. Johnson that, in his opinion, the Doctor's literary strength lay in writing biography, in which he infinitely exceeded all his contemporaries. 'Sir,' said Johnson, 'I believe that is true. The dogs don't know how to write trifles with dignity.' " R. Warner's *Original Letters*, p. 204   Date?

7. *Dictionary.* "I wish . . . that my work may please you [J.'s friend, Edmund Hector], as much as it now and then pleased me, for I did not find dictionary making so very unpleasant as it may be thought." *Letters* 1.42. (See, however, *John. Misc.* 1.410 ff.)

1755

8. *Dictionary.* *"BOSWELL. 'You did not know what you

were undertaking.' JOHNSON. 'Yes, Sir, I knew very well what I was undertaking,—and very well how to do it,—and have done it very well.' " *Bos.* 3.405

1779
9. *Dictionary.* *According to Mrs. Piozzi, "he really did not consider it as a great performance." *John. Misc.* 1.182   Date?
10. *Dictionary.* *J. to Mr. Thrale: "Alas, Sir . . . there are four or five hundred faults, instead of four or five." *John. Misc.* 1.182-3   Date?
11. *Epitaph on Levett.* *"Johnson said, that the remark of appropriation [*i.e.*, that the epitaph was appropriate and applicable to Levett alone] was just criticism." *John. Misc.* 2.373. (Tyers)   Date?
12. *Idler.* *According to Mrs. Piozzi, J. told her "that the character of *Sober* in the Idler [No. 31], was by himself intended as his own portrait; and that he had his own outset into life in his eye when he wrote the eastern story of Gelaleddin [No. 75]." *John. Misc.* 1.178. (Piozzi)   Date?
13. *Irene.* *His defence of *Irene* in its *Prologue.* See DRAMA 57 for excerpt.   1749
14. *Irene.* *Leaves room at a reading of *Irene:* "Sir, I thought it had been better." *Bos.* 4.5. (Langton's *Collection.* See also *ib. n* 1)   Date?
15. *Journey to the Western Islands.* *J. surprised at the small sale;[1] "for in that book I have told the world a great deal that they did not know before." *Bos.* 3. 325-6. (See also *supra* 2)   1778
16. *Latin Poems.* *According to Murphy, "Like Milton and Addison, he [J.] seems to have been fond of his Latin poetry." *John. Misc.* 1.459   Date?
17. *Letters.* To Mrs. Thrale: "Do you keep my letters? I am not of your opinion that I shall not like to read them hereafter; for though there is in them not much

---
[1] It was in reality considerable—4000 copies in a short time, according to Boswell. See *Bos.* 3.325 *n* 5

history of mind, or any thing else, they will, I hope, always be in some degree the records of a pure and blameless friendship, and in some hours of languour and sadness may revive the memory of more cheerful times."[1] *Letters* 1.361   1775

18. *Lives of the Poets.* "I have written a little of the Lives of the poets, I think with all my usual vigour." *John. Misc.* 1.86. (*Prayers and Med.s*)   1778

19. *Lives of the Poets.* "Written, I hope in such a manner as may tend to the promotion of Piety." *John. Misc.* 1.88. (*Prayers and Med.s*)   1779

20. *Lives of the Poets.* "Congreve . . . is one of the best of the little lives." *Letters* 2.160   1780

21. *Lives of the Poets.* *"The life of Cowley he himself considered as the best of the whole, on account of the dissertation which it contains on the *Metaphysical Poets*." *Bos.* 4.38   Date?

22. *Lobo's "Voyage to Abyssinia," Translation of.* *Boswell shows J. this early translation. "He said, 'Take no notice of it,' or 'don't talk of it.' He seemed to think it beneath him, though done at six-and-twenty. I said to him, 'Your style, Sir, is much improved since you translated this.' He answered with a sort of triumphant smile, 'Sir, I hope it is.'" *Bos.* 3.7   1776

23. *Parliamentary Debates.* *These *Debates*, according to Nichols, were "the only parts of his writings which gave him [J.] any compunction; but . . . at the time he wrote them he had no conception that he was imposing upon the world." The most rapidly composed of his writings except for the *Life of Savage*. *John. Misc.* 1.446-7. (Murphy. See also *ib.* 2.412)   1784

24. *Parliamentary Debates.* *"I saved appearances toler-

---

[1] Johnson, however, deprecated the fashion of publishing letters—at least, until the writer had died: "It is now become so much the fashion to publish letters, that in order to avoid it, I put as little into mine as I can." (*Bos.* 4.102.) "He [J.] did not choose they should be published in his lifetime; but had no objection to their appearing after his death." (*Bos.* 3.276. See also *Bos.* 2.58, 60.)

ably well; but I took care that the WHIG DOGS should not have the best of it." *John. Misc.* 1.379. (Murphy) Date?
25. *Political Pamphlets.* (*False Alarm* and *Thoughts on . . . Falkland's Islands.*) *J. prefers the *False Alarm:* "There is a subtlety of disquisition in the first, that is worth all the fire of the second." *Bos.* 2.147. (See also *John. Misc.* 1.173 for similar testimony) 1772
26. *Pope's "Messiah," Translation of.* *J.'s favourite line, "*Vallis aromaticas fundit Saronica nubes.*"[1] *Bos.* 1.272 1754
27. *Rambler.* *"Dr. Johnson said to an acquaintance of mine, 'My other works are wine and water; but my *Rambler* is pure wine.'" Rogers's *Table Talk*, ed. 1856, p. 10 Date?
28. *Rambler.* *"Of the allegorical papers in the Rambler, Labour and Rest [No. 33] was his [J.'s] favourite; but Serotinus [No. 165] . . . was by him considered as a masterpiece in the science of life and manners." *John. Misc.* 1.178-9. (Piozzi) Date?
29. *Rambler.* *Calls a *Rambler* essay "too wordy." *Bos.* 4.5. (Langton's *Collection*) Date?
30. *Rasselas.* *Boswell: "I have heard Johnson say, that if they [*Rasselas* and *Candide*] had not been published so closely one after the other that there was not time for imitation, it would have been in vain to deny that the scheme of that which came latest was taken from the other." *Bos.* 1.342. (See also *Bos.* 3.356) 1778
31. *Shakespeare, Edition of.* "To tell the truth, as I felt no solicitude about this work, I receive no great comfort from its conclusion; but yet am well enough pleased that the public has no farther claim upon me." *Letters* 1.123 1765
32. *Shakespeare, Edition of.* *His *Preface* not superior to Pope's:—"I fear not . . . the little fellow has done wonders." *John. Misc.* 1.184-5. (Piozzi) Date?

[1] The line should read "Mittit aromaticas vallis Saronica nubes."

33. *Vanity of Human Wishes.* *According to Mrs. Piozzi, J. thought his best lines were from *The Vanity of Human Wishes:*
    "The encumber'd oar scarce leaves the hostile
       [dreaded] coast,
    Through purple billows and a floating host."
John. Misc. 2.422. (Mrs. Rose)   Date?

34. *Vanity of Human Wishes.* *"When Dr. Johnson read his own satire, in which the life of a scholar is painted . . . he burst into a passion of tears one day." *John. Misc.* 1.180. (Piozzi)   Date?

35. *Vision of Theodore, the Hermit of Teneriffe.* *Percy "heard Dr. Johnson say, that he thought this was the best thing he ever wrote." *Bos.* 1.192   Date?

Johnston, Arthur

1. *Improves upon Buchanan. See BUCHANAN 2   1763
2. "Holds among the *Latin* poets of *Scotland* the next place to the elegant *Buchanan.*" *Wks.* 10.330. (*Jour. to W.I.*)   Composed 1774

Johnstone, Charles

1. *Chrysal; or the Adventures of a Guinea.* *J. recommends that it be printed. *Bos.* 5.275. (*Hebrides*, 1 Oct.)   1773

Jonson, Ben

1. "Then Jonson came, instructed from the school
    To please in method, and invent by rule;
    His studious patience, and laborious art,
    By regular approach, essay'd the heart:
    Cold approbation gave the lingering bays;
    For those who durst not censure, scarce could praise.
    A mortal born, he met the general doom,
    But left, like Egypt's kings, a lasting tomb."
Wks. 1.196. (*Drury-lane Prologue*)   1747

2. "This absurd labour of construing into rhyme was

countenanced by *Jonson* in his version of Horace."
Wks. 8.276. (*Idl.* 69) 1759

Journal des Savans

1. *J. does not think it well done. *Bos.* 2.39 1767

Junius

1. "One of the few writers of his despicable faction whose name does not disgrace the page of an opponent." *Wks.* 10.58. (*Falk. Isl.*) 1771
2. Attack on Junius. He attracts by force of novelty and vehemence against established authority. "As a rhetorician, he has had the art of persuading when he seconded desire; as a reasoner, he has convinced those who had no doubt before; as a moralist, he has taught that virtue may disgrace; and as a patriot, he has gratified the mean by insults on the high. . . . Let us abstract from his wit the vivacity of insolence, and withdraw from his efficacy the sympathetick favour of plebeian malignity; I do not say that we shall leave him nothing; the cause that I defend scorns the help of falsehood; but if we leave him only his merit, what will be his praise? It is not by his liveliness of imagery, his pungency of periods, or his fertility of allusion, that he detains the cits of *London*, and the boors of *Middlesex.* . . . They admire him . . . for contempt of order and violence of outrage, for rage of defamation and audacity of falsehood. . . . *Junius* is an unusual phænomenon, on which some have gazed with wonder and some with terrour, but wonder and terrour are transitory passions. He will soon be more closely viewed or more attentively examined, and what folly has taken for a comet that from its flaming hair shook pestilence and war, inquiry will find to be only a meteor formed by the vapours of putrefying democracy, and kindled into flame by the effervescence of interest struggling with conviction; which after having plunged its follow-

ers in a bog, will leave us inquiring why we regard it. Yet though I cannot think the style of *Junius* secure from criticism, though his expressions are often trite, and his periods feeble, I should never have stationed him where he has placed himself, had I not rated him by his morals rather than his faculties." *Wks.* 10. 67-9. (*Falk. Isl.*) 1771
3. *J. suspects Burke the author until B. denies it. See BURKE 2, 4 1775-9
4. *"He often delighted his imagination with the thoughts of having destroyed Junius." *John. Misc.* 1. 172. (Piozzi) Date?

Juvenal

1. *J. quotes Juvenal's "noble picture of inflexible virtue." (*Satires*, viii, ll. 79-84.) *Bos.* 5.361. (*Hebrides*, 26 Oct.) 1773
2. "The peculiarity of Juvenal is a mixture of gaiety and stateliness, of pointed sentences, and declamatory grandeur." *Lives* 1.447 1779
3. His "massiness and vigour." *Lives* 2.233 Ptd. 1780
4. Young's *Love of Fame, the Universal Passion* has "the morality of Juvenal with greater variation of images." *Lives* 3.394 1781

Kames, Henry Home, Lord

1. *Elements of Criticism.* *"Sir this book . . . is a pretty essay, and deserves to be held in some estimation, though much of it is chimerical." *Bos.* 1.393-4 1763
2. *"Keep him; ha, ha, ha! We don't envy you him." For context, see SCOTCH WRITERS 1 1768
3. *Elements of Criticism.* *"The Scotchman has taken the right method in his *Elements of Criticism*. I don't mean that he has taught us any thing; but he has told us old things in a new way." *Bos.* 2.89-90 1769
4. *Elements of Criticism.* *J. "thought very well of" it.

"Of other of his writings he thought very indifferently," etc. *John. Misc.* 2.16. (Hawkins's *Apophthegms*) Date?

Kelly, Hugh

1. *His *False Delicacy* "totally void of character."[1] *Bos.* 2.48   1768
2. *J. does not wish to be introduced to Kelly: "I never desire to converse with a man who has written more than he has read."[2] *John. Misc.* 2.6. (Hawkins's *Apophthegms*) Date?

Kempis, Thomas à

1. *"*Thomas à Kempis* (he observed) must be a good book, as the world has opened its arms to receive it."[3] A striking sentence quoted. *Bos.* 3.226   1778
2. *"He was, for some time, pleased with Kempis's, or rather John Gerson's tract 'De Imitatione Christi,' but at length laid it aside, saying, that the main design of it was to promote monastic piety, and inculcate ecclesiastical obedience." A favourite passage. *Wks.* 1.543. (Hawkins's *Life*) Date?

Kenrick, William

1. *"Sir, he is one of the many who have made themselves *publick*, without making themselves known." *Bos.* 1.498   Date?

King, William. (Of Christ Church)

1. "After this relation it will be naturally supposed that his poems were rather the amusements of idleness than

---

[1] "Ten thousand copies of it were sold before the season closed." See *Bos.* 2.48 n 2
[2] However, J. wrote a prologue for his comedy, *A Word to the Wise*, for the benefit of Kelly's widow. See *Bos.* 3.113; *John. Misc.* 1.181, 432
[3] J. read about half of it in Low Dutch at one time to test his mental faculties. *Bos.* 4.21

efforts of study; that he endeavoured rather to divert than astonish; that his thoughts seldom aspired to sublimity; and that, if his verse was easy and his images familiar, he attained what he desired. His purpose is to be merry; but perhaps, to enjoy his mirth, it may be sometimes necessary to think well of his opinions." *Lives* 2.31   1779

2. *Voyage to the Island of Cajamai* "is particularly commended." *Lives* 2.29   1779
3. *Art of Love.* "A poem remarkable, notwithstanding its title, for purity of sentiment." *Lives* 2.29   1779

Knolles, Richard

1. *Generall Historie of the Turkes.* *Hawkins says J. at times found "entertainment in turning over Knolles's voluminous and neglected history of the Turks."[1] *Wks.* 1.40   *cir.* 1735-6
2. *Generall Historie of the Turkes.* K. superior to all other English historians, and "in his history of the *Turks*, has displayed all the excellencies that narration can admit. His style, though somewhat obscured by time, and sometimes vitiated by false wit, is pure, nervous, elevated, and clear." Artful arrangement of multiplicity of events; entrance of new personages prepared; backgrounds to events sketched in; his descriptions "without minuteness, and the digressions without ostentation." Collateral events artfully interwoven with his main theme. "There is nothing turgid in his dignity, nor superfluous in his copiousness." Only his imaginary orations "tedious and languid." "Nothing could have sunk this author into obscurity, but the remoteness and barbarity of the people, whose story he relates." "This great historian." *Wks.* 6. 331-2. (*Ram.* 122)   1751

---

[1] According to Murphy, J.'s *Irene* is founded on a passage in K.'s *Historie of the Turkes. John. Misc.* 1.461-2. (See also *Wks.* 1.40)

La Bruyère, Jean De

1. *J. rates him below La Rochefoucauld. *John. Misc.* 1. 334. (Piozzi)   Date?
2. *J. "professed admirer of Boileau and La Bruyère" says Murphy. *John. Misc.* 1.416   Date?
3. "*Manners of the Age*, though . . . written without connection, certainly deserves great praise for liveliness of description and justness of observation." A forerunner of the *Spectator*. *Lives* 2.93   Ptd. 1780

La Rochefoucauld, François Duc de

1. *J. condemns Mrs. Piozzi for preferring La Bruyère to R., "who (he said) was the only *gentleman* writer who wrote like a professed author." *John. Misc.* 1. 334. (Piozzi)   Date?
2. *"One of the few *gentlemen* writers of whom authors by *profession* had occasion to be afraid." *John. Misc.* 2.304. (Seward)   Date?

Langbaine, Gerard. See RAPIN 1

Lansdowne. See GRANVILLE

Law, William

1. *Serious Call.* *"The finest piece of hortatory theology in any language." *Bos.* 2.122. (Maxwell's *Collectanea*. See also *Wks.* 1.564 *n*)   Date?

Lee, Nathaniel. For his collaboration with Dryden, see DRYDEN: *Duke of Guise*

1. "This great author." *Wks.* 5.133. (*Ram.* 20)   1750

Lewis, David

1. *J. praises highly verses by Lewis, and repeats them "with a noble animation." *Bos.* 4.307   1784

Lobo, Jerome

1. *Father Lobo's "Voyage to Abyssinia."* J. calls it in the preface to his translation, "curious and entertaining, and the dissertations that accompany it . . . judicious and instructive." Contains "no romantick absurdities or incredible fictions: whatever he relates, whether true or not, is at least probable. . . . He appears, by his modest and unaffected narration . . . to have copied nature from the life, and to have consulted his senses, not his imagination." *Wks.* 9.431
1735

London Chronicle

1. Aims of. See PERIODICAL WRITINGS 6   1757
2. *"The only news-paper he constantly took in." *Bos.* 2.103   1769

Longinus

1. L.'s praise of Demosthenes on the heroes of Marathon inferior to Dryden's eulogy of Shakespeare. *Lives* 1.412
1779

Lopez de Vega

1. *Verses "founded on a trivial conceit." *John.. Misc.* 1.193. (Piozzi)   Date?

Lucan

1. "Is distinguished by a kind of dictatorial or philosophic dignity, rather, as Quintilian observes, declamatory than poetical; full of ambitious morality and pointed sentences, comprised in vigorous and animated lines." *Lives* 2.77   Ptd. 1780

Lucas, Henry

1. *Earl of Somerset, The.* "He has compelled me to read his tragedy, which is but a poor performance, and yet may perhaps put money into his pocket; it contains

nothing immoral or indecent, and therefore, we may very reasonably wish it success." *Letters* 2.9   1777

Lucian

1. J.'s note on "Enter Apemantus" (*Timon of Athens*, I.i): "See this character of a Cynic finely drawn by Lucian, in his *Auction of the Philosophers.*" *Shak.* 6.177 *n* 3   1765

Lyttelton, George, First Baron

1. His "poems are the works of a man of literature and judgement, devoting part of his time to versification. They have nothing to be despised, and little to be admired." *Lives* 3.456   1781
2. *Account of a Journey into Wales.* Given "perhaps rather with too much affectation of delight." *Lives* 3.451   1781
3. *Blenheim.* Its blank verse "has neither much force nor much elegance." *Lives* 3.456   1781
4. *Dialogues of the Dead.* "Very eagerly read, though the production rather, as it seems, of leisure than of study,[1] rather effusions than compositions. The names of his persons too often enable the reader to anticipate their conversation; and when they have met, they too often part without any conclusion. He has copied Fénelon more than Fontenelle." *Lives* 3.451-2   1781
5. *Dialogues of the Dead.* *"Lord Lyttelton's Dialogues, he deemed a nugatory performance. 'That man, (said he,) sat down to write a book, to tell the world what the world had all his life been telling him.'" *Bos.* 2.126. (Maxwell's *Collectanea*)   Date?
6. *History of Henry II.* *"Johnson said, he thought his

---

[1] J. first wrote: "The production rather of a mind that means well than thinks vigorously." *Bos.* 4.58

style pretty good, but that he had blamed Henry the Second rather too much."[1] *Bos.* 2.38   1767
7. *Minor pieces.* "His little performances, whether Songs or Epigrams, are sometimes spritely and sometimes insipid. His epistolary pieces have a smooth equability, which cannot much tire because they are short, but which seldom elevates or surprizes." *Advice to Belinda* excepted: "Contains much truth and much prudence, very elegantly and vigorously expressed, and shews a mind attentive to life, and a power of poetry which cultivation might have raised to excellence." *Lives* 3.456-7   1781
8. *Progress of Love* and *Persian Letters.* "His *Progress of Love* and his *Persian Letters* were both written when he was very young; and, indeed, the character of a young man is very visible in both. The Verses cant of shepherds and flocks, and crooks dressed with flowers; and the Letters have something of that indistinct and headstrong ardour for liberty which a man of genius always catches when he enters the world, and always suffers to cool as he passes forward." *Lives* 3.446   1781
9. *Progress of Love.* "It is sufficient blame to say that it is pastoral." *Lives* 3.456   1781

Mackenzie, Henry

1. *The Man of the World.* *J. "thought there was nothing in it." *Bos.* 5.277. (*Hebrides*, 2 Oct.).   1773

Macpherson, James

1. *Ossianic Poems.* *"Dr. Blair . . . asked Dr. Johnson whether he thought any man of a modern age could have written such poems? Johnson replied, 'Yes, Sir, many men, many women, and many children.' " *Bos.*

---

[1] This was spoken to the king. For the *History's* "vulgar Whiggism," see *Bos.* 2.221

1.396. Repeated by Mrs. Piozzi, *John. Misc.* 1.321
cir. 1763

2. *Ossianic Poems: Fingal.* *"He [J.] denied merit to *Fingal*, supposing it to be the production of a man who has had the advantages that the present age affords; and said, 'nothing is more easy than to write enough in that style if once you begin.'" *Bos.* 5.388. (*Hebrides*, 10 Nov.)   1773

3. *Fingal.* "No better than such an epick poem as he could make from the song of Robin Hood; that is to say, that, except a few passages, there is nothing truly ancient but the names and some vague traditions." *Bos.* 5.164. (*Hebrides*, 8 Sept.)   cir. 1773?

4. *Ossianic Poems.* *J. does not believe in their authenticity: "I look upon M'Pherson's *Fingal* to be as gross an imposition as ever the world was troubled with. . . . As a modern production, it is nothing." *Bos.* 5.240-1. (*Hebrides*, 22 Sept. See also *ib.* 45, 95, 242, 387-9; 2.296-7, 309-10, 311, 347, 383; 4.252-3; and *Wks.* 10.462-3, for reiteration of this disbelief)   1773

5. *Ossianic Poems.* Letter to Macpherson calling the poems an imposture. *John Misc.* 2.446. Quoted also by Boswell with slight changes, *Bos.* 2.298   1775

6. *Ossianic Poems.* *"Sir, a man might write such stuff for ever, if he would *abandon* his mind to it." *Bos.* 4.183   Date?

7. *Fingal.* *"The poem of *Fingal*, he said, was a mere unconnected rhapsody, a tiresome repetition of the same images. 'In vain shall we look for the *lucidus ordo*, where there is neither end or object, design or moral, *nec certa recurrit imago.*'" *Bos.* 2.126. (Maxwell's *Collectanea*)   Date?

Madden, Dr. Samuel

1. A thought in *Timon of Athens* (I.i.108-9) "is better expressed by Dr. *Madden* in his elegy on Archbishop *Boulter.*" *Shak.*, Raleigh, 163   1765

2. *"I blotted a great many lines [of *Boulter's Monument*], and might have blotted many more, without making the poem worse." *Bos.* 1.318. See also *John. Misc.* 2.212, 267; *Lives* 2.131   1775?

Mallet, David

1. *"Why, Sir, Mallet had talents enough to keep his literary reputation alive as long as he himself lived; and that, let me tell you, is a good deal." *Bos.* 2.233
    1773
2. "As a writer he cannot be placed in any high class. There is no species of composition in which he was eminent. His Dramas . . . are forgotten: his blank verse seems to my ear the echo of Thomson." His works lived "by his personal influence; but which, conveying little information and giving no great pleasure, must soon give way, as the succession of things produces new topicks of conversation and other modes of amusement." *Lives* 3.410   1781
3. *Amyntor and Theodora*. Its "copiousness and elegance of language, vigour of sentiment, and imagery well adapted to take possession of the fancy. But it is blank verse." "Now lost in forgetfulness." *Lives* 3.406
    1781
4. *Eurydice*. J. knows not its merit, but has "heard it mentioned as a mean performance." *Lives* 3.402
    1781
5. *Excursion, The*. "A desultory and capricious view" of scenes of nature. "Not devoid of poetical spirit." Diction from Thomson. "He has Thomson's beauties and his faults." *Lives* 3.401   1781
6. *Life of Bacon*. "Written with elegance, perhaps with some affectation; but with . . . more knowledge of history than of science." *Lives* 3.404   1781
7. *Of Verbal Criticism*. A mere expansion of Pope. "More pertness than wit, and more confidence than knowl-

edge. The versification is tolerable, nor can criticism allow it a higher praise." *Lives* 3.401-2   1781
8. *Prologue of Thomson's "Agememnon"*. Superior to Thomson's *Prologue* to Mallet's *Mustapha*. *Lives* 3.406   1781
9. *William and Margaret*. "Contains nothing very striking or difficult." The charge of plagiarism has never been proved. *Lives* 3.401   1781

Mandeville, Bernard[1]

1. *"I read Mandeville forty, or, I believe, fifty years ago. He did not puzzle me; he opened my views into real life very much." *Bos.* 3.292. See also for Mandeville's influence, *ib.* 56 n 2; *Wks.* 1.263 n; *John. Misc.* 1.207; 2.20   1778
2. *J. influenced by Mandeville. "As a book however, he took care always loudly to condemn the Fable of the Bees, but not without adding, 'that it was the work of a thinking man.'" *John. Misc.* 1.268. (Piozzi)   Date?

Mandeville, Sir John

1. Quotes a passage from Mandeville "valuable for the force of thought and beauty of expression." *Dict.* (*History of the English Language*), ed. 1755   1755
2. *J. recommends his *Travels* for an account of China. *John. Misc.* 2.387. (Windham's *Diary*)   1784

Marana, I. P.

1. *Turkish Spy.* *"It told nothing but what every body might have known at that time; and . . . what was good in it, did not pay you for the trouble of reading to find it." *Bos.* 5.341. (*Hebrides*, 21 Oct.)   1773

---

[1] For the great influence of Mandeville on eighteenth century thought, see F. B. Kaye's article, *Studies in Philology*, 19.83-108

Marlowe, Christopher

1. *Tamburlaine.* An impropriety: "The god of love is mentioned . . . with all the familiarity of a *Roman* epigrammatist." *Wks.* 6.437. (*Ram.* 140)   1751
2. The song *Come Live with Me, and be my Love* "a beautiful little poem." *Shak.* 2.498 *n* 3   1765

Martial

1. *Mrs. Elizabeth Carter's father wrote to her in 1738: "You mention Johnson; but that is a name with which I am utterly unacquainted. . . . I a little suspect his judgment, if he is very fond of Martial." Pennington's *Carter*, Lon. 1816, 1.39   *cir.* 1738

Mason, William

1. *Colman's *Odes to Obscurity and Oblivion*, ridiculing Mason and Gray, "exposed a very bad kind of writing." *Bos.* 2.335   1775
2. *Elfrida.* "BOSWELL. 'Surely, Sir, Mr. Mason's *Elfrida* is a fine poem. . . . JOHNSON. 'There are now and then some good imitations of Milton's bad manner.'" *Bos.* 2.335. (See also *Caractacus*)   1775
3. *Inferior as a poet to Akenside. *Bos.* 3.32   1776
4. *Life and Letters of Gray.* *"I forced myself to read it, only because it was a common topick of conversation. I found it mighty dull; and, as to the style, it is fit for the second table." *Bos.* 3.31. See also GRAY 20, 21

   1776

5. *Mason as editor of Gray.* "A companion who was afterward to be his [Gray's] editor, and whose fondness and fidelity has kindled in him a zeal of admiration, which cannot be reasonably expected from the neutrality of a stranger and the coldness of a critick." *Lives* 3.424   1781
6. J. to Reynolds: "Mr. Mason's address [poetical *Epistle to Sir Joshua Reynolds*] to you deserves no great

praise; it is lax without easiness, and familiar without gaiety. Of his translation [of Du Fresnoy's Latin poem *De Arte Graphica*] I think much more favourably. . . . I find him better than exact; he has his author's distinctness and clearness without his dryness and sterility." *Letters* 2.286   1783

7. *Caractacus.* *"I have heard him [J.] . . . relate how he used to sit in some coffee-house there [at Oxford], and turn M—'s C-r-ct-u-s into ridicule for the diversion of himself and of chance comers-in. 'The Elf-da (says he) was too exquisitely pretty; I could make no fun out of that.'" *John. Misc.* 1.169. (Piozzi)   Date?

8. *According to Baretti, "Johnson always looked on him as a pigmy poet." *Letters* 1.317 *n* 2   Date?

Massillon

1. *Did not "go round the world." See FRENCH LITERATURE 2   1773

May, Thomas

1. "*May, Sandys,* and *Holiday,* confined themselves to the toil of rendering line for line, not indeed with equal felicity, for *May* and *Sandys* were poets, and Holiday only a scholar and a critick." *Wks.* 8.277. (*Idl.* 69)   1759

2. M's Latin poems superior to those of Cowley and Milton. *Lives* 1.12-13   1779

Metaphysical Poets.[1] See also COWLEY, DONNE, WALLER

1. (*Lives* 1) Their learning; to show it "their whole endeavour; but, unluckily resolving to shew it in rhyme, instead of writing poetry they only wrote verses." No

---

[1] For the use of the term "metaphysical poets" before Johnson, see A. H. Nethercot's article in *Mod. Lang. Notes*, 37.11-17.

ear; mechanical versifiers. Judged by Aristotle's dictum (poetry *"an imitative art"*) they were not poets: "they neither copied nature nor life; neither painted the forms of matter nor represented the operations of intellect." Judged by Pope's definition of "true wit," they were not wits. (19.) They seldom rose to J.'s higher conception of wit, as that "which is at once natural and new, that which though not obvious is, upon its first production, acknowledged to be just. . . . Their thoughts are often new, but seldom natural;" neither obvious nor just. But of wit "as a kind of *discordia concors*; a combination of dissimilar images, or discovery of occult resemblances in things apparently unlike . . . they have more than enough . . . their learning instructs, and their subtilty surprises"—one wonders, but is seldom pleased. (20.) Having "no regard to that uniformity of sentiment, which enables us to conceive and to excite the pains and the pleasure of other minds" they did not move the affections. Rather "beholders than partakers of human nature." (20.) The sublime likewise beyond their reach, lacking the grandeur of generality. (See GENERAL 9.) No limits to their hyperbole. (21.) But sometimes unexpected truth: "To write on their plan it was at least necessary to read and think." Not slavish imitators. (21.) "If their greatness seldom elevates their acuteness often surprises . . . genuine wit and useful knowledge may be sometimes found." (22.) Examples of their style. (23-34.) "In all these examples it is apparent that whatever is improper or vicious is produced by a voluntary deviation from nature in pursuit of something new and strange, and that the writers fail to give delight by their desire of exciting admiration." (35) 1779

Milbourne, Rev. Luke

1. His attack on Dryden's translation of Virgil: M.'s "outrages seem to be the ebullitions of a mind agitated

by stronger resentment than bad poetry can excite, and previously resolved not to be pleased." *Lives* 1.449   1779

Milton, John. (GENERAL CRITICISM)

1. *Hawkins and Towers assert that J. exulted in Lauder's supposed detection of Milton's plagiarism. Murphy refutes.[1] *John. Misc.* 1.398. (Murphy)   *cir.* 1750
2. "This mighty genius." *Wks.* 14.117. (*Preface* to Lauder's *Essay on Milton's* . . . *Paradise Lost*)
               1750
3. "That poet, whose works may possibly be read when every other monument of British greatness shall be obliterated." J., in his appeal to the public to aid the grand-daughter of Milton. *Wks.* 14.121. (*Postscript* to Lauder's *Essay on Milton's* . . . *Paradise Lost*)
               1750
4. "At length our mighty bard's victorious lays
Fill the loud voice of universal praise;
And baffled spite, with hopeless anguish dumb,
Yields to renown the centuries to come."
Wks. 11.346. (*Prol. to "Comus"*)   1750
5. J. writes a letter calling attention to the benefit performance for the grand-daughter of "our incomparable Milton." *Wks.* 14.123-4   1750
6. Milton an exception to that "striking contrariety between the life of an author and his writings" so frequently found. *Wks.* 5.88. (*Ram.* 14)   1750
7. J. drew 7.8% of the literary illustrations for his *Dictionary* (1755) from Milton. See ADDISON 5   1755
8. "The great Milton." *Shak.*, Raleigh, 1 56   1765
9. "Harry [Thrale, aged seven] will be happier now he goes to school and reads Milton." *Letters* 1.214
               1773

---

[1] Courtney points out that J. cherished a lock of Milton's hair which at one time was in Addison's possession. (*Bibliography*, 38)

10. *J. thinks that Milton's, rather than Pope's monument should be the first to be erected in St. Paul's. "I think more highly of him now than I did at twenty. There is more thinking in him and in Butler, than in any of our poets." *Bos.* 2.239   1773
11. *"Mr. Johnson pronounced a long eulogium upon Milton with so much ardour, eloquence, and ingenuity, that the Abbé [Roffette] rose from his seat and embraced him." *John. Misc.* 1.216. (Piozzi)   1775
12. M.'s precocity as a young poet referred to. *Lives* 1.3
    1779
13. (*Lives* 1) "What other author ever soared so high or sustained his flight so long?" (187.) "Milton would not have excelled in dramatick writing; he knew human nature only in the gross, and had never studied the shades of character" and the passions. Great book-learning, but "deficient in the knowledge which experience must confer." (189)   1779
14. *Of English poets, J. admires Milton next to Shakespeare. "Milton (says he) had that which rarely fell to the lot of any man—an unbounded imagination, with a store of knowledge equal to all its calls." *John. Misc.* 2.165. (? Cooke)   1784

Milton, John. (Versification and Style)

15. *Versification.* His licentious inversion of accents. (See Versification 2.) *Wks.* 6.93-6. (*Ram.* 86)   1751
16. *Versification.* Milton, whose ear was accustomed to the music of the ancient tongues and the softness of Italian, introduced series of proper names in an effort to counterbalance "the unfitness of our language for smooth versification." *Wks.* 6.105-6. (*Ram.* 88)
    1751
17. Elision of vowels. See Versification 5   1751
18. Milton's frequent use of "the hypermetrical or redundant line of eleven syllables" unsuited to heroic poetry. See Versification 6   1751

19. *Versification.* Founded on Greek and Latin poets: differences between the English heroic measure and that of Homer and Virgil make for insuperable difficulties "against which he has struggled with so much art and diligence, that he may at least be said to have deserved success." The hexameter of the ancients permitted a great variety of pauses, without the loss of harmony. "*Milton* was constrained within the narrow limits of a measure not very harmonious in the utmost perfection; the single parts, therefore, into which it was to be sometimes broken by pauses, were in danger of losing the very form of verse. This has, perhaps, notwithstanding all his care, sometimes happened." Milton's pauses examined, and those pauses in English heroic measure established which the ear justifies. (See VERSIFICATION 7.) Conclusion: "If the poetry of *Milton* be examined, with regard to the pauses and flow of his verses into each other, it will appear, that he has performed all that our language would admit; and the comparison of his numbers with those who have cultivated the same manner of writing, will show that he excelled as much in the lower as the higher parts of his art, and that his skill in harmony was not less than his invention or his learning." *Wks.* 6.115-21. (*Ram.* 90)   1751

20. M.'s use of imitative or "representative" metre: "That *Milton* understood the force of sounds well adjusted, and knew the compass and variety of the ancient measures, cannot be doubted, since he was both a musician and a critic; but he seems to have considered these conformities of cadence, as either not often attainable in our language, or as petty excellencies unworthy of his ambition; for it will not be found that he has always assigned the same cast of numbers to the same objects." True and false examples in M. A passage in which the sound counteracts the sense. "Those who are determined to find in *Milton* an as-

semblage of all the excellencies which have ennobled all other poets, will perhaps be offended that I do not celebrate his versification in higher terms. . . . Milton indeed seems only to have regarded this species of embellishment ["representative" metre] so far as not to reject it when it came unsought; which would often happen to a mind so vigorous, employed upon a subject so various and extensive. He had, indeed, a greater and a nobler work to perform; a single sentiment of moral or religious truth, a single image of life or nature, would have been cheaply lost for a thousand echoes of the cadence to the sense; and he who had undertaken to *vindicate the ways of God to man*, might have been accused of neglecting his cause, had he lavished much of his attention upon syllables and sounds." *Wks.* 6.145-51. (*Ram.* 94)   1751

21. *Style.* Milton "began to introduce the Latin idiom: and Browne, though he gave less disturbance to our structures in phraseology," etc. *Wks.* 4.612   1756
22. *His style of "eminent excellence." *Bos.* 3.280   1778
23. "Milton tried the metaphysick style only in his lines upon Hobson the Carrier. . . . The fashionable style remained chiefly with Cowley: Suckling could not reach it, and Milton disdained it." *Lives* 1.22   1779
24. "The sounding words and stately construction of Milton." His "grandeur." "All that is obsolete, peculiar, or licentious" in the "numbers" of *Paradise Lost* imitated by Philips. "Milton's verse was harmonious, in proportion to the general state of our metre in Milton's age, and, if he had written after the improvements made by Dryden, it is reasonable to believe that he would have admitted a more pleasing modulation of numbers into his work." *Lives* 1.317-8   1779
25. "The numbers of Milton, which impress the mind with veneration, combined as they are with subjects of inconceivable grandeur." See BLANK VERSE 9   1779
26. (*Lives* 1) *Diction.* Like a new language to the un-

accustomed reader. All his own. "But the truth is, that both in prose and verse, he had formed his style by a perverse and pedantick principle. He was desirous to use English words with a foreign idiom." More evident in his prose, for "such is the power of his poetry that his call is obeyed without resistance, the reader feels himself in captivity to a higher and a nobler. mind, and criticism sinks in admiration." Style "not modified by his subject": *Paradise Lost* and *Comus* exhibit same tendencies. " 'He wrote no language,' but has formed what Butler calls 'a Babylonish Dialect,' in itself harsh and barbarous, but made by exalted genius and extensive learning the vehicle of so much instruction and so much pleasure that, like other lovers, we find grace in its deformity."[1] (189-191.) "Copiousness and variety" of language, however; "he was master of his language in its full extent, and has selected the melodious words with such diligence that from his book alone the Art of English Poetry might be learned." (191.) *Versification.* M., "finding blank verse easier than rhyme, was desirous of persuading himself that it is better." (192.) Dangers of blank verse. (See BLANK VERSE 7.) But "I cannot prevail on myself to wish that Milton had been a rhymer, for I cannot wish his work to be other than it is; yet like other heroes he is to be admired rather than imitated." (194) 1779

Milton, John. (WORKS)

27. *Comus.* (See also *infra, Minor poems.*) (*Lives* 1) "Greatest of his juvenile performances." "The dawn or twilight of *Paradise Lost*" there. Shows system of diction already formed. (167.) Exhibits "his power of description and his vigour of sentiment, employed in the praise and defence of virtue. A work more truly

---

[1] cf. Dryden's reference to Milton's "antiquated words, and the perpetual harshness of their sound." Preface to *Sylvae. Essays of Dryden,* ed. Ker, 1.268

poetical is rarely found; allusions, images, and descriptive epithets embellish almost every period with lavish decoration. As a series of lines, therefore, it may be considered as worthy of all the admiration with which the votaries have received it. As a drama it is deficient. The action is not probable": "freaks of imagination" permissible in a masque, "but so far as the action is merely human it ought to be reasonable." (167-8.) Detailed analysis of the work. (168-9.) Dialogue unnatural and tedious. "The auditor therefore listens as to a lecture, without passion, without anxiety." (168.) Language poetical, sentiments generous, but "there is something wanting to allure attention." (169.) Songs "vigorous and full of imagery; but they are harsh[1] in their diction, and not very musical in their numbers. Throughout the whole the figures are too bold and the language too luxuriant for dialogue: it is a drama in the epick style, inelegantly splendid, and tediously instructive." (169)   1779

28. *Juvenile productions*. Excelled by many. *Lives* 1.87
   1779

29. *L'Allegro* and *Il Penseroso*. (See also *infra*, *Minor poems*.) (*Lives* 1) "I believe opinion is uniform; every man that reads them, reads them with pleasure." (165.) J.'s interpretation: they show how objects are coloured by mood, and how mood seeks out those things which coincide with it. (166-7.) "Through these two poems the images are properly selected and nicely distinguished, but the colours of the diction seem not sufficiently discriminated." J. questions whether characters do not resemble each other. Some melancholy in mirthful man. "They are two noble efforts of imagination." (167)   1779

30. *Latin poetry*. May's superior to Cowley's; Cowley's to Milton's. "Milton is generally content to express

---

[1] See under HARSH for note on J.'s use of this adjective.

the thoughts of the ancients in their language," Cowley puts his own thoughts into Latin. *Lives* 1.13 1779

31. *Latin poetry* (*Lives* 1) J. quotes Hampton with approval: "Milton was the first Englishman who, after the revival of letters, wrote Latin verses with classick elegance." (87. See also *ib.* 95, 96.) *Epitaphium Damonis.* "Written with the common but childish imitation of pastoral life." (97.) "In Latin his skill was such as places him in the first rank of writers and criticks." (154.) "The Latin pieces are lusciously elegant; but the delight which they afford is rather by the exquisite imitation of the ancient writers, by the purity of the diction, and the harmony of the numbers, than by any power of invention or vigour of sentiment . . . the elegies excell the odes, and some of the exercises on Gunpowder Treason might have been spared." (161-2) 1779

32. *Lycidas.* (See also *infra, Minor poems.*) For attack on elegiac pastoral, directed primarily, it would seem, against *Lycidas*, see PASTORAL 2 1750

33. *Lycidas.* "The diction is harsh,[1] the rhymes uncertain, and the numbers unpleasing. What beauty there is we must therefore seek in the sentiments and images." The inappropriateness and insincerity of these when pastoral and mythological. See ELEGY 4 1779

34. *Minor poems.* (See also under individual titles.) J. quotes passage by J. Warton in praise of *Lycidas*, *L'Allegro* and *Il Penseroso.* See DESCRIPTION 4 1756

35. *Minor poems.* (*Lives* 1) "The English Poems [1645], though they make no promises of *Paradise Lost*, have this evidence of genius, that they have a cast original and unborrowed. But their peculiarity is not excellence: if they differ from verses of others, they differ for the worse; for they are too often distinguished by repulsive harshness;[1] the combinations of words are new, but they are not pleasing; the rhymes and epi-

[1] For J.'s use of this word, see HARSH.

thets seem to be laboriously sought and violently applied." (162.) Tendency to "false approbation of his little pieces," and "to think that admirable which is only singular. All that short compositions can commonly attain is neatness and elegance. Milton never learned the art of doing little things with grace; he overlooked the milder excellence of suavity and softness."[1] (163)   1779

36. *Minor poems.* *J. and Hannah More discuss M.: "I accused him of not having done justice to the 'Allegro,' and 'Penseroso.' He spoke disparagingly of both. I praised Lycidas, which he absolutely abused, adding, if Milton had not written the Paradise Lost, he would have only ranked among the minor poets: he was a Phidias that could cut a Colossus out of a rock, but could not cut heads out of cherry stones." *John. Misc.* 2.195. (Referred to in *Bos.* 4.305)   1781

37. *On the Morning of Christ's Nativity.* J. quotes passage by J. Warton praising it. See DESCRIPTION 4   1756

38. *Paradise Lost.* Bk. II. ll. 879-882: "A beautiful passage." *Wks.* 14.89. (*Observ. on Macb.*)   1745

39. *Paradise Lost.* "This great poem." "This wonderful poem." *Wks.* 14.118-9. (Preface to Lauder's *Essay on Milton's . . . Par. Lost*)   1750

40. *Paradise Lost.* "It is now more than half a century, since the PARADISE LOST having broke through the clouds, with which the unpopularity of the author, for a time, obscured it, has attracted the general admiration of mankind; who have endeavoured to compensate the error of their first neglect, by lavish praises and boundless veneration. There seems to have arisen a contest, among men of genius and literature, who

---

[1] The antiquated diction of *Lycidas* was a familiar charge. (See T. Warton's ed. of Milton's *Minor Poems,* ed. 1791, p. 2, *n* 2.) Moreover, it is only just to remember that Milton's shorter pieces were quite overshadowed during the eighteenth century by *Paradise Lost.* (See *The Influence of Milton on English Poetry* by R. D. Havens, pp. 9, 419-21.)

should most advance its honour, or best distinguish its beauties. . . . Among the inquiries to which this ardour of criticism has naturally given occasion, none is more obscure in itself, or more worthy of rational curiosity, than a retrospection of the progress of this mighty genius, in the construction of his work; a view of the fabric gradually rising, perhaps from small beginnings, till its foundation rests in the centre, and its turrets sparkle in the skies; to trace back the structure, through all its varieties, to the simplicity of its first plan;" etc. *Wks.* 14.116-7. (*Preface* by J. to Lauder's *Essay on Milton's* . . . *Paradise Lost*) 1750

41. *Paradise Lost.* "His great Poem." *Shak.* 1.211 *n* 5
1765

42. *Paradise Lost.* "His wonderful poem." *Shak.*, Raleigh, 184 1765

43. *Paradise Lost.* (*Lives* 1) [a] "A design so comprehensive that it could be justified only by success." (121.) "A poem which, considered with respect to design, may claim the first place, and with respect to performance the second, among the productions of the human mind." (170.) Detailed analysis under heads of the Moral, Fable, Characters, the Probable and the Marvellous, Machinery, Episodes, Unity, Sentiments, Descriptions, Similes, etc. (171-80.) *Faults.* "The plan of *Paradise Lost* has this inconvenience, that it comprises neither human actions nor human manners." A unique situation—hence lack of sympathy in reader. What truths do apply to us are not new and therefore: "raise no unaccustomed emotion in the mind." (181-2.) Some ideas too sacred or awful: "Such images rather obstruct the career of fancy than incite it." (See SACRED POETRY 5.) But known truths made new by his genius and learning. *Paradise Lost* "a book of universal knowledge." But "the want of human interest in always felt." (183.) "*Paradise Lost* is one of the books which the reader admires and lays down,

and forgets to take up again. None ever wished it longer than it is. Its perusal is a duty rather than a pleasure. We read Milton for instruction, retire harassed and overburdened, and look elsewhere for recreation; we desert our master, and seek for companions."[1] (183-4.) [b] Plan inconvenient as it calls for the indescribable. Result: confused compromise between "pure spirit" and "animated body." (184-5.) [c] Allegory of Sin and Death unskilful:—"appears to me one of the greatest faults of the poem; and to this there was no temptation, but the author's opinion of its beauty." (185-6.) Absurdity results when allegorical figures are made agents. (See ALLEGORY 4.) [d] "Conduct of the narrative." "Satan is with great expectation brought before Gabriel in Paradise, and is suffered to go away unmolested." Inconsistency in report of creation. (186.) [e] Sentiments not always appropriate to the state of innocence. Some "anticipation." Inconsistency. [f] Unevenness inevitable: "What other author ever soared so high or sustained his flight so long?" (187.) [g] Imitation of Italian poets, especially of Ariosto's "levity" in the "Paradise of Fools." "A fiction not in itself ill-imagined, but too ludicrous for its place." (187.) [h] Play on words. M. delights too often in them; "his equivocations . . . his unnecessary and ungraceful use of terms of art." But these "at last bear so little proportion to the whole that they scarcely deserve the attention of a critick." (188.) *Summary:* "Such are the faults of that wonderful performance *Paradise Lost*; which he who can put in balance with its beauties must be considered not as nice but as dull, as less to be censured for want of candour[2] than pitied for want of sensibility." (188.) "The highest praise of genius is

---

[1] Chesterfield admitted to his son (letter of 4 Oct., 1752): "I cannot possibly read . . . Milton through. Keep this secret for me; for if it should be known, I should be abused by every tasteless pedant, and every solid divine in England."
[2] See CANDOUR for J.'s use of this word.

original invention . . . his work is not the greatest of heroick poems, only because it is not the first." M. not a borrower, however. "Of all the borrowers from Homer Milton is perhaps the least indebted." (194)
    1779
44. *Paradise Lost.* *Shakespeare's picture of a man, (*Ham.* III.4) preferred to Milton's (*Par. Lost.* IV. 300). *Bos.* 4.72-3   1781
45. *Paradise Regained.* "The great *Milton* . . . satirized it [the impiety of "judicial astrology"] in a very beautiful manner, by putting these reveries into the mouth of the Devil." *Shak.*, Raleigh, 156   1765
46. *Paradise Regained.* J. agrees with the general judgement: "in many parts elegant, and every-where instructive." The basis of *Paradise Regained* is narrow; "A dialogue without action can never please like an union of the narrative and dramatick powers. Had this poem been written, not by Milton but by some imitator, it would have claimed and received universal praise." "Too much depreciated." *Lives* 1.188
    1779
47. *Prose tracts. Of Education.* *"Education in England has been in danger of being hurt by two of its greatest men, Milton and Locke. Milton's plan is impracticable." *Bos.* 3.358. (See also *Lives* 1.99-100 where J. takes issue with Milton on the subject of education)
    1778
48. *Prose tracts.* (*Lives* 1) *A Smectymnuus pamphlet.* Style rough. "Controversial merriment" and "gloomy seriousness" of M. offensive. His malignity. (104.) *Areopagitica.* (See LIBERTY OF THE PRESS 3 for discussion.) *Pro Populo Anglicano Defensio*, etc. "Milton's periods are smoother, neater, and more pointed; but he delights himself with teasing his adversary as much as with confuting him." (113.) *Defensio Secunda.* "In this second Defence he shews that his eloquence is not merely satirical; the rudeness of his

invective is equalled by the grossness of his flattery. . . . Caesar when he assumed the perpetual dictatorship had not more servile or more elegant flattery." (118.) *Defensio contra Morum.* "No want of vehemence nor eloquence, nor does he forget his wonted wit." (119.) *Of True Religion*, etc. "Those who are not convinced by his reasons may be perhaps delighted with his wit." (148) 1779

49. *Samson Agonistes.* "It contains indeed just sentiments, maxims of wisdom, and oracles of piety, and many passages written with the ancient spirit of choral poetry, in which there is a just and pleasing mixture of *Seneca's* moral declamation, with the wild enthusiasm of the *Greek* writers. It is therefore worthy of examination, whether a performance thus illuminated with genius, and enriched with learning, is composed according to the indispensable laws of *Aristotelian* criticism: and, omitting at present all other considerations, whether it exhibits a beginning, a middle, and an end. The beginning is undoubtedly beautiful and proper, opening with a graceful abruptness, and proceeding naturally to a mournful recital of facts necessary to be known." But "at the conclusion of the first act there is no design laid, no discovery made, nor any disposition formed towards the subsequent event." The dialogue in which Manoah laments the fallen Samson, "as it might tend to animate or exasperate *Samson*, cannot, I think, be censured as wholly superfluous; but the succeeding dispute, in which *Samson* contends to die . . . is only valuable for its own beauties, and has no tendency to introduce any thing that follows it." The entrance of *Dalila* "produces a dialogue, in a very high degree elegant and instructive" but her visit has no "effect but that of raising the character of *Samson*." Succeeding events similarly sketched to the catastrophe which "is undoubtedly . . . just and regular . . . and the poem, therefore, has a beginning

and an end which *Aristotle* himself could not have disapproved; but it must be allowed to want a middle, since nothing passes between the first act and the last, that either hastens or delays the death of *Samson*. The whole drama, if its superfluities were cut off, would scarcely fill a single act; yet this is the tragedy which ignorance has admired, and bigotry applauded." *Wks.* 6.431-6. (*Ram.* 139) 1751

50. *Samson Agonistes. The sentiments,* "though much less liable to censure than the disposition of his plan, are, like those of other writers, sometimes exposed to just exceptions for want of care, or want of discernment." Anachronism, "unsuitableness of thoughts to the general character of the poem," "allusions to low and trivial objects" and "verbal conceits" illustrated from *Samson Agonistes.* However, "*Milton's* learning . . . and his invention, which required no assistance from the common cant of poetry, have preserved him from frequent outrages of local or chronological propriety." (For the principles of propriety of sentiment upon which these objections are based see SENTIMENT 1) *Wks.* 6.436-40. (*Ram.* 140) 1751

51. *Samson Agonistes. The language* "is through the whole dialogue remarkably simple and unadorned, seldom heightened by epithets, or varied by figures; yet sometimes metaphors find admission, even where their consistency is not accurately preserved." Examples. "The versification is in the dialogue much more smooth and harmonious than in the parts allotted to the chorus, which are often so harsh and dissonant, as scarce to preserve, whether the lines end with or without rhymes, any appearance of metrical regularity." Excellencies of *Samson Agonistes* "consist in the justness of diffuse reasonings, or in the contexture and method of continued dialogues" since the play lacks the "descriptions, similes, or splendid sentences" usual to tragedies. Passages quoted, "which seem to deserve particular

notice, either as containing sentiments of passion, representations of life, precepts of conduct, or sallies of imagination. . . . Such are the faults and such the beauties of *Samson Agonistes,* which I have shewn with no other purpose than to promote the knowledge of true criticism. The everlasting verdure of *Milton's* laurels has nothing to fear from the blasts of malignity; nor can my attempt produce any other effect, than to strengthen their shoots by lopping their luxuriance." *Wks.* 6.440-3. (*Ram.* 140) 1751

52. *Samson Agonistes.* "Too much admired. It could only be by long prejudice and the bigotry of learning that Milton could prefer the ancient tragedies with their encumbrance of a chorus to the exhibitions of the French and English stages; and it is only by a blind confidence in the reputation of Milton that a drama can be praised in which the intermediate parts have neither cause nor consequence, neither hasten nor retard the catastrophe." But "many particular beauties, many just sentiments and striking lines; but it wants that power of attracting attention which a well-connected plan produces." M. not good dramatist—book learning, but little experience in the world. *Lives* 1.188-9 1779

53. *Sonnets. Nos. XI* and *XII.* (*Lives* 1) "The first is contemptible,[1] and the second not excellent." (106.) *On His Deceased Wife.* "A poor sonnet." (116.) "The *Sonnets* . . . deserve not any particular criticism; for of the best it can only be said that they are not bad, and perhaps only the eighth and the twenty-first are truly entitled to this slender commendation." The sonnet unsuited to English language. See SONNET 2. (169)
1779

Mirror, The

1. *According to Boswell, J. spoke very well of it. *Bos.* 4.390 *n* 1 Date?

[1] It is, however, quoted by J. in his *Dict.* under *Sonnet.*

Molière

1. *The one French comic poet who goes "round the world." See FRENCH LITERATURE 2   1773
2. *"Moliere I think he had hardly sufficient taste of." *John. Misc.* 1.334. (Piozzi)   Date?

Montagu, Charles. See HALIFAX

Montagu, Mrs. Elizabeth

1. *An Essay on . . . Shakespear.* *"'It does *her* honour, but it would do nobody else honour. I have, indeed, not read it all. But when I take up the end of a web, and find it packthread, I do not expect, by looking further, to find embroidery. Sir, I will venture to say, there is not one sentence of true criticism in her book.' GARRICK. 'But, Sir, surely it shews how much Voltaire has mistaken Shakspeare, which nobody else has done.' JOHNSON. 'Sir, nobody else has thought it worth while. And what merit is there in that? You may as well praise a schoolmaster for whipping a boy who has construed ill. No, Sir, there is no real criticism in it: none shewing the beauty of thought, as formed on the workings of the human heart.'" Boswell points out that J.'s opinion is not biased by prejudice, "for Sir Joshua Reynolds has told me, that when the Essay first came out, and it was not known who had written it, Johnson wondered how Sir Joshua could like it."[1] *Bos.* 2.88-9   1769
2. *An Essay on . . . Shakespear.* *"Reynolds is fond of her book, and I wonder at it; for neither I, nor Beauclerk, nor Mrs. Thrale, could get through it."[2] *Bos.* 5.245. (*Hebrides*, 23 Sept.)   1773
3. *An Essay on . . . Shakespear.* Ironically referred to in letter to Mrs. Thrale:—"Having mentioned

---

[1] J., however, had considerable respect for her intelligence, not uninfluenced, perhaps, by her exalted social status. E.g., see *Bos.* 4.275
[2] Mrs. Thrale emphatically denies this, however, in a *Postcript* to her *Anecdotes*. See *John. Misc.* 1.351

Shakespeare and Nature, does not the name of Montague force itself upon me?" *Letters* 2.138   1780
4. *"Of Mrs. Montagu's elegant 'Essay upon Shakspeare,' he always said, 'that it was *ad hominem*, that it was conclusive against Voltaire; and that she had done what she intended to do." *John. Misc.* 2.307. (Seward)   Date?
5. *"When Shakspeare has got —— for his rival, and Mrs. Montagu for his defender, he is in a poor state indeed." *Bos.* 2.89   Date?

Montagu, Lady Mary Wortley

1. *Letters.* *"Those who know better of the world, would have rather possessed two pages of true history." *John. Misc.* 2.175. (Lady Knight's *Anec.*)   Date?
2. *Letters.* *"I have heard him [J.] say he never read but one book, which he did not consider as obligatory, through in his whole life (and Lady Mary Wortley's Letters was the book)." *John. Misc.* 1.319. (Piozzi)   Date?

Montesquieu, C. de Secondat de

1. *J. objects to his practice of supporting a strange opinion by quoting the customs of remote countries. He is, however, "really a fellow of genius too in many respects." *Bos.* 5.209. (*Hebrides*, 14 Sept.)   1773

Monthly Review

1. Compared with the *Critical Review, q.v.*   1767
2. *"The Monthly Reviewers are duller men [than the *Critical Reviewers*], and are glad to read the books through." *Bos.* 3.32   1776

More, Hannah

1. *Sir Eldred.* *J. flatters Miss More on her *Sir Eldred*, and "repeats all the best stanzas by heart." *John. Misc.* 2.184. (Hannah More)   1776

2. *"It is dangerous to say a word of poetry before her; it is talking of the art of war before Hannibal." *John. Misc.* 2.197   1782
3. *"The best of all the female versifiers." *Letters* 2. 328 *n* 3   1783
4. *"Johnson told me [Dr. Beattie] with great solemnity that Miss More was 'the most powerful versificatrix' in the English language." Forbes's *Beattie*, ed. 1824, p. 320. (*Bos.* 3.293 *n* 5)   1784
5. *Le Bas Bleu.* "Miss Moore has written a poem called Le Bas Bleu; which is in my opinion a very great performance." *Letters* 2.390   1784
6. *Le Bas Bleu.* *Hannah More writes that J. "tells me he longs to see me, to praise the Bas Bleu as much as envy can praise;—there's for you! . . . he said . . . there was no name in poetry that might not be glad to own it." *John. Misc.* 2.201-2   1784

Mulso, Hester. (Mrs. Chapone)

1. *J. repeats "with very apparent delight" verses by Miss M. *John. Misc.* 2.252. (Miss Reynolds) Date?

Murphy, Arthur

1. "A very judicious critick." J. agrees with a comment on *King Lear. Shak.*, Raleigh, 162   1765
2. *Zenobia.* *According to Mrs. Piozzi, J. told Murphy, who had submitted this tragedy to him for criticism, " 'that there was too much *Tig* and *Tirry* in it.' Seeing me laugh most violently, 'Why what would'st have, child?' (said he.) I looked at nothing but the dramatis [personæ], and there was *Tig*ranes and *Tiri*dates, or Teribazus, or such stuff. A man can tell but what he knows, and I never got any further than the first page.' " *John. Misc.* 1.332   *cir.* 1767?
3. *"I don't know (said he,) that Arthur can be classed with the very first dramatick writers; yet at present I

doubt much whether we have any thing superiour to Arthur." *Bos.* 2.127. (Maxwell's *Collectanea*)
Date?

Navagero

1. Included in list of important Italian authors. See ITALIAN LITERATURE 1   1755

Nemesianus

1. Since Virgil, "no shepherds were taught to sing by any succeeding poet till Nemesian and Calphurnius ventured their feeble efforts in the lower age of Latin literature." *Lives* 3.316   1781

Ogilvie, John

1. *J. can "find no thinking" in his poems. "BOSWELL. 'Is there not imagination in them, Sir?' JOHNSON. 'Why, Sir, there is in them what *was* imagination, but it is no more imagination in *him*, than sound is sound in the echo. And his diction too is not his own. We have long ago seen *white-robed innocence*, and *flower-bespangled meads*.'" *Bos.* 1.421   1763
2. *"When I asked Dr. Johnson's permission to introduce him, he obligingly agreed; adding, however, with a sly pleasantry, 'but he must give us none of his poetry.'" *Bos.* 1.423 *n* 1 by Boswell.   1763

Osborne, Francis

1. *"A conceited fellow. Were a man to write so now, the boys would throw stones at him." *Bos.* 2.193
    1772

"*Ossian.*" See MACPHERSON

Otway, Thomas

1. *"If Otway had written this play [Dodsley's *Cleone*, *q.v.*], no other of his pieces would have been remembered." *Bos.* 4.21. (Langton's *Collection*)   *cir.* 1758

2. (*Lives* 1) "One of the first names in the English drama." (241.) "Had not much cultivated versification, nor much replenished his mind with general knowledge. His principal power was in moving the passions." (247-8) 1779
3. *The Orphan.* "Has pleased for almost a century. . . . Its whole power is upon the affections, for it is not written with much comprehension of thought or elegance of expression. But if the heart is interested, many other beauties may be wanting, yet not missed." *Lives* 1.245 1779
4. *Poet's Complaint of his Muse.* Obscurity. "Little to commend." *Lives* 1.247 1779
5. *Venice Preserved.* "His last and greatest dramatic work." Still continues public favourite despite "want of morality in the original design, and the despicable scenes of vile comedy with which he has diversified his tragick action." Images stronger and language more energetic than in his *Orphan.* Public judgement right: "the work of a man not attentive to decency nor zealous for virtue; but of one who conceived forcibly and drew originally by consulting nature in his own breast." *Lives* 1.245-6 1779
6. *Venice Preserved.* *"Johnson," writes Northcote, "in his peremptory manner pronounced that there was not forty good lines to be found in *Venice Preserved.* Goldsmith asserted that, notwithstanding, it was of all tragedies the one nearest equal to Shakespeare. 'Poh!' said Johnson. 'What stuff in these lines!—
   "What feminine tales hast thou been list'ning to
   Of unair'd shirts, catarrhs and toothache got
   By thin-soled shoes?" '
'True', said Goldsmith; 'to be sure, that is very like to Shakespeare.' " S. Gwynne's *Memorials of an Eighteenth Century Painter*, p. 97. (Quoted in *Lives* 1.246 *n* 1) Date?
7. *"I once asked Dr. Johnson, if he did not think Ot-

way a good painter of tender scenes? and he replied, 'Sir! he is all tenderness.' " Dr. Burney, *Hist. of Music*, 1774, 3.598 *n*. (Quoted in *Lives* 1.248 *n* 1)
Date?

8. *According to Langton, "Johnson always appeared not to be sufficiently sensible of the merit of Otway." *Bos*. 4.21. (Dr. Burney calls this assertion "too *round*" and adds that J. once told him, "Sir, he is all tenderness." *ib. n* 1)
Date?

Ovid

1. A passage in Ovid, the beauty of which is accidental rather than inherent. *Wks*. 9.38-9. (*Adv*. 58)   1753
2. *"[J.] commended Ovid's description of the death of Hercules—doubted whether Virgil would not have loaded the description with too many fine words; that Virgil would sometimes *dare verba*." *Letters* 2.440. (App. D. From Windham's *Diary*)   1784

Paracelsus

1. Helmont and Paracelsus: "Wild and enthusiastic authors of romantic chymistry." T. Browne, *Works*, ed. Wilkin, 1835, 4.83 *n*   1756

Parnell, Thomas

1. *Hermit, The*. *An inaccuracy in. *Bos*. 3.392-3   1779
2. No great comprehension or fertility of mind. Not often original. "His praise must be derived from the easy sweetness of his diction: in his verses there is 'more happiness than pains'; he is spritely without effort, and always delights though he never ravishes; every thing is proper, yet every thing seems casual. . . . Of his other compositions [besides *The Hermit*] it is impossible to say whether they are the productions of Nature, so excellent as not to want the help of Art, or of Art so refined as to resemble Nature." (J. adds:— "This criticism relates only to the pieces published by

Pope [and not to his Posthumous Works]." *Lives*
2.54   1781
3. *Poems.* (*Lives* 2) In general J. accepts Goldsmith's criticism: "He bestows just praise upon *The Rise of Woman*, the *Fairy Tale*, and the *Pervigilium Veneris*; but has very properly remarked that in *The Battle of Mice and Frogs* the Greek names have not in English their original effect." (52.) *Night Piece on Death* inferior to Gray, says J., contrary to Goldsmith's judgement. *Elegy to an Old Beauty*, "perhaps the meanest" of P.'s performances. *Allegory on Man* "the happiest." (53.) *The Hermit.* "If there is some appearance of elaboration in *The Hermit* the narrative, as it is less airy, is less pleasing." (54)   1781
4. "Hic requiescit THOMAS PARNELL, S.T.P.
    Qui sacerdos pariter et poeta,
    Utrasque partes ita implevit,
    Ut neque sacerdoti suavitas poetæ,
    Nec poetæ sacerdotis sanctitas, deesset."
Bos. 4.54   Date?

Passeratius

1. Epitaph by P. highly praised. *Wks.* 9.442   1740

Percy, Bishop Thomas

1. *Reliques of Ancient English Poetry.* "A curious work lately printed."[1] *Shak.* 8.373. (This work referred to also in *Shak.* 8.446 *n* 5, and 447 *n* 6; and App. to vol. 8: note to vol. 2, p. 151, and *ib.* note to vol. 8, p. 281)
                                                                                                             1765
2. *J. prefers Mrs. Percy's judgement to her husband's. See SHENSTONE 1   *cir.* 1765

---

[1] The *Reliques* appeared the same year as J.'s *Shakespeare*. Percy stated that J., among others, importuned him to publish the *Reliques*, and that to J. he "owes many valuable hints for the conduct of the work." *Reliques*, ed. 1765, *Preface*, pp. ix and xiii. (See Courtney, *Bibliog.* p. 111; also Percy-Shenstone correspondence in *Quellen und Forschungen*, vol. 103 for frequent reference to J.'s interest in this work.)

3. *Hermit of Warkworth.* "Dr. Percy has written a long ballad in many *fits*; it is pretty enough." *Bos.* 2.136
                                                        1771
4. *Hermit of Warkworth.* *J. parodies this poem. *John. Misc.* 2.67-8. (Cradock. See also *ib.* 2.314-5 and *Wks.* 1.389-90)   *cir.* 1771?

Pergolesi

1. *La Serva Padrona.* *A burletta "not *unnatural*. It is a scene¹ that is acted in my family every day in my life." *John. Misc.* 2.411   Date?

Petrarch

1. Included in a list of important Italian authors. See ITALIAN LITERATURE 1   1755
2. His authority. See DANTE 1   1755
3. "This obligation to amorous ditties owes, I believe, its original to the fame of Petrarch, who, in an age rude and uncultivated, by his tuneful homage to his Laura, refined the manners of the lettered world, and filled Europe with love and poetry. But the basis of all excellence is truth: he that professes love ought to feel its power. Petrarch was a real lover," etc. *Lives* 1.6
                                                        1779
4. "Petrarch entertained the learned men of his age with the novelty of modern Pastorals in Latin," etc. *Lives* 3.317   1781

Petronius

1. Pope's lack of critical merit in mentioning Petronius among the great names of criticism in his *Essay on Criticism. Wks.* 15.475   1756

Petvin

1. *Letters on Mind.* Ridiculed as an example of the "terrifick" style. *Wks.* 8.144. (*Idl.* 36)   1758

---

¹ An old fellow is cheated by his servant.

Philelphe. See RENAISSANCE I

Philips, Ambrose

1. "He has added nothing to English poetry, yet at least half his book deserves to be read: perhaps he valued most himself that part which the critick would reject." *Lives* 3.325   1781

2. *The Freethinker.* "His happiest undertaking." "It . . . is little read; nor can impartial criticism recommend it as worthy of revival." Nothing indecent or licentious. *Lives* 3.322   1781

3. *"Namby Pamby" Poems.* "In his other poems [other than *Pastorals* and *To the Earl of Dorset*]" are "lines sometimes elegant; but he has seldom much force or much comprehension." *"Namby Pamby"* poems are "the pieces that please best." "The numbers are smooth and spritely, and the diction is seldom faulty. They are not loaded with much thought, yet if they had been written by Addison they would have had admirers: little things are not valued but when they are done by those who can do greater." *Lives* 3.324   1781

4. *Pastorals.* (*Lives* 3) "Which, flattering the imagination with Arcadian scenes, probably found many readers, and might have long passed as a pleasing amusement had they not been unhappily too much commended." (316.) Philips took Spenser for his model and "endeavoured to be natural, Pope laboured to be elegant." (319.) "The *Pastorals,* which by the writer of *The Guardian* were ranked as one of the four genuine productions of the rustick Muse, cannot surely be despicable. That they exhibit a mode of life which does not exist, nor ever existed, is not to be objected; the supposition of such a state is allowed to Pastoral." (324)   1781

5. *To the Earl of Dorset* (*"Letter from Copenhagen"*). "May be justly praised." *Lives* 3.324   1781

6. *Tragedies.* (*Lives* 3) *The Distrest Mother.* "Almost a translation of Racine's *Andromaque*. Such a work requires no uncommon powers." (314.) "No subject of criticism." (324.) *The Briton.* "Now neglected, though one of the scenes . . . is confessed to be written with great dramatick skill, animated by spirit truly poetical." (321.) *Humfrey, Duke of Gloucester.* "Only remembered by its title." (321.) Both tragedies are "not below mediocrity, nor above it." (324.) 1781

7. Translations from Pindar. See PINDAR 3   1781

Philips, John

1. "What study could confer Philips had obtained; but natural deficience cannot be supplied. He seems not born to greatness and elevation. He is never lofty, nor does he often surprise with unexpected excellence." *Lives* 1.320   1779

2. *Blenheim.* Poem of a scholar, not a soldier. Versification imitated from "all that is obsolete, peculiar, or licentious." Milton's virtues wanting. "Those asperities therefore that are venerable in the *Paradise Lost* are contemptible in the *Blenheim*." *Lives* 1.318   1779

3. *Cyder.* (*Lives* 1) "May be given this peculiar praise, that it is grounded in truth; that the precepts . . . are exact and just . . . at once a book of entertainment and of science." (319.) The mistake of using blank verse where images not grand enough to sustain it. (See BLANK VERSE 9.) "It is written with much art, though with few blazes of genius." (320)   1779

4. *Ode ad Henricum S. John.* "Gay and elegant," etc. *Lives* 1.318   1779

5. "*The Splendid Shilling* has the uncommon merit of an original design, unless it may be thought precluded by the ancient *Centos*. To degrade the sounding words and stately construction of Milton, by an application to the lowest and most trivial things, gratifies the mind

with a momentary triumph over that grandeur which hitherto held its captives in admiration; the words and things are presented with a new appearance, and novelty is always grateful where it gives no pain. But the merit of such performances begins and ends with the first author."*Lives* 1.316-7. "One excellence of *The Splendid Shilling* is that it is short. Disguise can gratify no longer than it deceives." (*ib.* 2.320)   1779-81

Pindar. See also PINDARIC VERSE

1. "The tempestuous Pindar." *Lives* 1.59   1779
2. "The verses of Pindar have . . . very little harmony to a modern ear; yet by examining the syllables we perceive them to be regular, and have reason enough for supposing that the ancient audiences were delighted with the sound." See PINDARIC VERSE 1   1779
3. A. Philips, in his translations of Pindar, found "all the obscurity of the Theban bard, however he may fall below his sublimity: he will be allowed, if he has less fire, to have more smoke." *Lives* 3.324-5   1781

Pitcairne, Archibald

1. *His Latin poetry overpraised. *Bos.* 5.57-8. (*Hebrides*, 18 Aug.)   1773

Pitt, Christopher

1. *Poems and Translations.* "I have not observed that any rise above mediocrity." *Lives* 3.278   1781
2. *Translation of "Aeneid."* (*Lives* 3) "I am sorry not to see [it] joined in the late publication with his other poems. It would have been pleasing to have an opportunity of comparing the two best translations that perhaps were ever produced by one nation of the same author." Pitt had advantage of Dryden's *Aeneid* and Pope's *Iliad* as examples. "Dryden leads the reader forward by his general vigour and sprightliness, and Pitt often stops him to contemplate the excellence of

a single couplet; ... Dryden's faults are forgotten in the hurry of delight, and ... Pitt's beauties are neglected in the languor of a cold and listless perusal; ... Pitt pleases the criticks, and Dryden the people; ... Pitt is quoted, and Dryden read." (279.) "This great work." (279)   1781

3. *Translation of Vida's "Art of Poetry."* In this, "he distinguished himself." *Lives* 3.277-8   1781

Politian[1]. See also RENAISSANCE, THE, I; ITALIAN LITERATURE I

1. "A name eminent among the restorers of polite literature." *Wks.* 6.358. (*Ram.* 127)   1751
2. "The learned Politian." *Lives* 1.87   1779

Pomfret, John[2]

1. P. "has been always the favourite of that class of readers, who without vanity or criticism seek only their own amusement. ... In his other poems [besides *The Choice*] there is an easy volubility; the pleasure of smooth metre is afforded to the ear, and the mind is not oppressed with ponderous or entangled with intricate sentiment. He pleases many, and he who pleases many must have some species of merit." *Lives* 1.302   1779

2. *The Choice.* "Exhibits a system of life adapted to common notions and equal to common expectations. ... Perhaps no composition in our language has been oftener perused." *Lives* 1.302   1779

Pope, Alexander. (COMPARED WITH DRYDEN.) See also *infra* 57, 58

1. *Boswell: "I told him [J.] that Voltaire, in a conversation with me, had distinguished Pope and Dryden

---

[1] In 1734 J. issued *Proposals* for an edition of Politian, but the work never appeared. See Courtney, *Bibliog.* 2
[2] Included in *English Poets* at J.'s recommendation. *Lives* 3.302

thus:—'Pope drives a handsome chariot, with a couple of neat trim nags; Dryden a coach, and six stately horses.' JOHNSON. 'Why, Sir, the truth is, they both drive coaches and six; but Dryden's horses are either galloping or stumbling: Pope's go at a steady even trot.'" *Bos.* 2.5   1766

2. *"He observed, that in Dryden's poetry there were passages drawn from a profundity which Pope could never reach." *Bos.* 2.85   1769

3. *Their Judgement.* Both possessed "integrity of understanding and nicety of discernment." "The rectitude of Dryden's mind was sufficiently shewn by the dismission of his poetical prejudices, and the rejection of unnatural thoughts and rugged numbers. But Dryden never desired to apply all the judgement that he had. He wrote, and professed to write, merely for the people; and when he pleased others, he contented himself. He spent no time in struggles to rouse latent powers; he never attempted to make that better which was already good, nor often to mend what he must have known to be faulty." Guided by the needs of the moment. Careless of future editions, "for when he had no pecuniary interest, he had no further solicitude. Pope was not content to satisfy; he desired to excel, and therefore always endeavoured to do his best: he did not court the candour, but dared the judgement of his reader, and, expecting no indulgence from others, he shewed none to himself. He examined lines and words with minute and punctilious observation, and retouched every part with indefatigable diligence, till he had left nothing to be forgiven." P. kept his pieces long in his hands. His "parental attention" to them continued after publication: in revised editions. "It will seldom be found that he altered without adding clearness, elegance, or vigour. Pope had perhaps the judgement of Dryden; but Dryden certainly wanted the diligence of Pope." *Their Knowledge:* "In acquired

knowledge the superiority must be allowed to Dryden. . . . His mind has a larger range, and he collects his images and illustrations from a more extensive circumference of science. Dryden knew more of man in his general nature, and Pope in his local manners. The notions of Dryden were formed by comprehensive speculation, and those of Pope by minute attention. There is more dignity in the knowledge of Dryden, and more certainty in that of Pope." *Prose style:* Both excelled in prose but differently: "The style of Dryden is capricious and varied, that of Pope is cautious and uniform; Dryden obeys the motions of his own mind, Pope constrains his mind to his own rules of composition. Dryden is sometimes vehement and rapid; Pope is always smooth, uniform, and gentle. Dryden's page is a natural field, rising into inequalities, and diversified by the varied exuberance of abundant vegetation; Pope's is a velvet lawn, shaven by the scythe, and levelled by the roller." *Genius:* Dryden superior, J. decides "with some hesitation." "It is not to be inferred that of this poetical vigour Pope had only a little, because Dryden had more, for every other writer since Milton must give place to Pope; and even of Dryden it must be said that if he has brighter paragraphs, he has not better poems. Dryden's performances were always hasty, either excited by some external occasion, or extorted by domestick necessity; he composed without consideration, and published without correction. What his mind could supply at call, or gather in one excursion, was all that he sought, and all that he gave. The dilatory caution of Pope enabled him to condense his sentiments, to multiply his images, and to accumulate all that study might produce, or chance might supply. If the flights of Dryden therefore are higher, Pope continues longer on the wing. If of Dryden's fire the blaze is brighter, of Pope's the heat is more regular and constant. Dryden often sur-

passes expectation, and Pope never falls below it. Dryden is read with frequent astonishment, and Pope with perpetual delight." *Lives* 3.220-3   1781
4. *"Of Pope as a writer he had the highest opinion." But his superior reverence for Dryden. *John. Misc.* 1.184-5   Date?

Pope, Alexander. (GENERAL CRITICISM)

5. J. drew 3.5% of the literary quotations for his *Dictionary* from Pope. See ADDISON 5   1755
6. *His genius.* (*Lives* 3) In youth, "thought himself the greatest genius that ever was." Danger in judgements passed in solitude, but "it was the felicity of Pope to rate himself at his real value." (89.) Genius referred to. (106, 217, 262, etc.) "Pope had, in proportions very nicely adjusted to each other, all the qualities that constitute genius. He had Invention . . . Imagination . . . Judgement . . . and he had colours of language always before him ready to decorate his matter with every grace of elegant expression." (For elaboration of these qualities, see GENIUS 23.) (247)   1781
7. P.'s greatness referred to. *Lives* 3.87, 184   1781
8. *Is Pope a Poet?* See POETRY 38 for J.'s emphatic answer: "If Pope be not a poet, where is poetry to be found," etc. "If the writer of the *Iliad* were to class his successors he would assign a very high place to his translator, without requiring any other evidence of genius." *Lives* 3.251-2   1781
9. *P.'s intellectual character:* (*Lives* 3) [a] *Experience.* Its effect on P.: "When he entered into the living world it seems to have happened to him as to many others that he was less attentive to dead masters: he studied in the academy of Paracelsus, and made the universe his favourite volume. He gathered his notions fresh from reality, not from the copies of authors, but the originals of Nature. Yet there is no reason to

believe that literature ever lost his esteem; he always professed to love reading." (216.) [b] *P.'s intellectual curiosity:* "His frequent references to history, his allusions to various kinds of knowledge, and his images selected from art and nature, with his observations on the operations of the mind and the modes of life, shew an intelligence perpetually on the wing, excursive, vigorous, and diligent, eager to pursue knowledge, and attentive to retain it." (216.) [c] *P.'s "Good Sense":* See GOOD SENSE 3. [d] *His genius.* See GENIUS 21. [e] *Memory:* "To assist these powers he is said to have had great strength and exactness of memory." 217.) [f] *Diligence:* "These benefits of nature he improved by incessant and unwearied diligence . . . and was never content with mediocrity when excellence could be attained . . . to make verses was his first labour, and to mend them was his last," etc. (217-8)   1781

Pope, Alexander. (VERSIFICATION AND STYLE.) See also under Pope's WORKS: *Iliad* and *Odyssey*

10. *Diction.* Examples of "barbarous, or impure words and expressions" in Pope. *Wks.* 9.188   1747
11. "From these lines [*Essay on Crit.* ll.366-73], laboured with great attention, and celebrated by a rival wit, may be judged what can be expected from the most diligent endeavours after this imagery of sound. The verse intended to represent the whisper of the vernal breeze, must be confessed not much to excel in softness or volubility; and the smooth stream runs with a perpetual clash of jarring consonants. The noise and turbulence of the torrent is, indeed, distinctly imaged, for it requires very little skill to make our language rough; but in these lines, which mention the effort of *Ajax*, there is no particular heaviness, obstruction, or delay. The swiftness of *Camilla* is rather contrasted than exemplified; why the verse should be

lengthened to express speed, will not easily be discovered. In the dactyls used for that purpose by the ancients, two short syllables were pronounced with such rapidity, as to be equal only to one long; they, therefore, naturally exhibit the act of passing through a long space in a short time. But the *Alexandrine*, by its pause in the midst, is a tardy and stately measure; and the word *unbending*, one of the most sluggish and slow which our language affords, cannot much accelerate its motion." *Wks.* 6.136-7. (*Ram.* 92)   1751

12. *J. denies that Pope excelled all in the art of condensation: "There is more sense in a line of Cowley than in a page (or a sentence, or ten lines,—I [Boswell] am not quite certain of the very phrase) of Pope." *Bos.* 5.345. (*Hebrides*, 23 Oct.)   1773

13. Even "the greatest master of numbers" unable to "fix the principles of representative harmony." J. uses the same sequence of syllables to illustrate tardiness and swiftness, except that the line imitating swiftness is the longer by one syllable.[1] *Lives* 3.232   1781

14. *Versification.* (*Lives* 3) "Among the excellences of Pope, therefore, must be mentioned the melody of his metre. By perusing the works of Dryden he discovered the most perfect fabrick of English verse, and habituated himself to that only which he found the best; in consequence of which restraint his poetry has been censured as too uniformly musical, and as glutting the ear with unvaried sweetness." J. suspects this to be "the cant of those who judge by principles rather than perception." (248.) No "superfluous rigour." But P. not careful of his versification to point where the difficulty would overbalance the advantage. Construction "not always strictly grammatical; with those rhymes

---

[1] "Flies o'er th' unbending corn, and skims along the main." (*Essay on Crit.* Pt. II, l. 373.) "The long majestick march, and energy divine." (*Imit. Horace*, Bk. II, Epist. 1, l. 269.)

which prescription had conjoined he contented himself . . . though there was no striking consonance; nor was he very careful to vary his terminations or to refuse admission at a small distance to the same rhymes." Alexandrines and triplets occasionally admitted in spite of Swift. (249.) A few double rhymes, "always, I think, unsuccessfully, except once in *The Rape of the Lock.*" Expletives early excluded, "but he now and then admits an epithet rather commodious than important", e.g., first six lines of *Iliad*. Sometimes "one verse seems to be made for the sake of another." French idioms sometimes vitiate his latter productions—perhaps from Bolingbroke.[1] (250.) "New sentiments and new images others may produce, but to attempt any further improvement of versification will be dangerous." See VERSIFICATION 32 1781

15. *Method of composition.* (*Lives* 3) "He was one of those few whose labour is their pleasure. . . . He laboured his works first to gain reputation, and afterwards to keep it. Of composition there are different methods. Some employ at once memory and invention" and write only when the production is finished. "The method of Pope, as may be collected from his translation, was to write his first thoughts in his first words, and gradually to amplify, decorate, rectify, and refine them. With such faculties and such dispositions he excelled every other writer in *poetical prudence*; he wrote in such a manner as might expose him to few hazards. He used almost always the same fabrick of verse; and, indeed, by those few essays which he made of any other, he did not enlarge his reputation. Of this uniformity the certain consequence was readiness and dexterity," etc. Especially in translating. (218-9.) "His poems . . . scarce ever temporary." (See OCCASIONAL WORKS 19.) Hence his productions never

---

[1] This remark not in first edition.

hasty. He let imagination subside; listened to criticism. (See CRITICISM 6.) (219-20) 1781
16. *"Sir, a thousand years may elapse before there shall appear another man with a power of versification equal to that of Pope." *Bos.* 4.46 Date?

Pope, Alexander. (WORKS)

17. *Dunciad.* *"He repeated to us, in his forcible melodious manner, the concluding lines of the *Dunciad.* While he was talking loudly in praise of those lines . . ." etc. *Bos.* 2.84. (See also *John. Misc.* 2.254, and *infra* 54) 1769
18. *Dunciad.* (*Lives* 3) P. "shewed his satirical powers by publishing *The Dunciad*, one of his greatest[1] and most elaborate performances." (145.) Satire has intended effect—characters blasted. (146.) "The prevalence of this poem was gradual and slow: the plan, if not wholly new, was little understood by common readers. Many of the allusions required illustration; the names" not easy to interpret by initial and final letters, and obscure even when printed in full. "The subject itself had nothing generally interesting; for whom did it concern to know that one or another scribbler was a dunce?" (146.) A later edition "made intelligible and diverting" by giving names of persons and notes on them. (150.) New edition of *Dunciad* with Cibber in Theobald's place: "Unhappily the two heroes were of opposite characters, and Pope was unwilling to lose what he had already written; he has therefore depraved his poem by giving to Cibber the old books, the cold pedantry and sluggish pertinacity of Theobald." (186.) Resulting inefficacy of his satire. (187.) P. takes hint from Dryden's *Mac Flecknoe*, "but the plan is so enlarged and diversified as justly to claim the praise of an original, and affords perhaps the best specimen that has yet appeared of personal satire ludi-

[1] See note to YOUNG 11.

crously pompous." J. not convinced that design was moral: revenge against Theobald, first motive. Petulance and malignity in this, but not very criminal. The value of satirical criticism: "he that refines the publick taste is a publick benefactor. [See SATIRE 6.] The beauties of this poem are well known; its chief fault is the grossness of its images. Pope and Swift had an unnatural delight in ideas physically impure, such as every other tongue utters with unwillingness, and of which every ear shrinks from the mention. But even this fault, offensive as it is, may be forgiven for the excellence of other passages; such as the formation and dissolution of Moore, the account of the Traveller, the misfortune of the Florist, and the crowded thoughts and stately numbers which dignify the concluding paragraph." (242.) Alterations, not always for the better. (242) 1781

19. *Dunciad.* *Mr. Langton tells J. "that Pope himself admired those [concluding] lines so much that when he repeated them his voice faltered: 'and well it might, Sir,' said Johnson, 'for they are noble lines.'" (Note by J. Boswell, Jun.) *Bos.* 2.84 n 2 Date?

20. *Elegy to the Memory of an Unfortunate Lady.* (*Lives* 3) "Poetry has not often been worse employed than in dignifying the amorous fury of a raving girl." (101.) "The illaudable singularity of treating suicide with respect." Verses in places have "vigorous animation" or "gentle tenderness; nor has Pope produced any poem in which the sense predominates more over the diction. But the tale is not skilfully told." Also inconsistency, and "inconsistency never can be right." (226) 1781

21. *Eloisa to Abelard.* It "may justly be regarded as one of the works on which the reputation of Pope will stand in future times." Regarding J. Warton's criticism of this poem, J. remarks: "There is not much profundity of criticism, because the beauties are sen-

timents of nature, which the learned and the ignorant feel alike." *Wks.* 15.477. (Review of J. Warton's *Essay on Pope*) 1756

22. *Eloisa to Abelard.* (*Lives* 3) "How much he has surpassed Prior's work [*Henry and Emma*] is not necessary to mention, when perhaps it may be said with justice, that he has excelled every composition of the same kind. The mixture of religious hope and resignation gives an elevation and dignity to disappointed love, which images merely natural cannot bestow. The gloom of a convent strikes the imagination with far greater force than the solitude of a grove." (105.) "The *Epistle of Eloise to Abelard* is one of the most happy productions of human wit": the subject would be hard to excel. (See SUBJECTS 15.) Their merit recommends their story to us. It is "undisputed history" and "the heart naturally loves truth." (See TRUTH 26.) "Their fate does not leave the mind in hopeless dejection." (235.) "The story thus skilfully adopted has been diligently improved. Pope has left nothing behind him which seems more the effect of studious perseverance and laborious revisal. Here is particularly observable the 'curiosa felicitas,' a fruitful soil, and careful cultivation. Here is no crudeness of sense, nor asperity of language." Its "sentiments which have so much vigour and efficacy." (236.) Its imagination. (See IMAGINATION 13) 1781

23. *Epic, P's Projected.* Pope "laid aside his Epick Poem, perhaps without much loss to mankind." See EPIC 9 1781

24. *Epitaphs,* Detailed analysis of P.'s. *Lives* 3.254-72 1781

25. *Essay on Criticism.* "The stupendous performance of a youth not yet twenty years old. . . . We cannot agree with him [Joseph Warton in *Essay on Pope*] in his censure of the comparison of a student advancing in science with a traveller passing the Alps, which

is perhaps the best simile in our language; that in which the most exact resemblance is traced between things in appearance utterly unrelated to each other. That the last line conveys no new *idea*, is not true; it makes particular what was before general. Whether the description which he adds from another author be, as he says, more full and striking than that of Pope, is not to be inquired. Pope's description is relative, and can admit no greater length than is usually allowed to a simile, nor any other particulars than such as form the correspondence." Pope's lack of critical merit in mentioning Petronius among the great names of criticism. *Wks.* 15.473-5. (Rev. of J. Warton's *Essay on Pope*) 1756

26. *Essay on Criticism.* (*Lives* 3) "A work which displays such extent of comprehension, such nicety of distinction, such acquaintance with mankind, and such knowledge both of ancient and modern learning as are not often attained by the maturest age and longest experience." (94.) Dennis's criticism analyzed. (See DENNIS 5.) Warburton sees in *Essay on Criticism* an order and connection not intended by author, for "almost every poem, consisting of precepts, is so far arbitrary and immethodical, that many of the paragraphs may change places with no apparent inconvenience." (99.) Reason for this. (See DIDACTIC POETRY 8.) "One of his greatest though of his earliest works . . . which if he had written nothing else would have placed him among the first critics and the first poets, as it exhibits every mode of excellence that can embellish or dignify didactick composition, selection of matter, novelty of arrangement, justness of precept, splendour of illustration, and propriety of digression." P. "never afterwards excelled it." "Alps" simile "is perhaps the best that English poetry can show." What constitutes a perfect simile. (See SIMILES 5.) "The simile of the Alps has no useless parts, yet affords a striking picture

by itself: it makes the foregoing position better understood, and enables it to take faster hold on the attention; it assists the apprehension, and elevates the fancy." (228-30.) Analysis of Pope's precept: "the sound must seem an echo to the sense." (See VERSIFICATION 33.) Its invention. (See GENIUS 23)   1781

27. *Essay on Criticism.* *J. attacks the couplet on true wit:[1] "a definition both false and foolish. Let wit be dressed how it will, it will equally be wit, and neither the more nor the less for any advantage dress can give it. . . . 'What oft was thought,' is all the worse for being often thought, because to be wit, it ought to be newly thought. . . . How can the expression make it new? It may make it clear, or may make it elegant; but how new?" D'Arblay, *Diary and Letters*, 2.108-9. See also WIT 7 for a similar attack on this couplet.
   1782

28. *Essay on Man.* *"There is reason to think, that Johnson conceived an early prejudice against the Essay on Man; and what once took root in a mind like his, was not easily eradicated." *John. Misc.* 1.374. (Murphy)
   cir. 1738?

29. *Essay on Man.* *Attacked by Crousaz "for some faults which it has, and some which it has not." *Bos.* 5.80. (*Hebrides*, 21 Aug.)   1773

30. *Essay on Man.* *J. defends a "low" expression (*Essay on Man*, iv. 224) :—"It is intended to be low: it is satire. The expression is debased, to debase the character." *Bos.* 5.83. (*Hebrides*, 21 Aug.)   1773

31. *Essay on Man.* (*Lives* 3) "He published the first part of what he persuaded himself to think a system of Ethicks." (160.) "The poem . . . a new kind." (161.) "Two memorable corrections" in first Epistle. (162.) "The *Essay* plainly appears the fabrick of a

---

[1] "True Wit is Nature to advantage dress'd,
  What oft was thought, but ne'er so well express'd."
(Pt. II, ll. 97-8)

poet [not simply transformed, as was claimed, from prose to verse]: what Bolingbroke supplied could be only the first principles; the order, illustration, and embellishments must all be Pope's." (163. cf. *Bos.* 3.403 for J.'s statement to the same effect.) Principles of *Essay* were not immediately examined: "philosophy and poetry have not often the same readers, and the *Essay* abounded in splendid amplifications and sparkling sentences . . . its flowers caught the eye which did not see what the gay foliage concealed, and for a time flourished in the sunshine of universal approbation. So little was any evil tendency discovered that, as innocence is unsuspicious, many read it for a manual of piety." (164.) "It is undeniable that in many passages a religious eye may easily discover expressions not very favorable to morals or to liberty." (165.) "A work of great labour and long consideration, but certainly not the happiest of Pope's performances. The subject is perhaps not very proper for poetry, and the poet was not sufficiently master of his subject." (242.) Examples of his weak reasoning. (243.) "This *Essay* affords an egregious instance of the predominance of genius, the dazzling splendour of imagery, and the seductive powers of eloquence. Never were penury of knowledge and vulgarity of sentiment so happily disguised. The reader feels his mind full, though he learns nothing; and when he meets it in its new array no longer knows the talk of his mother and his nurse. When these wonder-working sounds sink into sense and the doctrine of the *Essay*, disrobed of its ornaments, is left to the powers of its naked excellence, what shall we discover? That we are . . ." etc. (Summary of platitudes. 243-4.) "Surely a man of no very comprehensive search may venture to say that he has heard all this before, but it was never till now recommended by such a blaze of embellishment or such sweetness of melody. The vigorous contraction of some thoughts, the luxuriant amplification of others, the incidental illustrations, and sometimes the dignity, sometimes the softness of the verses, enchain philosophy, suspend criticism, and oppress judgement by overpowering pleasure. This is true of many paragraphs; yet . . . it contains more lines unsuccessfully laboured, more harshness of diction, more thoughts imperfectly expressed, more levity without elegance, and more heaviness without strength, than will easily be found in all his other works." 244-5)   1781

32. *Guardian.* (*Letter on Pastorals.* No. 40) (*Lives* 3) "A composition of artifice, criticism, and literature, to which nothing equal will easily be found." (107.) Its "unexampled and unequalled artifice of irony." Dexterity of his disguise. (319)   1781

33. *Homer, Translation of.* (See also *infra,* P.'s *Iliad* and *Odyssey.*) *J.'s answer to the charge that it "was not a good representation of the original": "Sir, it is the greatest work of the kind that has ever been produced." *Bos.* 3.257   1778

34. *Homer, Translation of.* "Since the English ear has been accustomed to the mellifluence of Pope's numbers," etc. *Lives* 1.453   1779

35. *Homer.* (*Lives* 3) "It is not very likely that he [P.] overflowed with Greek." But "minute enquiries into the force of words are less necessary in translating Homer than other poets, because his positions are general," etc. (113-4.) "The same general praise [see 41] may be given to both translations [*Iliad* and *Odyssey*]." (241.) Pope "had colours of language always before him ready to decorate his matter with every grace of elegant expression, as when he accomodates his diction to the wonderful multiplicity of Homer's sentiments and descriptions." (247.) "It is remarked by Watts that there is scarcely a happy combination of words or a phrase poetically elegant in the English language which Pope has not inserted into his

version of Homer. How he obtained possession of so many beauties of speech it were desirable to know." Perhaps he kept a regular collection "gleaned from authors, obscure as well as eminent." (251)   1781

36. *Homer, Translation of.* *The "learned critic [J.]" in Reynolds' *Fifteenth Discourse* (*Wks.* 1824, 2.152) remarks "that if Pope had not clothed the naked majesty of Homer with the graces and elegancies of modern fashions—though the real dignity of Homer was degraded by such a dress—his translation would not have met with such a favourable reception, and he must have been contented with fewer readers." *Lives* 3.240 *n* 1   Date?

37. *Iliad, Notes to.* "Though they were undoubtedly written to swell the volumes, ought not to pass without praise: commentaries which attract the reader by the pleasure of perusal have not often appeared; the notes of others are read to clear difficulties, those of Pope to vary entertainment." However, "too much of unseasonable levity and affected gaiety . . . too many appeals are made to the ladies, and the ease which is so carefully preserved is sometimes the ease of a trifler. Every art has its terms and every kind of instruction its proper style; the gravity of common criticks may be tedious, but is less despicable than childish merriment." *Lives* 3.240   1781

38. *Iliad, Translation of.* (See also *supra*, P.'s *Homer.*) Licences in the first lines of his *Iliad*, "which an easy writer must decline": inversions, a harsh metaphor, uncommon use of words, and padding. *Wks.* 8.309. (*Idl.* 77)   1759

39. *Iliad, Translation of.* "Considering into what hands Homer was to fall" the reader rejoices Dryden did not continue his translation of *Iliad*. *Lives* 1.389   1779

40. *Iliad, Translation of.* First book compared with Tickell's translation. *Lives* 2.309   Ptd. 1780

41. *Iliad, Translation of.* (*Lives* 3) "It is certainly the

noblest version[1] of poetry which the world has ever seen; and its publication must therefore be considered as one of the great events in the annals of learning. To those who have skill to estimate the excellence and difficulty of this great work, it must be very desirable to know how it was performed, and by what gradations it advanced to correctness," etc. (119.) "This great work." (128.) "The splendour and success of this work raised Pope many enemies." (136.) "That poetical wonder, the translation of the *Iliad*; a performance which no age or nation can pretend to equal." (236.) "Pope searched the pages of Dryden for happy combinations of heroick diction, but it will not be denied that he added much to what he found. He cultivated our language with so much diligence and art that he has left in his *Homer* a treasure of poetical elegances to posterity. His version may be said to have tuned the English tongue, for since its appearance no writer, however deficient in other powers, has wanted melody. Such a series of lines so elaborately corrected and so sweetly modulated took possession of the publick ear; the vulgar was enamoured of the poem, and the learned wondered at the translation." (238.) The objection that this version is not Homerical, that it "wants his awful simplicity, his artless grandeur, his unaffected majesty. This cannot be totally denied, but it must be remembered that 'necessitas quod cogit defendit,' that may be lawfully done which cannot be forborne. Time and place will always enforce regard." (See CRITICISM 23.) "Homer doubtless owes to his translator many Ovidian graces not exactly suitable to his character; but to have added can be no great crime if nothing be taken away. Elegance is surely to be desired if it be not gained at the expence of dignity. . . . To a thousand cavils one answer is sufficient; the purpose of a writer is to be read, and the criticism which would

---

[1] See VERSION.

destroy the power of pleasing must be blown aside. Pope wrote for his own age and his own nation: he knew that it was necessary to colour the images and point the sentiments of his author; he therefore made him graceful, but lost him some of his sublimity." (238-40)　　1781

42. *Iliad, Translation of.* (*Lives.* 3) *Versification.* Two unnecessary syllables in each of first six lines of *Iliad.* Alexandrines and triplets more frequent in his translations than in his original work. (249-50.) Pitt in his translation of the *Aeneid* "had an example [in Pope's *Iliad*] of an exact, equable, and splendid versification." (279)　　1781

43. *Juvenile poems. Silence:* "Composed . . . with much greater elegance of diction, music of numbers, extent of observation, and force of thought [than the *Ode on Solitude*]." *Wks.* 15.473　　1756

44. *Juvenile poems.* P.'s precocity. *Lives* 1.3; 3.90-1. *Ode on Solitude* and *Silence* examined, the latter highly praised. *Lives* 3.87-8　　1779-81

45. *Letters.* (*Lives* 3) Indifference of the public: insignificance of their matter. (158.) The collection "had, however, in some degree the recommendation of novelty. Our language has few letters, except those of statesmen. . . . Pope's epistolary excellence had an open field; he had no English rival, living or dead." Had the power of favouring himself in this collection: "And I know not whether there does not appear something more studied and artificial in his productions than the rest" except one studied letter by Bolingbroke. "Pope may be said to write always with his reputation in his head." (158-60.) "If the Letters of Pope are considered merely as compositions they seem to be premeditated and artificial." Pope's confessed "affectation and ambition" in his early letters. (208.) *A Letter to a Noble Lord.* "To a cool reader of the present time [it] exhibits nothing but tedious malignity." (179)　　1781

46. *Memoirs of . . . Scriblerus.* (In collaboration with Swift and Arbuthnot.) "If the whole [of the intended design] may be estimated by this specimen . . . the want of more will not be much lamented, for the follies which the writer ridicules are so little practised that they are not known; nor can the satire be understood but by the learned: he raises phantoms of absurdity, and then drives them away. He cures diseases that were never felt." Hence has been little read, or else forgotten by mankind, "as no man could be wiser, better, or merrier, by remembering it. The design cannot boast of much originality." *Lives* 3.182   1781

47. *Messiah, The.* "In his [J. Warton's] examination of the Messiah [in his *Essay on Pope*], he justly observes some deviations from the inspired author, which weaken the imagery, and despirit the expression." *Wks.* 15.470. (Review of J. Warton's *Essay on Pope*)
1756

48. *Messiah, The.* "That *The Messiah* excels the *Pollio* is no great praise, if it be considered from what original [Isaiah] the improvements are derived." *Lives* 3.226
1781

49. *Moral Essays.* The skill of reasoning poetically, "of uniting ornament with strength, and ease with closeness . . . Pope might have condescended to learn from him [Blackmore], when he needed it so much in his *Moral Essays*." *Lives* 2.254   Ptd. 1780

50. *Moral Essays.* Their imagination. See GENIUS 23
1781

51. *Moral Essays: Epistle to . . . Lord Bathurst.* (*Lives* 3) P. censured for his extravagant account of Kyrl, "the Man of Ross" and his incredible charities: "Narrations of romantick and impracticable virtue will be read with wonder, but that which is unattainable is recommended in vain." (172-3.) "When this poem was first published the dialogue, having no letters of direction, was perplexed and obscure. Pope

seems to have written with no very distinct idea, for he calls that an *Epistle to Bathurst* in which Bathurst is introduced as speaking." (173) 1781

52. *Moral Essays: Epistle to . . . Lord Bathurst* and *. . . to the Earl of Burlington.* In these, "Dr. Warburton has endeavoured to find a train of thought which was never in the writer's head. . . . In one [to Earl of Burlington], the most valuable passage is perhaps the elogy [*sic*] on Good Sense, and in the other the End of the Duke of Buckingham." *Lives* 3.245-6
1781

53. *Moral Essays: Epistle to Mr. Jervas.* Verses, "which certainly shew his power as a poet, but I have been told that they betray his ignorance of painting." *Lives* 3.108 1781

54. *Moral Essays: Epistle to Mr. Jervas.* *This, and the conclusion of the *Dunciad* "seemed to claim his highest admiration." *John. Misc.* 2.254. (Miss Reynolds) Date?

55. *Moral Essays: Of the . . . Characters of Men.* *"Johnson said, his characters of men were admirably drawn, those of women not so well." *Bos.* 2.84 1769

56. *Moral Essays: Of the . . . Characters of Men* and *. . . of the Characters of Women.* (*Lives* 3) They "are the product of diligent speculation upon human life; much labour has been bestowed upon them, and Pope very seldom laboured in vain." *Of the Characters of Women* compared with Boileau's *Satire* X; "it will then be seen with how much more perspicacity female nature is investigated and female excellence selected; and he surely is no mean writer to whom Boileau shall be found inferior. *The Characters of Men*, however, are written with more, if not with deeper, thought, and exhibit many passages exquisitely beautiful. 'The Gem and the Flower' will not easily be equalled. In the women's part are some defects: the character of Atossa is not so neatly finished as that of Clodio, and some of the female characters may

be found perhaps more frequently among men." (245.) *Of the . . . Characters of Men.* "Written with close attention to the operations of the mind and modifications of life." (173.) His favourite theory of the "ruling Passion" refuted. *Of the Characters of Women.* "Laboured with great diligence." (174-5)   1781

57. *Ode for . . . St. Cecilia's Day.* J. Warton, in *Essay on Pope* "justly commends the fourth [stanza], but without notice of the best line in that stanza or in the poem:
    Transported demigods stood round,
    And men grew heroes at the sound."
J.'s answer to Warton's objection that the measure in the "stanza of triumph," ("Thus song could reveal," etc.), is ridiculous and burlesque, since Addison uses the same measure in a comic scene in *Rosamond:* "both poets", writes J., "perhaps chose their numbers properly; for they both meant to express a kind of airy hilarity. The two passions of merriment and exultatation are undoubtedly different . . . but each is a species of joy; and poetical measures have not in any language been so far refined as to provide for the subdivisions of passion." (See VERSIFICATION 15.) Warton "observes very justly, that the odes both of Dryden and Pope conclude unsuitably and unnaturally with epigram." *Wks.* 15.472-3. (Review of J. Warton's *Essay on Pope*)   1756

58. *Ode for . . . St. Cecilia's Day.* (*Lives* 3) "The author is generally confessed to have miscarried, yet he has miscarried only as compared with Dryden [*Alexander's Feast*]; for he has far outgone other competitors. Dryden's plan is better chosen; history will always take stronger hold of the attention than fable: the passions excited by Dryden are the pleasures and pains of real life, the scene of Pope is laid in imaginary existence. Pope is read with calm acquiescence, Dryden with turbulent delight; Pope hangs upon the ear, and Dryden

finds the passes of the mind." (226-7.) Both odes lack "the stated recurrence of settled numbers" essential to metrical compositions. Pindar uncertain as a precedent. (See PINDARIC VERSE 6.) Detailed analysis of the *Ode*. (227-8) 1781

59. *Odyssey, Translation of*. (In collaboration with Broome and Fenton. See also *supra* P.'s *Homer*.) (*Lives* 3) "A very important event in poetical history." (77.) J. commends Spence's remarks on this translation as "commonly just." (143) 1781

60. *Pastorals*. Example from Pope of highly metaphorical passage,[1] unsuited to pastoral: "sentiments like these, as they have no ground in nature, are indeed of little value in any poem;" but particularly objectionable in pastoral. *Wks*. 5.242. (*Ram*. 37) 1750

61. *Pastorals*. J. Warton, in his *Essay on Pope*, very justly censures them, "considered as representations of any kind of life." (See PASTORAL 6.) Passages in Pope's imitation superior to the original: e.g., the lover in Theocritus wishes to be a bee that he may creep in the chaplet of his mistress; "Pope's enamoured swain longs to be made the captive bird that sings in his fair one's bower. . . . We more naturally desire to be that which she fondles and caresses, than that which she would avoid, at least would neglect. The superior delicacy of Theocritus I cannot discover," etc. "He [Warton] remarks, I am afraid with too much justice, that there is not a single new thought in the pastorals; and with equal reason declares, that their chief beauty consists in their correct and musical versification, which has so influenced the English ear, as to render every moderate rhymer harmonious." *Wks*. 15.469-70. (Review of J. Warton's *Essay on Pope*) 1756

62. *Pastorals*. *"Johnson said, his Pastorals were poor

---

[1] *Autumn*, ll. 89-92

things, though the versification was fine." *Bos.* 2.84
                                                                                           1769

63. *Pastorals.* (*Lives* 3) "As they well deserved they were read with admiration, and many praises were bestowed upon them and upon the Preface, which is both elegant and learned in a high degree." (90-1.) Suitable type for a young poet to begin on. (See PASTORAL 18.) "Close thought" in Pope's, however: "they have reference to the times of the day, the seasons of the year, and the periods of human life." Pope, probably justly, preferred the last. Unfortunate line in which the " 'Zephyrs' are made 'to lament in silence.' " No invention intended. "The imitations are so ambitiously frequent that the writer evidently means rather to shew his literature than his wit. It is surely sufficient for an author of sixteen not only to be able to copy the poems of antiquity with judicious selection, but to have obtained sufficient power of language and skill in metre to exhibit a series of versification, which had in English poetry no precedent, nor has since had an imitation." (224-5.) Patterned after Virgil. Pope laboured to be elegant, Philips to be natural. (319)
                                                                                            1781

64. *Prefaces and Dedications. Lives* 3.38, 90-1, 135, 137, 144   1781

65. *Rape of the Lock.* (*Lives* 3) "The most airy, the most ingenious, and the most delightful of all his compositions." (101.) "The soft luxuriance of his fancy was already shooting, and all the gay varieties of diction were ready at his hand to colour and embellish it. His attempt was justified by its success. *The Rape of the Lock* stands forward, in the classes of literature, as the most exquisite example of ludicrous poetry. Berkeley congratulated him upon the display of powers more truly poetical than he had shewn before; with elegance of description and justness of precepts, he had now exhibited boundless fertility of invention. . . . He

indeed could never afterwards produce any thing of such unexampled excellence. Those performances, which strike with wonder, are combinations of skilful genius with happy casualty; and it is not likely that any felicity, like the discovery of a new race of preternatural agents, should happen twice to the same man." (103-4.) "To the praises which have been accumulated on *The Rape of the Lock* by readers of every class, from the critick to the waiting-maid, it is difficult to make any addition." (232.) "Universally allowed to be the most attractive of all ludicrous compositions." (232.) Pope the inventor of a new race of supernatural beings. (See Originality 17.) "In this work are exhibited in a very high degree the two most engaging powers of an author: new things are made familiar, and familiar things are made new." (e.g., new race of "aerial people . . . is presented to us in a manner so clear and easy, that the reader . . . immediately mingles with his new acquaintance . . .," etc. And "the whole detail of a female-day is here brought before us invested with so much art of decoration that . . . every thing is striking . . .," etc. (233-4.) J. refutes Dennis's criticism that it wants a moral and hence is inferior to *The Lutrin*. "Perhaps neither Pope nor Boileau has made the world much better than he found it; but if they had both succeeded, it were easy to tell who would have deserved most from publick gratitude. The freaks, and humours, and spleen, and vanity of women . . . do more to obstruct the happiness of life in a year than the ambition of the clergy in many centuries." (234.) J. allows Dennis's charge that the machinery is superfluous—not "sufficiently intermingled with the action." Want of connection in other parts: *"ombre* might be spared"—"but what are such faults to so much excellence!" (235.) Its invention. (See Genius 23.) (247.) 1781

66. *Satires: Prologue to the Satires.* (*Epistle to Dr. Ar-*

buthnot.) (*Lives* 3) "In this poem Pope seems to reckon with the publick. He vindicates himself from censures; and with dignity, rather than arrogance, enforces his own claims to kindness and respect." (177.) Fragments are "wrought into one design, which by this union of scattered beauties contains more striking paragraphs than could probably have been brought together into an occasional work. As there is no stronger motive to exertion than self-defence, no part has more elegance, spirit, or dignity than the poet's vindication of his own character." Meanest passage, the satire on Sporus. (246) 1781

67. *Satires: Imitations of Horace.* (*Lives* 3) "This mode of imitation [see IMITATION 19] . . . seems to have been Pope's favourite amusement, for he has carried it further than any former poet." (176.) They "seem to have been written as relaxations of his genius . . . but what is easy is seldom excellent: such imitations cannot give pleasure to common readers." (See IMITATION 20.) *Sober Advice from Horace.* Published without P.'s name. "What he was upon moral principles ashamed to own, he ought to have suppressed." (176.) *First Epistle of the Second Book of Horace.* See *supra* 13 1781

68. *Satires: Satires of Dr. John Donne . . . Versified.* "A revival in smoother numbers of Dr. Donne's *Satires.* . . . Pope seems to have known their imbecility, and therefore suppressed them while he was yet contending to rise in reputation, but ventured them when he thought their deficiencies more likely to be imputed to Donne than to himself." *Lives* 3.177
1781

69. *Satires: Epilogue to the Satires.* (*Seventeen Hundred and Thirty Eight.*) (*Lives* 3) Too plainly showed his political partiality. (179.) "Very justly remarked by Savage that the second [*Dialogue*] was in the whole more strongly conceived and more equally supported,

but that it had no single passages equal to the contention in the first for the dignity of Vice and the celebration of the triumph of Corruption." (246)

1781

70. *Shakespeare, Edition of.* "For this part of his task, ["the observation of faults and beauties"] and for this only, was Mr. *Pope* eminently and indisputably qualified." *Shak. Proposals*, Raleigh, 7. (See also *Shak.*, Raleigh, 6, 21, 43-5. But cf. J.'s admission that Pope's *Preface* to Shakespeare is superior to his own: "The little fellow has done wonders." *John. Misc.* 1. 184-5)

cir. 1756

71. *Shakespeare, Edition of.* "Pope in his edition undoubtedly did many things wrong, and left many things undone; but let him not be defrauded of his due praise: he was the first that knew, at least the first that told, by what helps the text might be improved. If he inspected the early editions negligently, he taught others to be more accurate. In his Preface he expanded with great skill and elegance the character which had been given of Shakespeare by Dryden; and he drew the publick attention upon his works, which, though often mentioned, had been little read." *Lives* 3.139   1781

72. *Temple of Fame, The.* (*Lives* 3) Twenty-two "an early time of life for so much learning and so much observation as that work exhibits." The most reasonable of Dennis's remarks on this "is, that some of the lines represent *motion* as exhibited by *sculpture.*" (104-5.) Has, as Steele said, a thousand beauties. Every part splendid; great luxuriance of ornaments; "the original vision of Chaucer was never denied to be much improved; the allegory is very skilfully continued, the imagery is properly selected and learnedly displayed." Yet is little noticed because remote in scene and sentiments. (225-6)   1781

73. *Windsor Forest.* "On Windsor-forest, he [Warton] declares, I think without proof, that descriptive poetry

was by no means the excellence of Pope; he draws this inference from the few images introduced in this poem, which would not equally belong to any other place. He must inquire whether Windsor-forest has in reality any thing peculiar. The Stag-chase is not, he says, so full, so animated, and so circumstantiated as Somerville's. Barely to say, that one performance is not so good as another, is to criticise with little exactness. But Pope has directed that we should in every work regard the author's end. The Stag-chase is the main subject of Somerville . . . in Pope it is only incidental." *Wks.* 15.470-1. (Review of J. Warton's *Essay on Pope*)   1756

74. *Windsor Forest.* *Inferior in many respects as a youthful work to Miss Burney's *Evelina*. See BURNEY, FANNY 11   1779

75. *Windsor Forest.* (*Lives* 3) Addison's disturbance as a poet and politician at the last lines of *Windsor Forest:* "As a poet, he must have felt Pope's force of genius much more from many other parts of his works." (106.) "Pope cannot be denied to excel his masters [Denham and Waller] in variety and elegance, and the art of interchanging description, narrative, and morality." (225.) Dennis's objection: its "want of plan, of a regular subordination of parts terminating in the principal and original design." This inevitable in descriptive poems. (See DESCRIPTION 7.) But there may be too much diversity—e.g., story of Lodona and appearance of Father Thames "deserve least praise." (See MYTHOLOGY 31.) Its imagination. See IMAGINATION 13   1781

Prior, Matthew

1. *"Mrs. Thrale disputed with him on the merit of Prior. He attacked him powerfully; said he wrote of love like a man who had never felt it: his love verses were college verses; and he repeated the song 'Alexis

shunn'd his fellow swains,' &c., in so ludicrous a manner, as to make us all wonder how any one could have been pleased with such fantastical stuff. Mrs. Thrale stood to her gun with great courage, in defence of amorous ditties, which Johnson despised, till he at last silenced her by saying, 'My dear Lady, talk no more of this. Nonsense can be defended but by nonsense.'" *Bos.* 2.78   1769

2. *" 'There is nothing in Prior that will excite to lewdness. If Lord Hailes thinks there is, he must be more combustible than other people.' I instanced the tale of *Paulo Purganti and his Wife*. JOHNSON. 'Sir, there is nothing there, but that his wife wanted to be kissed when poor Paulo was out of pocket. No, Sir, Prior is a lady's book. No lady is ashamed to have it standing in her library.'" *Bos.* 3.192   1777

3. (*Lives* 2) His variety the cause of his popularity. "He has tried all styles, from the grotesque to the solemn, and has not so failed in any as to incur derision or disgrace." (201.) "His praise . . . that of correctness and industry, rather than of compass of comprehension or activity of fancy. He never made any effort of invention: his greater pieces are only tissues of common thoughts;[1] and his smaller, which consist of light images or single conceits, are not always his own." (Examples of his plagiarism.) (207.) "What he has valuable he owes to his diligence and his judgement. His diligence has justly placed him amongst the most correct of the English poets; and he was one of the first that resolutely endeavoured at correctness. He never sacrifices accuracy to haste, nor indulges himself in contemptuous negligence or impatient idleness: he has no careless lines or entangled sentiments; his words are nicely selected, and his thoughts fully expanded. If this part of his character suffers any abatement, it must be from the dis-

---

[1] 1st ed.: "were all tissues of sentiment."

proportion of his rhymes, which have not always sufficient consonance, and from the admission of broken lines into his *Solomon*." His rectitude of judgement secures him from the ridiculous or the absurd, but judgement cannot produce excellence. "Prior is never low, nor very often sublime. . . . Whatever Prior obtains above mediocrity seems the effort of struggle and of toil." Many vigorous, few happy lines. "He has every thing by purchase, and nothing by gift; he had no 'nightly visitations' of the Muse, no infusions of sentiment or felicities of fancy." (208-9.) *Diction*. "More his own than that of any among the successors of Dryden: he borrows no lucky turns or commodious modes of language from his predecessors." Phrases original, but sometimes harsh.[1] No elegances. "His expression has every mark of laborious study; the line seldom seems to have been formed at once; the words did not come till they were called, and were then put by constraint into their places, where they do their duty, but do it sullenly. In his greater compositions there may be found more rigid stateliness than graceful dignity." (209.) *Versification*. P. not negligent; he does not "increase the difficulty of writing by unnecessary severity, but uses triplets and alexandrines without scruple." Not successful in extending sense from one couplet to another. (209.) His imitation of Spenserian stanza so different that it is hardly an imitation, though J. is not sure "that he has lost any of the power of pleasing." Some poems show influence of "our Pindarick infatuation; but he probably lived to be convinced that the essence of verse is order and consonance." (209-10.) "His numbers are such as mere diligence may attain; they seldom offend the ear, and seldom sooth it; they commonly want airiness, lightness, and facility; what is smooth is not soft. His verses always roll, but they seldom flow." (210.)

---

[1] See HARSH for note on this word.

Summary. "In his private relaxation he revived the tavern, and in his amorous pedantry he exhibited the college. But on higher occasions and nobler subjects . . . he wanted not wisdom as a statesman, nor elegance as a poet." (211) Ptd. 1780

4. *Alma.* Professed imitation of *Hudibras.* Like it, left imperfect, but "imperfect, because it seems never to have had a plan." P. "appears . . . to have written the casual dictates of the present moment." Prior excelled Butler in versification, but was " 'inventore minor': he had not Butler's exuberance of matter and variety of illustration. The spangles of wit which he could afford he knew how to polish; but he wanted the bullion of his master." P., with little, "makes a fine shew." *Lives* 2.205 Ptd. 1780

5. *Carmen Seculare.* (*Lives* 2) "One of his longest and most splendid compositions . . . in which he exhausts all his powers of celebration. I mean not to accuse him of flattery." P. probably sincere, "and retained as much veracity as can be properly exacted from a poet professedly encomiastick." (184-5.) J. suspects it is seldom read through. (203) Ptd. 1780

6. *Country-Mouse and the City-Mouse, The.* (In collaboration with Halifax.) "In the detection and censure of the incongruity of the fiction [of Dryden's *Hind and the Panther*] chiefly consists the value of their performance." To readers a century distant not very forcible or animated. *Lives* 1.443 1779

7. *Epigrams and lighter pieces:* "are . . . sometimes elegant, sometimes trifling, and sometimes dull; among the best are *The Camelion* and the epitaph on *John and Joan.*" *Lives* 2.204 Ptd. 1780

8. *Henry and Emma.* "The greatest [? longest. See p. 550 *n*] of all his amorous essays." (211.) "A dull and tedious dialogue, which excites neither esteem for the man nor tenderness for the woman." (202-3)
Ptd. 1780

9. *Henry and Emma.* Surpassed by Pope's *Eloisa to Abelard.* See POPE 22   1781
10. *Love Verses.* (*Lives* 2) Less happy than tales. Pedantic. Have the "coldness of Cowley without his wit." (See AMOROUS VERSES 4.) "Even when he tries to act the lover without the help of gods or goddesses his thoughts are unaffecting or remote." (202.) "In his amorous pedantry he exhibited the college." (211)
Ptd. 1780
11. *Occasional Poems.* (See also *Carmen Seculare*). "Necessarily lost part of their value, as their occasions, being less remembered, raised less emotion." Inherent excellence of some, e.g., the burlesque of Boileau's *Ode on Namur.* A poor imitation of Spenserian antique style. (See IMITATION 17.) "Puerile" and "despicable" mythological fictions. (See MYTHOLOGY 21.) *Lives* 2.203-4   Ptd. 1780
12. *Prologues and Epilogues. Lives* 2.204   Ptd. 1780
13. *Prose Dedication of his Poems.* His "character" of Dorset praised. *Lives* 1.303   1779
14. *Solomon.* "The work to which he entrusted the protection of his name. . . . He had infused into it much knowledge and much thought; had often polished it to elegance, often dignified it with splendour, and sometimes heightened it to sublimity." But its fatal tediousness. (See AIM OF WRITING 22.) Subject sufficiently diversified, but lack of action and suspense. "Yet the work is far from deserving to be neglected. He that shall peruse it will be able to mark many passages, to which he may recur for instruction or delight: many from which the poet may learn to write, and the philosopher to reason." *Lives* 2.206-7
Ptd. 1780
15. *Tales.* Favourites. Great familiarity and great sprightliness: language easy, but seldom gross; numbers smooth, without appearance of care. Only four. These

analyzed. Probably not original. "But the merit of such stories is the art of telling them." *Lives* 2.201
Ptd. 1780

16. *Translations.* Version of Callimachus "sufficiently licentious; the paraphrase on St. Paul's Exhortation to Charity is eminently beautiful." *Lives* 2.205
Ptd. 1780

Rabelais, François

1. "The licentious *Rabelais*" ridicules the superstitions of astrology "with exquisite address and humour." *Shak.*, Raleigh, 156   1765

Racine, Jean

1. *Racine and Corneille, the two French tragic poets "who go round the world." See FRENCH LITERATURE
2   1773

Raleigh, Sir Walter

1. His historical writings: "deservedly celebrated for the labour of his researches, and the elegance of his style; but he has endeavoured to exert his judgment more than his genius, to select facts, rather than adorn them; and has produced an historical dissertation, but seldom risen to the majesty of history." *Wks.* 6.330. (*Ram.* 122)   1751

Ramsay, Allan

1. *J. refuses to learn his *Gentle Shepherd. Bos.* 2.220
1773

Rapin, Paul de

1. "It will not easily be imagined of *Langbane, Borrichitus,* or *Rapin,* that they had very accurately perused all the books which they praise or censure; or that, even if nature and learning had qualified them for judges, they could read for ever with the attention

necessary to just criticism. Such performances, however, are not wholly without their use; for they are commonly just echoes to the voice of fame. . . ." *Wks.* 6.139. (*Ram.* 93)　　　　　　　　　1751

Redi

1. Works commended. See ITALIAN LITERATURE 1
　　　　　　　　　　　　　　　　　　　　1755

Reed, Joseph

1. *"Sir, . . . I never did the man an injury; yet he would read his tragedy [*Dido*] to me." *John. Misc.* 2. 411. (Nichols's *Lit. Anec.*)　　　*cir.* 1767?

Richardson, Samuel

1. J. calls Richardson an author "who has enlarged the knowledge of human nature, and taught the passions to move at the command of virtue." *Wks.* 6.164. (*Ram.* 97)　　　　　　　　　　　　　1751

2. *" 'There is all the difference in the world between characters of nature and characters of manners; and *there* is the difference between the characters of Fielding and those of Richardson. Characters of manners are very entertaining; but they are to be understood, by a more superficial observer, than characters of nature, where a man must dive into the recesses of the human heart.' . . . In comparing those two writers, he [J.] used this expression: 'that there was as great a difference between them as between a man who knew how a watch was made, and a man who could tell the hour by looking on the dial-plate.' " *Bos.* 2.48-9
　　　　　　　　　　　　　　　　　　　　1768

3. *" 'Sir, there is more knowledge of the heart in one letter of Richardson's, than in all *Tom Jones*. . . . ERSKINE. 'Surely, Sir, Richardson is very tedious.' JOHNSON. 'Why, Sir, if you were to read Richardson for the story, your impatience would be so much fretted

that you would hang yourself. But you must read him for the sentiment, and consider the story as only giving occasion to the sentiment.' " *Bos.* 2.174-5   1772
4. *J. draws a character of Richardson, expressing "a high opinion of his talents and virtues." *Bos.* 5.395-6. (*Hebrides*, 11-20 Nov.)   1773
5. *Passages in Fanny Burney's *Evelina* "which might do *honour* to Richardson." See BURNEY, F. 5   1778
6. *After depreciating the talents of Fielding, J. "broke out into a noble panegyric on his competitor, Richardson; who, he said, was as superior to him in talents as in virtue; and whom he pronounced to be the greatest genius that had shed its lustre on this path of literature." *John. Misc.* 2.190. (Hannah More)
Date?
7. **Hawkins:* "Johnson was inclined, as being personally acquainted with Richardson, to favour the former opinion of his writings [i.e., that he was "a writer similar in genius to Shakespeare, as being acquainted with the inmost recesses of the human heart"], but he seemed not firm in it, and could at any time be talked into a disapprobation of all fictitious relations, of which he would frequently say they took no hold of the mind." *Wks.* 1.217   Date?
8. *French novelists compared to Richardson: "a wren was not an eagle." See FRENCH LITERATURE 8 Date?
9. *Clarissa Harlowe*. Letter to Richardson: "Though Clarissa wants no help from external splendour, I was glad to see her improved in her appearance, but more glad to find that she was now got above all fears of prolixity, and confident enough of success to supply whatever had been hitherto suppressed. [In the fourth edition, material omitted in earlier editions added. See Hill's note on this.] I never indeed found a hint of any such defalcation, but I regretted it; for though the story is long, every letter is short. . . . Clarissa is not a performance to be read with eagerness, and

laid aside for ever; but will be occasionally consulted by the busy, the aged, and the studious; and therefore I beg that this edition, by which I suppose posterity is to abide, may want nothing that can facilitate its use." *Letters* 1.21-2   1751

10. *Clarissa Harlowe.* J. suggests to Richardson that he suppress that part of the *Preface* "which seems to disclaim [R.'s authorship of] the composition. What is modesty, if it deserts from truth? Of what use is the disguise by which nothing is concealed?" J. wishes for an index to *Clarissa:* "Suppose that in one volume an accurate index was made to the three works—but while I am writing an objection arises—such an index to the three would look like the preclusion of a fourth, to which I will never contribute; for if I cannot benefit mankind, I hope never to injure them." *Letters* 1.34-5
    1753

11. *Clarissa Harlowe.* Richardson's "Lovelace" expanded from "Lothario" in Rowe's *Fair Penitent.* "But he has excelled his original in the moral effect of the fiction. . . . It was in the power of Richardson alone to teach us at once esteem and detestation; to make virtuous resentment overpower all the benevolence which wit, elegance, and courage naturally excite, and to lose at last the hero in the villain." *Lives* 2.67   Ptd. 1780

12. *Clarissa Harlowe.* *"He was a great admirer of Richardson's works in general, but of *Clarissa* he always spoke with the highest enthusiastic praise. He used to say, that it was the first Book in the world for the knowledge it displays of the human Heart. Yet of the Author I never heard him speak with any degree of cordiality."[1] *John. Misc.* 2.251. (Miss Reynolds)
    Date?

13. *Clarissa Harlowe.* *"It was not the two *last*, but the two *first*, volumes of Clarissa that he prized; 'For give me a sick bed, and a dying lady (said he), and I'll be

[1] E.g. see *Bos.* 5.395 and *John. Misc.* 1.273-4

pathetic myself: but Richardson had picked the kernel of life (he said), while Fielding was contented with the husk.'" *John. Misc.* 1.282. (Piozzi) Date?

14. *Sir Charles Grandison.* Letter to Richardson:—"You have a trick of laying yourself open to objections, in the first part of your work, and crushing them in subsequent parts. A great deal that I had to say before I read the conversation in the latter part, is now taken from me. *I wish however that Sir Charles had not compromised in matters of religion.*" *John. Misc.* 2.436   1754

Robertson, William

1. *R. uses "pretty words," but inferior to Hume and Clarendon. See SCOTCH WRITERS 3   1775
2. *"Sir, if Robertson's style be faulty, he owes it to me; that is, having too many words, and those too big ones." *Bos.* 3.173   Date?
3. *"The tinsel of Robertson." *John. Misc.* 2.10. (Hawkins's *Apophthegms*)   Date?
4. *History of Scotland.* *"Sir, I love Robertson, and I won't talk of his book." See SCOTCH WRITERS 1 for context.   1768
5. *History of Scotland.* *"The *verbiage* of Robertson. . . . It is not history, it is imagination. . . . You must look upon Robertson's work as romance, and try it by that standard. History it is not. . . . Robertson might have put twice as much into his book. Robertson is like a man who has packed gold in wool: the wool takes up more room than the gold. No, Sir; I always thought Robertson would be crushed by his own weight,—would be buried under his own ornaments. . . . I would say to Robertson what an old tutor of a college said to one of his pupils: 'Read over your compositions, and where ever you meet with a passage which you think is particularly fine, strike it out.'" *Bos.* 2.236-7   1773

6. *History of Scotland.* *A subject of his constant praise. *John. Misc.* 1.429-30   Date?

Rochester, John Wilmot, Second Earl of

1. *J. gives his poems to Mr. Steevens "to castrate for the edition of the poets, to which he was to write Prefaces." *Bos.* 3.191   1777
2. (*Lives* 1) "The glare of his general character diffused itself upon his writings. . . . This blaze of reputation is not yet quite extinguished; and his poetry still retains some splendour beyond that which genius has bestowed." (222.) "In all his works there is sprightliness and vigour, and every where may be found tokens of a mind which study might have carried to excellence. What more can be expected from a life spent in ostentatious contempt of regularity, and ended before the abilities of many other men began to be displayed?" (226)   1779
3. *Imitation of Horace*, on Lucilius: "not inelegant or unhappy," etc. Few adaptations "where the parallelism is better preserved than in this." Versification "is indeed sometimes careless, but it is sometimes vigorous and weighty." *Lives* 1.224   1779
4. *Minor poems. Lives* 1.225-6   1779
5. *Nothing.* "The strongest effort of his Muse." *Lives* 1.224-5   1779
6. *Songs.* "His songs have no particular character: they tell, like other songs, in smooth and easy language of scorn and kindness . . . with the commonplaces of artificial courtship. They are commonly smooth and easy; but have little nature, and little sentiment." *Lives* 1.224   1779

Roscommon, Wentworth Dillon, Earl of

1. *Essay on Translated Verse.* "When the sum of Lord Roscommon's precepts is collected it will not be easy to discover how they can qualify their reader for a better

performance of translation than might have been attained by his own reflections." If the mind is abstracted "from the elegance of the poetry," the precepts, boiled down, become commonplace. "Roscommon has indeed deserved his praises[1] had they been given with discernment, and bestowed not on the rules themselves, but the art with which they are introduced, and the decorations with which they are adorned," etc. *Lives* 1.236-7   1748

2. "We must allow of Roscommon . . . what is . . . very much to his honour, that he is perhaps the only correct writer in verse before Addison; and that if there are not so many or so great beauties in his compositions as in those of some contemporaries, there are at least fewer faults. Nor is this his highest praise; for Mr. Pope has celebrated him as the only moral writer of King Charles's reign." *Lives* 1.235   1748

3. "Of Roscommon's works the judgement of the publick seems to be right. He is elegant, but not great; he never labours after exquisite beauties, and he seldom falls into gross faults. His versification is smooth, but rarely vigorous, and his rhymes are remarkably exact. He improved taste if he did not enlarge knowledge, and may be numbered among the benefactors to English literature." *Lives* 1.239-40   1779

4. *Translations and minor verse.* *Lives* 1.237-8   1779

Rousseau, J. J.

1. *"Rousseau, and all those who deal in paradoxes, are led away by a childish desire of novelty." *Bos.* 1.441   1763

2.*"I think him one of the worst of men; a rascal who ought to be hunted out of society, as he has been. . . . I would sooner sign a sentence for his transportation, than that of any felon who has gone from the Old

---

[1] In the edition of 1748 "honours."

Bailey these many years. Yes, I should like to have him work in the plantations." *Bos.* 2.11-12   1766
3. *" 'Rousseau *knows* he is talking nonsense [about the superiority of the savage life], and laughs at the world for staring at him.' BOSWELL. 'How so, Sir?' JOHNSON. 'Why, Sir, a man who talks nonsense so well, must know that he is talking nonsense.' " *Bos.* 2.74
    1769
4. *Cause of decline of "infidel writers" such as Rousseau. See VOLTAIRE 11   1784

Rowe, Mrs. Elizabeth

1. "The copiousness and luxuriance of Mrs. Rowe . . . her brightness of imagery her purity of sentiments." Completed the great design, begun by Boyle, of employing "the ornaments of romance in the decoration of religion." *Wks.* 15.479-80. (Review of Elizabeth Harrison's *Miscellanies.* Quoted in *Bos.* 1.312)
    1756

Rowe, Nicholas

1. The delicacy, though effeminacy of Rowe. See SHAKESPEARE 59   1765
2. (*Lives* 2) Works "bear few marks of negligence or hurry." (70.) R. to be considered chiefly as a tragic writer and a translator. Failed ignominiously at comedy. "His occasional poems and short compositions are rarely worthy of either praise or censure." Seem "the casual sports of a mind" seeking amusement. (75.) *As a dramatist.* Not much art in the construction of his dramas. (75.) "He is not a nice observer of the Unities." (See DRAMA 53.) J. questions whether his plays show "any deep search into nature, any accurate discriminations of kindred qualities, or nice display of passion in its progress; all is general and undefined." (76.) *Tragedy of Jane Shore.* R. does not "much interest or affect the auditor, except in Jane Shore, who is

always seen and heard with pity. Alicia is a character of empty noise, with no resemblance to real sorrow or to natural madness. Whence, then, has Rowe his reputation? From the reasonableness and propriety of some of his scenes, from the elegance of his diction, and the suavity of his verse. He seldom moves either pity or terror, but he often elevates the sentiments; he seldom pierces the breast, but he always delights the ear, and often improves the understanding." (76)
Ptd. 1780

3. *Fair Penitent.* "One of the most pleasing tragedies on the stage." Still appears, and probably long will, "for there is scarcely any work of any poet at once so interesting by the fable and so delightful by the language. The story is domestick, and therefore easily received by the imagination, and assimilated to common life; the diction is exquisitely harmonious, and soft or spritely as occasion requires." The character of Lothario expanded by Richardson into Lovelace. (See RICHARDSON 11.) Fifth act: "the events of the drama are exhausted." *Lives* 2.67-8   Ptd. 1780

4. *Fair Penitent.* *Hannah More:*—"You would have enjoyed seeing him [J.] take me by the hand in the middle of dinner, and repeat with no small enthusiasm, many passages from the 'Fair Penitent,' &c." *John. Misc.* 2.197   1782

5. *Lucan, Translation of.* "One of the greatest productions of English poetry; for there is perhaps none that so completely exhibits the genius and spirit of the original. . . . His versification . . . seldom wants either melody or force." Occasional undue dilution of his author's sense. "But such faults are to be expected in all translations, from the constraint of measures and dissimilitude of languages." *Lives* 2.77
Ptd. 1780

6. *Royal Concert.* "Seems to have a better claim to longevity [than *Ulysses*]", because of its remote

fable. (See DRAMA 71.) *Lives* 2.68   Ptd. 1780

7. *Shakespeare, Edition of.* His *Life of Shakespeare* "not written with much elegance or spirit." *Shak. Pref.*, Raleigh, 43. For Rowe as Shakespearean editor, see *ib.* 6, 43   1765

8. *Shakespeare, Edition of.* "He has done more than he promised, and . . . without the pomp of notes or boasts of criticism, many passages are happily restored." His preface "cannot be said to discover much profundity or penetration." *Lives* 2.71   Ptd. 1780

9. *Tamerlane.* Exaggerated eulogy of King William. "Occasional poetry must often content itself with occasional praise." *Lives* 2.66-7   Ptd. 1780

10. *Tragedy of . . . Jane Grey.* Its violation of unity of scene in the middle of an act. See DRAMA 53
    Ptd. 1780

11. *Tragedy of Jane Shore.* (See also *supra* 2.) "The numbers, the diction, the sentiments, and the conduct, every thing in which imitation can consist, are remote in the utmost degree from the manner of Shakespeare; whose dramas it resembles only as it is an English story, and as some of the persons have their names in history. This play, consisting chiefly of domestick scenes and private distress, lays hold upon the heart. The wife is forgiven because she repents, and the husband is honoured because he forgives. This therefore is one of those pieces which we still welcome on the stage." *Lives* 2.69-70   Ptd. 1780

12. *Tragedy of Jane Shore.* *Hannah More: "He [J.] told me the other day, he hated to hear people whine about metaphysical distresses, when there was so much want and hunger in the world. I told him I supposed then he never wept at any tragedy but Jane Shore, who had died for want of a loaf. He called me a saucy girl, but did not deny the inference." *John. Misc.* 2.196-7
    1782

13. *Tragedy of Jane Shore.* *"Of the pathetic in poetry he [Johnson] never liked to speak, and the only passage I ever heard him applaud as particularly tender in any common book, was Jane Shore's exclamation in the last act, 'Forgive me! *but* forgive me!'" *John. Misc.* 1.283-4. (Piozzi) Date?

14. *Ulysses*, "which, with the common fate of mythological stories, is now generally neglected." See MYTHOLOGY 18 Ptd. 1780

Ryland, [? *John*]

1. J. criticizes his verses: "They seem to me rather to favour solitude too much," etc. See J.'s letter of July 24, 1783, printed in *Catalogue of the Johnsonian Collection of R. B. Adam.* 1783

Rymer, Thomas

1. For his petty Shakespearean criticisms, see *Shak. Pref.*, Raleigh, 14-15; 18 1765
2. His manner of criticism less pleasing than Dryden's. *Lives* 1.413 1779

Sallust

1. J. commends a biographical detail in the account of Catiline by Sallust, "the great master of nature." *Wks.* 5.384. (*Ram.* 60) 1750
2. *His historical characters trustworthy because he personally knew them. *Bos.* 2.79 1769

Salmasius

1. "A man of . . . sagacity of emendatory criticism, almost exceeding all hope of human attainment." *Lives* 1.111 1779
2. "Had been so long not only the monarch but the tyrant of literature." *Lives* 1.114 1779

Sandys, George

1. His translations. See MAY 1   1759

Sannazaro

1. *Pastorals.* Seeks pastoral novelty by removing "the scene from the fields to the sea." J. defends him against critics who say the sea is an object of terrour, and hence unsuited to pastoral: "the poet has a right to select his images, and is no more obliged to shew the sea in a storm; than the land under an inundation." *Wks.* 5.236. (*Ram* 36)   1750

Sarpi, Father Paul

1. *History of the Council of Trent.* "A work unequalled for the judicious disposition of the matter, and artful texture of the narration," etc. *Wks.* 4.326   1738
2. J. quotes a "memorable passage" from one of his letters. *Wks.* 4.327-8   1738

Satyr to His Muse

1. Anonymous attack on Dryden, showing "much virulence, and some spriteliness." *Lives* 1.374   1779

Savage, Richard

1. "The unfortunate and ingenious Mr. Savage." *Bos.* 1.164   1743
2. (*Lives* 2) "A man whose writings entitle him to an eminent rank in the classes of learning." (322.) His genius. (325, 326, 338, 358, 407, etc.) "Had he afterwards applied to dramatick poetry, he would perhaps not have had many superiors: for . . . he had treasured in his mind all the different combinations of passions and the innumerable mixtures of vice and virtue, which distinguish one character from another; and, as his conception was strong, his expressions were clear, he easily received impressions from objects, and very

forcibly transmitted them to others." (358.) "This at least must be allowed him . . . that he never contributed deliberately to spread corruption amongst mankind. His actions . . . were often blameable; but his writings, being the productions of study, uniformly tended to the exaltation of the mind, and the propagation of morality and piety. These writings may improve mankind when his failings shall be forgotten, and therefore he must be considered, upon the whole, as a benefactor to the world." (380-1.) "It is remarkable that the writings of a man of little education and little reading have an air of learning scarcely to be found in any other performances, but which perhaps as often obscures as embellishes them. His judgement was eminently exact both with regard to writings and to men. The knowledge of life was indeed his chief attainment." (430.) "Nor is there perhaps any writer who has less endeavoured to please by flattering the appetites or perverting the judgement. As an author therefore . . . if one piece which he had resolved to suppress be excepted, he has very little to fear from the strictest moral or religious censure." Though not altogether secure from criticism, "his works are the productions of a genius truly poetical, and, what many writers who have been more lavishly applauded cannot boast, that they have an original air, which has no resemblance of any foregoing work[1] . . . the versification and sentiments have a cast peculiar to themselves, which no man can imitate with success, because what was nature in Savage would in another be affectation . . . his descriptions are striking, his images animated, his fictions justly imagined, and his allegories artfully pursued . . . his diction is elevated, though sometimes forced, and his numbers sonorous and majestick, though frequently sluggish and encumbered. Of his style, the general fault is

[1] In first ed., "writer." *Lives* 2.433 *n* 3

harshness, and its general excellence is dignity; of his sentiments, the prevailing beauty is sublimity, and uniformity the prevailing defect." S. not always sufficiently instructed in his subject; works sometimes unfinished—but consider the circumstances of his life. "A great mind." (432-3) 1744
3. *Author to be Let.* (*Lives* 2) "Vigorous sallies of that sprightly humour which distinguishes *The Author to be let.*" (326.) "Of his exact observations on human life he has left a proof, which would do honour to the greatest names, in a small pamphlet called *The Author to be let,*" etc. (358-9) 1744
4. *Bastard, The.* "Vivacious sallies of thought", "pathetick sentiments." *Lives* 2.377, 381 1744
5. *Dedications.* Flattery with little art: "he seems to have written his panegyricks for the perusal only of his patrons, and to have imagined that he had no other task than to pamper them with praises however gross, and that flattery would make its way to the heart, without the assistance of elegance or invention." *Lives* 2.343-4. See also *ib.* 341, 360-2 1744
6. *Epistle to . . . Sir Robert Walpole. Lives* 2.363-4 1744
7. *London and Bristol Delineated. Lives* 2.424-6 1744
8. *Of Public Spirit.* (*Lives* 2) New poetical theme— colonies in uninhabited countries—suited to poetical treatment. (393.) His description of the miseries leading to exile "affords another instance of his proficiency in the important and extensive study of human life." (395.) "Not the most excellent" of S.'s works. "Many striking sentiments, majestick lines, and just observations," but language too unpolished, imagery not enlivened enough, plan too undigested. (397) 1744
9. *Preface to Miscellaneous Poems.* "Uncommon strain of humour," "gaiety of imagination," etc. *Lives* 2. 343 1744

10. *Progress of a Divine.* "Describes with that humour which was natural to him, and that knowledge which was extended to all the diversities of human life, his [a profligate priest's] behaviour in every station." *Lives* 2.388   1744

11. *Tragedy of Sir Thomas Overbury.* (*Lives* 2) Subject not wholly suitable: too recent to make necessary "fictions" of plan acceptable. (See DRAMA 55.) However, it affords "an uncommon proof of strength of genius and evenness of mind, of a serenity not to be ruffled, and an imagination not to be suppressed." If "not perfect, its faults ought surely to be imputed to a cause very different from want of genius," (i.e., his poverty.) (338-9.) "The rays of genius that glimmered in it, that glimmered through all the mists which poverty and Cibber had been able to spread over it." (341.) Its *Dedication.* (341)   1744

12. *Triumph of Health and Mirth.* Its gaiety, melody and agreeable allegorical "fiction." *Lives* 2.370   1744

13. *"Volunteer Laureate" poems.* (*Lives* 2) Repetitions; "forced conceptions and far-fetched images." (384.) But his elegy on the Queen, "a proof of . . . the power of his genius . . . his poem may be justly ranked among the best pieces that the death of princes has produced. By transferring the mention of her death to her birth-day he has formed a happy combination of topicks, which any other man would have thought it very difficult to connect in one view, but which he has united in such a manner that the relation between them appears natural; and it may be justly said that what no other man would have thought on, it now appears scarcely possible for any man to miss. The beauty of this peculiar combination of images is so masterly, that it is sufficient to set this poem above censure." Many other "delicate touches" in it. (407)   1744

14. *Wanderer, The.* (*Lives* 2) "Strong touches of that

ardent imagination which painted the solemn scenes of *The Wanderer.*" (326.) "It has been generally objected to *The Wanderer* that the disposition of the parts is irregular; that the design is obscure, and the plan perplexed; that the images, however beautiful, succeed each other without order; and that the whole performance is not so much a regular fabrick as a heap of shining materials thrown together by accident, which strikes rather with the solemn magnificence of a stupendous ruin than the elegant grandeur of a finished pile." This criticism "universal," and hence in a great degree probably just. "It was never denied to abound with strong representations of nature, and just observations upon life," etc. (365-6.) Its moral and religious tendencies. (See MORAL ELEMENT 3.) "Particular passages which deserve applause . . . the excellence of his description . . . the terrifick portrait of suicide . . . the artful touches by which he has distinguished the intellectual features of the rebels . . . a poem so diligently laboured, and so successfully finished . . . so valuable a performance," etc. (366-7) 1744

15. *Wanderer, The.* *J. points out passage, saying "These are fine verses." *Bos.* 4.288 1784

Scaliger, Joseph

1. See RENAISSANCE 1 1742

2. *Scaliger* surely influenced by literary patriotism in placing Virgil so far above Homer. *Wks.* 6.140-1. (*Ram.* 93) 1751

3. Latin poem on S. *Wks.* 11.389-90. For translation, see *John. Misc.* 1.410 *cir.* 1773

Scarron

1. The "despicable [epistolary] remains of *Voiture* and Scarron." *Wks.* 7.70. (*Ram.* 152) 1751

Scott, John, of Amwell

1. *His *Elegies* "are very well; but such as twenty people might write." *Bos.* 2.351   1775

Selden, John

1. *Table Talk. Better than any of the French *Ana*. *Bos.* 5.311. (*Hebrides*, 14 Oct.)   1773

Settle, Elkanah

1. Satirized for his stock elegies and epithalamiums. *Wks.* 8.47-8. (*Idl.* 12)   1758

Seward, Miss Anna

1. *J. approves of her verses on Lichfield. *Bos.* 4.331   1784
2. *Upon Miss Seward's mentioning *The Columbiade* by Madame du Bocage, J. remarks: "Madam, there is not any thing equal to your description of the sea round the North Pole, in your Ode on the death of Captain Cook." *Bos.* 4.331   1784

Shakespeare. (GENERAL APPRECIATION OF)

1. *J. told Boswell "that he read Shakespeare at a period so early, that the speech of the ghost in Hamlet terrified him when he was alone." *Bos.* 1.70   *Cir.* 1721?
2. "The great author." *Wks.* 14.66. (*Observ. on Macb.*)   1745
3. ". . . immortal Shakespeare rose;
   Each change of many-colour'd life he drew,
   Exhausted worlds, and then imagin'd new:
   Existence saw him spurn her bounded reign,
   And panting Time toil'd after him in vain.
   His powerful strokes presiding Truth impress'd,
   And unresisted Passion storm'd the breast."
   Quoted by Hawkins. *Wks.* 1.196. (*Drury-lane Prologue*)   1747

Shakespeare (Appreciation of) 469

4. Referred to as "great" author. *Wks.* 9.184   1747
5. "So great a poet." *Wks.* 14.479. (*Dedication to "Shakespear Illustrated,"* written for Mrs. Lennox)
   1753
6. J. drew 15.6% of the literary illustrations in his *Dictionary* (1755) from Shakespeare. See ADDISON 5
   1755
7. "Such was the power of our author's mind, that he looked through life in all its relations private and civil." *Shak.*, Raleigh, 178   1765
8. *No descriptive passage in Shakespeare equal to passage in Congreve's *Mourning Bride*; "but that is no reason for supposing Congreve is to stand in competition with Shakespeare." For this comparison, see CONGREVE 8, 9, 11   1769, etc.
9. *J.'s reply to Garrick, who suspects him of being "a little of an infidel" as regards Shakespeare: "Sir, . . . I will stand by the lines I have written on Shakespeare in my Prologue at the opening of your Theatre." *Bos.* 4.25. (Langton's *Collection*)   *ante* 1779
10. "Shakespeare he [Milton] may easily be supposed to like, with every other skilful reader." *Lives* 1.154
    1779
11. S., "the greatest [English] dramatist wrote without rules, conducted through life and nature by a genius that rarely misled, and rarely deserted him." *Lives* 1.410   1779
12. "Continues . . . the sovereign of the drama" by his power of pleasing. *Lives* 1.454   1779
13. "What is said of that mighty genius is true." (Referring to Gray's remarks in *Progress of Poesy*.) *Lives* 3.437   1781
14. *"The merit of Shakespeare was such as the ignorant could take in, and the learned add nothing to." *Letters*, 2.440. (App. D.: From Windham's *Diary*)
    1784

15. *J.'s most admired English poet. *John. Misc.* 2.165
    Date?
16. *Garrick "seized the very soul of Shakespeare . . . and . . . expanded its glory over the world." *John. Misc.* 2.333. (Stockdale) Date?
17. *"Corneille is to Shakespeare . . . as a clipped hedge is to a forest." *John. Misc.* 1.187. (Piozzi) Date?

Shakespeare. (ANALYSIS OF HIS WORK IN GENERAL)

18. *Anachronisms.* "Shakespeare deserts the manners of the age in which his drama is placed very often, without necessity or advantage." *Shak.*, Raleigh, 111-2. (See also *Shak.*, Raleigh, 115-6, and *Shak.* 7.288 *n* 1)
    1765
19. *Anachronisms.* "Though he so nicely discriminates, and so minutely describes the characters of men, he commonly neglects and confounds the characters of ages, by mingling customs ancient and modern, *English* and foreign." *Shak.*, Raleigh, 160   1765
20. *Anachronisms.* "He had no regard to distinction of time or place, but gives to one age or nation, without scruple, the customs, institutions, and opinions of another, at the expence not only of likelihood, but of possibility." Not the age's sole offender, however. *Shak. Pref.*, Raleigh, 21-2   1765
21. *Characters.* Shakespeare's tragedies "overstocked with personages." See *infra* 125   1745
22. *Characters.* (See also *infra*, *Dialogue* and *"Nature"*, *Truth to.*) [a] "Characters thus ample and general were not easily discriminated and preserved, yet perhaps no poet ever kept his personages more distinct from each other . . . it will be difficult to find, any [speeches] that can be properly transferred from the present possessor to another claimant. The choice is right, when there is reason for choice. [b] Other dramatists can only gain attention by hyperbolical or ag-

gravated characters, by fabulous and unexampled excellence or depravity, as the writers of barbarous romances invigorated the reader by a giant and a dwarf; and he that should form his expectations of human affairs from the play, or from the tale, would be equally deceived. Shakespeare has no heroes; his scenes are occupied only by men, who act and speak as the reader thinks that he should himself have spoken or acted on the same occasion: Even where the agency is supernatural the dialogue is level with life. Other writers disguise the most natural passions and most frequent incidents; so that he who contemplates them in the book will not know them in the world: *Shakespeare* approximates the remote, and familiarizes the wonderful; the event which he represents will not happen, but if it were possible, its effects would probably be such as he has assigned; and it may be said, that he has not only shewn human nature as it acts in real exigencies, but as it would be found in trials, to which it cannot be exposed." Shak. Pref., Raleigh, 13-14. (Johnson qualifies this, *ib.* p. 20: exceptions to the naturalness of his characters)   1765

23. *Characters.* "*Shakespeare* may be truly said to have introduced them both [character and dialogue] amongst us, and in some of his happier scenes to have carried them both to the utmost height." Shak. Pref., Raleigh, 36   1765

24. *Characters.* Their originality. See *infra* 59   1765

25. *Comedy and tragedy compared.* His natural disposition led him to comedy. "In tragedy he often writes, with great appearance of toil and study, what is written at last with little felicity; but in his comick scenes, he seems to produce without labour, what no labour can improve. In tragedy he is always struggling after some occasion to be comick; but in comedy he seems to repose, or to luxuriate, as in a mode of thinking congenial to his nature. In his tragick scenes there is

always something wanting, but his comedy often surpasses expectation or desire. His comedy pleases by the thoughts and the language, and his tragedy for the greater part by incident and action. His tragedy seems to be skill, his comedy to be instinct."[1] *Shak. Pref.*, Raleigh, 18-19   1765

26. *Comic scenes.* (See also *infra*, 31, 55, and 154.) The "reciprocations of smartness and contests of sarcasm" of his characters seldom very successful. "Their jests are commonly gross, and their pleasantry licentious. . . . There must . . . have been always some modes of gayety preferable to others, and a writer ought to chuse the best." *Shak. Pref.*, Raleigh, 22   1765

27. *Comic scenes.* Jests repeated. *Shak. Pref.*, Raleigh, 41   1765

28. *Contemporary allusions.* (See also *infra*, 51.) "I am always inclined to believe, that *Shakespeare* has more allusions to particular facts and persons than his readers commonly suppose." *Shak.*, Raleigh, 81. (See also *ib.* 87, 106)   1765

29. *Dialogue.* S., "the first considerable author of sublime or familiar dialogue in our language." *Wks.* 9.232. (*Shak. Proposals*)   1756

30. *Dialogue.* (See also *supra, Characters;* and *infra*, 47, 59 b.) "It will not easily be imagined how much *Shakespeare* excels in accomodating his sentiments to real life, but by comparing him with other authors. . . . The theatre, when it is under any other direction, is peopled by such characters as were never seen, conversing in a language which was never heard, upon topicks which will never arise in the commerce of mankind. But the dialogue of this author is often so evi-

---

[1] Perhaps, too, Johnson's low opinion of tragic acting influenced his choice. The more involved style and elevated diction of the tragedies were apt to be turned into rant and bombast on the eighteenth century stage. (See *Bos.* 2.92, and 5.38; *Wks.* 8.32; and DRAMA 1, note.) And there may be a further clue in his comment: "What is nearest us touches us most. The passions rise higher at domestic than at imperial tragedies." (DRAMA 69)

dently determined by the incident which produces it, and is pursued with so much ease and simplicity, that it seems scarcely to claim the merit of fiction, but to have been gleaned by diligent selection out of common conversation, and common occurrences." *Shak. Pref.*, Raleigh, 12-13   1765

31. *Dialogue (comic).* "There is a conversation above grossness and below refinement, where propriety resides, and where this poet seems to have gathered his comick dialogue. [See STYLE 12.] He is therefore more agreeable to the ears of the present age than any other authour equally remote, and among his other excellencies deserves to be studied as one of the original masters of our language." This true, generally speaking: "*Shakespeare's* familiar dialogue is affirmed to be smooth and clear, yet not wholly without ruggedness or difficulty." *Shak. Pref.*, Raleigh, 20   1765

32. *Didacticism.* J. wishes Shakespeare "had not ventured so near profaneness" at times. *Shak.*, Raleigh, 92

1765

33. *Didacticism.* "It is from this wide extension of design [his truth to general human nature] that so much instruction is derived. It is this which fills the plays of *Shakespeare* with practical axioms and domestic wisdom . . . from his works may be collected a system of civil and oeconomical prudence." *Shak. Pref.*, Raleigh, 12   1765

34. *Didacticism.* "His first defect is that to which may be imputed most of the evil in books or in men. He sacrifices virtue to convenience, and is so much more careful to please than to instruct, that he seems to write without any moral purpose. From his writings indeed a system of social duty may be selected, for he that thinks reasonably must think morally; but his precepts and axioms drop casually from him; he makes no just distribution of good or evil, nor is always careful to shew in the virtuous a disapprobation of the wicked;

he carries his persons indifferently through right and wrong, and at the close dimisses them without further care, and leaves their examples to operate by chance. This fault the barbarity of his age cannot extenuate; for it is always a writer's duty to make the world better, and justice is a virtue independent on time or place." *Shak. Pref.*, Raleigh, 20-1   1765

35. *Didacticism.* "He omits opportunities of instructing or delighting." See SHAKESPEARE 62   1765

36. *Didacticism.* Every reader of *Measure for Measure* indignant that Angelo should be spared. Isabella's plea for mercy contains questionable moral implication. *Shak.*, Raleigh, 80   1765

37. *Faults.* "We fix our eyes upon his graces, and turn them from his deformities, and endure in him what we should in another loath or despise . . . he has corrupted language by every mode of depravation. . . . He has scenes of undoubted and perpetual excellence, but perhaps not one play, which, if it were now exhibited as the work of a contemporary writer, would be heard to the conclusion." *Shak. Pref.*, Raleigh, 40-1   1765

38. *Faults.* Faults enumerated. *Shak. Pref.*, Raleigh, 20-4. See under *Anachronisms, Comic scenes, Didacticism, Plots, Style, Tragedies.*   1765

39. *Faults.* "*Shakespeare* with his excellencies has likewise faults, and faults sufficient to obscure and overwhelm any other merit." *Shak. Pref.*, Raleigh, 20   1765

40. *Faults.* "I am far from supposing that *Shakespear* might not sometimes think confusedly." *Shak.* 1.111 *n*   1765

41. *Faults.* J. in letter to Dr. Burney:—"I defend my criticism [of Shakespeare] in the same manner with you. We must confess the faults of our favourite, to gain credit to our praise of his excellencies. He that claims, either in himself or for another, the honours of

perfection, will surely injure the reputation which he designs to assist." *Bos.* 1.500   1765

42. *Faults.* *"Shakespeare never has six lines together without a fault. Perhaps you may find seven, but this does not refute my general assertion." *Bos.* 2.96
     1769

43. *Historical Dramas.* "The historical Dramas are now concluded, of which the two parts of *Henry* the Fourth, and *Henry* the Fifth, are among the happiest of our authour's compositions; and King *John, Richard* the Third, and *Henry* the Eighth, deservedly stand in the second class." *Shak.*, Raleigh, 153   1765

44. *Historical Dramas.* "His histories, being neither tragedies nor comedies are not subject to any of their laws; nothing more is necessary to all the praise which they expect, than that the changes of action be so prepared as to be understood, that the incidents be various and affecting, and the characters consistent, natural, and distinct. No other unity is intended, and therefore none is to be sought." *Shak. Pref.*, Raleigh, 24   1765

45. *How to read Shakespeare.* "Let him, that is yet unacquainted with the powers of *Shakespeare*, and who desires to feel the highest pleasure that the drama can give, read every play from the first scene to the last, with utter negligence of all his commentators. When his fancy is once on the wing, let it not stoop at correction or explanation. When his attention is strongly engaged, let it disdain alike to turn aside to the name of *Theobald* and of *Pope*. Let him read on through brightness and obscurity, through integrity and corruption; let him preserve his comprehension of the dialogue and his interest in the fable. And when the pleasures of novelty have ceased, let him attempt exactness, and read the commentators. Particular passages are cleared by notes, but the general effect of the work is weakened. The mind is refrigerated by interruption; the thoughts are diverted from the principal

subject; the reader is weary, he suspects not why; and at last throws away the book, which he has too diligently studied." *Shak. Pref.*, Raleigh, 61-2   1765

46. *How to read Shakespeare.* "Parts are not to be examined till the whole has been surveyed; there is a kind of intellectual remoteness necessary for the comprehension of any great work in its full design and its true proportions; a close approach shews the smaller niceties, but the beauty of the whole is discerned no longer." *Shak. Pref.*, Raleigh, 62   1765

47. *Judge each work as a whole.* "His real power is not shewn in the splendour of particular passages, but by the progress of his fable, and the tenour of his dialogue; and he that tries to recommend him by select quotations, will succeed like the pedant in *Hierocles*, who, when he offered his house to sale, carried a brick in his pocket as a specimen." *Shak. Pref.*, Raleigh, 12
    1765

48. *Love element in Shakespeare.* "Upon every other stage the universal agent is love. . . . To bring a lover, a lady and a rival into the fable; to entangle them in contradictory obligations, perplex them with oppositions of interest, and harrass them with violence of desires inconsistent with each other; to make them meet in rapture and part in agony; to fill their mouths with hyperbolical joy and outrageous sorrow; to distress them as nothing human ever was distressed; to deliver them as nothing human ever was delivered; is the business of a modern dramatist. For this probability is violated, life is misrepresented, and language is depraved. But love is only one of many passions; and as it has no great influence upon the sum of life, it has little operation in the dramas of a poet, who caught his ideas from the living world, and exhibited only what he saw before him. He knew, that any other passion, as it was regular or exorbitant, was a cause of happi-

ness or calamity."[1] *Shak. Pref.*, Raleigh, 13   1765

49. *Nature descriptions.* "He was an exact surveyor of the inanimate world; his descriptions have always some peculiarities, gathered by contemplating things as they really exist." *Shak. Pref.*, Raleigh, 39. (See also *infra*, 59 a)   1765

50. "*Nature*," *Truth to.* (See also *supra*, Characters, and 30, 48.) Invention "the first and most valuable" power of a poet. (*Wks.* 14.477.) "A very small part of the reputation of this mighty genius depends upon the naked plot or story of his plays. He lived in an age when the books of chivalry were yet popular, and when therefore the minds of his auditors were not accustomed to balance probabilities, or to examine nicely the proportion between causes and effects. It was sufficient to recommend a story, that it was far removed from common life, that its changes were frequent, and its close pathetic. This disposition of the age concurred so happily with the imagination of Shakespear, that he had no desire to reform it, and indeed to this he was indebted for the licentious variety, by which he has made his plays more entertaining than those of any other author. He had looked with great attention on the scenes of nature; but his chief skill was in human actions, passions, and habits; he was therefore delighted with such tales as afforded numerous incidents, and exhibited many characters in many changes of situation. These characters are so copiously diversified, and some of them so justly pursued, that his works may be considered as a map of life, a faithful miniature of human transactions; and he that has read Shakespear with attention will perhaps find little new in the crowded world. Among his other excellencies it

---

[1] Similarly, Warton lamented in 1756 this "epidemical effeminacy": "One would imagine, from the practice of our modern playwrights, that love was the only passion capable of producing any great calamities in human life: for this passion has engrossed, and been impertinently introduced into, all subjects." *Essay on Pope*, 5th ed., 1806, 1.258 *ff*. See also Warton's *Adventurer*, No. 113

ought to be remarked, because it has hitherto been unnoticed, that his *heroes are men*, that the love and hatred, the hopes and fears of his chief personages are such as are common to other human beings, and not like those which later times have exhibited, peculiar to phantoms that strut upon the stage. It is not perhaps very necessary to inquire whether the vehicle of so much delight and instruction be a story probable or unlikely, native or foreign. Shakespear's excellence is not the fiction of a tale, but the representation of life; and his reputation is therefore safe, till human nature shall be changed. Nor can he, who has so many just claims to praise, suffer by losing that which ignorant admiration has unreasonably given him. To calumniate the dead is baseness, and to flatter them is surely folly." (*Ib.* 479-81. Dedication to *Shakespear Illustrated*, written for Mrs. Lennox) 1753

51. "*Nature*," Truth to. "It is the great excellence of *Shakespeare*, that he drew his scenes from nature, and from life. He copied the manners of the world then passing before him, and has more allusions than other poets to the traditions and superstitions of the vulgar." This is a cause of his obscurity. *Wks.* 9.232. (*Shak. Proposals*) 1756

52. "*Nature*," Truth to. "*Shakespeare* is above all writers, at least above all modern writers, the poet of nature; the poet that holds up to his readers a faithful mirrour of manners and of life. His characters are not modified by the customs of particular places, unpractised by the rest of the world; by the peculiarities of studies or professions, which can operate but upon small numbers; or by the accidents of transient fashions or temporary opinions: they are the genuine progeny of common humanity, such as the world will always supply, and observation will always find. His persons act and speak by the influence of those general passions and principles by which all minds are agitated, and the whole

system of life is continued in motion. In the writings of other poets a character is too often an individual; in those of *Shakespeare* it is commonly a species." *Shak. Pref.*, Raleigh, 11-12   1765

53. *"Nature," Truth to.* "This therefore is the praise of *Shakespeare*, that his drama is the mirrour of life; that he who has mazed his imagination, in following the phantoms which other writers raise up before him, may here be cured of his delirious extasies, by reading human sentiments in human language, by scenes from which a hermit may estimate the transactions of the world, and a confessor predict the progress of the passions. His adherence to general nature has exposed him to the censure of criticks, who form their judgments upon narrower principles. *Dennis* and *Rhymer* think his *Romans* not sufficiently *Roman;* and *Voltaire* censures his kings as not completely royal. *Dennis* is offended, that *Menenius*, a senator of *Rome*, should play the buffoon[1]; and *Voltaire* perhaps thinks decency violated when the *Danish* Usurper is represented as a drunkard. But *Shakespeare* always makes nature predominate over accident; and if he preserves the essential character, is not very careful of distinctions superinduced and adventitious. His story requires Romans or kings, but he thinks only on men . . . a poet overlooks the casual distinction of country and condition, as a painter, satisfied with the figure, neglects the drapery." *Shak. Pref.*, Raleigh, 14-15
1765

54. *"Nature," Truth to.* Shakespeare's practice of mixing comic and tragic scenes true to nature. See *infra*, 90 *a*
1765

55. *"Nature," Truth to.* The vitality of his comic scenes in manners and words: "As his personages act upon

---

[1] "For he [Shakespeare] might as well have imagin'd a grave majestick *Jack-Pudding*, as a Buffoon in a *Roman* Senator." *On the Genius and Writings of Shakespear*, Letter I

principles arising from genuine passion, very little modified by particular forms, their pleasures and vexations are communicable to all times and to all places; they are natural, and therefore durable; the adventitious peculiarities of personal habits, are only superficial dies, bright and pleasing for a little while, yet soon fading to a dim tinct, without any remains of former lustre; but the discriminations of true passion are the colours of nature; they pervade the whole mass, and can only perish with the body that exhibits them. The accidental compositions of heterogeneous modes are dissolved by the chance which combined them; but the uniform simplicity of primitive qualities neither admits increase, nor suffers decay. The sand heaped by one flood is scattered by another, but the rock always continues in its place. The stream of time, which is continually washing the dissoluble fabricks of other poets, passes without injury by the adamant of *Shakespeare*." *Shak. Pref.*, Raleigh, 19   1765

56. *"Nature," Truth to.* Relied on direct observations of nature. See *infra*, 59 a   1765

57. *"Nature," Truth to.* His knowledge of human nature referred to. *Shak.* 1.319 *n* 3; 2.68, 189 *n* 8, 208 *n* 8; 3.372 *n* 2, etc. *Shak.*, Raleigh, 97, 104-5, 108, 108-9, 111   1765

58. **"Nature," Truth to.* Richardson's and Shakespeare's knowledge of the human heart. See RICHARDSON 7   Date?

59. *Originality.* (See also *infra*, under *Plots*.) [a] Relied on direct observation of mankind. "In this part of his performances he had none to imitate, but has himself been imitated by all succeeding writers. . . . *Shakespeare*, whether life or nature be his subject, shews plainly, that he has seen with his own eyes; he gives the image which he receives, not weakened or distorted by the intervention of any other mind; the ignorant feel his representations to be just, and the learned see

that they are compleat. [b] Perhaps it would not be easy to find any authour, except *Homer*, who invented so much. . . . The form, the characters, the language, and the shows of the *English* drama are his . . . he is the first who taught either tragedy or comedy to please. . . . To him we must ascribe the praise, unless *Spenser* may divide it with him, of having first discovered to how much smoothness and harmony the *English* language could be softened. He has speeches, perhaps sometimes scenes, which have all the delicacy of *Rowe*, without his effeminacy. He endeavours indeed commonly to strike by the force and vigour of his dialogue, but he never executes his purpose better, than when he tries to sooth by softness." *Shak. Pref.*, Raleigh, 37-40　　　　1765

60. *Plots.* (See also *infra*, "*Unities.*") "A very small part of the reputation of this mighty genius depends upon the naked plot or story of his plays." See *supra* 50　　1753

61. *Plots.* Shakespeare closely followed his sources, "instead of dilating his thoughts into generalities, and expressing incidents with poetical latitude." *Wks.* 9.234. (*Shak. Proposals*)　　　　1756

62. *Plots.* "The plots are often so loosely formed, that a very slight consideration may improve them, and so carelessly pursued, that he seems not always fully to comprehend his own design. He omits opportunities of instructing or delighting which the train of his story seems to force upon him, and apparently rejects those exhibitions which would be more affecting, for the sake of those which are more easy." *Shak. Pref.*, Raleigh, 21　　　　1765

63. *Plots.* Neglected endings: in many plays "he shortened the labour to snatch the profit. He therefore remits his efforts where he should most vigorously exert them, and his catastrophe is improbably produced or imperfectly represented." *Shak. Pref.*, Raleigh, 21　　1765

64. *Plots.* "His plots, whether historical or fabulous, are

always crouded with incidents, by which the attention of a rude people was more easily caught than by sentiment or argumentation; and such is the power of the marvellous even over those who despise it, that every man finds his mind more strongly seized by the tragedies of *Shakespeare* than of any other writer; others please us by particular speeches, but he always makes us anxious for the event, and has perhaps excelled all but *Homer* in securing the first purpose of a writer, by exciting restless and unquenchable curiosity and compelling him that reads his work to read it through." Shak. Pref., Raleigh, 32-3. See also *supra* 47   1765

65. *Plots.* Repetition of plot entanglements. Shak. Pref., Raleigh, 41   1765

66. *Style.* Examples of mean diction in *Macbeth*. See DICTION 2 b   1751

67. *Style.* His obscurity of diction the fault of an age of linguistic flux and the result of his "use of the common colloquial language." Wks. 9.232-3. (*Shak. Proposals*)   1756

68. *Style.* The "licentiousness" of Shakespeare's language. Wks. 9.235. (*Shak. Proposals*)   1756

69. *Style.* Shakespeare's "fulness of idea" and "that rapidity of imagination which might hurry him to a second thought before he had fully explained the first," causes of his obscurity. But to his audience, J. believes "that very few of his lines were difficult." Wks. 9.233. (*Shak. Proposals*)   1756

70. *Style: Narration.* "In narration he affects a disproportionate pomp of diction, and a wearisome train of circumlocution . . . instead of lightening it by brevity, [he] endeavoured to recommend it by dignity and splendour." Shak. Pref., Raleigh, 22-3   1765

71. *Style: Declamations* or set speeches, "commonly cold and weak, for his power was the power of nature; when he endeavoured . . . instead of inquiring what

the occasion demanded, to show how much his stores of knowledge could supply, he seldom escapes without the pity or resentment of his reader." *Shak. Pref.*, Raleigh, 23   1765

72. *Style: imperfect expression.* S. becomes "now and then entangled with an unwieldy sentiment" and leaves it imperfectly expressed. *Shak. Pref.*, Raleigh, 23   1765

73. *Style.* "The equality of words to things is very often neglected, and trivial sentiments and vulgar ideas disappoint the attention, to which they are recommended by sonorous epithets and swelling figures." *Shak. Pref.*, Raleigh, 23   1765

74. *Style: inopportune conceits or word-play.* "He no sooner begins to move, than he counteracts himself; and terrour and pity, as they are rising in the mind, are checked and blasted by sudden frigidity. A quibble is to *Shakespeare*, what luminous vapours are to the traveller; he follows it at all adventures; it is sure to lead him out of his way, and sure to engulf him in the mire. It has some malignant power over his mind, and its fascinations are irresistible. . . . A quibble is the golden apple for which he will always turn aside from his career, or stoop from his elevation. A quibble, poor and barren as it is, gave him such delight, that he was content to purchase it, by the sacrifice of reason, propriety and truth. A quibble was to him the fatal *Cleopatra* for which he lost the world, and was content to lose it." *Shak. Pref.*, Raleigh, 23-4. See also *supra* 26, 27, and *infra* 149   1765

75. *Style.* "The pathetick of *Shakespeare* too often ends in the ridiculous. It is painful to find the gloomy dignity of this noble scene [*Antony and Cleopatra*, IV, ix] destroyed by the intrusion of a conceit so far-fetched and unaffecting." *Shak.*, Raleigh, 180. See also *ib.* 183, 188-9, 199   1765

76. *Style.* "The work of a correct and regular writer is a

garden accurately formed and diligently planted, varied with shades, and scented with flowers; the composition of *Shakespeare* is a forest, in which oaks extend their branches, and pines tower in the air, interspersed sometimes with weeds and brambles, and sometimes giving shelter to myrtles and to roses; filling the eye with awful pomp, and gratifying the mind with endless diversity. Other poets display cabinets of precious rarities, minutely finished, wrought into shape, and polished into brightness. *Shakespeare* opens a mine which contains gold and diamonds in unexhaustible plenty, though clouded by incrustations, debased by impurities, and mingled with a mass of meaner minerals." Shak. Pref., Raleigh, 34   1765

77. *Style.* "He that will understand *Shakespeare*, must not be content to study him in the closet, he must look for his meaning sometimes among the sports of the field, and sometimes among the manufactures of the shop." Shak. Pref., Raleigh, 36   1765

78. *Style.* "He has corrupted language by every mode of depravation." Shak. Pref., Raleigh, 41   1765

79. *Style.* Originality of language, and smoothness of style. See *supra* 59 b   1765

80. *Style.* "The stile of *Shakespeare* was in itself ungrammatical, perplexed and obscure." Shak. Pref., Raleigh, 42   1765

81. *Style: Grammar.* "Shakespeare regarded more the series of ideas, than of words; and his language, not being designed for the reader's desk, was all that he desired it to be, if it conveyed his meaning to the audience." Shak. Pref., Raleigh, 47   1765

82. *Style.* "The expressions by which *Shakespeare* too frequently clouds his meaning." Shak., Raleigh, 89   1765

83. *Style.* Shakespeare "attends more to his ideas than to his words." Shak. 2.288 n 9   1765

84. *Style.* "Shakespeare has no great right to censure

poetical exaggeration, of which no poet is more frequently guilty." *Shak.* 7.305 *n* 4 1765

85. *Style.* "This is not an easy style; but is it not the style of *Shakespeare*?" *Shak.*, Raleigh, 195 1765

86. *Style:* "What authour of that age had the same easiness of expression and fluency of numbers?" See *infra* 108
1765

87. *Supernatural element.* Shakespeare "familiarizes the wonderful." See *supra* 22 b 1765

88. *Tragedies.* (See also *supra* 25.) "In tragedy his performance seems constantly to be worse, as his labour is more. The effusions of passion which exigence forces out are for the most part striking and energetick; but whenever he solicits his invention, or strains his faculties, the offspring of his throes is tumour, meanness, tediousness, and obscurity." *Shak. Pref.*, Raleigh, 22
1765

89. *Tragi-Comedies.* Shakespeare's success in tragi-comedy its justification, or perhaps an example of his triumph over defects. See DRAMA 75 1751

90. *Tragi-Comedies.* [a] The practice of "mixing comick and tragick scenes" defended. "*Shakespeare's* plays are not in the rigorous and critical sense either tragedies or comedies, but compositions of a distinct kind; exhibiting the real state of sublunary nature, which partakes of good and evil, joy and sorrow, mingled with endless variety of proportion and innumerable modes of combination; and expressing the course of the world." Although "contrary to the rules of criticism . . . there is always an appeal open from criticism to nature. The end of writing is to instruct; the end of poetry is to instruct by pleasing. That the mingled drama may convey all the instruction of tragedy or comedy cannot be denied, because it includes both in its alternations of exhibition and approaches nearer than either to the appearance of life." [b] J. refutes

the objection that since such a method interrupts the passions, it lessens "the power to move, which constitutes the perfection of dramatick poetry": experience does not prove this. "The interchanges of mingled scenes seldom fail to produce the intended vicissitudes of passion. Fiction cannot move so much, but that the attention may be easily transferred." Though there is occasionally "unwelcome levity," yet melancholy not uniformly pleasing to all, and "upon the whole, all pleasure consists in variety. . . . But whatever be his purpose, whether to gladden or depress, or to conduct the story, without vehemence or emotion, through tracts of easy and familiar dialogue, he never fails to attain his purpose; as he commands us, we laugh or mourn, or sit silent with quiet expectation, in tranquillity without indifference. When *Shakespeare's* plan is understood, most of the criticisms of *Rhymer* and *Voltaire* vanish away . . . the Gravediggers themselves may be heard with applause." *Shak. Pref.*, Raleigh, 15-18   1765

91. *"Unities," Shakespeare's observance of the.* Unity of action well preserved, though no "intrigue regularly perplexed and regularly unravelled . . . for this is seldom the order of real events, and *Shakespeare* is the poet of nature: But his plan has commonly what *Aristotle* requires, a beginning, a middle, and an end; one event is concatenated with another, and the conclusion follows by easy consequence." *Shak. Pref.*, Raleigh, 25   1765

92. *"Unities," Shakespeare's observance of the.* "As nothing is essential to the fable, but unity of action, and as the unities of time and place arise evidently from false assumptions, and, by circumscribing the extent of the drama, lessen its variety, I cannot think it much to be lamented, that they were not known by him, or not observed. . . . Such violations of rules merely positive, become the comprehensive genius of *Shakespeare*."

Shak. Pref., Raleigh, 29. For J.'s attack on "unities" see DRAMA: *Rules*   1765

Shakespeare. (INDIVIDUAL PLAYS)

93. *All's Well that Ends Well*. "This play has many delightful scenes, though not sufficiently probable, and some happy characters, though not new, nor produced by any deep knowledge of human nature. *Parolles* is a boaster and a coward, such as has always been the sport of the stage, but perhaps never raised more laughter or contempt than in the hands of *Shakespeare*. I cannot reconcile my heart to *Bertram*; a man noble without generosity, and young without truth; who marries *Helen* as a coward, and leaves her as a profligate: when she is dead by his unkindness, sneaks home to a second marriage, is accused by a woman whom he has wronged, defends himself by falsehood, and is dismissed to happiness. The story of *Bertram* and *Diana* had been told before of *Mariana* and *Angelo*, and, to confess the truth, scarcely merited to be heard a second time." *Shak.*, Raleigh, 103   1765

94. *Antony and Cleopatra*. Approaches the *genre* of history play: "There is not much nearer approach to unity of action in the tragedy of *Antony and Cleopatra*, than in the history of *Richard the Second*." *Shak. Pref.*, Raleigh, 17-18   1765

95. *Antony and Cleopatra*. "THIS Play keeps curiosity always busy, and the passions always interested. The continual hurry of the action, the variety of incidents, and the quick succession of one personage to another, call the mind forward without intermission from the first Act to the last. But the power of delighting is derived principally from the frequent changes of the scene; for, except the feminine arts, some of which are too low, which distinguish *Cleopatra*, no character is very strongly discriminated." Antony's diction "not distinguishable from that of others. . . . The eve..ts

... are produced without any art of connection or care of disposition." *Shak.*, Raleigh, 180   1765

96. *As You Like It.* "Of this play the fable is wild and pleasing. I know not how the ladies will approve the facility with which both *Rosalind* and *Celia* give away their hearts. To *Celia* much may be forgiven for the heroism of her friendship. The character of *Jaques* is natural and well preserved. The comick dialogue is very sprightly, with less mixture of low buffoonery than in some other plays; and the graver part is elegant and harmonious. By hastening to the end of his work *Shakespeare* suppressed the dialogue between the usurper and the hermit, and lost an opportunity of exhibiting a moral lesson in which he might have found matter worthy of his highest powers." *Shak.*, Raleigh, 86   1765

97. *Coriolanus.* "The Tragedy of *Coriolanus* is one of the most amusing of our authour's performances. The old man's merriment in *Menenius;* the lofty lady's dignity in *Volumnia;* the bridal modesty in *Virgilia;* the patrician and military haughtiness in *Coriolanus;* the plebeian malignity and tribunition insolence in *Brutus* and *Sicinius*, make a very pleasing and interesting variety: and the various revolutions of the hero's fortune fill the mind with anxious curiosity. There is, perhaps too much bustle in the first act, and too little in the last." *Shak.*, Raleigh, 179   1765

98. *Hamlet.* Variety its particular and distinguishing excellence. The incidents numerous. "The scenes are interchangeably diversified with merriment and solemnity; with merriment that includes judicious and instructive observations, and solemnity, not strained by poetical violence above the natural sentiments of man. New characters appear from time to time in continual succession, exhibiting various forms of life and particular modes of conversation. The pretended madness of *Hamlet* causes much mirth, the mournful distrac-

tion of *Ophelia* fills the heart with tenderness, and every personage produces the effect intended, from the apparition that in the first act chills the blood with horror, to the fop in the last, that exposes affectation to just contempt. The conduct [of the action] is perhaps not wholly secure against objections . . . some scenes . . . neither forward nor retard it. Of the feigned madness of *Hamlet* there appears no adequate cause, for he does nothing which he might not have done with the reputation of sanity. He plays the madman most, when he treats *Ophelia* with so much rudeness, which seems to be useless and wanton cruelty. *Hamlet* is, through the whole play, rather an instrument than an agent. After he has, by the stratagem of the play, convicted the King, he makes no attempt to punish him, and his death is at last effected by an incident which *Hamlet* has no part in producing. The catastrophe is not very happily produced; the exchange of weapons is rather an expedient of necessity, than a stroke of art. A scheme might easily have been formed, to kill *Hamlet* with the dagger, and *Laertes* with the bowl. The poet is accused of having shewn little regard to poetical justice, and may be charged with equal neglect of poetical probability. The apparition left the regions of the dead to little purpose; the revenge which he demands is not obtained but by the death of him that was required to take it; and the gratification which would arise from the destruction of an usurper and a murderer, is abated by the untimely death of *Ophelia*, the young, the beautiful, the harmless, and the pious." *Shak.*, Raleigh, 195-6   1765

99. *Hamlet.* "*Polonius* is a man bred in courts, exercised in business stored with observation, confident of his knowledge, proud of his eloquence, and declining into dotage. His mode of oratory is truly represented as designed to ridicule the practice of those times, of prefaces that made no introduction, and of method

that embarrassed rather than explained. This part of his character is accidental, the rest is natural. Such a man is positive and confident, because he knows that his mind was once strong, and knows not that it is become weak. Such a man excels in general principles, but fails in the particular application. He is knowing in retrospect, and ignorant in foresight. While he depends upon his memory, and can draw from his repositories of knowledge, he utters weighty sentences, and gives useful counsel; but as the mind in its enfeebled state cannot be kept long busy and intent, the old man is subject to sudden dereliction of his faculties, he loses the order of his ideas, and entangles himself in his own thoughts, till he recovers the leading principle, and falls again into his former train. This idea of dotage encroaching upon wisdom, will solve all the phænomena of the character of *Polonius.*" *Shak.,* Raleigh, 190-1   1765

100. *Hamlet.* *Shakespeare's picture of a man, (*Hamlet* III. iv), preferred to Milton's. (*Par. Lost,* IV. 300 *ff.*) *Bos.* 4.72-3   1781

101. *Julius Cæsar.* "Of this tragedy many particular passages deserve regard, and the contention and reconcilement of *Brutus* and *Cassius* is universally celebrated; but I have never been strongly agitated in perusing it, and think it somewhat cold and unaffecting, compared with some other of *Shakespeare's* plays; his adherence to the real story, and to *Roman* manners, seems to have impeded the natural vigour of his genius." *Shak.,* Raleigh, 179   1765

102. *King Henry IV.,* Parts I. and II. (See *supra* 43.) "Perhaps no authour has ever in two plays afforded so much delight. The great events are interesting, for the fate of kingdoms depends upon them; the slighter occurrences are diverting, and, except one or two, sufficiently probable; the incidents are multiplied with wonderful fertility of invention, and the characters

diversified with the utmost nicety of discernment, and the profoundest skill in the nature of man. The prince . . . is a young man of great abilities and violent passions, whose sentiments are right, though his actions are wrong; whose virtues are obscured by negligence, and whose understanding is dissipated by levity. . . . This character is great, original, and just. . . . But *Falstaff* unimitated, unimitable *Falstaff*, how shall I describe thee? Thou compound of sense and vice; of sense which may be admired but not esteemed, of vice which may be despised, but hardly detested. *Falstaff* is a character loaded with faults, and with those faults which naturally produce contempt. He is a thief, and a glutton, a coward, and a boaster, always ready to cheat the weak, and prey upon the poor; to terrify the timorous and insult the defenceless. At once obsequious and malignant, he satirises in their absence those whom he lives by flattering. He is familiar with the prince only as an agent of vice, but of this familiarity he is so proud as not only to be supercilious and haughty with common men, but to think his interest of importance to the duke of *Lancaster*. Yet the man thus corrupt, thus despicable, makes himself necessary to the prince that despises him, by the most pleasing of all qualities, perpetual gaiety, by an unfailing power of exciting laughter, which is the more freely indulged, as his wit is not of the splendid or ambitious kind, but consists in easy escapes and sallies of levity, which make sport but raise no envy. It must be observed that he is stained with no enormous or sanguinary crimes, so that his licentiousness is not so offensive but that it may be borne for his mirth. The moral to be drawn from this representation is, that no man is more dangerous than he that with a will to corrupt, hath the power to please; and that neither wit nor honesty ought to think themselves safe with such a companion when they see *Henry* seduced by *Falstaff*."
Shak., Raleigh, 124-5   1765

103. *King Henry IV.*, Parts I. and II. Compared with the three parts of *King Henry VI.* See *infra* 108   1765
104. *King Henry IV.*, Parts I. and II. *J. prefers Shakespeare in his moral aspects, e.g., "Iago's ingenious malice, and subtle revenge; or prince Hal's gay compliance with the vices of Falstaff, whom he all along despised. Those plays had indeed no rivals in Johnson's favour: 'No man but Shakespeare (he said) could have drawn Sir John.'" *John. Misc.* 1.283. (Piozzi)   Date?
105. *King Henry V.* (See also *supra* 43.)
      When he speaks,
 The air, a charter'd libertine, is still.
(I. i. 47-8.) "This line is exquisitely beautiful." *Shak.*, Raleigh, 127   1765
106. *King Henry V.* "This play has many scenes of high dignity, and many of easy merriment. The character of the King is well supported, except in his courtship, where he has neither the vivacity of *Hal*, nor the grandeur of *Henry*. The humour of *Pistol* is very happily continued; his character has perhaps been the model of all the bullies that have yet appeared on the *English* stage." In "the lines given to the chorus . . . a little may be praised and much must be forgiven." Their function questioned. "The great defect of this play is the emptiness and narrowness of the last act, which a very little diligence might have easily avoided." *Shak.*, Raleigh, 133   1765
107. *King Henry V.* Compared with the three parts of *King Henry VI.* See *infra* 108   1765
108. *King Henry VI.*, Parts I., II. and III. "These plays, considered, without regard to characters and incidents, merely as narratives in verse, are more happily conceived and more accurately finished than those of king *John, Richard* II., or the tragick scenes of *Henry* IV. and V. If we take these plays from *Shakespeare*, to whom shall they be given? What authour of that age

had the same easiness of expression and fluency of numbers? . . . Of these three plays I think the second the best. The truth is, that they have not sufficient variety of action, for the incidents are too often of the same kind; yet many of the characters are well discriminated. King *Henry*, and his queen, king *Edward*, the duke of *Gloucester*, and the earl of *Warwick*, are very strongly and distinctly painted." *Shak.*, Raleigh, 144-5 1765

109. *King Henry VI.*, Part 2. "This is one of the scenes [III. iii. Death of Cardinal Beaufort] which have been applauded by the criticks, and which will continue to be admired when prejudice shall cease, and bigotry give way to impartial examination. These are beauties that rise out of nature and of truth; the superficial reader cannot miss them, the profound can image nothing beyond them." *Shak.*, Raleigh, 138 1765

110. *King Henry VIII.* (See *supra* 43.) "This scene [IV. ii —"*Enter Katharine . . . sick.*"] is, above any other part of *Shakespeare's* tragedies, and perhaps above any scene of any other poet, tender and pathetick, without gods, or furies, or poisons, or precipices, without the help of romantick circumstances, without improbable sallies of poetical lamentation, and without any throes of tumultuous misery." *Shak.*, Raleigh, 150-1 1765

111. *King Henry VIII.* "The play of *Henry* the eighth is one of those which still keeps possession of the stage, by the splendour of its pageantry. . . . Yet pomp is not the only merit of this play. The meek sorrows and virtuous distress of *Catherine* have furnished some scenes which may be justly numbered among the greatest efforts of tragedy. But the genius of *Shakespeare* comes in and goes out with *Catherine*. Every other part may be easily conceived and easily written." *Shak.*, Raleigh, 152 1765

112. *King Henry VIII*. *Of all Shakespeare's characters, J. thinks Queen Katharine the most natural. He tells Mrs. Siddons: "whenever you perform it, I will once more hobble out to the theatre myself." *Bos.* 4.242
    1783
113. *King Henry VIII*. *"He advised Mrs. Siddons to play the part of Queen Catherine." *John. Misc.* 2.14. (Hawkins's *Apophthegms*)   1783?
114. *King John.* "The tragedy of *King John*, though not written with the utmost power of *Shakespeare*, is varied with a very pleasing interchange of incidents and characters. The Lady's grief is very affecting, and the character of the *Bastard* contains that mixture of greatness and levity which this authour delighted to exhibit." *Shak.*, Raleigh, 109   1765
115. *King John.* Compared with the three parts of *King Henry VI*. See *supra* 108   1765
116. *King Lear.* "The Tragedy of *Lear* is deservedly celebrated among the dramas of *Shakespeare*. There is perhaps no play which keeps the attention so strongly fixed; which so much agitates our passions and interests our curiosity. The artful involutions of distinct interests, the striking opposition of contrary characters, the sudden changes of fortune, and the quick succession of events, fill the mind with a perpetual tumult of indignation, pity, and hope. There is no scene which does not contribute to the aggravation of the distress or conduct of the action, and scarce a line which does not conduce to the progress of the scene. So powerful is the current of the poet's imagination, that the mind, which once ventures within it, is hurried irresistibly along." The seeming improbability of Lear's conduct and the instances of cruelty throughout the play accounted for on historical grounds. "But I am not able to apologize with equal plausibility for the extrusion of *Gloucester's* eyes, which seems an act too horrid to be endured in dramatick exhibition, and

such as must always compel the mind to relieve its distress by incredulity. Yet let it be remembered that our authour well knew what would please the audience for which he wrote. The injury done by *Edmund* to the simplicity of the action is abundantly recompensed by the addition of variety," and the re-enforcement of the main theme. Poetic justice not observed towards Cordelia, "contrary to the natural ideas of justice, to the hope of the reader, and, what is yet more strange, to the faith of chronicles." (For this plea for poetic justice, see DRAMA 33.) Lear, the injured father, stirs our compassions rather than Lear, the degraded king. *Shak.*, Raleigh, 159-62   1765

117. *King Lear.* "The description [of Dover Cliff] is certainly not mean, but I am far from thinking it wrought to the utmost excellence of poetry. He that looks from a precipice finds himself assailed by one great and dreadful image of irresistible destruction. But this overwhelming idea is dissipated and enfeebled from the instant that the mind can restore itself to the observation of particulars, and diffuse its attention to distinct objects. The enumeration of the choughs and crows, the samphire-man and the fishers, counteracts the great effect of the prospect, as it peoples the desert of intermediate vacuity, and stops the mind in the rapidity of its descent through emptiness and horrour." *Shak.*, Raleigh, 158-9   1765

118. *King Lear.* *J. rejects the description of Dover Cliff as inferior to the description of the temple in Congreve's *Mourning Bride:* "No, Sir; it should be all precipice,—all vacuum. The crows impede your fall. The diminished appearance of the boats, and other circumstances, are all very good description; but do not impress the mind at once with the horrible idea of immense height. The impression is divided; you pass on by computation, from one stage of the tremendous space to another. Had the girl in *The Mourning*

Bride said, she could not cast her shoe to the top of one of the pillars in the temple, it would not have aided the idea, but weakened it." *Bos.* 2.87   1769

119. *King Richard II.* "This play is one of those which *Shakespeare* has apparently revised; but as success in works of invention is not always proportionate to labour, it is not finished at last with the happy force of some other of his tragedies, nor can be said much to affect the passions, or enlarge the understanding." *Shak.*, Raleigh, 113   1765

120. *King Richard II.* Used to illustrate the lack of unity of the history play. *Shak. Pref.*, Raleigh, 17-18   1765

121. *King Richard II.* Compared with the three parts of *King Henry VI.* See *supra* 108   1765

122. *King Richard III.* "This is one of the most celebrated of our authour's performances; yet I know not whether it has not happened to him as to others, to be praised most when praise is not most deserved. That this play has scenes noble in themselves, and very well contrived to strike in the exhibition, cannot be denied. But some parts are trifling, others shocking, and some improbable." *Shak.*, Raleigh, 148. See also *supra* 43   1765

123. *Love's Labour's Lost.* "In this play, which all the editors have concurred to censure, and some have rejected as unworthy of our Poet, it must be confessed that there are many passages mean, childish, and vulgar; and some which ought not to have been exhibited, as we are told they were, to a maiden queen. But there are scattered, through the whole, many sparks of genius; nor is there any play that has more evident marks of the hand of *Shakespeare*." *Shak.*, Raleigh, 89   1765

124. *Love's Labour's Lost.* "The stile of the rhyming scenes in this play is often entangled and obscure." *Shak.*, Raleigh, 86   1765

125. *Macbeth.* "This tragedy like the rest of *Shakspeare's*

is perhaps overstocked with personages." *Wks.* 14.97. (*Observ. on Macb.*) 1745

126. *Macbeth.* "Touches of judgement and genius" illustrated. *Wks.* 14.100 1745

127. *Macbeth.* The Witches defended on grounds that to S.'s audience the bounds of probability not transgressed; "nor can it be doubted that the scenes of enchantment, however they may now be ridiculed, were both by himself and his audience thought awful and affecting." See CRITICISM 15 1745

128. *Macbeth.* Shakespeare's knowledge of human nature shown in Lady Macbeth's arguments for the murder. (I. vii. 28 *ff.*) *Shak.*, Raleigh, 170. (*Observ. on Macb.*) 1745

129. *Macbeth. I dare do all that may become a man, Who dares do more is none.* [I. vii.] "A line and a half; of which it may almost be said, that they ought to bestow immortality on the author, though all his other productions had been lost." *Shak.*, Raleigh, 171. (*Observ. on Macb.*) 1745

130. *Macbeth..* " '*Now o'er one half the world Nature seems dead.*' [II. i.] . . . This image . . . is perhaps the most striking that poetry can produce." This passage compared with Dryden's description of night in *The Indian Emperor* (III. ii.) : "Night is described by two great poets. . . . He that reads *Dryden*, finds himself lull'd with serenity, and disposed to solitude and contemplation. He that peruses *Shakespeare*, looks around alarmed, and starts to find himself alone. One is the night of a lover, the other, of a murderer." *Shak.*, Raleigh, 171-2. (*Observ. on Macb.*) 1745

131. *Macbeth.* The disgusting tautology of "*time and the hour*" avoided by J.'s emendation. *Wks.* 14.72. (*Observ. on Macb.*) 1745

132. *Macbeth.* The great poetry of passage beginning

"Come, thick night!" (I. v. 51 *ff.*), weakened by mean diction. See DICTION 2 b   1751

133. *Macbeth.* "This play is deservedly celebrated for the propriety of its fictions, and solemnity, grandeur, and variety of its action; but it has no nice discriminations of character, the events are too great to admit the influence of particular dispositions, and the course of the action necessarily determines the conduct of the agents. The danger of ambition is well described; and I know not whether it may not be said in defence of some parts which now seem improbable, that, in *Shakespeare's* time, it was necessary to warn credulity against vain and illusive predictions. The passions are directed to their true end. Lady *Macbeth* is merely detested; and though the courage of *Macbeth* preserves some esteem, yet every reader rejoices at his fall." *Shak.*, Raleigh, 177   1765

134. *Macbeth.* *"Many of Shakspeare's plays are the worse for being acted: *Macbeth*, for instance." *Bos.* 2.92. (cf. *Bos.* 5.38)   1769

135. *Macbeth.* J.'s imagination "heated" by thought of the weird sisters at Forres. "This to an *Englishman* is classick ground." *Wks.* 10.341. (*Jour. to W.I.*)
          Composed 1774

136. *Macbeth.* *"We talked of Shakspeare's witches. JOHNSON. 'They are beings of his own creation; they are a compound of malignity and meanness, without any abilities.'" *Bos.* 3.382   1779

137. *Macbeth.* *J. "forced . . . to prefer Young's description of Night to the so much admired ones of Dryden and Shakespeare." See YOUNG 6   Date?

138. *Measure for Measure.* "There is perhaps not one of *Shakespeare's* plays more darkened than this by the peculiarities of its Authour, and the unskilfulness of its Editors, by distortions of phrase, or negligence of transcription." *Shak.*, Raleigh, 75. See also *supra* 36
          1765

139. *Measure for Measure.* "Of this play the light or comick part is very natural and pleasing, but the grave scenes, if a few passages be excepted, have more labour than elegance. The plot is rather intricate than artful. The time of the action is indefinite. . . . The unities of action and place are sufficiently preserved." *Shak.*, Raleigh, 81   1765

140. *Merchant of Venice.* "The stile is even and easy, with few peculiarities of diction, or anomalies of construction. The comick part raises laughter, and the serious fixes expectation. The probability of either one or the other story cannot be maintained. The union of two actions in one event is in this drama eminently happy. *Dryden* was much pleased with his own address in connecting the two plots of his *Spanish Friar*, which yet, I believe, the critick will find excelled by this play." *Shak.*, Raleigh, 82   1765

141. *Merchant of Venice.* "The story is itself so wildly incredible, and the changes of the scene so frequent and capricious, that the probability of action does not deserve much care." *Shak.*, Raleigh, 82   1765

142. *Merry Wives of Windsor.* "The great fault of this play is the frequency of expressions so profane, that no necessity of preserving character can justify them. There are laws of higher authority than those of criticism." *Shak.*, Raleigh, 95   1765

143. *Midsummer Night's Dream.* "Wild and fantastical as it is, all the parts in their various modes are well written, and give the kind of pleasure which the authour designed. Fairies in his time were much in fashion." *Shak.*, Raleigh, 72   1765

144. *Othello.* "Othello is the vigorous and vivacious offspring of observation impregnated by genius." *Shak. Pref.*, Raleigh, 33   1765

145. *Othello.* "The beauties of this play impress themselves so strongly upon the attention of the reader, that they can draw no aid from critical illustration. The fiery

openness of *Othello*, magnanimous, artless, and credulous, boundless in his confidence, ardent in his affection, inflexible in his resolution, and obdurate in his revenge; the cool malignity of *Iago*, silent in his resentment, subtle in his designs, and studious at once of his interest and his vengeance; the soft simplicity of *Desdemona*, confident of merit, and conscious of innocence, her artless perseverance in her suit, and her slowness to suspect that she can be suspected, are such proofs of *Shakespeare's* skill in human nature, as, I suppose, it is vain to seek in any modern writer. The gradual progress which *Iago* makes in the Moor's conviction, and the circumstances which he employs to inflame him, are so artfully natural, that, though it will perhaps not be said of him as he says of himself, that he is *a man not easily jealous*, yet we cannot but pity him when at last we find him *perplexed in the extreme*. There is always danger lest wickedness conjoined with abilities should steal upon esteem, though it misses of approbation; but the character of *Iago* is so conducted, that he is from the first scene to the last hated and despised. [cf. FICTION 1 d.] Even the inferiour characters of this play would be very conspicuous in any other piece, not only for their justness but their strength. *Cassio* is brave, benevolent, and honest, ruined only by his want of stubbornness to resist an insidious invitation. *Roderigo's* suspicious credulity, and impatient submission to the cheats which he sees practised upon him, and which by persuasion he suffers to be repeated, exhibit a strong picture of a weak mind betrayed by unlawful desires, to a false friend; and the virtue of *Æmilia* is such as we often find, worn loosely, but not cast off, easy to commit small crimes, but quickened and alarmed at atrocious villanies. The Scenes from the beginning to the end are busy, varied by happy interchanges, and regularly promoting the progression of the story; and the narrative in the end, though it tells but what is known already, yet is necessary to produce the death of *Othello*. Had the scene opened in *Cyprus*, and the preceding incidents been occasionally related, there had been little wanting to a drama of the most exact and scrupulous regularity." *Shak.*, Raleigh, 200-1

1765

146. *Othello*. Note to V. ii. (the murder of Desdemona) :— "I am glad that I have ended my revisal of this dreadful scene. It is not to be endured." *Shak.*, Raleigh, 200

1765

147. *Othello*. *The moral in *Othello:* "In the first place, Sir, we learn from *Othello* this very useful moral, not to make an unequal match; in the second place, we learn not to yield too readily to suspicion. The handkerchief is merely a trick, though a very pretty trick; but there are no other circumstances of reasonable suspicion, except what is related by Iago of Cassio's warm expressions concerning Desdemona in his sleep; and that depended entirely upon the assertion of one man. No, Sir, I think *Othello* has more moral than almost any play." *Bos.* 3.40   1776

148. *Othello*. *Shakespeare in his moral aspects preferred. See *supra* 104   Date?

149. *Romeo and Juliet*. "This play is one of the most pleasing of our Author's performances. The scenes are busy and various, the incidents numerous and important, the catastrophe irresistibly affecting, and the process of the action carried on with such probability, at least with such congruity to popular opinions, as tragedy requires. Here is one of the few attempts of *Shakespeare* to exhibit the conversation of gentlemen, to represent the airy sprightliness of juvenile elegance. . . . *Mercutio's* wit, gaiety and courage, will always procure him friends that wish him a longer life; but his death is not precipitated, he has lived out the time allotted him in the construction of the play; nor do I doubt the ability of *Shakespeare* to have con-

tinued his existence. . . . The Nurse is one of the characters in which the Authour delighted: he has, with great subtilty of distinction, drawn her at once loquacious and secret, obsequious and insolent, trusty and dishonest. His comick scenes are happily wrought, but his pathetick strains are always polluted with some unexpected depravations. His persons, however distressed, *have a conceit left them in their misery, a miserable conceit.*" Shak., Raleigh, 188-9   1765

150. *Taming of the Shrew.* "The two plots are so well united, that they can hardly be called two without injury to the art with which they are interwoven. The attention is entertained with all the variety of a double plot, yet is not distracted by unconnected incidents. The part between *Catharine* and *Petruchio* is eminently spritely and diverting. At the marriage of *Bianca* the arrival of the real father, perhaps, produces more perplexity than pleasure. The whole play is very popular and diverting." Shak., Raleigh, 96   1765

151. *Timon of Athens.* "The play of *Timon* is a domestick Tragedy, and therefore strongly fastens on the attention of the reader. In the plan there is not much art, but the incidents are natural, and the characters various and exact. The catastrophe affords a very powerful warning against that ostentatious liberality, which scatters bounty, but confers no benefits, and buys flattery, but not friendship." Shak., Raleigh, 165-6. (cf. DRAMA 69, 72)   1765

152. *Titus Andronicus.* J. believes it is not by Shakespeare: "The colour of the stile is wholly different from that of the other plays, and there is an attempt at regular versification, and artificial closes, not always inelegant, yet seldom pleasing. The barbarity of the spectacles, and the general massacre which are here exhibited, can scarcely be conceived tolerable to any audience." Shak., Raleigh, 166   1765

153. *Troilus and Cressida.* "This Play is more correctly

written than most of *Shakespeare's* compositions, but it is not one of those in which either the extent of his views or elevation of his fancy is fully displayed. As the story abounded with materials, he has exerted little invention; but he has diversified his characters with great variety, and preserved them with great exactness. His vicious characters sometimes disgust, but cannot corrupt, for both *Cressida* and *Pandarus* are detested and contemned. The comick characters seem to have been the favourites of the writer, they are of the superficial kind, and exhibit more of manners than nature, but they are copiously filled and powerfully impressed." *Shak.*, Raleigh, 184   1765

154. *Twelfth Night.* "This play is in the graver part elegant and easy, and in some of the lighter scenes exquisitely humorous. *Ague-cheek* is drawn with great propriety, but his character is, in a great measure, that of natural fatuity, and is therefore not the proper prey of a satirist. The soliloquy of *Malvolio* is truly comick; he is betrayed to ridicule merely by his pride. The marriage of *Olivia*, and the succeeding perplexity, though well enough contrived to divert on the stage, wants credibility, and fails to produce the proper instruction required in the drama, as it exhibits no just picture of life." *Shak.*, Raleigh, 93
1765

155. *Two Gentlemen of Verona.* "It is not indeed one of his most powerful effusions, it has neither many diversities of character, nor striking delineations of life, but it abounds in γνῶμαι beyond most of his plays, and few have more lines or passages which, singly considered, are eminently beautiful." *Shak.*, Raleigh, 74   1765

156. *Two Gentlemen of Verona.* "In this play there is a strange mixture of knowledge and ignorance, of care and negligence. The versification is often excellent, the allusions are learned and just; but the author conveys his heroes by sea from one inland town to another

in the same country; he places the Emperour at *Milan* and sends his young men to attend him, but never mentions him more; he makes *Protheus*, after an interview with *Silvia*, say he has only seen her picture, and, if we may credit the old copies, he has by mistaking places, left his scenery inextricable. The reason of all this confusion seems to be, that he took his story from a novel which he sometimes followed, and sometimes forsook, sometimes remembred [*sic*] and sometimes forgot." *Shak.*, Raleigh, 74-5   1765

157. *Winter's Tale.* "This play, as Dr. *Warburton* justly observes, is, with all its absurdities, very entertaining. The character of *Autolycus* is very naturally conceived, and strongly represented." *Shak.*, Raleigh, 91   1765

Shebbeare, John

1. *Heroic Epistle to Sir William Chambers.* *J. allows Goldsmith "to read it to him from beginning to end." Praises its execution. *Bos.* 4.113   Date?

Sheffield, John, Duke of Buckingham

1. The "*Sheffields* of their time." See GRANVILLE 1   1751
2. (*Lives* 2) Impartial "criticism . . . discovers him to be a writer that sometimes glimmers, but rarely shines, feebly laborious, and at best but pretty. His songs are upon common topicks; he hopes, and grieves, and repents, and despairs, and rejoices, like any other maker of little stanzas: to be great he hardly tries; to be gay is hardly in his power." (175.) "His verses are often insipid, but his memoirs are lively and agreeable; he had the perspicuity and elegance of an historian, but not the fire and fancy of a poet." (177)
                                                        Ptd. 1780
3. *Essay on Poetry.* "The precepts are judicious, sometimes new, and often happily expressed;" but weak lines, and negligence. *Lives* 2.176   Ptd. 1780
4. *The Vision.* "A licentious poem, such as was fashion-

able in those times, with little power of invention or propriety of sentiment." *Lives* 2.170   Ptd. 1780

Shenstone, William

1. *" 'I admire him [J.]' says Farmer, 'and I pity him.' Johnson has found something to object to in the character of every one who came under discussion. 'Hurd, for instance, comes off badly, and Shenstone still worse: he pitys you for your opinion of the latter, indeed what he takes from *you*, he gives to your better half— Mrs. Percy's judgment is, he assures me (when there has been an equal opportunity of information) much to be prefer'd to her husband's!' " *Percy-Farmer Correspondence*, Brit. Mus. Add. MSS 28222, p. 49. (Quoted in *Ballad Criticism in Scandinavia and Great Britain*, by S. B. Hustvedt, pp. 206-7)   cir. 1765

2. *J. "would not allow him to approach excellence as a poet," or admit that he had "some power of thinking." *Bos.* 5.267. (*Hebrides*, 29 Sept.)   1773

3. *"Shenstone was a man whose correspondence was an honour." *Bos.* 5.268. (*Hebrides*, 29 Sept.)   1773

4. "*Love Pastorals.*" *J. "said, he believed he had tried to read all his *Love Pastorals*, but did not get through them." Of a stanza quoted by B.: "That seems to be pretty." (cf. *infra* 8.) *Bos.* 5.267. (*Hebrides*, 29 Sept.)
1773

5. "The general recommendation of Shenstone is easiness and simplicity; his general defect is want of comprehension and variety. Had his mind been better stored with knowledge, whether he could have been great I know not; he could certainly have been agreeable." *Lives* 3.359   1781

6. *Elegies.* "His conception of an elegy he has in his Preface very judiciously and discriminately explained." (See Elegy 7.) "His compositions suit not ill to this description [of elegy]. His topicks of praise

are the domestick virtues, and his thoughts are pure and simple, but wanting combination they want variety. . . . His *Elegies* have therefore too much resemblance of each other." Lines "sometimes . . . smooth and easy," but not always. Diction "often harsh, improper, and affected; his words ill-coined or ill-chosen, and his phrase unskilfully inverted." *Lives* 3.355   1781

7. *"Levities."* "His *Levities* are by their title exempted from the severities of criticism; yet it may be remarked in a few words that his humour is sometimes gross, and seldom spritely." *Lives* 3.357-8   1781

8. *Lyric poems.* (*Lives* 3) "Are almost all of the light and airy kind, such as trip lightly and nimbly along, without the load of any weighty meaning." (355-6.) *Rural Elegance*, an exception. Though irregular lines, and verbosity, yet has "philosophical argument and poetical spirit." (356.) "Of the rest I cannot think any excellent; *The Skylark* pleases me best, which has, however, more of the epigram than of the ode." (356.) *Pastoral Ballad.* J. regrets it is pastoral. (See PASTORAL 15.) Two passages quoted, "to which if any mind denies its sympathy it has no acquaintance with love or nature."[1] (356-7)   1781

9. *Moral poems. Lives* 3.358   1781

10. *Schoolmistress, The.* See IMITATION 23   1781

11. *"Shenstone holds amongst poets the same rank your dog holds amongst dogs; he has not the sagacity of the hound, the docility of the spaniel, nor the courage of the bull-dog, yet he is still a pretty fellow." *John. Misc.* 2.5. (Hawkins's *Apophthegms*)   Date?

Sheridan, Mrs. Frances

1. *Memoirs of Miss Sidney Bidulph.* *"I know not, Madam, that you have a right, upon moral principles,

---

[1] One of these stanzas was quoted by Boswell. See *supra* 4

to make your readers suffer so much [from the distresses of the heroine]." *Bos.* 1.390   *cir.* 1761?

Sheridan, R. B.

1. *"He who has written the two best comedies of his age [probably *The Rivals* and *The Duenna* are meant], is surely a considerable man." *Bos.* 3.116   *cir.* 1777

Sheridan, Thomas

1. *"Of Sheridan's writings on Elocution, he [J.] said, they were a continual renovation of hope, and an unvaried succession of disappointments." *Wks.* 11. 197. (Hawkins's *Apophthegms*)   Date?

Sidney, Sir Philip

1. J. quotes from *Arcadia* (Bk. I) under "confection," (*Dict.* 1755) but wrongly attributes it to Shakespeare. *Notes and Queries*, 8th S., 3.255   1755
2. Anachronism in his *Arcadia:* "confounded the pastoral with the feudal times." *Shak. Pref.*, Raleigh, 22   1765

Skelton, John

1. "Cannot be said to have attained great elegance of language." *Dict.*, 1755. (*Hist. of the Eng. Lang.*)
                                                                               1755

Smart, Christopher[1]

1. *Compared with Derrick. See **Derrick** 3   Date?

Smith, Edmund

1. *Pocockius.* *J. calls Smith's Latin verses on Pococke, the traveller, his best verses. *Bos.* 3.269   1778
2. *Pocockius.* Latinity open to objection, but J. does not "know where to find it equalled among the modern

---

[1] J. "wrote for some months in *The Universal Visitor*, for poor Smart, while he was mad." *Bos.* 2.345

writers. It expresses with great felicity images not classical in classical diction: its digressions and returns have been deservedly recommended by Trapp as models for imitation." *Lives* 2.12 1779
3. (*Lives* 2) Qualified to inform the understanding, but less power to move passions. (17.) "He had great readiness and exactness of criticism, and by a cursory glance over a new composition would exactly tell all its faults and beauties." (19) 1779
4. *Phædra and Hippolitus*. J. sides with popular verdict against Addison's eulogy. See DRAMA 70 1779
5. *To the Memory of Mr. John Philips*. "A poem, which justice must place among the best elegies which our language can shew, an elegant mixture of fondness and admiration, of dignity and softness." Some passages too ludicrous. But "every human performance has its faults." *Lives* 2.16-17 1779

Smollett, Tobias[1]

1. *A proposed epitaph for S. scorned by J.:—"'An English inscription would be a disgrace to Dr. Smollett'. . . . We were then shewn a Latin inscription. . . . Dr. Johnson sat down with an ardent and liberal earnestness to revise it." J.'s revisions quoted by Boswell. *Bos.* 5.366-7. (*Hebrides*, 28 Oct.) 1773

Somerville, William

1. Though he has not "reached such excellence as to raise much envy, it may commonly be said at least that *he writes very well for a gentleman*. His serious pieces are sometimes elevated and his trifles are sometimes elegant. . . . His subjects are commonly such as require no great depth of thought or energy of expression." *Lives* 2.318-9 1781

---

[1] Smollett, in 1759, at Johnson's request, petitioned successfully for the discharge of the latter's negro servant, Francis Barber, who had gone to sea.

2. *The Chace.* (*Lives* 2) "To this poem praise cannot be totally denied." S. knows his subject, "which is the first requisite to excellence." Though the subject is uninteresting to common readers, "he has done all that transition and variety could easily effect, and has with great propriety enlarged his plan by the modes of hunting used in other countries. [319.] With still less judgement did he chuse blank verse as the vehicle of *Rural Sports.*" (See BLANK VERSE 17) 1781
3. *Minor verses. Lives* 2.319 1781

Sophocles

1. *Oedipus.* *"Johnson did not seem to think favourably of it. . . . Johnson said, 'Œdipus was a poor miserable man, subjected to the greatest distress, without any degree of culpability of his own.' " *John. Misc.* 2.62.(Cradock[1]) 1763
2. *Oedipus Tyrannus.* "Stands amidst the foremost of the classical productions of antiquity. Of tragical writing it has ever been esteemed the model and the master-piece." J. commends "the grandeur of the subject," "the dignity of the personages." "The design is of the most interesting and important nature, to inculcate a due moderation in our passions, and an implicit obedience to . . . providence. . . . So sublime a composition could not fail to secure the applause, and fix the admiration of ages. The philosopher is exercised in the contemplation of its deep and awful morality; the critic is captivated by its dramatic beauties, and the man of feeling is interested by those strokes of genuine passion which prevail in almost every page —which every character excites, and every new event tends to diversify in kind or in degree. The three grand unities of time, place, and action, are observed with scrupulous exactness." Dramatic construction highly

---

[1] Cradock is not wholly reliable as a *raconteur.* See *John. Misc.* 2.61 *n* 1, 62 *n* 3, and 64 *n* 2

praised: each part necessary and admirably connected. "The principal objection ... is, that the punishment of Œdipus is much more than adequate to his crimes." But his character "by no means so irreproachable as some have contended." The rules of tragic art scarcely permit that a perfectly virtuous man should be loaded with misfortunes. "Had Sophocles presented to our view a character less debased by vice, or more exalted by virtue, the end of his performance would have been frustrated; instead of agonizing compassion, he would have raised in us indignation unmixed, and horror unabated . . . our indignation would have been transferred from Œdipus to the gods themselves. . . . By making him criminal in a small degree, and miserable in a very great one, by investing him with some excellent qualities, and some imperfections, he at once inclines us to pity and to condemn. . . . This is the doctrine of Aristotle and of nature, and shews Sophocles to have had an intimate knowledge of the human heart, and the springs by which it is actuated. That his crimes and punishment still seem disproportionate, is not to be imputed as a fault to Sophocles, who proceeded only on the ancient and popular notion of Destiny; which we know to have been the basis of Pagan theology." *Poems and Miscellaneous Pieces* by Thomas Maurice, 1779, pp. 149-51. (*Preface*, unsigned, written by J. for Maurice, to the latter's translation of *Oedipus Tyrannus*) 1779

Spectator, The. (See also ADDISON 32 and STEELE 1)

1. *"Johnson praised *The Spectator*, particularly the character of Sir Roger de Coverley. He said, 'Sir Roger did not die a violent death, as has been generally fancied. He was not killed; he died only because others were to die, and because his death afforded an opportunity to Addison for some very fine writing. We have the example of Cervantes making Don Quixote die.—

I never could see why Sir Roger is represented as a little cracked. It appears to me that the story of the widow was intended to have something superinduced upon it: but the superstructure did not come.'" *Bos.* 2.370-1   1775

2. *"It is wonderful that there is such a proportion of bad papers, in the half of the work which was not written by Addison; for there was all the world to write that half, yet not a half of that half is good. One of the finest pieces in the English language is the paper on Novelty [No. 626, by Grove], yet we do not hear it talked of." Sees no merit in No. 364 on travel. *Bos.* 3.33-4   1776

3. (*Lives* 2) "Written with less levity" than *The Tatler*. (92.) This the first English attempt of its kind to set up an "*Arbiter elegantiarum,* a judge of propriety," etc. (93.) Historical review of English periodicals. (94.) Influence of *Tatler* and *Spectator* on conversation: as Addison said, they "taught the frolick and the gay to unite merriment with decency—an effect which they can never wholly lose, while they continue to be among the first books by which both sexes are initiated in the elegances of knowledge." (95.) To their strictures on manners "they superadded literature and criticism, and sometimes towered far above their predecessors; and taught, with great justness of argument and dignity of language, the most important duties and sublime truths. All these topicks were happily varied with elegant fictions and refined allegories, and illuminated with different changes of style and felicities of invention." (95-6.) Character of Sir Roger: J. questions if A. "ever filled up his original delineation." (97.) "Essays thus elegant, thus instructive, and thus commodiously distributed." (98)
Ptd. 1780

4. Eighth volume of *The Spectator*, "perhaps more valuable than any one of those that went before it." A.'s

power of humour not lessened, but his seriousness increased. *Lives* 2.107-8   Ptd. 1780
5. J. calls No. 290 (by Steele) in praise of Philips's *The Distrest Mother*, "none of the best." *Lives* 3.314. See also *ib.* 315   1781

Spence, Rev. Joseph

1. *J. agrees with Boswell's description of Spence as merely "a pretty scholar." Boswell, in a note on this, writes that according to Langton, J. highly respected Spence's judgement in criticism. *Bos.* 5.317. (*Hebrides*, 15 Oct.)   1773
2. "A man whose learning was not very great, and whose mind was not very powerful. His criticism, however, [of Pope's version of *Odyssey*] was commonly just; what he thought, he thought rightly, and his remarks were recommended by his coolness and candour. In him Pope had the first experience of a critic without malevolence, who thought it as much his duty to display beauties as expose faults; who censured with respect, and praised with alacrity." *Lives* 3.142-3. See also *ib.* 1.414 and POETRY 3   1781

Spenser, Edmund.

For imitations of Spenser and for criticism of the Spenserian stanza, see under IMITATION and VERSIFICATION

1. "Augustus still survives in Maro's strain,
   And Spenser's verse prolongs Eliza's reign."
   Bos. 1.149   1741?
2. *According to Hawkins, J. formed his style through study of Spenser and others. *Wks.* 1.97   *cir.* 1741
3. *Shepheardes Calender*, ("September"), attacked: "studied barbarity" of language in opening lines, coupled with theological subject. *Wks.* 5.241-2. (*Ram.* 37)   1750
4. J. drew 2.9% of the literary illustrations in his *Dictionary* (1755) from Spenser. See ADDISON 5   1755

5. His smoothness and harmony. See SHAKESPEARE 59 b
1765

Sprat, Thomas. For *The Rehearsal* in which he is supposed to have collaborated, see BUCKINGHAM

1. Imitates Cowley: "Nothing therefore but Pindarick liberty was to be expected. There is in his few [poetical] productions no want of such conceits as he thought excellent; and of those our judgement may be settled by the first that appears in his praise of Cromwell, where he says that Cromwell's 'fame, like man, will grow white as it grows old.' " Of his prose works: "each has its distinct and characteristical excellence." *Lives* 2.38   1779
2. *History of the Royal Society.* "One of the few books which selection of sentiment and elegance of diction have been able to preserve, though written upon a subject flux and transitory." *Lives* 2.33   1779
3. *Misc. works. Lives* 2.32-3   1779
4. *"The tinsel of Sprat disgusted him." *Wks.* 1.271. (Hawkins's *Life*)   Date?

Statius

1. Sometimes guilty of hyperbolical exaggerations. *Lives* 1.415   1779

Steele, Sir Richard. See also SPECTATOR and TATLER

1. *Steele's *Essays* "are too thin . . . for an Englishman's taste: mere superficial observations on life and manners, without erudition enough to make them keep, like the light French wines, which turn sour with standing a while for want of *body*, as we call it." *John. Misc.* 1.187. (Piozzi)   Date?

Stepney, George

1. The "Stepneys . . . of their time." See GRANVILLE
1751

2. "Apparently professed himself a poet." "A very licentious [free] translator, and does not recompense his neglect of the author by beauties of his own. In his original poems, now and then a happy line may perhaps be found, and now and then a short composition may give pleasure. But there is in the whole little either of the grace of wit, or the vigour of nature." *Lives* 1.311   1779

Sterne, Laurence[1]

1. *Goldsmith calls Sterne " 'a very dull fellow.' JOHNSON. 'Why, no, Sir.' " *Bos.* 2.222   1773
2. *"Nothing odd will do long. *Tristram Shandy* did not last." *Bos.* 2.449   1776
3. *Miss Monckton "insisted that some of Sterne's writings were very pathetick. Johnson bluntly denied it. 'I am sure (said she) they have affected *me.*' 'Why (said Johnson, smiling, and rolling himself about,) that is, because, dearest, you're a dunce.' " *Bos.* 4.109   1781
4. *Sermons.* *"I did read them, but it was in a stage-coach; I should not have even deigned to have looked at them, had I been at large." Cradock's *Memoirs*, ed. 1826, p. 208. (Quoted in *Bos.* 4.109 *n* 1)   Date?
5. *Sermons.* *"*There* [in Sherlock, etc.] you drink the cup of salvation to the bottom; here [in Sterne] you have merely the froth from the surface." *John. Misc.* 2.429   Date?

Suckling, Sir John

1. "The fashionable [metaphysical] style remained chiefly with Cowley: Suckling could not reach it, and Milton disdained it." *Lives* 1.22   1779

---

[1] According to Steevens, J. remarked: "I was but once in Sterne's company, and then his only attempt at merriment consisted in his display of a drawing too indecently gross to have delighted even in a brothel." *John. Misc.* 2.320. (" In Murray's *Johnsoniana*, ed. 1836, p. 133," comments Hill on this passage, "*Sterne* is changed into *Hume*.")

Swift, Jonathan
1. "And Swift expires a driv'ler and a show." *Wks.* 11. 341. (*Vanity of Human Wishes*)   Composed 1748
2. "*Every man* (says *Swift*) *is more able to explain the subject of an art than its professors*; . . . This could only have been said by such an exact observer of life, in gratification of malignity, or in ostentation of acuteness. Every hour produces instances of the necessity of terms of art." *Wks.* 8.280-1. (*Idl.* 70)   1759
3. *"Swift has a higher reputation than he deserves. His excellence is strong sense; for his humour, though very well, is not remarkably good." *Bos.* 1.452   1763
4. *"Johnson, as usual, treated him with little respect as an authour." *Bos.* 2.65   1768
5. *"Swift is clear, but he is shallow. In coarse humour, he is inferior to Arbuthnot; in delicate humour, he is inferior to Addison. So he is inferior to his contemporaries; without putting him against the whole world." *Bos.* 5.44. (*Hebrides*, 16 Aug.)   1773
6. *"He [J.] attacked Swift, as he used to do upon all occasions." *Bos.* 2.318   1775
7. (*Lives* 3) Judge Swift's powers by their effects. In Queen Anne's reign, "he turned the stream of popularity against the Whigs, and must be confessed to have dictated for a time the political opinions of the English nation." His immense benefits to Ireland: they date their prosperity from his interference in their affairs. (50.) (See *ib.* 43.) "In his other works [other than *Tale of a Tub*] is found an equable tenour of easy language, which rather trickles than flows. His delight was in simplicity." Few metaphors. These "seem to be received rather by necessity than choice. He studied purity; and though perhaps all his structures are not exact, yet it is not often that solecisms can be found: and whoever depends on his authority may generally conclude himself safe. His

sentences are never too much dilated or contracted; and it will not be easy to find any embarrassment in the complication of his clauses, any inconsequence in his connections, or abruptness in his transitions. His style was well suited to his thoughts, which are never subtilised by nice disquisitions, decorated by sparkling conceits, elevated by ambitious sentences, or variegated by far-sought learning.[1] He pays no court to the passions; he excites neither surprise nor admiration; he always understands himself, and his reader always understands him." Knowledge of common words and things alone necessary. Reader "is neither required to mount elevations nor to explore profundities; his passage is always on a level, along solid ground, without asperities, without obstruction. This easy and safe conveyance of meaning it was Swift's desire to attain, and for having attained he deserves praise, though perhaps not the highest praise." Best mode for purely didactic purposes:—to impart new information; "but against that inattention by which known truths are suffered to lie neglected it makes no provision; it instructs, but does not persuade." (51-2.) "A man . . . with that vigilance of minute attention which his works discover." (56.) Swift's "unnatural delight in ideas physically impure." (See Pope 18.) "IN the Poetical Works of Dr. Swift there is not much upon which the critic can exercise his powers. They are often humorous, almost always light, and have the qualities which recommend such compositions, easiness and gaiety. They are, for the most part, what their author intended. The diction is correct, the numbers are smooth, and the rhymes exact. There seldom occurs a hard-laboured expression or a redundant epithet; all his verses exemplify his own definition of a good style, they consist of 'proper words in proper places.' " (65.) Some pieces gross,

---

[1] cf. *Lives* 3.51 *n* 3: "The Rogue never hazards a figure."

some trifling. But S. must have known their faults, for he "certainly wrote often not to his judgement, but his humour." (66.) *His originality:* "perhaps no writer can easily be found that has borrowed so little, or that in all his excellences and all his defects has so well maintained his claim to be considered as original." (66) 1781

8. *The "extraordinary prejudice and dislike of Swift, manifested on all occasions by Johnson" communicated to him by his warm friend, Dr. Madden, according to Percy. *John. Misc.* 2.211-2 Date?
9. *J.'s "invariable custom" to speak disparagingly of Swift. *John. Misc.* 2.330-1. (Stockdale) Date?
10. *Conduct of the Allies.* *" 'Sir, his *Conduct of the Allies* is a performance of very little ability.' 'Surely, Sir, (said Dr. Douglas,) you must allow it has strong facts.' JOHNSON. 'Why yes, Sir; but what is that to the merit of the composition? In the Sessions-paper of the Old Bailey there are strong facts. Housebreaking is a strong fact; robbery is a strong fact; and murder is a *mighty* strong fact; but is great praise due to the historian of those strong facts? No, Sir. Swift has told what he had to tell distinctly enough, but that is all. He had to count ten, and he has counted it right. . . . Why, Sir, Tom Davies might have written *The Conduct of the Allies.*' " *Bos.* 2.65 1768
11. *Conduct of the Allies.* Its success. "Yet, surely, whoever surveys this wonder-working pamphlet with cool perusal will confess that its efficacy was supplied by the passions of its readers; that it operates by the mere weight of facts, with very little assistance from the hand that produced them." *Lives* 3.18-19 1781
12. *Examiner, The.* Swift has the advantage in argument, but in wit, "I am afraid none of Swift's papers will be found equal to those by which Addison opposed him." *Lives* 3.16 1781
13. *Gulliver's Travels.* *"The miserable beings, whom

SWIFT has in his travels so elegantly described, as *supremely cursed with immortality*." *Adv.* No. 39,[1] 1st ed. (See Courtney, *Bibliog.* 39)   1753

14. *Gulliver's Travels.* **Gulliver's Travels* inferior to *Tale of a Tub. John. Misc.* 2.331. (Stockdale)
    Cir. 1770

15. *Gulliver's Travels.* *"I wondered to hear him say of *Gulliver's Travels*, 'When once you have thought of big men and little men, it is very easy to do all the rest'. . . . Johnson at last, of his own accord, allowed very great merit to the inventory of articles found in the pocket of *the Man Mountain*, particularly the description of his watch, which it was conjectured was his GOD, as he consulted it upon all occasions." *Bos.* 2.319   1775

16. *Gulliver's Travels.* (*Lives* 3) "A production so new and strange that it filled the reader with a mingled emotion of merriment and amazement." Eagerly read by high and low. "Criticism was for a while lost in wonder: no rules of judgement were applied to a book written in open defiance of truth and regularity. But when distinctions came to be made the part which gave least pleasure was that which describes the Flying Island, and that which gave most disgust must be the history of the Houyhnhnms." (38.) "He that had formed those images [of the Yahoos] had nothing filthy to learn." (63)   1781

17. *Gulliver's Travels.* "Those small poems [of Gay's] that please least are the pieces to which *Gulliver* gave occasion; for who can much delight in the echo of an unnatural fiction?"[2] *Lives* 2.284   1781

18. *History of the Four Last Years of the Queen.* *J. does not find it in his humour to agree with a friend praising Swift's style. The gentleman insists "that there

---

[1] Attributed to J.
[2] cf. J. Warton's prophecy: "Gulliver in the next century, will be as obscure as Gargantua." *Essay on Pope*, 2.6.

are *strong facts* in the account of the *Four last Years of Queen Anne:* 'Yes surely Sir (replies Johnson), and so there are in the Ordinary of Newgate's account.' "[1]
John. Misc. 1.187-8. (Piozzi)   Date?

19. *Journal to Stella.* *"Swift corresponded minutely with Stella and Mrs. Dingley, on his importance with the ministry, from excessive vanity—that the women might exclaim, 'What a great man Dr. Swift is!' "
John. Misc. 2.331. (Stockdale)   *cir.* 1770

20. *Journal to Stella.* The propriety of publishing these "diurnal trifles" questionable. "They have, however, some odd attraction: the reader, finding frequent mention of names which he has been used to consider as important, goes on in hope of information; and, as there is nothing to fatigue attention, if he is disappointed he can hardly complain." *Lives* 3.23   1781

21. *Journal to Stella.* *"There is nothing wonderful in the journal which we see Swift kept in London, for it contains slight topicks, and it might soon be written."
Bos. 4.177   Date?

22. *Letters,* (in vol. of Pope's *Letters*). "Pope may be said to write always with his reputation in his head; Swift perhaps like a man who remembered that he was writing to Pope." *Lives* 3.160   1781

23. *Memoirs of . . . Scriblerus.* See POPE 46   1781

24. *Miscellaneous prose tracts.* Briefly criticized. *Lives* 3.12, 13, 14, 19, 20, 48   1781

25. *Proposal for Correcting . . . the English Tongue,* etc. J. takes issue with Swift, in the latter's "petty treatise on the *English* language." *Wks.* 9.225. (*Pref. Dict.*)   1755

26. *Proposal for Correcting . . . the English Tongue,* etc. "Written without much knowledge of the general nature of language, and without any accurate enquiry into the history of other tongues." Stability of Acad-

---

[1] J. seems to doubt its authenticity in the *Lives* (3.27-8).

emy proposed by Swift, contrary to all experience. *Lives* 3.16   1781

27. *Tale of a Tub.* *"I doubt whether *The Tale of a Tub* be his; for he never owned it, and it is much above his usual manner." *Bos.* 1.452   1763

28. *Tale of a Tub.* *"I doubt if the *Tale of a Tub* was his: it has so much more thinking, more knowledge, more power, more colour, than any of the works which are indisputably his. If it was his, I shall only say, he was *impar sibi*." *Bos.* 5.44. (*Hebrides*, 16 Aug.) 1773

29. *Tale of a Tub.* *"*The Tale of a Tub* [said J.] is so much superiour to his other writings, that one can hardly believe he was the authour of it: 'there is in it such a vigour of mind, such a swarm of thoughts, so much of nature, and art, and life.'" *Bos.* 2.318-9   1775

30. *Tale of a Tub.* J. quotes Blackmore's attack on *Tale of a Tub*, and prefaces the quotation: "In these essays he [Blackmore] took little care to propitiate the wits, for he scorns to avert their malice at the expence of virtue or of truth." *Lives* 2.247   Ptd. 1780

31. *Tale of a Tub.* (*Lives* 3) "Charity may be persuaded to think that it might be written by a man of a peculiar character, without ill intention; but it is certainly of dangerous example." (10.) "This wild work." (10.) J. raises some doubts as to S.'s authorship of it. (10.) "The digressions relating to Wotton and Bentley must be confessed to discover want of knowledge or want of integrity.... But Wit can stand its ground against Truth only a little while." (11)   1781

32. *Tale of a Tub.* *"Johnson attributed the Tale of a Tub to Arbuthnot. He thought Swift not equal to it." (MS. note by Mr. Hussey in *Bos. John. Misc.* 1.374 *n*)   Date?

33. *According to Stockdale, J. said "that if Swift was really the author of *The Tale of a Tub*, as the best of his other performances were of a very inferior merit,

he should have hanged himself after he had written it." *Memoirs*, ed. 1809, 2.61. (Quoted in *Bos.* 1.452 n 2) Date?

Tacitus

1. *J. agrees with Boswell, that in spite of his acuteness, and his "terseness of expression, he was too compact, too much broken into hints, as it were, and therefore too difficult to be understood. . . . 'Tacitus, Sir, seems to me rather to have made notes for an historical work, than to have written a history.' " *Bos.* 2.189 1772

Tasso

1. Works commended. See ITALIAN LITERATURE 1 1755
2. *J. finds fault with a simile. *Bos.* 3.330 1778
3. *Gerusalemme Liberata.* Its supernatural machinery causes more curiosity than terrour: we know the outcome. *Lives* 1.386 1779
4. *Aminta.* "Easily imitated, and unworthy of imitation." See PASTORAL 14 1781

Tatler, The. See also under SPECTATOR and STEELE

1. J. to Mrs. Thrale: "Do you read the Tatlers? They are part of the books which every body should read, because they are the sources of conversation, therefore make them part of your library." *Letters* 2.352 1783

Temple, Sir William

1. *"Sir William Temple was the first writer who gave cadence to English prose. Before his time they were careless of arrangement, and did not mind whether a sentence ended with an important word or an insignificant word, or with what part of speech it was concluded." *Bos.* 3.257 1778

2. *"He [J.] once told me, that he had formed his style upon that of Sir William Temple, and upon Chambers's Proposal for his *Dictionary*." But Boswell thinks J. must have been mistaken—his style unlike Temple's. *Bos.* 1.218-9 . Date?

Theobald, Lewis

1. "My esteem of these critics." (Warburton and Theobald.) *Wks.* 14.74 1745
2. Warburton would "make two-and-fifty Theobalds, cut into slices!" See WARBURTON 6 *cir.* 1758?
3. "A man of narrow comprehensions and small acquisitions, with no native and intrinsick splendour of genius, with little of the artificial light of learning," but accurate and diligent. *Shak. Pref.*, Raleigh, 45 1765
4. "A man of heavy diligence, with very slender powers, first, in a book called *Shakespeare Restored*, and then in a normal edition, detected his [Pope's] deficiencies with all the insolence of victory." *Lives* 3.138 1781
5. "Poor Theobald, whom he [Pope in *Dunciad*] accused of ingratitude, but whose real crime was supposed to be that of having revised Shakespeare more happily than himself." *Lives* 3.145-6 1781
6. Pope in revised *Dunciad* gives to Cibber "the old books, the cold pedantry and sluggish pertinacity of Theobald." *Lives* 3.186 1781

Theocritus

1. His pastorals compared with Virgil's. See VIRGIL 12 a 1753
2. The "superior delicacy" of Theocritus to Pope questioned. See POPE 61 1756
3. *"Theocritus is not deserving of very high respect as a writer; as to the pastoral part, Virgil is very evidently superiour. He wrote when there had been a larger influx of knowledge into the world than when

Theocritus lived. Theocritus does not abound in description, though living in a beautiful country: the manners painted are coarse and gross. Virgil has much more description, more sentiment, more of Nature, and more of art." *The Dioscuri* (Idyl XXII, ed. Lang), particularly commended. "*The Sicilian Gossips* is a piece of merit." *Bos.* 4.2. (Langton's *Collection*) Date?

Thomson, James[1]

1. *"Thompson [*sic*], I think, had as much of the poet about him as most writers. Every thing appeared to him through the medium of his favourite pursuit. He could not have viewed those two candles burning but with a poetical eye." *Bos.* 1.453   1763
2. *"He allowed high praise to Thomson as a poet," but attacked his private character. *Bos.* 2.63   1768
3. *"Thomson had a true poetical genius, the power of viewing every thing in a poetical light. His fault is such a cloud of words sometimes, that the sense can hardly peep through." J. tells of reading Thomson aloud to Shiels, who expresses admiration. Whereupon J. announces: "Well, Sir . . . I have omitted every other line." *Bos.* 3.37   1776
4. (*Lives* 3) Thomson's early "poetically splendid" diction. (282.) "It may be doubted whether he was, either by the bent of nature or habits of study, much qualified for tragedy. It does not appear that he had much sense of the pathetick, and his diffusive and descriptive style produced declamation rather than dialogue." (293.) "As a writer he is entitled to one praise of the highest kind: his mode of thinking and of expressing his thoughts is original." (298.) His blank verse unlike Milton's or any other poet's. "His numbers, his pauses, his diction, are of his own growth, without transcription, without imitation . . . he

---

[1] Recommended by J. for the *English Poets. Bos.* 3.109

thinks always as a man of genius;" and sees with the eye of a poet. (See POETRY 41.) Blank verse properly used in *Seasons:* his thought would have been obstructed by rhyme. (See BLANK VERSE 18.) (298-9.) "The highest praise which he has received ought not to be supprest;" given by Lord Lyttelton:
"his works contained
'No line which, dying, he could wish to blot.'"
(301.) Mallet copies Thomson's diction. "He has Thomson's beauties and his faults." (401) 1781

5. *Castle of Indolence.* "Which was many years under his hand, but was at last finished with great accuracy. The first canto opens a scene of lazy luxury, that fills the imagination." *Lives* 3.293-4 1781

6. *Liberty.* (*Lives* 3) Thomson thinks it his noblest work, but Liberty's "praises were condemned to harbour spiders, and to gather dust; none of Thomson's performances were so little regarded. The judgement of the publick was not erroneous; the recurrence of the same images must tire in time; and enumeration of examples to prove a position which nobody denied, as it was from the beginning superfluous, must quickly grow disgusting." (289.) "*Liberty,* when it first appeared, I tried to read, and soon desisted. I have never tried again, and therefore will not hazard either praise or censure." (301) 1781

7. *Prologue to Mallet's "Mustapha".* "Not mean, but far inferior to that which he had received from Mallet for *Agamemnon." Lives* 3.406 1781

8. *Seasons, The.* (*Lives* 3) "The reader of *The Seasons* wonders that he never saw before what Thomson shews him, and that he never yet has felt what Thomson impresses. His is one of the works in which blank verse seems properly used." (See BLANK VERSE 18.) "His descriptions of extended scenes and general effects bring before us the whole magnificence of Nature, whether pleasing or dreadful. The gaiety of

Spring, the splendour of *Summer*, the tranquillity of *Autumn*, and the horror of *Winter*, take in their turns possession of the mind. The poet . . . imparts to us so much of his own enthusiasm that our thoughts expand with his imagery and kindle with his sentiments." Appeals also to the naturalist. (299.) "The great defect of *The Seasons* is want of method." This seems inevitable in description of natural objects. (See DESCRIPTION 8.) *Diction*. "His diction is in the highest degree florid and luxuriant, such as may be said to be to his images and thoughts 'both their lustre and their shade'; such as invests them with splendour, through which perhaps they are not always easily discerned. It is too exuberant, and sometimes may be charged with filling the ear more than the mind." (300.) These poems "improved in general" by subsequent revisions, "yet I know not whether they have not lost part of what Temple calls their *race*, a word which, applied to wines, in its primitive sense, means the flavour of the soil." (300-1.) *Winter*, "being of a new kind, few would venture at first to like, by degrees gained upon the publick." (285)   1781

9. *Tragedies. Lives* 3.288, 291, 293   1781

Thornton, Bonnell

1. *Ode on St. Cæcilia's Day.* (A burlesque.) *"Johnson praised its humour, and seemed much diverted with it." *Bos.* 1.420   1763

Tickell, Richard

1. *Project, The.* *"Sir, it has no power. Were it not for the well-known names with which it is filled, it would be nothing: the names carry the poet, not the poet the names." *Bos.* 3.318   1778

Tickell, Thomas

1. *As a biographer:* J. questions the utility of "the only circumstance by which Tickell has distinguished Ad-

dison from the rest of mankind, *the irregularity of his pulse.*" *Wks.* 5.385. (*Ram.* 60) 1750

2. "To Tickell, however, cannot be refused a high place among the minor poets; nor should it be forgotten that he was one of the contributors to *The Spectator.*" *Lives* 2.311 Ptd. 1780

3. *Epistle . . . to a Gentleman at Avignon.* "Stands high among party-poems: it expresses contempt without coarseness, and superiority without insolence. It had the success which it deserved, being five times printed." *Lives* 2.310 Ptd. 1780

4. *Iliad, Translation of.* (First book.) "The palm is now given universally to Pope; but I think the first lines of Tickell's were rather to be preferred." *Lives* 2.309 Ptd. 1780

5. *Kensington Garden.* "The versification is smooth and elegant, but the fiction unskilfully compounded of Grecian Deities and Gothick Fairies." See MYTHOLOGY 19 Ptd. 1780

6. *Minor pieces. Lives* 2.305, 307 Ptd. 1780

7. *On the Prospect of Peace.* J. thinks it unequal to the praise it received from Addison. "A piece to be approved rather than admired. But the hope excited by a work of genius, being general and indefinite, is rarely gratified." *Lives* 2.306-7 Ptd. 1780

8. *To Mr. Addison, on his Opera of Rosamond.* "They contain some of the most elegant encomiastick strains; and, among the innumerable poems of the same kind, it will be hard to find one with which they need to fear a comparison." *Lives* 2.305 Ptd. 1780

9. *To the Earl of Warwick, on the Death of Mr. Addison.* "Neither he nor Addison ever produced nobler lines than are contained in the third and fourth paragraphs, nor is a more sublime or more elegant funeral poem to be found in the whole compass of English literature." *Lives* 2.310 Ptd. 1780

Townley, James

1. *High Life Below Stairs.* *"Here is a Farce, which is really very diverting when you see it acted; and yet one may read it, and not know that one has been reading anything at all." *Bos.* 4.7. (Langton's *Collection*)
                                                                Date?

Trapp, Joseph

1. His *Prælectiones Poeticæ* recommended by J. for teaching the art of poetry. See POETRY 3   1748
2. *Aeneid, Translation of.* "His book may continue its existence as long as it is the clandestine refuge of schoolboys." *Lives* 1.453   1779

Tucker, Josiah. (Dean of Gloucester)

1. *"I look upon the Dean of Gloucester to be one of the few excellent writers of this period. I differ from him in opinion,"[1] etc. "He said he knew nobody whose style was more perspicuous, manly, and vigorous, or better suited to his subject." *John. Misc.* 2.187. (Hannah More)   1776

Vanbrugh, Sir John

1. *Provok'd Husband, The.* (In collaboration with Cibber.) *Goldsmith's *Good-natured Man* "the best comedy that had appeared since *The Provoked Husband*." *Bos.* 2.48   1768
2. *Provok'd Husband, The.* *"Even Sir Francis Wronghead is a character of manners, though drawn with great humour." (For context, in which J. distinguishes between characters of manners and of nature, see RICHARDSON 2.) *Bos.* 2.50   1768

Vida

1. His elegance referred to. *Wks.* 6.132. (*Ram.* 92)
                                                                1751

---

[1] He wrote tracts in favour of the American colonies.

Virgil. See also ANCIENT WRITERS
1. "Owed so much of his success to art and labour." *Wks.* 6.132. (*Ram.* 92) 1751
2. *Versification.* In the use of "representative metre," V. not less happy "than in the other graces of versification." See VERSIFICATION 8 1751
3. *Versification.* Examples of "representative metre" in Virgil. Blind reverence of the ancients, however, sometimes imagines such beauties. See VERSIFICATION 9 1751
4. *Love of fine words. See OVID 2 1784
5. *Aeneid.* Ornament in epic openings justified (see OPENING OF A WORK 2): the "dignity and magnificence" of the *Aeneid's* opening verses. *Wks.* 7.112. (*Ram.* 158) 1751
6. *Eclogues.* Example of ideas improper to pastoral from *Eclogue* VIII. *Wks.* 5.242. (*Ram.* 37) 1750
7. *Eclogues.* "The Pollio of Virgil, with all its elevation, is a composition truly bucolick, though rejected by the criticks; for all the images are either taken from the country, or from the religion of the age common to all parts of the empire." The *Silenus*—a disputable example of pastoral. "Neither can it well be defended as a fiction." *Wks.* 5.243. (*Ram.* 37) 1750
8. *Eclogues.* *"All the modern languages . . . cannot furnish so melodious a line as
'Formosam resonare doces Amaryllida silvas.' "
(*Eclogue* I.5.) *Bos.* 1.460 1763
9. *Eclogues.* *"The *Eclogues* I have almost all by heart." *Bos.* 4.218 1783
10. *Georgics.* *"The *Georgicks* did not give me so much pleasure [as did reading the *Aeneid*], except the fourth book." *Bos.* 4.218 1783
11. *Pastorals.* For a model for pastoral poetry, J. goes to Virgil, "from whose opinion it will not appear very safe to depart, if we consider that every advantage of

nature, and of fortune, concurred to complete his productions; that he was born with great accuracy and severity of judgment, enlightened with all the learning of one of the brightest ages, and embellished with the elegance of the Roman court; that he employed his powers rather in improving, than in inventing, and therefore must have endeavoured to recompense the want of novelty by exactness." *Wks.* 5.238-9. (*Ram.* 37. For an examination of pastoral poetry, in the light of a definition drawn from Virgil, see PASTORAL 2)

1750

12. *Pastorals.* (*Wks.* 9.68-76 [*Adv.* 92]) [a] His *Pastorals* examined "without any inquiry how far my sentiments deviate from established rules or common opinions": V. can hardly claim the praise of an inventor. "Greater splendour of diction, and elevation of sentiment" than in the pastorals of Theocritus, but less simplicity: "perhaps, where he excells *Theocritus*, he sometimes obtains his superiority by deviating from the pastoral character, and performing what *Theocritus* never attempted." However, J. agrees with Horace in applauding V.'s "elegance and sweetness." In all his pastorals is "a strain of versification which it is vain to seek in any other poet;" but all except the first and tenth, open "to considerable objections." (68-70.) [b] *Second pastoral:* "Though we should forget the great charge against it, which I am afraid can never be refuted, might, I think, have perished, without any diminution of the praise of its author; for I know not that it contains one affecting sentiment or pleasing description, or one passage that strikes the imagination or awakens the passions." (70.) [c] *Third Pastoral.* The quarrel carried on with "sprightliness and elegance," but the invectives "are too much degraded from the dignity of pastoral innocence." (70.) [d] *Fourth Pastoral.* "Splendid and pleasing" images, and "grandeur of language worthy of the first

of *Roman* poets" but supported by a wild fiction. (70.) [e] *Fifth Pastoral*. A model for pastoral elegies, yet "most of the images are of the mythological kind, and, therefore, easily invented; and . . . there are few sentiments of rational praise or natural lamentation." (71.) [f] *Sixth Pastoral*. "Rises to the dignity of philosophick sentiments and heroic poetry. The address to *Varus* is eminently beautiful." But "the fiction of *Silenus* seems injudicious," since Virgil mingles with it contemporary allusion. (71.) [g] *Seventh Pastoral*. "Not without some reproach to his inventive power," for similar in plan to the third pastoral. The prize adjudged without apparent reason. (71.) [h] *Eighth Pastoral*. Little more than a translation. (71.) [i] *Ninth Pastoral*. Contains, except for a few personal lines, "nothing that seems appropriated to any time or place, or of which any other use can be discovered than to fill up the poem." (72.) [j] *First and Tenth Pastorals*. "Sufficient to place their author above the reach of rivalry." Natural sentiments and "the genuine language of despair" in the tenth. J. prefers first pastoral, however, "which is equally natural and more diversified."[1] "The description of *Virgil's* happiness in his little farm, combines almost all the images of rural pleasure; and he, therefore, that can read it with indifference, has no sense of pastoral poetry." These two pastorals based on real occurrences. "The most artful fiction must give way to truth." (72-6)   1753

13. *Pastorals*. "In this week I read Virgil's *Pastorals*. I learned to repeat the *Pollio* and *Gallus*. I read carelessly the first *Georgick*." *Bos*. 2.288   1774

14. *Pastorals*. *His *Pastoral* writings compared with those of Theocritus. See THEOCRITUS 3   Date?

---

[1] One of J.'s juvenile compositions is a translation, in part, of this pastoral. See *Bos*. 1.51

Virgil. (Compared with Homer)

15. "The warmest admirers of the great *Mantuan* poet can extol him for little more than the skill with which he has, by making his hero both a traveller and a warrior, united the beauties of the *Iliad* and *Odyssey* in one composition: yet his judgment was perhaps sometimes overborn by his avarice of the *Homeric* treasures; and, for fear of suffering a sparkling ornament to be lost, he has inserted it where it cannot shine with its original splendor." e.g., Ajax's silent repulse of the advances made by Ulysses in the infernal regions appropriate to his character; but Dido's similar repulse of Aeneas in imitation of this, wholly out of keeping with her character. Thus Virgil "seduced by imitation." *Wks.* 6. 323-4. (*Ram.* 121)   1751

16. *"He said, the dispute as to the comparative excellence of Homer or Virgil was inaccurate. 'We must consider (said he) whether Homer was not the greatest poet, though Virgil may have produced the finest poem. Virgil was indebted to Homer for the whole invention of the structure of an epick poem, and for many of his beauties.'"[1] *Bos.* 3.193-4   1777

17. "The discriminative excellence of Homer is elevation and comprehension of thought, and that of Virgil is grace and splendor of diction. The beauties of Homer are therefore difficult to be lost, and those of Virgil difficult to be retained. The massy trunk of sentiment is safe by its solidity, but the blossoms of elocution easily drop away." e.g., the *Georgics* and the *Aeneid* lose in translation. *Lives* 1.447-8   1779

18. *J. has "great delight" in reading the *Aeneid* through, a book a night. "I do not think the story of the *Æneid* interesting. I like the story of the *Odyssey* much better; and this not on account of the wonderful things which it contains; for there are wonderful things

[1] For a debate between Johnson and Burke in which Johnson talked his best for Homer, and Burke for Virgil, see *ib.* 193, *n* 3

enough in the *Æneid*;—the ships of the Trojans turned to sea-nymphs,—the tree at Polydorus's tomb dropping blood. The story of the *Odyssey* is interesting, as a great part of it is domestick." *Bos.* 4.218-9   1783

Voiture, V.

1. The "despicable [epistolary] remains of *Voiture* and *Scarron*." *Wks.* 7.70. (*Ram.* 152)   1751

Voltaire

1. The King of Prussia's "skill in poetry and in the French language have been loudly praised by Voltaire, a judge without exception, if his honesty were equal to his knowledge." *Wks.* 4.536-7   1756
2. Referring to Voltaire: "It is the great failing of a strong imagination to catch greedily at wonders. He was misinformed, and was perhaps unwilling to learn, by a second enquiry, a truth less splendid and amusing." *Wks.* 4.556   1756
3. Example of petty Shakespearean criticism. See DENNIS 1   1765
4. Lack of understanding of Shakespeare's plan. *Shak. Pref.*, Raleigh, 18   1765
5. "Such censures [for violation of the "unities"] are suitable to the minute and slender criticism of *Voltaire*." *Shak. Pref.*, Raleigh, 29. See also *ib.* 33: an answer to Voltaire's expression of wonder that the English should prefer Shakespeare's "extravagances" to *Cato*.   1765
6. *"Has not stood his trial yet." See FRENCH LITERATURE 2   1773
7. *Histoire de Louis XIV*. *J. commends his method of collecting materials for this history. *Bos.* 5.393. (*Hebrides*, 11 Nov.)   1773
8. *"'Vir est acerrimi ingenii et paucarum literarum.'" *Bos.* 2.406. See also *John. Misc.* 2.308   1775

9. *Candide.* *"He said *Candide* he thought had more power in it than anything that Voltaire had written." *Bos.* 3.356   1778
10. "Voltaire, who loved a striking story, has told what he could not find to be true [in his *Siècle de Louis XV*]." *Bos.* 3.414   1779
11. *J.'s comment on the assertion that Voltaire, Rousseau and Hume are less read than formerly:—"All infidel writers drop into oblivion, when personal connections and the floridness of novelty are gone; though now and then a foolish fellow, who thinks he can be witty upon them, may bring them again into notice." *Bos.* 4.288   1784
12. *"Dr. Johnson used to think Voltaire's *Life of Charles XII of Sweden* one of the finest pieces of historical writing in any language." *John. Misc.* 2.306. (Seward. See also *Wks.* 11.204)   Date?
13. *"Voltaire, he said, was a good narrator, and that his principal merit consisted in a happy selection and arrangement of circumstances." *Bos.* 2.125. (Maxwell's *Collectanea*)   Date?

Waller, Edmund

1. Waller often attempted the "easy" style, but seldom successfully, "for he is too frequently driven into transpositions." *Wks.* 8.311. (*Idl.* 77)   1759
2. Cowley has many noble lines "such as the feeble care of Waller never could produce." *Lives* 1.59-60   1779
3. (*Lives* 1) His first poetic attempt "justifies the observation made by one of his editors, that he attained, by a felicity like instinct, a style which perhaps will never be obsolete. . . . His versification was in his first essay such as it appears in his last performance." Early formed "such a system of metrical harmony as he never afterwards much needed or much endeavoured to improve." (250-1.) W. "not so liberally supplied with grand as with soft images; for beauty

is more easily found than magnanimity." (283.) Delicacy; "certain nicety and caution;" seldom ludicrous or familiar. "He seems always to do his best, though his subjects are often unworthy of his care." (283.) "Genius now and then produces a lucky trifle." e.g., *To Amoret*, *On Love*, "which their excellency ought to secure from oblivion." (284.) In others of his "little poems" "sometimes his thoughts are deficient, and sometimes his expression." Verse not always musical. (284.) A "popular" poet: no abstruse images; understandable. (284.) "His thoughts are sometimes hyperbolical, and his images unnatural." (285.) Images of gallantry sometimes indelicate. (286.) Other faults: too remote applications, thought over-expanded, images not always distinct. (286.) "His sallies of casual flattery are sometimes elegant and happy . . . and sometimes empty and trifling." (287.) *Versification:* "As much of Waller's reputation was owing to the softness and smoothness of his numbers, it is proper to consider those minute particulars to which a versifier must attend." Excelled his contemporaries in smoothness, but "rather smooth than strong. [See also *ib.* 419.] . . . The critical decision has given the praise of strength to Denham, and of sweetness to Waller." (293. See also *Idler* 60 for Dick Minim's similar decision.) *Faults:* (See VERSIFICATION 20.) *General character of his poetry:* "elegance and gaiety. He is never pathetick, and very rarely sublime. He seems neither to have had a mind much elevated by nature, nor amplified by learning. His thoughts are such as a liberal conversation and large acquaintance with life would easily supply. They had however then, perhaps, that grace of novelty, which they are now often supposed to want by those who, having already found them in later books, do not know or enquire who produced them first. This treatment is unjust. Let not the original author lose by his imitators." (294-5.)

W. borrowed too much from the old mythology. (See MYTHOLOGY 10.) *Summary:* "But of the praise of Waller, though much may be taken away, much will remain, for it cannot be denied that he added something to our elegance of diction, and something to our propriety of thought." (296)   1779
4. Granville "copied the wrong as well as the right from his masters, and may be supposed to have learned . . . mythology from Waller." *Lives* 2.290

                                                                Ptd. 1780
5. W.'s descriptive art excelled by Pope. *Lives* 3.225

                                                                         1781
6. *Miscellaneous poems* briefly reviewed. *Lives* 1.250, 269-71, 276, 286-90, and AMOROUS VERSES 2   1779
7. *Panegyric to my Lord Protector.* Highly praised, not unjustly. "Such a series of verses had rarely appeared before in the English language." Lines: some grand, some graceful, all musical. Occasional feeble verse or trifling thought "but its great fault is the choice of its hero." *Lives* 1.289   1779
8. *Sacred poems.* The work of his old age. His poetical powers at eighty-two unimpaired, but the nature of their subject against them. See SACRED POETRY 4

                                                                         1779

Walsh, William

1. "The observation [on letter-writing] with which *Walsh* has introduced his pages of inanity, are such as give him little claim to the rank assigned him by *Dryden* among the criticks."[1] *Wks.* 7.71. (*Ram.* 152)

                                                                         1751
2. "To his Poems and Letters is prefixed a very judicious preface upon Epistolary Composition and Amorous Poetry." *Lives* 1.330   1779

---

[1] Hill notes: "In the reprint of the Preface in *Eng. Poets,* xvii. 333, these 'pages of inanity' have disappeared." *Lives* 1.330 *n* 4

3. "He is known more by his familiarity with greater men, than by anything done or written by himself . . . in all his writings there are pleasing passages. He has however more elegance than vigour, and seldom rises higher than to be pretty." *Lives* 1.330
 1779
4. "The sublime and pathetick Mr. Walsh." (J. is evidently ironical.) *Letters* 2.178 1780
5. His letters "seem written as exercises, and were never sent to any living mistress or friend." *Lives* 3.159
 1781
6. "A name yet preserved among the minor poets." *Lives* 3.93 1781

Walton, Izaak

1. J. once had the design of reviving Walton. See J.'s letter to the Rev. Dr. Horne, Apr. 30, 1774, printed in *Catalogue of the Johnsonian Collection of R. B. Adam.*
 ante 1774
2. *"He was a great panegyrist." *Bos.* 2.364 1775
3. *Lives.* "He talked of Isaac Walton's *Lives*, which was one of his most favourite books. Dr. *Donne's Life*, he said, was the most perfect of them." *Bos.* 2.363 1775

Warburton, William

1. *W.'s controversy with Crousaz.* J. deplores personal invectives used by both. *Wks.* 9.365. (See also Crousaz) 1743
2. "The learned Mr. *Warburton.*" *Wks.* 14.61. (*Observ. on Macb.*) 1745
3. "My esteem of these critics." (W. and Theobald.) *Wks.* 14.74 1745
4. *J. objects to placing Edwards, author of *The Canons of Criticism*, upon a level with Warburton: "Nay, (said Johnson,) he has given him some smart hits to be sure; but there is no proportion between the two men;

they must not be named together. A fly, Sir, may sting a stately horse and make him wince; but one is but an insect, and the other is a horse still." *Bos.* 1.263 *n* 3 by Boswell. See also *Shak. Pref.*, Raleigh, 49-50, for a similar comment upon the relative value of the two authors. *cir.* 1747

5. *As editor of Shakespeare:* "Detained by more important studies" from the elucidation of obscure passages. Warburton not less diligent or successful than Pope in his observation of faults and beauties in Shakespeare. But J. questions the value of such annotation. (See CRITICISM 38.) *Shak. Proposals*, Raleigh, 6-7
cir. 1756

6. *Dr. Burney to J.:—" 'But you think, Sir, that Warburton is a superiour critick to Theobald?' 'O, Sir, he'd make two-and-fifty Theobalds, cut into slices! The worst of Warburton is, that he has a rage for saying something, when there's nothing to be said.' " *Bos.* 1.329 *cir.* 1758?

7. Has "so much learning and sagacity." *Shak.* 6.186 *n* 1
1765

8. His "genius and learning," but J. attacks him as Shakespearean editor. *Shak. Pref.*, Raleigh, 47 1765

9. *As editor of Shakespeare.* Of a long note by W. on *Hamlet*, J. remarks: "This is a noble emendation, which almost sets the critick on a level with the authour." *Shak.* 8.188 *n* 6 1765

10. *J. tells George III that "he had not read much, compared with Dr. Warburton." *Bos.* 2.36 1767

11. *J. defends W. against Goldsmith. " 'Warburton,' said he [J.], 'may be absurd, but he will never be weak: he *flounders* well.' " *John. Misc.* 2.331. (Stockdale) *cir.* 1770

12. *"He has great knowledge,—great power of mind. Hardly any man brings greater variety of learning to

bear upon his point." *Bos.* 5.81. (*Hebrides*, 21 Aug.) 1773

13. *"When I read Warburton first, and observed his force, and his contempt of mankind, I thought he had driven the world before him; but I soon found that was not the case; for Warburton, by extending his abuse, rendered it ineffectual." *Bos.* 5.93. (*Hebrides*, 23 Aug.) 1773

14. J. refers to W. as "a great writer," quoting his opinion on Addison, however, as too extreme. *Lives* 2.127 Ptd. 1780

15. J. disagrees with W.'s criticism. *Lives* 2.145 and *n*; 3.99, 245, 271 1780-1

16. His analysis of Pope's *Essay on Criticism*. See POPE 26 1781

17. "Dr. Warburton, who excelled in critical perspicacity, has remarked that the preternatural agents are very happily adapted to the purposes of the poem [*Rape of the Lock*]." J. supports this view. *Lives* 3.233 1781

18. (*Lives* 3) "About this time [soon after Crousaz attacked Pope's *Essay on Man*] Warburton began to make his appearance in the first ranks of learning. He was a man of vigorous faculties, a mind fervid and vehement, supplied by incessant and unlimited enquiry, with wonderful extent and variety of knowledge, which yet had not oppressed his imagination nor clouded his perspicacity. To every work he brought a memory full fraught, together with a fancy fertile of original combinations, and at once exerted the powers of the scholar, the reasoner, and the wit. But his knowledge was too multifarious to be always exact, and his pursuits were too eager to be always cautious." His "haughty confidence" unconcealed. Adversaries treated with contemptuous superiority. "He seems to have adopted the Roman Emperor's determination, 'oderint dum metuant'; he used no allurements of gentle language, but wished to compel rather than per-

suade. His style is copious without selection, and forcible without neatness; he took the words that presented themselves: his diction is coarse and impure, and his sentences are unmeasured." (165-6.) Supplied the best notes to Theobald's edition of Shakespeare. (167.) Changes from attacker to defender of Pope: J. defends this as not necessarily hypocrisy: "surely to think differently at different times of poetical merit may be easily allowed." (167)   1781

19. *"If . . . I had written with hostility of Warburton in my *Shakspeare*, I should have quoted this couplet:—

'Here Learning, blinded first and then beguil'd,
Looks dark as Ignorance, as Fancy wild.'

You see they'd have fitted him to a *T*,' (smiling.)"¹ *Bos.* 4.288   1784

20. *"Of Warburton he always spoke well. He gave me, says he, his good word, when it was of use to me." *John. Misc.* 2.7. (Hawkins's *Apophthegms*. See also *Wks.* 11.213 for similar statement)   Date?

21. *"When a Scotsman was talking against Warburton, Johnson said he had more literature than had been imported from Scotland since the days of Buchanan." *John. Misc.* 2.15. (Hawkins's *Apophthegms*)   Date?

22. *"To Warburton's great powers he [J.] did full justice. He did not always, my brother says, agree with him in his notions; 'but,' said he, 'with all his errors, *si non errasset, fecerat ille minus.*'" *John. Misc.* 2.140-1. (Miss Hawkins)   Date?

23. *J. admires him, but cannot bear his style. *Bos.* 4.48   Date?

24. *"The table is always full, Sir. He brings things from the north, and the south, and from every quarter." *Bos.* 4.48   Date?

25. *"Warburton is perhaps the last man who has written

---

¹ J., however, in his *Shakespeare* often ridicules W.'s notes.

with a mind full of reading and reflection." *Bos.* 4.49
Date?

Warton, Joseph[1]

1. *Adventurer.* "He [Hawkesworth] and every other man mention your papers of Criticism with great commendation, though not with greater than they deserve." *Letters* 1.36   1754
2. *Essay on the Writings and Genius of Pope* reviewed by J. (*Wks.* 15.469 *ff.*) "This is a very curious and entertaining miscellany of critical remarks and literary history." (J. had already made this comment in the *Preface* to his *Dict.*, 1755.) In Warton's remarks on *The Rape of the Lock*, there is, says J. "no discovery of any latent beauty, nor any thing subtle or striking; he is indeed commonly right, but has discussed no difficult question." (476.) J. concludes review: "We intend to kindle, not to extinguish curiosity, by this slight sketch of a work abounding with curious quotations and pleasing disquisitions. He must be much acquainted with literary history, both of remote and late times, who does not find in this essay many things which he did not know before: and if there be any too learned to be instructed in facts or opinions, he may yet properly read this book as a just specimen of literary moderation."[2] (479)   1756
3. Pope's "learned commentator." *Lives* 1.329   1779
4. W. spoke of Addison's *Campaign*, "with harshness not often used by the good-nature of his criticism." *Lives* 2.128   Ptd. 1780
5. W.'s *Essay on the Writings and Genius of Pope*, "a book which teaches how the brow of criticism may be

---

[1] For his relations with J., see *Bos.* 2.41 *n* 1
[2] J. on the whole seems to agree with Warton's criticism, though issue is taken on many points. For J.'s criticism of particular passages, see Pope 21, 25, 47, 57, 61, 73; Description 4; and Milton 47. Dick Minim, the coffee-house critic, in *Idl.* 60, (*Wks.* 8.240-1) seems to have borrowed his opinions on Rowe, Addison's *Cato*, and Addison as a humourist, from Warton's *Essay*.

smoothed, and how she may be enabled, with all her severity, to attract and to delight." *Lives* 3.236. See also *Bos.* 1.448; 2.167 for praise of this *Essay.*   1781
6. J. defends Pope's *Pastorals* against Warton's charge of their lack of invention: not intended by author. *Lives* 3.224   1781
7. *"*Qui stupet* in statuis, applied to Joseph Warton's admiration of fine passages. His taste is amazement."[1] *Letters* 2.441 and *n* 2. (App. D.: From Windham's *Diary*)   1784

Warton, Thomas

1. *Obervations on the Faery Queen of Spenser.* J. commends its method: it directs attention "to the perusal of the books which those authours had read." See CRITICISM 16   1754
2. *History of English Poetry.* J. wishes that "what is undeservedly forgotten" of "antiquated literature" might be revived. "Warton has set a noble example,[2] may he have many to follow him, and none, unless it be you [Dr. Horne] and me, to overtake him." Letter to Rev. Dr. Horne, Apr. 30, 1774. Printed in *Catalogue of the Johnsonian Collection of R. B. Adam.*
     1774
3. *"When a well-known author [T. Warton, undoubtedly] published his poems in the year 1777: Such a one's verses are come out, said I: 'Yes (replied Johnson), and this frost has struck them in again. Here are some lines I have written to ridicule them: but remember that I love the fellow dearly, now—for all I laugh at him.[3]

[1] It is probably J. Warton whom J. called "an enthusiast by rule." (*Bos.* 4.33 and *n.*) Mme. D'Arblay describes how J entertained the company by taking off Dr. Warton's enthusiastic manner. (*Memoirs of Dr. Burney*, by Mme. D'Arblay, London, 1832, 2.82.)
[2] J. undoubtedly refers to Warton's *History of English Poetry* which began to appear in 1774.
[3] See *Bos.* 1.270 *n* 1

>   Wheresoe'er I turn my view,
>   All is strange, yet nothing new:
>   Endless labour all along,
>   Endless labour to be wrong;
>   Phrase that Time has flung away;
>   Uncouth words in disarray,
>   Trick'd in antique ruff and bonnet,
>   Ode, and elegy, and sonnet.' "

John. Misc. 1.190. (Piozzi)   1777

4. *"He observed, that a gentleman of eminence in literature[1] had got into a bad style of poetry of late. 'He puts (said he) a very common thing in a strange dress till he does not know it himself, and thinks other people do not know it.' BOSWELL. 'That is owing to his being so much versant in old English poetry.' JOHNSON. 'What is that to the purpose, Sir? If I say a man is drunk, and you tell me it is owing to his taking much drink, the matter is not mended. No, Sir, —— has taken to an odd mode. For example; he'd write thus:

>   "Hermit hoar, in solemn cell,
>   Wearing out life's evening gray."

Gray evening is common enough; but *evening gray* he'd think fine.—Stay;—we'll make out the stanza:

>   "Hermit hoar, in solemn cell,
>   Wearing out life's evening gray;
>   Smite thy bosom, sage, and tell,
>   What is bliss? and which the way?" '

BOSWELL. 'But why smite his bosom, Sir?' JOHNSON. 'Why to shew he was in earnest,' (smiling).—He at an after period added the following stanza:

>   'Thus I spoke; and speaking sigh'd;
>   —Scarce repress'd the starting tear;—
>   When the smiling sage reply'd—
>   —Come, my lad, and drink some beer.' "

Bos. 3.158-9   1777

---

[1] Undoubtedly Thomas Warton. See *Bos.* 3.158 *n* 3. Also a MS. note by Mme. Piozzi confirms this identification. See *Lond. Mercury* 5.291

Wasse, Christopher

1. J. censures his Greek and Latin verses. In English he "had no art or elegance of diction." *Bos.* 5.445. (*Journey into N. Wales*) 1774

Watts, Isaac

1. "A writer who, if he stood not in the first class of genius, compensated that defect by a ready application of his powers to the promotion of piety. . . . Dr. Watts was one of the first who taught the dissenters to write and speak like other men, by showing them that elegance might consist with piety." *Wks.* 15.480 1756
2. J. recommends that he be added to *The English Poets*, and calls him, "a man who never wrote but for a good purpose." *Bos.* 3.126. See also *Lives* 3.302, and *Letters* 2.275 *n* 4 1777
3. *"His poems are by no means his best works; I cannot praise his poetry itself highly; but I can praise its design." *Bos.* 3.358 1778
4. (*Lives* 3) The number and variety of his works "shew the intenseness of his industry, and the extent of his capacity." (306.) "As his mind was capacious, his curiosity excursive, and his industry continual, his writings are very numerous and his subjects various." (308.) "He was one of the first authors that taught the Dissenters to court attention by the graces of language." Heretofore, their coarseness and inelegance of style. "He shewed them that zeal and purity might be expressed and enforced by polished diction." (306.) "Whatever he took in hand was, by his incessant solicitude for souls, converted to Theology." Piety increasingly diffused over his works. "It is difficult to read a page without learning, or at least wishing, to be better. The attention is caught by indirect instruction, and he that sat down only to reason is on a sudden compelled to pray." (309.) "Few men have left behind

". . . such monuments of laborious piety. . . . His character, therefore, must be formed from the multiplicity and diversity of his attainments, rather than from any single performance; for it would not be safe to claim for him the highest rank in any single denomination of literary dignity: yet perhaps there was nothing in which he would not have excelled, if he had not divided his powers to different pursuits. As a poet, had he been only a poet, he would probably have stood high among the authors with whom he is now associated." (See POETRY 42 for J.'s reasons.) "But his devotional poetry is, like that of others, unsatisfactory." (See SACRED POETRY 9.) "It is sufficient for Watts to have done better than others what no man has done well. His poems on other subjects seldom rise higher than might be expected from the amusements of a Man of Letters, and have different degrees of value as they are more or less laboured, or as the occasion was more or less favourable to invention." (310.) *Versification.* "He writes too often without regular measures, and too often in blank verse; the rhymes are not always sufficiently correspondent. He is particularly unhappy in coining names expressive of characters. His lines are commonly smooth and easy, and his thoughts always religiously pure; but who is there that, to so much piety and innocence, does not wish for a greater measure of spriteliness and vigour? He is at least one of the few poets with whom youth and ignorance may be safely pleased"; etc. (311) 1781

5. *Miscellaneous works. Lives* 3.303, 308, 310   1781

6. *Poems for Children.* "Every man acquainted with the common principles of human action will look with veneration on the writer who is at one time combating Locke, and at another making a catechism for children in their fourth year. A voluntary descent from the dignity of science is perhaps the hardest lesson that humility can teach." *Lives* 3.308   1781

7. *Improvement of the Mind.* "Few books have been perused by me with greater pleasure." Radical principles of it in Locke's *Understanding* but "so expanded and ramified by Watts as to confer upon him the merit of a work in the highest degree useful and pleasing." Whoever instructs others is deficient in his duty, if he does not recommend this. *Lives* 3.309. (J. quotes from this work, *ib.* 251) 1781
8. *Improvement of the Mind.* *According to Hawkins, this work "was a very favourite book with him." *John. Misc.* 2.2 Date?

West, Gilbert

1. His learning evidenced by his poems and Pindaric dissertations. *Lives* 3.329 1781
2. "His *Imitations of Spenser* are very successfully performed, both with respect to the metre, the language, and the fiction; and being engaged at once by the excellence of the sentiments and the artifice of the copy the mind has two amusements together. But such compositions are not to be reckoned among the great achievements of intellect." See IMITATION 22 1781
3. *Institution of the Order of the Garter.* "For want of a process of events, neither knowledge nor elegance preserve the reader from weariness." *Lives* 3.332
 1781
4. *Odes of Pindar: First Olympick Ode.* "I . . . found my expectation surpassed, both by its elegance and its exactness. He does not confine himself to his author's train of stanzas, for he saw that the difference of the languages required a different mode of versification." Analysis of ode. "He is sometimes too paraphrastical." "West's version, so far as I have considered it, appears to be the product of great labour and great abilities." *Lives* 3.331-2 1781
5. *Odes of Pindar.* *J. praises this translation, but points out a "low" line. *Bos.* 4.28. (Langton's *Collection*)
 Date?

West, Richard

1. J. refers to "the powers which he shews in his letters, and in the *Ode to May*," and adds, "the judgement of every reader will confirm" West's opinion of Gray's *Agrippina*. *Lives* 3.423   1781

Whitehead, Paul

1. *"I would not take less [for a poem] than Paul Whitehead."[1] *Bos.* 1.124   cir. 1738
2. His *Manners* "a poor performance." *Bos.* 5.116. (*Hebrides*, 27 Aug.)   1773
3. "A small poet." *Lives* 3.180   1781

Whitehead, William

1. *Cibber's familiar style better than Whitehead's. "*Grand* nonsense is insupportable. Whitehead is but a little man to inscribe verses to players." *Bos.* 1.402   1763

Williams, Sir Charles

1. *J. speaks contemptuously of him. "He had no fame, but from boys who drank with him." *Bos.* 5.268. (*Hebrides*, 29 Sept.)   1773

Woodhouse, James. (The Poetical Shoemaker)

1. *"He spoke with much contempt of the notice taken of Woodhouse, the poetical shoemaker. He said, it was all vanity and childishness: and that such objects were, to those who patronised them, mere mirrours of their own superiority. 'They had better (said he,) furnish the man with good implements for his trade, than raise subscriptions for his poems. He may make an excellent shoemaker, but can never make a good poet. A

---

[1] Boswell states that J. undervalued Whitehead whenever his name was mentioned, and accounts for this prejudice on the ground that Whitehead "was a member of a riotous and profane club." *Ib.* 125

school-boy's exercise may be a pretty thing for a school-boy; but it is no treat for a man.' " *Bos.* 2.127. (Maxwell's *Collectanea*)   Date?

World, The

1. *"His opinion of *The World* was not much higher than of the *Connoisseur*," *q.v. Bos.* 1.420   1763

Wycherley, William

1. Granville "may be supposed to have learned obscenity from Wycherley." *Lives* 2.290   Ptd. 1780
2. "A man who seems to have had among his contemporaries his full share of reputation, to have been esteemed without virtue, and caressed without good-humour." *Lives* 3.91   1781

Yalden, Thomas[1]

1. "Of his poems many are of that irregular kind which, when he formed his poetical character, was supposed to be Pindarick." Imitated Cowley. *Lives* 2.301   1779
2. *Hymn to Darkness.* "Seems to be his best performance, and is for the most part imagined with great vigour and expressed with great propriety." Analyzed. *Lives* 2.301-2   1779
3. *Hymn to Light.* "Not equal to the other," etc. *Lives* 2.302   1779
4. *Other Poems.* "It is sufficient to say that they deserve perusal, though they are not always exactly polished, though the rhymes are sometimes very ill sorted, and though his faults seem rather the omissions of idleness than the negligences of enthusiasm." *Lives* 2.303
    1779

Young, Edward

1. *Y. "not a great scholar, nor had studied regularly

---

[1] Included in the *English Poets* on J.'s recommendation. *Lives* 3.302

the art of writing." *Bos.* 5.269. (*Hebrides*, 30 Sept.)
1773

2. (*Lives* 3) "He has no uniformity of manner." His changing style. "His numbers are sometimes smooth and sometimes rugged; his style is sometimes concatenated and sometimes abrupt, sometimes diffusive and sometimes concise . . . his thoughts appear the effects of chance, sometimes adverse and sometimes lucky, with very little operation of judgement." Did not improve by experience and self-correction. (393.) Accustomed to experiment. (396.) Young's poetry "abounds in thought, but without much accuracy or selection." Pursues an illustration "beyond expectation, sometimes happily . . . but sometimes he is less lucky [397-8]. . . . His conceits are sometimes yet less valuable. . . . He has the trick of joining the turgid and familiar [398]. . . . Antithesis is his favourite." (398-9.) *Versification.* His own. "Neither his blank nor his rhyming lines have any resemblance to those of former writers: he picks up no hemistichs, he copies no favourite expressions; he seems to have laid up no stores of thought or diction, but to owe all to the fortuitous suggestions of the present moment." Yet design once formed, it was probably patiently laboured. No certain model for his verses—not even copied from himself. No student of prosody—trusted to ear. "But, with all his defects . . . a man of genius and a poet." (399)   1781

3. *Complaint, The, or Night Thoughts.* *"Why, Sir, there are very fine things in them [the *Night Thoughts*]." *Bos.* 2.96   1769

4. *Complaint, The, or Night Thoughts.* *J. said "that there were very fine things in his *Night Thoughts*, though you could not find twenty lines together without some extravagance." *Bos.* 5.269-70. (*Hebrides*, 30 Sept.)   1773

5. *Complaint, The, or Night Thoughts.* "In his *Night

Thoughts he has exhibited a very wide display of original poetry, variegated with deep reflections and striking allusions, a wilderness of thought in which the fertility of fancy scatters flowers of every hue and of every odour. This is one of the few poems in which blank verse could not be changed for rhyme but with disadvantage." (See BLANK VERSE 19.) Its excellence "not exactness, but copiousness; particular lines are not to be regarded: the power is in the whole, and in the whole there is a magnificence like that ascribed to Chinese Plantation, the magnificence of vast extent and endless diversity." *Lives* 3.395-6   1781

6. *Complaint, The, or Night Thoughts.* *"I forced him one day, in a similar humour, to prefer Young's description of Night [i. 23] to the so much admired ones of Dryden [*Ind. Emp.* III. ii.] and Shakespeare [*Macb.* II. i. 49 *ff.*], as more forcible, and more general . . . 'but remember [replied J.] that taking the compositions of Young in general, they are but like bright stepping-stones over a miry road: Young froths, and foams, and bubbles sometimes very vigorously; but we must not compare the noise made by your teakettle here with the roaring of the ocean.' " *John. Misc.* 1.186-7. (Piozzi.) cf. SHAKESPEARE 130   Date?

7. *Conjectures on Original Composition.* *J. gives Young his criticism of this work, and "was surprized to find Young receive as novelties, what he thought very common maxims." *Bos.* 5.269. (*Hebrides*, 30 Sept.)
cir. 1759?

8. *Force of Religion.* Never popular. "Written with elegance enough, but Jane [Grey] is too heroick to be pitied." *Lives* 3.394   1781

9. *Last Day, The.* "Has an equability and propriety which he afterwards either never endeavoured or never attained. Many paragraphs are noble and few are mean, yet the whole is languid; the plan is too much extended, and a succession of images divides and weak-

ens the general conception: but the great reason why the reader is disappointed is that the thought of the LAST DAY makes every man more than poetical." See SACRED POETRY 10   1781

10. *Love of Fame, the Universal Passion.* *J. repeats two passages, and praises them highly. *Bos.* 5.270. (*Hebrides*, 30 Sept.)   1773

11. *Love of Fame, the Universal Passion.* "Is indeed a very great[1] performance." If it be a series of epigrams "it is what the author intended: his endeavour was at the production of striking distichs and pointed sentences; and his distichs have the weight of solid sentiment, and his points the sharpness of resistless truth. His characters are often selected with discernment and drawn with nicety; his illustrations are often happy and his reflections often just. His species of satire is between those of Horace and of Juvenal: he has the gaiety of Horace without his laxity of numbers, and the morality of Juvenal with greater variation of images. He plays, indeed, only on the surface of life; he never penetrates the recesses of the mind, and therefore the whole power of his poetry is exhausted by a single perusal: his conceits please only when they surprise." *Lives* 3.394   1781

12. *Lyrics.* "He had least success in his lyrick attempts, in which he seems to have been under some malignant influence: he is always labouring to be great, and at last is only turgid." *Lives* 3.395   1781

13. *Paraphrase on Job.* Not unsuccessful. "He indeed favoured himself by chusing those parts which most

---

[1] One cannot always be sure whether J. uses "great" or "greatest," as a term of commendation, or merely in the sense of extended in scope or length. *Love of Fame* is certainly long enough (over 2400 lines), but *Night Thoughts* is far "greater" in this respect. Instances where "great" and its derivatives do not seem to imply critical appreciation, are *Lives* 3.145, (the *Dunciad*, one of Pope's "greatest and most elaborate performances"); *ib.* 2.207 (Prior's "greater pieces are only tissues of common thoughts"); *ib.* 2.209; 1.313

easily admit the ornaments of English poetry." *Lives* 3.395   1781
14. *Resignation.* Y. in this "made . . . an experiment of a new mode of writing, and succeeded better than in his *Ocean* or his *Merchant.* It was very falsely represented as a proof of decaying faculties. There is Young in every stanza, such as he often was in his highest vigour." *Lives* 3.396   1781
15. *Tragedies.* (*Lives* 3) *Busiris.* "In *Busiris* there are the greatest ebullitions of imagination;" but it is "too remote from known life." (See DRAMA 73.) "*The Revenge* approaches much nearer to human practices and manners, and therefore keeps possession of the stage; the first design seems suggested by *Othello,* but the reflections, the incidents, and the diction are original." Moral observations sufficiently novel. (397.) *The Brothers.* "I may be allowed to say nothing, since nothing was ever said of it by the Publick." (397)
   1781